P9-CEV-609

SLANG

Lexical Works by Paul Dickson

Toasts

Words

Jokes

Names

Family Words

What Do You Call a Person From . . . ?

The Congress Dictionary (with Paul Clancy)

The Dickson Baseball Dictionary

The New Dickson Baseball Dictionary

War Slang

Labels for Locals

SLANG

The Topical Dictionary of Americanisms

PAUL DICKSON

Walker & Company
New York

Published by Walker Publishing Company, Inc., New York
Distributed to the trade by Holtzbrinck Publishers

All papers used by Walker & Company are natural, recyclable products made from wood grown in well-managed forests. The manufacturing processes conform to the environmental regulations of the country of origin.

Library of Congress Cataloging-in-Publication Data has been applied for.

ISBN-10: 0-8027-1531-1
ISBN-13: 978-0-8027-1531-9

Visit Walker & Company's Web site at www.walkerbooks.com

First U.S. edition 2006

3 5 7 9 10 8 6 4 2

Typeset by Westchester Book Group
Printed in the United States of America by Quebecor World Fairfield

A people who are prosperous and happy, optimistic and progressive, produce much slang; it is a case of play; they amuse themselves with the language.

—William Graham Sumner and A. G. Keller (sociologists), *Science of Society*, 1927

Life is our dictionary. Years are well spent in country labors; in town,—in the insight into trades and manufactures; in frank intercourse with many men and women; in science; in art; to the one end of mastering in all their facts a language by which to illustrate and embody our perceptions. I learn immediately from any speaker how much he has already lived, through the poverty or the splendor of his speech. Life lies behind us as the quarry from whence we get tiles and copestones for the masonry of to-day. This is the way to learn grammar. Colleges and books only copy the language which the field and the work-yard made.

—Ralph Waldo Emerson, *The American Scholar*, 1837

The official language of the state of Illinois shall be known hereafter as the American language, and not as the English language.

—State of Illinois, *Acts of Legislature*, chapter 127, section 178, 1923

CONTENTS

PREFACE

Twenty-odd years ago I got into a taxicab for a ride to the local airport and found that the elderly driver was a former carnival man. I told him I was fascinated with slang and hoped to put together a collection someday.

Rising to the bait, he gave me a fast backseat tutorial in carnival lingo. I stepped out of the cab with the feeling that a stamp collector must have when he buys a sheet of stamps and finds they contain some spectacular rarity. Most of the terms were traditional circus and carnival terms, but one was new to me and I liked it more than any of the others. The term was "hard flash," used to describe a carnival prize that is so appealing that a person will spend vast sums trying to win it. Hard flash could be anything from an immense stuffed animal to a lamp in the form of a large bronze palomino horse with a clock implanted in the side of its belly.

At that moment I became convinced that I should stop talking about writing a book on slang and actually do it. Writing it and getting such a book published became my own hard flash because I had been fascinated by slang from the time I was a little kid. I was brought up on radio and loved the talk of the hard-boiled radio private eyes and the double-crossing ex-cons they had to deal with, the bucolic banter of ballplayers who called an easily caught ball a "can of corn," and the "calls" of soda jerks and countermen at luncheonettes.

I was convinced there was a potentially popular and useful reference book begging to be created. It would be a topic-by-topic slang dictionary that would stand in contrast to the fine A-through-Z slang dictionaries then as now on the market. My first edition of *Slang* was published in 1990. I continued to collect slang examples and published a second edition in 1998, more than twice the size of the original. In this, the third edition, I have tossed out some expressions that are stale and added a lot that are fresh and new.

The first version now bears the whiff of ancient history and the second seems vaguely quaint, dating back to a time when "old school" was pejorative, 911 was just an emergency telephone number, and nobody had heard of Google (which was just getting started when the second edition of this book was published).

Back then, in 1998, you could still find a few people under forty who didn't say "no problem" in lieu of "you're welcome" and "like-speak" was still confined to people who had seen the movie *Clueless*.

Hark back to that simpler time when many small and even some medium-size cities had yet to be jolted by the powerful joe offered by Starbucks. But joe, along with jamoke and java, were suddenly the slang of the hard-boiled detective replaced by an Italianate vocabulary which was more Milan than Milwaukee. (This edition has a chapter on coffee slang and its major dialect, Starbuckian.)

The idea of a topical slang dictionary is not new, but it is one that has not been done in a long, long time. The last—and as far as I can tell, *only*—American topical slang book was Maurice H. Weseen's now-long-out-of-print *Dictionary of American Slang*, which is a marvelous book but primarily of historic interest today because it was published in 1934.

Weseen, an associate professor of English at the University of Nebraska, published his book at a time when the United States, and the rest of the English-speaking world, seemed to be defining itself through dictionaries and glossaries. The *Washington Post*'s review of Weseen's book on December 24, 1934, began: "The year 1934 should go down in history as the year of dictionaries. I suppose more dictionaries of various kinds have been published this year than in any previous 12-months in the history of the world." Among other things, the first major revision of Noah Webster's 1828 *Dictionary of the English Language* was published in a second edition by Merriam-Webster in 1934.

Two years later, H. L. Mencken published his definitive *The American Language* and it seemed that American slang, as distinguished from the slang of the British Isles, had a clear and bold new identity.

Weseen's book went into many printings but was never updated and went out of print when the immense amount of new World War II slang made it obsolete. It is still a good companion for reading James T. Farrell or John Dos Passos. Weseen's book has twenty topical slang categories, followed by a general section on American slang. The topical sections are still fun to browse because they give a good overall flavor for the topic at hand as it sounded during the Great Depression.

Despite and because of the fact that the idea has not been tried in such a long time, it was an attractive one. One major reason for a topical slang book is that most of us, I think, tend to approach slang topically rather than as a huge alphabetical body of words from many realms. If we are trying to decipher teenage slang, we don't want to have to wade through scores of terms used by the police, computer specialists, and GIs.

So here goes once more, with a tip of the hat to the carnival guy in the cab, Maurice H. Weseen and his original *Dictionary of American Slang*, and all the people who have helped with the compilation of all three editions of this work.

After a short introductory chapter on the subject of slang, there follow thirty separate chapters, each covering a separate area of slang by topic.

A number of people will be acknowledged for their help throughout the book, but three people were of such great assistance to this effort, I would be remiss if I failed to thank them and acknowledge their contributions here and now. They are the late Charles D. Poe, my researcher, the writer Joseph C. Goulden, and Randy Roberts, an archivist with the Tamony Collection at the University of Missouri, Columbia. For their suggestions and for making this a much better book, I also acknowledge Norman Stevens, Roberta Jacobson, and the old and new masters of this domain—the late Robert L. Chapman and Tom Dalzell.

Paul Dickson
Garrett Park, Maryland
April 2006

INTRODUCTION

SLANG 101: "IT AIN'T NO BIG THING"

Correct English is the slang of prigs who write histories and essays. And the strongest slang of all is the slang of poets.

—George Eliot, 1872

People seem to be fascinated by slang, and it is widely beloved in the abstract even by people who cringe when it is actually spoken. Some of the latter get all bent out of shape and start huffing about "double negatives" when someone says that something "ain't no big thing."

Well, it ain't.
So live with it.
Let it go.
Chill.
Slang is.
Period.
Game over.
Elvis has left the building.

Whether slang is in favor or out does not matter. It is renegade language that thumbs its nose at the very people who study and write about it. Slang is unruly, unrefined, irreverent, illogical, and it can be brutally frank and direct, or deceptively kind and euphemistic. Euphemism is the verbal trick that has been termed the deodorant of language, and slang has given us dozens of terms for drunkenness and insanity that are remarkably gentle.

The Quick and Dirty

What else is it besides euphemistic?

This is what amounts to the current conventional wisdom on the subject, or at least this slang watcher's beliefs about the nature of the beast.

Slang is as old as language itself, and American slang started on the Mayflower. Mario Pei, in *The Story of Language*, points out that the slang use of a term for a piece of pottery for the head, "crackpot," has counterparts in ancient languages, including Latin and Sanskrit. He also points out that Shakespeare used the slang of his time, and by doing so gave us such words as "hubbub," "fretful," "fireworks," and "dwindle."

Slang binds and identifies and thrives in groups with a strong sense of novelty and group activity. Solitary pursuits and repetitive work like farming and factory work produce little slang, but boxers, science-fiction fans, surfers, hospital emergency room workers, lifeguards, soldiers, high school students, and actors produce great gobs of it. Anyone who wants to go deep enough into any given self-defined subculture is going to find some kind of slang at work.

Slang is produced by living languages and the moment it stops being produced, the language in question is dead. It is also true that slang replenishes standard language. English words as diverse as "snide," "hold up," "nice" (as in "nice work"), "bogus," "strenuous," "clumsy," and "spurious" were regarded as slang not that long ago. Contemporary slang terms such as "sleazy," "hassle," and "gridlock" are headed for acceptance. Much slang has become so common that when we use it we forget that it is slang: "Pick up the *phone* and find out what time the *movie* starts. Better yet, *Google* the time."

It is all but impossible for an outsider to destroy slang, especially with the argument that it is improper, impolite, or politically incorrect. For most of the twentieth century a battle was waged against the word "*ain't.*" The anti-ain't-ers never had a chance. When, for example, during the Great Depression, they criticized the baseball great Dizzy Dean for using the a-word on his radio broadcasts, he all but liquidated their argument by pointing out, "Lots of people who don't say 'ain't' ain't eatin'."

On the other hand, one of the easiest ways to make a word or term stale is for the Oxford English Dictionary, *the mainstream media, or one of the other major arbiters of language to label it "fresh"* or *"the latest" or to declare it a real word.* The "Couric Rule"—named for the *Today* host Katie Couric—holds that once a word or term is uttered by any popular talk-show host trying to explain a term to her or his audience, the magic is gone. "Jiggy," "phat," and "fo' shizzle" are, as of this writing, hip-hop terms that are on the endangered list, but quite possibly they will be in again by the time you read this. "Bling" is forever kaput, and "def" was officially buried and given a eulogy by the Reverend Al Sharpton on Black Entertainment TV when the term gained entry into the *Oxford English Dictionary*.

The phenomena of political correctness and multicultural diversity run counter to slang. This is underscored by the case of a document still making the rounds that was created during the summer of 1989 by a group of young journalists who met at the University of Missouri as part of the Multicultural Management

Program. "The Dictionary of Cautionary Words and Phrases" lists terms that are to one degree or another derogatory and that are to be avoided in type. It includes a number of obvious slurs that anyone living in the last half of the twentieth century knows to be offensive. But how about these: airhead, babe, ball and chain, barracuda (when directed at a forceful woman), beefcake, Bible Belt, blue-haired, burly, buxom, Chinatown, codger, coot, cracker, dear (as in "He was a dear man" or "She is a dear"), dingbat, dirty old man, ditz, dizzy, Don Juan, and Dutch treat? The reasons for the offensiveness of these terms are spelled out: "airhead" is "an objectionable description generally aimed at women"; "buxom" is an "offensive reference to a woman's chest"; and "Dutch treat" "implies that Dutch people are cheap."

The list makes the point that even though these terms have been branded as offensive and may be dying out in print, they are still very much with us in spoken American.

The United States is particularly hospitable to slang, where it tends to be embraced rather than spurned. In 1914, the essayist George Fitch, in "Sizing Up Uncle Sam," wrote, "One of the most enthusiastic of American industries is the production of slang." American slang has been called one of the "success stories" of English, and according to one estimate, made in *Reader's Digest Success with Words*, there are some 35,000 American slang expressions. I—and others—suspect that that immense estimate may be on the low side.

It is not that hard to create slang, but it is hard to sustain a "new slang" in the absence of a group that continues to use it. Citizen's-band-radio slang (1975–77) and Valley Girl slang (1982–83) were short-lived despite receiving tremendous media attention. A few months after each peaked, they seemed to live on mostly in yellowing paperback quickies such as *The Official CB Slanguage Language Dictionary* and *How to Be a Valley Girl*.

On the other hand, echoes of Valley-speak came back with a vengeance in the 1995 film *Clueless*, which roared out of the box-office gate with a $16 million gross in its first five days. The film was Hollywood's attempt to package teenage slang, and press releases were actually sent out that contained a guide to some of the movie's slang. As Cher (played by Alicia Silverstone) explained in the release, "Just follow this simple glossary, and a world of chilling Baldwins and Bettys will open before you."

Very quickly—as Nathan Bierma wrote in the *Chicago Tribune* on July 20, 2005, on the tenth anniversary of the debut of the movie—"our language was, like, forever changed." Not only did *Clueless* bring us the ubiquitous "Whatever" (along with the gesture of joining thumbs and index fingers to form a W) and the rest of the Californicated way of speaking, which to adult ears was somewhere between heinous and cheesy, but it also brought an odd new syntax in which "all" and "like" became the salt and pepper of a new dialect. A line from the movie underscores the point: "This weekend he called me up and he's all, 'Where were you today?' and I'm, like, 'I'm at my grandmother's house.' "

If there is a high mortality rate with new slang, it is also true that terms that survive infancy tend to be absorbed into the standard language. The slang of the 1960s and 1970s is still very much with us. To be sure, there are few flower children around, and not many people can say groovy with a straight face. But there is a body of words and expressions, especially having to do with state of mind, that while clearly of the period, have assumed a role in current mainstream language.

The approximate period in which this slang came into being and showed strength was between 1965 and 1975. Some was old and borrowed, such as calling a job a gig, which was an old jazz term, but most of it was new, daring, and well publicized. It was also quickly adopted by the mainstream, a point that was made in a *Newsweek* story (February 3, 1969): "*Groovy. Beautiful. Out of Sight.* The jargon of the alienated, the oppressed, the discontented is becoming the idiom of Middle . . . America. Television writers babble like acid-heads, newspaper columnists sound like black militants and advertising copywriters echo the slogans of teenyboppers."

As the 1970s wore on, there were periodic declarations that the language of Haight-Ashbury and Woodstock was dying out, to be replaced by the banter of post-Watergate teens who called good-looking guys hunks and studs, deemed bad to be good, and called those who were "out of it" airheads.

Oddly, this was not to be. Much of the old slang hung on tenaciously, as those who had grown up with it grew older. Today middle-aged baby boomers work hard to keep it together: to be up front about their hang-ups, to avoid confrontations and rip-offs, and to maintain a hassle-free lifestyle. They strive to keep from getting uptight, strung out, or down on their kids, even if they've trashed their rooms. Heavy.

In the summer of 1996, Karl Vick dedicated a column in the *Washington Post* to the routine use of sixties drug-culture talk in official Washington. He quotes a Coast Guard admiral's alluding to an issue that had "a lot of people strung out," an FBI official's talking about "a real upper," and a Republican senator's mentioning people "freaking out."

Slang of the 1960s and 1970s continues in use to this day and has not encountered its equal despite the vast influence of the slang of rap, hip-hop, the World Wide Web, and all things wireless.

Slang often has as much to do with who says something as what they are saying. A simple word like "hot" has many conventional and slang meanings, depending on whether you are talking to a musician, police officer, electrician, florist, radiologist, cook, or basketball player. If a television talk-show guest talks about the green room, he's referring to the room in which guests wait to go on camera, regardless of its actual color. On the other hand, to a surfer on a California beach, the green room is the sought-for realm inside the curl of a wave. By extension, at some West Coast colleges, to be doing exceptionally well is to be in the green room.

Slang often is as much defined by context and word order (viz., "cowgirl" and "girl cow," "OK" and "KO," and "breaking ball" and "ball breaker") as by the expression itself. The word "say" is not slang unless it is used at the beginning of a sentence, in the sense of "tell me." This is as much true of the contemporary teenager who says, "Say, how much did that cost?" as it is in the line, "Oh, say, can you see, by the dawn's early light."

Much slang is being invented as we speak. In a February 7, 1993, article in the *Los Angeles Times* entitled "Beyond the Melting Pot—Gray Boys, Funky Aztecs, Honorary Homegirls," Lynell George wrote of Los Angeles as a crucible of new slang:

> L.A. has metamorphosed into a crazy incubator, and the children who live on these streets and submit to their rhythm rise up as exquisite hothouse flowers. They beget their own language, style, codes—a shorthand mode of communication and identification. It's more than learning a handy salutation in Tagalog, being conversant in street slang or sporting hip-hop-inspired styles. This sort of cultural exchange requires active participation and demands that one press past the superficial toward a more meaningful discourse and understanding.

George was of course right. Indeed, this similar paragraph could have been written about Miami, Chicago, New York City (especially the South Bronx, which is widely regarded as the crucible from which hip-hop sprang), or a dozen other cities.

Despite all of this, people still have a tough time defining slang.

Define or Decline

Consider the following questions:

> "Hey! No bullshit, but what the hell is slang anyhow?"
> "Could you please define slang?"
> "Can a suitable set of parameters be developed through which slang can be, first, identified and defined, and second, distinguished from conventional English, jargon, dialect, lingo, and argot?"
> "Wassup with all that?"

These four questions are one question posed in different idioms. Their impact is quite different because of how they are framed. Question 1 is expressed in simple old-school blue-collar working-class slang. It is both direct and rude. The second version is phrased in standard, or conventional, English. It is at once forthright and polite. The third question is excessively precise, and follows certain academic conventions. The fourth is urban street slang.

The four questions answer themselves up to a point by being examples. Slang, conventional English, and jargon sound different, and native speakers of English pretty much know which is which. But exactly how does slang distinguish itself from the other styles of expression?

In his monumental *The American Language*, H. L. Mencken grappled with this question and wrote, "The boundaries separating true slang from cant and argot are not easily defined," and "There is a constant movement of words and phrases from one category to another." Mencken's conclusion was that cant and argot belonged to the speech of small and cohesive groups, with cant having the extra characteristic of deceiving and mystifying outsiders. In the fourth edition of this work he says, "The essence of slang is that it is of general dispersion, but still stands outside the accepted canon of the language."

Mencken believed that slang was driven by exuberance and word-making energy. He compared slang's relationship to language to that between dancing and music.

What about jargon? The rough distinction that seems to work is that jargon is technical, professional talk that often, like cant, acts as a barrier to keep outsiders from understanding what is being said. But not always. For instance, medical doctors have a polysyllabic, Latinate jargon. Their bilateral probital hematoma is our shiner, black eye, or mouse. Some slang is jargon; for example, the slang and jargon of truck drivers overlap considerably. Perhaps the simplest definition of jargon was the one made by Mario Pei many years ago in the *Story of Language*: "the special terminology in use in any given walk of life."

Finally there is dialect, generally defined as a different manner of speaking a standard language, using a different but consistent grammar and set of distinct expressions and accents. By this definition black English, widely discussed and debated in the 1970s and dubbed Ebonics in the 1990s, qualifies as a dialect. At the same time, many of the words used in predominantly black rap music and hip-hop culture are slang, which is much more likely to be understood by a non-black teenager than by a middle-aged black person. One can, in fact, make the case that hip-hop slang and general teenage slang have so much in common that it is almost impossible to distinguish between them.

So if we can give slang a place, it occupies a perch between conventional English on one hand and private, in-group cants, jargons, and dialects on the other.

I Heard It on TV—Broadcasting Slang

How is slang faring in the first decade of the twenty-first century? In a time of prosperity, technological derring-do, conflict, and post-9/11 fear and anxiety, slang is as dynamic a force as it has ever been. Conflict is a catalyst for the creation of new slang, and English is still digesting slang terms arising from World War II. In addition, motion pictures, radio, and advertising have ensured a constant supply of new slang.

Now there are two new factors, television and the Internet, in place that over time will totally and completely overwhelm anything else in history as an integrator and disseminator of language. Television has become a great slang dispenser, soaking up words and phrases from one part of the population and repeating them for all of us to hear. Kids who have never been on a sled know what luge is, and people who have never sat in a Catskills hotel and witnessed a performance of a Brooklyn-born comic nevertheless know about shtick and schlock. For a moment in time we all knew enough CB (ten-four, good buddy) and Valley Girl talk (gag me with a spoon) to fake those slangs. We heard it on television.

This fact has not been missed by professional linguists and students of television. Frederick Mish, editorial director at Merriam-Webster, Inc., in Springfield, Massachusetts, points out that the electronic media have become a major influence on American English, especially when it comes to new words. "It overarches all the other influences and promulgates them. Whether you're talking about a new word or phrase from technology or cookery, it is likely to come to us through television," said Mish in an interview. Tom Shales, the *Washington Post* TV critic, has termed television "America's dictionary as well as its mirror."

One of the most dramatic cases of electronically transmitted slang occurred in the spring of 1989 when a gang of Harlem teenagers were arrested for the brutal beating and rape of a jogger in Central Park. Within hours of the arrest of the teenagers, the New York police were using the word "wilding" for the vile rampage and other acts of senseless violence. Although the police pointed out that they had never heard the term before that night, "wilding" spread into every nook and cranny of the English-speaking world within hours. Television, with assists from radio and the wire services, had put the term and its grotesque connotations into the minds of tens of millions.

Hearing is the key to the spread of new words. So much is said and written about the visual impact of television that we sometimes forget that the medium is equally auditory. This was crucial during the televised coverage of the Watergate and Iran *contra* hearings—what was spoken and "misspoken." Also during America's manned ventures into outer space, not only the images of the launches, the splashdowns, and costly animation were memorable, but also the voices of the astronauts, the reporters, and even the official NASA spokesmen. For a while we were all saying "A-okay" and counting down, 10–9–8–7 . . .

Television is a paradise. You can flip on Oprah or Dr. Phil and hear the latest in sensitive psychobabble, dial up the news and hear the latest in boardroom or diplomatic jargon, screen the new sitcoms for the next catchphrase, and catch a few innings of the ball game to listen for the latest nickname for spitballs (referred to, of late, as "wet ones"). Most Americans' source of police slang is cop shows ranging from *Dragnet* to *Hill Street Blues* to the blue talk heard on *NYPD Blue.* TV westerns of the 1950s invented a slang for the Old West with new terms such as "gunslinger" and "bounty hunter."

TV talk has affected us in so many quirky little ways. Decades ago kids used to dream of being asked to spell "relief" by their teacher so they could reply, "R–O–L–A–I–D–S." *Saturday Night Live* popularized the refrain of Hans and Franz, the Teutonic bodybuilders, "Ve're going to pump *you* up," and the Church Lady's "Isn't that special." Kids today probably cannot understand what was so special, just as my grown-up kids draw a blank when I try to tell them how I loved the Burns and Allen signature: "Say goodnight, Gracie." "Goodnight, Gracie."

Television creates slang in the form of rallying cries and catchphrases. "Where's the beef?" is long gone now, but it marked the winter of 1984 linguistically as it was repeated over and over by the late Clara Peller in a series of ads for the Wendy's hamburger chain and then was uttered as a rejoinder by Walter Mondale in the televised presidential debates. This kind of crossover into mainstream use is nothing new, but it was an especially dramatic example of how we mark time with catchwords and phrases in the television age. We can predict the appearance of a major new national pet phrase every few years—and many minor ones. It will be new one moment and emblazoned across a million T-shirts the next.

The most obvious impact has come with signature lines uttered by characters, comedians, and advertisers, such as the late Gilda Radner's chirpy "Never mind" on *Saturday Night Live* and Steve Martin's "Well, excuuuuuse me." Then John Belushi took the word "no" and extruded it into something that took three seconds to say, and it became his signature. If there were a Hall of Fame for such phrases, it would be hard to know where to begin. You'd have to consider "Would you believe?" (Don Adams as Maxwell Smart); "Book 'em" (McGarrett in *Hawaii Five-O*); Flo's endearing "Well, kiss my grits" (*Alice*); Jack Paar's "I kid you not"; Mork's "Nanu-nanu"; and the Fonz's "Aaaaaaaay!" There was a bunch from *Laugh-In,* including Arte Johnson's "Verrrrrry interesting!" and the ubiquitous "Sock it to me!" Then there was "Heeerrrre's Johnny," Tommy Smothers's "Mom always loved you best," and Charlie Brown's "Good grief," which appeared first in the comic strips but needed television to become a household term.

Certainly, "yucky" was in use before *Sesame Street,* but that show did for that article of slang what *The A-Team* did for "sucker." And speaking of *Sesame*

Street, it can be argued that this was the instrument by which the term "you guys," slang for males and females (as opposed to males alone as in *Guys and Dolls*), became popular. Shows such as *Star Trek* created their own vocabulary; *Star Trek* left a noun in its wake, "Trekkies," those who follow the show.

Radio was the first electronic medium to change the way we speak by transmitting buzzwords and catchphrases to a wide audience: "the $64 question" is a permanent part of the language—pushed to $64,000 by television—and people over sixty shudder nostalgically at the line, "Gotta straighten out that closet one of these days, Molly," from the *Fibber McGee and Molly* show. But television has really moved this dynamic into high gear and given it "may-jor mo-tion."

If we like how expressions sound, we remember them because they are our mental souvenirs, and we hang on to them for the same reason the Smithsonian hangs on to Archie Bunker's chair, the Fonz's jacket, and J.R.'s cowboy hat. Sometimes our mental souvenirs are actually the least funny element in a show. For all the great, funny lines from *M*A*S*H*, what we all will recall, even after the reruns have stopped, is the chilling phrase, "Incoming wounded." And scores of funny lines from *All in the Family* have been forgotten by people like me who can only remember that Archie called his son-in-law meathead and his wife dingbat.

So the big question is, Where's the magic? What makes a phrase memorable? It clearly defies full analysis, but timing appears to be terribly important. "Where's the beef?" would not have become so popular during the Iranian hostage crisis or during last days of the Vietnam War. It wouldn't have been an appropriate catchphrase or verbal souvenir of a time of crisis.

The process seems never-ending, as *Seinfeld*, *Buffy the Vampire Slayer*, *Friends*, *Sex and the City*, *The Sopranos*, and the reality shows keep delivering more slang.

Bada-bing.

A Web of Wordos

If television is never at a loss for words to go with its images, the Internet is awash in them. Potentially, the Net could be the greatest of all dispensers of slang and new English since the invention of movable type. The reason for this is simple: on the Net, almost any person, group, or subculture can reveal itself in a public place for the rest of the world to see. Not only can we see their jargon and slang in the context of their sites as they conduct their business, but there are hundreds—maybe thousands by the time you read this—of accessible online glossaries, dictionaries, and lexicons, and more appear every day. What's more, many of these dictionaries are updated weekly or even daily.

Many of the subgroups posting glossaries, heretofore apart from the mainstream, are for the first time widely visible. There is a growing online glossary of prisoner slang created by inmates around the country. There are at least five cyberpunk glossaries. Name it and there is probably an Internet slang glossary in place or abuilding—X-rated Esperanto, hard-boiled private eye lingo of the 1930s, American Civil War slang, plus special regional slangs of those involved in reenacting battles of the Civil War in Seattle or Boston.

In addition to the plethora of new, though traditional-style, glossaries, the Internet has generated some remarkable newfangled vehicles for the spread of new slang. In 1999 a man named Aaron Peckham created the site UrbanDictionary.com as an interactive repository for new phrases and words, and five years later he had more than 400,000 entries, and had attracted more than a million visitors. Peckham allows visitors to vote on terms' validity and veracity as they are placed on the site unedited. The material is raw and unfiltered, a lexical goldmine where the latest neologisms appear like fresh produce.

The Internet has become not only a preserver but also an enhancer of slang. For example, hundreds-of-years-old Cockney rhyming slang lay dormant even in the U.K. for much of the twentieth century until it resurfaced in the 1960s, aided by several books and movies—the most important being the brutal argot of the punks in Anthony Burgess's novel of the future, *A Clockwork Orange*. But it really went into high gear in cyberspace. Searches for Cockney rhyming slang on the Yahoo search engine in early 2006 yielded 164,000 hits, including scores of sites devoted entirely to the argot. Some recent contributions:

Gorillas in the Mist = pissed
Britney Spears = beers

If Cockney-style rhyming slang, called CRS on Web pages devoted to it, can be brought back from a former life in long-ago London, the Net can help pump other local slang in wholesale quantities into places distant from their origins. With the aid of radio and music videos, the slang that defines hip-hop (both the music and the lifestyle) becomes the slang of the young in the schoolyards and cafés of London almost as soon as it is created.

The Net was all but unknown when the first edition of this book was published, which underscores the point that slang is always issuing forth from new wellsprings. The second edition carried a separate section on Internet slang as distinguished from computer slang. Then, in 2003, the term "post-Internet" appeared, in reference to the fact that the old-school Internet of Yahoo, America Online, and Google was about to be a mere ingredient in a digital brew called the X Internet—for "extended Internet"—comprising the many links between the physical and digital worlds. And on it goes, a beam ever replenished by our lexical life.

AUCTIONESE

1

What's Your Pleasure?

In New York dealers call the items "cultural antiques," in Northern California the favorite word is "collectibles," in Dallas "new antiques." In Memphis and Madison, Wisconsin, they simply call the stuff junk—but they spell it, with verbal pinkie extended, J–U–N–Q–U–E.

—Wayne King, *The New York Times*,
August 22, 1970

How does one get a handle on the world of antiques, collectibles, and flea markets? Simple. At the auctions, where the auctioneers' slang is the most interesting and colorful of the trade.

Auctioneers are under a lot of pressure to be clever. They have to keep potential bidders not only entertained but also interested in what they are selling. This is especially true of country auctioneers, who may have to move such alluring treasures as an occasional box lot of rusted chains or a 1974 Dodge Dart without an engine. After all, you don't have to be too clever if you are offering a Monet, a Bentley, or John F. Kennedy's golf clubs.

In order to get a handle on the rich slang and pat phrasing of country auctioneers, as well as better understand how auctions work, I began collecting terms from auctioneers at auctions in Maine, New Hampshire, Massachusetts, Tennessee, and Connecticut over the course of a number of summers from 1982 to 2005.

I was helped by other auction buffs who tape-recorded or took notes on auctions that I was not able to attend. These regional auctions are authentic country and give a sense of the flavor of the larger whole. Since beginning in New England I widened my search and in recent months have been to, among others, a country auction in Hendersonville, Tennessee, and a farm auction in downstate Illinois.

Then another rich source of auctionese appeared, on the Internet, as exemplified by the phenomenon of eBay. In the early 1990s I began buying and selling online and became aware of this second tier of auction slang, some of which was the same but much new. In a live auction a shill works from the floor, but in an online auction he is often the seller, using an alternative registration and bidding name.

The following glossary is a primer on online and live-auction slang. There are those who insist that eBay will soon edge out the live auction, but until that day comes, remember that most fish you eat and the used car you buy were likely auctioned off privately, live, before they reached your fish market or used-car retailer.

Absentee bid. A bid that is made by a person not attending the auction and executed by someone working for the auctioneer. Some auctioneers do not accept them, while others encourage them. "Absentee bids are welcome and easily done" are the first words in an ad from James D. Julia, an auctioneer of Fairfield, Maine, in the August 1993 *Antiques and Collectibles*. It continues, "Simply fill out a form from our catalog, following all instructions, and use your fax, Visa or MasterCard to secure your bid. A 20% deposit (20% of your top offer) is required to process your absentee bid. This will confirm your bidding intentions and will not be charged to you unless you are delinquent in paying for a successful bid."

absentee bidder's table. At some sales, a place at the front where an employee of the auctioneer keeps track of the bids that have been left. "That's $175 at the absentee bidder's table."

accidental bid. A bid that is made when one swats at a fly, waves to a friend, or scratches one's nose. Largely mythological, the notion of executing such a bid puts fear in the minds of novice auction goers. Of course, it is another story if one "accidentally" raises one's bidding paddle and "accidentally" holds it high.

Some auctioneers go out of their way to allay bidders' fear of an accidental buy. "Don't worry, I know a bid," says one Yankee auctioneer. "Feel free to wave to your friends."

additions. Items included in an auction that are consigned by owners other than the person or company whose estate is being sold.

age. An older piece showing some signs of wear and tear, as in, "This piece has some age on it."

aggravation. Flaw. "This bottle is perfect except for a little aggravation in the neck."

agitation. Same as AGGRAVATION. The extent to which this term and "aggravation" can be applied was shown at a 1988 Rangeley, Maine, auction, where the glass covering a framed print was held together by several yards of masking tape. The auctioneer noted playfully that the glass had some agitation. Later in the same auction, a really decrepit child's chair was described as "agitated" with the explanation, "You'd have a lot of agitation if you were that old."

all for one money. The whole lot is sold together: "Here are five chairs all for one money." One of three ways of selling a lot; see also SO MUCH FOR ONE.

all in and all done. Final bid; last call.

all over the house. Too many bids at one price; need a higher bid to sort them out. "I've got fifty dollars all over the house. Somebody give me sixty dollars quick."

ancestral. Seldom-invoked term in auction ads that is only used when "early" and "old" do not convey the proper sense of antiquity. One of its rare appearances was in an ad for a 1985 Robert W. Skinner auction which contained the line, "Ancestral property from central and eastern Massachusetts families."

appraisal. An estimate, for a fee, of what real or personal property might bring if sold at auction, or, if appraised for insurance purposes, what it would cost to replace.

Arizona Windsor. Style designation for a funny-looking chair.

as is, where is. No claim is being made for the condition of an item and it must be removed from the premises by the buyer. A more colorful admonition: "Don't buy it if you haven't helt it, smelt it, and felt it."

auction fever. The belief on the part of the buyer that everything on the block is a bargain and that one would be foolish to set limits on one's bidding. Auctioneers encourage this malady.

auctioneer. The man or woman or team in charge of the event. Ambrose Bierce, in *The Devil's Dictionary,* defined it as "the man who proclaims with a hammer that he has picked a pocket with his tongue."

authentic Shaker. More often than not this term is used facetiously to mean "not authentic Shaker." A running gag, which has been ongoing during the last several decades as the prices on Shaker-made furniture and household objects have set higher and higher records, is to say that an item has "authentic Shaker" stamped on the bottom—something as likely as finding a coin dated 60 B.C. In context it usually comes up like this interchange recorded at a September 16, 1995, Rafael Osuna auction on Nantucket as a wooden box was presented:

POTENTIAL BIDDER: Is it Shaker?

AUCTIONEER: It says Shaker on the bottom. I wrote "authentic Shaker" on the bottom last week.

Backfield. The back of the hall: "I've got fifty dollars in the backfield." Some buyers like the backfield because it is easy to see who is in front of you making the bids.

ballroom auction. Sale of one or more properties, conducted in a hotel function room rather than on-site. Commonly used of real estate auctions held in motel function rooms.

Bay, the (online auction). eBay, as in, "I just got a laptop for twenty-five dollars. You gotta love the Bay."

believe he stole it. Auctioneer's pat response to a desirable item selling for a relatively low price.

Bible box. Generic name for table top or repository box for valuables.

bid retraction (online auction). The legitimate cancellation of a bid on an item by a bidder during an auction.

bid rigging (online auction). Fraudulent bidding by an associate of the seller in order to inflate the price of an item. Also known as SHILLING—and collusion.

bid shielding (online auction). Posting a high bid to put off other bidders, which you intend to withdraw near the end of the auction to let your lower bid made in another identity, or through a confederate, win.

bid siphoning (online auction). The practice of contacting bidders and offering to sell them the same item they are currently bidding on, thus drawing bidders away from the legitimate seller's auction.

bidder's choice. Term used when there are a number of items on the block. The winning bidder is allowed to take one or more of the items for the winning price. Whatever is left is auctioned separately.

bidder's paddle. Object on which the bidder's assigned number is written. The number must be recorded after every successful bid. Bidder's paddles can range from rather nice wooden or plastic affairs (which must be returned) to paper plates on which the numbers are written in crayon.

boat anchor. A heavy item with less than universal buyer appeal. Applied, for instance, to a monstrous old calculating machine at a Northport, Maine, auction. "Come on, folks, what am I bid? You can always use it for a boat anchor."

bumper (online auction). One who pushes the price of an item up without intending to win it. Some bump for fun, others in collusion with the seller. Report from an established eBay seller: "Some people bump to antagonize a buyer with deep pockets. I have an older friend who kept losing auctions to the same guy. He decided to bump up every auction that guy bid on, just to cost him a little money and get revenge."

buy-in. 1. (live auction) When a reserve has been set by the seller and no bidder reaches that reserve, the auctioneer buys in (or, "buys" from the auction in a cashless

buy-in. (*continued*)
transaction) for the seller. Often the other buyers do not know that a buy-in has taken place until the final list of prices realized is printed and the space next to the buy-in is blank. 2. (online auction) Also called a reserve. The fact that there is a reserve is apparent in the offering, but it is not revealed until the reserve is met.

buy it now (online auction). Allows sellers to buy something before the auction opens. Essentially turns an eBay auction into a traditional retail experience. An item may have a opening bid price of $5.00 and a "buy it now" price of $19.95. Once someone offers the $5.00 opening bid, the buy-it-now offer is removed.

buyer's premium. Fee charged to the buyer for the privilege of spending money, usually 10 percent of the gavel price. Some make no small point about not charging this fee: "Of course, no buyer's premium is ever charged," trumpets an auctioneer's ad in *Maine Antiques Digest.* An ad from Mike True in the *Maine Sunday Telegram* avoids the word "premium" for this practice, saying, "No buyer's penalty."

Can't cut it any closer. Point at which the auctioneer will take no more half or fractional increments in bidding. If the bid is for $160 and the auctioneer is asking for $170, he may accept $165 but can't cut it any closer so will not take $162.50.

cash or check. Means of payment at most auctions. Few auctioneers will take credit cards but most make it remarkably easy for the buyer, even those from out of state, to write a personal check.

catered. Food will be served at the auction.

change your tune. Something fine is coming up: "Change your tune for this one." Dan Andrews, an auctioneer who believes he was the first to use this phrase in this manner, often prefaces it with a loud "Whoa." Same as TIME TO OPEN YOUR EYES.

the chant. Patter used to create excitement and sell fast (more than a hundred bids per hour). Two-and-a-half-half-a-half-a-half-two-seventy-five-seventy-five-seventy-five-got-half-need-seventy-five-got-half-now-got-seventy-five-gimme-three-gimme-three-got-to-have-three . . .

character. Said of a piece showing signs of wear and tear.

chowder mug. Chamber pot. See THUNDER JUG / THUNDER MUG.

circular. Traditional term in the Northeast for a mailed auction notice and ad.

clean. Unadulterated. The term can be embellished, as when, at a Northport, Maine, auction, C. W. "Chas" Hare pointed to a Sheraton washstand and declared that it was "clean as a smelt."

clerking. The process of recording bids and totals and making sure that all bidders have paid for their purchases, or have "closed out."

closing out. Settling one's bill when one leaves the auction.

conditions of sale. The legal terms and provisions of an auction sale, which can be announced, posted, or printed in a catalog or on the back of the bidder's paddle. The conditions of sale cover such issues as protested bids, sales tax, absentee bids, buyer's premium, reserves, warranties, and the terms of payment.

cosmetically challenged. It works but it ain't pretty—way beyond a few scratches, dings, and dents.

country auction. "A true country sale," says a man who runs them, "is when the buyer and seller are allowed to make a fast deal without hidden reserves or other forms of protection. It will contain everything from period chests and fine jewelry to pots and pans and the outhouse door."

Did you want to buy it or rent it? Auctioneer's response to a low opening. Variations: "He's here to rent it"; "That's not a bid, that's the rental fee."

dings. Dents or scrapes. It is one of the terms used by auctioneers as well as used-car salespeople and it is almost always cast in the negative: "No dings. No nothing. Great shape."

distortion. Flaw or damage. A large L-shaped rip in an oil painting was termed a little distortion in a 1987 auction.

DOA. Dead on arrival. Nonfunctioning item. "This clock is DOA but it has a pretty face."

don't dwell, sell. Motto used by an auctioneer trying to get the action going. Also: *"Scream, holler, shout! Do something."*

don't shoot, I'll marry your daughter. Auctioneer's pat response to a loud noise made when a runner drops a large object. There are others. At a Nantucket auction peopled by well-heeled buyers, the auctioneer, Rafael Osuna, has been heard asking, "Who dropped their wallet?" after a large object has been dropped.

dusty. Untouched and not picked over, something still covered with the dust of an attic or barn loft. An ad for a George Morrill auction which appeared in *The Maine Sunday Telegram* on August 2, 1987, was headlined "Dusty Country Auction" and promised "Many wonderful dusty primitives and country items in old paint from the barns and attics . . ."

Dutch auction. 1. One in which the prices go down rather than up. In this day and age, this is a technique more likely to be employed by a used-car or stereo dealer than an auctioneer. A handbill for a 1991 Dutch auction from Audio Associates of Fairfax, Virginia, asks "What is a Dutch Auction?" and answers in part:

- Every display model in every store will be on sale!
- All models are on display now for your inspection.
- All prices for each of the four sale days are clearly marked on special Dutch Auction sale tags.
- The price on unsold models goes down every day!
- You decide the price that's right for you.
- Remember . . . all models are subject to prior sale.

2. (online auction) Auction in which the seller lists multiple quantities of an identical item. With multiple items up for sale, multiple bidders can win. Also, one bidder can try to buy more than one quantity. All winning bidders pay only the lowest successful winning-bid amount.

Dutch avoidance (online auction). Eschewing the Dutch auction by listing a single item and offering additional items for sale in the item description; this is a violation of eBay policy, but selling a duplicate item after the first has been auctioned off is legal. Often auctioning just one item at a time will lead to higher sales by creating the illusion of scarcity.

Early. Auctionese for "old." Explained in a July 1981 article in *The Washingtonian* on auctions and antiques: "An antique should be at least 100 years old. Presumably, an early one should be even earlier than that. But some alleged antique dealers consider anything before the Eisenhower era 'early.'" Sometimes an auctioneer will become redundant in an effort to make something seem appealing, such as describing an item as good, old, early. See also OLD.

early fire. Said of an eager bidding when the lot is first offered.

eBay University (online auction). A traveling classroom offering how-to seminars in buying and selling on eBay.

eBaysian (online auction). Adhering to eBay rules and values. These mostly reflect common sense: being honest with descriptions and contact information, avoiding prohibited items, etc.

end of day. Said of an unusual piece to indicate that it may have been made by a worker at the end of the day either to use up materials (say, some molten glass) or as a special personal item.

ended out. Added to. A chair leg that has been ended out is one that has been given fresh wood. Also, "pieced out."

estimate. An opinion—not an appraisal—of what price a property will bring at auction.

Fair room and fair warning. Coded reminder that if the bidder bids quickly, he or she can still make a tidy profit between what is paid and what the item can be sold

fair room and fair warning. (*continued*) for later. This item was passed along to the author from Paige McHugh of Cambridge, Massachusetts, after he had written an article on the secret language of auctioneers in the June 1990 issue of *New England Monthly.*

fair warning. The bidding is nearing a close, but you still have a moment in which to spend your money.

fast knock. To sell quickly, usually to the first bidder: "Do I have ten bucks. Got it. Sold." Used by auctioneers to get the attention of the crowd and get things moving.

feed. Auctioneer's term for the flow of goods being brought to the front for sale. A good auctioneer will control the feed so that the items are diverse and the best come up when the buyers are most eager to pay top dollar.

feedback roulette (online auction). Leaving one's eBay feedback at the last minute just before the ninety-day limit from the auction's end, to leave negative feedback, in the hope that the other party does not have time to retaliate in kind.

feeder. One who feeds goods to the auctioneer. See RUNNER.

finding story. Tale about how the item came to be in the auction. An account of a 1978 James Julia auction in *Maine Antique Digest* tells of a rare political banner that brought $1,150. Samuel Pennington wrote, "There even was a 'finding' story to go with this one, too. According to auctioneer Julia, the banner had been found by a man hired to clean out a Belfast hall. Part of his payment was that he could keep whatever he found in the hall—not a bad keep, this one."

Occasionally a finding story involves a treasure discovered at the town dump.

flake. Small chip, as in a perfect Depression glass decanter with a small flake.

flea-market kit. Kind name for a large pile of stuff that could never sell individually, say, a nonworking clock, five unwashed canning jars, four unrelated saucers, a padlock without a key, and a long run of clean *Poultryman* magazines. If this lot did not sell, a few other items would be added to make it an intermediate-level flea-market kit.

flow-blue. Desirable type of china decorated with blue designs whose color bleeds at the edges. It has also been known to "flow" from one place to another. At a 1987 Franklin county, Maine, estate auction a lot of flow-blue china that had attracted a lot of interest during the inspection period suddenly disappeared as the auction was about to start. A RUNNER found the plates at the bottom of a box of farming magazines just as he was putting it on the block. The magazines brought $5. The runaway china was offered separately and fetched $190.

folky. Describes an item with folk-art qualities, such as a great folky rug. Not to be confused with the noun "folkie" for a devotee of folk music.

Gallery. Building used for auctions and where sale goods are displayed prior to sale. Galleries are often also used to store recycled newsprint and snowplows.

gimmie what? Words of an auctioneer begging for an opening bid.

give 'em away for Christmas. Suggestion given by the auctioneer Clyde Allen when he was unable to move bidders up from $35 on a lot of augers.

going . . . going . . . gone. The auctioneer's sell line—but only in the movies. An auctioneer quoted in Joe Connolly's *How to Buy at Country Auctions* said, "Do you realize how long it takes to say that 400 times a night?"

gone. 1. Sold. 2. Missing, as in "a mug with a gone handle."

good. One of the most overly used words in auctionese. It seems to be a filler word used when the auctioneer is not sure what else can be said. At a July 1988 auction in the mountains of western Maine, a totally undistinguished painting was described as a "good early painting, quite good." It sold for $35 with its good frame.

good, early ware. Generic description of a whatsit that appears to have come from a kitchen.

good trade. Words used when a noteworthy sale has been made that favors the buyer.

gowser. An attractive oddity. In an article in the April 1981 issue of *Maine Antique Digest*, there was a report on a Plainfield, New Hampshire, auction conducted by William A. Smith during which an odd-shaped box came on the block. Smith called it a gowser and it sold for $45.

Hairlines. Network of small cracks in ceramic.

hall. Preferred name for any inside country auction venue that has served or often serves another function. For instance, the central Maine auction hall in Thorndike, Maine, was once a grain mill.

he ain't too drunk, let him bid against himself. Comment aimed at a bidder who has made two bids in a row. Heard at the Fryeburg, Maine, Agricultural Fair on October 6, 1989, by the legendary Raynor I. Razor Crossman at one of his last public auctions. Crossman died in early August 1991 at the age of eighty-seven.

he/she came early. Common comment when a bidder with paddle number 1, 2, or 3 gets a winning bid.

he'll be back. Said of someone who has just gotten a very good deal on something.

hernia special. Said of any item that is so heavy that it causes the RUNNERS holding it up to turn blue in the face.

hitters (online auction). Words that can be used to increase eBay search-engine traffic: vintage, punk rock, retro, mod.

honest. Not adulterated; pure. Often stated as "honest as can be."

horse. Bidder in a STALKING-HORSE AUCTION.

I can't buy 'em for that. Cry of despair of an auctioneer when he has put an item in the auction that he bought for more than it is about to be sold for.

I never would have thought of it. Commonly said when a half bid is made, especially when the bidding is low. "I've got five dollars, give me ten dollars, give me ten dollars. Okay, seven-fifty. I never would have thought of it."

if you was that old you'd have a lot more than chips. Said of a flawed item that is not moving.

important. Expensive.

infraction. A high-toned term for a chip. "There's been a small infraction here."

it's got some age on it. Old. Said for emphasis. See OLD.

it's no ______ but it's a good ______ anyhow. Phrase used to link an item being offered with a hot property: "It's no fifty-thousand-dollar decoy, but it's a good bird anyhow."

Jump bid. Bid that is suddenly much higher than the small increments being used by the auctioneer. It has a certain shock value and is often used by a serious bidder to get the bargain hunters out of the way.

junque. Blend word of junk + antique; a tongue-in-cheek element in many country auctions.

Kippers. In some parts of the country, members of a bidding pool are referred to as kippers. See POOL.

knockdown auction. Informal auction among members of a pool. See POOL.

Left bid. Bid left by a prospective buyer who has the auctioneer bid for him up to a certain limit.

let's show a little respect for this one. Something excellent is coming along.

like word (online auction). Deceptive trigger word such as "Picasso" for a modern painting or "like a Mathew Brady" for an old photo.

lookers. Auctioneer's derisive term for people who do not bid. "What's the matter, you all just lookers?"

looks like somebody missed the road to the dump. Candid admission of a low-quality lot. Quoted in a *Maine Sunday Telegram* account of a 1971 auction. A variation on this was "Throw it in the swamp," said of end of the auction of items attracting no bids or interest at an Earl Hare auction in Northport, Maine, in July 1986.

lot. Any and all auction items are called lots, whether they be a single item or a box full of kitchen utensils. This term has been used by auctioneers and others for so long that it turns up in such long-established idioms as "a lot" and "a bad lot."

lots per hour. Measure by which the speed of auction or auctioneer is judged. A fast auction is one at which items are knocked down at a hundred per hour.

Majolica. Colorful pottery style. Overheard at a Northport, Maine, auction as a piece was being offered:

FIRST WOMAN: What's majolica?

SECOND WOMAN: It's Italian for ugly.

married. Said of two incomplete pieces joined to form one—often bizarre—whole.

mongo (online auction). Garbage salvaged from streets and trash heaps.

Naru'd (acr; online auction). Not a registered user. An auction user term to describe users whose memberships have been discontinued.

new blood. One or more new bidders. Also, new fire. Typically, two or three bidders work an item to a certain level, when new blood enters the fray.

New Jersey. East Coast state beloved of Yankee auctioneers. It is a special place where the ugly looks good ("This would look great back home in New Jersey"). Mention of New Jersey can cause values to climb meteorically ("Just think what you'd have to pay for it back in Jersey"; or, in reference to an item stuck at $25, "Come on folks, you know you could get three-fifty for this back in Jersey"). It is believed that most people who buy New Jersey items at auction are from Massachusetts or Connecticut.

New Jersey tourist birds. Lesser decoys in the $15 to $25 range.

nibbling. Making repeated bids in an attempt to find / exceed the current highest bidders proxy.

no excuses to be made on this one. A good lot. Pet phrase of the auctioneer James E. Talbot of Turner, Maine. "Here's a Lincoln rocker. No excuses to be made for it. Let's start the bidding at fifty dollars."

no more partying, let's get with it. Said when an important bid was missed by a man who was talking.

no refund. no return. this isn't J. C. Penney. Caveat uttered at the beginning of a no-nonsense north-of-Boston country auction.

no-sale fee. A charge paid by the owner of property offered at auction with reserve when the property does not sell. Not all auction marketing firms use this fee.

nodi (acr; online auction). Notice of declared infringement. Claim made against online sellers who pirate images and descriptions from another seller. This is a reportable offense and can result in suspension of an account if committed more than a few times.

noise words (online auction). Words used in eBay descriptions that have no market value, such as "nice," "wow," etc.

nominal bid. Small bids that are normally rejected by auctioneers as a matter of policy. On the reverse of one auctioneer's bidding card is written: "Nominal bids: Small opening bids or very nominal advances made with the purpose of disparaging an item may be rejected by the Auctioneer. If there is no apparent interest in an item (appreciable opening bid), the item will be passed from the block by the Auctioneer."

no's. Auction notices commonly contain one or more of these (no children, no pets, no out-of-state checks, etc.). It has been suggested that the greater the number of no's, the tonier the auction.

not that well known in these parts. Said of an unknown painter or artisan who presumably is well known elsewhere. Heard at a Turner, Maine, auction of an Arizona desert scene painted by one Sterling Mock.

not words (online auction). Words like *"not,"* that, attract more attention to your auction item description. In his online auction glossary A. C. Dickson gives the example of "not Hermés" to describe an average handbag. First cousin to LIKE WORD.

nothing to hide. Without a problem or flaw.

nothing wrong with it but the price. Invitation to bid higher.

nothing wrong with it, it just needs a new home. Invitation to start bidding.

NWT. (online auctions). New with tags. It is one of hundreds of abbreviations used on eBay to stay within the fifty-five-character limit on the all-important title line. Among others: OJ = made in occupied Japan; ROTJ = relating to the George Lucas film *Return of the Jedi;* NRFSB = never removed from sealed box, ARC = advance reader's copy

Of the period. Short for "of the Colonial period," describing seventeenth-century goods. It is also used as an inspired bit of vagueness for a piece of indeterminate age: "Here's a sturdy ladderback chair—could be of the period. What's your pleasure?" Or, "I don't know if this is period, but it sure looks it."

old. Term of emphasis for something that is *really old.*

old blue (or other color) paint, the. Old or original paint. For reasons unclear, the word "the" is almost always attached to "old" when auctioneers talk about paint.

one hundred percent. Flawless; perfect.

Pass. To move on to the next item without selling the lot on the block. Items are usually passed when there is no bid or the bid is too low. One coastal Maine auctioneer announced at an auction that he would pass on any item that was not bid up to 20 percent of its value.

PayPal (online auction). Immediate-payment system created for eBay. Also the only way to buy and sell internationally quickly, short of using Western Union.

personality. Term used to describe the quality of an auction. On the National Public Radio Nightly Business Report for September 1, 1994, a report from the Continental Auction School in Mankato, Minnesota, an auctioneer described an auction with a bad personality (one prompted by nasty divorce) vs. one with a good personality (one for a beloved family).

phantom / phantom bid. A nonexistent bid acknowledged by the auctioneer to give an illusion that encourages other bidders to raise their own bids. An improper practice that is illegal in many jurisdictions. See also PICKIN' BIDS.

picker. One who finds selected items for resale or auction consignment; a middle person. Pickers bring items to auction but may also be at the auction where they have consigned goods, looking for bargains.

pickin' bids. Accepting a nonexistent bid to help jimmy up the price of a lot. The term seems to derive from the idea of pickin' bids out of thin air, or pickin' bids off the wall.

pinks (online auction). Nickname for eBay staffers who police discussion boards; their postings are in pink.

plant. A surrogate bidder often used when the real buyer does not wish to be identified. For example, a museum curator might choose not to bid in person because others might try to outbid him and then try to sell it to him/her later at an inflated price.

pool. Illegal informal agreement among dealers not to bid on an item so that another dealer gets the item at a low price. Those who sit on their hands are paid not to bid. For instance, Dan Andrews tells of selling a fine china closet for $950 but later learning that the dealer who got it for that had to pay $200 to the pool to get it at that price. Sometimes one dealer will bid for the whole pool, with one item going to one dealer and the next going to another. Dividing up a pile of pooled goods is often done at a *knockout auction* near the location of the legitimate auction.

As more collectors and independent dealers enter an auction, the effectiveness of the pool diminishes. The auctioneer Elsie Andrews adds that really good stuff tends to break up the pool; greed takes over. This is when you see a member of the pool trying to sneak in a bid from the door of the coat room.

pop it right out of here. Let's move this quickly.

pop off (online auction). When an eBay bid increases exponentially in the closing minutes of an auction. The most exciting of

Say, What's Illegal?

Warning! Warning!

Oddly, many in the auction world have been hard-pressed to demonstrate the fact that pooling is against the law. In an editorial in the Center Barnstead, New Hampshire, auction tabloid *Unravel the Gavel* (August 20, 1996) Cathy Greer wrote:

> Pooling is a federal offense, punishable by jail time and heavy fines . . . If you are still not sure what a "pool" is besides a favorite spot for a cool dip—then you have nothing to worry about. However, if you are approached at an auction and asked not to bid on certain items; if someone attempts to bribe or intimidate you not to bid—or if you are offered money to leave the auction, *do not* accept it. If the auction is in progress, go to one of the auction staff members such as the auction clerk or front desk and report it immediately.

pop off (online auction). (*continued*) these events take place in the last thirty seconds of an auction.

pos (acr). Piece of shit. Said of a lot that is no good and will be passed on. This is an inside joke between some auctioneers and their best customers who know that when the word "pos" is heard it does not mean the same thing as "pass" (although a pos is usually passed).

posteds. Specific printed or written ground rules for the sale which are displayed at the auction site. For example, here is one of the rules attached to a tent pole for a Clyde Allen auction in Carthage, Maine, on July 25, 1987: "In the event that two or more persons believe they have the purchasing bid, the item must be resold with only those persons participating."

power seller (online auction). An eBay seller who has been active on the site for at least ninety days, averages at least $1,000 a month in sales, ensures product delivery within three days, and receives at least 98 percent positive feedback.

prime time. The best time for selling, generally an hour to ninety minutes after the first half hour. This is the time for the best stuff.

probably. Adverb used to link an item to a possible provenance. For instance, almost any old sled that comes to the block in Maine is "probably" from South Paris (a former hotbed of sled creativity).

puffer. A bidder who is in league with the auctioneer bidding up prices; a SHILL.

puffing. A price-enhancing technique that may originate with a person employed by the seller to raise the price by fictitious bids. Puffing is forbidden by law and contracts resulting are void or voidable.

pulling-teeth time. One auctioneer's term for the first half hour of the auction, which comes before prime time. During this time, says the auctioneer who used the term, people gawk, sit on their hands, and generally forget that they have wallets. He stopped short of saying that this was a time when junk was offered, but said that he kept his really good stuff away from the first half hour.

pyramiding. An unorthodox ploy that uses false absentee bids and PHANTOM BIDS in succession to raise the bid several jumps between legitimate bids.

Quarter. Twenty-five dollars, as in, "Gimme a quarter and we'll start this one going." By extension, $50 is a couple of quarters.

quick knockdown. Method by which an auctioneer can adroitly mumble a few numbers and then award a plum to a friend or a partner. Illegal in most jurisdictions, it is almost impossible to prove in court.

Real wood . . . from a tree. Exasperated cry from an auctioneer unable to get an opening bid on a nice table.

real world. The area outside the auction room. "This rug would bring fifteen hundred in the real world, said the Nantucket auctioneer Rafael Osuna in a September 1995 auction. Let's start the bidding at $1,500.

reBay (online auction). The process of buying something on eBay and then reselling it on eBay; commonly said of books and CDs.

reflectoporn (online auction). When exhibitionists advertise shiny things on eBay and display their naked bodies as reflected on the items for sale. Tea pots, car bumpers, and mirrored objects are common carriers for this odd practice.

right. Pure and unadulterated; a piece that you don't have to worry about. Also, RIGHT AS RAIN, for emphasis.

right where we should've started. Said sometimes when the bidding reaches the point from which the auctioneer tried to start the bidding.

ring. 1. Groups of bidders who agree among themselves not to bid against each other, then later divvy up the properties they have purchased cooperatively. Same as a POOL and of just as much questionable legality. 2. In a livestock or vehicle auction, the area to which the current lot is brought for bidding.

ringman / ringperson. Auctioneer's helpers in livestock, vehicle, and other large-item auctions. They spot bids and relay them back to the auctioneer, usually shouting "Yep."

***Roadshow* effect.** The tendency for the prices of specific items to drop in value after they appear on the PBS show *The Antiques Roadshow,* because once they appear on television many similar items come onto the market. Appraisers on the show give a price they think an object will fetch at auction. The phenomenon was actually mentioned by one auctioneer on the show in 2005.

runner. The auctioneer's assistant, who helps spot bids, brings items to the front of the room, and holds items up for the audience to see.

Sameway. To the same person as the bid before. Instead of saying "Sold to number forty-two," the auctioneer may say, "Sold sameway."

sea captain's chest. Term used to describe the origin of pieces for sale, and to suggest age and quality, especially in New England. Similar terms are in use in other parts of the country, for example, in the West an item may have come out of a covered wagon. This is also common in Britain, where "sea captain" works as well. The linguist Fritz Spiegl wrote in a letter to the *Daily Telegraph* (May 19, 1999): "People with maritime heirlooms such as they take to *The Antiques Roadshow* invariably declare that they came from an ancestor who was a sea 'captain.' Never a bosun or midshipman."

second-chance offer. Along the lines of DUTCH AVOIDANCE, it allows sellers to sell to the under bidder when the winner disappears, but it is also a way to sell an identical item to the bidder who lost out.

sell ya one in a minute. Response made by the auctioneer Clyde Allen when asked, about five minutes before an auction was to begin, "You wouldn't have an extra chair for me?" (Like many on-site country auctions, this one required bidders to bring their own chairs.)

send it down the road. To get the bidding going. An auctioneer might say, "Gimme twenty-five dollars to send it down the road."

set/kick it in at ______. Injunction to start the bidding: "Do I have a hundred, do I have a hundred. Okay, let's set it in at fifty. Or "Fifty and go."

shill. Bidder who is working for the auctioneer to inflate bids.

shilling (online auction). Fraudulent bidding by the seller's using an alternate identity or an associate of the seller in order to inflate the price of an item. Also known as BID RIGGING and collusion.

sick. Term applied to glass that is cloudy, usually because it was used as a vessel for chemicals, or china that is stained or so weak that it lacks the characteristic ring you should get when you flick it with your fingernail.

signed. Said of anything with the maker's name on it, ranging from an oil painting to a soup strainer. An item that was not moving at an August 1986 auction at the Blue Goose Dance Hall in Northport, Maine, had the auctioneer making the plaintive cry, "But, folks, it's a signed Archibald."

smalls. Little items that are presumably appealing to out-of-state dealers and collectors without trucks. Smalls are good for the summer trade and the best of all are listed in the ads as "Shaker smalls" or "Indian smalls."

Smithsonian would pay thousands for this. One of the many bits of overblown nonsense used to get bidders moving. Used in an estate auction at the Blue Goose Auction Place and Dance Hall in Northport, Maine, on August 4, 1993, to describe an item that fetched a whopping $170.

sniping (online auction). Outbidding other buyers in the closing minutes or seconds of an auction, most commonly using a third-party service that specializes in this practice. eBay's policy on sniping is "Any bid placed before the auction ends is 'legal' on eBay." One technique snipers use involves opening eBay in several Internet browser windows simultaneously and synchronizing one's computer clock with eBay's to get bids in right under the wire. Sniping services have such names as Bidnapper, eSnipe, and Powersnipe. An alternative sniping format allows you to put a bid in before the auction opens, then to program the sniping system to put your bid in last.

so much for one, take 'em all. One way of selling a group of items. In this case you bid on one but are obliged to pay the same for the others. If one of a set of six chairs is sold this way for $20, the buyer has bought $120 worth of chairs. It differs from the next definition.

so much for one; take one, take all. The buyer of the first item can just take that item—$20 in the case of the aforementioned chair—or take the whole lot for $120. Also known as "choice and privilege," as in you can take your choice or have the privilege of taking them all.

soft close (online auction). An auction that continues to stay open as long as bids keep coming in. One eBay competitor keeps an auction open for an additional ten minutes if a high bid has come in during the last ten minutes. It is also known as a dynamic close.

sold! How country auctioneers conclude a transaction. Also, "Gone!"

stalking-horse bid. Process used to set a public starting price at large-item auctions (an entire farm or factory; a house). It is a technique often used when a court is the seller. A seller asks for bids to buy all or some of its assets. The high bid is determined and then used as a stalking horse by the seller, the court, which then holds a hearing to see if anyone wants to outbid the horse. If there is a higher bid, the bidder who submitted the horse is allowed to get back in the bidding. If no one exceeds the horse in court, the stalking-horse bid wins.

steal of the evening. Good trade. At a good country auction the auctioneer should deem something the steal of the evening about every half hour.

still plenty of money to be made on this one. An attempt to wake up the dealers in the crowd by pointing to resale potential.

string. Similar or same items that are offered consecutively.

Table tops. SMALLS.

ten-and-ten. The scheme by which both the buyer and the seller pay the auctioneer a 10 percent commission on a lot.

thanks for your help. Said when a bidder drops out after helping to get the bidding up to a level that pleases the auctioneer. Alternatively, "Appreciate the help."

this is not a rental, folks. Time-honored way of letting the audience know that the bids are too low.

three D's, the. Name for the main causes of consignment of goods for auction: death, debt, and divorce. Mrs. Virginia Weschler of the Weschler Auction house in Washington, D.C., says, "People move, get married, divorce, or their kids grow up, but the bedrock is people dying."

throw it in the swamp. Reaction to a lot that attracts no interest and no bids.

thunder jug / thunder mug. Chamber pot, from the noises created when they were used. There are auctioneers who will present the most decrepit example or the lid of one just to be able to say "thunder jug" in public. A variation on this is CHOWDER MUG. "Here's a beautiful chowder mug," says the auctioneer Rafael Osuna. "I mean, chamber pot."

time to open your eyes. Same as CHANGE YOUR TUNE.

times the money. You are bidding on one item in a lot but you must multiply that amount by the number of items in the lot when you settle up. For instance, you bid on one chair in a lot of six but you pay for all six.

tips. Everyone has tips for auction goers. Here are some that seem worthwhile:

- Read all warranties and conditions of sales.
- Don't be afraid to ask officials for help. They may alert you to an item's ballpark value.
- Turn on all cars or electrical equipment beforehand. These items are usually sold as is.
- Know the value beforehand so you don't overpay.
- Don't feel you have to win a bidding war. Be prepared to walk away.
- Check out the competition. Well-dressed bidders are often dealers willing to go higher than those casually attired and just looking for a bargain.

tray and table lots. Groups of glass and china. A step up from a box lot, a box of assorted items of little value, but not good enough to offer individually or as a set. The objects are offered generically, as in this line from a 1993 Richard W. Withington auction in Hillsboro, New Hampshire: "A large lot of Victorian glass and china to be sold in both tray and table lots."

treewood. Unknown wood. "What's it made of?" is the question from the floor. The auctioneer's answer: "Looks like treewood to me."

turnpike cruiser. A bedpan. Also referred to as a New York tureen.

20-percenter. Auctioneer who does not charge a buyer's premium but rather takes all of the traditional 20 percent commission from the seller. Besides the traditional 20 percent and the new TEN-AND-TEN scheme there are other variations. A sign noted in Clyde Allen's auction house in New Sharon, Maine, a few years back said, "20% commission—30% on Junk and left-over lawn-sale items."

Unfortunately, he isn't here. The last line of a story used by an auctioneer to get a piece of antique furniture over the $100 bid then on the floor. "A man was in here the other day and offered me two hundred sixty for it. Pleaded with me to let him have it, but I told him that it was advertised as part of the auction. Unfortunately, he isn't here tonight."

use it for packing. Suggestion made by an auctioneer having a hard time selling a homely brown quilt.

user I.D. (online auction). Trading name for all eBay members, both buyers and sellers.

Vendue / vendue sale. An auction, but more. In E. C. James's *I Remember Cape Cod*, there is this explanation:

Several times during the summer the Cape Cod Item and Bee, which came out on Thursdays, carried advertisements for "vendue sales" by which was meant auctions. These were no ordinary affairs by which householders sought to rid themselves of unwanted junk. Most of them represented, rather, the breaking-up of long-established homes through the death of their owners. A number of them included the property and effects of sea-faring men who had circled the globe in the sperm whale fishery or had sailed great clipper ships in the China tea trade.

Victorian. Having to do with the period 1837 through 1901, when Queen Victoria reigned. In most auction announcements this great period in history is reduced to the abbreviation "Vic."

video auction. Mail auction in which buyers view the lots on a VHS tape. A 1993 flyer for such an auction from Running Rabbit Video Auctions of Nashville offered 300 lots of antique marbles on a two-hour video. The cost of the auction tape was $15.

We're goin' the other way. One way of telling a bidder that he is bidding lower than the amount now on the floor.

what's it say here? Paul Revere. The kind of transparently bogus line used by country auctioneers to get the crowd into the action. The Revere name works well for silver or pewter bowls, as does Stradivarius for an old fiddle.

what's wrong with it? A challenge to the crowd to start bidding.

where's the pleasure? Who will make an opening bid?

whimsy. Something made as a hobby, to occupy a person's time, such as a carving made by a sailor on a long voyage. Often it is an odd or fanciful object such as an intricate carving of a chain made from one piece of wood. The word is currently popular among auctioneers, museum curators, and antique dealers to describe objects of uncertain utility but clear charm.

white goods. Refrigerators, stoves, washing machines, and other large appliances, regardless of their color. Some auctioneers will not handle them and will advertise a sale of "good antiques and household items: no white goods." Indeed, white goods have become a problem in the era of recycling. A headline in the July 20, 1991, Lewiston *Sun-Journal* stated, "Towns Must Join to Recycle White Goods."

winner's curse. Paying more for something than it is worth. The curse kicks in when the buyer realizes that all of the losing bidders estimated that the item had a lower market value.

Yellow chicken (online auction). Putting a popular item in the title of your auction that has nothing to do with what you are actually selling. The online version of the red herring.

you battin' a fly or are you bidding? Query used to determine whether a party is actually bidding. Also, "Is that a bid or are you waving at someone?" Or, "Are you bidding or scratching your nose?" See ACCIDENTAL BID.

you folks on this side are allowed to bid. Line used when only one side of the hall seems to be bidding.

you just can't seem to win. Said to a bidder who keeps dropping out before the next highest bid takes the item. Sometimes embellished by a line like "One more time you might get it."

you wanna stand up so everyone can see you? Used by a disgusted auctioneer after a bidder had asked to have a lot of good china put up early and then bid $25 when the auctioneer was trying to get an opening bid at $100.

you wouldn't want me to sell it for that if it was your mother's. Rafael Osuna's way of turning down a very low bid on a consigned item. Lines like this are reassuring to bidders who are also potential consigners.

you'll never see another one like this. Said of a particularly ugly painting at an Elmer Lyons auction in 1986. Confronted with a similarly ugly work which did not attract a single bid at a Nantucket auction, Rafael Osuna told his RUNNER to put it back facedown.

you're the expert. All-purpose disclaimer, usually followed by something on the order of, "You can tell if it's Louis XIV or Louis XV, I can't." Or, "Could be Shaker, but you're the expert."

yours. Auctioneer's way of saying that you have the high or winning bid.

AUTOMOTIVE SLANG

2

How to Speak Car Talk

Ever since the first car wheel put rubber to the road, cars have evolved a language of their own. Today, although just about everybody owns and drives a car, few know how to talk car-talk.

—Chrysler Corporation, booklet on Detroitese, 1959

If the automotive world is one that always seems to be in a constant state of flux and change, the informal language associated with the internal combustion engine is not. To be sure, new terms are always being coined, but the old terms endure. "Four on the floor" is still the accepted way of describing a four-gear car with stick shift on the floor, and a ragtop is still a convertible, just as it was when Ike was in the White House—and before: some of the slang from the late 1940s remains remarkably current. A 1949 *San Francisco Examiner* article on hot-rodders talks about skins, jugs, and bent-eights.

Car slang also has its own subsets and dialects. You will hear a different version of automotive slang from a used-car salesman, a race-car driver, a hot-rodder, or a mechanic. Even within auto racing there are distinct differences, depending on whether you are talking to a NASCAR or Indy competitor.

Here is a heavy sampling from all of those realms.

A-bone. Model A Ford, especially one that has been converted into a 1950s-style street rod.

air dam. A strip that hangs under the front grille of a race car, very close to the ground. It helps provide downforce at the front of the car.

air scoop. A forward-facing aerodynamic opening used to conduct cool outside air to some part of the vehicle such as the carburetor intake, the brakes, the radiator, or an oil cooler.

alki / alky. Methanol or alcohol used as a fuel.

anchors. Brakes.

apron. The portion of a racetrack that separates the racing area from the infield.

ark. One of many terms for a hulking older American car; also a canoe, BOMB, SLED, boat.

arching / arcing. Racing; going all out.

arm lot. Small used-car lot where cars are sold for almost nothing down and for which you pay enormous interest charges. They supposedly got this name because of the owners' strong-arm methods of collecting payment.

auto jumble. What they call flea markets in the British Isles; used increasingly to refer to swap meets in the United States where sports-car parts are sold and traded.

Back end. In car sales, the money to be made in high-interest financing and high-profit "options" such as paint sealants and rustproofing.

back haul. Return load a trucker hauls from his first destination back to his point of origin.

back light / backlite. Industry term for the rear window light.

back off. To throttle down while racing.

badge. Car's make.

badge engineering. A marketing practice of manufacturing one vehicle and selling it under a variety of brand names with superficial differences such as trim and name badges. For example, the Eagle Summit is a badge-engineered Mitsubishi Mirage. Likewise, the Mercury Topaz is a badge-engineered Ford Tempo.

bagel. A poorly maintained car, to a person looking at it for trade-in.

baldies. Drag-racing tires, which are supposed to lack tread; also badly worn tires.

balloon foot. A slow driver.

bam and scram. Hit-and-run accident, to radio traffic reporters and others.

banger. Trucker's term for a diesel engine cylinder. A six-banger is a vehicle with a diesel engine with six cylinders.

banking. The slope of a racetrack from the wall to the apron, generally measured in the corners.

banzai. All out.

bareback. Truck drivers' term for a tractor less its semi-trailer. See BOBTAIL.

barefoot. A car with worn-out tires.

barefoot pilgrim. Trusting car buyer who questions nothing.

barrel. 1. Engine cylinder. 2. Carburetor throat, alluded to in the term "four-barrel carburetor." 3. To speed.

base. Dealer's price.

B-back / beback / be-back. Derogatory name used by car salesmen for a potential customer who says he or she will return but clearly has no intention of doing so. From the time-honored departure line "I'll be back." A sign that occasionally shows up in the office of a used-car dealer reads "Be-backs never turn into greenbacks."

beach. To stop a truck or coast into a parking spot.

beached whale. Stolen car found stripped and up on blocks.

bear. Cop, to interstate truckers.

bear grease. Racing term—mostly NASCAR—for any packing material used to fill cracks and holes in a track's surface.

beater. Unreliable car.

beauty bolts. Exposed brightly finished bolt heads displayed for looks.

bedbugger. Moving van, especially in the slang of the long-distance trucker.

bedsteader. Sleepy truck driver.

beefer. A complaining consumer, in the lingo of the sales room.

been in service. Used-car and auto-auction term for a former police vehicle.

bent eight. V-8 engine.

big arm. Piston with a long stroke.

big banger. Big engine; one with large displacement.

big body. Large vehicles such as SUVs or older-model big cars.

big hat. State trooper, to a trucker.

big one, the. A multi-car pileup in a restrictor-plate (speed-controlled) race that

big one, the. *(continued)* may come near the end of the race in certain NASCAR venues (Daytona and Talladega). As many as twenty cars have been involved.

big three. The three major U.S. automobile manufacturers, Chrysler, Ford, and General Motors.

Bimmer. A BMW. In his "Dream Machines" column in the *Washington Post*, Brock Yates points out that "Beemer" is proper when referring to one of the company's motorcycles, although increasingly there are those who refer to the car as a "Beemer" or "Beamer."

binders. Brakes, especially those on a truck or race car.

bite. The adhesion of a tire to a road or track; traction.

bite a turn. To cut a corner, especially among truckers.

black box. Device housing electronic components. Many traditional mechanics do not go inside black boxes.

black-flagged. Said of a race car that has been waved off the track with a black flag because of a mechanical problem that endangers other drivers.

blindsided. To be hit mid-car by another driver who seemingly comes out of nowhere.

blow away / blow off. To defeat, pass, or win against a competitor in the world of auto racing.

blow lunch. Blow an engine.

blow off / blow off his doors. In racing, to pass a challenger.

blowed. NASCAR-ese for a world-class engine failure.

blower. Supercharger. Sometimes a turbocharger.

blown engine. 1. Engine with a supercharger, in racing circles. 2. All-inclusive term for a serious engine breakdown.

blown gasser. Supercharged car that is fueled by gasoline.

blue book. The value of a car given in *The Kelley Blue Book*, the guidebook listing standard prices for used cars. "I'll give you a hundred dollars over blue book for your Ford wagon."

bobtail. Said of a trucker when he drives a tractor without its semi-trailer, as in "He's runnin' bobtail." From the term for an animal whose tail has been bobbed, or cut off.

boll weevil. Novice truck driver.

bomb. 1. A bad car. 2. A large old car, lovingly addressed, as in "I had this great old bomb of a Caprice."

bondo / bondo'ed. Said of a car to which the product Bondo has been applied heavily to repair rusted or damaged areas.

boneyard. Junkyard.

book. A heavy metal contraption, usually orange in color, used to lock a vehicle wheel in place, and by clamping around it cause a car to remain in place. It is used to secure scofflaws' and other violators' vehicles so they cannot drive off and avoid paying fines.

boomcar. Vehicle with an extremely powerful stereo system being played with the volume and bass levels turned up and the car windows rolled down.

boondockin'. Trucker's practice of avoiding all major roads.

boondocks. Off the course, in racing.

booth. Where the papers are signed in closing a sale on a new or used car. It can be an office, cubicle, or desk.

boots. 1. Tires. 2. Tire inserts to reinforce the casing at weak points.

boss. Perfection.

Botts' dots. Raised reflective pavement markers that create a rumble when run over to alert drivers to tollbooths and other hazards. They are called Botts' dots because they were invented by Dr. Elbert Botts, who worked for the state of California in the 1950s. They are also known as IDIOT BUTTONS.

bow tie. Chevrolet, alluding to the shape of the company's logo.

box. Transmission.

box, the. The closing office. The glass-enclosed room at a car dealership where the final deal is made. Salespeople work to get the customer into the box.

bra. Covering used to prevent the front of a car from suffering damage from pebbles and other road debris. See CAR BRA.

brain bag. Briefcase, portfolio, or attaché case in which a truck driver carries trip reports, bills of lading, and the like.

brain bucket. Racing helmet. See also, GOURD GUARD.

brain fade. Racer's term for a momentary lack of attention leading to a mistake during a race.

brains blown out. Describing a car with a sunroof.

branch library. Describing a driver reading at the wheel.

brass hat. Sales term. A slightly used car; a demo.

brick. To get a customer to take a car immediately.

Brickyard, the. The Indianapolis racetrack.

BSR. Buzzes, squeaks, and rattles. Dreaded malady for new cars.

bucket. Contour seat for one person.

buff. Of a great-looking car. "That thing is totally buff."

build a fire. To run a rig at near top speed.

bull bar. Tubular chrome-plated steel bar in the shape of an inverted U adorning some four-by-four vehicles. First employed in areas where wandering wildebeasts and other large mammals were a danger; they became popular in the United States and Britain as a macho fashion accessory for four-by-four owners. They were banned in Britain on new vehicles produced after 2004 because of added dangers to pedestrians.

bull ring. A dirt racing track less than half a mile long. Bull rings are common in the American South.

bumblebee. Small foreign car.

bump, the. The process by which the sales manager sends the salesperson back to the customer to get a higher price on a car—to bump up the price.

bumper tag. 1. To drive close behind another car. 2. Touching other cars' bumpers in a game of tag in which one car is "it." This game is from the same era and state of mind as CHICKEN.

bumper thumper. Minor car accident.

buried / buried in your car. Describing a car owner who owes more on the car than its trade-in value. See UPSIDE-DOWN.

burn rubber. To accelerate so fast as to produce smoke and tire squeal.

bushing. Jacking up the price of a car after the buyer has signed an agreement to buy it. The classic bushing occurs when a salesman uses a high trade-in figure to estimate the final cost to the buyer, only to have the sales manager disallow the figure after the contract to buy has been signed.

busted lung. Spark plug that is not firing.

Cackle crate. Truck hauling live poultry.

California stop. Rolling stop, not a full stop—from the common belief that Californians are avid but bad drivers.

cam. Camshaft.

cancer. Rust or corrosion.

car bra. Close-fitting cover to protect the front end of a car from flying debris. Also known as a front-end mask, or BRA.

carcass. An old tire.

cat. Short for a Caterpillar-brand engine in a truck.

cement mixer. Vehicle that makes loud noises.

channel. To lower the floor by lowering the chassis.

charger. Aggressive car racer; one who gets to the front and stays there.

cherry. Older car in excellent condition; a nice vehicle.

chicken. Hot-rod game in which two cars drive toward each other on a head-on collision course; the first driver to turn away is the chicken. This game, more talked about

chicken. (*continued*)
than actually played, was part of the outlaw image of the fifties hot-rod culture, and it is still used as a metaphor for unreasonable automotive risk.

chizzler. A Chrysler engine, to a hot-rodder.

chop. To cut the top of a car down; to edit. Custom cars are sometimes "chopped and channeled" (cut down and lowered).

chop job. A strategic high-speed bump, in auto racing.

chop shop. Place where stolen cars are cut up for their parts, which are sold separately.

Christmas tree. 1. Electronic device using lights to signal the preparation and start of drag races. 2. An array of flashing lights atop a police car, tow truck, fire engine, and ambulance. 3. Car loaded with gadgets and gizmos.

chute. A racetrack straightaway.

clamshell. Large hinged rooftop luggage carrier that is easily installed and removed and opens to accept luggage like a giant clam.

clean deal. Car sale that does not involve a trade-in.

clunker. A worn-out vehicle or machine, especially a car. The term has been in use since the 1940s. See IRON.

coffin box. Sleeper added to a conventional truck cab, a.k.a. suicide box.

cold car / cold one. In the used-car business, a make, model, or year of car that is not popular and is hard to sell. A car can be cold for no apparent reason other than the fact that it is not moving.

collected. Said of an innocent victim of a bad race-car driver.

come in. The sudden rush of power around 30 mph in some turbocharged cars when the turbocharger comes into play.

commuter hooter. Traffic reporter for broadcast media.

cooler. Air conditioner.

cop caller. Truck with squealing brakes.

cop stop. A roadblock.

copilot. Cosigner, in car sales.

corn binder. Any tractor made by International Harvester.

corner. A curve in auto racing.

cowpath. Trucker's term for any inferior (i.e., narrow) two-lane blacktop road.

crank. 1. The crankshaft. 2. To start a car; to crank her up.

crash cage. The confines of a stock car used in racing. It consists of tubular steel formed into a cage that protects the driver when the car crashes.

crate. An unreliable car in poor repair.

creampuff. A used car in fine, clean condition that has customer appeal.

creeper. A board on wheels on which a mechanic lies to slide under and work on a car.

croak and choke. Adding credit and disability insurance to a car loan.

Cruise, the. Organized gathering of specialty-car owners in which cars are displayed in roped-off areas. Described by the *Washington Post* on June 22, 1993: "The phenomenon is called the Cruise and it's the rage among mostly middle-aged men who gather in local parking lots to show off the dream cars they could never afford in their youth."

cruising. 1. Driving slowly up and down a particular stretch of town or city street, or through a particular area of town. 2. Moving along at a good clip, such as "cruising down the highway."

crunch. A crash in racing.

cube. Short for cubic feet.

curb lizard. Used-car dealer term for one who drives slowly past the car lot, but never seems inclined to stop.

curbstoner. Used-car dealer who operates with a few cars, a telephone, and splashy ads.

Dagoed. Dropped front axle on a custom street car, giving it the classic high-in-the-back and low-in-the-front look. It is pronounced day-goed and derives from the ethnic slur for Italian.

Darlington stripe. The distinctive scrape on the right side of a stock car that every NASCAR driver eventually acquires on turn 3 at Darlington International Speedway in South Carolina. At the Turn Left Racing Web site devoted to NASCAR news this is explained: "You have to race so close to the wall to get around that track that if you are running right, you get the stripe. It lets you know that you are right on the edge. If you miss the stripe, you get the wrecker 'cause you hit the wall a bit too hard."

dash. The dashboard.

dashboard dining. Eating in one's car.

day cab. Trucker's term for a tractor without a sleeping compartment.

dead man. Racing-crew member who controls the flow of fuel into the tank of a racer, so called because if there is a fire or other problem he can bring the flow of fuel to a dead stop.

dead sled. Nonworking or abandoned car.

deadhead. Trucker's term for running empty, without a load.

death wish. A motorcycle, especially to a truck driver.

deathtrap. Car that has rusted through, is banged up, and probably has bad brakes and faulty steering.

deck lid. Lid of a trunk.

demo. Sales term for a demonstration vehicle.

detailing. Sales term. The art of touching up a car to hide minor damage and imperfections. It is commonly performed in getting a used car ready for resale. See DOCTORED and DOPING.

deuce. A 1932 Ford coupé ("deuce" = 2). Both the car and term have been given a long lease on life through the Beach Boys' hit "Little Deuce Coupe." The '32 Ford was long the hot-rodder's dream car for souping up and customizing.

Detroit. American, as in "car air conditioning was a Detroit idea."

diapers. Winter covering for front end of a vehicle to keep engine and radiator warm; a trucker's term.

diesel bear. Cop who deals only with interstate truckers.

dimple. Dent.

dinghy. Vehicle towed behind an RV (recreational vehicle).

dirt tracking. A controlled slide in auto racing. See DRIFT.

dirty air. The air used and exhausted by the lead car in a race.

DNF. Did not finish (NASCAR).

DNQ. Did not qualify (NASCAR).

doctored. Said of a used car with defects hidden by cosmetics.

dog. Lousy car; one that nobody wants, usually because it needs a lot of work; a junker.

doing the push-ups. Salesroom slang for the preliminaries: getting to know the customer; presenting the car.

donut. 1. Tire. 2. In NASCAR-ese: the black circle you see on the side of a car after it has rubbed alongside another car.

doping. Any method used to hide the flaws in a car being prepared for resale. Some of these are legal, some are not.

double nickel. The 55 mph speed limit.

down / downstroke. Down payment.

downsizing. Reducing the size and weight of a vehicle to achieve better fuel economy. The term came into prominence in 1977, when Detroit began talking like this: "I think when the downsizing gets going we're going to push them right out to the shores." (Henry Ford II, on foreign competition.)

DP. Down payment; deposit.

drafting. Driving or racing close to the tail of another car to take advantage of the vacuum created, to literally be "pulled" by the draft of the lead car. It gives the drafted car extra power without using extra fuel.

drift. To make a controlled slide in racing. See DIRT TRACKING.

drink. To consume fuel, as in, "That car drinks too much."

drive-off. Person who fills his or her tank at a self-service pump and then drives off without paying. A headline in the March 27, 2005, *Frederick News-Post*: "Economic Losses from Drive-Offs Huge."

drop in. Placing a brand-new engine in a car.

drop the hammer. To pop the clutch in drag racing.

dubs. Twenty-inch wheels. As in "rolling on dubs."

dusting. Trucker's term for driving with one wheel off the side of the road to throw up a cloud of dust; done to discourage tailgating motorist or traffic cop.

Eatin' concrete. To drive a truck down a highway.

e-class. Type of Mercedes-Benz. Even though an e-class is a Benz, in rap or hip-hop circles especially, e-class refers to any really expensive car, such as a Mercedes, Bentley, Rolls-Royce, BMW.

edgy car. Car that needs body work, interior work, etc. Automotive equivalent of the "handyman's special" in real estate.

EIRI. "Except in rare instances"—the official NASCAR term used to enforce decisions when there may not be a specific rule or regulation to cover such a decision.

emerjensen. Trucker's term for the emergency brake.

eskimo. Trucker's term for a driver who drives with the windows open in the winter.

ET. Elapsed time, in car racing.

everybody rides. Sales term for a van.

executive. Sales term. A car that has been used by the dealership; a fancy name for a demo. On occasion it has been implied that an executive car was driven by a Detroit executive of the company.

exotics. Unusual, usually foreign, cars. When a rental-car company offers a Porsche or Rolls, they are said to be offering exotics.

eye trouble. Truck driver's term for the inability to stay awake.

Face-lift. In the used-car trade, rolling back the odometer.

factory. Refers to a manufacturer, or means "as manufactured." In racing, a factory team is one sponsored and supported by a manufacturer. In NASCAR racing the term refers to one of the big three auto manufacturers. In that context "factory days" refers to the 1950s and '60s, when Ford, GM, and Chrysler actively and openly provided sponsorship, money, and technical support to their race teams.

fender-bender. Minor accident.

fiddle. Radio. A car with a good fiddle is one with a premium sound system.

fifty-fifty warranty. No warranty. It is a reference to an old gag that goes: "If it breaks in half, we will warrant that you own both halves."

fire. Heater, especially in used-car sales.

flag-to-flag. Race car that started in first place and finished in first place.

flat-out. As fast as possible.

flea. Car buyer out to get a tremendous bargain.

flypaper. A speed trap, called flypaper because so many people get trapped.

forked-eight. V-8 engine.

four-banger. Four-cylinder engine.

four-wheeler. A car, to a driver of an eighteen-wheeler.

4WD / 4 × 4 / four-by-four. Four-wheel-drive vehicle.

455 air-conditioning. Cooling obtained while driving with four windows open at 55 mph.

front-end bra. Nylon wire or plastic-mesh cover fitted to the front of a car to protect it from flying gravel and other minor road hazards.

frozen. Locked up or jammed.

fueler. Short for TOP FUELER.

full dresser. Motorcycle configured to turn heads—sporting plenty of chrome, gold-plating, etc.

full house. Car or engine loaded with all the accessories and performance gimmicks.

funny car. A vehicle used for drag races only but sporting a chassis that replicates a street car.

Garage mahal. Opulent parking structure. A play on Taj Mahal, it may have been coined by the *Wall Street Journal* in a July 18, 1994, article entitled "Call It Garage Mahal: Lowly Parking Area Becomes Attraction," about an $80 million garage with "seven underground levels, a polished granite lobby, brass sheathing on its benches and Mozart softly playing in the elevators."

gas guzzler. Car that drinks fuel. Also simply known as a GUZZLER.

Gasoline Alley. The garage/pit area at the Indianapolis Speedway.

gearhead. Auto enthusiast who actually works on his own car(s).

Georgia credit card. Siphon for stealing gas from other people's tanks. Joseph C. Goulden notes, "In Texas we call them Okie credit cards; in Southern California, they are Tijuana credit cards."

getting stale. Vehicle that has not been sold for forty-five or more days, in the jargon of used-car sales.

glass. Fiberglass.

glazed donut. A recapped tire.

gnarly. Most dangerous route, to off-roaders—a gnarly way up the mountain.

gobble. To drive fast; to "gobble" up the road.

goin' down. Trucker talk for a run from north to south.

goin' up. Trucker talk for a run from south to north.

Goodyear. To run over and kill an animal; from the tire brand name.

gourd guard. Crash helmet.

greasy side up. Trucker talk for a car or truck that has flipped over on its back.

green pea. Auto-sales slang for an inexperienced buyer.

grenade. To blow an engine.

grid. The alignment of cars for the start of a race.

gridlock. Initially a name for a mythical moment at which all the cars and trucks in Manhattan would be in a huge traffic jam and unable to move forward or backward. The term is on its way to becoming a conventional term for any severe traffic jam.

grind. 1. Car buyer who is able to negotiate a low price on a new car. 2. To work a price down: "To grind the salesman." 3. Also, to grind the gears.

grinder. A shopper who grinds the salesman down.

groove. The best route around a track.

ground effect. Items that make a car standing still look like it is in motion. SPOILERS (air dams) and the like create the illusion.

gumball machine. The lights on top of a police cruiser.

gut. To remove the upholstery and other items from a car.

guts. The interior of a car.

guzzler. Car that consumes a lot of gasoline.

Hairy. Of racetrack traffic that is thick and fast.

halo car. Lead car in a dealer's line of cars—the best, brightest, and most expensive.

hand-grenaded. Racer's term for a major league engine failure.

hand job. Trucker term for freight that must be unloaded by hand.

handshaker. Car with stick shift.

hang. Make a turn, as in "hang a left." Once considered a teenage or hot-rodder term, "hanging a left" has become general slang.

HANS (acr). Head and neck safety device. It came into use after the death of driver

HANS (acr). *(continued)*
Dale Earnhart at Daytona in 2001. The device fits around the shoulders and attaches to the driver's helmet, thereby limiting whiplash in a crash.

happy hour. NASCAR-ese for the last official practice session held before an event. It takes place the day before the race and after all qualifying and support races have been completed.

happy man. Car dealers' traditional term for finance companies or loan officers.

hat. 1. Crash helmet. 2. Vinyl roof on a car.

hauler. Car that is really fast; one that hauls ass.

header. An exhaust manifold that is designed for the free flow of exhaust gases.

heap. An unreliable car, usually dented; a crate.

hell driver. Auto stuntmen who crashed cars for a living at fairs and carnivals. The hell driver Lee ("Lucky") Lott destroyed 17,981 cars while plying his trade.

hides. Tires.

high-ball. 1. In sales, to give an estimate that is too high. For instance, a salesman may suggest a higher price for a trade-in than the customer will get after it has been "reappraised." 2. Technique by which a very high price is offered for a trade-in vehicle, with the extra amount made up by increasing the price of the new car. See also BUSHING.

hitch-itch. Restlessness that sometimes overcomes RV owners after too much time in one place; the itch to hitch up the tow vehicle to the RV and take off.

holdback. An allowance, typically 2 or 3 percent of the manufacturer's suggested retail price, that most manufacturers give the dealer after a car has been sold. Because of holdback, a dealer is able to sell a vehicle for invoice price or slightly less and still make a profit.

honey bear. Female cop, to interstate truck drivers. Sometimes also SUGAR BEAR.

honking. At top speed, in racing: "Boy was I honking." Hauling ass.

hooptie. An old beat-up car; say, an unrestored 1972 Oldsmobile.

hot car. 1. Stolen car. 2. Used car in great demand because of such factors as condition (a CREAM PUFF), mileage, make, model, or year.

hot rod. Older car significantly modified, through engine, chassis, and body changes, for looks, speed, and acceleration. The term was first featured in *Life* magazine in 1945 and is relevant to a hot-rod culture that is still very much alive, especially on the West Coast.

house. A car dealership.

house broken. Used-car-dealer slang for a car that does not leak water, oil, or any other fluid.

HOV. High-occupancy vehicle, usually one with three or more people inside. The term is used on interstate highways to indicate preferential lanes for rush-hour cars with more than one or two drivers. Since it is really a reference to car pools, HOV has been said to stand for "highly obtuse verbiage."

huffers and puffers. Turbochargers and superchargers.

hundred-mile coffee. Strong coffee, to truckers. A cup of this stuff presumably has the ability to keep a tired driver awake for another 100 miles.

hundred pointer. Car that has been restored to mint condition.

hungry boards. Side boards on dump trailer, gravel truck, or the like, enabling it to carry more cargo. They are so named because a trucker using them must be hungry for money.

Idiot buttons. Same as BOTTS' DOTS.

idiot lights. Red lights on the instrument panel that flash on to warn the driver of an engine, brake, or electrical problem. They are stand-ins for formerly standard gauges with needles, and presumably take less intelligence to understand. It also alludes to the fact that these lights have been known to go on when nothing is wrong.

igniter. Ignition distributor.

Indy. Of or relating to the Indianapolis 500 and the cars that race in it, which are Indy cars.

inswept. Narrowed at the forward end. Said of an automobile frame when the side elements are closer together at the forward end than at the rear.

iron. 1. Dog of a car; a CLUNKER. 2. Tire chains. 3. Any old truck.

iron orchard. Used-car lot.

it's been muddy. Sales and auto auction term for a vehicle that has water or flood damage.

Jack. Showroom nickname for a looker with no intention of buying.

jackknife. To fold like a jackknife blade closing. Usually used to describe a tractor-trailer truck gone out of control, with its trailer bent around or broken loose from the cab.

jack-off bar. Emergency brake handle, to truck drivers.

Jack the Bear. According to a 1994 NASCAR glossary: "When someone says his car is running like 'Jack the Bear,' it is moving at optimum efficiency."

jam jar. Car, in Cockney rhyming slang.

Jersey barrier. A low, reinforced-concrete wall wider at the base, tapering vertically to near mid-height, then continuing straight up to its top. The shape is designed to direct automotive traffic back toward its own lane of travel and prevent cars from crossing a median or leaving the roadway. Commonly used on new and reconstructed bridges and as a means of street closure for security reasons. There are so many of these barriers around Washington, D.C., that in 2004 *The City Paper* dubbed the capital Jersey Barrier City.

jick-jack. Fast talk, in the parlance of used-car salesmen.

jug. Carburetor.

June bug. Derisive term used by stock-car racers for the Indianapolis racing car. Sometimes called a WATER BUG.

junker. Car that is in bad shape, almost ready for the junk heap.

Kennie. A Kenworth truck, to those who like them.

Kenworthless. A Kenworth truck, to those who dislike them.

kidney buster. A hard-driving truck.

kissed by the Santa Fe. A car that was wrecked and then repaired, according to an article on auto showroom slang in *Newsweek* (August 7, 1989). The reference is to the Santa Fe Railroad.

knee-deep in rubber. Sales term for a used vehicle with ample tread left on the tires.

knock-off. Quickly removable wheel lug.

Laha (acr). Life, accident, and health insurance (pron. "la-ha").

land yacht. Large, elaborately styled U.S. car of the 1960s or 1970s.

lay. Leave, as in "lay rubber," meaning to accelerate so fast as to leave black rubber tire marks on the pavement.

laydown. A potential buyer of a new or used car who does not think or ask questions. "Give me twenty laydowns and I can sell twenty cars," says one dealer.

Le Mans start. A racing start in which drivers run across the track, jump in their cars, and start their engines. It is named for the famous French race where this start originated.

leadfoot. Person who drives fast, keeps a heavy foot on the accelerator.

leg-pisser. Customer with no intention of buying; tire kicker.

lemon. A bad car, specifically, a new one with mechanical problems, although it can be used to describe a used car. The term has been in use since at least 1905, when the percentage of cars that were lemons was a lot higher than today.

lemon law. Legislation allowing the buyer of a lemon some legal recourse.

Liddy light. The additional back-window brake light that has become standard equipment on all new cars. It was championed by Ronald Reagan's Secretary of Transportation

Liddy light. (*continued*) Elizabeth Dole and took its name from her childhood nickname, Liddy.

light the rug / light the tires. To make the tires smoke.

lipstick. Cosmetic changes made to a new-model car to give the illusion that it is different from the previous model.

loaded. Describing a car with many extras and options.

lollipop man. Racing-crew member who holds pole and sign ("lollipop") over the pit wall to show the driver the pit location and stopping point.

long block. To a mechanic, this is complete engine minus the oil pump and oil pan.

loop. To spin out in auto racing.

loose stuff. Debris on the apron and near the outside wall of a track.

lot lizard. Truck-stop prostitute.

low-ball. 1. To offer a car at a low price to pique a buyer's interest. When the deal is about to be consummated the seller will jack the price up. 2. To offer a car at an outrageously low price for a trade-in or sale to a used-car dealer.

low brakes. Condition in which the brake pedal must be pushed closer to the floor than normal to get the car to stop.

low-rider. A car using hydraulic suspension which can be adjusted so that it rides only a few inches above the pavement with the ability to "bounce" or "hop." Popularized in the group War's funky 1975 hit "Low Rider" and numerous hip-hop videos.

lump. The engine.

lunch. To blow an engine, especially in drag racing. "He just lunched his second engine this month." See BLOW LUNCH.

lunch money. A down payment on a car.

Mag. 1. Short for magneto. 2. Wheel cast from magnesium; a mag wheel.

main. Street where cars cruise; not necessarily Main Street.

make. Manufacturer.

mall assault vehicles. SUVs that, despite their rugged looks and toughness, are used for hauling kids and shopping.

marbles. Racer's term for track debris—pebbles, tire fragments, etc.

mashed-potato drive. Automatic transmission.

may-pops. Cheap tires used by low-end used-car dealers who know that they look fine but "may pop."

McTruck. Lincoln Mark LT, a very expensive pickup truck. When the *New York Times* reviewed this vehicle on October 9, 2005, it was headlined: "A McTruck for the McMansion."

Mexican overdrive. Coasting downhill.

mild ones. Older bikers who, according to an article in *USA Today* in June 1996, "go grey, not crazy." The term is a play on the movie title *The Wild Ones*, about a motorcycle gang invading a small town.

mill. An engine.

Monroney. Dealer slang for the window sticker on a new car which breaks down costs, fees, and charges. Named for Senator A. S. "Mike" Monroney, who wrote the Automotive Information Disclosure Act which mandated stickers beginning in 1958.

moth-eaten. Of a car from a harsh-weather state where snow, ice, and road salt have caused corrosion.

mountain-climbing job. Moving-truck term for a job in which furniture must be carried up one or more flights of stairs.

mouse house. Dealership in which customers (mice) are fed through an assembly-line sales operation, from salespeople to contract writers or closers.

mud doggin'. Driving a four-wheel-drive vehicle off the road for pleasure.

mud flaps. Large flaps behind the back tires of trucks to protect it and vehicles behind it from flying debris, mud, and snow.

mudding. Participating in a mud race.

The Monroney Code

Stickers have their own importance in the car culture, and if you keep your Monroney it may actually increase the value of the car at resale, especially in the case of a car that might acquire classic status. Stickers often baffle those not in the business. Here are a few clues to the code:

ABS Antilock brakes.

A/C Air conditioning.

ALS All-season tires.

AWD All-wheel drive.

cas Cassette with radio.

DOHC Dual overhead cam engine.

EFI Electronic fuel injection.

ETR Electronic-tuned receiver; means you get a digital readout of the radio station.

HD Heavy-duty, of cooling or shocks.

int Intermittent wipers.

OD Overdrive.

odo Odometer.

OHC Overhead cam engine.

P/B Power brakes.

P/S Power steering.

pwr Power, as in "o/s pwr dr & pass mrrs" (outside power door and passenger mirrors).

rr Rear, as in "rr seat air ducts."

SK&SC Seek and scan on the radio.

SOHC Single overhead cam engine.

sp/spd Speed, as in "4-sp auto trans" (automatic transmission).

SRS Supplemental restraint system—an airbag.

TC Traction control.

whl Wheel, as in "steering whl radio controls."

whls Wheels, as in alloy or "chrome whls."

murdercycle. Motorcycle, especially in the slang of the long-distance trucker.

muscle. Power in a car, as opposed to the illusion of power given by styling, names, racing stripes, etc.

muscle car. Car of the sixties and seventies designed to look and perform like a race car but designed for regular roads, such as the Ford Torino, Oldsmobile 442, and Dodge Charger. Some later cars fit the category—for example, the 1990 Mustang GT 25th Anniversary car. The Muscle Car Club's Web site (www.muscleclub.com) states that its members believe that "there is no substitute for cubic inches and no replacement for displacement" and that they are tied to an era when "the number of cubic inches was more important than the number of cupholders, and quarter mile times meant more than inches of ground clearance."

Nerdmobile. Any dull full-sized car; family car.

nerf. To nudge another vehicle with your vehicle.

nerf bars. Special bumpers used for pushing other vehicles.

no-parker. Any large car.

Ocean fenders. Rippled or dented fenders—with waves in them.

on the floor. A floor-shift mechanism, as opposed to one on the steering post. Depending on the number of forward gears, a car may be said to have three, four, or five on the floor. An automatic floor gear post can be said to be "automatic on the floor."

on the hook. In tow; at the rear of a tow truck.

open the tap. Open the throttle.

out of the chute / gate / hole. The start of a drag race.

outlaw. Race-car driver who runs in a nonsanctioned event.

Oval Office. The NASCAR Web site: "Think of [the Oval Office] as the 'principal's office' for NASCAR. This is the where drivers go to discuss what happened during the race. If NASCAR thinks a driver has done something they shouldn't have, they are called into the Oval Office."

Pacer. 1. Driver who drives on a racetrack at a predetermined speed before the green flag is dropped. 2. Car that sets the pace for a race.

packing. Adding extra charges to the base price of a car, for dealer prep, document prep, finance fees, etc.

parking lot. Traffic backup to truckers and other users of CB radio.

parting out. Selling a car for its parts. Often used as a lead-in in want ads under "Automobile Accessories." An ad from the *Arkansas Democrat Gazette* reads: "PARTING OUT Dodge 1984 SWB Pickup; no motor, trans or front cap. Whole $500 cash."

pee-on. Decal commonly seen on pickup trucks, featuring a demonic-looking boy peeing on a logo, symbol, or word. Common peeons have the boy watering the Ford oval, the Chevy bow-tie logo, or the words "the boss."

piece. Car that is a piece of junk; piece of shit.

pimpmobile. A large and showy car with lots of chrome, as would be used by a pimp.

pipes. Dual-exhaust system.

pit. Service area; place where one makes a "pit stop."

pit lizard. Groupie, NASCAR style.

pit road. The area where pit crews service the cars. Generally located along the front straightaway.

pit stall. The area along the pit road that is designated for a particular team's use during pit stops.

plug-in. Hybrid vehicle that can be plugged into electrical outlets for added power.

pop the clutch. To engage the clutch suddenly.

popcorn eater. Person who wanders through a lot or showroom with no focus on buying.

post. The steering column.

pot. Carburetor.

OvalSpeak Decoded

Oval stickers—used in Europe to identify a car owner's country of origin—are turning up everywhere. Decades ago they migrated to the United States as a means of identifying a European vehicle's country of origin: GB for Great Britain, IRL for Ireland, S for Sweden. Now people use the stickers to individualize their car. What makes the new ovals so much fun is that many are cryptic and require decoding. What is more, they tend to reflect where the car owner would like to be rather than where she is—beach towns more than hometowns.

Some examples of the black and white ovals most likely to be spotted inside and just outside the Beltway surrounding Washington, D.C.:

26.2 marathoner; 13.1 stands for half-marathoner

ACK Nantucket (Massachusetts, from its three-letter airline-baggage code)

ANA Annapolis (Maryland)

BI Block Island (Rhode Island)

BFLO Buffalo (New York)

BNL Barenaked Ladies (a Canadian band)

CC Cape Cod, Massachusetts

CKA Canada Kicks Ass

CUSE Syracuse University

DMB Dave Matthews Band

FDR Frederick (Virginia)

GC Grand Canyon

GOB Good Old Boy

HI Hawaii

HI Hatteras Island (North Carolina)

HJ Hand Job

JVD Jost Van Dyke (in the British Virgin Islands)

GSM Great Smokey Mountains

GSM Gay Single Male

HUNG Hungry Mother State Park (Virginia)

ID Irish Dancer

IHC I Hate Clowns

JHULAX Johns Hopkins University Lacrosse

KLP Key Lime Pie

KW Key West

LAX Lacrosse aficionado (Lacrosse is called Lax among its players).

LDS Church of the Latter-Day Saints

LMAO Laughing My Ass Off

MAC Macintosh user

MIZZOU University of Missouri

MV Martha's Vineyard

NEK Northeast Kingdom (Vermont)

NH Nag's Head

OBX The Outer Banks (North Carolina)

OINC Ocracoke Island (North Carolina)

PBV Proud Bush Voter

PKV Proud Kerry Voter

RB Rehoboth Beach (Delaware)

RDNK Redneck

RKBA The Right to Keep and Bear Arms

SG Sales God

SGLY Smile. God Loves You.

SKLS Skaneateles (New York)

SK8 Skateboarder

STFU Shut The Fuck Up

SWO Stupid White Oval

TI Topsail Island (North Carolina)

TKPK Tacoma Park (Maryland)

VEG Vegetarian

VH Van Halen

VRWC Vast Right-Wing Conspiracy

WAHM Work-At-Home Mom

W1 Bush won

W2 George W. Bush: Won again

WINE Hammondsport (New York)

power. Sales term for electrically operated windows, brakes, and seats.

preacher's car. Car lacking expensive options.

puke. Blow an engine. See LUNCH.

pull. To remove, especially in auto repairs, where components are always pulled—never lifted—from under the hood. "He pulled the radiator."

pull system. System in which the factory builds only cars ordered by customers at dealerships.

pump the chump. To push additional features such as rustproofing and other high-profit options in new-car sales.

Quarterback. Car-sales term for a person whom a buyer brings with her to help her negotiate the best deal, for instance when a young woman brings her father or boyfriend. Salespeople hate them.

Ragged edge. Racing term for the limit; to run on the ragged edge is to push oneself to the point where it is difficult to maintain control.

ragjob / ragtop. Convertible.

rags. Bad tires, to a truck driver.

rail job. Dragster built on bare frame rails, or one that has been created by stripping a car down to its frame.

rails. Frame of a dragster.

raked. Describes a car with a lowered front end—a classic hot-rod look.

R&R. In auto mechanics, remove and repair or remove and replace.

rap. Motor knock, or noisy misfire.

rat. Car that performs poorly.

rat rod. Hot rod with a raw ("ratty") look, such as primer paint and parts obviously not designed to fit together.

reefer. Refrigerated cargo trailer.

repro. A repossessed car. One who does the work of repossession is called a repo man.

rest cure. Practice of sending a car to the repair shop and having it returned to the customer without anything being done to it.

rice burner. Japanese motorcycle or car.

ride. Car.

ride the rails. Racing technique that calls for taking the outside course on the flats and the high part of the banked curves.

rims. Wheels.

roach. 1. Car buyer without credit or with bad credit. 2. Term used by automobile auctioneers to describe dealers who write bad checks.

road pizza. Mature road kill to truckers and other users of CB radio.

road tar. Truckstop coffee.

roller. 1. Rolls-Royce. 2. A car in stock; one that a buyer can come into a dealership and see, buy, and drive home in.

roller skate. Subcompact.

rolling stolens. Police term used to describe a stolen car still occupied by suspected car thieves.

rookie strip. The yellow stripe across the back of all Nextel Cup rookie cars, which allows drivers to recognize rookie drivers on the track.

rubber. Tires.

rubber baby buggy bumpers. The "softened" front bumper on NASCAR cars, designed to discourage unnecessary, and therefore dangerous, bump-drafting at the Daytona International Speedway and Talladega Superspeedway. Bump-drafting is the art of planting the front bumper of a 3,400-pound Cup car squarely into the rear bumper of the car in front, creating a momentary rise in engine RPM and speed for both. When properly executed, bump-drafting allows the two drivers involved to break out of the side-by-side packs typical of plate racing.

rubberneck. To slow down and turn one's head around to look at an accident or other roadside event.

rumble strips. Roughened areas in a road designed to make a high-pitched rumbling noise to warn drivers to slow down.

runnin' hot. Trucker term for running a truck without the right permits, overweight, or otherwise outside the law.

runnin' legal. The opposite of RUNNIN' HOT.

rust bucket. A car that is rusted through.

Saddle. Driver's seat to a trucker.

sailboat fuel. Trucker talk for the cargo in an empty trailer.

say hello. To give a competing race car a tap on the rear bumper to let the driver know that you intend to drive through his space—a means of telling him to move over.

scuff. Racing term for a tire that has been used at least once and is held for a future race.

shade-tree mechanic. One who works out of his house or barn rather than at a dealership, service station, or garage.

shaky side. Trucker CB term for the West Coast, so called because of the western proclivity for earthquakes.

shaved. A car stripped of ornaments.

shillelagh. Chevy engine, especially an old V-8.

shotty. Call made when someone wants the good seat in the car, the front passenger seat. Short form of "shotgun." Formerly, calling "shotgun" got you this spot. It is derived from the person "riding shotgun, on the stagecoach in westerns, who sat up front to the right of the driver and carried a shotgun in preparation for any sign trouble.

shunt. A crash, in car racing.

sig alert. Los Angeles radio traffic advisory system. People often assume the term is a blend of "signal" and "alert," but is actually named for Loyd Sigmon, who invented the computer-based warning system.

sissy bar. Backrest on a motorcycle that a rider can use to keep from falling off.

six-banger/six-holer. Six-cylinder engine.

skating. In auto sales, moving in quickly to take another's prospects, for example, grabbing the next person through the door when the person who is supposed to get that customer is fetching a cup of coffee.

skeeching. Holding on to the bumper of a slow-moving car on a snowy or icy street and getting pulled along. Also known as shagging.

skid lid. Motorcycle helmet.

skins. Tires.

sled. 1. Big car; also a tank, boat. 2. To drive in snowy conditions; to drive in winter. 3. In the world of automobile auctions, a sled is a vehicle badly in need of repair.

slicks. Wide, smooth-tread racing tires which have better grip on a dry track. They're useless in the wet, which is why NASCAR events don't run when it rains.

slide-ruler. Person coming onto a used-car lot or into a showroom with a strong interest in things like miles per gallon, displacement, and EPA ratings and who often carries a calculator. Not beloved. Worse still is the pipe-smoking slide-ruler.

slingshot. 1. A racing maneuver in which a car following in the draft of another gets a sudden burst of speed by using the vacuum of the draft. See DRAFTING. 2. Dragster in which the driver sits behind the rear wheels, like a rock in a slingshot.

slippery. Streamlined.

slipstreaming. Driving or racing close to the tail of another car to take advantage of the reduced air resistance. Also DRAFTING.

slow motion. Prospective car buyer who tends to think things over.

slug. 1. Piston. 2. Used car in need of major repairs.

slush / slush box. Automatic transmission.

sneakers. Tires.

snooze patrol. Cruise control.

snowballs. Traditional big, showy white-wall tires—the kind you'd put on a restored Packard.

soil sampling. Race-car driver who has landed in the tall grass.

solid citizen. Person with good credit in car sales.

souped up. Customized for greater power and speed.

spaghetti. Excess chrome or trim on a car.

special. One of several terms used in car sales for a vehicle that has been advertised or promoted but not necessarily reduced in price, such as cars offered in "sellathons."

speed bumps. Term for raised areas in road to make drivers slow down and observe low speed limits.

spinner. One who illegally sets back the true mileage on used cars to get them ready for market.

spinners. Hubcaps that spin, giving the effect of the whole wheel moving when it's stationary.

splash-and-go. Racing pit stop for fuel only.

spoiler. Metal strip used to control drag, downforce, and airflow. Primarily found on race cars, they appear under the front end and atop the back end (where the trunk would be on a sedan).

sport ute. SUV (for "sport utility vehicle").

spot. Immediate delivery, in car sales.

spotter. In NASCAR racing, the person located high above the racetrack who communicates with the driver. The spotter's job is to tell the driver the location of other drivers on the track, and to warn him of accidents or debris on the track.

sprinkle a load. To make quick stops to partially unload a tractor-trailer.

sputes. Sport utility vehicles.

squint. Tinted windshield glass.

squirrelly. Racing term describing a car that is given to sliding and lack of control. It is said to come out of turns "loose in the rear."

squirt. Windshield cleaning solution.

stacking. In sales, lining up more prospects than you can handle; for example, sending a prospect to the back lot to look around while grabbing a second prospect.

stagger. Practice of racing with different-size tires on oval tracks: slightly larger tires on the outside of the oval give the car the natural tendency to turn left.

'Stang. Ford Mustang.

stick. 1. Of a manual, as opposed to automatic, transmission (stick shift). 2. To a race-car driver, tire traction.

sticker. 1. A new tire; "sticker" is the manufacturer's paper label. 2. Of a car, short for "sticker (the undiscounted) price," so called because an itemized price list is stuck to one of the car's windows.

sticks. Furniture, in the context of collateral for a car loan.

stock. From the factory; taken from the normal stock.

stove bolt. Chevrolet six-cylinder engine.

straight-liner. Drag racer.

straw hat. Convertible.

stroked. Souped or hopped up; specifically, an engine in which the piston stroke length has been increased.

stroker. 1. The opposite of a CHARGER: a driver who never tries to set the pace and is simply content to win. 2. A racer who cannot afford to replace a blown engine but gets money and a chance to race the following week if he finishes. To finish, he "strokes along."

stroking. Describes a race-car driver who "lays back" in a race so as not to severely punish his car before the end of the event.

submarine. Car that has been damaged by flooding. The term came into prominence in late 1965 when, according to the March 1968 *Esquire*, some 30,000 cars were waterlogged by Hurricane Betsy and "many were reconditioned to hide water damage, [and] shipped out of state."

sugar bear. Female cop, to interstate truck drivers. Sometimes also HONEY BEAR.

sugar scoop. An indented surface leading to an AIR SCOOP.

summertime truck. A truck that is hard to start in the cold weather.

SUV. Sport utility vehicle.

swinging load. Carcass meat, to a truck driver.

Tank. Big car.

T-bone. 1. Model T Ford. 2. To take an accidental right-angle shot at the side of another car. T-bone wrecks killed the stock-car legend Tiny Lund in 1975 and ended the career of Bobby Allison in 1988.

T-bucket. Souped-up Model T Ford.

Texas rat. Used car originally owned by a long-distance driver.

three on the tree. Standard shift on a column, with three forward gears.

throw under a bus. Sales talk for selling someone a car or van with all the extras and options at full sticker price or better.

ticket. 1. A summons or citation. 2. Driver's license.

ticket taker. A driver with many traffic tickets.

Tin Lizzie. Ford Model T.

tired iron / tired rat. A beat-up car.

toad, the. Punning name for the car or other vehicle towed by an RV.

tool. To drive.

toothpick run. Trucker slang for a load of lumber.

top eliminator. Overall winner at a drag race, so called because he has eliminated all other drivers.

top fueler. State-of-the-art dragster.

tossing a rod. Blowing an engine; throwing a rod.

tourists. People who come to look at cars they cannot afford.

trailer queen. A classic car that has been restored but is never driven on the street and is taken from car show to car show on a trailer.

tranny. Transmission.

trans. Transportation, i.e., a vehicle of any sort, as in, "I'm dying for a pizza. Who's got trans?"

tub. The chassis of an Indy car, into which the driver fits.

turbo lag. The split second between slamming the accelerator to the floor and experiencing the takeoff of a turbocharged car.

turn. To generate or achieve a speed, as in "I turned eighty in the curve."

turtle shell. Trunk or trunk lid of a car.

tweak. 1. Small engine modification made to improve performance. 2. Modifications made by a manufacturer prior to a model's introduction. "Chrysler says it has 'tweaked' the design of its all new minivan, slated to make its debut next year" (*USA Today*, December 13, 1994).

200-mile tape. Duct tape so strong it can be used to hold a banged-up racer together to finish a race; racer's tape.

Unblown. Without a blower, or supercharger.

uncorked. Running without mufflers.

unglued. Blown, as in a "blown engine."

unhorsing. Getting a customer to give up his/her car for a long appraisal period so that the time can be used to sell the customer.

unloading. Losing part of a car, such as a dragster unloading a tire.

up. The next person through the door, as in, "This is your up." For a sales rep to take another person's walk-in is "snaking an up."

upside-down. Same as BURIED.

ute. Utility vehicle.

Vanity plate. License plate customized for the owner of the car using initials, nickname, spouse's name, etc.

ventilate the block. To throw a rod through the engine; to wreck the engine.

'Vette. Corvette.

volcano. Car that burns a lot of oil.

vulture. Trucker term for spotter plane looking for speeders.

Wagon. Station wagon.

waif. Inexperienced buyer, in car sales.

wail. To run fast and free.

walking the dog. Race-car driver who is running away from the field.

water bug. Same as JUNE BUG.

water dog. Trucker term for a truck with leaky water lines requiring frequent refilling.

waterslide. Wet highway, especially to a trucker.

wayback. The area behind the backseat in a station wagon or van.

wheel. To operate a car.

wheel kicker. A would-be buyer who is actually only interested in looking.

wheels. A car.

whiner. Car making an unpleasant noise.

whiskey rash. Disease afflicting cars belonging to habitual drunks. It is used in the used-car trade for a late-model car with numerous scrapes and dents acquired at different times.

wind. Air-conditioning, especially in an old, antique, or classic car.

windmill. Radiator fan.

window net. A mesh covering over a NASCAR driver's window to prevent a driver's arm from being exposed in a crash. Lowering the net after a crash is a signal from the driver that he is okay.

windows. Power windows, in used-car-dealer terminology.

winter-beater. Cheap, old car with dependable engine and heater driven during the worst of the winter while one's regular car is in storage.

wiped. To be beaten or overtaken in a race.

wired. With wire wheels.

wires. Wire wheels.

without shots. Out of warranty; car sold with no guarantees. Alludes to innoculations and injections (shots) against disease.

working for Exxon. Said of a truck that gets particularly bad mileage.

wrecker. A tow truck.

wrench. Mechanic, especially a racing mechanic.

wrinkle-rod. The crankshaft.

Yardstick. Mile marker along highway.

yell bell. Theft alarm.

yellowtail. A rookie driver, who may be required to race with a yellow back bumper to alert others to his inexperience.

YMMV. Your mileage may vary. A popular qualifier meaning "the outcome may be different under different conditions." It is sometimes used to talk about a promise not kept.

Z. To reinforce and lower the frame of your car, as in "That car's been z'd."

z-car. A high-performance car. From the 1970 Datsun 240Z and on through the Nissan 350Z, the Camaro Z-28, and the BMW Z4.

zephyr haul. Trucker's term for a light load.

zoomy. A wild street rod with open exhaust pipes.

AVIATION AND SPACE 3

Words from the Wild Blue Yonder

"Can You Talk the Language of the Age of Space?"

—Title of Air Force recruiting brochure, late 1950s

During World War II there was so much aviation slang used by American fliers and their RAF counterparts that the newspapers had to run occasional articles to point out that bombs were eggs, anti-aircraft balloons were pigs, planes were kites or crates, student pilots were kiwis, a routine flight was a milk run, and the cockpit was a pulpit.

Then, in the 1950s, jets, missiles, rockets, and satellites came into the picture and to a large degree aviation slang gave way to technical terminology. But this is not to say that there aren't plenty of ripe, colorful terms flying about out there. Here are examples from commercial, general, and military aviation as well as space exploration.

Ace face (military). Red lines on a pilot's face left by a tight-fitting oxygen mask.

air boss (Navy). On board a carrier, the head of the air department; he rules the flight deck.

air rage (commercial). Airborne equivalent of "road rage," referring to any out-of-control passenger.

aluminum cloud (military). The F-14 aircraft is so large that it is sometimes called this.

angels (military). Altitude, measured in thousands of feet. "Angels fifteen" means 15,000 feet above sea level. Also, a term lovingly used for the rescue helicopter by any aviator who has experienced an ejection and subsequent helicopter rescue.

A-OK (space). Fine; the best.

apex (acr; commercial). Advance purchase.

arcing around (Navy). Vigorous but aimless activity.

auntie (military). The prefix "anti," as in antimissile missile, used as a noun.

Back of the bus (commercial). Tourist class.

back to the taxpayers (military). Where you send a wrecked aircraft.

backout (space). Reversing a countdown because of a component failure or bad weather.

bag season (military). Cold weather or water conditions that require the wearing of anti-exposure gear, which is very restrictive, uncomfortable, and unpopular.

balloon meister. Official who instructs contestants in a ballooning competition on the exact requirements of the tasks they are to perform.

bandit (military). Dogfight adversary positively identified as a bad guy. Hostile aircraft.

bang one on. To make a bumpy landing, as opposed to GREASE IT.

barbecue mode (space). An orbiter taking a slow roll in space for thermal conditioning.

barber pole (commercial). A plane's maximum speed.

barf, beer, and a cigar (Navy). Fighter pilot's breakfast. Also "coke, smoke, and a puke."

belly landing. Landing without the benefit of wheels.

bent (military). Damaged or broken.

bingo (military). Minimum fuel for a comfortable and safe return to base. An aircraft can fly and fight past bingo fuel in combat situations, but at considerable peril.

bird (space and military). 1. Pilotless objects that fly, such as satellites and probes. 2. Helicopter.

bird watcher. Name given to those who lined the beaches around Cape Canaveral and the Kennedy Spaceflight Center to watch space launches. Sometimes also said of the press.

birdcage (commercial). The controlled airspace in the immediate vicinity of an airport.

birdman (Air Force). Pilot.

birds (military). Aircraft.

black box (commercial). A plane's flight-data recorder, which records all of a craft's functions—altitude, speed, and engine data—and the cockpit crew's conversations.

blow show (commercial). Airsickness, or a flight on which many passengers got sick.

blower (military). Afterburner, a device that injects fuel into a hot exhaust for extra thrust.

blowoff (space). The separation, by explosive force, of an instrument section or other package from a rocket vehicle.

blue letter (commercial). Letter of complaint about a flight attendant.

blue room (commercial). Lavatory on an airplane.

boilerplate (space). A metal replica of the flight model (e.g., of a spacecraft) but usually heavier and cruder for test purposes. This is an interesting transfer of an old newspaper term to a new realm. Its first meaning was syndicated material supplied to newspapers in plate form.

bootstrapping. The process which enables any device, such as a turbo pump, to feed back part of its output to create more energy and thus function independently. Etymology: from the notion of independence from the phrase "by one's own bootstraps."

borex (Navy). A dull, repetitive exercise (a busy, tense one might be a "sweatex").

bounce / tap (military). Unexpected attack on another aircraft.

bubbas (Navy). Fellow squadron members; anyone who flies the same aircraft as you do.

bucket shop (commercial). Place offering cheaper fares on major airlines; a consolidator.

bug smashers (commercial). Small private planes, especially when they are in congested areas.

bump (commercial). To remove a passenger with confirmed reservation because of overbooking. Domestic airlines must compensate a passenger who is bumped.

bumpee (commercial). One who has been bumped from a scheduled airline flight. A bumpee can be denied a seat because of overbooking or can volunteer to give up a seat for a reward, usually a free ticket.

bunt. Pilot slang for throwing the plane into a steep dive to avoid collision or other hazard.

burnout (military and space). The moment of final oxidization or combustion of fuel. Burnout velocity is the speed of a rocket or airborne vehicle at the moment it runs out of fuel. This term, which dates back at least to the early 1950s, turned up in the work context as "teacher burnout," "job burnout."

buzz. To fly low over an area, as in, "Let's buzz Toledo."

Caca, lala. Semi-acronyms for "collision alert" and "low-altitude alert," which appear as flashing signals on cathode ray tube (CRT) radarscopes.

carry-on (commercial). 1. Luggage carried aboard an airplane by the passenger. 2. A passenger carried onto a plane in a wheelchair.

catshot (Navy). A carrier takeoff assisted by a steam-powered catapult. A "cold cat," one in which insufficient launch pressure has been set into the device, can place the hapless aircraft in the water. A "hot cat," too much pressure, is less perilous, but can rip out the nose-wheel assembly or the launching bridle. These problems, once common, are practically unheard of today.

cattle class (commercial). Economy or coach class.

checking for light leaks (military). Taking a nap (refers to the eyelids).

cherry picker. Jointed crane with a small cupola at the end for lifting an astronaut into a space capsule.

cherubs (military). Altitude under 1,000 feet, measured in hundreds of feet ("cherubs two" means 200 feet).

chicken switch (space). An abort switch or any other control that stops the mission.

chicks in tow (military). Fighters lined up for midair refueling.

Chinese landing. Landing with one wing lower than the other. This would appear to be based on the fact that "one wing low" sounds like a Chinese name, rather than on an ethnic slur.

claw (commercial). First-time flyer.

cockpit queen. Female flight attendant who spends a lot of time socializing with the pilots.

cod (acr; naval). Carrier onboard delivery, a plane that delivers mail and other supplies to an aircraft carrier.

combat dump (military). A bowel movement before flying. Also, "sending an admiral to sea."

conk out. Sudden loss of an engine during a flight.

controlled flight into terrain (commercial). A perfectly flyable plane hitting the ground.

counting the rivets (commercial). When another aircraft comes too close.

crashbait (commercial). Frequent flyer.

crawlerway (space). Heavily reinforced road built for transporting space vehicles and rockets.

Dayside (space). The portion of a planet or the moon illuminated by the sun's light.

deadheading (commercial). For a crew member to fly (free) as a passenger, either to return home or to catch a flight to which he or she is assigned. One is only considered to be deadheading when in uniform, so going on vacation in civvies does not count.

deal (commercial). Any passenger who needs special assistance, such as a child traveling alone or someone in a wheelchair. The gate agent will go to the plane when the door opens on arrival and ask the flight attendant, "Got any deals?"

decay (space). Loss of energy.

deep space (space). Beyond Pluto.

dirt dive. To research a skydive on the groud.

doghouse (space). In the vernacular of the early days of rocket flight, the moundlike housing for instruments on an otherwise smooth skin of a rocket.

dogleg (space). Change in launch trajectory to achieve a better orbit.

dogs (commercial). Passengers.

doolie (Air Force). Air Force academy cadet.

double ugly (military). Fond nickname for the enormously capable but less than beautiful F-4 Phantom. See also RHINO.

drift factor (military). If you have a high one, you aren't reliable.

driver (Navy). Pilot.

drone (Military). Unmanned aircraft.

drop zone. A center for skydivers.

dry run (military and space). A practice or rehearsal.

Elephant (Navy). Big shot; officer above the rank of Navy captain.

empty kitchen (commercial). Derogatory name given to female pilots by males—presumably from the fact that the woman is in the cockpit of a plane rather than at home in her kitchen.

empty leg (commercial). An empty flight between two consecutive scheduled stops.

envelope. 1. In military aviation, the maximum performance parameters of an aircraft; flying at the edge of the envelope can be both exciting and dangerous. 2. In ballooning, another name for the balloon.

equipment (commercial). The plane. If you are told that there has been a slight delay in the arrival of the equipment, it means your plane is late.

exotic. Fuel that delivers a great deal of power for its weight and volume.

eyeball instrumentation. Visual inspection.

Fangs out (military). When a pilot is really hot for a dogfight.

fangs sunk in floorboard (military). When a fighter pilot boresights on a kill but ends up getting shot himself.

fare jumping (commercial). The tendency of online airfares to rise in a very short time period. In an article on the topic, the *Baltimore Sun* (April 17, 2005) noted: "One first class fare on Expedia increased $748, from 641.19 to $1,389.19 in less than 30 seconds."

fat Albert (Air Force). Wide-bodied jumbo jet.

feet wet/dry (Navy). The former means "over water," the latter "over land."

fifi (commercial). An Airbus plane (made in France).

flat-hatting (Navy). Unauthorized low-level flying and stunting. It is thrilling, sometimes fatal, and usually career-ending if one is caught.

fly by wire (military and space). To fly by autopilot.

flyby. A spacecraft passing within the vicinity of a planet or other object.

flying coffin. Dilapidated aircraft.

footprint (space). The space taken up by a spacecraft after it has landed.

frequent-dyer program. Free flight coupons which funeral directors receive after they have shipped a certain number of bodies (known as ship-outs).

furball (military). A confused aerial engagement with many combatants. Several aircraft in tight air-combat maneuvering (ACM).

Gas burner (Navy). Unproductive, long-winded officer.

geese. 1. (commercial) Passengers (pejorative). 2. (military) Bombers in formation, in World War II slang.

gizmo (military). Piece of technical gear. Also: doodad, thingamabob, or hoo-ha.

go juice (military). Jet fuel.

go–no go (space). The decision to launch or not launch; the point of no return.

go-round. An aborted landing.

goo (military). Bad weather that makes it impossible to see; in the clouds.

good up (military). Screw up.

grav field (space). Gravitational field.

grease it. Pilotese for a smooth landing.

green apple (military). The control knob for the cockpit's emergency oxgen supply.

greenie board (Navy). Prominently displayed squadron scoreboard where the landing-signal officers rate the pilots' carrier landings. Any color other than green is bad. Also called the "weenie board."

ground stop (commercial). Airport delay during which planes at an airport are not allowed to depart if they are bound for destinations experiencing bad weather.

Hangar queen (military). An aircraft that suffers chronic "downs." Hangar queens are often pirated for spares for the squadron's other aircraft, so when the aircraft leave the carrier at the end of the cruise, the maintenance officer normally flies the hangar queen because he knows which parts have been taken, such as the "queen's" ejection seats.

hawk (commercial). Passenger who causes trouble. Sometimes called a VULTURE.

high warble (Navy). Unduly agitated.

hit the silk (military). To bail out.

holding hands (military). Flying in close formation.

hummer (military). Any ingenious machine—plane, car, or weapon—whose actual name can't be recalled. Also "puppy," "bad boy." The E-2 Hawkeye early-warning aircraft is also nicknamed "hummer," in reference to the sound of its turboprop engines.

Icing. The phenomenon of ice accumulating on aircraft.

in the drink (military). Down at sea.

Indian night noises (Navy). The ominous creaks, pops, and shudders of an aircraft in flight.

Indians (commercial). Small private planes. Same as BUG SMASHERS.

irates (commercial). Angry, unruly passengers who vent their frustrations on airline personnel.

Judy (Navy). Radio call signaling that your quarry is in sight and you are taking control of the intercept.

jump-seat sniffer (commercial). Derogatory "STEW talk" for a passenger who chases female flight attendants, who sit in the plane's jump seats. This term was first given wide circulation in Jay David's *Sex and the Single Stewardess*. Also LOBBY LOCUST.

Kick the tires and light the fires (military). Formerly, to bypass or severely shorten the required routine of physically inspecting the aircraft prior to flight. Current meaning: "Let's get this aircraft preflighted and outta here, pronto."

kiss 'em (commercial). The pilots' final announcement to passengers before landing, thanking them for flying.

kiwi. Grounded pilot.

K-ops (acr; space). "One thousand (K) operations per second." Measurements relevant to space exploration call for much use of the letter K, which stands for "kilo," one thousand in the metric system of measurement. For example, "K-gal" means one thousand gallons.

LAX (commercial). The three-letter baggage-ticket code of Los Angeles International Airport. Other airport codes that have been adopted for conversation are ORD for O'Hare Airport in Chicago and MIA for Miami.

layover (commercial). Time spent by a member of a flight crew in a city other than that person's home base.

leapex (Navy). A jump-through-your-ass project, exercise, or drill. Something silly that needs to be done *now*!

leather or feather (commercial). "The choice between filet mignon and chicken cordon bleu that pilots are offered on board" (*Newsweek*, July 3, 1989).

lobby locust (commercial). Term used by female flight attendants for a man who hangs around hotel lobbies trying to pick them up. See JUMP-SEAT SNIFFER.

lost the bubble (military). Got confused or forgot what was happening.

lox (acr; military aviation and space). Liquid oxygen.

loxing (military and space). The job of loading liquid oxygen into the fuel tanks of a missile or space vehicle.

LTA (ballooning). Lighter than air.

Mad dog (commercial). A nickname for a Douglas MD-88, a 142-passenger plane.

mark one eyeball. Human sight. This term came into play during the moon landings, which were helped considerably by the "mark one eyeball."

Marsdoggle (space). A blend of "Mars" and boondoggle, a wasteful and highly expensive mission to Mars.

Martin-Baker fan club (Navy). If you eject, you're a member—the reference is to the Martin-Baker company, the manufacturer of ejection seats. An official list of members is maintained.

meatball / the meatball. Nickname for the NASA seal as it was first designed in 1959. After an official seal was designed, this emblem proposed by James Modarelli, the head of Lewis's Research Reports Division, was used as the more informal of the two. The sphere represents a planet, the stars symbolize space, and the red chevron signifies aeronautics (the latest design in hypersonic wings in 1959) with an orbiting spacecraft around the wing. In 1992, administrator Dan Goldin brought NASA's meatball back from retirement in order to invoke memories of the glory days of the Apollo Project and to show that "the magic is back at NASA."

metsat (space). Meteorological satellite, for short.

milk run (military). Routine mission flown repeatedly.

miracle flight (commercial). A wheelchair-bound passenger who gets to the front of the line and then leaps to his or her feet after boarding.

motorman's pal (space). A tube attached to the lining of a space suit used for collecting urine samples during flight. The allusion is to the device strapped to the leg of male streetcar workers on long runs.

my fun meter is pegged (military). Sarcastic comment for "I am not enjoying this."

Nasa (acr). Never a straight answer, used traditionally by reporters covering NASA, the National Aeronautics and Space Administration.

near space. Near the earth.

nerd bird. Flight between two locations with high employment in electronics and information technology—Austin to San Jose, for example.

NMA (commercial). "Not my aisle," used when there is a problem in another flight attendant's aisle.

no-fly list. Post-9/11 term for list of those who are not allowed to fly on airlines.

no joy (military). No other aircraft in sight.

no-load (military). An underachiever.

no-op. A plane that will not operate; a flight that has been canceled.

no-show (commercial). A passenger who does not appear for a flight on which he or she holds a reservation.

nose-picking speed (Navy). Pointlessly slow.

NRSA (commercial). "Nonrevenue space available." Means nonpaying passengers such as deadheading crew can get a free ride. They may board only after paid seats have been filled.

nugget (military). A first-tour aviator.

nylon letdown (military). Ejection and subsequent parachute ride.

Offline (commercial). Travel on a carrier other than the one that sold the passenger the ticket.

open jaw (commercial). Describes a trip and the ticket for that trip with different destination and departure points.

opportunity to excel (military). A disagreeable job, absent the time or resources needed to complete it properly.

Padlocked (military). To have a BANDIT firmly in your sights.

passing gas (military). What an aerial tanker does—literally, it passes gasoline in midair.

PAX (commercial). A passenger, from the ticket code for "passenger."

penalty box (commercial). An inactive runway where incoming aircraft wait until a gate becomes available.

pinkie (Navy). A landing made at twilight between official sunset or sunrise time and true darkness. It counts officially as a night landing, but is cheating, and is many senior officers' preferred type of "night" landing.

piss quiz. A surprise urine test for drugs.

pit (commercial). The belly of the plane, where baggage is stored.

plumber (military). An inept pilot.

pod. Detachable compartment of a spacecraft.

power puke / power barf (military). Projectile vomiting, a symptom of airsickness.

puffer machine. Airport machine that sucks in the air around passengers and within seconds determines whether they've been in contact with explosives. Used by the Transportation Security Agency.

puke (military). Someone who flies a different kind of aircraft than you; for example, a fighter puke or an attack puke.

punch out (military). To eject.

push, the (commercial). Time of maximum traffic at the airport; for example, the late-afternoon rush hour at the beginning of the Thanksgiving weekend.

push the envelope. To reach beyond the boundaries; to stretch or exceed known limits. Tom Wolfe popularized this term in his 1979 book *The Right Stuff*: "Pushing the outside, probing the outside limits, of the envelope seemed to be the great challenge and satisfaction of the space flight."

PZ. Prohibited zone over which balloons are restricted from flying, such as prisons.

Quiet sun. Condition of the sun when it is relatively free of sunspots and other factors that interfere with radio transmission.

Rabbit (commercial). System of white strobe lights that flash in sequence to give a pilot the illusion that a white ball is guiding him up the runway.

ramp (commercial). The giant paved area around the gates where jets are parked. Formerly called the tarmac.

redcoats (commercial). Passenger service agents, the senior employees who wear red jackets and patrol the terminal to help passengers with problems.

red-eye (commercial). A late-night flight, commonly a midnight flight between the West and East Coasts, as in "I came in on the red-eye from L.A."

retros (space). Braking rockets, or retrorockets.

rhino (military). Nickname for the F-4 Phantom. See also DOUBLE UGLY.

roach coach (commercial). Flight to the tropics.

road warriors (commercial). Frequent business travelers.

rocket science / scientist. A measure of intelligence, or lack thereof, needed for a task: "You don't have to be a rocket scientist to . . ."; "It's not rocket science."

rockoon. Blend of "rocket" and "balloon," it describes a rocket launched from a balloon.

rotation (commercial). When a plane's nose wheel lifts off the runway.

Sardine class (commercial). Coach or tourist class.

scramble (military). To take off in a hurry.

scrub. To cancel or to back out of a countdown.

seat pitch (commercial). Jargon for leg room.

sending an admiral to sea (Navy). A bowel movement before flying. See COMBAT DUMP.

sierra hotel (Navy). "Shit hot," the pilot's favorite and all-purpose expression of approval. In Navy communications, the letter *S* is "sierra" and *H* is "hotel."

ROCKET SCIENCE 101

The term "rocket science" saw use as early as October 10, 1957, in the *New York Times*, in reference to the Army missile team in Huntsville, Alabama. Later Wernher von Braun was often identified as America's leading rocket scientist. The saying "It's not rocket science" was probably inspired by an oft-quoted full-page ad run in the *New York Times* in 1957, a reprint of an October 15 editorial in *Missiles and Rockets* directed toward President Eisenhower. It ends with this line: "You don't have to be a scientist, Mr. President, to solve this problem. You must be a leader."

skygod. Superior skydiver, but a term that can also be used disparagingly for a jumper with more ego than ability.

slam dunk (commercial). Landing technique that allows the plane to stay above traffic until the last minute, at which point it quickly drops to land.

smallsat (space). Small satellite.

smoking hole (military). An airplane crash site.

souls on board / SOB (commercial). The number of people aboard a plane, passengers and crew.

soup. Fog.

space cadet. Early nickname for space enthusiasts. Initially used by the U.S. Army's missile development group to describe themselves, it is still used to describe those who want a full-fledged manned program and a return to the moon. The term dates to a children's book of the same name by Robert Heinlein and given a big boost from the syndicated television show *Tom Corbett, Space Cadet*, which premiered in 1955. It was set in the year 2355.

space junk. Debris in earth orbit.

spacetug. Utility vehicle for servicing orbiting space stations.

spaghetti suit. The long underwear worn by astronauts, which is composed in part of tubes that carry cool water.

spam in a can. Human in a space vehicle. The original *Mercury* astronauts, who were willing to sit atop a rocket booster in a tiny capsule to be sent into space, let it be known that this was how they felt.

splashdown. The landing of a space vehicle in the ocean.

squawk code. A code assigned to each aircraft, which allows it to dial up and onto the radar system, where it can be identified and watched by Air Traffic Control.

starship. Interstellar vehicle.

static line. Type of skydiving jump in which a rope attached to the plane automatically pulls the chute cord.

stew (commercial). Stewardess.

stew zoo (commercial). An apartment where a lot of female flight attendants live, or a hotel where they lay over.

stick shaker. An alerting device in a cockpit that indicates if a stall condition may be in the offing.

stick-throttle interconnect (military). Mock-tech term for a pilot (also called just a "stick").

stuff. Clouds or weather, to any pilot.

Three-pointer. Aircraft landing in which the three sets of wheels all touch down at the same time; a good landing.

tiger (military). An aggressive pilot.

tinman. Aluminum space suit.

tits machine (Navy). According to a collection of military aviation slang on the Internet, this is "a good, righteous airplane.

tits machine (Navy). (*continued*) Current airplanes need not apply. This is a nostalgic term referring to birds gone by. By all accounts the F-8 Crusader was a tits machine."

touchdown. Landing of a manned or unmanned spacecraft on the surface of the moon, a planet, or on its return to earth.

trick-or-treat (military). If you don't make this pass, you will fail.

TSA. Transportation Security Agency, an agency established in 2001 immediately following the 9/11 attacks to safeguard United States transportation systems and ensure safe air travel. Others think TSA stands for "thousands standing around"; "take your shoes off, asshole"; "taxpayers screwed again"; "totalitarian security assholes"; "too stupid already"; and more.

turn-around / turn-around flight (commercial). Flight that returns a crew or crew member his or her base on the day of departure.

UDIWOF. Upside Down in the Weeds on Fire—in other words, not good.

unk. Unknown.

unobtanium. Facetious though useful term, in the early days of the American space program, for a substance that "either theoretically cannot exist or that cannot be produced because technology is insufficiently advanced."

upgrade (commercial). To move from tourist to first class.

VIP. Very Inspected Person. Term TSA screeners use for the randomly chosen "selectees" who are given a major search.

vomit comet. Any flight or mission that induces nausea. The ultimate vomit comet may have been the KC-135 aircraft used to film the movie *Apollo 13*, in which weightlessness was simulated and filmed by going into a steep dive from a steep climb at high altitude.

vulture (commercial). A troublesome passenger. Also known as a HAWK.

WAG (military). Wild-ass flying guess.

Warthog (military). Universal nickname for the A-10 Thunderbolt II close air support aircraft.

water walker (Navy). High performer.

week in the barrel. Astronaut's slang for periods of time spent publicizing and marketing the space program, especially in the home districts of key members of Congress.

wet lease (commercial). Leasing agreement for an aircraft that includes the crew and supporting services.

white-knuckler. 1. Short-haul commuter airline flight. 2. Any flight on which there is turbulence or a close call.

worm. NASA logo in which the name is spelled out in an angular script that has a wormlike appearance. It has battled the traditional MEATBALL logo at the highest level of the space agency.

wrong side of the curtain (commercial). Tourist or economy class.

XTAL. NASA-ese for crystal. Over time the National Aeronautics and Space Administration has developed thousands of acronyms and abbreviations. For reasons unclear, many of them shorten words using the letter X. Others include XFER for transfer, XFD for cross feed, XPNDR for transponder, and XMT for transmit.

Zero-dark-thirty (military). Technically a half hour after midnight, but commonly used to describe any event that is scheduled to take place after midnight and before sunrise.

zero g (military and space). Zero gravity, the state of weightlessness.

zip fuel (military and space). High-energy jet fuel.

zoombag (military). Flight suit.

4

BUREAUCRATESE

The Talk of the White-Collar Bailiwick

The purpose of Newspeak was not only to provide a medium of expression for the world-view and mental habits of the devotees . . . but to make all other modes of thought impossible.

—George Orwell, *1984*

The language used is bureaucratic gobbledygook, jargon, double talk, a form of officialese, federalese and insurancese, and double speak. It does not qualify as English.

—Judge Jack B. Weinstein, ordering the government to simplify Medicare forms, July 11, 1984

The classical language of public health and health care is a throwback to a time gone by. Rooted in bureaucratic jargon such as "needs assessment" and military terms such as "surveillance," "targeting," and "intervention," it represents a striking paradox. It not only fails to capture the essence of our work, but it also has the potential to break down and fracture the trust between our profession and the public that is necessary for our work to make a difference. The challenge is to simplify the language that we use, to clarify it, get rid of bureaucratic jargon and paradoxical acronyms so that it is more humane and more in synch with inspiring hope.

—Richard Aronson, medical director of the Maternal and Child Health program of the Maine Bureau of Health

Most people think of bureaucratese as a feature of communication by the federal government, but it is spoken and written, with variations, in many other places. It seems to be used anywhere that people are sorted into departments and divisions and communicate with each other through memos and interoffice mail.

It is the linguistic fuel of state and local government, think tanks, and consulting firms, educational administration, nonprofit organizations, and much of corporate America. Increasingly, bureaucratese is the lingo of white-collar America. Subdivisions of this lingo have emerged in education (educanto), planning (plannish, or urbabble, in the case of urban planning), the government (bureaucratese, clerk-speak, governmentese, officialese, or, as the late, ever-provocative San Francisco columnist Herb Caen put it, bureaucrapese), and specific agencies of government (statese at the State Department).

It is proliferating, seeming to grow and reinforce itself with each new leap in communications technology. Its breeding grounds are telephone lines and computer screens and, increasingly, the Internet, and it reproduces through copy and fax machines. Even television plays a role in the proliferation as it covers events like Watergate and the 1986–87 Iran *contra* hearings, in which many of the key roles were played by people who spoke it fluently.

Some basic points on bureaucratese:

- This slang does not always sound like a slang, but rather, a pompous version of standard English. It is, however, slang in the classic sense of a language particular to a certain group that is *not* used by others and not intended for widespread dispersal. It also fits the definition of jargon, so it can be called a hybrid.
- It dotes on adding extra syllables ("utilize" for "use," "orientate" for "orient") and loves to turn nouns into verbs; for instance, to assign a job to a person is to "task" that person. It hates simple words such as money and cash, in favor of terms such as resources, funds, allocations, appropriations, and relies heavily on what one critic has termed "reductive prefaces": debrief, disensus, disadvantaged, disequilibrium, and disincentive.
- This slang is accompanied by extended metaphors and colorful clichés. Someone who tries to save a doomed project is accused of "trying to rearrange the deck chairs on the *Titanic*," and someone who tries to grasp the elusive is said to be "trying to nail jelly to the wall." The most colorful of these expressions are saved for things that cannot be accomplished or portend disaster: herding cats; opening a can of worms; boiling the ocean.
- Its uses have a penchant for the passive voice, the collective "we," and acronyms.
- Bureaucratese thrives on repetition of key words. If a local government agency is charged with reducing traffic congestion to qualify for federal money by getting more people to walk, it embraces "pedestrianism." It then dutifully suggests a "pedestrial task force study group" to look at the idea of an annual "pedestrian conference," urging formation of "citizen pedestrian advocacy groups," and talks a lot about "enhanced pedestrian facilities." It loves certain words such as "diversity" and "community" and can turn a simple universally understood word such as "school" into "community of learners."
- Bureaucratese has been much maligned and criticized since it first began to proliferate during World War II. A number of people, including Jimmy Carter, tried to control it. Despite this, it chugs along in true bureaucratic style and seems to get the job done—that is to say, "it has displayed and demonstrated an

ongoing efficacy when confined to certain logical parameters." The latest in a long line of contributors are those bureaucrats and policy wonks who came into power with Bill Clinton, who taught us to think in terms of "lifelong learning occupational development," which means training for a new job.

• It is not limited to the United States but thrives wherever English is spoken. In Australia, a group called the Plain English Association sends out a Christmas carol in officialese each year to underscore the problem. The 2005 carol was a translation of "O Come All Ye Faithful" (*Sydney Daily Telegraph* of December 9, 2005).

> It would be appreciated if persons pertaining to belief and not insignificant states of gladness would proceed by appropriate means to the location of Bethlehem in observance of the personage whose natal event coincided with his recommended appointment as the supreme monarch of angels. It would be further appreciated if persons proceeding to the said location would be in triplicate adorement pursuant to his sovereign status as Christus Deus.

• Like a virus, it will infect seemingly unlikely subjects such as radio and television weather forecasters. Suddenly and without warning perfectly fine words like "thunderstorms," "rain," and "snow" became "thunderstorm activity," "rain situations," and "snow events."

Acceptable. Possibly acceptable. When used in terms like "acceptable level of unemployment," it means acceptable to those using the term (that is, those who have a job).

activate. Start.

alarmist. Anyone who rocks the boat or questions an important decision.

apologist. One who takes a position that you don't like on an issue or industry.

apples and oranges. That which defies comparison.

appropriate judgmental standards. Good rules.

at this point in time. Now. This phrase came into its own during the Watergate hearings, when one suspected that witnesses used it to give themselves extra time to think.

Back burner. Metaphor of delay or dismissal, as in "Let's put that one on the back burner and get back to it later." The back burner amounts to bureaucratic limbo.

backdoor spending. Spending that is provided for outside the normal channels of appropriations.

backgrounder. Session in which a ranking official gives information on the proviso that it is not quoted directly or attributed to an individual.

bailiwick. Realm or area of responsibility, as in "That is not my bailiwick."

ball of wax. The entire situation; the whole enchilada.

ballpark figure. Estimate.

bandwidth. Time, in the sense that there are those who have no more bandwidth for a problem.

basically. In short.

big picture. Larger considerations.

bird dog. To put something aside; to make no decision. In other quarters, this means to sniff something out, but in bureaucratese

bird dog. (*continued*)
one can bird dog a project that is going nowhere.

boil the ocean. Phrase signifying that a job is impossible.

boondoggle. A project or program that wastes taxpayers' money. This interesting term was created in about 1930 by an American scoutmaster, Robert H. Link, to describe a handmade object of leather, wicker, pipe cleaners, or whatever. From this it became a word for the trivial or wasteful.

brainstorm. A collective attempt to be creative and find new ideas or solutions. As a verb, brainstorm describes group rather than individual thought.

broadbrush. Crude; rough.

buy. To approve, as in "I'll buy that." This term is never used with money—that kind of buying is "procuring."

Can of worms. A mess, problems.

causal factors. Reasons.

charged. Ordered to; told to.

clearance mechanisms. What it takes to get an okay.

coequal. Equal.

cognitive skills. Book learning.

cola (acr). Cost-of-living adjustment. Heard in debates and hearings on Social Security, the civil service, and congressional pay. William Safire has noted that in a legislative context a "cola freeze" is not a way to serve a soft drink.

community. Group of people *not* linked geographically; for example, the handicapped community, the gay community.

copy. To send a copy; "Copy me on that memo." It replaces the prephotocopy-era verb "to carbon."

counterfactual. Untrue, as in a counterfactual proposition, or a lie.

counterintuitive. Surprising, not what you'd expect (unless you thought about it).

CYA. Cover your ass. An almost universal trait in government and politics to make sure that one's decisions are authorized, in writing, or cannot be traced at all, so that you cannot be held responsible for them.

Data. Anything in writing (numbers, figures, facts, graphs, etc). A precise term that has lost its precision through overuse.

day one. The beginning; the first day. "I could have told you from day one that this would not work."

debrief. To get information from someone. This term emerged from the Pentagon and spread into other monolithic buildings, along with PREBRIEF.

deliverable. Fancy word for work.

destabilize. Overthrow or destroy.

detention center. Jail.

developing nation. A nation that may be developing economically and technologically, standing still, or mired in decay. Formerly undeveloped or underdeveloped nations.

dialogue. Conversation.

disadvantaged. Poor. A 1965 Jules Feiffer cartoon character tells how he went from being poor to being poor but needy. Then they told him that it was self-defeating to think of himself as needy, so he became deprived. Then they told that he was underprivileged, and finally he was disadvantaged. The character summed it up, "I still don't have a dime, but I have a great vocabulary."

discipline. Occupational specialty. To ask "What is your discipline?" is the bureaucratic equivalent of the singles bar question "What's your sign?"

disensus. Lack of consensus.

disequilibrium. Out of whack; not in balance.

disincentive. Anything that tends to reduce motivation.

doable. Workable.

domicile. Home.

double dipper. Person who takes dual compensation from the government. Typically, but not always, a military retiree who takes a paying government job while receiving a military pension.

dysfunctional. Not working.

End-result. Result.

end-user. Recipient.

etched in sand. Flexible.

etched in stone. Cannot be changed, but often stated in the negative: "This plan is not exactly etched in stone."

ethically disoriented. Educanto for a cheater.

excessive resource use. Waste.

exercise. Take or make, such as exercising an option or exercising one's opinion.

expertise. Experience. This term has come to encompass all things and has become totally divorced from the idea of knowledge that a true expert possesses.

Facilitate. To ease.

facility. Thing; place.

fallback position. A defeat.

feedback. Reaction to, as in "I'd like some feedback on Friday's meeting."

finalize. To end.

fine-tune. To work out the details.

freeze. To stop or hold in place—from a nuclear freeze to a COLA freeze.

full-court press. All-out pressure applied by a member of Congress on a government agency.

functional. Working.

functional utilization. Actually being used.

fund. Pay for.

funding. Money. Funding is almost always spoken of in terms of increased or decreased funding.

fungible. Interchangeable, as in "All shopping centers are fungible."

fuzz. To blur on purpose; to make less direct.

FY. Fiscal year.

Gag rule. Reference to a debate-limiting rule, by its opponents.

God squad. Top federal officials who decide which endangered species will be protected. The God squad is formally known as the Endangered Species Committee and gets its nickname in part from the fact that it alone has the authority to override the Endangered Species Act, thereby "playing God." Membership on the committee is reserved for those wearing specific "hats," including the secretary of agriculture, the secretary of the Army, the administrator of the Evironmental Protection Agency, and the chairman of the president's Council of Economic Advisors. The God squad meets infrequently and only to discuss the most serious of issues. When it began meeting at the end of 1991 to consider the case of the northern spotted owl, it was the first time it had convened in thirteen years.

good. Fair to poor, as in "Good try, but let's try to do it right this time."

goo-goos (acr). Forces of and for *go*od *go*vernment.

green fees. Taxes on gaz-guzzling cars, coal-burning power plants, and the like, which are intended to keep the planet green.

Hands off. Not involved, as in "President Reagan had a hands-off management style."

hands on. Involved; participating.

herding cats. Impossible task.

heretofore. Before.

human resources. People at work. This used to be known as the "workforce."

hurry-up spending. The practice of federal agencies to "use it or lose it," spend down their budgets in the final days of the fiscal year, "practically shipping the money out of the Treasury in wheelbarrows" (former Senator William Cohen, R–Maine).

I can live with. Said of something that is mediocre or arrived at through compromise; a lukewarm okay.

impact. Effect, such as a school impacted by dwindling population.

implement. Do.

implementation. Doing.

in the loop. Knowing what is going on; not left out of the loop.

in view of. Since.

incent. The people brought in by Bill Clinton use this as a verb, as in "incenting companies to create new jobs."

incentivize. To create an incentive.

indicated. Said. "You indicated that you would empty the garbage."

information-processing center. Typing pool.

infrastructure. Originally, bridges, sewers, roads. Now it refers to anything that can be used to increase productivity.

inoperative. Broken; not working.

interconnect. Connect.

interdependent. Dependent.

interdisciplinary. Anything involving people with different backgrounds.

interpersonal. Between humans.

intervention. Interference.

irrespective. Regardless.

is of the opinion that. Believes.

K–12. Educanto for the period from kindergarten through the twelfth grade, the last year of high school (pron. "K through twelve").

Laundry list. List of things to accomplish.

let's discuss. Memo notation from a superior that means a junior should come down to his office.

low profile. Something that is being kept out of the limelight.

Maximize. Make the most of.

media center. Library.

methodology. Method.

Mickey Mouse. Meager results requiring substantial effort; petty concerns.

micromanage. To manage down to the last detail and leave little for subordinates to decide.

mobile-response unit. Police car, ambulance, or fire truck.

motivationally deficient. Lazy.

multidisciplinary. Diverse. A committee with people from various departments or interests is invariably described as a multidisciplinary task force.

Needless to say. Needs to be said (if it were actually "needless to say," it would not be said).

neonatal unit. Nursery for newborns.

Off-load. Unload.

on the fence. Bureaucratic code term describing a person with a job who is doing virtually nothing.

one would think. I think.

OTE. Overtaken by events. Said of a program, report, or concern that has been rendered obsolete by time.

outreach. Reaching the consumer.

overcrowded. Crowded.

oversight. A mistake; a screwup.

Paper pusher. Self-deprecating term for one in a bureaucracy. The term is sometimes useful when things go wrong: "Don't ask me, I'm just a paper pusher."

paper trail. Evidence left by a bureaucrat to prove that he or she acted in a particular way in dealing with a situation.

past history. History.

pencil in. To tentatively schedule something. It rests on the fact that pencil can be erased. "Pencil in lunch for Wednesday."

phase in. Start; implement.

phase out. Stop; dismantle.

phase zero. The beginning of something.

plum. A political appointment; a job given out by the president.

policy. Predetermined response.

prebrief. Brief in advance of a meeting or event.

Say What?

A June 20, 1996, article in the *Washington Post* described a federal worker on the fence:

> Public Health Service physician James D. Felsen starts each day at the office with a cup of coffee. After coffee he reads a newspaper, checks his mail and telephones friends. Felsen saves his Styrofoam coffee cups, because they help him keep track of how many days he has gone to his office in the huge federal Parklawn Building in Rockville [Maryland].
>
> He has constructed an arch out of the used cups in his office. The first row stretches from the floor on one wall up to the ceiling and down to the floor on the opposite side. He is half-way through the second row.

Felsen had been doing this for three years at an annual salary of $117,000—including a valued-employee $15,000 bonus.

preplanning. Planning.

prioritize. To decide what is most important; to assign priorities to things.

private sector, the. Business; anything that is not part of the government, which is the public sector.

proactive. Advance planning.

procedural safeguards. Defined by Don Ethan Miller in his *Book of Jargon*, as "red tape."

process. Work or activity, as in the "planning process" or the "information process."

procurement. Buying; getting hold of.

program. Almost anything. In 1962 Senator Stephen M. Young of Ohio defined a program as "any assignment or task that cannot be completed in one phone call."

programitis. The notion that for every problem there is a government program that will solve it.

project. See PROGRAM.

promulgate. Announce; issue an order; start something.

prune. A political appointee with experience; an appointee who has held the job for a while. It is a play on the term PLUM in that a prune is a plum with time on the job.

public sector. The government—federal, state, and local.

qualitative. Having to do with quality and things that cannot be measured.

quantification. Putting a number on something.

quantitative. Having to do with numbers.

quick fix. Nonexistent solution. In the context of the bureaucracy it is common to state that there is "no quick fix" when a problem cannot be solved by money.

R and D. Research and development.

redundancy of human resources. Too many employees.

reinventing the wheel. To study something that has already been studied; usually stated negatively by those opposed to the action in question.

reskilling. Retraining. This term may have been invented by Governor John R. McKernan of Maine, who in 1967 said to a reporter, "That tells you right off the bat that we need serious reskilling of our workforce."

revenue shortfall. One of several clever ways of saying that there is a deficit without saying the word. If "deficit" is used, it is never "our deficit," but rather, "the deficit."

revise to reflect. Revise.

revolving door. The movement of higher-level managers and executives between public- and private-sector employment. It is typically used to describe high government officials who take jobs in the private sector after two years as, say, a "deputy undersecretary."

RFP. Request for proposals, which is a notice to bid for a government contract.

RFQ. Request for quotations.

rif / riff (acr). Reduction in force. A cutback in staff, or a layoff, used in connection with the federal workforce, including the military, and crops up as agency budgets are trimmed and riffing becomes rife.

riffed. To have lost one's job.

root cause. Cause.

Sanitary landfill. A dump.

sanity check. Reviewing a report or data to make sure it makes sense.

scenario. Hypothetical case; a prediction.

seed money. Money used to start something.

selected out. Fired.

shortfall. Not enough. A budgetary shortfall is a shortage of money.

signage. Signs.

significant contribution. Contribution.

silver bullet. A tax break or loophole that benefits a particular interest group, as in "a silver bullet for the oil industry."

sleaze factor. That component of an administration or political party that is corrupt, unethical, controversial, scandal-ridden, or otherwise under a cloud.

state of the art. Not out of date; current.

subject matter. Subject.

sunset legislation. Legislation that specifies the periodic review of, or stated date of demise for, a program or agency.

sunshine rule. Rule that opens a previously closed proceeding to public scrutiny.

surviving spouse. A widow or widower.

Take a fix / take a reading. To try to figure something out; to attempt to frame an answer.

target. 1. To aim or earmark. 2. Goal.

task. 1. Job. 2. To assign work.

task force. A temporary committee.

tasker. Memo or other device used to communicate the assignment of a task.

thrust. Direction.

time frame. A period of time.

trickle-down. A downstream benefit from a law or a program after it has benefited and been filtered through its prime beneficiary.

turkey farm. Bureaucratic equivalent of Siberia: a desk with no duties.

Underutilized. Used rarely.

unsubstantiated rumor. Rumor.

up to speed. Current.

utilization. Use.

utilize. To use.

Verbalize. To say.

viable. Workable. This term came into its own when bureaucratese was criticized for its dependence on the word "feasible."

visualize. See.

Watchdog. Term used to describe the OVERSIGHT function of commissions, committees, and certain agencies, notably the General Accounting Office, the investigatory arm of Congress.

when deemed appropriate. When okay.

whistle-blower. One who reveals corruption or mismanagement in an organization.

wiggle room. Feature of a public statement that sounds authoritative but is really so vague that the speaker can later change positions and still use the same words. Writing about such statements in the *Washington Post*, Susan Trausch reported on March 16, 1986, "The phrase 'cautious optimism' has about a mile of wiggle room on either side. So does 'tentative acceptance' and 'he is leaning in that direction.'"

window. Opportunity.

wired. Describes a grant, contract, or job whose winner is predetermined: "They said it was open to new bidders, but we thought it was wired from the beginning." Also, well connected.

within the framework of. Within.

Your court. Your problem now, from the tennis metaphor "the ball is now in your court."

Zero fund. To not pay for; fail to appropriate money for something.

zero-sum game. Conflict in which one player's gain is the other's loss. Usually initiated by one who will be able to say "My gain is your loss."

BUSINESS AND FINANCE 5

Buzzwords for Big Shots

That guy [a broker] is no lamb at this game, and right now he's a bull on a lot of cats and dogs I'd never suggest you own. He doesn't get hung up in many pups, though, and some of his hot issues in recent years have been real yo-yos.

—Sylvia Porter, "Your Money's Worth,"
September 17, 1964

It has been long argued that slang tends to thrive in informal environments. So how come the highly structured, formal realm of money management is as slangy as any baseball dugout or high school locker room? In this realm the gray institutions of fiscal responsibility are known as Fannie Mae, Ginnie Mae, Sally Mae, Freddy Mac, and the Fed.

Acapulco spread. Transaction with multiple commissions that is so complicated and exhausting that it will "send the broker winging off to a Mexican vacation" (*Wall Street Journal*).

accordion management. Quickly increasing and decreasing the size of a workforce by using temporary workers.

air-pocket stock. A security whose value has dropped sharply, as an airplane when it hits an air pocket.

alligator spread. A transaction in which the commissions eat up the profit.

arbs. Arbitrageurs, those who speculate in the stock of companies with announced or rumored deals.

asset stripping. Buy a company, sell the assets, dump the employees.

at the market. The current price of a security.

audits from hell. Excruciatingly detailed random tax audits staged to determine patterns of taxpayer compliance with the law.

Baby Bells. The regional telephone companies created as a result of the breakup of Ma Bell—the American Telephone & Telegraph System.

baby bond. Bond sold in denominations of less than the amount of $1 million.

back-end load. A sales charge paid when selling shares in a mutual fund.

back off. Sudden sinking of a stock price after a rise.

bag job. Describing a security bought on what turns out to be a false rumor.

bang for the buck. Value or excitement for the money spent.

bar. One million dollars.

basis point. One hundredth of one percent.

basket case. A company or economy in trouble.

bazillion. Indefinite enormous number.

bean counter. An accountant; a statistician.

bear hug. The embrace that a large company puts on a another (not always smaller) company that it is taking over. "Big companies buy little companies and usually end up destroying the very thing they coveted the small company for" (*Forbes* magazine).

bear market. One that is going down; a market driven by uncertainty or pessimism or both.

bear raid. Heavy selling of a stock to force its price down so that large quantities can be purchased at the depressed price.

beard. To act as a front for another.

bed and breakfast. Selling a security and buying it back quickly to minimize capital gains taxes.

bedbug letter. Letter from the Securities and Exchange Commission informing company of problems or bugs in its registration statement.

belly up. Out of business; bankrupt. See WENT TOES.

beta. A measure of the volatility of a fund using a known index such as the Standard & Poor's 500. A value of over 1.0 means the fund is aggressive and risky, while a value under 1.0 indicates a more stable or conservative fund.

Big Blue. IBM.

big board. The New York Stock Exchange.

Big D. Economic depression, as in "Is This Just a Recession—or the 'Big D'?" (headline, *Newsweek*, January 21, 1991).

bigee. Something or someone important.

BIMBO (acr). Buy-in/management buyout, transaction in which both incoming and existing management are involved in the acquiring group.

birdseed. Insignificant amount of money.

black book. 1. A preplanned defense against a takeover. 2. A database, such as a brokerage firm's black book on junk bonds.

black hole. The discrepancy in the global balance of payments.

black knight. Predator who mounts a hostile takeover of a company.

Black Monday. October 19, 1987, when the stock market crashed.

blackout. A provision in a planned merger banning both parties from negotiating with others.

blind pool. A war chest that a company can tap in the event of hostile takeover bids or for any other purpose. It is blind because investors commit to it before they know how the money will be used.

blow back. To sell a new issue quickly. This is usually not popular with the underwriter who brought it.

blowout bid. An offer to buy out a company that far exceeds the real value of the company, as measured by the value of its outstanding stock. A blowout bid is one that is meant to scare off rival buyers—to avoid the hassle of a bidding war.

blue chip. Common stock in a major corporation with a long-standing ability to generate profits and dividends.

blue-sky laws. State laws created to protect the public from securities fraud. Supposedly the phrase was coined when a judge likened the value of a stock to the value of a piece of blue sky.

Bo Dereks. Bonds maturing in the year 2010, from Bo Derek's role as the perfect woman in the movie *10*.

boiler room. Room in which fast-talking salespeople use the phone to sell securities or commodities, for outrageous commissions or markups, that usually are overpriced and have poor investment characteristics.

boot. Cash thrown in with stock in an acquisition deal; a cash sweetener.

box. One's own holdings. To sell short against one's own portfolio is known as "selling short against the box." See SHORT.

brass ring. Wall Street partnership.

breakup value. The value of a company after a takeover and it is broken up and the component parts are sold off.

Buck Rogers. Securities that enjoy a sudden rise in a short period of time.

bucket shop. Dishonest brokerage house that gambles with its clients' stocks, bonds, and other holdings without permission.

bucketing. Broker arranging a trade for a customer at a higher price than a market open to all bidders would produce.

bull market. One that is going up.

burbed-out. Looking very middle-class, suburban.

burn rate. The speed with which high-tech and Internet companies consume cash resources.

burn someone down. To hand out a worthless stock tip.

Cafeteria plan. Benefit plan that allows an employee some alternative choices (like selecting dishes in a cafeteria).

callable. Describes certain bonds and preferred stocks that can be redeemed, or called, by the issuer before maturity.

candy-store problem. Situation involving a great variety of good choices.

car. A futures contract, a legal commitment to receive a commodity at some point in the future: "a throwback from the days when commodities were transported in railway cars" (*Lamont's Glossary*).

cascade. To send information through a company.

cash cow. Enterprise that creates a lot of surplus cash flow, as opposed to paper profits. For instance, in the newspaper business the newest cash cow is personal want ad columns. Widely used, the term is being milked to death.

category killers. Huge retailers in specialized consumer areas who because of their buying power can offer lower prices than other retailers; Home Depot and Circuit City are two examples.

cats (acr). Certificates of accrual on Treasury securities. One of several financial "felines," including tigrs (Treasury investment growth receipts) and lyons (liquid yield option notes). These are house names for zero-coupon (which pay interest on maturity) "stripped" Treasury bonds. They are said to be stripped because the interest is separated from the principal and sold separately.

cats and dogs. Stocks of unproven value that cannot be used as collateral, among other things.

CBOE. Chicago Board of Exchange.

CEO. Chief executive officer; the boss. William Safire has pointed out that in olden times the boss was called the president or chairman.

chainsaw. To disrupt or destroy a business deal.

Chinese Wall. Term characterizing the procedural barriers that prevent information known to people in one part of the business from becoming known to those in another part, to avoid conflicts of interest.

churn. To cause a client to buy and sell securities imprudently in order to generate commissions for the broker. Churning is an illegal practice, by a broker or financial adviser, of frequently buying and selling stocks, bonds, and mutual funds simply to generate commissions.

closed fund. A mutual fund that no longer lets in new investors. This usually happens when the fund has grown so large that it no longer can reach its objectives.

cold call. A sales call made to a stranger, often at night, to sell securities.

comfort letter. Letter from an accountant saying that there is no false or misleading information in a financial statement.

contrarian. Person who thinks that the market will move in the opposite direction, up or down, from where the majority believes it is moving.

corner. To take control of the price of a

security or commodity by obtaining a major interest in it. See SQUEEZE.

Crazy Mary. Community Psychiatric Centers, whose stock market symbol is CMY.

creeping takeover. Gradual accumulation of large amounts of the shares in a company through purchases on the open market.

crooked E. The Enron Corporation, after 2002, when it was forced to declare the largest bankruptcy in American history, making its logo of a tipped letter *E* particularly apt.

cut a melon. For a company to declare a large stock dividend.

Damager. Manager.

dawn raid. Quick buy of substantial amounts of a company's stock on the market before the market becomes aware that something is going on.

day order. An order given to a broker that is good for just one day.

dead-cat bounce. Small increase in the market averages after a substantial drop.

death cross. Situation where long-term and short-term averages converge, seen as evidence that security values will decline.

deduck. A tax deduction.

deep pockets. A reliable source of money.

diddly-squat. Nothing; a big zero.

dish. Bribe, in international business slang.

dividend-capture. Investment strategy in which stocks are bought just before they declare dividends and are sold immediately thereafter.

dog. Enterprise that costs more to operate than it produces in income. The opposite of a cash cow.

dot-bombs. Failing dot-com companies; also known as dot-coma, dot-goner, and dot-compost.

downsize. Euphemism used to describe layoffs; perhaps one of the most reviled bits of nineties jargon.

DRIP (acr). Dividend reinvestment plan, where cash dividends from stock are automatically reinvested into the purchase of new shares of that same stock.

drop-dead fee. Money paid to those who have backed a raider if the raid fails; a kill fee.

duck. Any deduction from one's paycheck.

duckets. Money.

dummy. A member of a board of directors who has no direct interest in the company but represents someone who does; a human proxy.

dump. To unload goods in a foreign country at a very low price, to prevent a domestic oversupply.

Enron / Enronate / Enroned / Enronize. To destroy an organization by fraud and deception in the manner of the Enron Corp.

equities. Ownership interest possessed by stockholders in a corporation. Stocks.

ERISA (acr). Employee retirement income security plan.

ESOP. Employee stock ownership plan.

ethics deficit. Corporate corruption.

ex-dividend. Without dividend; a stock that is sold as "ex-dividend" is sold after the dividend has been credited to the previous owner. See DIVIDEND-CAPTURE.

Face card. A business leader.

Fannie Mae. Nickname of the Federal National Mortgage Association.

fast track. The path of quick ascent to the top of the corporate heap.

Fed, the. The board of governors of the Federal Reserve System and the Federal Reserve Banks. Also called THE SYSTEM.

Fed time. The half hour between eleven-thirty and noon, eastern standard time, when Federal Reserve banks are, by tradition, most likely to buy and sell securities.

fifo (acr). "First in, first out," an accounting term used in areas ranging from computing interest to computing inventory value. Lifo stands for "last in, first out." Filo stands for "first in, last out."

fill or kill. The stock-trading equivalent of speak or forever hold your peace.

fixed-income investment. Bonds, certificates of deposit, and other instruments that pay a fixed rate of interest, as opposed to stocks where payments vary with a company's profits.

floor. The huge trading area of the New York Stock Exchange.

footsie (acr). The British FT-SE 100, an index of share prices of the 100 largest U.K. companies.

friendly takeover. Purchase of a company that is welcomed or unopposed.

front-end load. A sales charge paid when shares of a mutual fund are bought.

front run. For a broker to load up his friends and favorite customers with a stock, hype it, and then sell it to later customers at a higher price. Illegal.

Garbitrageur. Derogatory blend of garbage and arbitrageurs, for those who manipulate rather than simply speculate in stock of companies with announced or rumored deals.

get face. To gain respect.

get off the dime. To get a business deal moving.

get someone's motor running. To sell one's business ideas to another.

get the gate. To be laid off.

GIC. Guaranteed investment contract, an investment product issued by an insurance company where a rate of return is guaranteed for one to seven years, as long as the insurance company has the financial ability to make the payments.

gilt edge. Term used to describe the highest-quality stocks and bonds. The term originated in the British government-securities market.

glass ceiling. The invisible but real limit on women's ascendance in most business hierarchies.

go blooey. A company or stock about to go under.

go naked. To sell an option without owning the security to which it is linked or a stock one does not own.

go public. To sell the shares of a private company to the public.

Godfather offer. A takeover offer so generous that management can't refuse without fear of shareholder lawsuits.

golden handcuffs. Packaged perks and forms of delayed compensation that keep executives locked into their jobs. To qualify for these benefits, which include annuities and stock-purchase plans, the executive must stay in place for a defined period of time.

golden parachutes. Generous compensation packages, usually a combination of money and benefits, for executives that provide them with substantial benefits to allay their fears in the event that the company is being taken over or they are fired.

goose job. Forcing up the value of a stock by strategic purchases.

grave dancer. Someone who profits from another person's business misfortune.

gray knight. An opportunistic bidder intervening in a hostile takeover; less noble than a white knight.

gray market. Retail operation that falls into the gray area between the legitimate and the illegal, or black, market.

grease. Extraordinary amount of commission on the sale of a stock, resulting from the fact that the stock the firm acquired for sale to customers was cheap. This is usually legal.

green weenie. An unpleasant surprise: "Imagine what a weenie must look like when it is left in a refrigerator (which is unplugged) and forgotten for six months. A green weenie in business wheeling and dealing lingo is an unpleasant surprise discovered belatedly as part of a transaction or deal" (Ron Sturon, *Green Weenies and Due Diligence: Insider Business Jargon—Raw, Serious and Sometimes Funny*).

greenmail. Money paid by a takeover target to a raider to avert a takeover; blackmail of a different sort and color. It is usually paid in terms of a highly inflated stock price.

greenmailer. One who stages a raid in order to be paid to call it off.

GRIT (acr). Grantor retained income trust, an irrevocable trust to which a residence is transferred for a term of years, with the grantor retaining the use of the residence for that term.

GTC order. Order to buy or sell a stock that is "good till canceled."

Haircut. In lending, the difference between the value of a loan and the value of the collateral used to secure that loan.

halo effect. The blessing bestowed on a particular stock once it has been purchased by an important player.

hickey. Broker's loss from a customer's failure to deliver a check on a purchase (usually because the price went down by the payment date) or to deliver stock on a sale (for the opposite reason).

Hokeys. Nickname for bonds of the Home Owners Loan Corp.

home run. Large capital gain in a stock in a short period of time.

hoovering. Acquiring stocks as if one were sucking them up with a vacuum cleaner (Hoover is a famous vacuum-cleaner brand).

hot new issue. A new stock or bond that is met with heavy demand, driving up the market price when it is first offered publicly.

hung up. Describes a situation in which one cannot sell a security without taking a large loss.

hushmail. Unethical situation in which stock is bought from the director of a company by a raider at a substantial premium in return for the silence of that director.

hype. Excessively exaggerated positive news on a stock.

Iced. A business deal settled once and for all.

ink slinger. The person who signs his or her name to a contract; the person ultimately responsible.

insiders. Top executives, directors, and large stockholders associated with a given stock. The buying and selling of insiders is watched carefully as a judge of the health of a stock.

IPO. Initial public offering.

James Bond. A security due in the year 2007, a nickname inspired by the code number of the famous fictional spy.

January effect. Uncanny tendency for stocks with a low amount of capital to take off during the first month of the year.

junk bond. Bonds that offer higher yields at the cost of higher risks. They have gained added notoriety because they have fueled takeover bids by providing leverage to assist in financing transactions.

Kick it out. To liquidate a security without regard to price.

killer bees. Firms and outside individuals used to help fight off a takeover, including law firms, PR firms, and proxy solicitors.

killer technology. An invention or new technology that renders another invention or technology obsolete.

knockout. Share or shares of Coca-Cola, whose New York Stock Exchange symbol is KO.

Lady Macbeth strategy. Takeover tactic in which a third party pretends to be a white knight, then joins the hostile bidder.

lamb. Inexperienced investor; one given to buying and selling on rumor and questionable tips.

leads. A list of prospects from which a broker works making, cold calls. Brokers sometimes pay for leads, or obtain them from some business or industry related to the stocks they're selling.

lemons and plums. Bad deals and good in the lingo of those involved in corporate buyouts. All deals begin as plums.

lettered stock. Restricted stock that cannot be sold unless registered with the SEC.

liar's poker. A game played by bond traders using the serial numbers on dollar bills instead of cards; made popular by the bestselling book of the same name.

libor / libid (acr). London interbank offer rate and London interbank bid rate.

lifo (acr). "Last in, first out." See FIFO.

lilo (acr). "Last in, last out." See FIFO.

load. The fee or commission an investor pays to buy an investment, such as shares in a mutual fund. A front-end load is charged when you buy the product; a back-end load is charged when you take your money out before a specified time. "No-load" funds don't charge either fee, and some mutual funds with loads waive them for IRAs and Keogh accounts.

lollipop. An offer by a company to buy shares from stockholders at a premium, thus avoiding a hostile takeover. Also known as a sugar pill, the opposite of a POISON PILL, but accomplishes the same thing.

London fix. Price given twice each business day by London bullion dealers to set the value of an ounce of gold.

long. A bullish position in which one holds securities in anticipation that they will go up in price. By extension, anything that one has possession of: "This company is long on goodwill and short on cash."

loonie. The Canadian dollar, because of the loon on the $1 coin.

lyons (acr). Liquid yield option notes. See CATS.

Ma Bell. The American Telephone & Telegraph Company.

Mad Dog. McDonnell Douglas, a nickname that plays off its stock symbol, MD.

magic bullet. Specific, fail-safe solution to a business problem.

Manny Hanny. The Manufacturer's Hanover Trust Co.

Mart brothers. Wal-Mart and Kmart.

melon. Large stock or cash dividend. See CUT A MELON.

meltdown. The October 1987 market crash.

mentor. Senior executive who takes on a younger protégé.

mil / millie. One million.

milk. To pull as much money as possible out of a company or security.

mommy track. Female career path that is interrupted and slowed by having children.

mortgage-backed. A security whose value is based on a pool of home mortgages.

motors. Shares of General Motors stock.

mouse-milking. Term for an effort that seems too great for the results it generates; for instance, a broker spending a lot of time on a very small account.

mullets. Brokers' derogatory term for customers.

munchkin. A person of low status in a corporation.

New-issue whore. Brokerage client who wants to get the hot new issues to make a quick profit. See WHORE.

noise. Stock market movement caused by phenomena not reflective of general sentiment. Programmed trading—trading triggered by computer programs—is a prime source of noise.

no-load fund. A mutual fund that sells its shares at net asset value without a sales charge. They're the most popular type among people who do their own investing.

noon balloon. Midday rally.

noon swoon. Midday sell-off.

Odd lot. 1. A lot of less than a hundred stocks, or a bond with less than $100,000 in principal value. 2. Anything out of the ordinary.

odor lucri. Latin for the smell of money; expectation of gain.

Pac-Man defense. Named after the popular video game, it describes a move in which a target company turns around and tries to swallow the company that is trying to acquire it. Sometimes it works simply because it is an audacious move that scares away the pursuer. It is so named because a key element in Pac-Man is the ability of the pursued to turn on its pursuer.

pals (acr). Passive activity losses, tax shelters that use debt and depreciation to create a loss, which is then deducted against income.

paper profit. An unrealized profit on a security that is still being held.

pard. Business partner.

pencil whipping. Falsifying records, in the parlance of the white-collar criminal.

penny stock. An inexpensive security, usually under five dollars a share; many in this class sell for under a dollar and are priced in pennies.

people churner. Boss who drives out talent.

people pill. Defensive tactic to ward off a takeover in which management threatens to quit in the event of a takeover, leaving the company without experienced leadership.

pigs (acr). Passive income generators; syndicated investments whose earnings are designed to be sheltered by PALS.

pink sheets. Listing of over-the-counter (OTC) stocks that are not always listed in the newspapers. Pink sheets list all traded OTC stocks.

pip. The smallest unit of any given currency: cent, pfennig, etc.

pit. Where commodities are traded, as opposed to a floor, where stocks and bonds exchange hands.

plastic. Credit card(s).

plateauing. Moving sideways in a corporation.

plunge. Reckless speculation.

point. Unit for valuing stocks; one point equals a dollar.

poison pill. Making a takeover so unattractive, by diluting a company's stock, that someone attempting a hostile takeover passes it up. See LOLLIPOP.

porcupine provisions. Legal provisos made to deter takeovers.

privatize. The opposite of going public; converting a publicly owned company into a private one by buying up shares.

product. Goods. "Anyone can talk about computers, but can he move product?"

prudent-man rule. Common-law standard for assessing the degree of care a trustee or other fiduciary agent must show to meet the standard of a man of discretion and intelligence seeking preservation of capital and reasonable profits.

puddle / pool. Item in a company's overall inventory.

puds (acr). Nickname for bonds of public utility districts.

pups. Cheap, inactive stocks; dogs.

push money. Extra money paid to a salesperson to aggressively sell certain merchandise.

Qtip (acr). Pronounced like the small swab you stick in your ear, it stands for "qualified terminal interest property"—a trust.

quants. Computer technologists working in the financial industry, designing sophisticated investment strategies and computer models; the folks who made "program trading" possible.

quick-and-dirty. A business transaction done rapidly and carelessly.

Rag out. To dress in an expensive business suit.

raider. One who swoops down and buys other companies by acquiring large amounts of stock.

ratchet. An incentive arrangement in which managers get a bigger share of equity if the venture performs well.

red herring. Prospectus that cannot be used to confirm the sale of a security because it still lacks clearance from the Securities and Exchange Commission to become the final prospectus, so called because such documents have a legend so stating, along with two red lines running down the left side and the top of the cover only.

regs. Regulations (written or unwritten) of a company.

reits (acr). Real estate investment trusts (pron. "reets"). Mutual funds invested in real estate whose earnings go directly to shareholders and avoid corporate taxation.

rep. Representative, as in "sales rep."

repo. An agreement to sell a government bond for cash together with an agreement to repurchase the bond (on a special later date) at a higher price, reflecting the interest charged for the loan of the cash for a specified period.

resistance level. Dollar level at which a stock or bond seems to stop rising in a rally.

retread. Employee trying out a new career area.

rig. To manipulate a stock.

rightsize. To lay off workers, a term that makes "downsizing" seem downright Draconian.

ring the register. Take a profit.

RIPP (acr). A reduction-in-personnel plan; a layoff, as in a five-hundred-person RIPP.

road kill. Company that has been steamrollered by the competition.

roll-ups. Procedure whereby limited partnerships are converted into publicly traded entities.

round lot. A hundred shares, or a multiple of a hundred shares, in the case of stock. A $1 million value for a bond priced at $5,000.

run one's rhymes. To give a sales pitch.

Safe harbor. Relief from regulation. Attempts have been made in Congress to allow small companies to have a safe harbor in discussing their future prospects while being relieved from shareholder suits if those prospects do not work out.

Sallie Mae. Nickname of the National Student Loan Marketing Association.

Santa Claus rally. Rise in stock prices between Christmas and New Year's Day.

scenery. A board of directors selected for their status and respectability.

scorched earth. Destructive anti-takeover measures a company takes to make itself less attractive to raiders.

screwed, blued, and tattooed. Cheated on a business deal.

seagull model. Term used to describe a consultation in which the consultant flies off, makes a couple of passes over his client, drops a strategy on the client, and returns home.

seat. Membership in a commodity or securities exchange.

securitization. When a financial institution changes an asset—such as loans, credit card loans, and home mortgages—into a security that can be traded.

shake out. A period of market activity or crisis that causes small investors to drop out of the market.

shallow river running fast. Describes a stock, stocks, or the whole market moving in response to rumors.

shark. One who attempts a hostile corporate takeover; an avaricious raider.

shark repellent. Any measures that a target company uses to fend off a SHARK; for instance, changing a company's rules to require stockholder approval before a takeover can be accomplished.

short. To sell stocks one does not own, borrowing to make delivery in anticipation of buying the stocks back after a drop in value. In contrast, to be LONG is to actually own stock.

showstopper. Legal move made to thwart a hostile takeover.

skunk works. Backroom corporate think tank convened to foster new ideas.

slam dunk. A stock, usually a new issue, that is supposed to have a quick rise when it opens, so that it can be rapidly sold. A "sure thing."

slob (acr). What else but a secured lease obligation bond?

smidge. Small amount of price: ⅛ of a point (i.e., ⅛ of one dollar), for instance.

soft landing. Economic turn of events that avoids recession but achieves a slower period of growth without inflation.

spiff. Extra money paid to a salesperson to aggressively sell certain merchandise.

spot price. In international trade, the price of a currency delivered today as opposed to at a future, or forward, date.

squeeze. To control the price of a security. See CORNER.

squib. A tiny advertisement; a mention of the company or a product name.

Stalingrad. To snow under with paperwork—as Michael M. Thomas explains in *Hard Money,* "Russian winter with subpoenas instead of snowflakes."

Steadman. Term that has become mutual fund industry slang for dreadful performance, as in "the fund pulled a Steadman." What Charles A. Jaffe wrote in the *Washington Times* on September 7, 1995, gives an idea how bad Steadman funds are: "If you were to list the 10 worst-performing funds the past 10 years, all four Steadman funds would be there." Named for Charlie Steadman, who, according to *Kiplinger's Personal Finance Magazine* in 1999, "burned through investors' assets at a rate unseen in the fund business since the Great Depression."

steenth. Short for 1/16 of a point, in spoken stock-and-bond reports.

story stock. Stock that is more dependent on a good story than on its balance sheet.

street name. The name of a brokerage house or bank that is put on a stock registration for the benefit of the client who owns it. This makes it easier to buy and sell stock.

stripped. Said of a financial instrument whose interest has been separated from its principal and sold separately. See CATS.

suboptimal. A failure.

sucker rally. Name for a stock rise in the midst of a bear market, when sophisticated investors steer clear of the market.

suit. Top administrator or woman; anyone who is in charge. Term implies use of authority, not necessarily wisely.

swooner. Stock that is particularly sensitive to good or bad news.

System, the. See the FED.

Tabbed. Well dressed.

take-away. Measure of success for a business meeting. "I had great take-away from our meeting with the sales reps."

take the spear in the chest. To accept full blame for something.

tape watcher. Small investor who monitors his or her investments by watching the transaction tape, in a brokerage office or on cable TV; the Financial News Network runs the tapes continuously.

tapped out. Out of available cash; bankrupt.

target. Object of a takeover bid.

teeny. One sixteenth of a point.

Texas disease. Epidemic savings-and-loan failure.

thou. One thousand.

thunderbolt thinker. Person with sudden insights that create new business and profits.

tigrs (acr). Treasury investment growth receipts. See CATS.

tin parachute. Plan guaranteeing employees severance pay—the poor cousin of the GOLDEN PARACHUTE.

top tick. The highest price of the day, as in "to buy a stock at top tick."

toxic waste. Bonds that go beyond junk bonds.

triple witching hour. One of the four Fridays in each year on which options and futures contracts expire.

turkey. A lousy deal.

twiggy bond. Thin coverage—from Twiggy, a very thin fashion model of the 1960s–1970s.

Ultra. Consumer who demands the best of everything; the upper end of upscale.

up tick / uptick. Securities transaction made at a price higher than the last one.

Velvet. An easy or quick profit.

vulture fund. Pool of investment money used to purchase distressed real estate as cheap prices.

Walk in. Brokerage customer who simply walks into the office without an appointment.

walks the walk. Person or company which does what it promises ("talks the talk.")

war babies. Defense stocks.

wash tub. Bond issued by the Washington Suburban Sanitary District.

went toes. Synonym for BELLY UP.

whisper number. Unofficial and always unattributed earnings estimate.

whisper stock. Stock in a company that is believed or rumored to be ripe for a major play.

white bread. Dull, unimpressive transaction.

white knight. A friendly suitor who intervenes in a hostile takeover and saves the target company and its assets. An opportunistic second bidder is a GRAY KNIGHT.

white space. Area of opportunity such as an underserved market.

white squire. A WHITE KNIGHT who buys less than a majority interest in the takeover-target company.

whore. Customer who wants the hottest new-issue stock coming out so that it can be sold quickly at a profit. Also known as NEW-ISSUE WHORE.

widget. Any unspecified product; commonly used in hypothetical scenarios: "Say I've got two million widgets and not enough trucks hired to haul them."

wild duck. An innovative employee who has a different perspective.

window dressing. Anything done to make a mutual fund or stock look good just prior to the end of a period, to improve the quarter or year-end reports sent to stockholders.

with ice. When issued.

wooden ticket. A fictitious trade in an issue that a broker promised to sell, but couldn't get anyone to buy. He will quietly try to cancel the transaction later on.

Xd. Ex-dividend. It refers to security after its current dividend has been paid.

Yankee bond. Foreign bond issued in dollars and registered for sale in the United States.

yard. A billion of anything—dollars, yen, units.

yo-yos / yo-yo stocks. Pricey volatile issues that fluctuate wildly in price.

Zero. A zero-coupon bond or one on which interest is not paid until maturity.

zero out. To legally avoid paying taxes.

zero tick. A security transaction in which the sale price is identical to the previous transaction.

zinger. Paid stock promotion masquerading as an unbiased report.

zombies. Companies that continue to function even though they are bankrupt.

6

COMPUTERESE

What Do You Say to a Chiphead?

The Chipheads Are (Sigh) Winning.

—Headline in the *San Francisco Examiner*,
January 3, 1983

The personal computer (PC) created a revolution. It also created an odd means of expression through which almost everything got renamed. The TV screen became a monitor, writing became word processing, and a list of options became a menu. Not enough to label something portable, computers came out as laptops, palmtops, notebooks, and the odd subnotebook.

It also embraced an odd proclivity for misnomer: floppy disks are hard, hard copy is floppy, peripherals are central, and global searches are intensely localized. As if to tweak the noses of the language purists, the computerists have converted large numbers of nouns into transitive verbs as they format, access, array, input data, output data, interface, download, and upload.

Many familiar nouns were used for other objects, yielding no little confusion among those who don't know a computer mouse from Mickey Mouse or a byte from a bite and think that a hard drive is leaving work at rush hour.

Computer slang is, in a word, quirky. Traditionally, this country has created great slang. Whether you were talking about lumberjacks, hoboes, GIs, or short-order cooks, you were talking about groups of people each with a rich, colorful slang. But then came the computer revolution, headed by computer nerds, and it generated a less than dynamic slang—at least at first. But as computers got smaller and cheaper, all sorts of people got into the act, and soon there was a burgeoning slang that featured terms created by outlaw hackers, computer gamers, and the new geek elite.

Here is a heavy sampling, including some that no longer sound like slang to those who are at home in the world of bits, bytes, K's, and modems.

Speaking of modems, this device is the one that made possible a new universe, the World Wide Web and the Internet. Seemingly overnight, the Web and the Net developed their own culture with their own language and upstaged computers. Chapter 19, "Net-speak," contains this new slang, which is growing at supersonic speed.

AAC. Alter all commands, one of the many letter codes used by hackers and programmers. Dozens more are salted through this chapter.

AAR. Alter at random.

AB. Add backwards.

abend (acr). An abnormal or abortive end. This is what can happen when a machine is fed bad input data or shut down before it completes a routine.

abterm (acr). Abnormal termination. See ABEND.

AFFB. A force five belch, allegedly a humorous hacker initialism.

AFVC. Add finagle variable constant.

AIB. Attack innocent bystander, to hackers who speak in initialisms.

algy. Algorithm for short.

alpha. Preliminary testing.

antidote. Program or programs used to protect computers from a computer virus. These programs tend to have apt names such as Vaccine, Flu Shot, and Syringe.

apple orchard. IBM corporate headquarters in Armonk, New York, a site that was once an apple orchard.

architecture. The selection and interrelationship of components that make up different kinds of computer systems.

ascII (acr). American Standard Code for Information Interchange; the 128-character standard used by most computers.

AT. It originally stood for Advanced Technology, an IBM Corp. PC model that used an 80286 chip. Now, any 80286 chip.

AWTT. Assemble with Tinker Toys.

BAB. Bourbon and branchwater.

BAC. Branch to Alpha Centauri.

back door. A hole in computer security deliberately left by designers. Also known as a TRAPDOOR.

BAF. Blow all fuses.

bag biter. Something or someone that has created problems.

banana problem. Not knowing when to bring an activity to a close. It comes from the old joke about the child who knew how to spell banana but didn't know when to stop.

bandwidth. The capacity, measured in cycles per second, of a circuit or other medium that carries information, like the "bus" of a computer. The higher the bandwidth, the more information can be processed. By extension, "Bill Gates is a high-bandwidth kind of guy."

barf. To fail or malfunction.

baud. Measurement, in bits per second, of the speed by which computers move data from one place to another.

BDC. Break down and cry.

BDT. Burn data tree.

bead. A small program module.

bells and whistles. Unessential but often alluring features. Sometimes the words "and gongs" is added for emphasis.

beta. The final stages of development before a product is released to market. "The software is in beta" means it is in advanced development (after alpha, or preliminary development). In the software industry, beta has been known to last a year or more. "Her baby is in beta" means she is expecting soon.

beta test. The first tests of new software outside the company that developed it, where the company did the alpha testing.

big iron. Mainframe computers. This term was in common use at IBM.

bit (acr). A compression of the words binary digit, it is the smallest unit of digital information, represented by an 0 or a 1.

black box. Small piece of equipment that will make everything work right.

black-box approach. To accept computed results without questioning the method used to get those results.

blem. Problem, possible shortening of blemish.

blue. An IBM computer, from the Wall Street nickname "Big Blue" for IBM. A "true-blue shop" is a computer center where all the equipment comes from IBM.

blue collar. Computer working in a factory.

blue-speak. Jargon of those who work for IBM which is a sizable language unto itself. The tenth edition of the *IBM Jargon and General Computing Dictionary*, published in 1990 by IBM U.K., contained more than 1,400 entries. More than a mere glossary, its editor called it "a window on the IBM culture." Some examples were also contained in the September 27, 1993, issue of *BusinessWeek*.

boat anchor. Old computer of dubious utility. A Silicon Valley Web site takes the definition one step further: "Unused, obsolete cpu kept around to leverage acquisition of a new machine at the beginning of the fiscal year. 'Fred's office floor was cluttered with boat anchors.'"

bogon. A person who is bogus or says bogus things. A bogon is also a mythical subatomic particle bearing the unit charge of bogosity. These related terms were brought to national prominence by *The Hacker's Dictionary* (see "Sources").

bogosity. The degree to which something is bogus. See BOGON.

bomb. To fail or malfunction. Bombing is less than crashing; that is, a program may bomb, but a system crashes.

boot. To start. To restart is to reboot. The term is short for bootstrapping alluding to the bootstrap loader, a small program that when moved into memory will load the rest of the system.

bootstrap. A small program that gets the computer up and running, from the image of pulling oneself up by the bootstraps.

boudoir. An area containing a coupled processor and memory. An area where the processors and memory elements are separated is called a dance hall.

box. A computer.

bozotic. Absurd, from Bozo the clown.

BPS. Bits per second; see BAUD.

breadboard. A board on which experimental electronic circuits can be laid out.

bridgeware. Hardware or software that serves as a bridge between two kinds of system.

bsod (acr). The dreaded "blue screen of death," which shows itself when there has been a major failure or crash.

bug. An error, defect, or problem; cleaning up such a program is called DEBUGGING. A Navy computer pioneer, Grace Hopper, has claimed that the term was coined in 1945 by her team, working on the Mark II, the first large-scale American computer, when a glitch occurred after a two-inch moth got stuck in one of the Mark II's relays. The term had been used before to describe an error or failure, but this was its first application to computers. Hopper taped the original bug to the page of her logbook for the day on which it was dislodged from the machine.

bulletproof. Said of a program that is safe from both hackers and the inept.

burst. To tear printer paper along its perforated line, as in "Print and burst that report, please."

byte. Eight bits. It is the standard unit of computer information. See CHARACTER.

Card. 1. A printed circuit. 2. A cybernetic age ago this term referred to the punched computer cardboard card bearing the timeless admonition: "Do not bend, fold, spindle or mutilate."

careware. Type of shareware for which part of the registration fee goes to charity.

casters up. A dead computer, a reference to the wheels on a frame holding equipment.

CBNC. Close but no cigar.

CH. Create havoc.

Say What?

In 1993 when a new regime took over at IBM, the company vowed to get rid of some of the language that was particular to that company. First off the bat, it banished the IBMism LOB (line of business.) Here are other examples of blue-speak that have escaped from the inside:

all blue. Describes a customer that has bought all of its equipment from IBM.

blue glue. What binds IBM components together.

boil the ocean. To attempt something too ambitious, as in "He's really boiling the ocean on that problem."

drink from a fire hose. To be at the receiving end of a flood of information.

eat one's lunch. To consume personal time on work.

exterior wet conditions. Rain. This term was once used by an IBM division to explain why it had not conducted a fire drill.

flatten. To resolve an issue, as in "We have to flatten this before tomorrow's meeting."

goat-roping. A gathering of the key players needed to resolve an issue, as in "We'll have to have a goat-roping on this PC pricing strategy."

hypo. A high-potential employee, generally destined for management.

IBM-ois. French version of blue-speak.

milk a mouse. To pursue a trivial issue.

nonconcur. To disagree.

open kimono. To go "open kimono" is to reveal everything to another.

panoota (acr). To guess, to estimate. From "pull a number out of the air."

pay for the coffee. To suffer mild pressure.

reswizzle. To improve something, as in "Frank's boss asked him to reswizzle his foils." Synonym: To tweak.

ROJ. Retired on job, applied to those not pulling their loads.

sheep-dip session. Sales seminar.

side sucker. Program that uses a large amount of system resource.

slope shoulders. To refuse to take responsibility for a problem.

tip of the ice cube. Visible part of something very small and insignificant.

tired iron. Old data-processing euipment.

uncork. To make an internal problem public.

character. A letter, number, symbol, or space. A character is equivalent to one BYTE. *The Hacker's Dictionary*, by Guy L. Steele et al., points out that there is an elaborate hacker vocabulary for the various keyboard symbols; for instance, the number symbol, #, is called a "hash mark, mesh, crunch, pig-pen," and some names for the exclamation mark, !, are, "excl, exclam, bang, shriek, wow."

chip. An integrated circuit on a wafer slice, usually made from silicon.

chiphead. Computer enthusiast. Of this term Sandy Grady wrote in the *San Francisco Examiner* (January 3, 1983): "The human race, you see, is now divided into Chipheads and Squareheads. The Chipheads—and there are millions of them—think computers are changing the world. A Chiphead will rhapsodize endlessly about his Atari or Osborne or IBM. A Chiphead swears computers are the greatest things since food and sex."

chips and salsa. Hardware and software.

chomp. To fail or lose or, as stated in *The Hacker's Dictionary* (see "Sources"), "to chew on something of which more was bitten off than one can."

chrome. Fancy, flashy features.

client. 1. A personal computer. 2. One of the class of powerful small computers called workstations.

closed architecture. Equipment designed to work only with the accessories made by the same company.

CMD. Compare meaningless data.

CML. Compute meaning of life.

CNB. Cause nervous breakdown.

code bloat. Growth of systems resource requirements caused by the addition of features and functionality in software.

code warrior. A writer of code, the building blocks of software.

coffee break. Unscheduled failure.

COLB. Crash for operator's lunch break.

cold fault. Any malfunction or fault that is apparent as soon as the machine is turned on.

compu-speak. Jargon of chipheads; cyberbabble.

computer virus. See VIRUS.

connectivity. The ability of computers to talk to each other; generally applied to communication among different computer architectures. (Interestingly, software people usually say "connecTIVity"; hardware people usually say "CONnectivity.")

The "connectivity conspiracy" is the tendency of manufacturers to come up with new products that are not compatible with old ones.

core dump. To unload a computer's main memory or, by extension, to get something off your chest. See DUMP.

CPU. Central processing unit, the electronic brain of a computer system.

cracker. One who is adept at breaking into computer systems: a hacker with a criminal bent.

crapplet. A badly written or profoundly useless applet, which is a small program written in Java.

CRASH (acr). Continue running after stop or halt.

crash. 1. To stop working; to freeze up. 2. A major malfunction resulting in the loss of information.

creeping featurism. The tendency for a complicated program to become more so as new features are added.

crippleware. Software infected with a VIRUS or viruses, as in "I had better things to do than sort through 650 megs of crippleware looking for the problem."

cruftware. Cruddy soft- or hardware.

crufty. 1. Bad, poorly built. 2. Yucky, such as catsup smeared on one's keyboard.

crunch. To process or compute routinely.

CS. Crash system.

CSL. Curse and swear loudly.

cursor. Movable screen symbol—usually a vertical dash or a small square—that indicates where the next character will appear.

cuspy. Excellent.

CVG. Convert to garbage.

cybercrud. Cybernetic bullshit; hype.

cyberizing. Bringing someone into the electronic universe.

cyberphobe. One with a fear of the computer.

cyberpunk. High-technology enthusiast with, as a writer for the *Los Angeles Times* put it, "futuristic ideas and outlaw nature."

Daughterboard. A small circuit board directly attached to the MOTHERBOARD.

DDT. A debugging program, from the name of the famous insecticide.

dead-tree edition. The paper version of a manual or publication that is available in both paper and electronic forms.

deadlock. Stoppage created when two computer processes wait for the other to do something. In some circles this is referred to as a "deadly embrace."

debugging. See BUG.

default. A preset value for a variable. For instance, the default in a word-processing program might be for two spaces after a period.

diddle. To work aimlessly; not seriously.

digerati. A group of people who are especially knowledgeable about the digital revolution (cf. "literati").

digizine. CD-ROM–based periodical.

disk farm. Massive data-storage facility, such as those maintained by the National Aeronautics and Space Administration.

display. The CRT, or monitor.

dithering. The substitution of black and white dots for shades of gray, in computer graphics. It can be used to make curving patterns less jaggy.

DLN. Don't look now. Like the next two entries, it is one of the many three- and four-letter codes used to convey nontechnical comments and insults.

DMPE. Decide to major in phys ed.

DOC. Drive operator crazy.

docs. Documentation; the instruction manual.

dogwash. Crisis, in hacker-speak, as in "Is this a real dogwash?"

dongle. Any silly device hanging from or attached to a computer. It comes from a small device, seldom used these days, that attached to one of the ports of the computer to prevent nonauthorized people from pirating programs.

down. Describes a system that has crashed; is out of order; isn't functioning.

downsizing. The process of moving from big computer systems to smaller ones, also called "rightsizing." This is the same "downsizing" that was applied to firings in the 1990s (and called dumbsizing by those who are suddenly out of work).

DPMI. Declare programmer mentally incompetent.

DPR. Destroy program.

DTC. Destroy this command.

DUD. Drive user to drink (free service of Windows).

dump. See CORE DUMP.

DW. Destroy world.

DWIM. Do what I meant.

EBRS. Emit burned resistor smell.

ECO. Electrocute computer operator.

EIAO. Execute in any order.

EIL. Execute infinite loop.

electronic bulletin board. Information offered on a computer not attached to a network. Each bulletin board stands alone and has its own phone number.

electronics hobbyist. Term used facetiously and euphemistically for and by those who have gotten into cybernetic mischief, such as illegally breaking into a system.

elegant. Describing a solution that is uncluttered and smooth; not clumsy. See KLUDGE.

EMIF. Erase most important file.

encrypt. To scramble information with a code or password so that other people can't read it.

end-user. The person who buys and/or uses the computer, known as a USER in other realms.

ENF. Emit noxious fumes.

EPB. Execute program bug.

EPI. Execute programmer immediately.

ethernet. A local-area-network standard that uses radio frequency signals carried by coaxial cables.

execute. To run a program.

expert system. A program that mimics the intelligence of a human expert in a specific field of knowledge, such as mining or medicine.

Face time. Face-to-face meeting held with an actual person.

feep. The soft beeping sound that a computer terminal makes when it is booted.

firmware. Elements of a computer system that are neither hardware or software, usually a program burned into ROM.

F-key. Collective term for the key on a computer keyboard that can be given different interpretations depending on the program one is using (pron. "F-key"). The letter *F* in F-key refers to the word function.

flavor. Variety.

FLI. Flash lights impressively.

floor sort. A split-open box of computer cards—now largely obsolete.

floppy disk. An encapsulated sheet of plastic that is used to store information. Because of the stiff plastic jacket in which they are locked, they are not the slightest bit floppy. The larger five-inch version is long gone and the smaller three-inch floppy is becoming quickly obsolete.

flyback. The time it takes for the cursor to go from the end of one line on a computer monitor to the beginning of the next.

footer. Words that may appear at the bottom of each page in a word-processed document. See also HEADER.

footprint. Floor or desk space taken up by a computer or printer.

freeware. Copyrighted software available free of charge.

freeway. Public-domain software.

friction feed. A method of moving paper by pressing rollers against the page and spinning them.

frobnitz. An unspecified physical object; a widget.

fry. To fail; to become inoperable. *The Hacker's Dictionary:* "Said especially of smoke-producing hardware failures."

FSM. Fold, spindle, and mutilate.

FUD / FUD factor (acr). Fear, uncertainty, and doubt. The term is used in the context of recommending or buying potentially unknown hardware or software.

fuzzification. The process of making fuzzy.

fuzzify. To convert to FUZZY LOGIC. To convert back to crisp, nonhuman logic is to defuzzify.

fuzzy logic. Logic based on the premise human reasoning does not rely on statements' being clearly true or false; thus a model of computer reasoning based on the kind of imprecision found in human reasoning.

Garbage. Unwanted data. To amass this data in a separate file, disc, or buffer to make room for more is to make a "garbage collection."

gateway. The connecting computer link that translates between two different kinds of computer networks.

GCAR. Get correct answer regardless.

GDP. Grin defiantly at programmer.

gearhead. Programmer.

gig. GIGABYTE, or one billion BYTES of data.

gigabyte. About 1 billion BYTES, often abbreviated GB.

GIGO (acr). Garbage in, garbage out; solutions from bad data will also be bad.

glitch. A flaw. It differs from BUG in that bugs tend to appear in software whereas glitches appear in hardware. A loose wire is

glitch. (*continued*)
a glitch—an interesting distinction, given the fact that the first BUG was in hardware. Also, a sudden interruption in electric service.

global. A global search covers an entire file; for example, it looks for all instances of a given name.

gooie. Phonetic rendition of the acronym GUI, or graphical user interface.

graunch. A devastating error.

gray market. The not-quite-legal buying and selling of computers through nonauthorized dealers.

gritch. To complain; believed to be a blend of gripe + bitch.

grok. To understand, a verb that made its terrestrial debut in Robert A. Heinlein's *Stranger in a Strange Land*.

gronk. To clear a machine that has been jammed, or WEDGED.

gronk out. To stop working.

gronked. Inoperative. It can be applied to people when they are sick or exhausted.

groupware. Network software.

growzy. Describing a computer that is slow to respond to commands. Said to be a blend of grumpy + drowsy.

gubbish. Junk; bad data. A blend of garbage + rubbish.

GUI (acr). Graphical user interface (pron. "GOOIE").

gulp. Multiple bytes (a pun).

guru. An expert, one possessing not only wizardlike skill but also a history of serving as a knowledge resource for others.

gweep. User.

Hack attack. A period of frenzied programming.

hacker. 1. Historically, one who enjoys getting into the details and creative side of computing, as opposed to one who simply uses a computer. For hackers, there are even special greetings, such as "How's hacking?" and farewells, such as "Back to hacking." 2. A genius programmer. 3. One devoted to the computer enterprise to the point of excluding normal social and working life. 4. A malefactor who can range from a fun-loving but irritating prankster to a bona fide cybercriminal. It is the association of such activities with the word "hacker" that infuriates the good hackers.

hair. Difficulty.

handshake. An introductory exchange of electronic signals.

hang. To wait—sometimes interminably, as in a DEADLOCK or "deadly embrace."

hard copy. Printed version of what appears on the computer screen; printout.

hard disk. Rigid platter used for storing computer data magnetically. The speed and storage capacity of a hard disk is much greater than that of a floppy disk. Unlike a floppy disk, a hard disk is seldom removable.

hard-wired. A circuit designed to do one specific task. By extension, said of a person with a very narrow and rigid view of his or her job, as in "Those folks at the Department of Motor Vehicles are really hard-wired."

hardware. 1. Equipment: the computer, disk drivers, monitor, etc. 2. Broadly, physical capital; the physical machinery necessary for computation.

hash. Unwanted or meaningless data.

header. Words that may appear at the top of each page of a word-processed document. See also FOOTER.

heat sink. Piece of metal with small fins that draws heat away from computing chips that get hot.

hedgehog. Person whose abilities are limited to one machine or program.

home. The starting position for the cursor on a document; usually in the upper left-hand corner.

home page. The main point of entry into a multimedia program, usually with icons representing the largest categories into which the contents have been divided.

host. The controlling unit in some computer networks; usually refers to a MAINFRAME computer, one of the huge processors—fewer and fewer these days—set in large frames.

housekeeping. Routine chores—cleaning up files, getting rid of unneeded material, backing up, etc.—that have nothing to do with computing per se.

hungus. Large, unmanageable, humungous (from which it appears to derive).

hygiene. Steps taken to prevent systems from being infected by a computer virus. A tenet of computer hygiene is not trusting foreign data or other people's machines.

IB. Insert bug.

icon. A command in pictorial form pioneered by Apple Computer and adopted by Microsoft Windows. Click a mouse on it and the program or document opens.

IDE. Integrated-drive electronics, a type of interface for controlling hard drives.

IFM. Is it a full moon?

incantation. Any particularly arbitrary or obscure command that one must mutter at a system to attain a desired result.

ISC. Insert sarcastic comments.

Jitter. Brief instability of a signal—not enough to cause a crash.

joystick. An input device, used primarily in computer games, that allows one to give the computer directions by tilting a stick. Like its namesake, the aviator's joystick of World War II, it is a reference to the erect male member.

JTZ. Jump to Twilight Zone.

juice a brick. To recharge a big nicad battery.

K / kilobyte. A thousand BYTES. Often used as a unit to measure how much information a computer can store at one time. It is also used to measure the size of a file or program. One K equals 1024 letters or characters. K is always upper case.

keyboard plaque. Buildup of dirt and crud found on computer keyboards

keyboard vittles. Food particles that are in the crevasses of computer keyboards.

killer app. An applications program that is so compelling that it makes people begin lusting to own a PC. Spreadsheet programs were early killer apps.

KISS (acr). Keep it simple, stupid, a long-established bit of computer dogma and graffiti.

kludge / kluge. 1. A clumsy solution to a problem; a jury-rigged piece of hardware (pron. "klooje"). 2. A clever programming trick intended to solve a particularly nasty problem in an expedient, if not clear, manner. It is the opposite of "elegant," a term sometimes used to describe a skillful, neat hardware or software solution

LAP. Laugh at programmer.

lapware. Software designed for very young children.

launch. To start an application.

learning curve. The time it takes to learn something in the computer world.

liveware. People, especially technicians and users, found in the vicinity of computer systems.

logic board. Apple-speak for MOTHERBOARD.

logic bomb. A computer virus whose effects are triggered and felt when a certain result is specified during routine computation.

LPA. Lead programmer astray.

Macro. A program within a program.

magic. Too complicated to explain, as in "How does it do that?" Answer: "Magic."

mailbomb. To send or urge others to send massive amounts of e-mail to a single system or person, especially with the intent of crashing the recipient's system.

mainframe. A large computer rapidly becoming obsolete with the growing efficency and power of minicomputers. The name comes from the big bulky frame holding the machine.

masquerading. Assuming the identity of another to get into a system.

master-slave arrangement. When one device (a slave) is controlled by another to

master-slave arrangement. (*continued*) which it is connected (a master). Master-slave arrangements are found in disk-drive arrays and other hardware configurations.

MAZ. Multiply answer by zero.

MDE. Mindless data entry.

meatware. The human body.

megabyte. A million bytes; also, a meg.

menu. List of actions available in an application.

mickey. Unit of displacement for—what else?—a computer mouse; smallest measurable unit of mouse movement.

micro. A personal, or micro, computer. Generally speaking, a microcomputer implies a single user (oddly, a minicomputer has many users).

mindshare. To discuss an idea or issue, as in "Let's mindshare on that one."

mini. A minicomputer; a midrange machine between a personal computer and a MAINFRAME.

mips (acr). Millions of instructions per second; a measure of a computer's processing capability.

mnemonic. A way of naming something that helps you remember its purpose, as in Alt-F-S, which is a keyboard File Save command in Windows.

moby. Immense, like Herman Melville's *Moby-Dick*.

mode. State of being. For instance, "night mode" is "The state a person is in when he is working at night and sleeping during the day" (*The Hacker's Dictionary*).

modem (acr). modulator-demodulator, a piece of hardware that allows two computers to "talk" to each other over a phone line.

modem pilot. PC operator who engages another in simulated aerial combat by modem.

monospacing. Uniform and equal spacing between the letters of words, as produced by a typewriter.

morph. To undergo transformation from one set of graphic characteristics to another on screen by use of computer technology; from "metamorphosis."

motherboard. Circuit board to which the main processor chip, memory, and slots for additional cards are attached to form the guts of a computer. See LOGIC BOARD.

mouse. A small electromechanical box with a button or buttons on it which is attached to a computer by a tail-like cable. As it is moved across a desk, the cursor moves across the computer screen. A button on the mouse is "clicked" to give commands.

MTBF. Mean time between failure—how long it takes for a chip or other element of hardware to break down.

multitasking. The ability to run several programs at once. Now used for people.

mung. To change irrevocably or to destroy, as in "I really munged that program." In *The Book of Jargon*, Don Ethan Miller points out that this term began as an acronym from "mushed until no good."

MW. Malfunction whenever.

MWT. Malfunction without telling.

N. A number, usually a large one.

neat hack. 1. Clever technique or deed. 2. Practical joke.

nerd pack. Plastic shirt-pocket protector pack for keeping pens and pencils.

nerdling. Immature hacker.

newbie. A new computer user.

nibble. Half a byte; a four-bit word. Sometimes written "nybble," presumably to match BYTE.

number crunching. Repetitive, routine numerical calculating. A computer or person employed to do this kind of work is sometimes called a number cruncher.

OBC. Omit backup copies.

off-the-shelf. Standard program or piece of equipment that has not been customized or tailored for a specific group of users, nor does it need to be. The military uses the acronym cots, for "common off-the-shelf."

OML. Observe Murphy's Law, which holds that "anything that can go wrong, will." It is used as a reminder that these machines and their operators are disaster-prone.

open architecture. Describing an expandable system that allows for the easy replacement and upgrading of circuit boards. It also implies that you can use boards made by third parties.

orphan. 1. Computer system that gets no software support from its parent company. Orphans usually result when a manufacturer has gone out of business or because the company has abandoned a line of computers. Some half-forgotten orphans are the Apple Liza and everything with the names Kaypro, Morrow, Sinclair, and too many others. 2. Odd programs and bits of software that are in your computer. An article in the *Montgomery (Maryland) Journal* (on a new program) to clean computers of odd files, carried the headline "Windows Cleaner-Upper Finds and Kills Orphans."

Paste. To insert into a computer document an item such as text, graphics, records from a database, and numbers from a spreadsheet that has been cut or copied from elsewhere.

PEHC. Punch extra holes in cards, now used ironically in the post-punch-card era.

percussive maintenance. Whacking an electronic device to try to get it to work.

peripherals. Anything that connects to the computer, including disk drives, monitors, and printers. Defined by John Held as "what you discover you also need if you go to buy a personal computer" (*Washington Post*).

pessimal. Terrible; the opposite of optimal.

phage. A program that modifies other programs or databases in unauthorized ways.

phreaking. The art of cracking into telephone networks.

pixels. Tiny dots that make up the images on a computer screen. The greater the number of pixels, the better the quality of the image.

pizza box. Low-profile desktop computer, usually with a monitor on top.

planar / planar board. IBM-speak for MOTHERBOARD.

plokta (acr). Press lots of keys to abort. To press random keys in an attempt to get some response from the system. One might plokta when the abort procedure for a program is not known, or trying to figure out if the system is just sluggish or really in bad shape.

plug-and-play. Term meaning that you add the card or peripheral; the computer automatically figures out how to make it work with your system.

p-mail. Physical mail, as opposed to e-mail. Also called snail mail.

pnambic. Relating to a process whose apparent operations are, in part or in whole, false. It is an acronym formed from a line in *The Wizard of Oz*: "Pay no attention to the man behind the curtain."

PNRP. Print nasty replies to programmer.

ports. Connectors through which the computer sends and receives data to and from other computers, printers, and keyboards.

power user. Someone who may not be as proficient as a hacker but knows how to get the most out of his computer and software, and is experienced and adept at problem solving.

prompt. Signal from the computer that it is ready to take a command. A prompt can take various forms, from a blinking cursor to a full question stated in plain English.

propeller heads. Programmers.

put more lipstick on the pig. To make cosmetic changes on a software program to make it more appealing to consumers.

QBE. Query by example. A technique by which a user shows a program how to ask questions of a database to get information.

RA. Randomize answer.

RAM. (acr). Random-access memory. Chips on which data are stored temporarily as the computer is working. The information is wiped out when the machine is turned off. See ROM. Also known as memory.

RCB. Read commands backwards.

RDA. Refuse to disclose answer.

reality check. The simplest kind of test of software or hardware; doing the equivalent of asking what 2 + 2 is and seeing if you get 4.

release. A particular version of a piece of software, such as Windows 2000 or XP.

resident. Existing in memory, generally taken to mean in RAM, and therefore not permanent.

rich-text format. A type of file format readable by most major word processing programs.

ROD. Roll over and die.

ROM (acr). Read-only memory. Computer chips on which permanent information is stored. Unlike data in RAM, data in ROM is installed by the manufacturer and cannot be altered.

RPM. Read programmer's mind.

RRSGWSSNK. Round and round she goes, where she stops, nobody knows.

RTDD. Read the damn documents, i.e., the instruction manual.

RWDF. Rewrite disk, destroying fat.

RYFM. Read your fucking manual.

RYT. Rotate your tires. See SYW.

Sagan. A large quantity of anything, from astronomer Carl Sagan, who will always be recalled for the uttering of the words "billions and billions" on his television series *The Cosmos*.

SAI. Skip all instructions.

salami attack / salami technique. Computer crime in which the culprit instructs the computer to do his dirty work a small slice at a time (hence salami). Typically, such an attack is mounted when the malefactor instructs the computer to transfer a few cents from hundreds of accounts and deposit them in his account. For instance, a few seldom-noticed cents might be deducted from every monthly service charge.

SCCA. Short circuit on correct answer.

screen dump. A printout of the image that appears on-screen.

screen-saver face. Look of extreme boredom.

screwdriver shop. Computer retailer who assembles computers on the spot, usually selling at prices below comparable name-brand equipment.

scroll. To move up or down through text on a screen.

scrub. To clean or purge a file of unneeded data.

SCSI (acr). Small computer system interface, a method of connecting PERIPHERALS to a computer (pron. "scuzzy").

send storm. A deluge of private messages received while a user is trying to do something else online.

serial port. A PORT, or connection, on the back of a PC that allows data transfer, one bit at a time.

SFH. Set flags to half-mast.

SFT. Stall for time.

shareware. A program that is distributed freely under the assumption that anyone who uses it will pay for it (that is, it is not freeware or public-domain software).

shelfware. Unused software on a shelf in its original shrink wrap.

shovelware. Often-useless software dumped onto a CD-ROM or computer software bundle to fill space.

Silicon Valley. Area south of San Francisco that has attracted many semiconductor and computer manufacturers. Similarly, there is Silicon Beach in Southern California and several Silicon Prairies in the Midwest (Urbana-Champaign, Illinois, for one). The nickname for the area between Detroit and Ann Arbor has been called Automation Alley because of the concentration of robotics firms in the area.

slave. Machine that is under control of another. See MASTER-SLAVE ARRANGEMENT.

smoke test. Test in which one turns on a machine and gives it a passing grade if it does not smoke, spark, or burst into flames.

snarf. To grab, especially to grab a large document or file for the purpose of using it with or without the author's permission.

sneaker net. Human alternative to a local area network in which humans run from one machine to another bearing floppy disks.

social engineering. In the world of computer criminality, this is conning someone with access to a network into divulging a password.

software. 1. Lengthy, complicated codes of instructions, called programs, that tell the machinery how to accomplish certain tasks. 2. In the larger economic world, software can be anything we think of as being a valuable idea.

soho (acr). Small office, home office; a large market segment for computers.

SOS. Sign off, stupid.

spaghetti code. Program written without a coherent structure.

spazz. To behave erratically.

spike. A sudden surge of electric current that can create computer havoc. Same as SURGE.

splash. To shoot something down; to cancel, especially a new program.

spoofer. One who fools a system into believing it is being accessed by an approved user.

SQL. Structured query language; a specialized way of getting information from a database, generally, one stored in a larger computer. Sometimes pronounced "sequel."

steel collar. Industrial robot in the sense that blue collar stands for industrial worker.

stoned. Computer virus that revealed itself ca. 1992 which erases everything on your machine and leaves the screen proclaiming "Your computer is now stoned. Legalize marijauna."

superprogrammer. A prolific programmer; one who can code exceedingly well and quickly. Not all hackers are superprogrammers, but many are.

surge. A spike or sudden burst in power that can literally fry computer chips.

SYW. Spin your wheels (see RYT).

TARC. Take arithmetic review course.

task bar. A thin strip along the bottom of the computer screen. In Windows 95, the start button is located here.

tech-mech. Engineer or techie who "sold out" to the military or a large corporation.

techie. Technician.

technoslut / technotrash / technoweenie. Brilliant technician who is a social disaster.

template. A "master" document for a word processor, or spreadsheet, or other application that is used as the starting point or a rough draft.

thrashing. The act of randomly hitting keys in the hope that you will trigger a covert possibility in a computer program.

three-finger salute. Process of simultaneously striking the three keys "ctrl," "alt," and "delete" in order to restart your computer after it freezes up.

tiled. Arrangement of open windows so that they do not overlap.

TILO. Turn indicator lights off.

time bomb. Outlaw term. Instructions built into a program that cause destruction of data at a particular time in the future.

time sink. A project that consumes boundless amounts of time.

TN. Take a nap.

TPDH. Tell programmer to do it himherself.

trackball. A ball nested in a laptop computer that takes the place of the ball in a conventional mouse. One moves the onscreen cursor by moving the ball.

transparent. A process not obvious to the user.

trapdoor. In computer crime parlance, a gap in a program, created by accident or

trapdoor. (*continued*)
deliberately, that allows access to that program by bypassing its security system. It may be designed on purpose by somebody who has legal entry but plans to make an illegal foray later, or who doesn't want to take the time to jump through all the security loops every time he launches the program. See also BACK DOOR.

trash 80. Affectionate name for the old Tandy TRS computer.

trojan horse / trojan. Any secret set of illegal instructions built into an existing program. The affected program acts normally until the hidden commands are triggered or a certain date and time are reached (for example, Friday the 13th at noon). There is a mad ingenuity at work here, including one known as "notroj," which according to the *New York Times* of May 19, 1987, "pretends to be a program that guards against trojans. It's actually a time bomb that will wipe out your hard disk after it is more than 70% full."

TRQ. To-read queue.

TSR. Terminate and stay resident. Said of a program that stays in memory (RAM) after it has been executed. By remaining in memory, it is readily available for the user to run it again.

TTA. Try, try again.

tweak. To fine-tune; to make a slight adjustment.

tweak freak. A computer techie obsessed with finding the root of all tech problems, regardless of their relevance.

Up. Working, or up and running. A machine is often said to be up after it has been DOWN (CRASHED).

UP. Understand program.

upgrade. The new improved version (usually of something you were told was the new improved version in the first place).

user. One who works with the computer but does not get into the innards of programs. Not a hacker. See END-USER.

user-friendly. Industry jargon for easy to use. User-friendly computers usually have many menus. Especially user-friendly equipment is, according to the *IBM Jargon and General Computing Dictionary*, "user-cuddly."

Vactor. Synthetic actor used in computer animation. A blend of—take your pick—video + actor or virtual + actor.

vanilla. Ordinary; standard; the usual flavor, such as a piece of equipment with no special features.

vaporware. 1. Software that does not exist yet but which is often announced by a software company and discussed and given coverage in the trade press. It has been termed a realm of hype and illusion where promises and deadlines are sometime things. After Microsoft missed three target delivery dates for Windows 95 after its initial announcement in February 1994, there was a period when folks were alluding to the new operating system as vaporware. 2. Hardware that has yet to materialize on the market but is promoted as if it were about to revolutionize the computer industry.

VAR. Value-added reseller. Generally, a person who puts together computer systems complete with software, hardware, and peripherals.

variable. In software, a data element that can be changed.

virtual. Not physical but behaving as if physical; a simulation.

virus. Program or instruction created to cause mischief. A virus may clog a system with useless information or erase or alter existing information. Like true biological viruses, they spread and cause the electronic equivalent of epidemics.

Vulcan nerve pinch. Any taxing hand position required to reach all of the appropriate keys for certain commands. Inspired by the reboot for a Mac II computer, which involves simultaneously pressing the "control" key, the "command" key, the "return" key, and the "power on" key.

WA(H)G. Wild-assed (h)airy guess.

wallpaper. Lengthy printouts that give more information than will ever be used.

-ware. All-purpose ending for computer goods. In her book *Word Watch*, Anne H. Soukhanov points out that there is a trademarked program for do-it-yourself divorces called Divorceware, which shows how far we have come from the simple business of hardware, as in hardware store. With the advent of computers hardware begat software, which begat, among other things, vaporware, crippleware, careware, freeware, fontware, liveware, groupware, and firmware. Wetware, in the newest wrinkle of Silicon Valley lingo, refers to those who operate the machinery and to the combination of knowledge and character that they bring to their tasks.

warm boot. To restart a computer using the "ctrl-alt-del" key combination.

wave a dead chicken. To go through the motions even though you are sure that the results will be futile.

wedged. To get stuck.

wetware. 1. The human brain and its DNA code. 2. Humans when using computers. As opposed to SOFTWARE or HARDWARE.

WIBNI. "Wouldn't it be nice if . . . ?" in hacker-speak.

window. A section of the screen showing a document.

wirehead. Fanatic tinkerer and fixer addicted to computers to the extent that other things in life are neglected.

wizard. Illustrated, detailed, step-by-step instructions on how to accomplish a task. An old Windows 95 term that has survived as a generic term.

wonky. Broken.

word wrap. The ability of a word-processing program to drop a word to the next line rather than allow a word to be broken at the end of a line. The text is literally wrapped around to the next line and eliminates the need for the carriage return at the end of each line. In Notepad, in Windows, the word-wrap function must be turned on; otherwise words will run off the right side of the screen.

worm. A rogue program that endlessly duplicates itself, thereby causing the infected system to bog down. Unlike a virus, a worm does not attach itself to a program; it survives independently.

WSWW. Works in strange and wondrous ways.

wykiwyl (acr). An acronym-like coinage, prounounced "wicky-will," for "what you know is what you like."

wysiwyag (acr). "What you see is what you almost get."

wysiwyg (acr). "What you see is what you get" (pron. "wizzy-wig"). It refers to the alleged ability to view a display and see exactly what will be printed in terms of typography and graphics.

wysln. "What you see looks natural" (pron. "wizz-lin").

Yo-yo mode. Condition of a system that is alternately UP and DOWN (working and not working).

Zap. To erase.

zipperhead. One with a closed mind.

zorch. To move quickly.

7

CRIME, PUNISHMENT, AND THE LAW

Words You Don't Hear on the Outside

The slang—or, as it used to be called, "cant"—of thieves, gypsies, vagabonds and their fellows has enriched the English language and its literature since Shakespeare's time.

—Geoffrey Nunberg, *New York Times Book Review*, "Voice of the Yegg and the Grifter: Language of the Underworld," May 2, 1982

Most of the early works on slang in English were concerned with the cant of criminals. For instance, *The Tom and Jerry Flash Dictionary*, published in London in 1825, contained an elaborate slang listing that included no less than sixty orders of coves, or receivers, of foreign goods, including footpads, rumpadders, twirlers, maces, pab priggers, cadgers, dubsmen, and swaddlers.

Then as now, crime is a rich area for the collector of slang. Today there are really four sets of slang associated with crime and punishment: that of the criminal, that of prison, that of the police—these three covered in this chapter—and the slang of drugs, covered in a separate chapter.

Although there are differences in these various slangs, they are all interrelated and aided, amended, and augmented by characters in television series such as Andy Sipowicz and his pals on *NYPD Blue*, the various manifestations of *Law & Order*, *CSI: Crime Scene Investigation*, *Hill Street Blues*, *The Sopranos*, and *Homicide: Life on the Street*.

All day. A life sentence, in the lingo of prisoners.

all day and night. A life sentence to prison.

armor. Weapons, to a convict.

Baby-dolling. Sending kids out to collect money for a bogus charity or cause with false credentials, such as a typewritten letter from a "coach" asking for money for football uniforms.

baby raper. Inmate term for older convict who has committed a sexual offense against a minor or whose crime is unknown.

badge. A cop, guard, correctional officer.

badge-heavy. Describing a self-important cop; or one who gets carried away with his or her authority.

bag. 1. Police term for a uniform; to be sent back to the uniformed ranks after being a plainclothes officer is known as going back "into the bag." 2. To arrest, as in "bag him."

B&W / black-and-white. Police car. This term varies from city to city according to the local police colors.

banger. A knife. Also called a burner or a shank.

baton. Nightstick.

beagle. A detective.

beat. Diluted, as in a "beat drug," a drug that has been cut.

beat the bricks. To get out of prison.

belch. To inform or testify.

BFR. Big fucking rock, in police reports, alluding to a primitive burglary tool.

big con. Confidence game or trick, normally requiring an elaborate setup, that nets the con artist big money.

bit. A prison sentence.

blaster. Gunman.

blocks. Prison cellhouses.

blotter. Police-station ledger.

blue flu. A police sick-out; a strike action in which police call in sick.

blue-light bandit. Criminal who impersonates a police officer to commit a crime.

body pack. More than three dead bodies, in police parlance.

bolo (acr). Police shorthand for "be on the lookout for."

bonaroo. One's best clothes, in prison parlance, as in "I've got my bonaroos all ready for my next visit."

bones. Dominoes, a very popular game in prison.

boneyard. In prison talk, the family (conjugal) visiting area.

book. 1. Life sentence, in the sense that one has had the book thrown at one. 2. To arrest.

boost. To shoplift.

boss. A guard, to prison convicts—some say it stands for "sorry son of a bitch" spelled backward.

bottle baby. Derelict.

bounce. Police vernacular for a brainstorming session.

bow-and-arrow squad. A police unit not allowed to carry firearms.

breakdown. Shotgun.

bricks. The outside or on the outside, as in "on the bricks."

bridal suite. Room where police who work late or extra shifts can take a nap.

broadway. The first floor of some tiers of cells in prison. A wide area where convicts come and go and may occasionally be housed if the prison is particularly crowded.

broom. Policeman who keeps the station house clean and acts as an errand boy.

brownie. A traffic cop, in the eyes of the police who deal with crime.

bubs. The blue flashers, also called bubbles, on the tops of police cars.

bucket, the. Jail.

bucket of blood. Violent tavern requiring routine police visits.

bug. 1. Police term for a criminal without compassion or empathy. 2. A crazy person, in prison talk.

buggin'. Police slang for goofing off.

bull. Guard, in slammerese.

bullet. Sentence of one year in prison.

bunkie. In slammerese, the person with whom a prisoner shares a double bunk bed.

burn. To shoot.

bus ride. A court appearance, to a person in prison.

bus therapy. Unnecessary transporting of a prisoner as a form of punishment.

bush gang. Prison gang that works outside cutting brush and doing other jobs. It has been termed a chain gang without the chains.

buy down. Term when convicted criminals are willing to forfeit as much of their ill-gotten estate as possible to the authorities in hopes of getting a reduced sentence.

buy you a suit. Phrase used to tell a police officer that there is a bribe forthcoming if a violation is overlooked. Also, "give you a hat."

buzz. In the parlance of the police, to flash your badge when you are off-duty.

Cadillac. Prison coffee with cream and sugar; smooth, rich, and creamy.

cage. Prison cell.

calendar. A year, in prison talk.

canned. Imprisoned.

cannon. A pickpocket.

cap. In prison lingo, the amount of marijuana that fits into a ChapStick cap.

carry-out rape. Police term for abduction and rape.

catcher. Sexually passive or submissive prison convict, often victimized.

cellie / celly. One's cellmate.

chalk. Home-made alcohol, or PRUNO.

chester. Child molester, in the vernacular of prison convicts.

chicken hawk. Child molester.

chi-mo. Child molester.

chill. Kill.

chinaman. Convict who washes his clothes in the sink instead of using the prison laundry.

chop shop. Garage where stolen cars are disassembled in preparation for being sold on the used-parts market.

clavo. A prison stash or collection. "He has a huge clavo of jelly beans."

Club Fed. Federal penitentiaries, especially to inmates of other institutions.

code 7. Work break or meal, to most police, part of a larger number code.

coin wrestler. One who dives into public fountains for coins thrown by tourists for luck; usually homeless men working late at night.

cold gun. A gun that has been worked on to disguise its origins, as opposed to a HOT, or stolen, gun.

collar. To arrest.

collars for dollars. When corrupt police purposely wait until a shift's end to make an arrest. The time it takes to process a suspect can guarantee as much as twenty-four hours' overtime pay.

convict. Career criminal, to a fellow convict.

cooping. Of police officers, sleeping or relaxing on the job.

cop killers. Armor-piercing bullets.

cop's cop. A compliment among members of the New York City Police Department. This came to light in 2000 when Baltimore hired a new police commissioner, Edward T. Norris, from New York City. Norris brought with him a vocabulary that included widespread use of the word "cop," which was regarded as derogatory by some old-timers. Norris told the *Baltimore Sun* that "cop's cop" was a "real term of endearment" in New York. He was told that the Baltimore eqivalent was "He's a real *po*-lice."

corner. In prison a corner is a group a man hangs out with. "Lots of times, even a loner is hooked to a certain corner, so within that you've got 'strong corners,' 'weak corners,' etc. Once you know all the corners, where they are, and what their guidelines are, then you get an easy feel for the pulse of a prison" (Fannie Martin, *Committing Journalism*).

corset. Bulletproof vest.

crate. A carton of cigarettes in prison.

crib. One's cell.

crib burglar. A burglar who breaks into and robs homes and apartments.

***CSI* effect.** Expectation by juries that prosecutors in criminal cases will have the same kind of slam-dunk forensic evidence common to television shows such as *CSI: Crime Scene Investigation*, *Crossing Jordan*, and the like. Prosecutors claim that this effect has made convictions harder to attain.

cut. To attempt suicide behind bars.

Say What?

Caveat: "convict" vs. "inmate"

An inmate in a Colorado prison wrote to the author:

> Even though the terms are generally interchangeable, in many systems "inmate" carries a negative connotation, while "convict" implies a career criminal or one who is attuned to the nuances of prison life. This is called being "down"—"Bob is a real down dude."
>
> The importance of words is never more obvious than in prison—the wrong word, or even saying one the wrong way, can get an inmate killed.

Glossaries of prison terms have underscored the point. A Web site entitled "Prison Slang 101" contains this definition: "Inmate: Derogatory term for prisoners. Used by guards and administrators, or other inmates who are called fish (first-timers and new arrivals who don't know the lingo yet)—or kiss-asses, 'lops,' fools, dingbats, and assorted other goofball inmates."

Daddy. Pimp.

dance hall. Execution chamber.

dead presidents. Money in bills. "Open your wallet and show me some dead presidents."

dead time. Time spent in jail that does not count against a sentence. For instance, time spent for contempt or not cooperating with a grand jury is often dead time.

deck. A pack of cigarettes, to a prison convict.

deuce. Police term for drunk or drunk driver.

Deuce, the. The block of Forty-second Street between Seventh and Eighth avenues in New York City, to police and criminals alike. This was once considered to be the area with the greatest incidence of crime in the nation.

deuce-deuce. A .22-caliber gun.

devastator. An exploding small-caliber bullet.

digger. A pickpocket.

dime / dime ya. To inform on someone; to DROP A DIME.

dimed out. In prison, telling on someone. "The rat, he dimed me out."

dinger. Burglar alarm.

dip. In a pickpocket operation, the dip is the person who removes the wallet. The SETUP is the person who prepares the victim, usually by bumping into him.

dirty. Describing a bad prison reputation.

divorce. To police, a domestic shooting.

DMZ. Demilitarized zone. Street or area of a city that separates a high-crime area from one with an average or low crime rate. In New York City, the DMZ of the Upper East side is Ninety-sixth Street.

do a piece of work. Whack, hit, or pop, in gangland; to kill.

DOA. Dead on arrival.

doghouse. Prison watchtower.

doin' doors. Corrupt police talk for kicking in doors at known drug locations without a warrant solely to steal cash and drugs. Also known as hittin' spots, or a drug raid.

drive-by. A crime committed from a moving vehicle such as a drive-by shooting.

drop a dime. 1. Police term for calling in information on a specific crime. 2. In prison, to inform on someone. "He dropped a dime on his bunkie."

DRT. Dead right there. More emphatic term than DOA.

drum. Jail cell.

duck pond. A spot where an officer can write a lot of tickets with little effort. It's also known as a hole, a cherry patch, or a cash register.

dump truck. A lawyer who makes an easy deal at the expense of the client.

dumping ground. A police precinct, usually in a poor, crime-ridden neighborhood, where the department sends officers with discipline problems.

E85. Police slang or code language for a girlfriend.

equalized. Armed.

eyeball van. Police term for surveillance vehicle with one-way glass.

Face the heat. To take responsibility, in prison parlance.

feero. Fire bug; an arsonist.

fence parole. An escape, in slammerese.

56. Police term for time off.

finger. 1. A police informer. 2. To identify someone as a suspect; to inform on someone.

fireworks. Gunplay; shoot-out.

fish. A new prisoner.

five-finger discount. Shoplifting.

five-O. Street slang for "cops," taken from the television show *Hawaii Five-O*.

fix. 1. A stationary post for a police officer. 2. Trouble (to be in a fix).

flake. To plant false evidence.

flip. To turn on; to give evidence to the police or to prison authorities.

floater. Police term for a body found in water.

fly. To escape from prison.

fooled out. To make a mistake.

four-five. A .45-caliber gun.

four-to-four. Police beat from four in the afternoon until midnight, but it may also include time to unwind at a bar that closes at four A.M. In *One Police Plaza*, William J. Caunitz describes one of these shifts, saying, "The session lasted until four in the morning. Policemen's wives have dubbed these tours the 'four-to-fours.'"

freeway dancer. Police term for people who dash across major highways in the dark.

freeworld. 1. The outside, to a prisoner. 2. Manufactured cigarettes, as opposed to hand-rolled, or "tailor-made."

fresh kills. New homicides, to a detective.

GAC. "*G*ot *a*way *c*lean," in police-speak.

gank. 1. To rob or rip off. 2. A fool or easy mark.

Gat. Gun.

gate money. The small sum of money the state gives a prisoner upon his release.

gauge. Shotgun, especially to police.

gee. A guy in prison.

get busy. Street slang for robbing someone.

get paid. Street slang for committing a successful robbery.

get small. To get away, to disappear, especially for a suspect, as in "He got small in a hurry."

gimmie. Police term for a handgun, from the robber's demand "Gimme . . ."

G-joint. Federal prison.

gladiator fight. Prison fight staged for the benefit of others, such as guards.

gladiator school. Maximum-security prison.

glass beat / glass post. Police term for a beat where there are a lot of stores with large plate-glass windows.

go on the box. To take a lie-detector test.

GOA. Gone on arrival, variant on DOA.

gold tin. Detective's badge, as opposed to TIN, which is the name for a uniformed policeman's badge. To "get the gold tin" is to be promoted to detective.

gonzales. The game of blackjack.

gooners. Prisoners' term for corrections officers.

Gray Bar Motel / Hotel. Jail.

grounder. In his book *Close Pursuit: A Week in the Life of an NYPD Homicide Cop* (see "Sources"), Carsten Stroud writes that this term is used by the New York Police Department for "a homicide case that can be solved with relative speed and simplicity." The opposite of a grounder is a "mystery" or a "queer one."

Hair bag. 1. Veteran cop, to other cops. 2. A PERP, especially since *Hill Street Blues* and augmented by *NYPD Blue*.

hard time. 1. Sentence with no parole in sight. 2. Sentence to hard labor.

heat. 1. Gun. 2. Pressure on a suspect.

heeled. Carrying a gun.

he-she. Transvestite, to the police.

hit. Shoot.

hit man. Gang assassin.

hitch. Prison sentence.

hold your mud. Criminals' talk for not blabbing to the police or feds when arrested; one who does not rat on others holds his mud. In James Mills's *Underworld Empire*, a man is described as "an old-time crook, who holds his mud."

holding. Carrying a gun.

hole. 1. Solitary confinement. 2. The subway, to an urban police officer in a city that has one.

hook down. "The guard is coming," in prison talk.

hook 'n' bookin'. Handcuffing and arresting, in police-officer talk.

horse. Person who smuggles money or drugs into prison. Also known as a MULE.

Horsemen. In Canada, the Royal Canadian Mounted Police.

hot. Stolen.

hot prowl. Police talk for a prowler in an occupied home.

hot shot. Police emergency call meaning "shots fired."

house. Prison cell.

hugger-mugger. According to Joseph Wambaugh, in *Echoes in the Darkness*, a man who "picks on plain or homely women, turns on the charm and gives them some cuddles while he picks their purses."

husher. Device used to mask conversation between the judge and attorneys in jury trials.

IBM. For "Italian business man," in the parlance of the FBI. It refers to someone associated with the Mafia.

in a crack. In trouble, especially in prison.

in-house lawyer. Convict paralegal. See JAILHOUSE LAWYER.

in the free. Prison term for out of jail; on the street.

ink. Tattoos in jail.

inside / outside. Inside and outside the walls of a prison.

iron pile. Prison weight-lifting equipment.

Jacket. 1. A criminal record. 2. The reputation (good or bad) of a prisoner or convict. Prisoners can put false jackets on other prisoners to discredit them.

jailhouse lawyer. A prisoner who assists others in filing legal actions. As explained on a convict-controlled Internet site (devoted to prison slang): "Some are quite knowledgeable, others know enough to get themselves or others into trouble. Jailhouse lawyers are important because most prisoners have limited access to law libraries, little legal knowledge, and there are all too few lawyers able to assist prisoners."

jailin'. 1. Someone who's in the hole (a.k.a. in jail). 2. Attitude to doing jail time. Seth Morgan in his book *Homeboy* writes, "Jailin' was an art form and lifestyle both. The style was walkin' slow, drinkin' plenty of water, and doin' your own time; the art was lightin' cigarettes from wall sockets, playin' the dozens, cuttin' up dream jackpots, and slowin' your metabolism to a crawl, sleepin' twenty-four hours a day. Forget the streets

jailin'. (*continued*)
you won't see for years. Lettin' your heart beat the bricks with your body behind bars was hard time. Acceptin' the jailhouse as the only reality was easy time."

jakes. Police term for uniformed police.

jocker. Aggressive homosexual male prisoner.

John Law. The police.

joint. Prison.

jolt. A long prison sentence, as in "I got a life jolt."

jug. 1. To attempt to cut the jugular vein. 2. Jail; the joint.

juice. Good prison connections; penitentiary pull.

jump-outs. Teams of arresting officers who commonly jump out of hiding or out of a patrol car.

Kazoonie. Passive homosexual male prisoner.

keep. Prison.

keeping six. Safecracker's code for a lookout; one who watches for the police and other interlopers.

keeping the peek. In prison, activity of a lookout, watch for the guards, etc.

keester. To hide contraband in the rectum. Prisoners keester money, drugs, and even weapons.

KG. Police term for "*k*nown *g*ambler."

kick 'em. To release a suspect, in police talk.

kit. Items for taking drugs, in prison talk.

kite. 1. Letter to, from, or within prison, as in "to float a kite." Inside, kites are often contained on small pieces of folded paper. 2. Specifically, a written request for services within the joint, such as a request for dental or medical services.

klepto. Kleptomaniac.

knocked. Arrested.

Kojak light. Portable flashing red light that police can throw up on the roof of an unmarked car to mark it. The term comes from the television cop Kojak, who used such a light.

Lajaras. Hispanic street slang for New York cops. It derives supposedly from the name O'Hara.

launder. To legalize illegal money.

lay chickie. To act as a lookout.

lay paper. Pass worthless checks.

lay the track. Have sex in prison.

lemac. A Camel Brand cigarette, in slammerese. It is the word "camel" spelled backward.

lockdown. The policy of confining a group of prisoners or an entire prison to cells. Generally done in response to unrest or emergency, although some lockdowns are instituted for extended periods of time. The term has also been employed in an extended sense to describe inner-city confinement of kids by parents fearing street violence.

loid. To open a lock with a credit card or other piece of plastic. The term predates credit cards and harks back to the time when burglars used thin strips of celluloid.

Mafias. Dark sunglasses, in prison lingo.

mainline. What prisoners call the general population.

man, the. The warden.

mark. 1. Victim. 2. Someone who wants to be a gang member.

maxin'. Prison slang for serving maximum time. By extension, hanging out, as one must do while serving a long sentence.

maytag. Prison slang for a male convict unable to protect himself from homosexual rape.

minute. Prisoners' term for a short sentence. A life sentence is ALL DAY.

Mirandize. To warn a suspect of his or her constitutional rights under the Supreme Court's Miranda decision.

moe. Married homosexual in prison.

mole. Convict secretly working for THE MAN.

money bus. Armored truck.

monster. Prisoners' term for HIV, as in "He has the monster."

mooch. Target of a scam.

mooner. Person who gives police a hard time and is believed to be most pesky during a full moon.

mother's day. Day on which welfare checks arrive and women are more vulnerable to robbery.

motor. Tattoo gun, in prison.

mug. 1. Rob and beat. 2. To take a police or prison photo, or mug shot.

mule. In prison, a person who carries things—usually contraband—for others, either around the prison or in prison. See HORSE.

mushfake. Contraband in prison.

mustard chucker. Pickpocket who preys on tourists and others by "spray[ing] a victim with mustard. He apologizes profusely and helps to remove it while an accomplice steals the victim's wallet" (*New York Times*, July 13, 1989).

Mutt and Jeff act. Interrogation technique in which one police officer, Mutt, is the bad cop (heavy and hostile), and the other, Jeff, is good-natured and friendly.

Ninja rock. A three-eighths-inch-thick cube-shaped piece of white porcelain used—originally by Southeast Asian gangs—to break into cars.

Off. To kill.

on ice. In the morgue.

on the arm. A free meal or other item, in police terminology. Writing in the *New York Times* (February 15, 1970), David Burham said that this expression "might be a play on the expression 'the long arm of the law.'" A character in Vincent Patrick's *Pope of Greenwich Village* says, "He wasn't that greedy at all. He was putting next to nothing into his pocket. It was all bar bills and seven-course dinners on the arm."

on the grain and drain train. To be in solitary confinement in prison. Refers to the old notion of "bread and water."

on the muscle. Said of a nervous suspect, by police.

one-percenters. Term used by outlaw or outcast bikers (motorcyclists) to show that they represent the worst 1 percent of the population.

Paper. 1. Parking ticket. 2. To issue a ticket. 3. Acid (LSD), in drug parlance.

paper hanger. Check forger, to police; a bad-check passer.

patch. The proceeds of a crime that are given to corrupt police to keep the perpetrator from going to jail. A patch is much more costly than a simple bribe or payoff, since it involves the total haul.

pavement princess. Prostitute.

perp. Perpetrator.

phone's off the hook. Convict talk for "the guard is listening."

phony collar. Unjust arrest.

PI. Prison industries.

piddling. Crafting items out of matchsticks, toothpicks, and other humble objects in prison. An item in the *Houston Post* for March 23, 1989, speaks of a death-row convict known for his piddling ability.

piece. A revolver.

pile. Weights in prison, as in the iron pile.

pine-box parole. Prison term for dying in the joint.

pinner. A marijuana cigarette the size of a toothpick, in slammer-ese.

pitcher. Sexually dominant, aggressive, in the lingo of prison.

place, the. Prison.

plant. Police stakeout.

playing on ass. Gambling without money—if a prisoner loses, "it's his ass."

pocket man. Criminal holding the money after a robbery or other crime.

pop caps. To open fire, in police parlance.

popcorn machine. The light(s) on top of a police car.

potty watch. Special prison watch when someone is suspected of eating, or concealing

potty watch. (*continued*) in the anal cavity, drugs or other contraband items, such as money.

pp. Short for "penitentiary pull"; influence in prison.

present the bill. Nicaraguan slang for a death threat to government deputies in the National Assembly.

press your bunk punk. Prison command meaning "Lie down on your bed and shut up."

priors. Previous prison terms; having several priors may lead the judge to give a convict the maximum sentence.

pruno. Homemade alcohol, fermented juice, the classic prison drink.

pulling someone's card. Finding out about another prisoner, in prison talk.

punch job. Safecracking job in which the dial of the safe has been removed.

punk. 1. To sodomize. 2. Victim or willing partner in a homosexual arrangement.

put his papers in. For a policeman to retire.

put your pen to the wind. By convicts, to tell an officer to go ahead and write a disciplinary report. By officers, to tell prisoners to go ahead and file a grievance.

Rabbit. A convict who has escaped or is planning to do so.

raisin jack. Homemade booze, in prison.

rap. Talk, especially in prison.

rap sheet. Criminal record.

rape kit. Material used to collect evidence from a victim of sexual attack.

reefer. The six-button tunic worn by police in cold weather.

ride on. A drive-by shooting.

ride-out. Automotive scam in which the perp intentionally slams into the car of an apparently wealthy person in hopes of making an injury claim and getting a fat settlement.

road dog. Prison term for a good friend made in prison.

roll. To take fingerprints, in police-speak.

roller. A police car.

roscoe. Gun. This term is dated, common to gangster movies of the 1940s, but is still used with tongue in cheek. (There is a sizable slang vocabulary from these movies, which is still toyed with. Some examples: "shamus" for private eye, "mug" for man or his face, "big house" for prison, etc.)

rough off. To steal; to rip off.

rounder. Street criminal who operates around bars, clubs, and hotels, selling drugs, setting up high-stakes poker games, etc. So called because they are always *around* to make the deals.

Safe. The vagina, where women prisoners may hide contraband.

S&J. Sentence and judgment.

S&W. Short for Smith & Wesson.

satch. Paper that has been impregnated with heroin or LSD and mailed into prison in an envelope.

Saturday night special. Cheap handgun.

scratch. A traffic citation.

screw. Prison guard.

SCUM. Semi-acronym for street crimes unit.

second-story man. Burglar.

setup. The person who sets up a pickpocketing—the DIP is the one who actually takes the wallet.

shakedown. Search in prison.

shank. 1. Handmade prison weapon, generally a stabbing instrument. 2. To stab.

shine on. To ignore, in prison parlance.

shit watch. Convict suspected of hiding drugs in his anus or ingesting them will be placed on a shit watch.

shiv. Knife.

shoe. Plainclothes detective.

short. Describes somebody with little prison time to do.

short con. A confidence game requiring little preparation and involving small stakes.

shot. Friend in prison.

signal C. Coffee or coffee break, in patrol car parlance.

signal 12. Someone who is dead, in police parlance.

size the vic. To observe or size up a victim from a distance.

skell. Police name for a derelict or habitual drunk. The term was used by detectives on the television show *NYPD Blue* for street punks. Many believed that the term was created for the show, but the *Oxford English Dictionary* listed earlier uses. The first use cited in the *OED*'s entry for "subway": "1982 *N.Y. Times Mag.* 31 Jan. 21/3 'Other New Yorkers live there, eating yesterday's bagels and sleeping on benches. The police in New York call such people 'skells.'" *Ibid.*, "These 'skells' are not merely down and out. Many are insane, chucked out of New York hospitals."

skinner-diddler. Prison slang for a person who has committed a sex crime, usually against a child. Also hedge-hopper and child lover.

slammer. 1. Prison. 2. In illegal boiler-room sales swindles, the high-pressure salesperson who gets the mark to part with his money.

slim jim. Thin, flexible strip of metal used by car thieves to yank open the lock on a car door.

smurfing. Money-laundering procedure whereby currency is exchanged at various banks in amounts slightly less than those that must be reported to federal authorities. These amounts change, but when all transactions of $10,000 or more had to be reported, many transactions took place involving $9,999.

snitch. An informant; a rat.

songbird. Informer.

spit on the sidewalk. To commit a minor crime.

spitter. Police slang for a pickpocket.

squat. An intentional accident in which two cars bump each other so that a fraudulent injury claim can be made.

squeal. Complaint, in police parlance.

squirrel. Mentally ill convict.

squirrel chaser. 1. Any police officer assigned to patrol parks. (2) Park police.

stall. Person who distracts a victim in a robbery. The "hook" is the person who takes the money or goods.

staties. State police.

stay down. Engage in a fight to prove one's manhood, in Texas prison talk.

step back. Incarceration. A prosecuter may waive "step back" in certain arraignments. It comes from the words of judges who tell some defendants to step back and be escorted to prison.

stepson. Convict under the control of another.

stinger. Prison convict's appliance used to heat water, which may be created by attaching live electrical wires to a metal plate.

stir. Prison.

stooge. A person working for the prison administration.

straight eight. Shift in which patrolman puts in eight hours with no overtime.

strapped. Armed, in the parlance of street gangs.

straps. Street slang for guns.

street. The outside world, as in "on the street."

swag (acr). Stolen without a gun, in police talk.

swallow. Female operative who obtains secrets for sex.

swap paint. What one car does to another when it is sideswiped.

system, the. The entire corrections and jurisprudence bureaucracy; to convicts it is the enemy.

Tailor-made. Factory-rolled cigarettes, in prison.

10/13. Police radio code for an officer in trouble who needs immediate help. One of the "ten" codes: 10/6 stands for "Shut up, you're jamming the frequency," and 10/98 means "This car is ready for a new assignment."

Thirsty Third. New York police nickname for the 46th Precinct's Third Squad, in recognition of its members' penchant for drinking on the job.

13½. The sum total of twelve jurors, one judge, and a half chance at a fair trial, often featured in tattoos seen in prison.

three hots and a cot. In the lingo of the streets, the food and lodging afforded by jail.

throw bricks. Commit a felony.

throwaway. Clothing worn by a mugger and discarded immediately after committing the crime, to confuse pursuers.

tin. Policeman's badge; by extension, a policeman. See also GOLD TIN.

TNT. Police ticket and towing patrol (T 'n' T).

tombstoning. Using the identity of the deceased to commit fraud.

tree jumper. Rapist in the lingo of prison.

trey-eight. A .38-caliber gun.

turn. To change sides from gangster to informer.

turn out. To rape or make into a "punk," in prison language.

turning on the Christmas lights. Festive flashing of a patrol car's emergency lights.

turnkey. A guard who is there just to open doors, who cares about nothing other than doing his or her shift, in prison talk.

24/24. Prison slang for all day.

24/24 rule. "The most important hours in the investigation of any murder are the last twenty-four hours in the victim's life and the first twenty-four hours after the body has been discovered" (Carsten Stroud, *Close Pursuit: A Week in the Life of a NYPD Homicide Cop*).

UTL. Police radio term for "unable to locate."

Vesting. Process by which an inmate's good time for good behavior becomes irrevocable and cannot be taken.

vic. A duped customer, such as one to whom a bogus drug has been sold (victim).

vice-mail. The use of telephone voice-mail messages to defraud.

Wad cutter. Bullet.

wagger. A flasher, to police.

Waldorf Astoria. Solitary confinement in prison.

walk-alone. A prisoner who cannot exercise on a yard with other prisoners. San Quentin's death row has a yard for "walk-alones" to exercise together.

walls. The joint; prison.

waste. Kill.

whack / whack in the mouth. To execute, in gangland.

white-powder bar. Lawyers who defend the top-level drug dealers.

wire. The fence surrounding a prison.

wired. 1. Carrying a recording device or microphone. 2. Armed.

Yard hack. Guard in a prison yard.

yard-in. Command given to return to prison cell. Closing of the recreation yard.

yard-out. Prison recreation yard opens.

yellow sheet. Same as RAP SHEET.

yoking. A form of mugging in which a male victim is grabbed from behind and put in a headlock and has his wallet taken from his jacket pocket.

Zippers. Scars.

zip to five. Parole time of zero to five years.

8

CUBE-SPEAK

The Postdigital Talk of the Modern Office, a.k.a the Cube Farm

As geek chic takes hold of the technology-obsessed culture, geek-speak seeps into everyday language.

—Michiko Kakutani, "When the Geeks Get Snide: Computer Slang Scoffs at Wetware," *New York Times*, June 27, 2000

In the white-collar workplace of the 1990s, the trend was to have rows and rows of small, doorless spaces separated by chest-high partitions, creating cubes. These cubes were at once disposable, elastic, and temporary enough so that they could be totally reconfigured over a weekend. Whether called departmentalization, nonterritorial design, or dejobbing, it added up to a sense of working in an odd new atmosphere characterized by downsizing, outsourcing, and a steady loss of perks and benefits. The new term for these environments was "cube farms."

Along with it came a special jargon to describe a world in which face-to-face communication was increasingly replaced with digital discussion and where the most important person in the office was not a person in a suit but the information technology, or IT, guy. Such coinages are an Internet-spawned phenomenon of slang that has been been minted by clever people. New expressions get passed everywhere by e-mail and then end up on cube farms the next morning. They appear in e-mailed lists with names like "Lexicon Valley," "New Words for the Week," "A Quick Lesson in Cyber-Slang," and "Cubicle-Ville Has a Whole New Language." The lists are republished in free weekly newspapers and sometimes get printed out and tacked onto analog bulletin boards (the kind made of cork) and published in newspapers from Los Angeles to London.

An example of this sort of entry: "**404** Someone who is clueless. From the Web error message, '404 Not Found,' which means the document requested couldn't be located. 'Don't bother asking John. He's 404.' "

What makes cube-speak unusual is that the words are deliberate coinages that end up being used by larger and larger groups of people. Historically, coinages of this kind have gathered little traction and have quickly perished, but other coinages did not have the Internet or so many willing accomplices in the mainstream media.

Cube-speak had many parents, but one, Gareth Branwyn, stands out as the Johnny Appleseed of this slang because of his column, "Jargon Watch," in *Wired* magazine, along with a book of the same name that came out in 1997 (New York: Hard Wired Books). The book was based on the deluge of submissions of expressions, figures of speech, and other binary bon mots that Branwyn received from the cube farms of America. "Cube farm," the book explains, refers to the typical American workplace with each worker assigned to his or her own cubicle. Words taken from *Jargon Watch* were copied and recopied and quickly lost any association with his book or column.

Another important source for these terms is several small collections of deliberate coinages created for the "Style Invitational" column, which appears in the Sunday edition of the *Washington Post* and is widely circulated on the Internet (see also "Sources").

Here is a basic course in cube-speak.

Adminisphere. The rarefied organizational layers above the rank and file that make decisions that are often profoundly inappropriate or irrelevant.

alpha geek. The most knowledgeable, technically proficient problem solver in an office or work group, as in "I dunno, ask Rick. He's our alpha geek." This term has actually become so widespread that the listing of the American Speakers Association made it the top word of the year in 1996 and it was runner-up to "soccer mom" in word-of-the-year balloting by the American Dialect Society. The term is showing up in more and more newspaper articles as a virtual job description: "Stute, a 34-year-old alpha geek, has been piecing together his hacker profile system for more than 12 years" (*Dallas Morning News*, October 22, 2003).

ambimousetrous. Able to use the mouse well with either hand.

assmosis. The process by which some people seem to absorb success and advancement by kissing up to the boss rather than working hard.

Batmobiling. Putting up emotional shields. Refers to the retracting armor that covers the Batmobile, as in "She started talking marriage and he started batmobiling."

beepilepsy. The brief seizure people sometimes suffer when their beepers or cell phones go off, especially in vibrator mode. Characterized by physical spasms, goofy facial expressions, and stopping speech in midsentence.

benoftmue (acr). Big event no one foresaw that messes up everything, as in "Due to the recent benoftmue, our group had to reorg again" (pron. "ben-ofta-moo").

betamaxed. When one technology is overtaken in the market by an inferior one that is better marketed, as happened when VHS bested beta as a video-recording format.

bio break. Recess in a meeting for biological purposes such as using the restroom or smoking.

bithead. Highly competent computer professional.

bleeding edge. Well beyond the leading edge.

blowing your buffer. Losing one's train of thought. Occurs when the person you are speaking with won't let you get a word in edgewise or has just said something so astonishing that your train of thought gets derailed. "Damn, I just blew my buffer!"

bozone. The substance surrounding stupid people that stops bright ideas from penetrating. From Bozo the Clown.

brain fart. A by-product of a bloated mind producing information effortlessly. A burst of useful information.

business provocative. Sexy attire to get attention at work.

buzzword bingo. Concept of a competition taking place in a meeting where employees track the buzzwords uttered by top executives on an electronic bingo card. One is declared a winner when one completes a line.

buzzword-compliant. Describes a piece of writing that is littered with jargon and buzzwords.

Canfusion. Bewilderment that results from staring too long at the free drinks in the kitchen cooler, trying to decide whether to have a Coke, Pepsi, Diet Coke, diet Pepsi, caffeine-free Diet Coke, etc.

career-limiting move / CLM. Action that would most likely get you fired or seriously demoted. Trashing your boss while he or she is within earshot is a serious CLM.

catering vultures. People who flock to an unattended catering site to pick through the remains of meeting food. These vultures are quite benevolent and reduce the amount of waste we produce.

caught in a loop. Repeating the same thing over and over.

chainsaw consultant. Outside expert brought in to reduce the employee head count.

chair trap. When you trap yourself in your office chair by accidentally hitting the pneumatic seat adjustment, causing it to drop suddenly, thereby locking your legs under your chair.

chief ponytail guy. Alpha geek with appropriate hair.

chip jewelry. Old computers destined to be scrapped or turned into decorative ornaments. "I paid three grand for that Mac SE, and now it's nothing but chip jewelry."

compunicate. To communicate with someone in the same room via instant message instead of in person.

crop dusting. Surreptitiously farting while passing through a cube farm, then enjoying the sounds of dismay and disgust; leads to PRAIRIE-DOGGING.

cube farm / cubefarm. Office filled with cubicles. An article in the December 19, 2004, *Toronto Star* mentions a section of the city as serving the automatons of "the Younge Street cubefarms." The term was also announced by the CBC on July 26, 2004, as one of the latest words to be accepted by the Canadian edition of the *Oxford English Dictionary*.

Dancing baloney. Animated gifs and other web f/x that are useless and serve simply to impress clients. "This page is kinda dull. Maybe a little dancing baloney will help."

deboning. Removing stitched-in subscription cards and card-stock ad pages from a magazine to make it easier to read.

decafalon. The grueling event of getting through the day consuming only things that are good for you.

digital hygienist. Person who vets employee e-mails for obscene jokes and complaints about the company.

Dilberted. To be exploited, oppressed, and screwed over by one's boss, from the hapless comic strip character.

door dorks. People who stand in your doorway to talk with you, rather than entering your office.

doortag browsing. Act of browsing nametags on doors while in a different building, in the hopes of spotting someone famous (or maybe just somebody you've conversed with frequently via e-mail, but never met).

Doppler effect. The tendency of stupid ideas to seem smarter when they come very quickly (*Washington Post* Style Invitational).

Dorito syndrome. Feelings of emptiness and dissatisfaction triggered by addictive substances that lack nutritional content. "I just spent six hours surfing the Web, and now I've got a bad case of Dorito syndrome."

drailing. E-mailing while drunk; blend of drunk + e-mailing.

drinking from a fire hose. To get overwhelmed with the amount of information being presented.

Eat your own dogfood. Use the product you're developing in your day-to-day operations.

egosurfing. Scanning the Net, databases, print media, or research papers looking for a mention of your name.

Elvis year. The peak year of something's popularity, as in "Barney the dinosaur's Elvis year was 1993."

e-mauling. Stalking someone via e-mail.

Facemail. Backward means of communication, clearly inferior to voice mail or e-mail. Involves actually walking to someone's cube and speaking to him or her face-to-face.

fatkins. Disciples of Atkins who have taken the "all the fat you can eat" idea to lunatic extremes.

fiber media. Material printed on paper. Used disparagingly, as in "Yeah, I used to be a writer in fiber media, but now I'm a content provider in cybermedia."

fire drill. Crisis (usually imagined) that requires immediate and sustained attention.

fish bowl. Unused, obsolete monitor kept around to leverage acquisition of a new monitor at the beginning of the fiscal year.

flame. An angry message, often a personal attack, posted on the Net. Also, the verb for posting such a message.

flight risk. An employee suspected of planning to leave a company or department soon.

Geek. A person who is socially inept but a whiz with computers. Increasingly, as computers are considered vital to our lives, geek takes on a very positive meaning.

geek appeal. Sex appeal in the world of electronic gadgetry. In reviewing new equipment, *Network Computing* magazine rates things 1 ("undeniably unimpressive") through 5 ("exudes geek appeal").

geek chic. Fashion inspired by computer geeks—heavy black-rimmed glasses, nerd packs (shirtpocket plastic sleeves for pens and pencils), etc.

generica. Fast-food joints, strip malls, and subdivisions, as in "We were so lost in generica that I couldn't remember what city it was."

glazing. Corporate-speak for sleeping with your eyes open. A popular pastime at conferences and early-morning meetings. "Didn't he notice that half the room was glazing by the second session?"

glibido. All talk and no action (*Washington Post* Style Invitational).

GOOD job. A "get-out-of-debt" job. A well-paying job people take in order to pay off their debts, one that they will quit as soon as they are solvent again.

granular. Generally, and rather peculiarly, used in tandem with the verb "to get," as in "We need to get granular on this issue," meaning to examine the fine details.

Graybar land. The place you go while you're staring at a computer that's processing something very slowly while you watch the gray bar creep across the task indicator. "That cad rendering put me in graybar land for like an hour."

gray matter. Older, experienced businesspeople hired by young entrepreneurial firms looking to appear more reputable and established.

Hall hogs. Herd of people blocking a hallway, usually after a meeting or conference, loudly discussing things too important to be discussed at the meeting—and being totally impervious to anyone trying to pass through their gauntlet—while also disturbing people in nearby offices trying to get some work done.

high dome. Egghead, scientist, Ph.D.

hipatitis. Terminal coolness (*Washington Post* Style Invitational).

Idea hamsters. People who always seem to have their idea generators running.

in the plastic closet. Said of someone who refuses to admit to having cosmetic surgery (*Washington Post* Style Invitational).

innoculatte. An expression that suggests that you are taking coffee intravenously, you are running so late.

intaxication. Euphoria created by a tax refund—lasting only until you recall that it was your money to begin with.

irritainment. Entertainment and media spectacles that are annoying, but you find yourself unable to stop watching them.

Karmageddon. As originally defined, "It's like, when everybody is sending off all these really bad vibes, right? And then, like, the earth explodes and it's, like, a serious bummer" (*Washington Post* Style Invitational).

keyboard plaque. Disgusting buildup of dirt and crud found on some people's computer keyboards.

kubris. Extreme arrogance of the kind that allows a multimedia auteur to think he is Stanley Kubrick.

Martian genius. A person who comes up with a brilliant but not elegant, obvious, or direct solution of a problem.

meatspace. Physical world, as opposed to cyberspace—also known as the "carbon community."

meeting seconds. Compressed minutes for a quick meeting, such as, "1. Bob is going to Taiwan. 2. No new showstopper bugs. 3. Pizza was late."

milk henge. Collection of half-used milk cartons sitting on the kitchenette counter.

monkey testing. Giving a product to a novice without any introduction or instructions. From the old American Tourister ads, where they "monkey-tested" their luggage by giving it to a gorilla to play with.

mouse potato. Wired generation's version of the couch potato.

muffin top. Visible tummy spilling over hipster jeans.

multi-threaded. Able to do more than one thing at a time. This term is a compliment and is the opposite of single-threaded.

munge. A computer program that performs mundane, repetitive tasks.

Nerd. A socially inept person. Some geeks consider nerds as geek wannabes without the technical ability for full geek status.

net. To summarize, as in "I was really impressed by Jon's ability to net the entire meeting down to four key points."

net it out. Give me the bottom line; get to the point. As in "net it out for me."

net storm. Unexplainable multiple network failures in a specific building or region. Usually transient, but rarely fixed through human intervention. "No one was able to get onto corpnet due to the net storm."

net.god / net.goddess. Someone who has been online from the beginning and knows everything.

nonlinear. Inappropriately intense negative response. "I told him we didn't have any Starbucks gazebo blend and he went totally nonlinear."

Obfun. Obligatory fun. Team-building exercises that are not optional, usually scheduled on top of the normal team meetings.

offline. Outside the confines of a mass meeting, so as not to take up the time of those attendees not directly concerned with an issue. "Let's take this conversation offline."

ohnosecond. That minuscule fraction of time in which you realize that you've just made a big mistake.

open-collar workers. Folks who work at home or telecommute.

osteopornosis. Degenerate disease.

Percussive maintenance. The fine art of whacking the crap out of an electronic device to get it to work again.

ping. To send a brief e-mail. "I'll ping Jim about revising the schedule." Derives from Internet jargon, where one computer can ping—or send a message to—another computer, asking it to respond to verify the connection.

plug-and-play. New hire who doesn't need any training.

prairie-dogging. In a cube farm, heads popping up over the tops of cubicles trying to see what's going on when something loud happens. An article in *Crain's Detroit Business,* December 6, 1999, quotes an architect who maintains that carefully planned cubes encourage "effective 'prairie dogging.'" This word appeared originally in Gareth Branwyn's "Jargon Watch" column in *Wired* magazine.

Ramp up. Technical term appropriated for general usage, meaning to gear up, to reinforce, and, in a sense, to gird oneself for greater effort.

random. Describing an idea that is poorly thought out or an action that is ill considered. Most commonly used in the exclamation "That's so random!" which according to current computer lore is an expression that Bill Gates uses frequently.

randomize. To divert someone from his or her goal with tertiary tasks or niggling details, as in "Marketing has totally randomized me by constantly changing their minds about the artwork."

ROM-brain. A person who just talks and doesn't listen, from read-only memory on a computer, which cannot be overwritten.

Salmon day. The experience of spending an entire day swimming upstream, only to get screwed in the end.

sarchasm. The gulf between the author of sarcastic wit and the person who doesn't get it (*Washington Post* Style Invitational).

schedule chicken. Setting an unattainable schedule in the hopes that another team will slip first and buy you more time. From the fifties teenage game "chicken," where two cars drive toward each other in a test of nerves to see who will chicken out first and swerve away.

scope creep. The tendency of projects to expand beyond their original scope.

screen-saver face. The look one gets when one has been bored to the point of shuttering off his brain.

scrow. To work seventy-hour weeks to meet an unrealistic deadline.

seagull manager. A manager who flies in, makes a lot of noise, shits over everything, and then leaves.

server. Fictional central computer designed to provide employees with a surefire excuse for failing to meet deadlines. "I would have finished, but the damn server's been down all morning."

shelfware. Software that remains unused on a shelf in its original shrink wrap.

showstopper. A really big bug. A function, object, or issue important enough to jeopardize a ship date or schedule in order to correct or include. "They're offering Dove bars to anyone who finds a showstopper in the latest beta."

siliwood. The coming convergence of movies, interactive television, and computer. Blend of silicon + Hollywood.

single-threaded. Not able to do two things at once, as in "He's single-threaded; he can't chew gum and walk at the same time." The opposite of MULTI-THREADED.

slipping. Euphemism for abjectly failing to hit a deadline.

smart guy. The ultimate compliment. "He doesn't shower often, but he's a real smart guy. Okay, let's hire him."

sneaker net. A method of moving data from one personal computer to another using people in sneakers carrying disks, CDs, or flash drives.

spacordi. The mass of cords strewn underneath your desk (just add sauce).

square-headed spouse. Computer.

Starfleet Academy programmer. One

who is long on theory and short on experience.

stress puppy. A person who seems to thrive on and even enjoy being stressed out and whiny.

swiped out. An ATM or credit card that has been used so much its magnetic strip is worn away.

Take-away. Impressions gleaned from a meeting or message.

thrashing. Never getting anything done because you are trying to do too much.

total disconnect. Extremely low-bandwidth human interaction. "It was a total disconnect. I spent half an hour explaining how this stuff worked, and he just didn't get it."

tourists. People who are taking training classes just to get a vacation from their jobs. "We had about three serious students in the class; the rest were tourists."

trash-sitters. People who come into a meeting late and then sit on the trash receptacles instead of at the table. Usually done in an attempt to remain aloof from the rest of the participants.

triority. The three important jobs your boss wants you to do at once.

Um-friend. A sexual relation of dubious standing or a concealed intimate relationship, as in "This is Dale, my . . . um . . . friend."

under mouse arrest. Getting busted for violating an online service's rule of conduct. "Sorry I couldn't get back to you. AOL put me under mouse arrest."

uninstalled. Euphemism for being fired.

Verbing. Corporate urge to turn perfectly good nouns into verbs, as in "databasing a survey."

Wall crawlers. Shy employees who walk down the hallways with a shoulder pressed against the wall and their eyes cast downward.

wim (acr). Any sort of party or employee morale builder, usually held during business hours; from the Windows NT group's "weekly integration meetings."

wombat (acr). Waste of money, brains, and time.

Yellular. Speaking with a raised voice in response to a bad cellphone connection, in the misguided hope that talking louder will improve the connection, as in "I'm so embarrassed. I went totally yellular at a restaurant last night."

DRUGS

9

The Spacy Talk of the Junkie, Cokehead, Druggie, Pothead, and Gen Rx-er

"To which we must now add drugs."

—Anthony Burgess, quoted in the *Times Literary Supplement*, December 5, 1986, in response to the assertion that slang's chief stimuli are liquor, money, and sex

It is rare that the focus of a page-one story in the *New York Times* is pegged to a matter of slang, but that was the case on August 4, 2005, when the newspaper ran a piece with a Rome, Georgia, dateline entitled "Cultural Differences Complicate a Georgia Drug Sting Operation."

What had happened was that forty-nine convenience store clerks and owners in rural northwest Georgia were charged with knowingly selling materials that would be used to make methamphetamines. The evidence was caught on tape as undercover government agents came in and bought the over-the-counter cold medications, matches, and cooking fuel in a can to "finish up a cook"—a term used in the preparation of meth.

Seems that all but five of the forty-nine defendants were Indian immigrants who, their defenders claimed, did not understand the drug slang used by the agents. To them, said the *Times*, " 'cook' is no more sinister than a barbecue."

The article underscored the point that while there is little that is subtle about today's illegal drug trade, it possesses a slanguage that is at once direct, street-smart, and composed of a vast and dazzling collection of synonyms and coded words. In defense of the Indian store clerks, it could be argued that most native speakers not part of the culture of meth would just as likely have ended up in handcuffs had they found themselves in the same situation.

What follows is a major haul of drug slang from many sources, including the office of the White House drug czar. The fact that the list is far from complete underscores the extent to which the drug culture has left its footprint on the larger culture.

A. 1. LSD. 2. Amphetamine.

ab. Short for abscess—the result of using dirty needles and/or adulterated drugs.

abandominiums. Abandoned row houses where drugs are used.

Abe. $5 worth of drugs, an allusion to the fact that Abraham Lincoln is pictured on the $5 bill.

abolic. Veterinary steroid.

Acapulco gold. Powerful marijuana from southwest Mexico, somewhat gold in color.

ace. 1. A single pill. 2. Marijuana; PCP.

acid. LSD.

acid head. LSD user.

AD. Short for drug addict. According to Jonathan Green, in his *Dictionary of Contemporary Slang*, the letters have been reversed to avoid confusion with the law's DA, for district attorney.

Adam. Methamphetamine.

African black / African bush / African woodbine. Marijuana cigarette.

agonies. Withdrawal symptoms.

a-head. Amphetamine user.

Ah-pen-yen. Opium.

aimies. Amphetamine; amyl nitrite.

AIP. Heroin from Afghanistan, Iran, and Pakistan.

air blast. Inhalant.

airhead. Marijuana user.

airplane. Marijuana.

Alice B. Toklas. Marijuana brownie, named for Gertrude Stein's companion, who was renowned for this dopey confection.

all-American drug. Cocaine.

all lit up. Under the influence of drugs.

all star. User of multiple drugs.

alpha-ET. Alpha-ethyltryptamine.

ames. Amyl nitrite.

amidone. Methadone.

amoeba. PCP.

amp. 1. Amphetamine. 2. Accelerated heart rate associated with meth use.

amp joint. Marijuana cigarette laced with some other form of narcotic.

amped-out. Fatigue after using amphetamines.

amping. 1. Accelerated heartbeat. 2. Being high on amphetamines.

amt. Dimethyltryptamine.

Anadrol. Oral steroid.

anatrofin. Indictable steroid.

Anavar. Steroid taken orally.

angel dust / angel hair / angel mist. PCP.

Angie. Cocaine.

Angola. Marijuana.

animal. LSD.

animal trank / animal tranquilizer. PCP.

ant trafficker. One dealing in very small quantities.

antifreeze. Heroin.

anywhere. Holding or possessing drugs, as in the query "Are you anywhere?"

apple jacks. Crack.

Aries. Heroin.

aroma of men. Isobutyl nitrite.

artillery. Equipment for injecting drugs.

ashes. Marijuana.

assassin of youth. Marijuana, from the 1930s film of the same name.

asskash. Narcotics concealed in the rectum, usually in a condom or metal capsule. Blend of ass + cache.

atom bomb. Heroin mixed with marijuana.

atshitshi. Marijuana.

attic. Slurred rhyme of "addict."

Aunt Hazel. Heroin.

Aunt Mary. Marijuana.

Aunt Nora. Cocaine.

Aunti / Aunt Emma. Opium.

Aurora borealis. PCP, a hallucinogen.

B 1. Benzedrine. 2. Amount of marijuana to fill a matchbox.

babe. Drug used for detoxification.

baby / baby bhang. Marijuana.

baby habit. Occasional use of drugs.

baby T. Crack.

babylon. The outside world. A Rastafarian term used primarily by members of Jamaican gangs, as is BACK IN THE BOX.

babysit. Guide someone through their first drug experience.

back door. Residue left in a pipe.

back in the box. To be back in operation again after being arrested on a drug charge.

back to back. Smoking crack after injecting heroin or using heroin after crack.

backbreakers. LSD and strychnine.

backjack. Injecting opium.

backtrack. Allow blood to flow back into a needle during injection.

backup. Prepare vein for injection.

backwards. Depressant.

bad. Crack.

bad bundle. Inferior-quality heroin.

bad go. Bad reaction to a drug.

bad seed. Peyote, heroin, marijuana.

bag. 1. A measure of narcotics according to its retail value; hence, a nickel bag is a $5 amount. 2. Container for drugs.

bag bride. Crack-smoking prostitute.

bag man. Person who transports money.

baggies. Plastic bag for small quantities of narcotics.

bagging. Using inhalant.

baldhead. Undesirable; outsider.

bale. Marijuana.

ball. Crack.

balling. Cocaine taken vaginally.

balloon. Heroin supplier.

ballot. Heroin.

bam. Depressant; amphetamine.

bamblacha. Marijuana.

bambs. Depressant.

bang. To inject a drug; inhalant.

bank. Money. To say that one has bank is to say that one has a lot of money.

bank bandit pills. Depressant.

bar. Marijuana.

barb. Depressant.

Barnes man. New York street slang for a major drug dealer. According to Carsten Stroud, in *Close Pursuit: A Week in the Life of an NYPD Homicide Cop*, the term comes from the name of a famous Harlem dealer, Nicky Barnes.

barrels. LSD.

base. 1. Freebase. 2. Cocaine; crack.

base crazies. Searching on hands and knees for crack.

baseball. Crack.

basehead / base head. 1. One addicted to freebasing cocaine. In his autobiography, *Long Time Gone*, the musician David Crosby described himself as a basehead for fifteen harrowing years of his life. 2. Person who BASES.

bash. Marijuana.

basuco. Cocaine or coca paste residue sprinkled on marijuana or regular cigarette.

bathtub speed. Methcathinone.

batt. IV needle.

battery acid. LSD.

bazooka. 1. Cocaine paste that is said to have an "explosive" effect on the user. 2. Synthetic drug. 3. Cocaine; crack.

bazuco / bazko. Highly addictive powder containing cocaine, kerosene, ether, and sulfates that can be rolled into a cigarette for smoking.

bazulco. Cocaine.

be off. To abstain: to be off drugs.

beam me up, Scotty. 1. Mixture of PCP and crack, from the original *Star Trek* line calling for transmogrification back to the ship. 2. Crack dipped in PCP.

beamer. Crack user.

beans. Amphetamine; depressant; mescaline.

beast. 1. Police. 2. LSD.

beast, the. Heroin.

beat artist. Person selling bogus drugs.

beat bag. Quantity of heavily cut (diluted) narcotics.

beat vials. Vials containing sham crack to cheat buyers.

beautiful boulders. Crack.

bebe. Crack.

bedbugs. Fellow addicts.

beemers. Crack.

beeper boy. Dealer using electronic equipment in sales effort.

behind the scale. To weigh and sell cocaine.

beiging. Chemicals altering cocaine to make it appear a higher purity.

belly habit. The stomach pains that accompany withdrawal from continued heroin use.

belt. 1. The "kick" of a narcotic. 2. Effects of drugs.

Belushi cocktail. A mixture of cocaine and heroin, a reference to the late comedian John Belushi, who was killed with such a mixture.

belyando spruce. Marijuana.

bender. Drug party.

bennies. 1. Benzedrine. 2. Amphetamine.

benz / benzo. 1. Mercedes-Benz. 2. Amphetamine.

Bernice / Bernie / Bernie's flakes / Bernie's gold dust. Cocaine.

B-40. Cigar laced with marijuana and dipped in malt liquor.

bhang. Marijuana, Indian term.

big bag. Heroin.

big bloke / big C. Cocaine.

big D. LSD.

big 8. one-eighth kilogram of crack.

big flake. Cocaine.

big H / big Harry. Heroin.

big man. Drug supplier.

big O. Opium.

big rush. Cocaine.

biker's speed. Meths.

Billie hoke. Cocaine.

bindle. 1. Paper in which drugs are wrapped and folded. It comes from a hobo slang term for a bedroll that is carried folded up (a once common term for a tramp was a bindle stiff). 2. Small packet of drug powder; heroin.

bing. Enough of a drug for one injection.

binge. Defined in a 2005 Meth Glossary compiled by Utah drug and court officials as "using again and again to maintain a meth high. Each rush diminishes in intensity until a high is no longer attainable. During the final stages of a binge, the user may become delusional, paranoid and 'sketched out,' and may become violent."

bingo. To inject a drug.

bings. Crack.

birdie powder. Heroin; cocaine.

bird's eye. A small amount of narcotics.

biscuits. 1. Methadone. 2. Fifty rocks of crack.

bite. Arrest.

bite one's lips. To smoke marijuana.

biz. Bag or portion of drugs.

BJs. Crack.

black. Opium.

black acid. LSD; LSD and PCP.

black and white. Amphetamine.

black bart. Marijuana.

black beauties. Depressant; amphetamine.

black birds. Amphetamine.

black ganga / black gold. High-potency marijuana.

black gungi. Marijuana from India.

black gunion. Marijuana.

black hash. Opium mixed with hashish.

black mo / black moat. Highly potent marijuana.

black mollies. Amphetamine.

black mote. Marijuana mixed with honey.

black pearl. Heroin.

black pill. Opium pill.

black rock. Crack.

black Russian. Hashish mixed with opium.

black star. LSD.

black stuff. Heroin.

black sunshine / black tabs. LSD.

black tar. 1. Heroin. 2. Potent Mexican heroin with a tarry look.

black whack. PCP.

black widow. Black capsule carrying amphetamines.

blacks. Amphetamine.

blanco. Heroin.

blanket. Marijuana cigarette.

blanks. Low-quality drugs.

blast. 1. A line or snort of cocaine. 2. To smoke marijuana; to smoke crack.

blast a joint / blast a roach / blast a stick. To smoke marijuana.

blasted. Under the influence of drugs.

blizzard. White cloud in a pipe used to smoke cocaine.

block. Marijuana.

block busters. Depressant.

blonde. Marijuana.

blotter / blotter acid / blotter cube. LSD.

blow. 1. Cocaine; to inhale cocaine; to smoke marijuana. 2. A snort or sniff of cocaine.

blow a fix / blow a shot. The needle misses the vein and the injection is wasted in the skin or muscle.

blow a stick. To smoke marijuana.

blow blue. To inhale cocaine.

blow coke. To inhale cocaine.

blow one's roof. To smoke marijuana.

blow smoke. To inhale cocaine.

blow the vein. 1. To use too much pressure on a weak vein, causing it to rupture. 2. The injection misses the vein and is wasted.

blow up. Crack cut with lidocaine to increase size, weight, and street value.

blowcaine. Crack diluted with cocaine.

blowing smoke. Marijuana.

blowout. Crack.

blue. Depressant; crack.

blue acid. LSD.

blue angels. Depressant.

blue barrels. LSD.

blue birds. Depressant.

blue boy. Amphetamine.

blue bullets. Depressants.

blue caps. Mescaline.

blue chairs / blue cheers. LSD.

blue de Hue. Marijuana from Vietnam.

blue devil / blue dolls. Depressants.

blue heaven / blue microdot / blue mist / blue moons. LSD.

blue sage. Marijuana.

blue sky. Heroin.

blue sky bond. High-potency marijuana from Colombia.

blue tips. Depressant.

blue vials. LSD.

blunt. Marijuana inside a cigar; marijuana and cocaine inside a cigar.

boat. Marijuana laced with PCP.

bo-bo. Marijuana

bobo. Crack.

bobo bush. Marijuana.

body packer / body stuffer. Person who ingests crack or cocaine to transport it, or to avoid prosecution.

bogart a joint. Salivate on a marijuana cigarette; refuse to share a marijuana cigarette.

bolasterone. Injectable steroid.

Bolivian marching powder. Cocaine.

bolo. Crack.

bolt. Isobutyl nitrate.

bomb. Crack; heroin; large marijuana cigarette; high-potency heroin.

bomb squad. Crack-selling crew.

bomber. Marijuana cigarette.

bombido. Injectable amphetamine; heroin; depressant.

bombita. Amphetamine; heroin; depressant.

bombs away. Heroin.

bone. Marijuana; $50 piece of crack.

bonecrusher / bones. Crack.

bong. Type of pipe used to smoke marijuana.

bonita. Heroin.

boo / boom. Marijuana.

boom car. Drug dealer's car with loud, expensive stereo system.

boomers. Psilocybin or psilocin.

boopers. Amyl nitrite.

boost. 1. To inject a drug. 2. To steal.

boost and shoot. Steal to support a habit.

booster. To inhale cocaine.

boot. To inject a drug.

boot the gong. To smoke marijuana.

booted. Under the influence of drugs.

botray. Crack.

bottles. Crack vials; amphetamine.

boubou. Crack.

boulder. Crack; $20 worth of crack.

boulya. Crack.

bouncing powder. Cocaine.

box lab. Small, mobile meth lab.

boxed. In jail.

boy. Heroin.

bozo. 1. Ration of drugs, often an ounce. 2. Heroin.

brain ticklers. Amphetamine.

break night. Staying up all night until day-break.

breakdowns. Forty-dollar crack rock sold for $20.

brewery. Place where drugs are made.

brick. One kilogram of marijuana or crack.

brick gum. Heroin.

bridge up or bring up. Ready a vein for injection

britton. Peyote.

broccoli. Marijuana.

broker. Go-between in a drug deal.

brown. Heroin; marijuana.

brown bombers / brown dots. LSD.

brown crystal / brown rhine / brown sugar. Heroin.

brownies / browns. Amphetamine.

bubble gum. Cocaine; crack.

buck. Shoot someone in the head.

bud. Marijuana. One expensive strain of California pot is known as Mendo Bud, for Mendocino. This term came into vogue during the countercultural era.

buda. A high-grade marijuana joint filled with crack.

Buddha grass. Strong marijuana sold by bar girls in Saigon during the Vietnam War.

buffer. Crack smoker; a woman who exchanges oral sex for crack.

bugged. 1. Annoyed. 2. To be covered with sores and abscesses from repeated use of unsterile needles.

bule. Marijuana.

bull. Narcotics agent or police officer.

bullet. 1. A line or snort of cocaine. 2. Isobutyl nitrite.

bullet bolt. Inhalant.

bullia capital / bullion. Crack.

bullyon. Marijuana.

bumblebees. Amphetamine.

bump. Crack; fake crack; boost a high; a $20 hit of ketamine.

bundle. Heroin.

bunk. Fake cocaine.

burese. Cocaine.

burn. To cheat; to sell bogus drugs. A source who knows about such things says, "A burn artist is a dope dealer who consistently sells catnip for pot, Accent [the commercial flavor enhancer] for speed, coffee for heroin, etc. Don't take up the trade; you could get shot."

burn bag. A quantity of bogus drugs sold as real.

burn one. To smoke marijuana.

burn the main line. To inject a drug.

burned. To purchase fake drugs.

burned out. Collapse of veins from repeated injections; to be permanently impaired from drug abuse.

burner. Gun, usually a handgun.

burnese. Cocaine.

burnie. 1. Half-smoked marijuana cigarette. 2. Marijuana.

burnout. 1. State of being addled by and dependent on marijuana. 2. Heavy abuser of drugs.

burros. Derogatory but common name given to people who carry cocaine and other drugs across the Mexican border on their persons.

bush. Cocaine; marijuana.

businessman's LSD / businessman's trip / businessman's special. Dimethyltryptamine.

bust caps. To inject a narcotic. In military slang, the same term is used for firing a weapon.

busted. Arrested.

busters. Depressants.

busy bee / butt naked. PCP.

butter. Marijuana; crack.

butter flower. Marijuana.

buttons. Mescaline.

butu. Heroin.

buzz. 1. A marijuana high. 2. Under the influence of drugs.

buzz bomb. Nitrous oxide.

C

C. Cocaine.

C, the. Methcathinone.

C joint. Place where cocaine is sold.

cabbage head. An individual who will use or experiment with any kind of drug.

caballo. Heroin ("horse" in Spanish).

cabello. Cocaine ("hair" in Spanish).

caca. Heroin.

cactus / cactus buttons / cactus head. Mescaline.

cad / Cadillac. One ounce.

Cadillac. PCP.

Cadillac cops. Drug Enforcement Agency and other enforcers who drive rental luxury cars.

Cadillac express. Methcathinone.

cafeteria use. Use of various drugs simultaneously, particularly sedatives or hypnotics.

caine. Cocaine; crack.

cakes. Round disks of crack.

Cali. Marijuana.

California cornflakes. Cocaine.

California sunshine. LSD.

cam trip. High-potency marijuana (from Cambodia).

Cambodian red / cam red. Marijuana from Cambodia.

can. One ounce of marijuana.

Canadian black / canamo / canappa. Marijuana.

canceled stick. Marijuana cigarette.

C&M. Cocaine and morphine.

candy. Cocaine; crack; depressant; amphetamine.

candy bar. Cocaine joint.

candy c. Cocaine.

cannabinol. PCP.

cannabis tea. Marijuana.

cap. Crack; LSD.

cap up. Transfer bulk-form drugs to capsules.

capital H. Heroin.

caps. Crack; heroin; psilocybin or psilocin.

carburetor. Crack STEM attachment.

carga. Heroin.

carmabis. Marijuana.

carne. Heroin.

carnie. Cocaine.

carpet patrol. Crack smokers searching the floor for crack.

carrie / carrie nation. Cocaine.

cartucho. Package of marijuana cigarettes.

cartwheels. 1. Amphetamines. 2. A feigned illness, fit, or spasm enacted by an addict to get drugs legally from a physician.

Casper the ghost. Crack.

cat. Methcathinone.

cat valium. Ketamine.

catch a buzz. Smoke marijuana.

catnip. Marijuana cigarette.

caviar. Crack.

cavite all star. Marijuana.

C-dust / Cecil / C-game. Cocaine.

chalk. Methamphetamine; amphetamine.

chalked up. Under the influence of cocaine.

chalking. Chemically altering the color of cocaine so it looks white.

chandoo / chandu. Opium.

channel. Vein into which a narcotic is injected.

channel swimmer. One who injects heroin.

charas. Marijuana from India.

charge. Marijuana.

charged up. 1. Marijuana intoxification. 2. Under the influence of drugs.

Charley. 1. Heroin. 2. Cocaine.

chase. To smoke cocaine; to smoke marijuana.

chaser. Compulsive crack user.

chasing the dragon. 1. Smoking a mixture of heroin and cocaine. 2. Crack and heroin.

chasing the tiger. To smoke heroin.

chasing the white nurse. Addicted to morphine or cocaine.

cheap basing. Crack.

check. Personal supply of drugs.

cheeba / cheeo. Marijuana.

chemical / chewies. Crack.

chiba chiba. High-potency marijuana from Colombia.

Chicago black / Chicago green. Marijuana.

chicken powder. Amphetamine.

chicken scratch. Searching on hands and knees for crack.

chicle. Heroin.

chief. LSD; mescaline.

chieva. Heroin.

China cat. High-potency heroin.

China girl / China town / China white. Fentanyl.

Chinese number 3. Variety of heroin processed in Hong Kong and sold by Chinese merchants.

Chinese molasses / Chinese tobacco. Opium.

Chinese red. Heroin.

chip. Heroin.

chipper. Weekend junkie.

chipping. Using drugs occasionally.

chippy. Cocaine.

chippying. Light narcotic sampling.

chira. Marijuana.

chocolate. Opium; amphetamine.

chocolate chips. LSD.

chocolate ecstasy. Crack made brown by adding chocolate-milk powder during production.

cholly. Cocaine.

chorals. Depressant.

Christina. Amphetamine.

Christmas rolls. Depressant.

Christmas tree. Marijuana; marijuana mixed with crack; depressant; amphetamine.

chronic. Marijuana. From the concept "chronic user."

chucks. Hunger following withdrawal from heroin.

churus. Marijuana.

cid. LSD.

cigarette paper. Packet of heroin.

cigarrode cristal. PCP.

citrol. High-potency marijuana from Nepal.

CJ. PCP.

clap. Shoot.

clear up. Stop drug use.

clicker. Crack and PCP.

climax. Crack; isobutyl nitrite; heroin.

climb. Marijuana cigarette.

clips. Rows of vials heat-sealed together.

closet baser. User of crack who prefers anonymity.

cloud / cloud nine. Crack.

cluck. Crack smoker.

coasting. Under the influence of drugs.

coasts to coasts. Amphetamine.

coca. Cocaine.

cocabucks. Cocaine money, in the same sense that oil money has been called petrodollars.

cocaine blues. Depression after extended cocaine use.

cocaine industrial park. State-of-the-art facility for the manufacture and distribution of cocaine.

cochornis. Marijuana.

coco rocks. Dark brown crack made by adding chocolate pudding powder during production.

coco snow. Benzocaine used as cutting agent for crack.

cocktail. Cigarette laced with cocaine or crack; partially smoked marijuana cigarette inserted in regular cigarette.

cocoa puff. To smoke cocaine and marijuana.

coconut / coconuts. Cocaine.

coffee. LSD.

coke. Cocaine; crack.

coke bar. Bar where cocaine is openly used.

coke bugs. Nickname for cocaine hallucination in which bugs infest the user's body.

coke oven. Drug joint.

coked. Under the influence of or addicted to cocaine.

cokie. Cocaine user.

cola. Cocaine.

cold turkey. 1. The act of completely and suddenly quitting drugs, as in "go cold turkey." The term is also used for getting off tobacco or alcohol. 2. Sudden withdrawal from drugs.

coli / coliflor tostao / colly weed / Colorado cocktail / Colombian. Marijuana.

columbo. PCP.

Columbus back. Marijuana.

come down. Experience the effect of a drug wearing off.

come home. End an LSD trip.

comeback. Benzocaine and mannitol used to adulterate cocaine for conversion to crack.

conductor. LSD.

connect. Purchase drugs. The connection is a supplier of illegal drugs.

contact lens. LSD.

convert. One newly addicted to drugs.

cook. 1. Mix heroin or cocaine with water. 2. Heat a drug to prepare it for injection.

3. To manufacture drugs, especially meth, in batches.

cook down. Process in which users liquefy heroin in order to inhale it.

cooker. 1. A receptacle in which drugs are heated before injection. 2. To inject a drug.

cookies. Crack.

cooler / coolie. Cigarette laced with cocaine.

coolie mud. Cheap grade of opium or heroin, often derived from residues.

cop. 1. To buy drugs. 2. To obtain drugs.

copilot. Amphetamine.

copilots. Amphetamines, so called because of truck drivers who have been known to use them on long trips.

copping zones. Specific areas where buyers can find a way to purchase drugs.

coral. Depressant.

coriander seeds. Cash.

cork the air. To inhale cocaine.

corn. Marijuana.

Corrinne. Cocaine.

cosa. Marijuana ("thing" in Spanish).

coso. Small package of BAZUCO.

'cotics / cotics. 1. Narcotics for short. 2. Heroin.

cotton. Currency.

cotton brothers. Cocaine, heroin, and morphine.

courage pills. 1. Heroin. 2. Depressant.

course note. Bill larger than $2.

cozmo's. PCP.

crack. Form of cocaine that is highly addictive and relatively cheap. It is smoked by the user.

crack attack. Craving for crack.

crack back. Crack and marijuana.

crack cooler. Crack soaked in wine cooler.

crack gallery / crack spot. Place where crack is bought and sold.

crack house. Building in which crack cocaine is sold and used.

cracker jacks. Crack smokers.

crackers. LSD.

crackhead. One addicted to crack.

crank. Meth or methamphetamines; amphetamine; methcathinone.

cranking up. To inject a drug.

crankster. Someone who uses or manufactures meth.

cranny. Marijuana.

crap / crop. Low-quality heroin.

crash. 1. To collapse in exhaustion after a bout of heavy drug use—especially amphetamines. 2. Sleep off the effects of drugs.

crazy weed. Marijuana.

credit card. Crack stem.

crib. Crack.

crimmie. Cigarette laced with crack.

crink. Methamphetamine.

cripple. Marijuana cigarette.

cris / crisscross / Cristina. Meth.

croak. Crack and meth.

Crop, the. The agricultural side of the marijuana business. As one close observer writes from his rural Northern California home, "When people in the Emerald Triangle speak of the Crop, they do it reverently, and they ain't talkin' about apples, grapes, or corn."

cross tops / crossroads. Amphetamine.

crown crap. Heroin.

crumbs. Tiny pieces of crack.

crunch and munch. Crack.

crying weed. Marijuana.

crypto. Methamphetamine.

crystal / crystals. Meths in crystalline form; PCP; amphetamine; cocaine.

crystal joint. PCP.

crystal meth. Meth.

crystal tea. LSD.

cube. One ounce; LSD.

cubes. 1. Demerol. 2. Marijuana tablets.

culican. High-potency marijuana from Mexico.

cupcakes. LSD.

cura. Heroin.

cushion. Vein into which narcotics are injected.

cut. Adulterate drugs.

cut-deck. Heroin mixed with powdered milk.

cyclones. PCP.

D. LSD.

DA. Drug addict. See also AD.

dabble. 1. To experiment with drugs; to be in the early stages of addiction. 2. To use drugs occasionally.

dama blanca. Cocaine.

dance fever. Fentanyl.

dawamesk. Marijuana.

dead on arrival. Heroin.

deadhead. Heavy marijuana user who is a follower of the Grateful Dead.

deca-duabolin. Injectable steroid.

deck. One to fifteen grams of heroin, also known as a BAG; packet of drugs.

deeda. LSD.

delatestryl. Injectable steroid.

demo. Crack stem; a sample-size quantity of crack.

demolish. Crack.

DET. Dimethyltryptamine.

detox. Detoxification for short; the process of getting off drugs, even if only temporarily.

Detroit pink. PCP.

deuce. Two dollars' worth of drugs; heroin.

devil, the. Crack.

devil's dandruff. Crack.

devil's dick. Crack pipe.

devil's dust. PCP.

devilsmoke. Crack.

dew. Marijuana.

dews. Ten dollars' worth of drugs.

dexies. Amphetamine.

diambista. Marijuana.

dianabol. Veterinary steroid abused by humans.

diet pills. Amphetamine.

dihydrolone. Injectable steroid.

dimba. Marijuana from West Africa.

dime. Crack; $10 worth of crack.

dime bag. Ten dollars' worth of drugs.

ding. Marijuana.

dinkie dow. Marijuana.

dip. 1. A small amount; a single dose. 2. Crack.

dipping out. Crack runners taking a portion of crack from vials.

dirt. Heroin.

dirt grass. Inferior-quality marijuana.

dirty basing. Crack.

disco biscuits. Depressant.

disease. Drug of choice.

ditch. Marijuana.

ditch weed. Marijuana of inferior quality, Mexican.

Dixie Cup people. Those workers and couriers in the international drug trade with so little importance that they can be used once and thrown away like a paper drinking cup.

djamba. Marijuana.

DMT. Dimethyltryptamine.

do. Consume a given drug, as in to "do" amphetamines.

do a joint. To smoke marijuana.

do a line. To inhale cocaine.

do a number. Make and smoke a marijuana cigarette.

DOA. PCP; crack.

doctor-shop. To try to get drugs legally by prescription.

dog. Good friend.

dog food / doggie. Heroin.

dollar. One hundred dollars' worth of drugs.

dolls. Depressant.

domes. LSD.

domestic. Locally grown marijuana.

domex. PCP and methamphetamine.

dominoes. Amphetamine.

Don Jem / Dona Juana / Dona Juanita. Marijuana.

doobie / dubbe / duby. Marijuana cigarette, as in "He taught her to roll doobies." The seventies rock group the Doobie Brothers took its name from this slang term. In 1993 the former drummer for the group, John Hartman, launched a lawsuit against twenty police departments in California that had turned him down for employment because of his former drug use. He lost and was clearly not aided in his effort by the name of the group.

doogie / doojee / dugie. Heroin.

dooley. Heroin.

dope. Heroin; marijuana; any other drug.

dope fiend. Crack addict.

dope-smoke. To smoke marijuana.

dopium. Opium.

doradilla. Marijuana.

dose / dots. LSD.

doub. Twenty-dollar rock of crack.

double bubble. Cocaine.

double-clutch. To take more than one's share of a communally shared marijuana cigarette.

double cross. Amphetamine.

double dome. LSD.

double rock. Crack diluted with procaine.

double trouble. Depressant.

double ups. A $20 rock that can be broken into two $20 rocks.

double yoke. Crack.

dove. Thirty-five-dollar piece of crack.

dover's powder. Opium.

downer / downers. 1. Barbiturates. Any drug used to slow the nervous system. Sometimes used to bring user down from a high. 2. Depressant.

downie. Depressant.

draf weed / drag weed. Marijuana.

draw up. To inject a drug.

dream. Cocaine.

dream gum / dream stick. Opium.

dreamer. Morphine.

dreams. Opium.

dreck. Heroin.

dropper. To inject a drug.

drowsy high. Depressant.

druggie. User.

dry high. Marijuana.

duct. Cocaine.

due. Residue of oils trapped in a pipe after smoking BASE.

duji. Heroin.

dummy. PCP.

durabolin. Injectable steroid.

durog / duros. Marijuana.

dust. Heroin; cocaine; PCP; marijuana mixed with various chemicals.

dust bunny. Person showing effects of ANGEL DUST.

dust of angels / dusted parsley. PCP.

dusting. Adding PCP, heroin, or another drug to marijuana.

dymethzine. Injectable steroid.

dynamite. 1. Powerful narcotic. 2. Mixture of heroin and cocaine.

dyno / dyno-pure. Heroin.

Early girl. Marijuana that comes in before the main crop.

earth. Marijuana cigarette.

easing powder. Opium.

eastside player. Crack.

easy score. Obtaining drugs easily.

eating. Taking a drug orally.

ecstasy. Methamphetamine.

egg. Crack.

eight ball. One-eighth ounce of drugs or methamphetamines (see CRANK).

eight-track. Two and a half grams of cocaine.

eightball. Crack and heroin.

eighth. Heroin.

el diablito. Marijuana, cocaine, heroin, and PCP.

el diablo. Marijuana, cocaine, and heroin.

electric Kool-Aid. LSD. This term came into play in Tom Wolfe's book *The Electric Kool-Aid Acid Test*, which featured a group of LSD consumers known as the Merry Pranksters.

elephant. PCP.

embalming fluid. PCP.

emergency gun. 1. Homemade hypodermic syringe often made of a pointed medicine dropper or a medicine dropper tipped by a pin. 2. Instrument used to inject other than syringe.

endo. Marijuana.

enoltestovis. Injectable steroid.

ephedrone. Methcathinone.

Equipose. Veterinary steroid.

erth. PCP.

esra. Marijuana.

estuffa. Heroin.

ET. Alpha-ethyltryptamine.

evil. Cocaine.

explorers club. Group of LSD users.

eye opener. 1. First ingestion or injection of the day. 2. Crack; amphetamine.

Factory. Place where drugs are packaged, diluted, or manufactured.

faith. Addiction.

fall. Arrested.

famous dimes. Crack.

fantasia. Dimethyltryptamine.

farm-to-arm. Describing an operation in which the same people grow, process, and sell a drug. For instance, a Mexican heroin grower who controls the pushers who retail it on the streets of Chicago.

fat bags. Crack.

fatty. Marijuana cigarette.

feed bag. 1. Taking narcotics by mouth as opposed to by injection. 2. Container for marijuana.

fi-do-nie. Opium.

fields. LSD.

fiend. Someone who smokes marijuana alone.

fifteen cents. Fifteen dollars' worth of drugs.

fifty-cent bag. Fifty-dollar quantity of drugs.

fifty-one. Crack.

finajet / finaject. Veterinary steroid.

fine stuff / finger / fir. Marijuana.

fire. To inject a drug; crack and meth.

fire it up. To smoke marijuana.

first line. Morphine.

fish scales. Crack.

five-C note. A $500 bill.

five-cent bag. Five dollars' worth of drugs.

five-dollar bag. Fifty dollars' worth of drugs.

fives. Amphetamine.

fizzies. Methadone.

flake. Cocaine.

flame cooking. Smoking cocaine base by putting the pipe over a stove flame.

flamethrowers. Cigarettes laced with cocaine and heroin.

flash / flat blues. LSD.

flat chunks. Crack cut with benzocaine.

flea powder. Low-purity heroin.

Florida snow. Cocaine.

flower / flower tops. Marijuana.

fly Mexican airlines. 1. To smoke marijuana flying. 2. Be under the influence of drugs.

following that cloud. Searching for drugs.

foo-foo dust. Cocaine.

food. Marijuana.

foolish powder. Heroin; cocaine.

footballs. Amphetamine.

45-minute psychosis. Dimethyltryptamine.

fraho / frajo. Marijuana.

freebase. 1. To purify cocaine with the aid of ether. 2. To smoke the pure cocaine thus produced. 3. To smoke cocaine or crack.

freeze. Cocaine; renege on a drug deal.

French blue. Amphetamine.

French fries / fries. Crack.

frios. Marijuana laced with PCP.

Frisco special / Frisco speedball. Cocaine, heroin, and LSD.

friskie powder. Cocaine.

frosty. High.

fry. Crack.

fry daddy. Crack and marijuana; cigarette laced with crack.

fu. Marijuana.

fuel. Marijuana mixed with insecticides; PCP.

G. 1. One thousand dollars, or 1 gram of drugs. 2. An unfamiliar male.

gaffel. Fake cocaine.

gaffus. Hypodermic needle.

gage / gauge. Marijuana.

gagers / gaggers. Methcathinone.

galloping horse. Heroin.

gamot. Heroin.

gange / gangster. Marijuana.

gangster pills. Depressant.

ganja. Marijuana from Jamaica.

gank. 1. Bad drugs. 2. Fake crack.

garbage. Inferior-quality drugs.

garbage heads. Users who buy crack from street dealers instead of cooking it themselves.

garbage rock. Crack.

gash. Marijuana.

gasper / gasper stick. Marijuana cigarette.

gate. House or apartment.

gato. Heroin.

gauge butt. Marijuana.

GB. Depressant.

gee. Opium.

geek. 1. Crack addict. 2. Crack and marijuana.

geeze. 1. To inject narcotics. 2. To inhale cocaine.

geezer. To inject a drug.

geezin a bit of dee gee. 1. Injecting smack. 2. Heroin.

generation Rx / gen. Rx. Teenagers who use prescription painkillers, mainly Vicodin and OxyContin, to get high. It is a play on the term Generation X.

geronimos. Barbiturates.

get a gage up. To smoke marijuana.

get a gift. Obtain drugs.

get down. To inject a drug.

get high. To smoke marijuana.

get lifted. Be under the influence of drugs.

get off. To inject a drug; get high.

get one's wings. To start using heroin.

get the wind. To smoke marijuana.

get through. Obtain drugs.

Ghana. Marijuana.

GHB. Gamma hydroxy butyrate.

ghost. LSD.

ghost busting. 1. Smoking cocaine. 2. Searching for white particles in the belief that they are crack.

gick monster. Crack smoker.

gift-of-the-sun. Cocaine.

By the Number

420—Time to Get High

On April 20, 2005 (4/20), a number of news outlets, including National Public Radio and the *Houston Chronicle*, revealed that this was the annual Get High Day observed at 420 parties and rock concerts being staged across the country. According to the *Chronicle*, the city would host a number of 420 celebrations, including an eight-band concert sponsored by NORML (National Organization for the Reform of Marijuana Laws), which would start at 4:20 P.M.

Denise Witner, host of a Web site on "Parenting Adolescents" that works to decode teenage slang, investigated the origin of the term and reports: "According to Steven Hager, editor of *High Times*, the term '420' originated at San Rafael High School in 1971 among a group of about a dozen pot-smoking wiseacres who called themselves the Waldos, who are now pushing 50. The term was shorthand for the time of day the group would meet, at the campus statue of Louis Pasteur, to smoke pot. Intent on developing their own discreet language, they made 420 code for a time to get high, and its use spread among members of an entire generation."

420 is not the only number that means something in the drug culture. A few others, in numerical order:

007s Methylenedioxymethamphetamine (MDMA)

100s Lysergic acid diethylamide (LSD)

151 Crack cocaine

2-for-1 sale A marketing scheme designed to promote and increase crack sales

24-7 Crack cocaine

25s Lysergic acid diethylamide (LSD)

3750 Marijuana and crack rolled into a joint

40 OxyContin pill

40-bar OxyContin pill

420 Marijuana use

45-minute psychosis Dimethyltryptamine

51 Combination of crack cocaine with marijuana or tobacco

69s Methylenedioxymethamphetamine (MDMA)

714s Methaqualone

80 OxyContin pill

giggle smokes. Marijuana cigarettes.

gimmick. Drug-injection equipment.

gimmie. Crack and marijuana.

gin. Cocaine.

girl. Cocaine; crack; heroin.

girlfriend. Cocaine.

give wings. Inject someone or teach someone to inject heroin.

glacines. Heroin.

glad stuff. Cocaine.

glading. 1. The inhalation of easily obtainable household and industrial products, such as Glade, from which the term gets its name. Also known as huffing and bagging. 2. Using inhalant.

glass / glass gun. Hypodermic needle.

glo. Crack.

gluey. Person who sniffs glue.

go-fast. Methcathinone.

go into a sewer. To inject a drug.

go on a sleigh ride. To inhale cocaine.

go loco. To smoke marijuana.

God's flesh. Psilocybin or psilocin.

God's medicine. Opium.

gold. Marijuana; crack.

gold dust. Cocaine.

gold star. Marijuana.

golden dragon. LSD.

golden girl. Heroin.

golden leaf. Very high-quality marijuana.

golf ball. Crack.

golf balls. Depressant.

golpe. Heroin.

goma. Opium; black tar heroin.

gondola. Opium.

gong. 1. Gun. 2. Marijuana; opium.

goob. Methcathinone.

good and plenty. Heroin.

good butt. Marijuana cigarette.

good fellas. Fentanyl.

good giggles. Marijuana.

good go. Proper amount of drugs for the money paid.

goods. Drugs.

goofball. Cocaine and heroin; depressant.

goofers. Depressant.

goofy's. LSD.

goon / goon dust. PCP.

gopher. Person paid to pick up drugs.

goric. Opium.

gorilla biscuits. PCP.

gorilla pills. Depressant.

got it going on. Fast sale of drugs.

graduate. Completely stop using drugs, or progress to stronger drugs.

gram. Hashish.

grape parfait. LSD.

grass / grass brownies / grata. Marijuana.

gravel. Crack.

gravy. 1. To inject a drug. 2. Heroin.

gray shields. LSD.

grease. Currency.

great tobacco. Opium.

green. Inferior-quality marijuana, PCP, or ketamine.

green double domes. LSD.

green dragons. Depressant.

green frog. Depressant.

green goddess. Marijuana.

green gold. Cocaine.

green goods. Paper currency.

green leaves. PCP.

green single domes / green wedge. LSD.

greens / green stuff. Paper currency.

greeter / greta. Marijuana.

griefo / griff / griffa / griffo. Marijuana.

grit / groceries. Crack.

G-rock. One gram of rock cocaine.

ground control. Guide or caretaker during a hallucinatory experience.

G-shot. Small dose of drugs used to hold off withdrawal symptoms until full dose can be taken.

gum / guma. Opium.

gumdrop. Barbiturate.

gun. 1. Hypodermic syringe; needle. 2. To inject a drug.

gungun. Marijuana.

gutter. 1. A vein into which a drug is injected. 2. A vein, to a heroin addict.

gutter junkie. Addict who relies on others to obtain drugs.

gyve. Marijuana cigarette.

H. Heroin.

H and C. Heroin and cocaine.

habit. Addiction.

hache. Heroin.

hail. Crack.

hairy. Heroin.

half / half piece. Half ounce.

half a C. $50 bill.

half a football field. Fifty rocks of crack.

half G. Five hundred dollars.

half load. Fifteen bags (decks) of heroin.

half moon. Peyote.

half piece. Half an ounce of heroin or cocaine.

half track / hamburger helper. Crack.

hand-to-hand. Direct delivery and payment.

hand-to-hand man. Transient dealers who carry small amounts of crack.

hanhich. Marijuana.

happy cigarette. Marijuana cigarette.

happy dust. Cocaine.

happy flakes. Any powdered narcotic.

happy powder / happy trails. Cocaine.

hard candy. Heroin.

hard line / hard rock. Crack.

hard stuff. Opium; heroin.

hardware. Isobutyl nitrite.

harpoon. Hypodermic syringe.

Harry. Heroin.

has. Marijuana.

hash. Hashish.

hash bash. Rally or event for the legalization of marijuana.

hats. LSD.

have a dust. Cocaine.

have the slows. To be very high.

haven dust. Cocaine.

Hawaiian. Very high-potency marijuana.

Hawaiian sunshine. LSD.

hawk. LSD.

hay. Hashish or marijuana.

hay burner. Smoker of marijuana.

hay but / hay butts. Marijuana cigarettes.

haze. LSD.

Hazel. Heroin.

HCP. PCP.

he-man. Fentanyl.

head drugs. Amphetamine.

headlights. LSD.

heart-on. Inhalant.

hearts. Amphetamine.

heaven dust. Heroin; cocaine.

heavenly blue. LSD.

heeled. Having plenty of drug money.

Helen / hell dust. Heroin.

hemp. Marijuana.

henpecking. Searching on hands and knees for crack.

Henry. Heroin.

Henry VIII. Cocaine.

her. Cocaine.

herb. Marijuana.

Herb and Al. Marijuana and alcohol.

Herba. Marijuana.

hero / hero of the underworld / heroina / herone / hessle. Heroin.

high beams on / high beams. 1. High on cocaine. 2. The wide eyes of a person on crack.

hikori / hikuli. Peyote.

hillbilly heroin. OxyContin.

him. Heroin.

Hinckley. PCP, an allusion to the craziness of John Hinckley, the man who shot President Ronald Reagan.

hippie crack. Inhalant.

his (acr). Heroin in a straw. The powder is tapped into the straw and heat-sealed at either end, then sold.

hit. 1. A puff, injection, swallow, or snort that gets a drug into one's system. 2. To adulterate drugs prior to selling them. 3. A purchase. 4. Crack; marijuana cigarette; to smoke marijuana.

hit the hay. To smoke marijuana.

hit the main line / hit the needle / hit the pit. To inject a drug.

hitch up the reindeers. 1. To inhale cocaine. 2. Inject drugs.

HMC. 1. Her majesty cocaine. 2. Mix of heroin, morphine, and cocaine.

hocus. Opium; marijuana.

hog. PCP.

holding. Possessing drugs. The mid-1960s rock group Big Brother and the Holding Company used the word in this sense. The band was Janis Joplin's vehicle to fame and glory.

hombre. heroin.

homegrown. Marijuana.

honey. Currency.

honey blunts. Marijuana cigars sealed with honey.

honey oil. Ketamine; inhalant.

honeymoon. Early stages of drug use before addiction or dependency develops.

hong-yen. Heroin in pill form.

hooch. Marijuana.

hook / hooked. To addict to drugs.

hooter. Marijuana; cocaine.

hop / hops. Opium.

hophead. Heroin addict.

hopped up. Under the influence of drugs.

horn. To inhale cocaine; a crack pipe.

horning. Heroin; to inhale cocaine.

horse. Heroin.

horse heads. Amphetamine.

horse tranquilizer. PCP.

hot dope. Heroin.

hot heroin. Poisoned to give to a police informant.

hot load / hot shot. 1. A very potent dose of heroin that may be lethal. 2. Lethal injection of an opiate.

hot rolling. Liquefying meth into an eye dropper for inhalation.

hot stick. Marijuana cigarette.

hotcakes. Crack.

house fee. Money paid to enter a crack house.

house piece. Crack given to the owner of a crack house or apartment where crack users congregate.

how do you like me now. Crack.

hows. Morphine.

hubba / hubba, I am back. Crack.

hubba pigeon. Crack user looking for rocks on a floor after a police raid.

hubbas. Small, pea-sized amounts of crack cocaine.

huff. Inhalant.

huffer. 1. Person who inhales vapors from solvents and other chemical compounds to get high. 2. Inhalant abuser.

hulling. Using others to get drugs.

hunter. Cocaine.

hustle. Attempt to obtain drug customers.

hustler. Seller.

hyatari. Peyote.

hype. 1. Hypodermic syringe. 2. Heroin or other addict.

hype stick. Hypodermic needle.

Ice. 1. A smokable form of amphetamines that first hit the streets of Hawaii and California in the latter half of 1989. It is similar to crack, but the high lasts longer and it would appear to be even more addictive than crack. 2. Cocaine; methamphetamine; smokable amphetamine.

ice-cream habit. 1. A minimal addiction; nonsevere habit. 2. Occasional use of drugs.

ice cube. Crack.

ice-tong doctor. Physician who prescribes or sells narcotics illegally.

idiot pills. Depressant.

ily. Marijuana.

in. Connected with drug suppliers.

in-betweens. Depressant; amphetamine.

Inca message. Cocaine.

Indian boy / Indian hay. Marijuana from India.

Indica. Species of cannabis found in hot climates. Grows 3.5 to 4 feet.

indo. Marijuana; a term from Northern California.

Indonesian bud. Marijuana; opium.

inner itch. To have a craving for narcotics.

instant zen. LSD.

interplanetary mission. Travel from one crack house to another in search of crack.

iron cure. Treatment of narcotic addiction by unyielding regime of abstinence.

isda. heroin.

issues. Crack.

J. Marijuana cigarette.

jab job. To inject heroin into the blood.

jab stick. Syringe.

jack. To steal someone else's drugs.

jack-up. To inject a drug.

jackpot. Fentanyl.

jag. Keep a high going.

jam. 1. Overdose. 2. Amphetamine; cocaine.

jam cecil. Amphetamine.

Jane. Marijuana.

jar wars. Controversy over drug testing that involves the use of urine samples.

jay / jay smoke. Marijuana cigarette.

jee gee. Heroin.

Jefferson airplane. Used match that has been cut in half to hold a partially smoked marijuana cigarette, an allusion to the eponymous band and the fact that the split match looks a bit like an airplane.

jellies. Depressant.

jelly. Cocaine.

jelly baby / jelly bean. Amphetamine.

jelly beans. Crack.

jet. Ketamine.

jet fuel. PCP.

Jim Jones. 1. Marijuana cigarette dipped in PCP, from the name of the crazed cult leader. 2. Marijuana laced with cocaine and PCP.

jive. Heroin; marijuana; drugs.

jive doo jee. Heroin.

jive stick. Marijuana.

Johnson. Crack.

joint. Marijuana cigarette.

jojee. Heroin.

jolly bean. Amphetamine.

jolly green. Marijuana.

jolly pop. Casual user of heroin.

jolt. 1. Cocaine. 2. To inject a drug. 3. Strong reaction to drugs.

Jones. Heroin.

Jonesing. Need for drugs.

joy flakes. Heroin.

joy juice. Depressant.

joy plant. Opium poppy.

joy pop. To inject a drug.

joy popper / joy popping. Intermittent user or use of hard drugs.

joy powder. Heroin; cocaine.

joy smoke. Marijuana.

joy stick. Marijuana cigarette.

ju-ju. Marijuana cigarette.

Juan Valdez / Juanita. Marijuana.

juggle. Sell drugs to another addict to support a habit.

juggler. Teenaged street dealer.

jugs. Amphetamine.

juice. 1. Steroids. 2. PCP.

juice joint. Marijuana cigarette sprinkled with crack.

juke. Holdup.

jum. Sealed plastic bag containing crack.

jumbos. Large vials of crack sold on the streets.

junk. 1. Addiction narcotics. 2. Cocaine or heroin.

junkie / junky. An addict.

Kabayo. Heroin.

kabuki. Crack pipe made from a plastic rum bottle and a rubber spark-plug cover. Also LAMBORGHINI.

kali. Marijuana.

kangaroo. Crack.

kaps. PCP.

karachi. Heroin.

kaya / Kentucky blue. Marijuana.

keyster plant. Drugs hidden in a person's rectum.

KGB (acr). Killer green bud.

K-hole. Periods of ketamine-induced confusion.

kibbles and bits. 1. A combination of the stimulant Ritalin and the painkiller Talwin, a reference to a heavily advertised dog food called Kibbles 'n Bits. 2. Cocaine scraps. 3. Small crumbs of crack.

kick. 1. Getting off a drug habit. 2. An inhalant.

kick stick. Marijuana cigarette.

kicked by the horse. Addicted to heroin.

kiddie dope. Prescription drugs.

kiff. Marijuana.

killer / killer weed. Marijuana and PCP.

kilter / kind. Marijuana.

king ivory. Fentanyl.

King Kong pills. Depressants.

king's habit. Cocaine.

kit. Equipment used to inject drugs.

Kleenex. Methamphetamine.

klingons. Crack addicts.

knocker. Addict—one who knocks him or herself out with narcotics.

kokomo / kryptonite. Crack.

kumba. Marijuana.

L. LSD.

LA. Long-acting amphetamine.

lace. Cocaine and marijuana.

lady / lady caine / lady snow. Cocaine.

lakbay diva. Marijuana.

Lamborghini. Crack pipe made from a plastic rum bottle and a rubber spark-plug cover. Also KABUKI.

lason sa daga. LSD.

laugh and scratch. To inject a drug.

laughing gas. 1. Nitrous oxide. 2. Marijuana.

laughing weed. Marijuana.

lay. An ounce of narcotics.

lay-back. Depressant.

lay-out. Equipment for taking drugs.

LBJ. LSD, PCP, or heroin.

leaf. Marijuana or cocaine.

leapers. Amphetamine.

leaping. Under the influence of drugs.

lemonade. 1. Heroin. 2. Poor-quality drugs.

lens. LSD.

lib (librium). Depressant.

lid. One ounce of marijuana.

lid poppers. Amphetamine.

light stuff. Marijuana.

lightning. Amphetamine.

lima. Marijuana.

lime acid. LSD.

line. Cocaine.

Lipton tea. Inferior-quality drugs.

lit / lit up. Under the influence of drugs.

little bomb. Amphetamine; heroin; depressant.

little smoke. Marijuana; psilocybin/psilocin.

LL. Marijuana.

llesca. Marijuana.

load. Twenty-five bags of heroin.

loaded. High.

loaf / lobo. Marijuana.

locker room. Isobutyl nitrite.

locoweed. Marijuana.

log. 1. PCP. 2. Marijuana cigarette.

logor. LSD.

loused. Covered by sores and abscesses from repeated use of unsterile needles.

love. Crack.

love affair. Cocaine.

love boat / lovely. 1. PCP. 2. Marijuana dipped in formaldehyde.

love drug. Methamphetamine; depressant.

love pearls / love pills. Alpha-ethyltryptamine.

love trip. Methamphetamine and mescaline.

love weed. Marijuana.

lovelies. Marijuana laced with PCP.

LSD. Lysergic acid diethylamide.

lubage. Marijuana.

Lucy in the sky with diamonds. LSD.

'ludes / luding out / luds. Quaaludes or taking quaaludes.

M

M. 1. Morphine. 2. Marijuana. 3. Meth.

machinery / macon. Marijuana.

magic dust. PCP.

magic mushroom. Psilocybin and psilocin.

magic smoke. Marijuana.

mainline. To inject a drug.

mainliner. Person who injects into the vein.

make up. Need to find more drugs.

mama coca. Cocaine.

Manhattan silver. Marijuana.

marahoochie. Marijuana.

marathons. Amphetamine.

mari. Marijuana cigarette.

marshmallow reds. Depressant.

Mary / Mary and Johnny / Mary Ann / Mary Jane / Mary Jonas / Mary Johanna / Mary Warner / Mary Weaver. Marijuana.

Maserati. Crack pipe made from a plastic rum bottle and a rubber spark-plug cover. Also LAMBORGHINI, KABUKI.

matchbox. One quarter ounce of marijuana, or six marijuana cigarettes.

matsakow. Heroin.

Maui Wowie / Maui Wauie. Marijuana strain that may or may not have come from Hawaii.

max. Gamma hydroxy butyrate dissolved in water and mixed with amphetamines.

maxibolin. Oral steroid.

mayo. Cocaine or heroin.

MDA (acr). Miracle drops of acid—actually meth.

MDM / MDMA. Methamphetamine.

Medusa. Ethyl chloride.

meg / megg / meggie. Marijuana.

merk. Cocaine.

mesc / mescal / mese. Mescaline.

messorole. Marijuana.

meth. Methamphetamine.

meth head. Regular user of meth.

meth monster. Person who has a violent reaction to meth.

methatriol. Injectable steroid.

Mexican brown. Heroin; marijuana.

Mexican horse / Mexican mud. Heroin.

Mexican red. Marijuana.

Mezc. Mescaline.

Mickey Finn / Mickeys. Depressant.

microdot. LSD.

midnight oil. Opium.

Mighty Joe Young. Depressant.

Mighty Mezz. Marijuana cigarette.

Mighty Quinn. LSD.

mind detergent. LSD.

minibennie. Amphetamine.

Mira. Opium.

miss. To inject a drug.

Miss Emma. Morphine.

missile basing. Crack liquid and PCP.

mission. Trip out of the crack house to obtain crack.

mist. 1. PCP. 2. Crack smoke.

mister blue. Morphine.

MJ / MO / MU. Marijuana.

modams / mohasky. Marijuana.

mojo. Cocaine or heroin.

monkey. 1. Drug dependency. 2. Cigarette made from cocaine paste and tobacco.

monkey dust / monkey tranquilizer. PCP.

monos. Cigarette made from cocaine paste and tobacco.

monte. Marijuana from South America.

mooca / moocah. Marijuana.

moon. Mescaline.

moonrock. Crack and heroin.

mooster / moota / mutah / mooters / mootie / mootos / mota / mother / moto. Marijuana.

more. PCP.

morf. Morphine.

morning glory. First "hit" of the day.

morning wake-up. First blast of crack from the pipe.

morotgara. Heroin.

mortal combat. High-potency heroin.

mosquitoes. Cocaine.

mother's helper / mother's little helper. 1. Valium. 2. Depressant.

mouth worker. One who takes drugs orally.

movie-star drug. Cocaine.

mow the grass. To smoke marijuana.

mud. Opium or heroin.

muggie / muggle. Marijuana.

mujer. Cocaine.

mule. Carrier of drugs.

munchies. Hunger attack after marijuana use.

murder 8. Fentanyl.

murder one. Heroin and cocaine.

mush-mind. Marijuana user whose mind has become muddled by it.

mushrooms. 1. Psilocybin or psilocin. 2. Name for innocent bystanders who get hurt or killed in urban drug shoot-outs.

mutha. Marijuana.

muzzle. Heroin.

Nail. 1. Hypodermic needle. 2. Marijuana cigarette.

nailed. Arrested.

nebbies. Depressant.

nemmies / nimbies. (1) Nembutal. (2) Depressant.

new jack swing. Heroin and morphine.

new magic. PCP.

New York barricade. A two-by-four nailed across the door of a crack house.

nice and easy. Heroin.

nickel / nickel bag. 1. Five dollars' worth of drugs. 2. Heroin.

nickel deck. Heroin.

nickel note. Five-dollar bill.

nickelonians. Crack addicts.

niebla. PCP.

nimbies. Depressant.

nix. Stranger among the group.

nod. Effects of heroin.

noise. Heroin.

nose candy / nose powder / nose stuff. Cocaine.

nose drops. Liquefied heroin.

nubs. Peyote buttons.

nugget. Amphetamine.

nuggets. Crack.

number. Marijuana cigarette.

number 3. Cocaine.

number 8. Heroin.

O. 1. Opium. 2. OxyContin.

OC. OxyContin

ogoy / oil / old Steve. Heroin.

on a mission. Searching for crack.

on a trip. Under the influence of drugs.

on ice. In jail.

on the bricks. Walking the streets.

on the nod. Under the influence of narcotics or depressant.

on the pipe. Freebasing cocaine.

one and one. To inhale cocaine.

one box tissue. One ounce of crack.

one-fifty-one. Crack.

one way. LSD.

OP. Opium.

ope. Opium.

optical illusions. LSD.

orange barrels / orange cubes / orange haze / orange micro / orange wedges. LSD.

oranges. Amphetamine.

outerlimits. Crack and LSD.

owsley / owsley's acid. LSD.

ox / oxy / oxy-cotton. OxyContin.

Oz. Inhalant.

ozone. PCP.

P. Peyote.

pack. Heroin or marijuana.

pack of rocks. Marijuana cigarette.

pakalolo / Pakistani black / Panama cut / Panama gold / Panama red. Marijuana.

Panatella. Large marijuana cigarette, a reference to a type of cigar.

pane. LSD.

pangonadalot. Heroin.

panic. 1. Shortage of heroin—"There's panic in needle park." 2. Drugs not available.

paper / paper acid. LSD.

paper bag. Container for drugs.

paper blunt. Marijuana within a paper casing rather than a tobacco leaf casing.

paper boy. Heroin peddler.

parabolin. Veterinary steroid.

parachute. 1. Crack and PCP, smoked. 2. Heroin.

paradise / paradise white. Cocaine.

parlay. Crack.

parsley. Marijuana.

paste. Crack.

pat. Marijuana.

patico. Crack (Spanish slang).

PCP. Phencyclidine.

P-dope. Twenty to 30 percent pure heroin.

peace / peace tablets. LSD.

peace pill / peace weed. PCP.

peaches. Amphetamine.

peanut. Depressant.

pearls. Amyl nitrite.

pearly gates. LSD.

pebbles. Crack.

peddler. Drug supplier.

pee wee. Crack, or $5 worth of crack.

peg. Heroin.

pellets. LSD.

pen yan. Opium.

pep pills. Amphetamine.

Pepsi habit. Occasional use of drugs.

perfect high. Heroin.

perico. Cocaine.

perks. Percodan.

perp. Fake crack made of candle wax and baking soda.

Peruvian / Peruvian flake / Peruvian lady. Cocaine.

peth. Depressant.

peyote. Mescaline.

P-funk. 1. A synthetic form of heroin that was first discussed before a national audience September 1989 at a hearing of the Senate Judiciary Committee on New Trends in Narcotics. 2. Heroin or crack and PCP.

phennies / phenos. Depressant.

pianoing. Using the fingers to find lost crack rocks—which might resemble someone playing the piano.

piddle. Hospital, especially one used to treat addicts. The term is an old one and is based on a slurred pronunciation of "hospital."

piece. One ounce of cocaine or crack.

piedras. Crack (Spanish for "rocks").

piles. Crack.

pill ladies. Elderly females who sell OxyContin and other drugs that have been prescribed to them legally.

pillow. Any opiate.

pimp. Cocaine.

pimp your pipe. Lend or rent your crack pipe.

pin. Marijuana.

pin gon / pin yen. Opium.

ping-in-wing. To inject a drug.

pink blotters / pink robots / pink wedge / pink witches. LSD.

pink hearts. Amphetamine.

pink ladies. Depressant.

pipe. 1. Crack or marijuana pipe. 2. Vein into which a drug is injected. 3. To mix drugs with other substances.

pipero. Crack user.

pit. PCP.

pixies. Amphetamine.

plant. Hiding place for drugs.

pocket rocket / pod. Marijuana.

poison. Heroin or fentanyl.

poke. Marijuana.

polvo. Heroin or PCP.

polvo blanco. Cocaine (Spanish for "white powder").

pony. Crack.

poor man's pot. Inhalant.

pop. To inhale cocaine.

poppers. Isobutyl nitrite or amyl nitrite.

poppy. Heroin.

posse. Jamaican gang often dealing in marijuana and crack, or both.

pot. Marijuana.

potato. LSD.

potato chips. Crack cut with benzocaine.

pothead. Regular marijuana user; one who has become addled by the weed.

potten bush. Marijuana.

powder. Heroin or amphetamine.

powder diamonds. Cocaine.

power puller. Rubber piece attached to crack STEM.

pox. Opium.

PR. Panama red, a type of marijuana. See also PAKALOLO.

prescription. Marijuana cigarette.

press. Cocaine; crack.

pretendicia / pretendo. Marijuana.

primo. Crack or marijuana mixed with crack.

primobolan. Injectable and oral steroid.

primos. Cigarettes laced with cocaine and heroin.

Proviron. Oral steroid.

pseudocaine. Phenylpropanolamine, an adulterant for cutting crack.

puff the dragon. Smoke marijuana.

puffer. Crack smoker.

pulborn. Heroin.

pullers. Crack users who pull at parts of their bodies excessively.

pumping. Selling crack.

puppy. Gun.

pure. Heroin.

pure love. LSD.

purple. Ketamine.

purple barrels / purple haze / purple flats / purple ozoline. LSD.

purple hearts. Phenobarbital, LSD, amphetamine, or a depressant.

push. Sell drugs.

push shorts. To cheat or sell short amounts.

pusher. 1. One who sells drugs. 2. Metal hanger or umbrella rod used to scrape residue in crack pipe stems.

Q. Depressant.

quacks. Quaaludes.

quad. Depressant.

quarter / quarter bag. Twenty-five dollars' worth of drugs.

quarter moon. Hashish.

quarter piece. One quarter ounce.

quas. Depressant.

Queen Ann's lace. Marijuana.

quicksilver. Isobutyl nitrite.

quill. Meth; heroin; cocaine.

Racehorse charlie. Cocaine; heroin.

rad weed. Marijuana.

ragweed. Inferior-quality marijuana or heroin.

railroad weed. Marijuana.

rainbows. Depressant.

rainy-day woman. Marijuana.

Rambo. Heroin.

rane. Cocaine or heroin.

rangood. Marijuana grown wild.

rap. 1. A criminal charge. 2. To talk with someone.

raspberry. Female who trades sex for crack or money to buy crack.

rasta weed. Marijuana.

ratboy. Street slang for a person (human "laboratory rat") who is skilled at testing the strength of various drugs.

rave. Party drug designed to enhance a hallucinogenic experience.

raw. Crack.

razed. Under the influence of drugs.

ready rock. Cocaine, crack, or heroin.

recompress. Change the shape of cocaine flakes to resemble a "rock."

recycle. LSD.

red. Under the influence of drugs.

red and blue / red bullets. Depressant.

red caps. Crack.

red chicken. Heroin.

red cross. Marijuana.

red devil. 1. Seconal. 2. Depressant.

red dirt. Marijuana.

red dragon. Opium. This term emerged from Chinese-American gang slang.

red eagle. Heroin.

red flag. Method of injecting heroin in which the needle is put into a vein and the plunger is drawn back until blood is drawn into the bulb. This ensures a hit in the vein rather than in the muscle.

red phosphorus. Smokable speed.

Red Rum. A powerful brand of heroin that killed the rock musician Jonathan Melvoin, of the group Smashing Pumpkins, in July 1996. Red Rum is "murder" spelled backward. The weekend after Melvoin's death the market for packets stamped "Red Rum" were in high demand on Manhattan's Lower East Side. Rather than scare potential buyers, a heroin death will signal to other users that the brand is of high purity.

reds. Depressant.

reefer. Marijuana.

regular P. Crack.

reindeer dust. Heroin.

Rhine. Heroin.

rhythm. Amphetamine.

riding the wave. Being under the influence of drugs.

rig. Paraphernalia for injecting or smoking drugs.

righteous bush. Marijuana.

ringer. Good hit of crack.

rings. Guns and bullets.

rippers. Amphetamine.

roach. Butt of a marijuana cigarette.

roach clip. A holder for smoking a marijuana cigarette right down to the end.

road dope. Amphetamine.

roca. Crack (Spanish for "rock").

rock / rock attack / rocks / rocks of hell / Rocky III. Portion of crack cocaine, as in "The boy had twenty-one rocks of cocaine in his possession with a street value of a thousand dollars."

rock house. Place where crack is sold and smoked.

rock star / rock head / rockette. Female who trades sex for crack or money to buy crack. See RASPBERRY.

rocket. Marijuana cigarette.

rocket caps. Dome-shaped caps on crack vials.

rocket fuel. PCP.

roid rage. Aggressive behavior caused by excessive steroid use.

roller / rollers. 1. Police, from the fact that patrol cars roll through open-air drug markets slowly. 2. Vein that will not stay in position for injection.

rolling. Methamphetamine.

roofies. Rohypnol, a powerful prescription sedative known as the date-rape drug because it can cause blackouts with complete loss of memory.

rooster. Crack.

root. Marijuana.

rope. 1. Marijuana. 2. Marijuana cigarette. 3. Rohypnol (see ROOFIES).

rosa. Amphetamine.

rose marie. Marijuana.

roses. Amphetamine.

Rox / Roxanne. Cocaine; crack.

royal blues. LSD.

roz. Crack.

R's and T's. A combination of the stimulant Ritalin and the painkiller Talwin.

ruderalis. Species of cannabis found in Russia that grows to a height of one to two and a half feet.

runners. People who sell drugs for others.

running. Methamphetamine.

rush. 1. Intense orgasm-like sensation that follows an intrevenous injection. 2. Isobutyl nitrite.

rush snappers. Isobutyl nitrite.

Russian sickles. LSD.

Sack. Heroin.

sacrament. LSD.

salt. Heroin.

salt and pepper. Marijuana.

Sam. Federal narcotics agent.

sancocho. To steal (also Spanish for "slew").

sandoz. LSD.

sandwich. Two layers of cocaine with a layer of heroin in the middle.

Santa Marta. Marijuana.

sasfras. Marijuana.

satan's secret. Inhalant.

satch. Papers, letter, cards, clothing, etc., saturated with drug solution (used to smuggle drugs into prisons or hospitals).

satch cotton. Fabric used to filter a solution of narcotics before injection.

sativa. Species of cannabis that thrives in a cool, damp climate and grows up to 18 feet high.

scaffle. PCP.

scag / scat / scate. Heroin.

schmeck / schoolboy. Cocaine.

scissors. Marijuana.

score. Purchase drugs.

scorpion. Cocaine.

Scott. Heroin.

Scottie / Scotty. Cocaine, crack, or the high from crack.

scramble. Crack.

scrambler. Street term for a hustler or, occasionally, a drug dealer.

scratch. Money.

script. A prescription given to a drug user who has faked physical illness or emotional distress to get it.

scruples. Crack.

seccy. Depressant.

seeds. Marijuana.

seggy. Depressant.

sen. Marijuana.

seni. Peyote.

sernyl. PCP.

serpico 21. Cocaine.

server. Crack dealer.

servin'. Selling, as in "servin' rock."

sess. Marijuana.

7-up. Cocaine; crack.

sewer. Vein into which a drug is injected.

sezz. Marijuana.

shabu. Ice.

shake. Useless or poor-quality leaves of a marijuana plant.

shaker / baker / water. Materials needed to freebase cocaine, including a shaker bottle, baking soda, and water.

sharps. Needles.

she. Cocaine.

sheet rocking. Crack or LSD.

shermans / sherms. PCP or crack.

shit. Heroin.

shmeck / schmeek. Heroin.

shoot / shoot up. To inject a drug.

shoot the breeze. Nitrous oxide.

shooting gallery. Place where drugs are used.

shot down. Be under the influence of drugs.

'shrooms. Psilocybin or psilocin; short for "mushrooms."

siddi. Marijuana.

sightball. Crack.

silly putty. Psilocybin or psilocin.

silver bike. Syringe with chrome fittings.

simple simon. Psilocybin or psilocin.

sinse. Marijuana.

sinsemilla. 1. Seedless, as applied to marijuana, specifically the unpollinated female plants. 2. The name of the powerful Northern California seedless variety of marijuana.

sixty-two. Two and a half ounces of crack.

skee. Opium.

skeegers / skeezers. Crack-smoking prostitute.

skid. Heroin.

skid-drop. A means by which a large load of drugs is dropped from the air by means of a cargo skid attached to a parachute.

skied. Be under the influence of drugs.

skin popping. Injecting drugs under the skin.

skunk. Marijuana.

slab. Crack.

slam. To inject a drug.

slanging. Selling drugs.

sleeper. Heroin or depressant.

sleet. Crack.

sleigh ride. Drug spree.

slick superspeed. Methcathinone.

slime. Heroin.

smack. Heroin.

smack weed. Pot cured in heroin.

smears. LSD.

smoke. Heroin and crack, crack, or marijuana.

smoke Canada. Marijuana.

smoked out. Under the influence of drugs.

smoking gun. Heroin and cocaine.

snap. Amphetamine.

snappers. Isobutyl nitrite.

sniff. To inhale cocaine, inhalant, or methcathinone.

snop. Marijuana.

snort. To inhale cocaine; use inhalant.

snot. Residue produced from smoking amphetamine.

snot balls. Rubber cement rolled into balls and burned to release a hallucinatory gas.

snow / snow bird / snow cones / snow soak / snow white. Cocaine.

snow ball. Cocaine and heroin.

snow pallets. Amphetamine.

snow seals. Cocaine and amphetamine.

society high. Cocaine.

soda. Injectable cocaine used in Hispanic communities.

softballs. Depressant.

soles. Hashish.

soma. PCP.

sopers. Depressant.

space base. Crack dipped in PCP; hollowed-out cigar refilled with PCP and crack.

space cadet / space dust. 1. Mixture of PCP and crack. 2. Crack dipped in PCP.

space ship. Glass pipe used to smoke crack.

spark it up. To smoke marijuana.

sparkle plenty / sparklers. Amphetamine.

Special K / special la coke. Ketamine.

speed. Meth; amphetamine; crack.

speed ball. 1. A mix of heroin and cocaine, which is what killed the twenty-three-year old actor River Phoenix in 1993. 2. Amphetamines used as an enhancer of personal performance, as in "Getting there by copter he would only have to swim one way, cutting time in half. With the aid of a speed ball and flippers, he could improve that by twenty-five percent" (Jay Richard Kennedy, *The Chairman*).

speed boat. Marijuana, PCP, or crack.

speed for lovers. Methamphetamine.

speed freak. Habitual user of meth.

spider blue. Heroin.

spike. 1. To inject a drug. 2. Needle.

splash. Amphetamine.

spliff. 1. A joint or portion of marijuana. 2. Marijuana cigarette.

splim. Marijuana.

split. 1. Half and half. 2. To leave.

splivins. Amphetamine.

spoon. 1. One-sixteenth ounce of heroin. 2. Paraphernalia used to prepare heroin for injection.

sporting. To inhale cocaine.

spray. Inhalant.

sprung. Said of a person just starting to use drugs.

square grouper. A bale of marijuana, when it washes ashore in south Florida.

square mackerel. Marijuana, in Florida.

square time Bob. Crack.

squirrel. 1. A person smoking cocaine, marijuana, and PCP. 2. LSD.

SS. Skin shot: injection into skin rather than directly into the vein.

stack. Marijuana.

star. Methcathinone.

star dust / star-spangled powder. Cocaine.

stash. Place to hide drugs.

stash areas. Drug storage and distribution areas.

steerer. One who does not sell drugs but guides or steers potential buyers to places where they are sold.

stem. 1. Glass pipe for smoking crack or ICE. 2. Cylinder used to smoke crack.

stems. Marijuana.

step on. 1. To cut or adulturate a drug by doubling its weight and halving its purity. If fifteen pounds of a drug is "stepped on" twice, it becomes sixty pounds. 2. To dilute drugs.

stick. Marijuana cigarette.

stick-up boys. Those who rob drug dealers.

stink weed. Marijuana.

stoned. Under the influence of drugs.

stoner. Habitual user of marijuana.

stones. Crack.

stoppers. Depressant.

STP. PCP.

straw. Marijuana cigarette.

strawberry. 1. Prostitute who will trade sex for cocaine. 2. Female who trades sex for crack or money to buy crack. See RASPBERRY.

strawberry fields. LSD, an allusion to the Beatles song "Strawberry Fields Forever."

strung out. 1. Condition resulting from habitual use of drugs. 2. Heavily addicted to drugs.

stuff. Heroin.

stumbler. Depressant.

sugar. Cocaine; LSD; heroin.

sugar block. Crack.

sugar cubes / sugar lumps. LSD.

sugar weed. Marijuana.

sunshine. LSD.

super acid. Ketamine.

super C. Ketamine.

sweet Jesus. Heroin.

sweet Lucy. Marijuana.

sweet stuff. Heroin; cocaine.

sweets. Amphetamine.

swell up. Crack.

T. Cocaine or marijuana.

tab / tabs / tail lights. A dose of LSD.

taima. Marijuana.

taking a cruise. PCP.

takkouri. Marijuana.

tamal. Small packet of the drug BAZUCO.

tango & cash. Fentanyl.

tar. Opium or heroin.

tardust. Cocaine.

tarred and feathered. Addicted.

taste. Heroin; small sample of drugs.

tax / taxing. 1. Price paid to enter a crackhouse. 2. Charging more per vial depending on the race of a customer or if the customer is not a regular.

tea / tea 13. Marijuana. Why 13? In her trendy, punky *Modern English,* Jennifer Walters asserts that the number 13 alludes to the fact that M, for marijuana, is the thirteenth letter of the alphabet.

tea party. To smoke marijuana.

teardrops. Doses of crack packaged in the cut-off corners of plastic bags.

tecate. Heroin.

tecatos. Hispanic heroin addicts.

teeth. 1. Bullets. 2. Cocaine or crack.

tension. Crack.

Tex-Mex / Texas pot / Texas tea. Marijuana.

Thai sticks. Bundles of marijuana soaked in hashish oil or marijuana buds bound in short sections of bamboo.

THC. Tetrahydrocannabinol.

thing. Heroin, cocaine, or the main drug interest at the moment.

thirst monsters. Heavy crack smokers.

thirteen. Marijuana.

thoroughbred. Drug dealer who sells pure narcotics.

thrusters. Amphetamine.

thumb. Marijuana.

tic tac. PCP.

ticket. LSD.

ticket agent. Dealer in hallucinogenic drugs.

tie. To inject a drug.

tin. Container for marijuana.

tissue. Crack.

T-man. Federal narcotics agent.

TNT. Heroin or fentanyl.

toilet water. Inhalant.

toke / toke up. To inhale cocaine or smoke marijuana.

tolly. Street name for toluene, a hydrocarbon solvent.

toncho. Octane booster that is inhaled.

tool. Gun.

tooles. Depressant.

tools. Equipment used for injecting drugs.

toot. 1. Cocaine. 2. To inhale cocaine.

tooties. Depressant.

tootsie roll. Powerful form of Mexican heroin.

top gun. Crack.

topi. Mescaline.

tops. Peyote.

torch. Marijuana.

torch cooking. Smoking cocaine base by using a propane or butane torch as a source of a flame.

torch up. To smoke marijuana.

torpedo. Crack and marijuana.

toss up. Female who trades sex for crack or money to buy crack. See STRAWBERRY, RASPBERRY.

totally spent. To have a methamphetamine hangover.

toucher. User of crack who wants affection before, during, or after smoking crack.

tout. Person who introduces buyers to sellers.

toxy. Opium.

toy. Container for narcotics.

toys. Opium.

TR-6s. Amphetamine.

track. To inject a drug.

tracks. Marks left in the skin from continued injection of drugs into the veins.

tragic magic. 1. Mixture of PCP and crack. 2. Crack dipped in PCP.

trails. LSD-induced hallucination that moving objects are leaving multiple images or trails behind them.

tranqu. Depressant.

trap. Hiding place for drugs.

travel agent. LSD supplier.

trays. Bunches of vials.

trey. Three bucks' worth of drugs, often a half-inch vial of crack.

trip. LSD or alpha-ethyltryptamine.

triple-nine. A form of morphine base.

troop. Crack.

trophobolene. Injectable steroid.

truck drivers. Amphetamine.

tubo. Crack and marijuana.

tuie. Depressant.

turd. Secreted narcotics, usually hidden in the rectum.

turf. Place where drugs are sold.

turkey. 1. A fake capsule containing only sugar or chalk that is sold as a powerful drug. 2. Cocaine or amphetamine.

turnabout. Amphetamine.

turned on. 1. Introduced to drugs. 2. Under the influence of a drug.

tutti-frutti. Flavored cocaine developed by a Brazilian gang.

tweak mission. On a mission to find crack.

tweaker. Crack user looking for rocks on the floor after a police raid.

tweaking. Drug-induced paranoia.

tweek. Meth-like substance.

tweeker. Methcathinone.

twenty. A $20 rock of crack.

twenty-five. LSD.

twist / twistum. Marijuana cigarette.

two for nine. Two $5 vials or bags of crack for $9.

Ultimate. Crack.

uncle. Federal narcotics agent.

Uncle Milty. Depressant.

unkie. Morphine.

unmarried. An addict with no regular connection. See CONNECT.

up against the stem. Addicted to smoking marijuana.

uppers / ups / uppies. Amphetamines. Drugs used to stimulate the nervous system.

ups and downs. Depressant.

using. Taking narcotics.

utopiates. Hallucinogens.

uzi. 1. Crack. 2. Crack pipe.

V. Valium, a depressant.

vipe. To inhale marijuana smoke.

viper. Marijuana smoker.

viper butts / viper's weed. Marijuana.

vitamin A / vodka acid. LSD.

VS. Vein shooter.

Wac. Mixture of PCP and marijuana.

wack. PCP.

wacky weed. Marijuana.

wake ups. Amphetamine.

wasted. 1. Under the influence of drugs. 2. Murdered.

water. 1. PCP. 2. Meth.

wave. Crack.

wedding bells. LSD.

wedge. LSD.

weed. Marijuana.

weed hound. Since the 1920s, one with a craving for marijuana.

weed tea. Marijuana.

weightless. High on crack.

wheat. Marijuana.

when-shee. Opium.

whippets. Nitrous oxide.

white. Amphetamine.

white ball. Crack.

white boy. Heroin.

white Christmas. Cocaine.

white cloud. Crack smoke.

white cross. Meth or amphetamine.

white dust. LSD.

white ghost. Crack.

white girl. Cocaine or heroin.

white-haired lady. Marijuana.

white horizon. PCP.

white horse / white junk / white lady. Cocaine; heroin.

white lightning. LSD: a term borrowed from alcohol, where it means powerful, homemade booze or moonshine.

white mosquito. Cocaine.

white nurse. Heroin.

white owsley's. LSD.

white powder. Cocaine or PCP.

white-powder bar. Collective term for lawyers representing the higher level of drug seller.

white snow / white sugar / white tornado. Crack cocaine.

whites. Amphetamine.

whiz bang. Cocaine and heroin.

wild cat. Methcathinone and cocaine.

window glass / windowpane. LSD.

wings. Heroin or cocaine.

wisdom weed. Marijuana.

witch / witch hazel. Heroin or cocaine.

witch, the. Heroin.

wollie. Rocks of crack rolled into a marijuana cigarette.

wonder star. Methcathinone.

wool the jacket. To become addicted.

woolah. A hollowed-out cigar refilled with marijuana and crack.

woolas. 1. Cigarette laced with cocaine. 2. Marijuana cigarette sprinkled with crack.

woolies. Marijuana and crack or PCP.

wooly blunts. Marijuana and crack or PCP.

working. Selling crack.

working half. Crack rock weighing half a gram or more.

working man's cocaine. Meth.

works. Drug user's equipment for injecting drugs.

wrecking crew. Crack.

X-arm. Arm preferred by an addict for injection.

X-ing. Taking methamphetamine.

Xmas. Period of euphoria following narcotic ingestion.

XTC. Methamphetamine.

Ya ba. A pure and powerful form of meth from Thailand; "crazy drug."

yahoo / yeaho. Crack.

Yale. Crack.

ye olde Peruvian marching powder. Mock elegant nickname for cocaine.

yeh. Marijuana.

yellow / yellow bullets. LSD; depressant.

yellow bam. Meth.

yellow dimples. LSD.

yellow jacket. 1. A barbiturate. 2. A depressant.

yellow submarine. Marijuana.

yellow sunshine. LSD.

yen. Opium.

yen pop. Marijuana.

yen shee suey. Opium wine.

yen sleep. Restless, drowsy state after LSD use.

yerba. Marijuana.

yerba mala. PCP and marijuana.

yesca / yesco. Marijuana.

yeyo. Cocaine (Spanish term).

yimyon. Crack.

Z. One ounce of heroin.

zacatecas purple. Marijuana from Mexico.

zambi. Marijuana.

zen. LSD.

zeppelin. Cigar containing secreted narcotics.

zero. Opium.

zig zag man. LSD, marijuana, or marijuana rolling papers.

zip. Cocaine.

zol. Marijuana cigarette.

zombie. 1. Heavy marijuana user. 2. PCP. 3. Heavy user of drugs.

zooie. A tool to hold the butt of a marijuana cigarette. See ROACH.

zoom. 1. Marijuana. 2. Mixture of PCP and marijuana.

zoomar. Powerful narcotic.

zoomers. Individuals who sell fake crack and then flee.

10

FANTASY, THE FUTURE, SCIENCE FICTION, POTTERDOM, AND CYBERPUNK

Coming to Terms with Parallel Worlds

Listen to a fan's speech. It's a foregone conclusion if he uses words such as faned, fapan, fanac, sercon, Neffer, vombic, fout, slan, neohood, grok. By the way, a female fan is a "fanne."

—"Amazing World of the Fen," *San Francisco Examiner*, October 13, 1968

Bink, dweezle, frakkin' geek, scrod, skag, skeekin', sokkin', dithead.

—"Internet Glossary of Slang in 2054," cyberpunk swearwords

The vocabulary of *Harry Potter and the Sorcerer's Stone*, with words such as Quidditch and Snape and Slytherin and Filch, sounds as if it could have been extracted from some long-lost verse of Lewis Carroll's "Jabberwocky."

—Valerie Kuklenski, "For All You Muggles Out There . . ." *Los Angeles Daily News*, November 16, 2001

Most slang concerns itself with the real world, of what is or what was. However, there is a small but growing corner of the slang universe reserved for what will be or could conceivably be or was in a parallel universe unknown to muggles (mere mortals in the world of Harry Potter). Science fiction ("ess-eff," not "sigh-fi," to its serious fans), futurism, fantasy, and cyberpunk—the newest and determinedly nasty in-your-face child of science fiction and the Net—generate their own odd terminologies.

At the other end of the spectrum from cyberpunk is the growing fascination with the fantasy worlds of J. K. Rowling's Harry Potter, C. S. Lewis's Narnia books, and J. R. R. Tolkien's classic *The Lord of the Rings* trilogy. These are old-school fantasies, where good and evil wrestle for control of an imaginary world.

Here is a smattering from some of these netherworlds.

Ace of spades (cyberpunk). Solo term for death in combat. To "draw the ace" is to die in battle.

alf (acr). Alien life form. The Alf of television fame was named with this science fiction acronym in mind.

APA / -apa. 1. Amateur press association or amateur press alliance, which are cooperative efforts to publish FANZINES, or in this case, *apazines*. As one versed in APA ways explains, "Minac [minimum activity] is generally two pages per issue. Each author pays to print his pages, and the O.E. [official editor] collates and distributes the APA when each issue is ready." 2. As a suffix, it is used in words like "Bobapa"—an APA where all discussion relates to Bob.

apogee (cyberpunk). The best. The greatest.

apparate (Potterism). To disappear in one spot and reappear in another within an instant. Much the same as the "Beam me up, Scotty" of *Star Trek*.

Bake-brain (cyberpunk). General-purpose derogatory term indicating someone with limited or damaged mental faculties (frequently due to excessive use of neural cyberware).

bem (acr). Bug-eyed monster of science fiction. The bible of bems is *Barlowe's Guide to Extra-Terrestrials*, by Wayne Barlowe and Ian Summers, which contains such fine examples as the Abyormenite, Denu, Ixtl, Pnume, Thrint, and Unhjinian.

Benji (cyberpunk). A robot dog or robohound.

Bertie Bott's Every Flavor Beans (Potterism). Wizard candy, which comes in flavors ranging from chocolate, coconut, and peppermint to sprouts, liver, grass, ear wax, and tripe. Other Hogwarts treats: Butterbeer (buttery nonalcoholic drink), Drooble's Best Blowing Gum, Chocolate Frogs, Pumpkin Pasties, Cauldron Cakes, and Licorice Wands.

big crunch. The hypothesized contracting of the universe by implosion and the flip side of the "big bang" of creation. The general estimate is that if it takes place, it is still some 110 billion years off.

big dark (cyberpunk). Space.

biosoft (cyberpunk). Software that can plug straight into a jack that goes into a person's head, to give them, for example, fluency in Spanish or an understanding of electronics.

bitty box (cyberpunk). A primitive, underpowered, or generally useless computer or other electronic device.

biz (cyberpunk). Crime.

black clinic (cyberpunk). A medical facility that specializes in the implant of illegal or unregistered cyberware.

black ice (cyberpunk). Illegal countermeasure software that causes physical harm or death to an intruder.

bloc (cyberpunk). A powerful group with universal grasp, such as the aerospace bloc or the pharmaceutical bloc.

BNF. Big name fan; one known in fannish circles.

boggart (Potterism). A shape-shifter that takes on the likeness of your worst fears.

booper (cyberpunk). A robot.

booster (cyberpunk). Any member of a gang that affects cyberware, leather clothing, and random violence.

Boswash. Futurists' term for the emerging supercity sprawling between Boston and Washington. For those who believe the city will stretch from Portland, Maine, to Portsmouth, Virginia, the name is Portport. The Chicago-to-Pittsburgh supercity has been called Chipitts, and the sprawl from San Francisco to San Diego, Sansan.

bount (cyberpunk). Bounty hunter.

brain potato (cyberpunk). A braindance addict.

braindance (cyberpunk). A direct connection to a virtual reality via neural link. Used for recreation, criminal rehabilitation, and training exercises.

bruce (cyberpunk). Pronunciation of the hacker acronym BRS (big red switch). 1. To deactivate a machine. 2. To kill someone or render them senseless.

BTL chip (cyberpunk). "Better than life" chip (also called "DreamChips"). An illegal cyberdata chip that provides the user with a combination of artificial reality coupled with direct stimulation of different centers of the brain.

buttonhead (cyberpunk). A person addicted to stimulating the pleasure centers through interface sockets.

CE. A close encounter. A CE3 is a close encounter of the third kind, celebrated in the film of the same name. The third kind is a contact of a human with a UFO and its occupants. CE2s involve UFOs that interact with the environment, and CE1s are encounters that are close and detailed enough to rule out misinterpretation of some other stimuli.

cement poisoning (cyberpunk). What a person dies of after being pushed off a multistory building and hitting the sidewalk. Also known as deceleration trauma.

character. The playing piece that most people use in role-playing games. "You enter these games through the persona of a character," says the writer and fantasy-game designer Mike Stackpole. "If you play well, your character will develop into a 'real' person who will leave you no doubt about how he or she would handle a situation."

Chinese take-out (cyberpunk). Anything extremely jumbled or messy, as in "That riotgun made his chest look like Chinese take-out."

chit. Playing piece in role-playing games.

choob (cyberpunk). Jerk; nerd; weirdo.

chopping (cyberpunk). The process of cracking a stolen credcard or credchip—punkese for credit card or credit chip.

chrome (cyberpunk). 1. Flash, glitter, bells and whistles, tinsel. Material used to spice up the appearance of something. 2. Sexy features on a program, not needed for functionality but radiating style, such as a guillotine instead of a trash-can icon. 3. Generic reference to cyberware.

clamhead look. Describing Star Trekkers who wear Klingon haircuts.

clubzine. Fanzine published by a science fiction club.

combat drugs (cyberpunk). Designer drugs for military use.

-con. A suffix to indicate a convention, such as Worldcon, Lunacon, Swampcon (in Baton Rouge), Amigocon (El Paso), Onceuponacon, Kublacon, Deepsouthcon, Mythcon, Loscon (Los Angeles), Okcon (Tulsa), Armadillocon (Austin), and Pretty Goodcon. The names of these conventions underscore the urge to pun and play with words that is at work in organized science-fiction fandom. See also NONCON.

concom. Convention committee, the people who organize and produce the cons.

condom. Those who attend conventions; the world of conventions.

cortex bomb (cyberpunk). A small, implanted explosive device (usually in the skull) that detonates in response to a timer or remote signal. Usually implanted against the wearer's will to keep him under control. Most cortex bombs will detonate automatically if tampered with.

crudzine. "A worthless fanzine," according to Robert Runte's "Fanspeak Glossary."

cyberaxe (cyberpunk). Any musical instrument—although typically a guitar—that is equipped with a cybernetic interface.

cyberculture. Society served by automation.

cybermetrician. Person with a highly advanced level of rapport with computers.

cyberpsychosis (cyberpunk). A psychotic aberration suffered by excessive users of cyberware.

cyberpunk. A science fiction movement led by a group of young writers who, according to Michael Dirda, writing in the *Washington Post*, "share a liking for hard-edged, high-tech, razzle-dazzle visions of the future, especially a grim future where computers, drugs, and cybernetics rule." The dust jackets on recent editions of Rudy Rucker's 1982 novel *Software* contain this claim: "The astonishing cyberpunk novel that started it all." By most accounts, the best

Sup Zombie?

Cyberpunk has its own sublingo, which goes beyond the terms such as derms, flatline, meat puppet, razor boy/girl, sensetapes, and other terms listed in this glossary. It also comprises a motley assortment of gang and cop slang, motorcycle slang, some of the slang of the military, French slang, Russian cant, nonstandard Spanish and Japanese slang of all sorts, but especially motorcycle slang. Thus, ammo (ammunition), bakuto (Japanese: gambler), B&E (cop slang for breaking and entering), organiskaya (the Russian mafia), boga (in vogue from Spanish), 'ricain, (French slang for American), and bourgie (low-class, from the French bourgeoisie) are all part of the lingo. There are many terms for low-life scum, including yono (from the Korean *yonomoseki*), and garbage, including gomo (from the Japanese). The cyberpunks even have their own term for nihilist, which is zombie—about the closest that this hard-edged subculture gets to humor.

example of the genre is Bill Gibson's *Neuromancer.*

cyborg. Human fitted with electronic parts.

cybot. Cybernetic robot; a robot capable of making decisions.

Daddy / daddie (cyberpunk). According to the Jes Wulfsberg Nielsen's "Shadowrun & Cyberpunk Glossary" on the Internet: an "add-on" chip; a cyberdata chip containing a programmed skill that augments existing skills or provides new ones. These chips provide "instant" training of a normally unknown ability such as flying a jet.

D&D. The game dungeons and dragons.

derms. Dermal patches that introduce drugs into a person's system, a term with ties to cyberpunk.

die of the measles (cyberpunk). In military parlance, an assassination that makes the death appear to be of natural causes.

dirtgirl (cyberpunk). An earth woman; derogatory.

disruptors (Trektalk). Energy weapons.

DM. Dungeon master; in D&D, person who designs adventures for others to engage in.

dock (cyberpunk). 1. To meet someone. 2. To have sex.

'dorph (cyberpunk). 1. Street slang for synthetic endorphins (painkillers produced naturally by the human body), a designer drug that increases healing powers, limits fatigue, and produces a "rush" similar to a second wind. 2. A synthetic analogue for endorphins. Used to suppress pain and shock. Addictive.

doughboy / doughgirl (cyberpunk). Someone who is wearing too much armor.

dozmo. Irritating or boorish science fiction fan.

drekky/drek (cyberpunk). Common curse word (archaic "shit").

drig (cyberpunk). Copulation. Expletive.

drobe. One who attends science fiction conventions in costume.

DSPSG (Trektalk). Disgusting, slobbering Patrick Stewart groupie, an allusion to the commander in *Star Trek*, Jean-Luc Picard, played by Patrick Stewart.

duck (cyberpunk). A person who carries more weapons than could possibly be needed.

dweegs. Dorks with guns. Fan David C. Kopaska-Merkel says that this is a reference to "pubescent males or those with arrested development who brandish weapons (more often than not fakes) at conventions,

dweegs. (*continued*)
angering the management, and commonly causing the convention to be banned from the only good convention hotel in town." Extremely pejorative.

Earth grazer. Asteroid that comes close—that is, within several million miles—of earth.

egoboo. Ego boost, in the world of science fiction.

encounter. In the realm of UFOLOGY, one of three levels of extraterrestrial contact. See CE.

ETI. Extraterrestrial intelligence.

exobiota. Extraterrestrial life.

exosociology. Futurists' term for that aspect of sociology dealing with extraterrestrial civilization.

exotic (cyberpunk). An obviously biosculpted individual, usually with nonhuman features such as fangs, fur, a tail.

Faaan. A fanatical science fiction devotee. Often called "triple-A fan."

'face / face / eye-face / I-face (cyberpunk). The interface. Jacking into the Net.

fafia (acr). Forced away from it all. A fan may fafiate from fannish activities because of bad press or any of a hundred other reasons. See also GAFIA.

fanac. Blend of fan activity fan + activity (pron. *fan*-ac) in the realm of science fiction. A prime example of fanac is publishing a FANZINE.

fandom. The science fiction subculture.

faned. Fan editor, for short.

fannish. Relating only to science fiction fans; of the realm.

fanzine. A blend of fan + magazine, these are simple science fiction periodicals that may be stenciled or photocopied.

fan-speak. How science fiction fans speak. It is made of up initialisms, acronyms, blended words, obscure in-jokes, and standard terms used in special ways.

fate to be meat (cyberpunk). Someone bound for the body banks. "It is his fate to be meat."

Federation (Trektalk). Short version of the United Federation of Planets, consisting of 150 planets and colonies, including Earth. Encompassing a wide variety of life-forms, the Federation is the chief political organization of a mere 5 percent of the Galaxy.

fen. Plural of fan. Once said to be obsolete, it still shows up in print and is all over the Web.

FIAWOL. Fandom is a way of life—science fiction initialism for one of the two camps of fandom. The second camp is represented by the idea of FIJAGH.

FIJAGH. Fandom is just a goddamned hobby.

filk music (SF). Originally a typo for "folk music." Singing filksongs is now a popular activity. They are generally parodies of folk or popular songs with science fiction or fantasy lyrics. In writing about this phenomenon, the *Wall Street Journal* reported that there are two forms of filk: bardic filk, in which people sing together, and chaos filk, when a group of fans sing whenever so moved.

fixed pie. The view of the earth's future that contends there is a known limit to the planet's resources.

flatline. To be slain while hacking into a system in cyberspace. This is the most severe form of dealing with an intruder.

fletcher (cyberpunk). A flechette pistol, SMG, or rifle.

flickercladding (cyberpunk). A synthetic plastic material impregnated with fiber-optics and temperature gauges designed to respond to skin temperature, a twenty-first-century version of the mood ring, but worn as clothing, according to Jes Wulfsberg Nielsen's "Shadowrun & Cyberpunk Glossary," on the Internet.

fossil (cyberpunk). 1. An elderly person. 2. Someone who refuses to give up old ways. 3. Any old or obsolete item.

foxtrot uniform (cyberpunk). Fucked up.

frob (cyberpunk). To alter control settings in a random or mischievous fashion.

FRP. Fantasy role playing. An expert authority, Michael Stackpole, says, "This is the generic term used to describe all of the role-playing games, though purists stick to RPG for that designation."

FTL. Faster than light, as in FTL travel.

Gafia (acr). Getting away from it all. "To gafiate means to abandon science fiction and return to the mundane world," writes Michael Dirda in the *Washington Post.* See also FAFIA.

gagh (SF). From *Star Trek*, a Klingon delicacy (live worms). In fandom and at conventions it is made from noodles or occasionally from cooked squid.

gamer. One who plays role-playing games.

geek (cyberpunk). To kill or die.

genre. The style or setting of a particular story or series within the larger universe of SF, Sword and Sorcery, Hard SF, Fantasy, Romance, Mystery and Horror, etc.

get-a-lifer. Hardcore *Star Trek* fan; one needing to get a life.

GM. Game master, the director of role-playing games. A definition given by Chaosium, Inc., a distributor of such games, says that the GM "is one player who acts as the story's narrator and coordinator, describing the game world to the players, presenting the evening's objective, and controlling the actions of all the bad guys."

go-go-gang (cyberpunk). A biker gang.

gobstones (Potterism). Wizardly version of marbles. Pieces squirt noxious liquid in a player's face when a point is lost.

Golden Age. The 1940s and early 1950s, the period in which some of the greatest science fiction writers (Arthur C. Clarke, Isaac Asimov, and Robert Heinlein) were writing their classics.

goto (cyberpunk). A dossier, usually illegally compiled.

grab gee (cyberpunk). To spend time in a gravity field.

grav or gee (cyberpunk). 1. Gravity. 2. Weight. 3. A measure of importance.

Gringotts (Potterism). Wizards bank.

grognard. Experienced war gamer; a compliment.

grok. To be, to love, to understand, to have cosmic awareness, etc. The verb is Martian and comes from Robert A. Heinlein's *Stranger in a Strange Land.* The term has spread outside the realm of science fiction, where it is still used but is considered passé.

grrl. Female science fiction fans and fictional characters known for their toughness. As a character named Red Monster puts it in one glossary of Sci-fi terms, "Like a girl, only without the sugar and spice. We are not darling little pink-ruffled girls, we are shit-kicking taking-crap-from-no-one grrls."

Gumby from Monty Python (cyberpunk). An act of minor but conspicuous stupidity, as in "pulling a gumby."

Hard (cyberpunk). 1. A flattering term, like cool, hip, tough, etc. 2. A target wearing an exoskeleton. 3. Any heavily armored object or position.

hard science / hard SF / hard. Science fiction that is hardware-intensive or in which the magic and fantasy obey the laws of science. With the advent of the NEW WAVE in the 1960s, hard science fiction was deemed to be conservative and "Old Wave."

heroic fantasy / heroic fiction / HF. A genre of fantasy fiction that mixes monsters, barbarians, and pretty women.

hexed (cyberpunk). 1. Having a cyberpsychosis. 2. Being obsessed with the Net.

hibernaculum. Place where a human is put into artificial hibernation for travel into deep space.

High Frontier. Term characterizing space as a vast human habitat.

hotdogger (cyberpunk). Inexperienced netrunners; derogatory.

howler (Potterism). Letter that, when opened, howls and screeches at the reader.

Hugo. The most famous award in the world of science fiction, it is awarded by the World Science Fiction Convention and is voted on by members of that convention. It is named after Hugo Gernsback, the "father of modern science fiction."

hyperspace. Space containing more than three dimensions. A realm in which vehicles move faster than light. It was made popular in the movie *Star Wars*.

IDIC. (Trektalk). Abbeviation for "infinite diversity in infinite combination"—a Star Trekker tenet of life.

ish. "Issue," in the world of science fiction literature; often used as a suffix. NEXTISH, for instance, is the next issue of a FANZINE.

Jack (cyberpunk). 1. Jack in, or enter cyberspace. Jack out, or leave cyberspace. 2. A direct neural interface connection (usually in the skull) for a cyberdeck.

jander (cyberpunk). To walk in a casual or arrogant manner; to strut.

jazzed (cyberpunk). Equipped with reflex-enhancing cyberware.

Kibble card (cyberpunk). Government food ration card. Kibble is a food product of the future resembling dry cat or dog food.

kleptoid (cyberpunk). Thief or prowler.

Klingon (Trektalk). 1. Belligerent humanoid warriors originally from the planet Qo'noS. 2. Language of about two thousand words created by Marc Okrand, a writer. It is the language of the alien Klingons of Star Trek and there are now Klingon language camps for those hoping to master the guttural, totally fabricated tongue. Here is a bit of Klingon from Ian Spelling's "Inside Trek" column in the *Washington Times* (October 10, 1994): "ja'chuqmeH roj-Hom neH jaghla," which in English would be "The enemy commander wishes a truce in order to confer."

knight bus (Potterism). Emergency vehicle for the transport of wizards and witches.

knut (Potterism). Bronze wizard money: twenty-nine knuts to a sickle.

kranston maneuver (cyberpunk). To become spacesick to the point of vomiting.

Leaky Cauldron (Potterism). A London pub catering to wizards and witches; invisible to Muggles.

leash (cyberpunk). A corporate safeguard implanted into an employee to ensure loyalty and continued service. Cortex bombs and sabotaged chipware are common examples.

LGM. Little green men.

lifeboat ethic. The moral code based on the belief that an individual or nation can justify not aiding less fortunate individuals or nations because of widespread shortage and deprivation. Some believe that this "ethic" will lead to wars of redistribution.

light sailing. A means of spaceship propulsion in which a giant sail is used to catch powerful solar winds.

lizard brain (cyberpunk). A cold, calculating, unemotional person, somebody always running in pure floating point mode, such as Mr. Spock, of *Star Trek*, as viewed by the cyberpunks.

Martian Statue of Liberty. An idea that first appeared in Arthur C. Clarke's *Profiles of the Future.* The inscription on the base of this imaginary structure reads: "Give me your nuclear physicists, your chemical engineers, your biologists and mathematicians."

matchbox (cyberpunk). A sleep cube or coffin.

meat puppet (cyberpunk). A person who has had a neural cutout so they do not have to be conscious of what is happening to their body. Generally used to describe prostitutes, who use the cutouts to be "elsewhere" while their johns thrill themselves. In Ocelot's *Definition of Slang Used in Cyberpunk*: "A prostitute whose consciousness is wired into a braindance/simstim unit while customers have sex with her."

meatball (cyberpunk). Someone augmented with grafted muscle.

megacharacters. Characters in a role-playing game who have become "too tough" and possess many weapons and powers.

metalhead (cyberpunk). A full 'borg conversion.

Mirror of Erised (Potterism). A mirror in which Harry Potter sees his parents, not his reflection. Erised is desire spelled backward.

monkey trick (cyberpunk). A job in which a monkey—an expendable person—is not expected to survive.

monster fodder. A role-playing-game term for characters who are often used as guinea pigs to test traps and other hazards.

monty haul. Derogatory term for a role-playing game in which there are incredible rewards for trivial actions. It is a play on the name of Monty Hall, host of the once-popular *Let's Make a Deal* television quiz show.

moontel. Lodging on the moon.

mother ship. Term used in science fiction and UFO writing for a large spaceship from which smaller craft emerge.

mudblood (Potterism). Person born to nonmagic parents.

mudboy (cyberpunk). An earth man; derogatory.

muggles (Potterism). Mere mortals without magical powers.

In his column for the *Daily Telegraph* of May 12, 2001, John Morrish had some etymological clues for this word, given new meaning by J. K. Rowling: "A 'muggle' was once a Kentish word for tail, and a 'muggling' was a man with a tail. But perhaps the most common previous use for 'muggles' was as a Jazz Age term for marijuana."

munchkin. Derogatory role-playing-game term for immature players who dwell on boring war stories.

mundane. A person with no knowledge of science fiction; nonfan. Interestingly, one of the cyberpunk dictionaries defines this as "A non-magician, or non-magical."

Nebula. The second most famous award in the world of science fiction (after the HUGO). It is awarded by and voted on by members of the Science Fiction Writers of America (SFWA).

neofan. A new science fiction fan who sometimes displays excessive enthusiasm.

netfet / net fetishist (cyberpunk). Derogatory term for a netrunner who can only relate to life in the Net.

New Wave. Label for the "soft" science fiction of the 1960s, which deemphasized science and technology and emphasized values, politics, sociology, psychology, and social experimentation.

nextish. See ISH.

noncon. A "nonconvention"—a science fiction gathering that is too small to be a convention.

normals. Fantasy gaming for characters without special powers who must constantly be rescued. Akin to MONSTER FODDER.

nowism. Short for "now chauvinism." The tendency to export present-day forms, conventions, technology, or morality to a future setting where they are inappropriate or unlikely.

NPC. A nonplaying character in fantasy gaming. "The players may interact with this character, in most cases to resort to combat, hence initiating role playing," says Michael Stackpole, who adds, "Munchkins kill NPCs."

OME. "Oh my Eru," a substitution for "OMG" ("oh my God"). Eru Iluvatar is the over-god J. R. R. Tolkien's Middle Earth.

one and twenty (cyberpunk). The twenty-first century.

output (cyberpunk). Boyfriend.

overcook (cyberpunk). To go too fast.

Pan Galactic Gargle Blaster (SF). From *The Hitchhiker's Guide to the Galaxy*, a strong alcoholic concoction composed of many different alcohols. It is served at some sci-fi conventions along with edibles with names like Atomic Jello (Jello cubes containing alcohol) and Romulan Ale (a blue alcoholic beverage, popularized by *Star Trek*).

parallel universe / parallel world. Science fiction setting or premise in which the world is presented as it would be if a key historical or biological event had gone differently.

parsec. A parallax second, which is the equivalent of 3.26 light-years.

parselmouth (Potterism). Wizard who can talk to snakes. Harry Potter is a parselmouth.

planet X. A tenth planet in the solar system, which was once suspected but not proven. It is now used in a mocking, tongue-in-cheek context. The late futurist Ralph Hamil had this to say about a name for planet X: "Over the years, astronomers have postulated a 'Hades' and a 'Oceanus' among other names suggested for the hypothetical planet. 'Charon' and 'Prosperine' are other alternatives from science fiction." Martin Kottmeyer adds that "Nemesis" is the hypothetical planet involved in dinosaur-extinction theories.

platform 9 3/4. The boarding point at London's King's Cross station for the Hogwarts Express, which takes Harry Potter and his friends to Hogwarts School of Witchcraft and Wizardry.

popsicle (cyberpunk). A frozen corpse, usually found in a drifting space wreck.

porky. (cyberpunk) Someone who loves or collects weapons; from a "porcupine."

posergang (cyberpunk). Any group whose members affect a specific look, or bodysculpt job.

propars. Futurists' blend of professional + parents.

prozine. A commercial science fiction magazine, published to make money—a blend of profit + magazine. A longtime fan, David C. Kopaska-Merkel, says, "Not all are published by major publishing houses (e.g., *Aboriginal SF*), but all have slick covers [and] advertising, and at least purport to make a profit."

puppets (cyberpunk). Street gang members who have, overtly or covertly, sold out to a major corporation or organized crime syndicate.

Quakers (cyberpunk). Missiles or rockets.

quidditch (Potterism). Most popular sport of the wizard world, a hybrid of soccer and rugby played in the air on broomsticks with flying balls.

Rad (cyberpunk). 1. Radiation. 2. A dose of radiation.

railway thinking. A way of thinking about the future in which events repeat themselves.

ramscoop. A spacecraft that operates on hydrogen, which it scoops up in space and converts to energy.

razor boy / razor girl (cyberpunk). A cybernetically augmented thug. The name comes from the addition of razorblade claws (retractable or not) in the fingers. Augmentation includes eye replacement for sighting, direct computer links, etc.

reality junkies (cyberpunk). Addicts of virtual reality, braindance, the Net, or video games.

recycling (cyberpunk). Environmentally friendly act of killing someone and taking the corpse to a body bank.

rimbo (cyberpunk). A gun-toting sex kitten; blend of rambo + bimbo.

ripperdoc (cyberpunk). Surgeon specializing in implanting illegal cyberware.

rockerboy / -girl (cyberpunk). A musician or performer who uses his or her art to make political or social statements.

RPG. Role-playing game. Literature from Palladium Books of Detroit, distributor of the "megapopular" *Teenage Mutant Ninja Turtles* game, defines an RPG in its sales literature as "not a traditional board game. In fact, it has no playing board, no deck of cards, no spinner, nor even playing pieces. Instead the players have a book of rules with background information about adventure in a fictional world." See also FRP.

rules lawyer. Derisive role-playing-game term for a player who memorizes rules so carefully that he or she can cite verbatim specifics in arguments.

S&S. Short for Swords and Sorcery, a genre of fantasy fiction that mixes monsters, barbarians, and pretty women. It is also known as HF, for "heroic fiction" or "heroic fantasy." The Conan the Barbarian series epitomizes this science fiction genre.

saving roll / saving throw. The use of dice to simulate fate in role-playing games.

SETI. Search for extraterrestrial life.

sci-fi. What science fiction is called outside the world of science fiction. "Sci-fi," pronounced "sigh-fi," is used ironically by fans. See SF.

screamsheet (cyberpunk). A slick, flimsy newspaper printed at a data terminal.

sensetapes. (cyberpunk). The equivalent of videotapes, which allow the user to get the sensations of actors within the teleplay. Most tapes represent very rich, upper-class life situations so the hopeless can experience what they will never know in life.

sercon. SF-fan term; blend of serious + constructive.

SF. Science fiction, although some insist that it stands for "speculative fiction" or "science fantasy." The faithful say SF rather than "sci-fi" and pronounce it "ess-eff."

Shadowrun. Role-playing game set in the years 2050, 2060, or 2070 (depending on the game edition) following a great cataclysm that has brought use of magic back to the world. The language and literature that surround the game are central and help define cyberpunk.

shortwire (cyberpunk). To burn out, flame out, splash down, and generally crash, mentally.

shredder (cyberpunk). A minigun or auto-cannon.

sickles (Potterism). Currency of the witch and wizard world, along with knuts and galleons. Sickles are silver and there are seventeen of them to a galleon.

sidewalk outline (cyberpunk). A recently deceased person, or one who is expected to die soon. The reference is to the chalk outline drawn around a dead body at a murder scene by the police.

skeleton (cyberpunk). All the collected electronic records kept on a person; their electronic identity.

skiffy. Science fiction (sci-fi).

skyball (cyberpunk). A satellite (usually for surveillance).

slam (cyberpunk). To assault or beat up, as in "Let' go slam some 'dorphers." See 'DORPH.

slammit on (cyberpunk). 1. To get violent. 2. To attack someone without reason.

slash. A type of science fiction involving romantic or sexual involvement between two characters of the same sex. The term originates from early Star Trek fandom, namely "Kirk/Spock" stories. The term "slash" comes from the slash (/) between the names of the characters involved.

slash and hack. Term used in role-playing-game circles for the play of beginners whose characters turn into traveling butchers who kill monsters and take treasure. Also known as "shoot and loot" or "trash for cash."

slice 'n' dice (cyberpunk). A monofilament cyberweapon not unlike the suburban weed-whacker, usually mounted in the tip of a finger, which is used as a garrotte or whip. It will cut through almost all organic material and most plastics.

smof (acr). Secret master of fandom. Fannish word defined by an insider as "Mysterious and shadowy, but not as much as they might like; smofs supposedly run fan groups and put on conventions. It has either complimentary or pejorative connotations, depending on usage."

snitch (Potterism). The gold darting winged ball in the game quidditch. Whoever captures the snitch wins the game.

solar wind (cyberpunk). Hot air, i.e., basically bullshit.

solo. Role-playing game that can be played by one person working against a programmed text.

sorting hat (Potterism). Talking wizard's hat that announces the house assignments for first-year Hogwarts students.

space opera. A science fiction story written especially for action and excitement and intergalactic adventure. Analogous to "horse opera" for old-fashioned cowboy movies.

space western. Space opera in which Martian or Jovian town looks and sounds like Dodge City.

spaceship ethic. The moral code based on the concept that the earth is a large vehicle

spaceship ethic. (*continued*) or spacecraft whose survival depends on cooperation by the passengers.

speculative fiction. Term used to refer to both science fiction and fantasy. It can also include literary fiction that uses science fictional or fantastic elements.

spill (cyberpunk). 1. To spend money. 2. To confess or inform on others.

splatterpunk. A movement that combines the SF and horror genres and unites the nihilism of punk with hyperviolent action.

squib (Potterism). One who, despite having been born into a wizarding family, has little or no magical ability.

suitcase war. One waged by people who leave small thermonuclear devices in other people's countries.

system hacker. A role-playing-game participant who uses loopholes and words like "sometimes" in the rules to do outlandish things. "You can generally see them coming, and can modify situations to disallow most of their nonsense," says Mike Stackpole.

Tachyon. Theoretical particle that fuels much science fiction in that it moves faster than light and cannot go any slower.

tag (cyberpunk). 1. Name, handle, or trademark. 2. To grab or take something.

taking sake (cyberpunk). Working for Japanese business or criminal concerns.

terraforming. Reengineering the atmosphere or terrain of planets to make them ready for human habitation.

Third Industrial Revolution. A technological revolution that frees us from the confines of earth. The first two revolutions freed us from physical slavery and repetitive tasks.

tiger team (cyberpunk). Computer experts that test system security by attempting penetration.

***Titanic* analogy.** False perception of the earth as "unsinkable," in the sense that the *Titanic* was regarded as unsinkable before it sank.

transphotic. Faster-than-light travel.

Trekker. *Star Trek* fan. In his *Fanspeak Glossary* (see "Sources") Robert Runté points out that this term is used for more restrained or older fans, while TREKKIE tends to be used for the more fanatical or younger fan.

Trekkie. Fan of the *Star Trek* phenomenon: two television series, five movies, books, and more. Hotter than ever!

trid (cyberpunk). Three-D successor to video.

trog (cyberpunk). Short for troglodyte. A derogatory term meant to indicate that an individual is subhuman or extremely ugly or misshapen.

twitcher. 1. Fantasy gamer who is so excited by a subject that he explodes with energy and chatter and is given to long, one-sided "conversation." 2. (cyberpunk) Taser and, by extension, any electricity-based weapon.

Ufology. The study of unidentified flying object (UFO) reports.

uforia / ufomania. Zest for UFOs or conviction that aliens are visiting our world.

user interface (cyberpunk). Anything used to snort, inject, or otherwise ingest drugs, a borrowing of a term that is key to straight computer use.

VR-cade (cyberpunk). A virtual reality, braindance, or video-game arcade or parlor.

Waldo. Mechanical hands, coined by Robert A. Heinlein in a story of the same name. The main character was named Waldo, who had severe physical disabilities so he needed several "waldoes" to keep him going.

warp factor (Trektalk). The unit measuring faster-than-light travel: Warp factor 1 is the speed of light; warp factor 5 is 214 times the speed of light.

weefle (cyberpunk). An inexperienced netrunner; derogatory.

wetwork (cyberpunk). Assassination.

white hole. The hypothetical location from which matter and energy emerge after being sucked into a black hole.

Whovian. Fan of the long-running British science fiction television series *Dr. Who*. In a television special on the phenomenon it was stated: "Denver is the center of Whovian activities in America.

wild card. Futurists' term for an event that defies conventional forecasting—for instance, the emergence of AIDS.

Wilson (Cyberpunk). Netrunner slang for someone who you consider stupid, crazy, or a screwup.

wizworm (cyberpunk). Slang for a dragon.

wormhole (Trektalk). Space tunnel; a shortcut from one part of the galaxy to another.

Xenology. The study of extraterrestrials.

X/O. Trek code for crossover: a story that includes *Star Trek* characters and characters from other shows, or characters from more than one *Star Trek* show.

Zine. Small fan magazine.

zonedance (cyberpunk). Convincing others to dance to your tune. As explained in the *Definition of Slang Used in Cyberpunk*, compiled by Ocelot, "Dancing turned into a dominance game. The dancer tries to persuade, by charisma, talent, or violence, other dancers within his zone to conform to his movements. Challenging because other dancers are often listening to other music via cyberaudio."

FOOD AND DRINK

11

Words and Phrases from Haute to Not So Hot

Ah, the menu—what contortions of language it embodies, what culinary sleights of hand it conceals, what glories of the kitchen it celebrates and how mysterious it can be.

—Stanley Dry, *Food & Wine*, March 1984

"Couple a blues with," says Pete, the counterman and owner of the Deluxe Diner in Rumford, Maine.

"Couple a blues comin' up," says a female voice from the kitchen. As Pete draws coffee from a forty-year-old coffee machine that he fired up at 3 that morning (for his 4 A.M. customers), the waitress, Rose, appears with two monster homemade blues—blueberry muffins—and several pats of real butter.

On this summer morning the blues are selling well, and a few minutes later Pete asks for one "with wheels," meaning that it is to be put in a paper bag "to go."

There are a lot of good reasons to stop at this diminutive diner, which is tucked into a tiny lot on Oxford Street. The food is first-rate, the prices are what big-city folk payed in the 1970s, and Pete Duguay, the owner, makes sure you feel at home even when it's early and the sky is as black as his coffee.

The atmosphere is just about as traditionally diner-ish as you can find, and it sounds like a diner, from the sizzle of the ancient grill to the banter as the waitress trades barbs and pleasantries with the largely male patrons who line the row of stools. Then there are the calls—or abbreviated orders—that are hurled about and are as much a part of the diner culture as bread pudding, squeaky stools, and neon-rimmed clocks.

Calls are those distinct forms of communication that allow those behind the counter to pass orders around with a degree of efficiency and good humor that is typically American. The rules are easy: make it flip and make it easy to hear so there is no confusion and no need to repeat. For this reason, "down" means toasted and mayonnaise is always mayo. Odd sound effects are allowed. I ordered a turkey sandwich in a Delaware diner not long ago and the waitress passed on the order by making loud gobbling noises to her cook.

Aside from gobbles, short-order calls can be disconcerting if one is not prepared for them. A friend who was born in Scotland and moved to the United States as a young man loves to tell the story of the first time he ate in an American diner and heard a waitress call across the room and tell her counterman to "burn the British." He recalls, "I didn't realize she was asking for a toasted English muffin and for one very quick moment I thought I'd stumbled on some hotbed of anti-British feeling."

The lingo is fairly easy to master and many examples such as Pete's are easily heard if you get off the interstate. These calls were born of an earlier America and nurtured in diners, lunch counters, and soda fountains and hang on in the older traditional diners, but now are much less commonly heard than in earlier decades of the twentieth century. Perhaps it was because these terms were colorful and not always that appetizing that they became increasingly unwelcome. In his *Dictionary of American Food and Drink*, John F. Mariani explains, "The vitality of lunch-counter speech—*cat's eye* for tapioca, *baby* for glass of milk, *jerk* for ice cream soda, and *Adam and Eve on a raft* for fried eggs on toast—had a raciness about it that many people sought to put an end to in the 1930s."

Fact is, much of the lingo survived the 1930s as did places like the Deluxe Diner, which has occupied the same spot since 1928. Diner slang is just a small part of the rich brew of food slang from all over the world. English is a liberal language that seems predisposed to welcoming words from other languages. The point at which we speakers of American English are most open-minded would seem to be when we are most open-mouthed. We devour dishes, and words, such as pasta, empanadas, souvlaki, quiche lorraine, havarti, caldo verde, tabbouleh, yakitori, and osso bucco.

The reason for this linguistic liberalism, which has been especially strong since World War II, is simple. Some things are better said with the original word or phrase or a reasonable approximation. A wok is a wok and to call it "a shallow pan used for quick stir-frying" is an unwieldy description, not a name.

In this international stew, much new food terminology comes from foreign languages, but American food and drink slang comes through loud and clear on the lips of patrons, barkeeps, and pizza delivery guys.

Here is the slang of food and drink—some old, some new, and all in use and in your face.

AC. American cheese.

al desko. Dining while sitting at one's desk (from "al fresco").

all the way. A sandwich served with all the fixins: lettuce, mayo, onion, etc.

amateur night. 1. To heavy drinkers, New Year's Eve—when everyone is drinking. 2. In some restaurants, the night when the patrons order the most recognizable wines and foods.

amuse-bouche. A small complimentary appetizer offered at some restaurants.

antifreeze. Alcohol, illegal or legal.

apron. A bartender.

Baby. Menu-ese for young, as in "baby kiwi" or "baby bok choy."

back. On the side. "Scotch, soda back" would be straight scotch with soda water on the side.

back of the house. The kitchen, in a restaurant.

B&B. 1. Bed-and-breakfast. 2. Bread and butter. 3. Benedictine and brandy.

bang / banger. Straight booze, usually vodka, on ice, which the bar customer bangs ceremoniously on the bar before downing.

baptize. To add water to a drink.

barfly. One who spends much time at a bar drinking.

barkeep. Bartender.

BB. Back booth, in a restaurant.

beef darts. In a pizza joint, game played during slow times, in which workers hurl pinches of raw beef against a wall.

beergoggles. Perception influenced by the consumption of alcohol, as in "He was handsome, but I was wearing beer goggles."

behind the stick. To tend bar.

big three. In the burger realm, McDonald's, Burger King, and Wendy's.

binder. Constipating food.

birthday cake. Pizza with too many items on it.

bite. Small meal or snack.

BJ. Bug juice—any sugary, noncarbonated fruit drink.

black. Black coffee.

blind pig. Tavern that opens after the legal closing hour; any illegal bar.

blood pie. Pizza with extra sauce; also called a hemorrhage.

blue plate special. A special low-priced meal, usually changing daily.

blues. 1. Blue fish. 2. Blue crabs.

bondage pie. Pizza with S&M (sausage and mushroom).

bones. Barbecued ribs.

bootie food. Food that goes right to the butt.

booze. Liquor, an old slang term that is as commonly used today as ever.

booze cruise. Short boat trip on which there is plenty of music and drinking.

bouncer. 1. Bad check, in a restaurant. 2. Person employed to keep order in a bar or nightclub.

bowl of red. Chili con carne.

brainfreeze. Piercing headache experienced after consuming frozen or cold food or beverage. This term was trademarked by the 7-Eleven franchise in 1994 to describe the effects of its Slurpee frozen drink.

branwagon. The drive toward healthier eating, a blend of bran (such as oat or wheat) + bandwagon.

brew-ha. Beer.

brew pub. A bar-restaurant where beer is brewed on the premises.

brewski. Beer.

brown bag. 1. Paper bag or wrapping for a meal. 2. To bring one's lunch in a brown paper bag, as in, "Let's brown bag it tomorrow and go to the park."

bubble and squeak. Mashed potatoes and shredded beef.

bucket o' blood. Tough bar or saloon.

Budhead. Beer drinker.

bug juice. Noncarbonated fruit drink.

bullshot. Vodka mixed with beef broth.

burger. Hamburger.

burger joint. Place where the specialty is hamburgers.

busdog / busgod. Unisex terms to replace male "busboy."

bust some suds. To drink some beer.

buzzmaker. A particularly potent mixed drink.

Cage. Service bar.

campers. Slow-eating restaurant patrons.

cancer ward. Smoking section of an eating establishment.

carp. In the pizza business, anchovies; also called guppies, penguin food, smellies.

carry-out. Place that sells food to be taken from the premises.

cattle fries. Fried bull testicles, in Texas.

CB. Cheeseburger.

chaser. Hard liquor thrown back after a beer or other less potent drink. See RINSE.

chew and screw. Restaurant patron who eats and leaves without paying the bill. Also known as MASTICATE AND VACATE.

chicken-fried. Describing a flour-covered steak or other piece of beef that has been cooked in deep hot fat, in the manner of fried chicken.

chili mac. Chili con carne mixed with macaroni or other pasta.

chili size. Chili con carne served over a hamburger patty in a dish.

chilly. A beer.

chocoholic. Person with a passion for anything chocolate.

chow down. To eat.

chugalug. To drink without pausing to finish a gulp.

church key. Beer-can opener. This term is at least thirty-five years old and should have been eliminated by the pop-top can, but it is still heard.

comfort food. Food with nostalgic, pleasant overtones: mashed potatoes for some, chicken soup for others.

cooler. 1. A wine concoction, usually combining wine, carbonated water, and fruit juice. 2. A BOUNCER.

country style. Food served family style, as described on the menu at Country Line Barbecue: "You get a big platter of meat (beef, ribs, brisket, and sausage), and generous bowls of potato salad, cole slaw and beans. It's all for one and one for all."

cowboy. Short-order-cook slang for a Western omelette.

crack a tube. To open a beer can.

crispy. Hungover.

cuke. Cucumber.

Dagwood. Enormous sandwich, from the multilayered constructions of Dagwood Bumstead of the comic strip *Blondie* fame.

damages. The bill in a restaurant.

DD. Designated driver.

DDK. Designated drunk.

dead one. An empty beer or liquor bottle.

deli. 1. Delicatessen. 2. In the style of a delicatessen, such as deli-sized sandwiches.

demi-veg. Part-time vegetarian.

designer ketchup. Ketchups made from unusual ingredients such as cranberries, plums, or mushrooms. A 1991 *Boston Globe* blind tasting of designer ketchups yielded a winner: Heinz Tomato Ketchup. A plum ketchup was adjudged to taste like "sweet black mud."

destroy. To top a pizza with everything: "Destroy it!"

dirty. Slightly burned, as in dirty potato chips, which have dark spots from overcooking.

ditch. Water, in the sense that "Jack ditch" is a call for Jack Daniel's and water.

do lunch. Have lunch with someone.

doggy bag. A bag provided by restaurants to hold a patron's leftovers. Despite the

doggy bag. (*continued*) face-saving name, the contents of a doggy bag are usually destined for human as opposed to canine consumption.

Dominoid. Employee of Domino's Pizza.

down. Anything toasted, in short-order-cook slang. "Whiskey down" is slang for toasted rye—a play on rye whiskey.

draggings. Waitstaff term for diners who linger at the table.

dry. A brew of beer with higher alcohol content than standard.

DQ. Dairy Queen.

Early-bird special. Restaurant meals that are reduced in price for those who are seated early.

easy over. See ONCE OVER EASY.

Edgar Allan. Pizza with pepperoni (p) and onions (o): a play on Poe.

86. To be out of something; "Eighty-six on the lemon pie." This is one of the few survivors of an elaborate restaurant code that obtained before World War II. For instance, 95 stood for a customer leaving without paying, and 400W stood for maple syrup.

em. An empty beer, wine, or liquor bottle.

empty calories. Foods with little nutritional value.

extreme beer. Over-the-top brew, with an alcohol content of 20 percent or higher, aged in used bourbon casks, and infused with nontraditional ingredients such as ginger or chocolate.

eyetalian. See ITALIAN.

Fast food. Food that is cheap, standardized, and quickly dispensed. Most fast-food restaurants are chains with plenty of parking.

fat farm. Camp or resort where one goes to diet and exercise.

fat pill. A pastry or other food that is very high in calories and seemingly has the effect of a pill taken to make one fatter.

FBI. Franks and beans, in short-order-cook slang. What does the I stand for? Nothing. FBI sounds better than FB.

fern bar. Establishment characterized by light wood, hanging plants, and good illumination. No longer hip, they are still very much with us.

FGTs. Fried green tomatoes, in short-order parlauce.

five B's. Name used in parts of New England for Boston baked beans and brown bread.

flapper. Square table in a restaurant because they often have flaps that can be extended to seat more patrons.

flat food. Vending-machine food.

flat-lined. To be totally drunk.

flexitarian. A vegetarian who occasionally eats meat.

flight. Three different two-and-a-half-ounce samplings of wine offered for a flat price. Trendy way of getting a sip of three expensive wines.

fluff and fold. In restaurant parlance, this is an injunction to take special care of a patron or tableful of patrons.

flyers and fungus. Pepperoni and mushroom pizza. Pepperoni slices are called flyers because they can be thrown like Frisbees.

foam. Beer.

foodie. Someone who has an intense interest in foods and cuisine. In the eighties, one who was quick to discover *grazing*, talked about "food as fashion," and was among the first to try out new restaurants.

fool. A pureed fruit dessert mixed with sugar and cream.

frankenfood. Genetically engineered food.

free-range. Describing chicken or other fowl that is raised outside rather than in a factory farm. These birds are preferred by people who have ethical problems with the treatment of fowl in factory-like coops. Free-range eggs are the eggs laid by these fowl.

freegan. Person who only eats what they can get for free; a play on the word "vegan."

frickles. Fried pickles, a dish with a following in parts of the South.

frogs' eyes. Tapioca pudding.

front of the house. Dining area of a restaurant.

frontloading. Drinking a lot in a short period of time before going to an event where liquor will not be served, such as the ballet.

froth. Beer.

full house. Lettuce, tomato, and mayo.

Garbage. Restaurant adjective for leftovers used in another dish. It is not as nasty as it sounds: a *USA Today* article on the new California cuisine featured a restaurant specializing in "garbage salads" using leftover shrimp, avocados, etc.

getting stiffed. Waitstaff term describing when a party leaves no tip or a very small tip.

gin 'n It. A British drink consisting of two parts gin to one part Italian vermouth, served at room temperature. In other words, a lukewarm martini.

give good wrist. To pour generous drinks.

GJ. Grapefruit juice.

going all the way. Chocolate cake with chocolate ice cream.

golf ball. Small area in the middle of the pizza left free of toppings so that items don't pile up in the middle when pizza is cut.

gop (acr). On a pizza, green peppers, onions, and pepperoni.

gorp. "Trail mixture" of peanuts, raisins, and candy such as chocolate or yogurt chips. It has been claimed that the term began as an acronym for "good old raisins and peanuts," but many would side with William Safire, who thinks that the acronym story is bunk. Safire has written, "To me, the word seems formed like Lewis Carroll's creation of *chortle* by combining *chuckle* with *snort*; *gorp* is a wedded *snort* and *gulp*."

grapes of wrath. Wine.

grazing. Ordering a series of appetizer-sized portions rather than one large entrée. One can graze a meal's worth at a single restaurant or at several.

greasy spoon. Restaurant at the low end of the scale in terms of food, cleanliness, and decor; a dive.

green chop. Coleslaw, in some rural regions of Maryland.

greenhouse look. Restaurant or bar with immense windows and lots of greenery.

grinder. Sandwich served on Italian bread sliced sideways. This is one of a number of names for the same thing, with this one being popular in parts of southern New England. Other regional names include hero, hoagie, Italian, torpedo, submarine, and wedge.

ground hog. Today as always, the preferred nickname for a steam-operated still.

growing a beard. Restaurantese for food that has not been picked up from the serving line and is getting cold.

gumbo. A tasty stew of okra, vegetables, and meat or seafood.

guppies. Anchovies, on pizza.

Happy camper. In the context of bars and restaurants, this term refers to one who is intoxicated; however, "not a happy camper" is an angry customer.

happy hour. Period before dinner during which bars attempt to promote themselves, often with reduced drink prices.

harmless. Latte made with decaf espresso.

hemorrhage. Pizza with extra tomato sauce.

hero. Sandwich served on Italian bread sliced sideways. The term, by the way, was invented in the 1930s by the legendary food writer Clementine Paddleford of the New York *Herald Tribune*, who insisted that you had to be a hero to eat one. But one wordsmith, Bruce Boston, says "hero" is actually a Greek's pronunciation of their own stacked sandwich, the gyro.

hoagie. The same thing as a HERO, SUBMARINE, or TORPEDO.

hold. To leave something out, as in "Roast beef, hold the gravy."

SAY WHAT?

National restaurant franchises have made "pancakes" the preferred term for flat rounds of batter fried on a griddle, but it's not the only current term. Some people in the Northeast call them "griddlecakes," and others call them "hotcakes." "Flapjacks" is holding its own in the South and West. In the North's upper tier, they are "wheatcakes."

Doughnuts are "crullers" to some natives of New York and New England; a "fried cake" in the North; a "fossnock" or "fatcake" to someone in the heart of Pennsylvania Dutch country; and in Berlin, New Hampshire, a doughnut hole may still be called a "comfy."

What do you call a rich, flaky pastry filled with fruit or soft cheese and topped with icing? A Danish pastry, right? Well, don't be too sure. In New York City, it's likely to be simply a "Danish"; a "bear claw" in the West; a "maple bar" in the Northwest; and in the Midwest it is likely to be a "Bismarck."

If you cut a potato into long strips and deep-fry them, there's little disagreement about what you call the result. French fries. But ask people what they call potatoes sliced into flat circles and fried up—that's a different story. In many Eastern diners they are "fresh fries," while in the Northeast they are "home fries" or sometimes "pan fries." But someone from an upper Midwest state like Minnesota might come out with "American fries."

A quick and dirty way to tag a New Yorker, by the way, is to ask how he or she orders at a place that sells pizza by the slice. A "slice," of course, as in, "Lemme have a soda and a slice."

You order ice cream in the town or city where you grew up and ask for a cone dipped in tiny multicolored or chocolate flecks of candy. How exactly do you place your order? They are "jimmies" in Boston and Northern New England, "sprinkles" in New York and Connecticut, and "ants" in Rhode Island; west of the Hudson they have several names, including "shots" and "cake decorations." Incidentally, in the United Kingdom folks call them "hundreds and thousands."

hooter. Same as SHOOTER.

hopping. Moving around in search of food or companionship, as in restaurant hopping, bar hopping, or table hopping.

hungchow. Any food that is constipating; a BINDER.

hush puppy. Deep-fried cornmeal dumpling.

Idiot oil. Booze.

in-and-out. Martini mixed by pouring a small amount of vermouth into the pitcher, swizzling it around, pouring it out, and adding gin.

in the ozone. Restaurant term for a table where the patrons have had too much to drink.

in the trees / in the weeds. 1. Describing a kitchen that is running way behind. 2. A waiter's term for having too much work to do in an evening.

inhale. To eat quickly, as if one is breathing in one's food.

Irish sweetener. Alcoholic substance added to coffee, often Irish whiskey or brandy.

Italian. Long sandwich served on Italian bread. In the Northeast it is often pronounced "eye-talian."

Jew stew. Chicken soup.

jigger. Bar glass holding one half ounce of liquor, used for measurement.

junque food. So-called adult fast food, a $7.95 hamburger touted as "our deluxe gourmet burger."

Kittie bag. Same as doggy bag, only smaller.

knock back. To drink aggressively, as in "knock back two beers."

Lardon. French for bits of bacon or fat pork, used to upscale the notion.

leaded. Caffeinated coffee.

liquid bread. Beer, especially dark brews.

lite. Low in calories; lighter than normal.

little ears. A pasta called orecchiette.

lizards. Green peppers, on pizza.

lo-cal. Low in calories.

lone bone. Single rib, in barbecue parlance.

long list. A restaurant's full listing of wines in stock.

long neck. A beer bottle with a long neck. There is a certain bravado associated with carrying one around a bar, especially a Lone Star long neck in a Texas bar.

low 'n' slow. Preferred method of barbecue preparation: cooked at a low heat for a long period of time.

Martooni. Martini.

masticate and vacate. Describing a restaurant patron who eats and runs without paying. Also known as CHEW AND SCREW.

mayo. Mayonnaise.

meat and three. Meat dish with three vegetable side dishes. Common in the southern United States.

meat market / meat rack. Singles' bar where the primary objective seems to be to get laid.

medley. Upscale MENU-ESE for a mixture or combination, as in "a medley of baby vegetables."

megadiner. One of the new breed of diners that can seat as many as 500, in contrast to the classic forty-seaters built in the 1930s through the 1950s.

menu-ese. Derogatory term for the overblown descriptions of simple food found on some menus, as in "Fresh Fruit Salad—transported in a pineapple boat for the highest vibration, and your transmutation with yogurt on the side for accent, or dressing sprinkled with coconut . . . $6.35" (a real example).

merry Christmas. In short-order-cook slang, tuna on toast with lettuce and tomatoes.

microbrew. Beer from a small brewery producing beer for local consumption.

mud pie. An ice cream concoction that is intensely chocolate.

munchies. A craving for food.

mystery meat. Food, usually from an institutional cafeteria, that defies identification.

Neat. Straight liquor, not on the rocks.

nibbling. Sipping a drink slowly.

nightcap. Drink taken late at night.

nosh. To munch or snack; from Yiddish.

noshery. Delicatessen or snack bar where one goes for appealing food.

OD. To overeat; from "overdose."

OJ. Orange juice.

on the rocks. A drink served with ice.

on wheels. To go. Sometimes stated as "put wheels on that."

once over easy. To turn over and cook lightly on the other side, usually of fried eggs. Eggs can also be "medium—over hard" and other variations.

open dating. An easily read date telling when a product was packed and when it must be pulled from the shelf.

oyster shooter. Shot glass containing a fresh oyster, popular in the Northwest. An article in the August 5, 2005, *Portland Tribune,* "O is for Oregon and Oysters," stated that shooters are offered along the course of the Newport, Oregon, marathon. "One year a woman ate 26 oyster shooters during the race—one for every mile."

PB. Peanut butter.

PBD. Peanut butter and dill pickle sandwich.

PBJ. Peanut butter and jelly. In some parts of the South, a popular drink is the "PBJ shake," a peanut butter and jelly milkshake.

penguins. Waitstaff dressed in black and white.

pig out. To overeat.

pistol. Pastrami in short-order-cook slang.

pit cheese. Mix of items found in the pit, a trough that underlies individual bins of pizza items. From time to time, pit cheese is collected and items are sorted and returned to their proper bins.

pit stop. Place where one goes for food and a trip to the restroom, on a car trip.

placer. Customer who places a hair or something as objectionable in his food so that he can complain and not have to pay for the food.

plate. To present artistically—to compose a dish with glazes, purees, garnishes, and the like.

pork out. To overeat. See PIG OUT.

pork popsicle. Barbecued rib.

pot luck. 1. Meal made of whatever is on hand. 2. A dinner to which everyone brings a dish.

power breakfast / power lunch. A meeting at which policy makers discuss business or politics over their meal.

Rabbit food. Raw vegetables.

repeaters. Beans.

Republican pizza. a pizza with GOP.

rinse. CHASER.

roach coach. Small truck selling prepared food; common around industrial areas where there are no cafeterias.

road ribber. Those who go on the road to sell barbecue ribs at chili cookoffs, barbecue festivals, and the like. According to an article in the December 1992 *Food Arts* magazine, some road ribbers can make up to $20,000 a weekend.

rocks glass. Glass for the cocktail called an old-fashioned.

Rocky Mountain oysters. Testicles of bull or other male animal that have been breaded and fried. Also known as bull fries,

Pop Quiz

How would you ask for a carbonated beverage in different regions of the United States if you wanted to be sure to be understood? A "soda" would be understood in the Northeast and "pop" would work in the North from New Hampshire to Washington State, and especially in the Midwest, where it is "pahp." In parts of New England, such as Massachusetts and Manchester, New Hampshire, you could score with "tonic." In the South, plain old "cold drink" will do just fine. An older person from the Midatlantic states might call it "dope," and in Oklahoma and parts of Tennessee, "Coke" is generic for any soft drink.

cattle fries (term preferred in Texas), prairie oysters, and swinging steaks. According to *Travel Matters* magazine, a Severence, Colorado, restaurant calls them "headless and tailless shrimp."

roots and berries. Derogatory characterization of natural foods or food consumed by vegetarians.

ruckus juice. Moonshine.

Sack. A bag of ten—count 'em, ten—burgers from the White Castle chain of stores.

scarf. To eat quickly. The term is often used in connection with fast food. William Safire is of the opinion that this word came from an African American usage of the 1930s for food, "scoff."

set-up. Tableware, in a restaurant.

shooter. 1. Straight shot meant for consuming in one gulp. 2. House drink that is usually sweet and easy to consume quickly. These shooters are common to summer beach bars and often feature a fruit liqueur, such as DeKuyper Peachtree Schnapps, Southern Comfort, or tequila. These drinks often have names that are as wild as their formulas. The writer Joe Goulden brought back a copy of the *Beachcomber* free newspaper from the Delaware coast a few years ago that contained a "shooter survey" rating such libations as the Blood Clot, Midnight at the Oasis, 57 Chevy with Hawaiian Plates, Sex on the Beach, the Russian Quaalude, Deep Throat, the Chocolate Virgin, and Daphnie Divine's Deluxe Dixie Daiquiri. From the other coast comes the Bay Bridge Commuter Shooter, combining vodka, gazpacho, horseradish, Tabasco, a prawn, and lime juice. See also OYSTER SHOOTER.

shopping-list menu. Menu that not only lists the dishes but also informs the patron what went into it, including the garnish ("garnished with a sprig of spring parsley").

short dog. 1. Single can of beer. 2. Small, cheap bottle of wine.

short stack. Two pancakes. See STACK.

shot. A small, measured quantity of liquor, usually two ounces, give or take a half ounce.

shot glass. A small glass or other vessel for measuring liquor, usually one and a half or two ounces.

sinker. Heavy, dense version of a dish, especially baked goods. The term brings back the memory of a heavier-'n-lead stack of blueberry pancakes served in Maine, where they are called "sinkas."

skinny. Latte made with one percent or nonfat milk.

skirt. Ring of ice cream sticking out around the edges of a scoop on a cone.

slab. Full rib portion, usually a dozen.

slider. Midwesternism for small burgers, such as those one can get at the White Castle chain—they go down real easy.

smoothie. Blended drink.

s'mores. A confection made by melting chocolate and marshmallows over a graham cracker, blend of some + more. A traditional campfire treat, they are so popular that there are several brands of s'mores on the market.

smothered. Covered.

sparg. Asparagus.

splash. A small amount of water or soda, as in "bourbon with a splash."

spritzer. White wine and soda water.

sproutsy. A vegetarian.

spud. Potato.

stack. A pile of pancakes or toast.

starters. 1990s menu-ese for appetizers.

starver. A customer who orders a pizza, then claims he didn't order it, but will buy it at a discount.

sticks. Food sliced into long, sticklike shapes—fried mozzarella sticks or batter-dipped zucchini sticks, for instance.

stinking rose. Garlic, among garlic lovers.

stoner. Customer who calls for a pizza or other call-out food but has a hard time recalling his address.

straight up. Without ice, as in "whiskey straight up."

submarine. Sandwich served on Italian

submarine. (*continued*)
bread sliced longitudinally. Known also as a HERO, HOAGIE, ITALIAN.

suds. Beer.

sunny side up. Eggs that are fried on one side only, not turned over.

surf 'n' turf. Generic name for meat and seafood on the same platter.

swill. Beer.

swine on a stick. Barbecued pork rib.

Tabhead. Person on a diet, from Tab, the diet cola.

table from hell. Term used in the restaurant business for a table of people who are drunk and abusive.

T&T. Tanqueray (gin) and tonic.

tater. Potato.

teen / teenie. Martini.

Tex-Mex. Type of food that is influenced by traditions on both sides of the Texas-Mexico border.

three-martini lunch. Codeword for the excesses of expense-account dining. It has recently become emblematic for the kind of common business lunch that began to fall out of favor with growing health consciousness and awareness of need to keep one's wits about one while discussing business. However, such lunches are still fairly common.

thunder thighs. Quadruple grande whole-milk latte with chocolate syrup and extra whipped cream.

to go. Food that is taken out of a restaurant for consumption elsewhere.

torpedo. See SUBMARINE.

trash fish. Cheap, unpopular whitefish.

tray. Name for the paper boats in which traditional Carolina barbecue is served.

trons. The restaurant staff in some places—shortening of WAITRON.

tube steak. A hot dog.

twist. Twist of sliced lemon peel in a drink: tonic with a twist.

Umbrella room, the. Fake fancy-restaurant name for a sidewalk food cart, as in "Let's grab a quick lunch at the Umbrella Room." This term was collected in New York City by Joseph C. Goulden, who reports that it is popular there.

unleaded. Decaffeinated coffee.

Veggies. Vegetables.

veggy. 1. A vegetarian. 2. A sandwich made with vegetables and cheese.

vegucation. Education about vegetarianism.

vergus. Menu-ese for the juice of unripened grapes.

V's. Vegetables.

vulture pie. Badly constructed pizza, suitable only for vultures or for eating by employees.

Waitron. Term for WAITSTAFF.

waitstaff. Male and female waiters, taken as group.

walking. A to-go order, in short-order terminology, as in "grilled cheese walking."

wall box. Miniature jukeboxes affixed to the wall of booths in a diner.

wasabi. Pistachio-green Japanese mustard that is a staple of sushi bars and is increasingly used to coat peanuts and peas served as a bar snack. According to Wikipedia, "Almost all sushi bars in America, and most in Japan, serve imitation wasabi because the real product is extremely expensive. Imitation wasabi is usually made from horseradish, mustard, and green food coloring, often as a powder to be mixed with water to make a paste."

watering hole. A bar.

wedge. See SUBMARINE.

western. Omelette, or a sandwich containing an omelette, filled with ham, green pepper, and onions.

wet dog. A bad wine with a chemical smell.

whiskey. Short-order call for rye bread—a play on rye whiskey.

with wings. To go.

wolf down. To eat quickly.

wood-finished. Scotch or bourbon embellished by being stored in casks originally used to age port, sherry, and other products.

working the line. Cooking at a restaurant stove.

works, the. Everything; all the extras. A pizza called "The Works" on sale at Foodee's in Concord, New Hampshire, features tomato sauce, mushrooms, pepperoni, green pepper, onions, three cheeses, and hamburger or sausage.

wreck 'em. Scramble eggs, in short-order-cook slang. "Wreck two" is an order to scramble two eggs.

Zapper. Microwave oven.

zip-code wine. A wine-trade term for a French wine from a shipper who has an impressive address but whose grapes do not come from that region.

zombie food. Unacceptable food that has been brought back to acceptability with the aid of irradiation or other sterilization techniques.

12

GAMING SLANG

Coming to Terms with the Track, the Table, the Wheel, the Slots, and the Bingo Jackpot

The chalk horse bolted, ignored driving and it was a blanket history. [Translation:] "The favorite wouldn't run straight, ignored the jockey's whip and crossed the finish line side by side with about 50 other bums."

—"Turfmen Have Own Mysterious Lingo," *San Francisco Chronicle*, April 21, 1971

In 2003, about 83,000 people laid out real money to play poker online. By the end of 2005 that number had risen to 1.9 million. During this same short period cable television embraced poker as a competitive and telegenic subject deemed to be the fastest-growing spectator sport in America. Toss into that mix the mushrooming of tribal casinos, state lotteries, off-track betting, big-money events such as the World Series of Poker, and the ever-expanding gambling economies of Las Vegas, Reno, Atlantic City, and the Gulf Coast, and it can be said that we have moved into new territory when it comes to games of chance.

Not surprisingly, the lingo of gambling has burgeoned. Poker slang has been expanded with the growth of the new poker favorite, Texas hold 'em, which seems to be a game of endless new lingo. In these games—there is also Omaha hold 'em and other variations—players receive two to four hole cards—cards dealt facedown so that they cannot be seen by other players—and five community cards—cards dealt in the middle of the table and shared by all players. Usually there are betting rounds after the hole cards have been dealt, then again after three upcards ("flop") are dealt, after a fourth upcard ("turn") is dealt, and finally after a fifth upcard ("river") is dealt. Hold 'em is the game that is played in the casinos, online, and on television. The old cinematic poker that you see in movies such as *The Cincinnati Kid* is old school—the five-card draw is not played at the casinos or on cable. The old-fashioned poker games are simply too slow.

Here then is a sampling of gambling slang.

Across the board (horseracing). A win, place, or show bet.

action. 1. How many people are betting how much and on what team. 2. In poker, money that is being bet. "No action" means a hand or game has few bettors and fewer raisers. "Gimme some action," when heard at the poker table, is a plea for calls and raises.

all in. When a poker player puts all of his playable money and chips into the pot during the course of a hand.

American Airlines. Ace, in poker.

Backside. The stable area of a racetrack.

bad beat. When a poker hand that is seemingly unbeatable is beaten—for example, a full house being beaten by four of a kind.

bangtail (horseracing). A tail bobbed or tied short, but also a nickname for a horse, among old-school track writers and habitués.

baseball (horseracing). Daily-double play in which a bettor pairs an entry in one race with all the horses in the other.

beard. One who places bets for a friend with a bookie who has cut off the friend for not paying, for snitching to police, or for having won too much.

bible. The *J.K. Sports Journal*, a publication with sports-betting information, published in Los Angeles.

big dime. A $10,000 bet.

big nickel. A $5,000 bet.

big slick. An ace and a king, in poker.

bingo. 1. One of the world's most popular games. It goes by different names in different places—housie in the U.K., for example. 2. To win at the game of bingo.

bingo bladder. Illness stemming from the inability to leave the game.

blind switch. Describes a racehorse trapped behind or between other horses so that it has no running room.

BM. See BOOKIE / BOOKMAKER.

boat people. Casino-employee slang for gamblers arriving by the busload.

boat race. Fixed horse race.

bookie / bookmaker. Broker who for a fee accepts bets on sporting events with the hope that he can pay the winners off with the losers' money and have money left as his profit.

bucket. Casino-employee term for the place where a gambler's markers are kept.

bugboy (horseracing). Apprentice jockey, from the asterisk with which newspapers have traditionally identified them in entry lists.

burned out. Casino-employee slang term for when a player has gambled away all the credit extended by the house.

Cage. Cashier's area, in a casino.

caller. Person who draws the numbers in bingo and calls them out to players.

casino feet. Condition afflicting those who stand at slot machines for many hours at a time, soreness and swelling of the feet and legs.

chalk / chalk horse. The favorite horse in a race.

chicken and feathers gambler. A gambler who is fat with money one day and the next day has nothing left but feathers, to a casino employee.

chips. The traditional method of covering bingo numbers. Chips are translucent, so that a checker can read the numbers covered while verifying a win.

churn (sports wagering). The effect of betting and rebetting money on a sports event.

clock a player. When a casino employee records the size and frequency of a patron's bets. The heaviest bettors receive the most complimentary services.

cold call. In poker, calling both a bet and raise at the same time, as opposed to calling a bet then later calling a raise made after the call.

colors. Silks worn by jockeys denoting ownership of a racehorse. Silks are the jacket and cap worn by a jockey.

Bingo!

Bingo callers—"housie" callers in Britain—have traditionally used nicknames to embellish the numbers they are calling. Also, some bingo-hall players will call these out on their own as a way of verifying the call and as a totem of sorts. A report on a Florida bingo hall in the *St. Petersburg Times* ("Battle with the Numbers," June 5, 1998) tells of a woman working her bingo cards in a church bingo hall: "At 11, she yells 'Chicken legs.' At 22 she quacks." A common nickname for 22 is "two little ducks," presumably because the two 2's resemble ducks'—or swans'—necks and heads.

These terms come from both sides of the Atlantic and some of them allude to things British but are still common in the United States. For example, 10 will sometimes be accompanied with "Downing Street" or "Den," for the address of the British Prime Minister. The numerical nicknames are becoming less common today with the advent of computer-generated numbers in larger bingo halls, but they are still used by many and are being preserved on the countless bingo sites online, viz.:

1 Kelly's eye

2 one little duck

5 man alive

7 lucky for some

8 one fat lady

9 doctor's orders

10 current P.M.'s den

11 chicken legs

13 unlucky for some

16 sweet sixteen

17 dancing queen (from the ABBA song)

21 royal salute

22 two little ducks

23 Lord Is My Shepherd

24 two dozen

25 duck and dive

30 dirty Gertie

37 more than eleven

41 life's begun

44 ducks

45 halfway there

50 Hawaii Five-O

51 tweak of the thumb

55 speed limit

59 engine 59

62 tickety boo

63 tickle me

64 the Beatles' number ("Will you still love me when I'm 64?")

65 old-age pension.

66 clickety-click

71 bang on the drum

76 trombones

77 Sunset Strip

79 one more time

81 stop and run

86 between the sticks

87 fat lady with a crutch

88 two fat ladies

90 top of the shop

cover. When a number that appears on one's bingo card is called, to cover it with either a chip or a dot of ink from a dauber. A player running a streak of bad luck will claim to be unable to "cover anything."

cover all. A bingo game in which, to win, you must cover every square on a card. These games usually pay the largest prizes.

cover the spread. In sports wagering, when the favored team wins the game by more than the spread.

cowboys. Kings, in poker.

cuppy. The quality of the track surface when it breaks under a horse's hooves.

cushion. The surface of the racetrack, in horse racing.

Dabber / dauber. A round pad atop a bottle of ink used to mark paper bingo cards as numbers are called. The colorful inks are translucent, so that the numbers can be read after they have been dabbed or daubed.

daily double. Picking the winning horses or dogs in consecutive races in track betting.

dead man's hand. In poker, a pair of aces and a pair of eights. Gambling lore has it that Wild Bill Hickok was shot and killed holding this hand.

dead money. Money contributed to the poker pot by players who have folded.

declare. To withdraw a horse from a race.

derog. Casino-employee term used when a credit check of a gambler turns up derogatory information about the player's gambling.

dime. A $1,000 sports bet.

dog. The underdog in a sporting event, according to the odds. The dog will be "plus" the points.

dollar. In sports wagering, a $100 bet.

door card. Ticket stub or receipt purchased when playing bingo, in some locales. The door card proves that you bought your cards that day at that location.

draft. An annual party at which fantasy league participants gather to select players to fill the rosters of their imaginary sports franchises.

ducks. Twos, in poker.

Exacta. In track betting, picking the top two finishers in a race in the exact order.

eye in the sky. Camera or employees hidden above the ceiling to spot cheaters at a casino.

Favorite. Team in a sporting event picked to win; the favorite will be "minus" the points.

fish. Poker player who loses money. According to an old saw, "If you can't spot the fish at the table, you are the fish."

fishhooks. Jacks, in poker.

flipping markers. Casino-employee slang for when a gambler pays off a debt at one house by borrowing from another. Also known as rolling markers.

flop. In seven-card Texas hold 'em, the three cards dealt facedown in the center of the table, then flipped after the first round of bets. The other "community" cards that are dealt with subsequent betting rounds are the "turn card" and the "river."

four corners. A special bingo game that is won by covering the four corner squares of the card. Other popular special configurations include the forms of certain letters such as X, L, and T.

futurity. Race in which the horses are entered before they have been born.

Game. 1. Single round of bingo. 2. A licensed organization's regularly scheduled bingo sessions (i.e., "St. Norbert's has one of the oldest games in the city").

gaming. Euphemism for gambling.

George / Georgette. Casino-employee nicknames for male and female big tippers.

getting down. Placing a bet, in sports wagering.

go through the screen. To check a gambler's credit history on the casino's computer terminal (the screen).

gold card. Casino-employee slang for card given to high-rolling gamblers by some casinos entitling them to unlimited free room-service privileges. They are nevertheless expected to tip for the services.

grind. A casino gambler who makes small bets.

guerrilla gambling. Combination of smart play and hit-and-run tactics thought to be a way to beat the casinos at their own games.

gumbo. In horseracing, a very muddy running surface on a racetrack.

Hedge. In sports wagering, to bet the opposite of your original bet in order to reduce your liability.

Idiot factor / i-factor. Casino-employee slang for the fact that a sizable number of gamblers make fundamental mistakes when playing a game like blackjack or baccarat, thus increasing the house's win.

irons. Stirrups.

Jackson five. In poker, a jack and a 5.

juice. 1. In sports wagering, a fee, generally 10 percent, charged on losing bets; also known as VIGORISH, or VIG. 2. In casino-employee talk, friends in high places.

Kicker. The highest card in your hand that goes with a pair; used to break a tie.

Kojak. King-jack pocket cards, in poker.

Ladies. In poker, two or more queens.

laydown. 1. (poker) To fold a hand. 2. (sports wagering) To bet.

laying off. A bookie betting with another bookie for the purpose of having roughly equal amounts of money bet on games, in order to protect against losses.

laying the points. In sports wagering, betting the favorite; the point spread will be subtracted from the favorite's final score.

limits. A bookie's upper and lower range. Most legal Nevada bookmakers take bets between \$5 and \$9,900.

line. The point spread; a handicap rating that serves to balance the strengths of opposing teams, generally expressed in points. The favorite is minus the points while the underdog is plus the points. The purpose of the line is to get half the bettors to wager on one team and half on the other.

lizard. In casino poker, small cards; the low cards—2, 3, 4—in hi-lo stud. A favorite hand of some Texas and Omaha hold 'em players, who look for lizards on the "flop" while fearing the appearance of big cards.

low-five account. Casino-employee slang for when a gambler's bank account has a balance in the low five figures, say, between \$10,000 and \$30,000. Other types of balances in gamblers' accounts: high six, medium four.

lowball. A version of poker in which the weakest hand wins. A perfect lowball hand would be 5-4-3-2.

Maiden. A horse of either sex that has not won a race.

marker. Casino-employee slang for an IOU, the voucher, similar to a check, that a gambler gives to the casino in exchange for credit. The house later redeems the marker at the gambler's bank.

middle. Sports-wagering slang for winning both sides of a game. For example, if you bet the underdog +3½, the favorite −2½, and the favorite wins by 3, you've middled the book.

money man. A wealthy person who backs a bookmaker financially in case of heavy losses.

monster. A poker hand with a high possibility of winning.

morning glory. Horse that runs well in workouts, but not in races.

morning line. Probable odds posted by the racetrack's handicapper at the time entries are drawn.

muck. In poker, the pile of discards.

mudder. A horse that races well over a wet or soft track.

Nickel. In sports wagering, a \$500 wager.

no-limit. Poker game in which there is no maximum allowed bet.

number one player. A casino's best customer—one who bets at least \$300 to \$500 per bet and who thinks little of winning or losing several hundred thousand dollars in a weekend.

nut / the nuts (poker). 1. The "lock" hand, usually a sure thing. 2. The best possible hand of a given class. The "nut flush" is the highest possible flush, but would still lose to, say, a full house.

nut player. Tight poker player who only plays the best hands.

On the rim. On credit.

on tilt. Describes a frustrated poker player playing recklessly. It alludes to the game-ending "tilt" of pinball, which occurs when the player has been too rough with the machine.

overs and unders. A bet in which one wagers that the combined total score of both teams will be, depending on the bet, more or less than a bookie's predicted total.

Pari-mutuels (horseracing). The mutuels system, whereby winning bettors get all money wagered by losers after the house percentage is deducted; from Paris ("Paree").

parlay. Wager placed on two or more teams or propositions, all of which must win against the point spread in order for the bet to pay off. Parlay gives higher payoff odds but is generally considered a "sucker bet."

pay wholesale. Casino-employee parlance for settling a credit account for less than the full amount.

payouts. Money owed by the bookie to winning bettors.

pick 'em. Line on a sporting event when the teams are considered even, no points to either side; also known as "straight up."

picture frame. A game of bingo won by covering all the squares around the edge of a card.

play and pay. In casino slang, a good gambler from the standpoint of the house: no matter how much is played, the player covers the losses.

pocket. 1. (poker) Facedown cards that only the player can see. 2. (horseracing) Getting boxed in.

pocket rockets. A pair of aces, in poker.

poker paranoia. Condition that occurs when a poker player has a spell of bad luck and becomes convinced that others, including members of his own family, are jinxing him.

postage stamps. A bingo game won by covering the four squares in each corner of the card.

prod (horseracing). An illegal electrified tool used to stimulate a horse, similar to a cattle prod.

public, the (sports wagering). Infrequent or recreational bettors who often bet with their hearts, not their heads.

punter (horseracing). A bettor.

push. 1. (sports wagering) A tie game when adjusted with the LINE; when this occurs, no money is exchanged. 2. (blackjack) Tie between the player and the dealer. The player neither wins nor loses.

Railbird. Person who hangs out and watches poker from behind the rail around the poker room.

rake. In casino poker, the percentage of each round of bets taken by the house. It's how the casino makes its money off poker games.

Reno syndrome. Term used by some doctors in gambling centers to describe the person who does not eat for a day or two and then gobbles down a seven-course dinner or plows through the buffet line.

RFB. Patron given free room, food, and booze while gambling at a casino. Other free services, or comps, include limousine service and free tickets to casino shows.

river. The fifth and last "community" card dealt faceup in a hold 'em poker game. To spike at the river is to hit the winning hand on the fifth card and to drown at the river is to lose on the fifth card.

rocks. In casino poker, cautious players who fold early, and have a tendency to stay in a game only if they have a NUT hand. Chronic "rocks" are sometimes called "granite." Rocks typically don't play unless they have a pair of aces or ace and king as their hole, or beginning, cards.

rounder. Professional gambler who frequents high-stakes events.

route. A relatively long horse race.

rush. Winning streak, in poker.

Sandbag. To play a strong poker hand as if it were only a mediocre one.

sanitary ride. Describes a horse that did not try its best in a race, or a jockey who took the animal wide to avoid tight spots or flying mud, harming its chances of winning.

seagull (horseracing). Bettor who hangs around the big bettors to see where their money is going and then using the information to place a $2 bet.

shed row. The stable area of a racetrack.

shoe. In blackjack, a box that holds multiple decks of cards.

short stack. Poker player with the fewest chips at the table. To be "short-stacked" is to be playing with a only a small amount of money, thus limiting one's risk and reward.

sided. When large numbers of bettors wager a lot of money on one team, leaving the bookmaker vulnerable to a big loss, he is said to be "getting sided." "A bookie's greatest fear, besides the police," according to one wagering glossary on the Web.

snake. In casino poker, the table circuit of house dealers: thirty minutes dealing hold 'em and stud poker at three tables, and then a thirty-minute break.

snowmen. Pair of 8's, in poker.

soft hand. Blackjack hand that includes an ace, which can be counted as either a 1 or 11.

speed limit. Pair of 5's, in poker.

spin. In roulette, one game with a split bet. Also, a bet on two numbers.

spotter. A casino employee who monitors the action on the floor and detects cheats.

stick. A jockey's whip; to whip.

straight-up bet. In roulette, a bet on one single number.

street bet. In roulette, a bet on three numbers.

subway tickets. Cards dealt from the bottom of the deck, in poker.

superfecta (track betting). Picking the top four finishers in a race in the exact order; can be bet for as little as 10 cents.

superstiff. Casino patron who does not even tip the cocktail waitress when she serves him free drinks; the cheapskate's cheapskate.

Table hopper. Gambler who moves from table to table in a casino.

take down. To disqualify a horse after it has finished in the money.

taking the points. In sports wagering, betting the underdog; the points will be added to the underdog's final score.

tap out. To go broke.

tell. Body language or other personal mannerism that gives other poker players clues to what you have in your hand.

Texas hold 'em. A seven-card-stud poker variation. Each player gets two cards facedown (the hole), and three cards (the flop) are dealt facedown in the center. After the first bets, based on hole cards, the flop cards are turned and there's a second round of bets. Then the "turn" card is dealt faceup, followed by wagering. After that, the river card is dealt faceup, and the final bets are made. The winner is the player who makes the best five-card hand from the two hole cards and the five on the board.

third baseman. Blackjack player on the left-hand side of the table and so the last to be able to ask for a hit.

time-warp syndrome. Ailment of gamblers who have lost track of time in a casino and do not know if it is day or night and, in extreme cases, what day of the week it is.

toke. To tip, in casino parlance.

Tom. A poor tipper, at a casino.

tout (horseracing). 1. To give or sell betting advice. 2. One who does so.

treys. In poker, 3's.

Pocket Cards

Some Texas hold 'em nicknames for two-card "hole" combinations dealt facedown.

A + A American Airlines, pocket rockets, or sticks

A + K big slick

A + J Ajax

A + 3 Baskin-Robbins

K + Q the marriage (or the divorce, if it doesn't hold up)

K + 9 the dog

Q + J Oedipus Rex or Maverick

Q + 3 A San Francisco busboy

J + 5 Motown

9 + 8 Oldsmobile

8 + 8 Little Oldsmobile

5 + 7 Heinz

3 + 9 Jack Benny

3 + 3 Crabs

10 + 2 Doyle Brunson, because Brunson, a poker icon, won back-to-back World Series of Poker in 1976 and '77 holding that hand

9 + 5 Dolly Parton

7 + 6 76 trombones

10 + 4 Highway Patrol

trifecta. In track betting, picking the top three finishers in a race in the correct order.

TTO. This trip only. Means that a gambler's credit will only be extended temporarily by the casino.

turfite. A racetrack habitué or one whose life is defined by the track.

Underlay. In sports wagering, when the odds on a proposition are in favor of the house.

upcard. Blackjack dealer's card that is dealt faceup.

Vig / vigorish. The bookmaker's "service charge." You have to bet $11 to win $10. If you bet $110 and win, you get $210 in return, not $220. If you bet $100 and win, you get $190.90 in return. If you tie, you get your entire bet back. If you lose, you get zip. The bookmakers profit if more people lose than win or if exactly half the bettors win.

Walk hots. To cool a horse down after a race or workout.

walking on eggs (horseracing). Describing a horse that is sore.

walking sticks. In poker, 7's.

walking with chips. Casino-employee term for when a gambler gets chips from a casino on credit, cashes them in, and then walks out of the casino, essentially taking an interest-free loan.

walkover. A horse race with only one starter because of scratches. The starter is required to gallop the required distance to win the race.

win-place-show. In track betting, the traditional bets for first, second, and third.

wise guys. Professional bettors, in sports wagering.

witch stick. Lucky stick that some bingo players put on their tables to improve "reception" of winning numbers.

Zeroing out. When a casino gambler pays the outstanding balance on a credit account.

13

HIP-HOP AND LIKE THAT

An Earful of Urban Culturez

Hip-hop. The very word sparks fear, distaste, and misunderstanding in many an adult. With the baggy clothes, the swagger, and the misogyny and profanity in many popular rap songs, hip-hop represents everything adult educators don't want in schools. Yet this same pop-culture phenomenon—more than 30 years old and still gaining in global popularity—can spark a vital enthusiasm for learning in kids we educators can tap into if we treat it with the same respect that we ask our students to give nineteenth-century poets.

—Kenneth Smith, teacher, Threshold *magazine, Winter 2006*

Hip-hop hasn't just reached the mainstream, it owns it.

—Kristi Turnquist, The Oregonian, *October 8, 2004*

Inspired by rap music (which is also referred to as hip-hop), hip-hop refers to a body of music dominated by fast, clearly spoken, or rapped, lyrics that consist of rhymed couplets. In addition, hip-hop describes a host of urban subcultures, certain kinds of graffiti art, a fashion of wearing loose, brightly colored clothing, sneakers or clunky shoes, and a street-dance style done standing up with lots of rhythmic kicks, hops, stamps, and angular arm movements.

But it is even more than all that. It has become a phenomenon adopted by the young the world over, in which new words and phrases are coined faster than the mainstream can keep up. For a "def" (cool) rapper, the trick is to eliminate a term from your vocabulary once the "street elite" collectively determine that the term has gone too mainstream.

Indeed, the term "def" had become so mainstream by 1993 that the rap community held a funeral for the word—replete with a eulogy by the Rev. Al Sharpton—to lament its inclusion in the *Oxford English Dictionary.* By 2006, seventy terms defined with a connection to hip-hop appeared in the electronic edition of the *Oxford English Dictionary.*

A more recent example: by October 30, 2005, "bling" had become so mainstream that the *Washington Post* could title an article on robes of the Ottoman Empire "Out of Turkey: Sultans of Bling" and an ad in the *Las Vegas Review/Journal* for September 22, 2005, could say of a sequin shrug, "This is bling." By the end of 2005, Robin D. Givhan wrote in the December 28 issue of the *Washington Post*, in an article entitled " 'Bling' Isn't Cool—Can You Dig It?" that use of the term had become as annoying as a "nervous tic." Givhan explained this particular case of verbicide: "The word *bling* has been overused by every two-bit jeweler selling cubic zirconium. It had been worn out by virtually all fashion publicists—who for the last five months have been chirping, 'Bling in the New Year!'—and by every morning TV host trying to make the umpteenth holiday shopping segment sound fun and nifty."

Hip-hop is an ever-changing language in which a word or phrase can quickly change meaning, go out of style, or carry multiple meanings. "The language is very transitory," Tom Dalzell, the author of *Flappers 2 Rappers: American Youth Slang* told a *New York Times* reporter. "When you take a snapshot of what's being said in October, it may not be said a month later. The really powerful words move around quickly now. MTV and VH1 are the greatest levelers of slang today" (January 5, 1997).

Many of these terms will be dated by the time you read this, so think of this compendium as a look into the slang of hip-hop as it is evolving and affecting the larger worldwide culture.

Ac / ack. The Acura Legend.

Afrocentric rap. Genre that speaks specifically and exclusively of the social and political concerns of the African American community.

aggie. Angry.

ahizzead. Ahead. Snoop Dogg often inserts "izz" or "izzle" in the words he uses, for example, "hizzouse" for house. "Cheat on your man, ma, that's how you get ahizzead."

all gravy. Fine; good.

all that. Cool, good.

alternative rap. Genre that incorporates nontraditional (for rap) samples from other recordings and subject matter.

amped. Worked up, excited.

audi 5000. I am outta here.

Back in the day. Old-school times.

banging. Really good; awesome.

bank. Money, cash. Also known as, change, cheddar, duckets, flow, loot, Benjamins, and pape.

B-boy / B-girl. Early-eighties abbreviation for break-dance boy or girl; later, any street kid who is considered cool or hip.

beats. Music; tunes.

beef. Disagreement or conflict.

Benjamins. Dollars, from the image of Benjamin Franklin on the $100 bill. "It's all about the Benjamins."

bet. For sure, as in "I'll pay you back. Bet."

bite. To steal another's ideas, lyrics, beats, or style, as in "Get your own idea and stop bitin' mine."

blazin'. Extremely good.

bling bling / bling. 1. Flashy material wealth; or having material wealth, especially jewelry. Term coined by the New Orleans rap family Cash Money Millionaires in the late 1990s. The *Oxford English Dictionary* included "bling" in the 2003 edition.

2. Jewelry of the sort that sets off alarms in airports.

blingage. Jewelry, as in "Check my blingage."

blinglish. The influence of hip-hop on language.

blow up. To become famous.

blow up the spot. To expose to everybody; make public.

bomb. Impressive thing, person, or event.

boo. Term of endearment for a boyfriend or girlfriend, as in "She used to leave school early just to see her boo."

bootylicious. Hot, sexy. Attributed to the rapper Snoop Dogg in the 2003 *Oxford English Dictionary*, occasioning one music writer to note in 2004, "Anyone uttering that hip-hop expression today would be mocked as a person who is sooo not cool."

bounce. To leave.

break dancing. Street-dance style that includes spinning on the floor on various parts of the body: head, hand, knee, back and—most extraordinarily—the neck. An early observer of break dancing, Ken Tucker, writing in the *San Francisco Examiner* of October 18, 1983, noted, "You haven't lived until you've seen someone move to music while dancing on his neck."

brizzles. Women, broads. "I got a living room full of brizzles."

bubblegum rap. Genre of radio-friendly, highly commercialized rap that avoids the harsh language and moral ambiguity of other forms. Often derided by "true hip-hoppers."

buck-fifty. A cut from a razor blade, which used to cost $1.50.

buck wild. Uncivilized person or behavior; crazy.

buff. To remove graffiti.

bugged / bugging out. Stressed.

buggin'. Weird behavior, agitated.

bum-rush. To invade, break down the doors; a reversal of "bum's rush," for eject.

bust a cap. To shoot someone.

bust it. No more delay. Let's do this. Let's get started. "Bust a move," the title of a Young MC hit, means to make a move *now*.

butta. To be smooth; nice, like butter, as in "That's a butta jacket."

buttas. Things that are really cool; admirable objects.

Cake. Money.

camos. Camouflage-patterned clothing.

cardio-hip-hop. Aerobics blended with hip-hop dancing; also called street jam.

cats. Men, enemies.

cheddar. Money. Cheddar Bob is a character in the 2002 film *8 Mile*.

cheese. Money.

chickenhead. A dim-witted or silly girl.

chill. Cool; something that is relaxed and cool.

chill out. To relax and take it easy.

clique. West Coast equivalent of CREW.

clockin'. Bringing in, as in "clockin' dollars."

crazy. Extreme, as in "The millionaire had crazy dollars."

cream. Money.

crew. Organized group or team of rappers, DJs, dancers, or graffiti artists who work together.

crunk. Blend of crazy + drunk, although there are other explanations such as this one appearing on rapdict.org. "Originally, this term comes from the words crazy and funk. As opposed to popular opinion, crunk has had no relation to being coked up and drunk until recently. Because of its similarity of terminal sound with the word drunk many rappers have used it in reference with being crazy and under the influence. This and the intrinsical association with hard partying has brought about its association with alcohol."

crunk juice. A heavy drink, made popular by Lil Jon—a mixture of Red Bull and Hennessey.

cutting. Method used by DJs to segue from one record to another without missing a beat.

D, the. Detroit.

da bomb. Mid-nineties term for "the best."

dead presidents. Money. Most American dollar bills have a former president of the United States on them.

deep. A group with a large number of members.

def. Early-eighties term meaning good, new, wonderful. Replaces cool. The claim has been made that it derived from "definite" and "death." It was a common term in rap music lyrics. An article in the *New York Times* ("Words to Rap By," August 22, 1988) quotes Robert Farris Thompson, a professor of African and Afro-American art at Yale University: "The rappers are saying 'def' derived from 'death' meaning terrific . . . when in the forties boppers said: You kill me, you send me to heaven."

digits. Telephone number. "He has listed digits."

dime piece. Cute.

dis / diss. To speak ill of someone; to show disrespect, to insult; short for dismiss; often used in the past tense, as in "I dissed him."

disrespezzy. Disrespect.

dog / dogg / dawg. 1. Feet. 2. Buddy; best friend, partner, as in "Michael Jordan, my dogg, uses his dogs and hands to earn big bucks."

doggin'. Being disrespectful.

dollar cab. The bus, or subway or streetcar in some cities.

dome. head or mind.

dome piece. head.

dope. 1. Superb, outstanding, as in "That's a dope Porsche." 2. To clown, to make fun of, mock or ridicule. This term is widely labeled as outdated, but as one blogger put it, "Sometimes it can be revived and sound cool, but very few can pull it off."

double deuce juice. Twenty-two-ounce can of malt liquor or cold beer.

down. 1. To be a part of a group or action. 2. To agree, as in "I'm down with that."

down low / DL. Quiet, as in "The couple kept their marriage plans on the d.l. for months."

dragon. Bad breath.

drama. Trouble; dangerous situation.

drop. Convertible car.

duckets. Money.

dukey rope. Fat gold chain.

Ebonics. Black English.

essay. Describing anyone of Hispanic origin who lives the hip-hop life. From the abbreviation for South America.

Fa shizzle / fo shizzle / for shizzle. A Snoop Dogg coinage, so co-opted that a 2003 issue of *Fortune* could carry this ad: "Sunday the Mortgage Bankers Association hooks it up for shizzle at its ninetieth Annual Convention and Expo in San Diego." Ben Rayner, who discovered the line, noted in his piece "Shizzle Has Fizzled; Someone Alert the Suits" that the highlight of the meeting in San Diego was a debate between Bob Dole and Al Gore mediated by the CNN commentator Greta Van Susteren.

fake da funk. Pretend.

fat. Living well.

fat caps. Nozzle from cans of cooking spray or spray glue; graffiti artists often put them on spray-paint cans to make the spray wider.

flava. Style. "He has mad flava." This term made news in the fall of 2002 when an internal *CNN Headline News* memo was made public which urged its anchors to use more "cutting edge" slang terms such as "flava" and "ill." According to a report in *Parade* magazine (December 29, 2002), the memo contained a glossary with the following instructions: "Please use this guide to help all you homeys and honeys add a new flava to your tickers and dekos."

flossin'. Showing off.

fly. Good-looking, attractive, fashionable.

fly girl. Early-eighties term for the female version of a B-BOY. One who is fly is hip, desirable, fun.

forty / 40. 40-ounce malt liquor.

four-one-one / 411 / the 411. Information. "What's the four-one-one on him?" Popularized by the rapper Mary J. Blige in 1992 with the release of *What's the 411?*

fresh. Good, new, stylish.

front. To put up a front, dissemble ("He frontin', so forget him"), to try to be something you're not; to try to pass off someone else's stuff as your own.

fugly. A blend of fucking + ugly.

G / gee. Gangsta, for short; homey. An honorific by one male friend of another.

game, the. The music business.

gangbangers. Gang members taking part in criminal activity.

gangsta. 1. A gang member. 2. Of or relating to gangs, gang members, or their lifestyle. 3. Of or relating to GANGSTA RAP, its performers, and its fans.

gangsta rap. Rap featuring aggressive, misogynistic, brutal lyrics, and often focusing on the violence of gang culture. The genre is informed by the South Central Los Angeles street gang experience. At its best, it offers harsh, unforgiving social commentary.

gat. Gun.

get crunk. To have a good time.

getting over. Succeeding, sometimes at other people's expense.

getting up. In the graffiti subculture, getting well known and respected by other artists.

G-funk. Gangsta funk; gangsta raps backed up by melodic samples and background music.

ghetto. 1. Something undesirable, low class; parochial. 2. Something excellent.

ghetto bird. 1. Police helicopter. 2. Person who lives in the ghetto.

got it going on. Doing good.

got the vapors. Trying to absorb someone's fame or creative juices, as in "He got the vapors."

graf. Graffiti.

green. Money.

green language. Correct language used in job interviews and on other occasions when hip-hop terms are inappropriate.

grill. 1. A person's face, with an emphasis on the teeth. "Guard your grill" is a warning to protect your face from getting punched. 2. Gold molded to fit a person's teeth. In early 2006 "Grillz," an ode to platinum- and diamond-encrusted teeth, was the top-playing song on the *Billboard* list.

Hard. Authentic, tough, muscular, as in "Jive me them hard jams every time."

hata. Someone who is jealous.

heads. People.

hella. Very. "New York City was hella-cold last winter." Derived from "a hell of a lot." Examples: hella-cool, hella-funny, hella-crazy, hella-stupid, etc.

herb. To steal.

hip-hop. Street-level movement comprising music, fashion, politics, and social consciousness, African American in origin but currently the nation's most influential cultural movement across the board. Includes, but is not limited to, rap. The name hip-hop stems from some nonsense syllables in rap's first national hit, 1979's "Rapper's Delight," by the Sugar Hill Gang.

hip-pop. Hip-hop that has crossed over to pop. Often used derisively.

ho / hoe. Woman of questionable morals, short for "whore"; anyone (male or female) with low or nonexistent sexual morals. Ludacris rapped: "You doin' ho activities with ho tendencies."

holla. Good-bye.

holla back. Call me later.

homeboy. Close male friend.

homegirl. Close female friend.

homes. Neighbor, friend; from HOMEBOY, slang for companion.

homeslice. Close friend.

homey. Close friend.

homo-hop. LGBT hip-hop.

hoochie. Oversexed.

hood, the. The neighborhood—usually an inner-city neighborhood. A neighborhood where a gang is in control.

hoodie. Oversized, hooded sweatshirts, usually with a zip front and drawstring. They suddenly became fashionable and they are not cheap, many selling for over $100.

hoodrat. Female, generally sexually promiscuous, and not upwardly mobile.

hoopdee / hooptie. Junky car. Also, a beat-up car.

hoops. Basketball.

hot mess. To look very bad.

hot minute. Fast.

house. 1. Have a major success, gain great acclaim, putatively from "bringing the house down." 2. To defeat. "Evander Holyfield housed Mike Tyson in their last fight."

house music. Invented in Chicago but popularized in Europe, house is basically an outgrowth of disco, although no one really rallies to that dreaded word, which is why some claim that rap was created.

hurban. Blend of hispanic + urban, a radio format that is a mix of Latin, hip-hop, and other urban styles.

hype. Bigger than life; great.

hyped. Energetic, exciting.

Ice creams. Jewelry, especially diamonds.

ill. 1. Good, awesome, admirable. 2. Depending on time and context, bad or off your rocker, as in "You Be Illin'," the title of a Run-DMC hit. 3. Drunk.

illed on. Cursed out or humiliated in a sport, especially basketball.

I'm all that. I'm the most, I'm the best.

I'm down with that. I agree with that. I think we should do that.

I'm vexed. I'm ticked off.

izz Latin. Related to pig Latin: a word is transformed by removing most of the trailing syllables and replacing them with "-izzle" or by dropping "-izz" into the middle of words in front of vowels to form -izza, -izze, -izzi, -izzo, and -izzu. The rapper Snoop Dogg is generally credited as the originator of this practice in rap, although hip-hop Web sites maintain that E-40 was doing it on his albums long before him.

Jack. 1. To jack someone is to rob him or steal his car with him in it. 2. Jack Daniel's whiskey. 3. Telephone or cell phone.

jacked. Messed up.

jam. A musical performance, record, or party ("That's a def jam").

Jesus piece. A chain with (a crucifix) on it.

jet. To leave or go; to run or leave fast.

jigga. Gigolo.

jiggy. Get creative; mix it up. The term became so overused that by 2000 Nicole Volta Avery could warn in the *Detroit Free Press*, "Using this word is the ultimate badge of uncoolness." Her article "Saying the Right Thing Means Not Trying Too Hard" (August 3, 2000) noted that there was nothing worse than baby boomers "acting like a brand new playa."

jimmy. Penis.

jimmy hat. Condom.

junk in the trunk. Describes a good-looking rear end.

Keepin' it real. 1. To stay black. 2. To be yourself. 3. To stay cool, as in "He shaved his head because he wanted to keep it real."

kicks. Shoes.

Lamp. To take one's ease—possibly from the image of leaning against a lamppost.

lampin'. Hip.

livin' large. Living in luxury; doing well.

locking. A street-dance style that includes full leg splits, pointing, clapping, and swinging arm movements.

loot. money.

lucci. money.

Macadacious. Hyped.

mack daddy. In seventies vernacular, a mack was a sharp-dressing, cool-acting pimp. At present it means less a pimp and more someone who is simply sharp and cool. To be a mack daddy is to be the mackest of them all.

mad. 1. Beautiful. 2. Very. 3. A lot, as in "Michael Jordan has mad skills," or "We couldn't move because the dance floor was mad crowded."

man-ho. Gigolo.

man up! Exhortation to be tough, to face the situation.

modo. Ugly; claimed to be a shortening of the name of Quasimodo.

monster cables. Heavy gold chains.

New jack. Newcomer, rookie.

new school. Hip-hop culture after 1990, although the actual cutoff date depends on whom you ask.

nitro. Very good.

Off the hook. Extremely exciting.

OG. Original gangsta.

old school. 1. Hip-hop culture prior to 1985; see NEW SCHOOL. 2. Something retro, vintage, or classic—anything from sneakers to playground basketball rules.

on the serious tip. Speaking seriously now.

on the strength. Really great, as in "His show was on the strength."

Papers. Cash, paper money.

partay. Party.

peace. All right, calm. "The crowd around me was excited, but I was peace."

peace out. Good-bye.

pearl. To leave.

peep. To watch, pay close attention to, scrutinize.

peeps. 1. People. 2. To look at, to be aware of, as in "Ayo, did you peep the Knicks game?"

phat. Something that's good to the extreme. So out of favor that Robin Givhan could write in the *Washington Post* that the use of "bling" had become "as persistent as a dry cough and as annoying as old people who say 'phat' and 'You go, girl!' "

pimp. 1. Over the top; very cool. 2. To adorn or embellish, in the sense that the MTV show in which old cars are customized is called *Pimp My Ride.* Few terms better underscore the ability of the hip-hop culture to redefine the meaning of a word—from that of a man running prostitutes to a word that appears in family newspapers in the context of flashy cars. "Pre-Fabbed and Furious: The Chevy Cobalt Is a Ride That Is Already Pimped to the Hilt," ran a headline in *Express*, a *Washington Post* publication, on August 24, 2005.

pimped chariot. Rehabbed car.

PJs. The projects.

playa / playah. 1. Someone who is "true to the game." 2. Black playboy—from the fact that *Players* is a black-oriented adult men's magazine.

played. Used, dumped. "You got played by her."

popping. Robotic style of street dancing characterized by freezing the joints in sequence and isolating various parts of the body.

poser. Someone who pretends to be someone he is not.

posse. Your group of friends. The people you hang with.

props. Short for "propers" or "proper respects." To give someone their props is to pay respect or credit. "You get mad props for that."

props against. Disrespect.

Phat City

The extent to which "phat" became the poster word for the acceptance of rap and hip-hop slang is underscored by a special twelve-page brochure, produced by Merriam-Webster, to show how the word made its way into *Merriam-Webster's Collegiate Dictionary* (11th edition). It cited "phat" used in context in *Essence,* ESPN, *Sports Illustrated,* and the *New York Times Magazine,* in which David Brooks talks about the "phat spoilers" on his Dodge Grand Caravan.

"Phat" had already appeared in the *Oxford English Dictionary* as a term of approbation and appeared in headlines in the *New York Times* ("A Phat, Fly Thing," May 29, 1994).

A major online source for hip-hop slang is the Rapdict.org Web site, which defines "phat" in its first meaning as "Rich like butter, really good, extremely well put together." It then suggests that the term was created as an acronym: "If a girl was phat, she had Plenty o' Hips And Thighs, in other words, PHysically ATtractive; old slang. Think 60's or early 70's here."

The *Oxford English Dictionary*'s take on the acronyms is that they "are likely to be later rationalizations" and that the term is a respelling of the word fat. It remains true that the lore of slang is heavy with assertions that common terms contain hidden acronyms that explain them. Thus, "put it in my pocket" is the etymology for pimp, according to some.

punked. To be embarrassed by someone else.

Raggedy. Broken down.

roll. To move, travel, or walk from one point to another, as in "Puffy rolled out of the limo and into the club."

roll up. To sneak up on someone.

Scandalous. Dirty behavior that should not be publicized.

school. 1. To show superiority by teaching someone a lesson. 2. A specific era in hip-hop history. There have been many discussions about the difference between the OLD SCHOOL and the NEW SCHOOL.

scratching. Manipulating a record turntable by hand to create a sound with little or no resemblance to the original recording.

scrub. A worthless guy; slacker; loser.

shitkickers. Combat-style boots.

shook. Scared.

shorty. Girlfriend; potential girlfriend; term of endearment.

sick. Awe-inspiring move, lyric, drawing, etc. that is amazing to the point of indescribability.

signs. Hand gestures gang members use to identify themselves, similar to the alphabet for the deaf.

sketch out. To act strangely.

sketchy. Weird, shady.

skills. Talents.

slammin'. Great; extremely impressive.

slo yo roll. Calm down.

slob. An insult to a rival gang member.

smashin'. Fashion.

smoke. To shoot and kill with a gun.

stack up. Make money.

stain. Annoying person; useless person.

step to. Challenge.

straight that. Similar to right on, but with more attitude. When you say "Straight that," you not only say you agree with whatever is being said, but you dare anybody else to disagree.

street dance. Any dance evolving out of American urban street culture, especially those styles inspired by rap music, popping, locking, break dancing, and hip-hop.

stupid. Beyond all common sense or reason. Extreme.

stupid fresh. Light, humorous side of hip-hop.

Tag. A given graffiti artist's signature, often illegible to the unpracticed eye.

that's five thousand. From a video game in which 5,000 points entitle you to move on to the next screen. "That's five thousand" means to go to the next phase or to move on.

thugged out. Tough-looking; threatening in dress and demeanor.

tighten up. Calm down.

timbs. Timberland boots, especially the tan work boots favored by rap stars.

tool. Someone who tries too hard to belong.

toy. 1. A beginning graffiti writer or someone with limited skills. 2. To purposefully write over another graffiti artist's work, known as toying someone out.

trick. Derogatory term to describe a woman.

trifling. Worthless; not worth the time of day.

tru dat. Right on. Smooth, fresh, phat, obese, mad, deft, good (of graffiti or anything else).

Vibing. A good feeling.

vickies. Women's underwear, an allusion to the Victoria's Secret catalog.

vogueing. Fashion-model runway moves and gestures combined with dancing.

Wack / whack. So stupid it's not worth dealing with; embarrassing. Poor quality, bad. Short for whacky. Crazy, or out of line, as in "The way my boss treated me was really wack."

walk you down. To catch up to someone who is ahead of you, whether on the street, financially, or in terms of fame, etc.

wax. Impressing, beating someone badly in a competitive duel, as in "He waxing them and they hate it."

what up? What's up? What's happening?

wheels of steel. Turntables.

whip. A car. Perhaps from the old gag: A: "Can I drive you home?" B: "You have a car?" A: "No. A whip."

wigger. 1. Derogatory term for white person who adopts black styles. 2. Someone who wears a wig.

word / word up. Truth. Often used as a punctuation of another's thoughts, much as "right on" once was. If someone says something you strongly agree with, you reply, "Word."

XXX throwdown. Sex orgy.

Ya feel me. Do you understand?

you buggin'. You're acting crazy.

you got it goin' on. You've got it together, you're really def.

Z. Often used in place of S, as in *Boyz in Da Hood.* By 2002, Maureen Tkacik could write in the *Wall Street Journal* (December 30, 2002): "'Z' is becoming the new 'S'—that is to say, ubiquitouz." She reported that Target Stores, citing just one example, had shelves labeled Kool Toyz, a karaoke machine called Loud Lipz, and a doll house called Dinky Digz.

Zerp. Slang for syrup, such as Robitussin. Also, sizz-zerp.

JAVA-SPEAK

14

Slang of the Twenty-first-Century Coffeehouse

At M.E. Swing Coffee Roasters, if you want a 20-ounce cup of java, you had better be prepared to call it by its proper name: a jumbo. At Cosi, it's a gigante. At Bread and Chocolate, a molto grande. At Starbucks, ask for a venti—rhymes with 20—and that's what you get. At the Seattle's Best stand at the Smithsonian's Arts and Industries Building, 20 ounces makes a royal entrance under the vaunted moniker of a grande supremo—not, of course, to be confused with a grande, which, despite the fact that *grande* means "large" in Italian, is, most everywhere, a 16-ounce medium. Refreshingly, McDonald's, Dunkin' Donuts, Quartermaine Coffee Roasters and Firehook Bakery all still call a spade a spade. Ask for a large and you get a large 20-ounce cup of piping hot joe.

Got it?

—Michael O'Sullivan, "Naming Names Can Be a Tall Order,"
Washington Post, February 28, 2003

Coffeehouses now either outnumber or vie with the tavern roster in many American business districts. With them has come a culture as distinct as the traditional bar culture, replete with its own lingo. The adoption of this new coffeehouse lingo has been accelerated by the television sitcoms *Friends* and *Frasier*, which have been very successful on both sides of the Atlantic. Frasier moved from a bar (*Cheers*) to a coffeehouse. Then there were movie scenes such as the one where the actor Steve Martin, playing Harris K. Telemacher, in the 1991 film *L.A. Story*, ordered a "half double decaffeinated half-caf with a twist of lemon."

More than a decade later, Telemacher's line is no longer so funny because we are deep into the cult of coffee, where the excessive is now normal. Coffee beans allowed to cure by India's monsoons are prized, as are acquired tastes such as Kopi Luwak, coffee from the Indonesian island of Sumatra, an area well known for its excellent coffee. It has a unique flavor, explained by Mia Stainsbury: "You might have heard of Kopi Luwak coffee sold at Urban Fare. It's collected from the droppings (the icky kind) of the coffee-bean-munching luwaks, the tree-dwelling animals found in Java, Sumatra, and Sulawesi. They can only digest the outer layer [of the bean], so the rest of the bean passes through, undigested and apparently enhanced by their stomach acids, giving it a $600-a-pound, gourmet flavour. The beans are retrieved and (we hope) washed" (*Vancouver Sun*, November 20, 2002).

By 2005 the price of this coffee had dropped to a mere $75 a pound on Web sites that do not shy away from lauding the luwak's role in coffee production. A typical line: "The resulting coffee is said to be like no other. It has a rich, heavy flavour with hints of caramel or chocolate." Then there is Vietnam's popular "weasel coffee," or "coffee weasel"—*ca phe chon*, *chon* meaning "weasel"—which works on the same concept as kopi luwak, except that it involves a weasel rather than a luwak. A variant of this coffee is artificially processed by subjecting the unroasted beans to enzymes that purport to duplicate the effects of the weasel's digestive system.

We have come a long way since 1998, when Primer Pret à Manger, a London chain, felt compelled to put out a simplified coffee menu which demystified the new drinks:

The Menu
Latte—the milky one
Cappucccino—the foamy one
Mocha—the chocolaty one
Espresso—the small one

Here is a look at this emerging lingo, informed by personal visits to the Bean Bag, Caribou, Green Mountain, Seattle's Best, Torrefazione, Coffee People, Peet's, Stumptown Roasters, Brewed Awakenings, Dunkin' Donuts, Seattle Gourmet (and their drive-thru espresso stands), Elliot Bay, Starbucks, and others.

Addshot. Used by BARISTAS when relaying an order that requires an additional shot of espresso. "Frappuccino with an addshot" means a FRAPPUCCINO with a shot of espresso added.

americano. Espresso mixed with hot water.

Barista. Espresso bartender. "In a warehouse choked with enough *eau de caffeine* to make a slumbering panda leap up and tap dance, two dozen of this region's finest baristas—a.k.a those hip folks manning your local coffee bar—are grinding, frothing and plotting their way toward nothing less than global supremacy" (*USA Today,* February 19, 2003).

big brew. 7-Eleven's 24-ounce infusion of caffeine.

biodiversity. A blend of many types of coffee.

black eye. Espresso mixed with brewed coffee.

Café noir. Black coffee.

cake in a cup. Double cream, double sugar. Also called a double double.

cap. Short for CAPPUCCINO.

cappuccino. Espresso mixed with frothy steamed milk; it is widely believed to be so named because of its resemblance to the color of the brown monk's robe of the Capuchin Friars.

cause coffee. Any coffee tied to a political or environmental cause. Bird-friendly coffees are grown under canopies of native trees that provide shelter and sustenance for migrating birds. Fair-traded coffees are purchased (usually from smallholder farms) at a "fair" price, one that should permit farmers to adequately sustain their families and their farms. Eco-OK coffees are certified by an arm of the Rainforest Alliance to meet a range of balanced environmental and economic criteria intended to assure the long-term health of both land and people.

COD. Coffee of the day; mainly at Starbucks.

coyote. Middleman in the transfer of beans from the third world to the developed world. Third-world coffee farmers are often at a deep disadvantage in supply-and-demand equations.

crappuccino. Poorly made but expensive (in the $4 range) coffee drink. Term first reported by the *DailyCandy* Web site.

cuppa. "Cup of," in the lingo of diners and hash houses, as in cuppa joe, cuppa java, cuppa mud, cuppa jamoke, cuppa murk.

cupper. Coffee aficionado, first cousin to the serious wine enthusiast.

cupping. Tasting and spitting, as opposed to drinking. Caribou coffee describes the process on its Web site: "Coffee is ground into a porcelain or glass cup and hot water is poured over the top. The coffee steeps for a few minutes and the grounds rise to the top, forming a crust. When the crust is broken with a silver spoon, the cupper evaluates the coffee's aromas. After the coffee cools for a bit, the cupper samples the liquid, evaluates the flavors, and spits the coffee out to avoid caffeine intake."

customology. Name created by Starbucks for teaching patrons the language of the coffeehouse. Promulgated by a series of "Customology 101" press releases.

Double cupping. Putting one paper cup into another to protect tender fingers from hot coffee; increasingly rare practice, as JAVA JACKETS are supplied.

double down. Call in which the second order is identical to the one preceding.

dry. Foamy. A dry cappuccino is one that is more foam than milk.

Eggspresso / egg espresso. Egg scrambled by an espresso machine without oil or butter.

estate coffee / estate-grown coffee. Coffee from a particular estate dedicated to one type of coffee.

extra hot. Describes a drink in which the

Taster's Terms

A growing list of terms used to describe coffee gives the vocabulary of the wine lover a run for its money—for example: bitter, bland, bright, brisk, burnt, caramelly, carbony, chaffy (a taste reminiscent of sawdust), chocolaty, dead, delicate, dirty (a mustiness reminiscent of eating dirt), dry, earthy, flat, fragrant, fruity, grassy (an aroma and flavor reminiscent of a freshly cut lawn), harsh, mellow, muddy (thick and dull), musty, nutty, rioy (starchy, like pasta water), rough, rubbery, shallow, sharp, snappy, soft, sour, spicy, sweet, tangy, thin, turpeny (turpentine-like), vibrant, watery, wild, winey . . .

milk has been steamed to a temperature higher than 170 degrees Fahrenheit (between 160 and 170 degrees is normal); mainly Starbucks.

Frap. Any drink based on Starbucks' frappuccino coffee drink. Loosely, refers to any iced coffee or espresso drink.

frap rush. When fraps are ordered in bunches, usually right after the local high school has let out.

frappuccino. A coffee drink made in a blender, developed and sold by Starbucks, combining coffee, milk, sugar, ice, and other miscellaneous ingredients.

full city / full city roast. Very dark roast.

Grande. Medium: between a tall (small) and a large (venti); mainly Starbucks.

gutless wonder. Cappuccino made with decaf, nonfat milk, and artificial sweetener; a drink on TV's *Frasier*.

Hammerhead. Espresso mixed with brewed coffee.

harmless. Decaf.

high-test. A cup of regular (not decaffeinated) coffee.

Jamoke. Blend of java + mocha (pron. ja-*moh*-kee). Diner and luncheonette slang.

java. Brewed coffee.

java jacket. Paper sleeve that is slipped onto a hot paper cup.

jitterati. Those who need constant supply of caffeine to meet deadlines.

joe. Old-school diner slang for coffee. Also, java, jamoke, sludge, silt, bilge, murk, mud, and a shot-in-the-arm.

Latte art. Creating designs in latte foam with the steamer. "Espresso is the blackboard while milk is the chalk," one latte artist told the *Vancouver Sun* (November 20, 2002).

latte factor. Coined by the American financial analyst David Bach, it refers to cash wasted on those seemingly insignificant purchases we make every day such as a drink or snack in a café, which, though small, over time add up to a significant amount of money.

lattenomics. Term created by the *Economist* magazine (January 15, 2004) to measure the valuation of world currencies based on the relative price of a Starbucks tall latte in various countries. Called the Starbucks Index, it has achieved some measure of success as an economic measure.

lungo. Italian for "long"; used to describe a stretched expresso made by letting twice as much water as usual run through the espresso machine. A caffè lungo must not be mistaken for a café AMERICANO, which is an espresso with a little hot water in it. A lungo is richer but more bitter.

Macchiato. Starbucks drink that is mostly milk foam, with a shot of espresso. The caramel macchiato is its most popular incarnation.

No fun. Latte made with decaf coffee and nonfat milk; also called a "skinny harmless" or a "why bother."

no whip. No whipped cream. See also WHIPLESS.

On a leash. To go, in a disposable cup with handles.

on wheels. An order to go.

Park it. An order to stay.

Quad / quad jammer. Four shots of espresso; also known as a double double.

Red eye. Drip coffee with a shot of espresso.

ristretto. Short shot of espresso.

Schizo. A cup of coffee made with equal parts of caffeinated and decaffeinated coffee. A barista might order "an iced tall schizo skinny hazelnut cap with wings," which translates as "a small iced hazelnut cappuccino with one shot of regular and one of decaf, plus skim milk with foam, to go."

skinny. A latte or other drink made with skimmed milk.

solo. A single shot of espresso. Compare "doppio" (two shots) and "triplo" (three).

shock it. Instruction to add a few ice cubes to a hot coffee or espresso drink to cool it down to a more immediately drinkable temperature.

short and dry. What to ask for if you want to minimize the amount of milk relative to coffee in a latte or cappuccino.

shot. A single shot of espresso: the amount found in an espresso cup. A double is two shots.

shot in the dark. A regular coffee with a shot of espresso in it. Also called a speed ball. I've also been told that in L.A. this is called a red eye, and elsewhere a bellman, boilerhouse, and depth charge.

split shot. A half-caf espresso shot.

Starbuckian. Term used to describe the language used in Starbucks coffee shops. A number of such terms—Starbucksian, Starbuckese, Starbonics—are listed on a variety of Web sites dedicated to deciphering the language and ritual of Starbucks worldwide. Of all of these terms, Starbuckian is the most popular. It is a noun and also an adjective, as in the Starbuckian practice of rapid expansion.

steamer. A steamed-milk drink made with a flavored syrup.

Tall. Twelve-ounce cup—small; mainly Starbucks.

Basic Starbuckian

In 2001 the quirky, hip BBC online service h2g2, which "explains life, the universe and everything else," noted the growth of Starbucks outside the United States and published a guide to the rituals of ordering at the chain's coffee shops. Its summing-up of the universal language of ordering at Starbucks:

• No matter how well you study this entry, or how much of a veteran Starbucks customer you are, you may be sure of one thing when ordering your drink: you will order it incorrectly. Some way, somehow, you will say something that is out of line, and the counter person will look down on you. Some ways to avoid this are as follows:

• Always order the "tall" size. This saves you from having to pronounce "grande" (pron. "grand-ay") and "venti" (no matter which way you pronounce this—"ven-tay," or "ven-tee"—the barista will correct you with whatever form you didn't use! Tread very carefully when ordering this size).

• Make your drink as simple as possible. If you don't reel off a list of requirements in your order, the barista cannot correct you on the order you said it in. For example, if you were to order a "tall, skim, mocha with no whipped cream," invariably, the barista would tell his colleague behind the bar to make a "tall, no whip, skim, mocha." However, if you order a "tall latte" you can rob them of this satisfaction.

• Give up on all espresso drinks and order the coffee of the day. This is whatever coffee they are brewing the regular Christian way for that day. If you want to sound really cool, order a "COD."

thunder thighs. A double-tall mocha made with whole milk and topped with extra whipped cream.

triple. Three shots of espresso, for those for whom a double just doesn't offer enough of a jolt.

Unleaded. Decaf—the opposite of HIGH-TEST.

Vanilla steamer. Steamed milk with vanilla syrup; mainly Starbucks.

venti. A twenty-ounce cup at Starbucks, unless you're ordering a cold drink, in which case it is a twenty-four-ounce cup, to make room for ice. Venti is Italian for "twenty."

virgin. Decaf, in some coffeehouses. Works well with certain calls—e.g., "tall virgin on wheels."

Wet. Drink made with steamed, not foamed, milk.

whipless. Hold the whipped cream.

why bother? See NO FUN.

with legs. A cup packed to go.

with room. With space left at the top of the cup either to add cream or prevent spills while driving 70 mph down the freeway with a latte between one's legs!

with wings. A cup with handles.

without. Without foam.

15

MEDIA AND PUBLISHING SLANG

Words from Those Who Fill the Printed Page, the Airwaves, and, Increasingly, Cyberspace

Midway Signs Limey Prof to Dope Yank Talk

—*Chicago Tribune*, October 18, 1924, headline announcing the arrival in the United States of Sir William Craigie to begin work on *A Dictionary of American English*

The first journalist I asked about the slang of her trade insisted that there was no such thing. A few hours later she called back and said that she was wrong, and proceeded to reel off a bunch of terms. Seems that she had gone to lunch with a group of coworkers who had discussed the premise that there was no journalism slang, and the terms began to come forth.

This underscores the unwritten first law of slang and jargon: people in traditional occupations are seldom aware that their speech is just as quirky and slangy as that of most others.

Most teenagers and rock musicians are aware of their slang, but that is because it is ever-changing and brash and they seek to set themselves apart. Journalistic slang is so ingrained in history and in the craft that it may appear invisible to its practitioners.

Above the fold. Of a newspaper story that is important enough to merit placement above the fold of a full-sized front page.

ACE. Assistant city editor of a newspaper.

activity. TV weather word that means nothing but sounds important. "We can expect some thunderstorm activity in the next seventy-two hours." Newspapers still refer to them as plain old thunderstorms.

actualities. A reborn radio term for "what is actually happening," a snippet of on-the-scene reporting or a view of an event unfolding before the camera's eye, which the producer hopes will transcend verisimilitude and achieve verity.

ad jack. Small ad promoting a feature of the newspaper, used as a filler, placed under a paid ad to "jack" it up, to fill a hole.

advancer. Story written in advance of an event such as a play or state fair.

agate. Tiny newspaper type—"Let's run the survivors' names in agate." Agate is actually a proper name for a type 5.5 points in size, but has come to mean all small type, including 6-point type, nonpareil.

A-matter. Newspaper copy that can be written in advance of a story or interview.

another pretty face. A derogation of local anchormen.

ARC. Advance reader's copy, a roughly bound galley preview a book—a pre-first edition—often with hundreds of errors. Increasing numbers of collectors look for ARCs.

art. Any kind of illustration for a book or article.

astonisher. An exclamation point. Proofreaders call it a bang, bing, yell, shout, hurrah, backbone, and slam.

AstroTurf letter. A letter to the editor produced by Internet-based letter-writing campaigns initiated by groups that provide the text or the talking points, post a letter on their Web site inviting supporters to copy it, and send it off to their local newspaper under their own name. The opposite of grassroots, newspapers generally do not publish these letters.

Balloon. A story promoted on page one over the name of the newspaper.

banner. 1. A headline running across more than half of the newspaper page at the top. 2. Ad or headline running across a Web page.

bastard. Last word in a paragraph that ends up at the top of the following column. Once prohibited in newspapers by eagle-eyed editors, they now pop up regularly thanks to computerized page layout. See ORPHAN, WIDOW.

bastard title. Title standing alone on a separate page preceding the text.

beat / run. When a reporter is detailed to cover a group of news sources, he is said to have a beat. "He covers the city hall beat."

bird feed. A transmission via satellite. "Feed" is a transmission; "bird" is a satellite, from the "Early Bird" designation of Telstar.

bite / snatch. A short piece of film that precedes the main broadcast, as in "Give us a bite of Carter."

bite a dog. Create a story.

blacksmith. A below-par reporter or writer, i.e., one who pounds out copy or news stories.

blad (acr). Book layout and design. It is used to describe a prepublication sample of the book used for marketing and publicity.

blargon. Blog + jargon.

blawg. Blend of blog + law; a blog about legal affairs.

bleg. Blend of blog + beg; blog that asks for help or money.

blog. Web sites that allow users to post their own messages or respond to others'. Similar to journal entries, they appear chronologically on a single site, which can make it easier to exchange messages than via e-mail or discussion boards. It is a shortening of the more formal term "web log."

blogger. A person who owns or writes for a web log.

blogosphere. The world of blogs; this term may be an invention of the media rather than a word actually used by bloggers.

blogroll. List of links in the sidebar of a blog, often linking to other blogs

blurker. One who reads many blogs but leaves no evidence of himself such as comments behind.

BOM. Business office must. A story generated by the business side of the paper, often to please an advertiser.

break. 1. Division before a new paragraph, in a newspaper. 2. Occurrence of a news event, as in a breaking story.

break page. The page on which a story is continued.

brite. An upbeat story that usually doesn't jump.

broadsheet. Describing full-format newspapers associated with serious journalism as

broadsheet. (*continued*)
contrasted to the smaller tabloid format. which has long been associated with sensationalism.

buckeye. Derogatory term for an ad visually unsophisticated or lacking in taste.

budget. Listing of the day's or week's stories scheduled for a given section of the newspaper.

bulldog. The first morning edition of an evening newspaper and the first night edition of a morning newspaper. Also, advance edition of the Sunday paper, which in some cities can be bought late on Saturday.

burn. To give away or compromise a source.

Carry. What a story can support in terms of headline size, art, and sidebars.

cartouche. Decorative panel or border enclosing a legend or other graphic; usually oval-shaped.

checkbook journalism. Controversial method of news gathering in which news sources are paid for telling their story to the press.

Chinese. Term describing the TV or motion picture camera technique of panning while moving away from the subject.

churn rate. The number of subscribers a newspaper must replace or resell each year. The average churn rate for metropolitan dailies is about 70 percent, meaning that if you were to maintain a readership of 500,000 you have to get 350,000 back each year.

circle wipe. Video effect in which the image first appears as a small dot in the center of the screen, then grows to full size while covering the preceding scene.

CNN effect. Name given to the negative effect on the economy caused by too many people staying home and watching a crisis unfold on cable television.

cold copy. In broadcasting, announcement read unrehearsed.

copy. Manuscript text to be set in type or broadcast.

cough button. Announcer's switch in a broadcast studio allowing him or her to cut off the mike momentarily.

country-club journalism. A cynical view of journalism, that real competition in the world of journalism is limited because of the many shared ideas, backgrounds, and associations of the owners.

crawl. In TV production, titles and credits that move up or down or left to right on the screen. Usually seen at the conclusion of a program. Also called title crawl, title roll, crawling title, creeper, and creeping title.

crib. Plagiarize.

crick. Critic.

cub. Novice reporter.

Dead. Copy is called dead after it has been set and proofread. Type that has been used and is not to be used again is dead.

delicious. Blargon for a social bookmarking service that allows users to share their bookmarked sites with others. To delicious (v.) someone in blargon is to add them to your delicious (adj.) bookmarks.

desk. A newspaper department, i.e., the city desk, sports desk, copy desk, etc.

deskman. A term loosely descriptive of both copy readers and editors.

Dewey Beats Truman. Any wrongheaded news story. An allusion to the *Chicago Tribune* banner headline of Election Day 1947, when the paper, sure that Thomas E. Dewey had beaten Truman, jumped the gun in printing page one. On Thursday, October 12, 1986, a day before the Dow fell 190.58, *USA Today* went to press with "Despite superstition, stocks do pretty well on Fridays the 13th."

dingbat. 1. In printing, any typographical ornament. Also, flubdub. 2. A printer's slang term for an ornament, or flourish, used to decorate the composition.

double truck. Two-page ad laid out like one page with no gutter down the middle between the pages.

drooling. Unrehearsed talk to fill out allotted program time.

dummy. A proposed or planned example of a new publication or layout. Something that can be used for advertiser or editorial comment or opinion.

dummy type. Type of a certain font and size laid to show how a designed space will look. It has no meaningful content.

Ear. In newspaper layout, the little box appearing at the top corners of page one, on either side of the paper's name on broadsheet papers. Ears can be used for such things as weather, sports scores, announcements of stories inside the paper, ads, or promotions. Boston's famous *Mid-Town Journal*, in the 1950s, a paper that cost five cents, had a classic ear: "Our paper is so valuable, people steal it."

early fringe. Period before prime time, in TV parlance.

eighty percenter. A *USA Today* term for a story done in advance and awaiting a news peg, as in "Let's do an eighty-percenter on the Rolling Stones and put a top on it when the tour opens."

Etaoin Shrdlu. A name invented by linotype operators, who used it as a temporary "slug," or story name. The letters were chosen by running a finger down the left two vertical rows of the linotype keyboard (don't look for it on your keyboard—linotypes have a special keyboard). Sometimes, however, Etaoin wasn't so temporary, and his name inadvertently made its way into print. Despite its passing from the scene around 1977, old-time newspaper people regarded old Etaoin as a person. James E. Farmer, who wrote about his demise for the *Indianapolis Star*, noted in a letter to the author, "I was the one to note his passing—due to printing technology—and to try to give him a decent burial."

evergreen. An article that could run at any time, such as "Will We Ever Find a Cure for the Common Cold?"

exclusive. Overworked term that usually means nothing more than "We think we were there first and nobody else was interested."

eyewitness news. Term used in television for news operations that hardly ever have reports from eyewitnesses.

Feed. Network lingo for live or taped segments sent from one location to another, by phone lines if audio, or by satellite if video.

fishback. Magazine term for a reference to an earlier article, as "First reported in the October 1996 issue, p. 22."

five W's and an H. Journalism's basic questions: who, what, when, where, why, and how?

flag. Newspaper term for nameplate or logotype appearing atop page one.

fluff. Soft inconsequential material posing as news—for instance, a local news story on a network entertainment show used by the station.

folo. A secondary article on the same subject as the main article.

frankenbite. Sound bite "improved" by selective editing.

friar. A spot of too little ink, resulting in faintness.

frontmatter. All material in a book or publication that precedes the actual text.

Gawk shows. Daytime talk television featuring the bizarre—*Jerry Springer* is the perfect example.

gimper. A human-interest "sob" story about an incurable disease, loss of life, or severe injury: "Let's do this gimper. It's got a wheelchair case in it."

go hunting. In TV, a command to the cameraman to use his judgment in finding a good camera shot.

gonzo. Form of journalism based on the notion that the best nonfiction is better than any fiction and that "with an expense account anything is possible."

graf. Paragraph, in the newsroom.

green book. Any book published on environmentally friendly paper.

grip. Studio stagehand, a.k.a. cable puller, dolly pusher, floor man, gopher.

gutter. In printing, two inner margins of facing pages of a publication. A.k.a. "back margins."

guys in pajamas. Bloggers as a group; the cyber-equivalent of calling newspaper people "ink-stained wretches."

Happy news. Television. Local news format which emphasizes the upbeat and features good-looking, personable, joking anchorpeople.

hard news. Newsworthy event that needs no embellishment or hyping—a midair collision, a presidential election.

harlequins. Heavyset decorative type elements.

hat trick. In hockey, scoring three goals in one game. In the media, appearing on *Meet the Press*, *Face the Nation*, and *This Week with George Stephanopoulos.*

head. Headline. The longer form is rarely used. The different-level headlines are identified by numbers. Subhead is short for subheadline. A good headline is called "a great head."

hed. Old-school rendering of "head" to avoid confusion with the word "head" in copy.

hickey. Printer's slang for ornament.

honeymoon. Period of at least a few months after an election during which Congress and the press refrain from criticizing the president, governor, mayor, or other elected official.

horse. To read proof without the aid of a copy holder.

hot corner. At *USA Today*, the lower right-hand corner of page one, which carries a hot, often offbeat item with a color picture.

HTK. Head (hed) to come; used during layout when a story headline was yet to be written. TK signals that these letters are not part of the text.

human interest / HI. The quality in a story that makes it good newspaper copy even though it contains no news. Such a story paints an interesting picture of life.

hype. Excessive promotion; used pejoratively. The double whammy comes when the term "so-called" is used with hype.

Inverted pyramid. At one time, the standard way of writing all news stories, with the FIVE W'S AND AN H in the lead sentence or paragraph. Today, more news stories are presented as feature stories.

island position. 1. An ad surrounded entirely by editorial material. 2. In broadcasting, a commercial with programming on either side.

Jimmy Olsen photo. A photo of great importance and moment, named for the photographer on the *Daily Planet*, Clark Kent/Superman's paper. The *Washington Post* (January 13, 1991): "Almost 23 years ago, a Jimmy Olsen photo from Vietnam played its own role in our history. It was a picture of the bleeding and dead Marines sprawled on a tank retreating from Hue in the Tet offensive of 1968. When then senator Eugene McCarthy saw the photo, he said later, he knew that 'that was the turning point.' The opposition to the war that formed around McCarthy's presidential candidacy drove Lyndon Johnson from the White House."

journalese. The particular code in which journalists slant or peg a story.

j-school. Journalism school.

jump, jump-over/run-over. The part of a story that is continued on a later page. Also used as a verb. "Jump the yarn over onto page seven."

jump-head. The headline that appears above a JUMP.

Kotex. Derogatory term for giveaway weekly with little or no hard news.

Lead / lede. The first line or paragraph of an article or broadcast news item intended to seduce the reader into reading the whole article. "The lead is to a newspaper writer what a home run is to a ballplayer—the sum total of his art, the feather in his cap, the pat on his back" (Thomas Collins, *Newsday*). All newspapers write the word "lede," to avoid confusion with "lead"—the metal—which in this day of electronic composition is still used in terms like "extra lead" for more space.

Allegedly Said What?

A Decoder for Deciphering the News

adult. Dirty, as applied to bookstores, magazines, and movies.

alleged. Word used by people in the news business to prevent lawsuits and drive the rest of us crazy, as in "The alleged murder took place when the victim was shot in the back."

arguably. Impossible to substantiate, as in "He is arguably the best National League left-handed pitcher ever from Connecticut with three consonants in his middle name."

bureaucrat. Term used to describe a public servant when the story is about red tape, excessive regulation, or anything else negative. The same person becomes a civil servant in a positive story.

by all accounts. Term used when details are sketchy and no direct quote can be found.

cannot be independently confirmed. Said of rumor that is so juicy that it cannot be left out of the story.

cannot be ruled out. Term used with the highest grade of pure space-filling speculation.

claimed responsibility. Confessed to a crime, often a heinous one involving more than one death. "A terrorist group today claimed responsibility for taking the lives of 54 innocent people."

craggy. Ugly (of faces).

crusty. Obnoxious.

densely wooded area. Where most badly decomposed bodies are found; target for small planes in trouble.

ebullient. Crazy; off the wall.

emotional. Required adjective to describe reunions and homecomings.

fragile shoreline. Where all oil spills wash up.

freewheeling. Chaotic; confused: "In a freewheeling interview the candidate lashed out against the high cost of dry cleaning, frequent-flier programs, diet colas, supermarket shopping carts with defective wheels, and the proliferation of nuclear weapons."

golf ball. Unit of measurement for size of hailstones.

guru. Authority who has not made an ass of himself in the last six months, or, in the case of financial gurus, the last two weeks.

hardworking. Plodding and dull.

he'll be missed. Words uttered by television anchors in announcing the death of someone he has never heard of prior to the broadcast.

indefatigable. A real pest; someone who calls the reporter at home during the World Series to complain about something.

irreverent. Swears and shouts a lot.

labor of love. Province of eccentrics and borderline crazies: "His campaign to save old outhouses is strictly a labor of love."

message. Three or four ads on television, as in "We now pause for this message."

militant. Fanatical. The veteran journalist Bob Skole says: "Term to describe terrorists that some pompous media use for fanatical murderers of innocent civilians, on the theory that one man's terrorist is another man's freedom fighter. To such media, there are no terrorists, only militants or activists. Except, as in the case of the BBC, when terrorists [the London underground bombers] blow up local civilians."

modest. Applied to most houses and many salaries. It has been observed that journalese has decreed that all houses be either modest or stately.

myth. A notion we have been pushing for years, but we are now ready to drop.

no explanation was offered. We forgot to ask; there was nobody there but the cleaning crew.

noted authority. Anyone whose name appears on the reporter's address book.

obscure. Fact not known to the reporter before working on the story. "She was charged under the provisions of an obscure law making it illegal to bury people alive."

observers. Cabbies, bartenders, bellhops, and camel tenders, to name a few. Not to be confused with thoughtful observers or veteran observers.

once thought to be. "What we erroneously reported last Wednesday."

only time will tell. Sign-off line beloved by television reporters covering summit conferences and unresolved municipal issues. "Will the town dump continue to be open on Sundays? Only time will tell."

outgoing. A happy drunk.

outspoken. Very noisy; abusive; a pain in the neck.

presumably. Codeword telling the reader that the writer is about to make a wild-assed guess.

reportedly. We have no idea if this is so, but it sounds good.

Rubenesque. Fat.

ruddy-faced. Drunk.

self-evident. "I just figured this out myself."

sources say. Person or persons sitting across from the reporter in the newsroom said it.

spry. Any senior citizen who is not in a wheelchair or coma (John Leo, "Journalese for the Lay Reader," *Time*).

summit. Any meeting attended by people above the clerical or secretarial level.

twisted wreckage. Place from which survivors emerge miraculously.

unexpected. We told you yesterday that this wouldn't happen.

visibly moved. Crying or sobbing on the part of a public official or VIP. Regular people merely cry.

well-manicured lawns. Used to describe neighborhoods with high-priced houses.

world class. Puffed-up term for someone or something that is good.

leg man. Old-fashioned reporter who makes his or her living from calf muscles.

lobster shift. Late-night or early-morning working shift, commonly from 11 P.M. to 7 A.M., 12 P.M. to 8 A.M., or 1 A.M. to 9 A.M. Used in both daily print and broadcast media. According to press lore, the term comes from the fact that people on this shift live their lives backwards, like lobsters, which sometimes move in reverse.

Man bites dog. Story that works because it is a reverse of the predictable—dog bites man.

masthead. Statement of name of paper, its ownership, place of publication, subscription rates, etc., usually on editorial page.

match. Story written to cover a story that was missed but that one of your competitors covered.

ME. Managing editor.

media circus. Event that, to the consternation of reporters with notepads, has drawn more than one television camera. For television people a media circus is any event that attracts one of the major network anchors and features an open bar and free buffet.

mike stew. Unwanted, extraneous background sound picked up by the microphone.

morgue. The place or room where dead copy is kept, where cuts of pictures are filed, a collection of references, clippings, etc. Increasingly electronic.

MOS. Man on the street, a target for quick impromptu interviews.

Mountweazel. A bogus entry purposely inserted in a dictionary or encyclopedia as a means of protecting copyright; now also refers to those individuals who spend countless hours hunting for these entries. It dates from the 1975 edition of the *New Columbia Encyclopedia* and its entry for Lillian Virginia Mountweazel, a photographer born in Bangs, Ohio, in 1942 only to die at the age of thirty-one in an explosion while working on assignment for *Combustibles* magazine.

MSM. Mainstream media, to bloggers and other outsiders.

Nipo (acr). Night police reporter, in the parlance of the newsroom.

noodling. Background music that plays as the titles and credits come on.

Obit. Obituary.

off its feet. Badly set type, said to be off its feet when not standing up straight and thus making only a partial impression.

off-lead. Newspaper's second most important news story of the day, traditionally appearing either in the top left corner or directly below the lead on the right.

off the record. An arrangement with the media not to use the information discussed—unless it is obtained elsewhere.

op-ed page. A page that features commentary, ideas, illustrations, etc., positioned opposite the editorial page.

orphan. A short line appearing at the bottom of a page, or a short word or part of a word appearing on a line by itself at the end of a paragraph. Compare WIDOW.

Pablum. Like the eponymous cereal, writing that is soft, bland, oversimplified.

pack journalism. The phenomenon of reporters chasing after the same stories, using the same or similar leads and, by consensus, deciding what will be the news of the day.

paint it red. Write a story as sensationally as possible.

peacock. To appear on televised news conferences. Washington reporters will often miss off-camera briefings at the White House but will appear at on-camera briefings to preen like a peacock.

peewee. Very short bit of news used to fill space in a newspaper; a filler.

pennysaver. Free paper filled with classified ads.

photo opportunity. Also photo op, or, as the congressional press gallery monitors advise, PO. This means generally that a politician, often with diplomat or other bigwig in tow, will emerge or briefly invite cameras into an otherwise closed meeting, for photos and TV pictures only, not for comments. However, reporters often pose or shout questions anyway. Once restricted to the political arena, athletes, actors, rock stars, and others are now offering photo ops.

pi. Still sometimes heard in reference to jumbled type. In Boston's old newspaper district, a small back street has the official name of Pi Alley. According to local lore, when a stick or case of type was dropped and the letters were a total mess, or "pied," printers would dump the type out a window and into the alley instead of going through the tedious job of sorting out the type and recasing it.

piece. An article.

piece of manpower. A network term for "star."

'plosive. Contraction of explosive, used for sounds sometimes produced in a mike when letters such as B or P are overstressed.

printhead. Print journalist, to TV journalists.

Reefer. In a newspaper, a front-page reference to inside contents. It is the word "refer" pronounced with emphasis on the first syllable.

rim. In a newsroom, the outer edge of the copy desk, around which copyreaders sit, as opposed to the "slot" or inner edge presided over by the executive in charge of that desk.

river. Undesirable streak of white space running down through several lines of type because certain words in each line happen to end at the same point, making the space between words line up vertically.

roser (acr). Radio on-scene report.

running story. One that goes on and on, such as the O. J. Simpson trial.

Scandal sheet. Tabloid specializing in trysts, love nests, people with their paws in cookie jars, gossip, weaknesses, and more.

scoop. Information obtained by or given to a single reporter, who thereby "scoops" his competitors.

screamer. 1. A BANNER headline, often exceptionally bold and large. 2. An exclamation point.

second coming head. The largest headline type that a given newspaper can use—an allusion to the notion that this would be the type size used for the Second Coming of Christ.

second-day lede. Newspaper story running on the day after an event such as an airline crash, which can no longer lead with "Plane Crashes" but needs something like "Pilot Error Suspected in Yesterday's Crash."

see you in the aim. See you in the morning. Aim = A.M.

segue. TV term for a transition (pron. segway).

shout. An exclamation point. Also called screamer or shriek.

silly season. Period when hard news is not easy to find, usually late in the summer, when Congress is adjourned, the president is on vacation, and the financial markets are in low gear. Also known as squirrel season—when the nuts are out.

skinback. Story that makes up for a missed "truth." Real-life example: newspaper runs series saying that local schools are slipping; the outcry is so great that it runs a story saying that other data suggest that the schools are, in fact, improving.

skybox. Box at top of a front page of a newspaper.

slop. Anything set in type that does not make it into the paper in a particular edition.

slot. The center of the various news departments (or DESKS) on a newspaper The man or woman in charge of a desk is said to be in the slot.

slug. An identifying mark or label for a story. It may be the briefest possible description, such as "hotel fire." Also called catchline, slugline, guide, and guideline. Originally, slugs were pieces of lead that held the type in place on printing presses.

snipe. In outdoor advertising, strip of copy added, often at an angle across a corner, over a poster ad, providing an additional message such as names or slogans.

sob sister / slobby. A reporter (usually a woman, but the term is not changed when it refers to a man) skilled in the art of painting a sympathetic picture of a figure prominent in the sensational news. She or he ghosts the stories you read that carry the byline of the most recent murderess.

sound bite. A short, pithy statement carried by the electronic media. It has become a valuable tool in election and reelection campaigns, as a good sound bite can serve as an unfiltered spot commercial. By contrast, statements that show up in the print media do not have the same effect and may, in fact, end up in an editorial opposing the candidate.

spec. Working without a guarantee that your story will be accepted and paid for.

spike. To kill a story. From the spike on the slot man's or city editor's desk, where the day's copy was pinned.

spin. Partisan interpretation, such as that given to the press by a politician's press secretary.

split, the. Local news, from the fact that many papers put local news in a separate section following national news.

splog. Blend of spam + blog: fake or misleading comments posted on a blog.

spot. Originally a speakeasy, now any bar. "There's a new spot across the street."

spot buy. In broadcast advertising, the purchase of available commercial time; less than full program sponsorship.

stand-upper. Television term for a report in which the correspondent stands, with microphone in hand, and delivers a segment of the news, with a prop like the U.S. Capitol in the background.

stet. "Let it stand." Used in print media to restore something that has been deleted. In electronic media the term stet is often spoken as a code for restoring something to the original.

stock footage. Motion picture footage or television videotape retained on file that can be used in more than one production. Also called stock shot, library footage, library shot, library material, archive material, or file film.

stringer. Reporter or broadcaster who generally works as a local-area freelance correspondent for a newspaper, newsmagazine, wire service, or broadcast organization. A stringer is paid by the assignment or for the stories he or she originates and gets accepted. A lucky stringer may be paid a regular retainer.

subhead. The small headlines that appear in the body of the story and below the main headline.

sudoku. Number puzzle that originated in Japan, which has become a staple of daily newspapers along with the crossword puzzle.

swing man. The copyreader who relieves the copy chief.

Tab. A tabloid newspaper.

take. In print journalism, a page, as in "Give me a couple of takes on the judge's record with murder trials."

talking heads. Politicians or analysts talking on television—a sure channel-switcher for viewers, TV producers feel. On February 21, 1992, President George H. W. Bush, under fire for a slumping economy, said, "Let's not listen to the gloom and doom from all those intense talking heads who are happy only when they say something negative."

tally light. Red TV camera light indicating when the camera is on. Also, camera cue light or cue light.

thirty. The end. In the old days, 30 was written at the end of a reporter's copy. The *Bulletin of the National Press Club* still lists the names of members who have died under the number 30, but this slang expression is very rarely used in speaking.

thumbsucker. An article speculating on the significance of a news event. Slate.com goes further, calling it a "derogatory reference to [a] story that ponders a bit of news and doesn't introduce any."

tickler. File system where notices of upcoming news events are stored.

TK. "To come," in journalese; used for material not yet in place. "The piece is all done, but his age is still TK."

tokem. TK, as pronounced in many newsrooms: "Joe is calling in his tokem on the fire story."

toy department. Media sports departments.

trained seal. A magazine staff writer who works on salary.

tube buster. A newspaper story so hot that it will burst the plaster tube wrapper that so many papers come in today.

Update. Local TV news term for a promotional line such as "Find out at 11:00—new hope for the dead" or "Verdict at 10:00."

Visibility. What politicians need to get elected—speeches and positions that get them exposure in the media.

vlog. A video blog—a blog used to display various forms of video.

voice-over. Spoken commentary accompanying a film being shown.

voice wrap. The use of a newscaster's voice to introduce and to close a piece of film or tape.

voicer. Radio broadcast for a report read without embellishment.

Walkup. A story that runs the day before or the day of a major scheduled news event, for example, the Opening Ceremonies of the Olympic Games.

Wally Journal. The *Wall Street Journal*.

weekender. Newspaper story scheduled to run on an upcoming weekend, usually Sunday.

whiparound. In broadcast news, a technique in which an anchorman introduces the three successive reporters in one long breath, as the cameras cut from one to the other.

widow. Printer's term for a short, paragraph-ending line appearing at the top of a page or column. Compare ORPHAN.

wipe. In television production, a transitional technique between shots using a boundary electronically created to separate images as one is replaced by another via a moving line, an expanding or contracting circle, or another of several hundred geometric wipe patterns.

wire. Newspaper story that comes in from a wire news service such as the Associated Press. The term is still very much in use, even though all the telegraph wire has been replaced by transmissions via satellite, microwave, and the phone line.

wood. Filler material in early editions of a newspaper.

write around a hole. To write a newspaper story around a key piece of information that is not yet available.

writethru. Wire-service term for a story that has been completely rewritten so that the original should be discarded.

16

MEDICAL AND EMERGENCY ROOM SLANG

Words You Don't Want to Hear from Your Hospital Bed

The range and number of these [slang] terms suggests the extensiveness of the verbal aggression towards patients among medical personnel. These terms are all used "backstage," never in the presence of a conscious patient.

—Lois Monteiro, "Not Sticks and Stones, but Names," *Maledicta*, Summer 1980

There are three medical languages. The first is the highly technical, Latinate tongue that has been called "medicant." In this scientific tongue a headache is cephalalgia, sweating is diaphoresis, vomiting is emesis, and the inability to tell time is horologagnosia.

There also is a stuffy, bureaucratic jargon: measurements and characteristics become parameters, doctors and nurses become generic providers, and patients are turned into consumers. Much of this terminology has been imposed by the insurance industry. The folks who insure your health like you to cozy up to terms like "payer," "vendor," and "third-party providers." Former Surgeon General C. Everett Koop has said, "I'm still old-fashioned enough to think of myself as a physician, not a provider. And I think of my patients as patients, not consumers." But some insurers have abandoned "provider" for the even more distant HCP—health-care provider.

The third medical language is blunt, irreverent, and not meant for public consumption. It is pure slang—the slang of doctors, nurses, and hospital technicians, especially those in the emergency room (ER) in North America and the accidents and emergency departments (A&E) in the United Kingdom. This slang is lusty and irreverent—most likely partially a defense that helps medical personnel deal with the constant exposure to medical emergencies and physical suffering.

Acute lead poisoning. Gunshot wound.

acute MI. Acute monetary insufficiency.

AGA. Acute gravity attack—patient fainted or fell over.

AGMI. Ain't gonna make It. Will not survive.

albatross. Chronically ill patient who will remain with a doctor until one of them expires.

ALC. *A la casa*—send the patient home.

angel lust. Male cadaver with an erection.

ART. Assuming room temperature—dead.

ATS. Acute thespian syndrome—faking illness.

ax. A surgeon.

Aztec two-step. Diarrhea acquired in Latin America.

Baby catcher. Obstetrician.

bag. To administer oxygen through a mask.

banana. Patient with jaundice.

banana bag. Intravenous solution containing a liquid multivitamin that gives the fluid a bright yellow color. Used in undernourished patients.

BBA. Baby born in ambulance (U.K.).

beached whale. Obese patient.

beans. Kidneys.

big C. Cancer.

blade. Surgeon.

bloods. Blood tests.

blown mind. Gunshot wound to the head.

blue blower. Patient with severe lung disease.

blue pipe. Vein.

bobbing for apples. Using the finger to unclog a severely constipated patient.

boogie. A tumor.

bordeau. Urine with blood in it.

bounceback. Patient who keeps returning to the hospital.

box. To die.

brat diet (acr). Bananas, rice, apple sauce, and toast—a common prescription for infant diarrhea.

bright lights / bright lights and cold steel. Surgery.

bronk. To undergo bronchoscopy.

brothel sprouts. Genital warts.

bubar (acr). Buggered up beyond repair, an acronym reserved for victims of surgical incompetence (U.K.).

buff up. To ready a patient for release.

bug juice. Antibiotics.

bugs in the rug. Pubic lice.

bull in the ring. A blocked large intestine.

bury the hatchet. Accidentally leaving a surgical instrument inside a patient.

C & T Ward. Place where comatose patients are placed in a hospital—it stands for "cabbages and turnips."

cabge (acr). A coronary artery bypass operation (pron. "cabbage").

callbellectomy. The desire to surgically remove overused call bell from patient's hand.

Captain Kangaroo. Chairman of a pediatrics department.

cath. To catheterize.

celestial transfer. Passage from life to death.

chrome-induced ischemia. Describing a patient who develops inexplicable chest pains when arrested and handcuffed to a wheelchair.

circling the drain. Said of patients who are getting sicker and are close to death.

code azure. Message to other medical professionals to do nothing extraordinary to save a very ill patient who will die shortly no matter what is done. It is the opposite of the official code blue, which mobilizes the staff in an effort to save someone.

creepers. The elderly—a reference to walkers and wheelchairs.

crispy critter. A patient with severe burns.

crock. 1. Complainer. 2. Hypochondriac.

cut and paste. To open a patient, discover that there is no hope, and immediately sew him up. Well, almost immediately. Sometimes young surgeons practice surgical techniques for a while first.

Deep fry. Cobalt therapy.

Delhi belly. Intestinal upset acquired overseas.

departure lounge. Geriatric ward.

diagnose and adios. Said of treatment that is long on analysis but short on treatment.

digging for worms. Varicose vein surgery.

dirtball. Patient who enters the emergency room filthy and smelling badly.

dishwasher. Sterilization machine.

ditzel. Small, unidentified mass seen on an X-ray.

doc. Doctor, to a doctor. For instance, firms that help M.D.'s with the financial side of their practice are known as "doc watchers."

doc-in-the-box. Small medical facility, usually in a shopping center, where one can go for treatment without an appointment.

domino transplant. A rare organ transplant in which a person is given a new heart and lungs.

DNR. Do not resuscitate: order on patient's chart to tell medical staff that the patient is terminally ill and does not want anyone to try to bring him back to life if he dies. The British eqivalent is DNA, for "do not attend."

door handle. British medical slang for a patient who recalls an additional symptom or malady as he is walking out the door.

DOW. See MI.

dowager's hump. Manifestation of osteoporosis.

Dr. Feelgood. A doctor who is indiscriminate about prescribing drugs.

drooler. A catatonic patient.

DSB. Drug-seeking behavior, referring to patients with bogus complaints seeking narcotics.

duck. Portable urinal for bedridden male hospital patients. Before these were made of plastic, they were known as glass or porcelain ducks.

dump. Patient that nobody seems to want.

dwelly belly. Slang for Hispanic patients with abdominal pain, from the Spanish word for pain, *duele*.

dwindles, the. Advancing old age.

Eating in. Intravenous feeding, as in "Two-oh-four-B will be eating in tonight."

eating the bill. Providing care for indigent patients who are not covered by insurance, as in "We ate the bill on that guy."

ECU. Eternal care unit, as in "Gone to the ECU"—dead. A play on ICU intensive-care unit.

ER. Emergency room.

Fanger. Oral surgeon.

fascinoma. A "fascinating" tumor; any interesting or amusing malignancy.

finger wave. Rectal exam.

flatline. To die.

flea. Internists, so called because they are the last ones to leave a deceased person, the last ones to admit that a patient who has suffered a cardiac arrest is actually dead; they keep trying when all hope for survival is long since past.

FLK. Funny-looking kid. Used in the newborn nursery.

FLP. Parents of an FLK.

fluids and electrolytes. Consumed at happy hour.

fluorescent light therapy. Treatment for a patient who offends the triage nurse and is made to sit for long periods in the harsh light of the waiting room.

fluttering-eye syndrome. Patient faking unconsciousness.

four F-er. A gallbladder patient: "fat, forty-ish, flatulent female."

frequent flier. ER repeat customer.

Freud squad. Psychiatrists.

full moon. Full ER or overcrowded waiting room.

Gag clause. Managed-care policy often interpreted as forbidding doctors to tell patients about treatment options for which the plan will not pay.

gasser / gas passer. Anesthetist.

gatekeeper. HMO parlance for an internist or family-practice doctor whose role is to keep costs low by allowing only a certain number of patients to go to specialists.

GGF1. Granny (or grandpa's) got a fever and a basic set ("1") of tests should be done. This term was used in the first episode of the television show *ER* in 1994 in that immortal set of lines: "Give him D-5. N.S. cc's. Do a head CT. Non-contrast. Get Psych Services down here for a consult. Do a GGF1."

GLM. Good-looking mother. Used in pediatrics especially to describe a nice-looking parent.

GOK. "God only knows" what disease the patient has.

gomer. A complaining, irksome patient. Medical lore holds that this began as an acronym for "get out of my emergency room." However, William Safire has suggested that it may have come from the Scottish dialect word "gomeral," for simpleton. In a *New York Times* (May 13, 2001) article about "Hospital Lingo," Sheilendr Khipple wrote that the word "is now sharply discouraged due to a new sensitivity to image of doctors in reaction to the uncaring image presented by HMOs."

gone camping. Of a patient in an oxygen tent.

gone to . . . Hospital euphemism for dying. A staff member at a Virginia hospital reports that it is "gone to Chicago" where he works.

goober. Tumor.

goombah. Large unidentified mass seen on an X-ray.

gorked. Anesthetized.

GPO. Good for parts only.

grapes. Hemorrhoids.

gravity-assisted concrete poisoning. Said of one who jumped or fell from height.

GSW. Gunshot wound, as per TV's *ER*. Alan Baragona of the American Dialect Society has questioned using a five-syllable abbreviation for the three-syllable term, although it is quicker to write in a report.

Hammer. Local anesthetic.

handbag positive. Elderly confused female patient lying on hospital bed clutching handbag.

head. A brain-injury patient. Usage: "I've got a head I've got to deal with."

head whack. Head injury.

hey docs. Alcoholics handcuffed to wheelchairs in big-city medical wards who, at the sight of a white coat, bleat out in chorus, "Hey, doc!"

HIBGIA. Had it before, got it again.

hit and run. The act of operating quickly so as not to be late for another engagement.

hits. New patients.

HIVI. Husband is village idiot.

hole in one. A gunshot wound in the mouth or other bodily oriface.

hospitalitis. Malaise of patients who have been in the hospital too long.

HSP. Heart-sink patient—one who causes the doctor's heart to sink the moment the patient walks in the door (U.K.).

Ivy pole. Rack from which intravenous equipment hangs.

Jennings effect. Phenomenon of large numbers of people quitting smoking or attempting to quit after a celebrated person

Jennings effect. (*continued*) dies because of a pack-a-day cigarette habit. Named for ABC's Peter Jennings, who died in 2005. Name will change when the next tobacco-related death occurs.

Journal of Anecdotal Medicine. Oft-cited imaginary source of medical wisdom.

jungle rot. Fungus infection of the crotch area.

Knife-happy. An overly enthusiastic surgeon.

Leeches. Staff whose job involves taking blood.

liver rounds. A staff party, so called because of liver-damaging alcohol.

LOLFOF. Little old lady found on floor. Used in emergency medicine especially.

loop the loop. Flamboyant surgical rearrangement of the intestines.

loose change. A dangling limb in need of amputation.

lunger. Patient with obvious lung disease.

M&Ms. Morbidity and mortality conferences.

Melody Hill anemia. Drunk on cheap wine. The name of any cheap wine can be used.

MGM syndrome. Faker putting on a good show.

MI. Normally this stands for myocardial infarction, but a Florida doctor explains that some acute MIs are not admitted to hospitals as "hospitals use MI to mean monetary insufficiency." An alternative to MI is DOW, which stands for "deficiency of wallet."

molar masher. Dentist.

Montezuma's revenge. Diarrhea, especially when touched off by foreign food or a trip to a less-developed nation such as Mexico.

Mount Saint Elsewhere. Inferior hospital for welfare charges and the terminally ill.

Neuron. neurologist.

not even in the ball game. Confused senile patient.

O sign. Comatose patient with mouth open wide. See also Q SIGN.

OBS. Obvious bullshit.

OFIG. One foot in the grave.

oids / roids. Steroids.

old-timer's disease. Alzheimer's disease.

OPD. Obnoxious personality disorder.

organ recital. A hypochondriac's medical history.

PAFO. Pissed and fell over (U.K.).

pan. To pass out bedpans.

parentectomy. To remove parents from a situation to improve child's condition.

pecker checker. Urologist.

PEP. Pharmaceutically enhanced personality. One who is either stoned or medicated.

percussive maintenance. The sharp blow that cures faulty medical equipment.

pet arm. A useless appendage resulting from paralysis.

phlebitis. Flea bites.

pink cheater. Latex finger cover used in gynecological and proctological examinations.

pink puffer. Patient breathing rapidly due to lung disease.

pit, the. The emergency room.

player. Same as GOMER.

plumber. Urologist.

PMSB. Poor miserable son of a bitch, as explained by a neurologist: "This PMSB comes in complaining of a thousand things, and rightfully so!"

PPPP. Particularly piss-poor protoplasm—a patient in bad shape.

preemie. Premature infant.

psychoceramic. Same as a CROCK.

Q sign. An O SIGN with the patient's tongue hanging out—a worse prognosis.

quackpractor. Chiropractor.

quad. Quadraplegic.

Rear admiral. Proctologist Reinhold Aman, the editor of *Maledicta*, has noted that this term was given a boost when President Carter was operated on for hemorrhoids by Dr. William Lukash, who held the rank of rear admiral.

red pipe. Artery.

reeker. Smelly patient.

rheumaholiday. Rheumatology.

road map. Injuries incurred by going through a car windshield face-first.

roasted goober. A tumor after intensive cobalt treatment.

rock. A stable patient.

rocket room, the. Unit where there are many deaths (transfers to heaven).

rooters. Indigents and hangers-on who gather in big-city emergency rooms in order to be entertained by legitimate cases.

rule of five. When more than five of the patient's orifices are obscured by tubing, the patient has no chance of survival.

Scope. To undergo endoscopy.

scratch and sniff. A gynecological examination.

shadow gazer. Radiologist.

short-order chefs. Morgue workers.

shotgunning. Ordering a vast battery of tests in the hope that at least one of them will provide some kind of a clue as to what is actually wrong.

shrink. Therapist or psychologist. Short for the earlier "head shrinker."

SICU. Surgical intensive-care unit (pron. "sick-U").

sieve. Intern or resident who will admit persons to his or her sevice for the most minor illnesses. Contrast with WALL.

silver goose / silver stallion. Proctoscope.

slasher. General surgeons.

smilin' mighty Jesus. Spinal meningitis.

snake. To run a fiber-optic scope into a patient's bodily orifice.

SOB. Short of breath, in ER-speak.

soufflé. A patient who has jumped or fallen from a high place, that is, a sidewalk soufflé.

speed bump. Hemorrhoid.

spostas. Those who are "sposta" be somewhere else, like court, and want a written excuse from a medical authority for not being there.

spots and dots. Traditional set of childhood diseases—measles, mumps, and chickenpox.

squash. Brain.

stamp. Skin graft.

stat. Short for *statinum*, Latin for "immediately." A key word in all television medical dramas.

stirrups. Apparatus used when women get gynecological exams or are delivering a baby.

sturgeon. Surgeon.

Tail-light sign. Said when a patient (usually elderly) is dropped off at an emergency room by relatives or friends who drive off, forcing the patient to be admitted to the hospital.

TATT. Tired all the time (U.K.).

TEC. Dead; short for "transfer to eternal care."

TEETH. Tried everything else, try homeopathy (U.K.).

tern. Intern.

Thorazine shuffle. The slow, lumbering gait of psychiatric patients who have been given large doses of phenothiazines.

3H enema. An enema that is "high, hot, and a hell of a lot." Given to selected patients who have given the staff a hard time.

three P's. Term some doctors use to refer to the pill, permissiveness, and promiscuity.

three-toed sloth. Patient with diminished capacities, usually from long-term alcoholism.

TMB. Too many birthdays—person dying of old age.

tooth-to-tattoo ratio. Visual determination of basic intelligence. A positive ratio (more teeth than tattoos) is generally better.

tough stick. A person whose veins are hard to find when blood needs to be drawn.

train wreck. A patient with several serious medical problems.

TSS. Toxic sock syndrome, of a patient with low hygienic standards.

tube. Used as a verb, as in "I'm going to tube the patient in 419." Means to insert a breathing tube into the patient's airway to help him or her breathe.

tubed. Died, as in going down the tubes.

turf. To move a patient, as in "Turf that woman in the ER to obstetrics."

TWA. Third world assassins. Slang for the allegedly poor medical care delivered by physicians who went to medical school in foreign countries.

twitch. Hypochondriac.

UBI. Unexplained beer injury.

VBT. Very bad thing.

vedgy. A patient requiring intensive care, incapable of movement.

vegetable garden. Ward for those in comas.

Velcro. Family or friends who accompany patients everywhere.

V-fib. Paramedic lingo for ventricular fibrillation. It means that the heart has stopped pumping and is merely quivering in what might be called death throes.

VIP. Very intoxicated person.

vitals. Pulse, blood pressure, and other vital signs.

WADAO. Weak and dizzy all over.

wall. Intern or resident adept at not admitting patients to his or her sevice. Compare with SIEVE.

wallet biopsy. Finding out how much care a paying patient can afford. If a patient fails a wallet biopsy in a private hospital, he gets transferred to a public hospital. Defined by David Olive, author of *Business Babble: A Cynic's Dictionary of Business Jargon*, as "a preoperative procedure performed in private hospitals to determine the likely duration of a patient's stay."

ward X. The morgue.

whale. Grossly obese patient.

wig picker. Same as SHRINK.

witch doctor. Specialist in internal medicine.

WNL. Will not listen. Said of the patient who will not take medical advice.

WWI. Walking while intoxicated; play on DWI, driving while intoxicated.

YOYO. You are on your own.

Zap. To administer electroshock therapy.

zebra. An outlandish or unlikely diagnosis. According to Sheilendr Khipple, "A medical school aphorism holds, 'If you're walking down Fifth Avenue and you hear hoofbeats, you think of horses, not zebras,' meaning that a common diagnosis is more likely to be correct than a rare one" ("Hospital Lingo: What's in a Bed Plug?," *New York Times*, May 13, 2001).

zorro belly. Patient with many scars on stomach indicating earlier surgery.

MENTAL STATES 17

Cutting with a Dull Tool, Too Much Cuckoo in the Clock, and Other Fulldeckisms and Marbles Metaphors

But the first time I heard that idea, it was from the eminent prosecutor, Mister Shanley, and when Richard Shanley says something, and it sounds good to me, I start wondering if maybe all of a sudden I'm not traveling with a full sea bag anymore.

—George V. Higgins,
The Judgment of Deke Hunter

I have frequently remarked that the Americans, who generally treat business in clear, plain language, devoid of all ornament, and so extremely simple as to be often coarse, are apt to become inflated as soon as they attempt a more poetical diction. They then vent their pomposity from one end of a harangue to the other, and to hear them lavish imagery on every occasion, one might fancy that they never spoke of anything with simplicity.

—Alexis de Tocqueville, *Democracy in America*

Mental illness, oddness, and offness is a fertile area for slang. There are scores of slang terms for various states of mental aberration. Without leaving the D's, we have daffy, dippy, dotty, dingy, and dingaling, and the B's include bananas, beany, birdy, buggy, bugs, bughouse, and bonkers.

This lexicon can be cruel, yet, paradoxically, it is kinder than the proper language of psychiatry. To be branded as loopy or wifty seems less dire than being labeled neurotic. In fact, the trend seems to be toward metaphoric description as opposed to a single word. There is nothing new about this. People have had bats in their belfries, snakes in their heads, and bees in their bonnets for generations, but what is new is that we seem to be in the midst of a bumper harvest of metaphors for being a bit "off." It is by far the biggest and fastest-growing metaphoric harvest of recent decades, and there are vast collections of these terms floating around. A gigantic collection on the Internet carries the name "fulldeckisms," from the saying "not playing with a full deck."

If slang for mental states started out as a means of folk expression, it has crept up the social scale to the point where a columnist in the *Times Literary Supplement* reporting on eccentric behavior among executives at HarperCollins publishers "made it sound as if the publishers of the Bible had gone one horseman short of an apocalypse." In his column in the *Toronto Globe and Mail*, Robert Fulford talks of "rococo" examples along the lines of "He's a flying buttress short of a cathedral." Fulford, by the way, calls them "marbles metaphors," from the classic "missing a few . . ." or "lost his marbles."

The expressions that follow have certainly been influenced by what have been termed "Westernisms," or "ruralisms," folksy bucolic similes and metaphors along the lines of "dumber than a barrel of hair." Considerable creative powers have been expended on coming up with a new way of saying that a person, well, . . .

A

Has an **apartment** to let.

Has an unfurnished **attic**.

B

Only **baba** and no **lu**.

Got **beamed up** and forgot to come down.

No **beans** in his pod / No **beans** in her pot.

Doesn't know how many **beans** make five.

Belt doesn't go through all the loops.

Gone around the **bend**.

Too many **birds** on his / her antenna.

The **blender** doesn't go past "mix."

All **booster,** no payload.

Swallowed the **bottle** instead of the pills.

Bow is unstrung.

No room at the **brain inn**.

Brain is stuck in first gear.

Brain cells never divided.

Her **bread** ain't done.

Two **bricks** shy of a load.

A **bubble** off of plumb (or out of level).

He's not the brightest **bulb** on the Christmas tree.

Out where the **buses** don't run.

Missing a few **buttons**.

C

Not **cable**-ready.

Car isn't hitting on all cylinders.

No **cheese** on the taco.

Gone **crackers**.

A few **chips** short of a bag of Wavy Lays.

The **computer's** on but there's no prompt.

Not **computing** with a full disc.

No **comics** with the bubblegum.

Her **cornbread** ain't cooked in the middle.

A few **croutons** short of a Caesar salad.

A **cup and saucer** short of a full place setting.

All the **cups** aren't stacked in the cupboard.

D

The **date** on his/her carton has expired.

Dealing with a **dead battery**.

A **dial tone**.

Missing a few dots on her **dice**.

His **dipstick** doesn't quite touch the oil.

Temporarily **disconnected**.

Left his **dresser drawers** open.

Doesn't have all her **dogs** on one leash.

One **doughnut** shy of a dozen.

Dow-Jones average is off a few points.

Cutting with a **dull tool**.

E

Over the **edge**.

Elevator doesn't run to the top floor.

Running on **empty**.

empty suit. Person of authority lacking authority and /or intelligence and/or conviction. From the *Washington Times* of November 13, 1990: "If President Bush doesn't identify himself with something, he'll be written off as an empty suit." Writing in the *Washington Post*, Mark Shields wrote on the eve of the 1994 election: "To call Rep. Michael Huffington, the Republican state nominee [California], an empty suit is to libel the nation's garment industry."

Enchiladas have lost their chili.

Coming in on three **engines**.

Not much to show for four billion years of **evolution.**

F

Too much **fee-fye** and not enough **fo-fum**.

About due for a **fill-up**.

No **fish** on the hook.

Fishing without bait.

No batteries in the **flashlight**.

A **flying buttress** short of a cathedral.

All **foam** and no beer.

Ready to join the **frogs** on the lily pad.

A few **fries** short of a Happy Meal.

Not playing with a **full deck**.

G

Missed the last **gas station** on the highway of life.

From the shallow end of the **gene pool**.

Goalie for the dart team.

No **grain** in the silo.

Has a **guest** in the attic.

H

One tree short of a **hammock**.

Her **hard drive** is full.

Her **hat** is on too tight.

Has had his **hat** blocked with him still in it.

Driving with one **headlight.**

Has lived too long at the **high-tension wire cafe**.

Off her **hinges**.

Playing **hockey** with a warped puck.

No one **home** in the dome.

One **horseman** short of an apocalypse.

Nice **house**, nobody home.

One **hushpuppy** short of a barbecue platter.

Hunting in an empty forest.

I

Two **ice cubes** short of a full tray.

IQ of a salad bar.

IQ of an ice cube.

IQ of three below houseplant.

J

His **jogging trail** doesn't go all the way around the lake.

No **juice** in the cable.

K

He's a few **kilocycles** short of his assigned frequency.

Not **knitting** with both needles.

Has a **knot** in his kite string.

L

No **lead** in the pencil.

A **leak** in the think tank.

No **leaves** in the tea.

No **lemon** in his lemonade.

The **lights** are on but there's nobody home.

A few **loons** in the bin.

Member of the **loony** book club.

A **low-watt bulb**.

Lunch box (presumably a play on "out to lunch").

M

Missing a few **marbles**.

Couldn't find his way through a **maze** even if the rats helped him.

Hangin' out with **Mr. Peanut**.

Microdeckia: micro/small + deck of cards.

Too much **motor** for her axle.

Too much **multi** in the personality.

Puts **mustard** on her fruit loops.

N

Nutty as a fruitcake.

Nuttier than a squirrel's breakfast.

O

Has only one **oar** in the water.

She has both **oars** in the water, but they're on the same side of the boat.

Overdrawn at the memory bank.

P

A mind like **Paul Revere's** ride—a little light in the belfry.

No **paint** on the canvas.

Cuts out **paper dolls**.

A few **peas** short of a casserole.

Plays **piano** in a marching band.

Half the **pickets** are missing from his fence.

A few **pickles** short of a jar.

Somebody blew out her **pilot light**.

Somebody pulled his **plug**.

A dim **porch** light.

A thruppence short of a **pound**.

Puppies not woofin'.

Q

Running two **quarts** low.

R

Serves the **racquet** instead of the ball.

His **receiver** is off the hook.

Driving in **reverse**.

His **Rice Krispies** don't snap, crackle, and pop.

Off his **rocker**.

Not present at **roll call**.

Has a **room** for rent.

She forgot to put her **sail** up.

Two **sandwiches** short of a picnic.

A **screw** loose.

In one too many **scrimmages** without a helmet.

Ain't traveling with a full **sea bag**.

Few **shingles** missing from his roof.

Has all of his **shit** in one sock.

Her **skylight** leaks a bit.

One **slice** short of a loaf.

His **Slinky's** kinked.

Living in an incompatible **solar system**.

Abducted once too often by **space aliens**.

Splinters in the windmills of his mind.

On the highway of life, she is a **stalled vehicle**.

No **strings** in the racquet.

No **students** in the class.

He fell out of the **stupid** tree and hit every branch on the way down.

T

One **taco** short of a combination platter.

On her **team**, they're one player short.

A few **termites** in the attic.

He has a few loose **tiles**.

Driving with her **top** down.

The gates are down, the lights are flashing, but the **train** isn't coming.

Is out of his **tree**.

On a **trip** with no luggage.

No **turning ballerina** in the jewelry box.

Runs a **typewriter** without a ribbon.

U

Off in the **upper story**.

Born **upstairs** over a vacant lot.

Her **upstairs** ain't fully furnished.

V

Volunteers as a bowling ball.

W

Two **wafers** short of communion.

All **wax** and no wick.

Running with one **wheel** in the sand.

No **wheels** on the golf cart.

The **wheel** is running but the hamster is dead.

No **wick** in the candle.

No **wind** in the windmill.

Not **wrapped** too tightly.

Y

Too much **yardage** between the goalposts.

No **yoke** in the egg.

18

NAUTICAL SLANG

At Sea with the Language

Every seaman, whether naval, Merchant Marine, or yachtsman, knows that when he steps aboard a vessel he is stepping into another existence and wishes it to remain that way.

—Gershom Bradford, *The Mariner's Dictionary*, quoted in the *St. Petersburg Times*, December 9, 1984

What distinguishes nautical slang from other slang is that so much of what was once specialized slang and jargon is now standard English. From stem to stern, port and starboard, dozens of terms are now and have long been found in conventional dictionaries along with the notation "naut."

Much of this slang and terminology came ashore long ago. I spent three years in the U.S. Navy in the early 1960s, where I was well indoctrinated in the slang of the sea. Imagine my surprise when I came out of the Navy and found nautical images in a brokerage house where I went to work for a year. There people routinely jumped ship, produced boilerplate, and went full speed ahead . . . trying, of course, not to go overboard in the process.

This is not to say that this traditional slang is safe from the onslaughts of verbal reform and political correctness. During the 1970s the United States Navy attempted to purge itself of its traditional slang. The shipboard mess was officially renamed enlisted dining facilities, the galley of yore became a kitchen, and the brig became a correctional facility. In deference to the genderless society, the Department of Defense ruled in 1979 that a ship would be it and not she and that it would be "crewed" and not "manned."

In 1984, a good year to lash out against such things, then secretary of the navy John F. Lehman, Jr., condemned "the bureaucratization of naval language" and ordered all naval facilities to return to traditional terms by January 1, 1985. Halls were once again passageways and toilets, heads.

Here is a selection of today's un-"reformed" nautical slang, whether it be from the U.S. Navy, the World Cup, or the works of Tom Clancy.

Admin suite. In a foreign port, a hotel room rented for onshore partying.

air boss. Head of the aviation department on an aircraft carrier.

airdale / airedale. Any person in the air (aviation) department aboard an aircraft carrier. If this was once derogatory—an Airedale is a dog, after all—it is used with some pride by those in the air wing of a carrier.

all hands. The entire crew of a ship.

anchor. Lowest-ranking man or woman in the class at the U.S. Naval Academy.

ash can. Depth charge.

Back-seater. F-14 radar-intercept officer, who sits behind the pilot, in naval aviation.

basement. Hangar deck of an aircraft carrier where the aircraft are kept when not in service.

battlewagon. Battleship.

BB-stacker. Ordnanceman, in the Navy.

beach, the. Ashore, whether it be Cannes or Norfolk.

before the mast. The enlisted sailors whose quarters are traditionally in the forecastle, near the bow of a ship.

belay that. Stop that.

bellhop. Sailor's term for a Marine, especially one in dress uniform. Sometimes stated as "seagoing bellhop."

big chow. Meal served before a big day, in the Navy, for instance, before a major aircraft carrier attack.

bilge. The proper meaning of this term is that portion of a ship below the water line. The slang use of this term refers to bad food or bad information. At the U.S. Naval Academy it means to flunk out. Bill O'Neill reports that there is a gate at the Naval Academy known as the bilge gate, which is "one small gate that lads being bounced out of the academy pass through; hence no middie will walk out that gate, though civilians use it. A middie will step into the roadway and stroll out the big gate, instead."

bilge rat. Boiler technician or other belowdecks sailor.

bilge water. Soup.

bird farm. Aircraft carrier.

bird hatching. Fathering more than one child; term coined by Admiral Hyman Rickover.

bitter end. The end of an anchor line, which goes around the bitt.

black shoe. A member of the regular seagoing navy, as opposed to naval aviators, who are allowed to wear brown shoes.

blue shirt. Aircraft handler on an aircraft carrier.

blue thunder. Expensive speedboats used by government drug agents to intercept drug smugglers' boats.

blue-water ops. Aircraft carrier flight operations beyond the reach of land.

blue-water sailor. Boater who heads for the open seas, as opposed to those who stay close to the coast.

bluejacket. Sailor.

boat candy. Women who adorn boats, often in scanty attire.

boat nanny. A person hired or otherwise compensated (in beer, for instance) for cleaning someone else's craft.

boat pox. Gelcoat blisters on Fiberglas boats.

boomer. 1. Submarine with nuclear missiles. 2. Member of the nuclear-powered Navy.

boondocker. Basic U.S. Navy boot for some forty years, up to their phasing out in 1997. They were tough and unforgiving, and by the Navy's own admission the service was losing people from foot problems created by the boots.

boot. Sailor fresh from boot camp.

bow bunny. Bikini-clad woman adorning the bows of a boat.

Bravo Zulu. Job well done, in Navy slang.

brightwork. What must be polished, mostly brass and teak.

brig rat. Prisoner serving time in the brig, a naval prison.

bubble-chaser. Aviation-hydraulics technician.

bubble-head. Submariner, to a surface sailor.

bullet-stopper. Marine, in Navy slang.

bunk. A sailor's bed.

Cag. Commander of the air group, the chief pilot on an aircraft carrier.

can. 1. Destroyer; short for tin can. 2. Can buoy or a can-shaped channel marker.

captain of the head. Sailor in charge of cleaning toilets.

cat. The catapult used to launch planes on an aircraft carrier.

Charlie Noble. Smokestack of a ship's galley.

chauffeurs. Name that Navy F-14 Tomcat radar-intercept officers call their pilots.

cigarette boat. Very fast cigarette-shaped speedboat popular in south Florida and the vessel of choice for dealers in illegal drugs.

Cinderella liberty. A Navy or Marine Corps pass that expires at midnight.

cloth man. Sailboater, to a powerboater. Also known as a rag bagger.

coasties. Members of the Coast Guard.

coffee grinder. Winch for controlling certain types of sails on yachts. Also simply known as a grinder.

conn. Control of the ship. An officer of the deck on a Navy vessel will "take the conn" when taking responsibility for the ship's course and speed.

Crabtown. Annapolis, Maryland.

Cracker Jack. Familiar sailor's uniform of bell-bottoms and a blouse with a square flap—the same as that found on the Cracker Jack popcorn candy box.

Crotch, the. The U.S. Marine Corps.

crow. The sleeve insignia eagle that marks petty officers in the U.S. Navy. To get one's crow is to get a promotion to petty officer.

cryppies. Cryptologists.

cumshaw. That which is obtained by bribery or other illegal means.

Daisy chain. A collection of boats tied together for interboat socializing. Often seen in PLAYPEN.

dead horse. A debt, to a Navy man.

deck ape. 1. Enlisted sailor assigned to deck or gunnery duties. 2. In pleasure and sport boating, a crew member who does the hard work with lines and sails.

deep-six. To throw away or kill, as in "deep-sixing a project." Its traditional meaning is to drown, alluding to a person who is six fathoms deep.

Dilbert dunker. Contraption of the modern U.S. Navy used in training to simulate the action of an airman ditched at sea.

dirt sailor. One assigned to ground combat operation, such as Navy hospital corpsmen assigned to Marine units in Iraq.

dirtbag. A less-than-adequate sailor.

dolphins. The U.S. Navy submariner's badge.

Dutchman. A plate covering a crack or other imperfection.

Easy. Carefully.

ego alley. Waters where wave-blasting powerboats go to show off.

end on. Head-on.

event 1,000. The code word for any incident in which men are trapped in a submarine stranded on the bottom, and search and rescue operations are to be initiated.

Feather merchant. Civilian, to uniformed Navy men.

fender belly. Term for a fat, potbellied sailor, usually a "lifer," such as an old Navy chief petty officer.

field day. Day, or portion thereof, set aside for cleaning up a Navy vessel or base.

fish. Torpedo.

flag plot. Navy term for a command center. It comes from the fact that a naval officer above the rank of captain is allowed to fly a flag showing his or her rank. A flag officer.

flattop. Aircraft carrier.

floating coffin. An unsafe ship.

floating palace. A large and comfortable ship.

fouled. Jammed or obstructed, as a fouled line or prop.

four-oh / four-point-oh. Outstanding; used to express the highest degree of admiration. It comes from the highest rating, 4.0, that one can achieve on a Navy fitness report.

four-oh sailor. Human perfection. In John Barron's *Breaking the Ring*, a character defines a 4.0 sailor as "a guy who can walk on water without getting his shoes wet."

four striper. Navy captain.

Freshwater Navy. The Coast Guard.

Galley yarn. A rumor in the Navy; one that originates—metaphorically or actually—in the ship's kitchen or galley.

geedunk. Navy or Marine term for ice cream, candy, or junk food.

gertrude. Underwater telephone, used for communication between submarines. The term shows up in Tom Clancy's *The Hunt for Red October.*

ghosts. Imperfect sonar images.

Gitmo. Guantanamo Beach, Cuba; specifically, the U.S Navy base there.

glory hole. Quarters for chief petty officers aboard Navy ships.

gouge. 1. To cheat. 2. The answer or solution. 3. The latest inside information—the skinny.

grinder. 1. Large winch for raising and lowering sails. 2. Person positioned just left of the mast who controls such winches. A 1984 article on the crew of the America's Cup contender *Liberty* in *USA Today* termed this the "most brutal physical position" on a twelve-meter yacht. 3. A Marine Corps parade ground.

gummer's mate. Dental technician.

Hash mark. Stripes worn on the sleeves of Navy enlisted men, representing years of service. Each stripe represents an enlistment.

head. 1. Toilet. 2. Compass heading. This sets up a basis for confusion, as in the query "Quartermaster, where is your head?"

heavier metal. A larger, more powerful warship—a cruiser in heavier metal, to a destroyer crew.

Say Where?

Those Vulgar Tubes, by Joe J. Simmons III, a scholarly study of the disposal of human waste at sea aboard European ships of the fifteenth through seventeenth centuries, contains a list of some of the names given to shipboard facilities over the years, including the eponymous "vulgar tubes." The list:

Beakhead
Forestage
Garderobe
Head
Pissdale
Quarter gallery
Roundhouse
Sanitary
Seat-of-ease
Steep-tub
Stern-turret
Toilet box

holiday. An imperfection; a spot left unfinished or uncleaned.

Hollywood shower. A full shower with the water running nonstop, a rarity on most Navy vessels, where freshwater conservation measures are normally in effect and the procedure is to lather up, shut off the water, wash, and then turn on the water to rinse off. A line from Tom Clancy's *The Hunt for Red October*: "A Hollywood shower is something a sailor starts thinking about after a few days at sea."

hook. The anchor.

hooligan. Not seamanlike; something that has been sloppily slapped together.

hot bunk. The use of the same bed by more than one sailor, depending on who is standing watch.

huff duff. High-frequency direction finder; from HFDF.

hydraulic sandwich. Liquid lunch.

Irish pennant. Loose rope or loose thread on a sailor's uniform.

Jarhead. Member of the Marine Corps, to a sailor—who is likely to be called swabbie in return, from swabbing the decks.

jet jockey. Pilot.

joe. Coffee.

Julie. The system that activates the Navy's sonar buoys. As James W. Canan was doubtlessly pleased to report in his book *The Superwarriors*, it was named Julie "after a Philadelphia stripteaser who had a reputation for turning passive boys into active boys."

jump. To leave; to jump ship is to leave without permission.

jury-rig. To repair or put together in an emergency; to slap together.

Keel-haul. To punish, an allusion to the long-outlawed practice of punishing a sailor by dragging him by rope under the keel of the ship.

Lay day. A day off from racing, as can be requested by either boat during the America's Cup series.

liberty. Overnight leave. Compare CINDERELLA LIBERTY.

liberty hound. One who finagles extra time off; one who takes all the time off allowable.

lights out. Radar is off, in the U.S. Navy.

Mast. Ship captain's hearings before which sailors are brought and punished for minor infractions.

mat. The main deck of an aircraft carrier.

mating dance of the lead-bottomed money-gobblers. Phrase used to describe the positioning of boats for the start of the America's Cup and other major races.

Med, the. The Mediterranean Sea, in the parlance of the sailors of the Navy's Sixth Fleet.

Mickey Mouse rules. Petty rules and regulations. In his marvelous book on nautical terminology, *Salty Words*, Robert Hendrickson writes, "One theory holds that World War II U.S. Navy Military Indoctrination Centers, or MIC's, where undisciplined sailors were restrained, gave their initials to this expression for petty rules."

monkey fist. Knot put at the end of a heaving line, often with a small piece of lead or other weight in the middle of the knot to allow it to be thrown more easily.

mosquito boat. Motor torpedo boat, or PT boat.

mothballs. In reserve.

mother / mom. An aircraft carrier, to the pilots whose planes have been launched from it.

mousing. Lashing across a hook to keep it from slipping.

mule. Handler on the flight deck of an aircraft carrier.

mustang. Navy slang for an officer who worked his way up through the ranks.

Navy shower. Water-conservation practice in which a sailor wets down for a few seconds, turns off the water and lathers up, and then enjoys a few more seconds of freshwater to rinse off. A HOLLYWOOD SHOWER is preferable.

no-wake zone. An area where boats are to operate at low speed so as to create no wake.

NUB. Nonusable body; seasick sailor, for example.

nuke. Sailor in the U.S. Navy who serves aboard a nuclear sub or other nuclear-powered vessel.

nun buoy. A buoy shaped like a nun's hat.

OD. Officer of the deck, in the Navy. The OD is in charge of the ship and is the representative of the captain.

old man, the. The captain, the skipper.

our concrete brethren. Members of the Air Force, to those in Naval aviation. From the fact that Air Force pilots land on concrete runways while their seagoing counterparts land on carrier decks.

Paddles. The landing signal officer on an aircraft carrier who helps guide incoming aircraft onto the carrier deck.

padre. Chaplain in the Navy.

paint. Scanned by radar.

painter. A line in the bow of a boat used to make the vessel fast to a dock or another vessel.

pepper report. Navy ammunition report.

PFDs. Personal flotation devices; may be lifejackets, life rings, or cushions.

pipes. Boatswain (pron. bos'n). The boatswain transmitted captain's orders by means of different note pattern played on his pipe.

pitman. Same as SEWERMAN.

plank owner. Traditional name for a member of a ship's original crew—one who trod its deck timbers, or planks, when they were still new—that is still used in the plankless nuclear age.

playpen. Enclosed area for powerboats to moor and party: An article on party boats on Lake Michigan described Chicago's playpen as "the water between approximately Navy Pier and Oak Street Beach—long the migratory playground of young boaters, because the breakwater takes the edge off the waves" (*Chicago Tribune*, July 20, 2003).

pointy end. Name used by aircraft-carrier pilots to describe the "front end of the boat."

porkchop. Navy supply officer. According to *The Random House Dictionary of the English Language*, porkchop is a traditional metaphor for a "livelihood, especially one acquired with little effort."

poster boy. A sharp-looking and knowledgeable sailor.

purple shirt. Member of an aircraft carrier flight-deck fueling crew.

Quarters. Living areas on a ship.

Racer tracers. Groupies who follow sailboat racers around the world.

rag-bagger. Sailor, to a powerboater.

rail meat. In competitive sailing, crew used for ballast only.

rates. Deserves, in the U.S. Navy.

razor blades. A scrapped ship—presumably it has been converted to razor blades.

red lead. Ketchup.

red shirt. Emergency-crew member on the deck of an aircraft carrier.

reefer ship. A supply ship with refrigeration facilities.

rock stars. Pro sailors; egomaniacs to weekend boaters.

romper. A ship which has moved—romped—more than ten nautical miles ahead of its convoy and is unable to rejoin it.

roof. The flight deck of an aircraft carrier.

rubber duckie. An inflatable rubber boat that is towed behind a ship to confuse radar-guided missiles; a decoy.

Screw. The propeller.

scuttlebutt. 1. Drinking fountain. 2. Gossip and rumor.

seagull. 1. Navy term for one who follows the ship or fleet—applied to spouses and prostitutes alike. 2. Chicken served on a Navy vessel.

seaweed. Spinach.

secure. To put away or tie down.

sewerman. Crew member on a large sailboat who is in charge of sails belowdecks—the sewer—where sails must be unpacked and repacked during a race.

shellback. Sailor who has crossed the equator; hence, one with some experience.

Sherwood Forest. Missile room, on a U.S. submarine.

ship over. To reenlist in the Navy.

ship's husband. The yacht basin antonym of the golf widow.

shooter. The catapult officer on an aircraft carrier.

sick bay. Medical area on a Navy ship.

Silent Service. Sobriquet of the modern submarine force. According to Admiral I. J. Galantin, in *Take Her Deep!*, the name was "bestowed by a long-forgotten reporter, or [refers to] some ingrained idea about classified information to which other branches of our armed forces were less sensitive."

SINS (Navy). Situational inertial navigation system.

six-pack license. License that allows a civilian to captain a boat as a commercial enterprise as long as there are no more than six passengers on inland waters.

skate. In the Navy, a goof-off; someone who doesn't work hard or get much accomplished.

skins. Waterproof oilskin outerwear.

skipper. Commander of a unit or ship.

skunk. To a submariner, an unidentified surface contact.

skylarking. Goofing off, Navy style.

slop chute. 1. A ship's garbage chute. 2. Canteen where beer is sold.

snipe. Navy seaman working belowdecks in the engineering department.

soup. Fog.

splice the mainbrace. To have a drink; head off for happy hour. Although this term dates back to the British Navy and the era of wind and sail, when it indicated getting a ration of grog, it is used playfully today by people conscious of its anachronistic quality.

spud locker. Place where food, including potatoes, is kept. Aircraft-carrier pilots refer to crashing into the back end of a ship as "hitting the spud locker."

squid. Sailor.

stamps. Mail clerk on a Navy ship.

stink-potter. Powerboat owner, to a sailor.

straphanger. Boat owner's guest who knows nothing of sailing.

stray dogs. Married male powerboat owners who prowl about the waterways looking for women.

striker. A sailor training in a specific area; trainee.

stripes. An officer in the Navy, because of the gold stripes worn on the Navy dress uniform.

swab / swabbie / swab jockey. Ordinary seaman.

Tadpole. Frogman not yet fully qualified; one still in training.

tailhook. Aircraft carrier–based pilot.

three sheets to the wind. Drunk; also, all sheets flapping (sheets are lines that control the sails).

tin can. Navy destroyer.

tin fish. Torpedo.

trice. Raise with a line.

two-foot disease / two-foot-itis. Mock affliction that infects recreational boat owners who are always looking for a vessel that is two feet longer than the one they have.

Under the gun. Under armed guard.

Vice boats. Big powerful muscle boats of the type first made popular on the *Miami Vice* television show.

vulture's row. The island area of an aircraft carrier where mechanics, plane pushers, and others concerned with flight operations congregate during deck landings.

Weasels. Men with great boats but with personalities such that no woman would ride with them.

WET. Weekend training, in the Naval Reserves.

white-blue-white. Marine summer dress uniform: white cap, blue tunic, and white trousers.

working blues. Navy slang for a black shirt with matching pants.

XO. The executive officer, or second in command, on a naval vessel.

Yellow sheet. An aircraft spotter on an aircraft carrier. They control BLUE SHIRTS.

yeoman. In the Navy, a petty officer with clerical duties.

Z-gram. The terse, no-frills style of memos and orders pioneered by Admiral Elmo Zumwalt during his tenure as chief of naval operations.

NET-SPEAK

19

An Increasingly Wireless Web of Words

The word "Internet" may have been the most important new term of the 1990s for the simple reason that it may have been the most important development of the 1990s.

Predictably, the Net is not only spinning off its own rich slang but also becoming a great carrier of American slang. The lexicographer Anne H. Soukhanov, author of the new book *Word Watch: The Stories Behind the Words of Our Lives* (see "Sources"), was asked in 1995 what she thought were the most important trends in the English language today. "There are two," she replied. "American English in its everyday form is turning into something equivalent to vulgar Latin. And the slang vocabulary of American English, thanks to the Internet, is expanding all around the world." An important component of this American slang onslaught is the Internet slang itself, especially the three-letter acronyms (or TLAs) common to online communications. The Internet and online messaging are awash in these acronyms and initialisms.

AFK. Away from keyboard.

angry fruit salad. Web site with too many bright colors

anonymous remailer. A computer that takes e-mail messages, strips the sender's name and e-mail address, and sends them on their way.

applet. Temporary software applications built into the Internet that allow the user to use such tools as elaborate computer animation without owning the software. Applets have been likened to a park bench which is used by one person after another.

archie. Program that searches archives for particular software titles.

ASL? Query asking for age, sex, and location.

B2B. Business-to-business; refers to a subcategory of commercial Web sites.

backbone. A high-speed line or series of connections that forms a major path within a network.

BAK. Back at keyboard.

bandwidth. Originally a technical term referring to the amount of data per unit time a computer or transmission line can handle; Netters use it as a general description of Net traffic, as in "That was a real waste of bandwidth."

bandwidth hugger. Someone who fights spam. According to a junk e-mail glossary in the October 2005 issue of *Inc.* magazine, "So called because he won't yield any system capacity [bandwidth] to junk e-mail."

barney. Temporary, opportunistic Internet users. These are people who are online only for the length of a free access offer from AOL or MSN.

bit barfing. Overwhelming Web visitors with extensive information.

bit spit. Any form of digital correspondence—text, fax, image—or the act of sending same. "Did you bit-spit that file to Joe?"

black hole. An e-mail account that automatically deletes everything that goes into it.

bogosity. The quality of being bogus, or something that is bogus—the Internet stand-in for "bullshit."

bozo filter. Program that identifies e-mail from unknown senders and files it in an electronic mailbox. Same as TWIT FILTER.

BRB. Be right back.

browser. Generic term for a program that accesses and displays files available on the Internet.

BTDT. Been there, done that.

BTW. By the way.

bulletin board system. A computerized service that connects with your computer by modem and allows you to upload and download files, leave messages (e-mail), and talk to other users. Sometimes called a host system.

Chat. An area of the service where a group of users can type messages to each other in real time—to talk in type. Each message is seen by all the users of a virtual "chat room."

chat group. A number of Internet users who communicate with each other simultaneously.

chicken-boner. A spammer (see SPAM). According to one junk e-mail glossary, "While [the spammer] sees himself as a cyber entrepreneur, he is really just a beer-drinking, chicken-bone-chewing lowlife" (*Inc.*, October 2005).

client. A client can be a personal computer or one of the class of powerful small computers called workstations.

client server. Many small computers linked together to swap information and do work.

cobweb. A Web site that is never updated.

community network. A network devoted to local public-interest information and the discussion of local issues.

cybercrime. Internet crime.

cybercrud. Obfuscatory tech talk.

cyberhustler. Marketeers who buy rights to domain names which have not been renewed and then sell space on the sites to advertisers who get to use it as a billboard viewed by those searching for information offered by the original owner. Often used by pornographers.

cyberporn. Online pornography.

cybersleep. Term created on August 7, 1996, when America Online crashed, leaving its 6 million subscribers in the lurch, or a state of cybersleep.

cyberslut. Woman willing to exchange sexual messages electronically.

cyberspace. The popular word for describing computerized communications. When you enter a bulletin board, you're in cyberspace. The term was coined by the novelist William Gibson to describe the area of interaction between a virtual-reality system and a hacker's brain . . . something not currently accessible on the Internet.

cybrarian. Librarians using the Internet in their work.

Dialer. Program that automatically dials a telephone number through a modem and connects one machine with another.

domain. The part of an e-mail address to the right of the @ sign.

Subscribers are identified by a series of letters and symbols that look something like this: skip@asu.edu. That's the Internet address for Skip Brand, a graduate student and chief Internet guru at Arizona State University.

download. To move a file via modem from a bulletin board or another computer to your computer.

E-mail. Electronic mail that can be sent and received by your computer via modem.

e-mailbox. The electronic address to which e-mail is sent.

e-mailer. User of e-mail.

emoticon. Symbols that use punctuation marks to suggest facial expressions in order to denote emotion in a message. See box, "Punc Speak."

Not everyone is as enamored of the symbols as those who send them—Chet Raymo of the *Boston Globe*, for one. Writing in the May 22, 1995, issue, he said: "Then there is the pretentious tendency of e-mailers to use only lowercase type, unconventional punctuation, and those breathlessly silly combinations of punctuation marks called emoticons—typographical smiley faces and frowny faces that are supposed to convey human feeling."

e-tailing. Electronic retailing.

evil twin. Wireless networks that pretend to offer free Wi-Fi connections to the Internet but are actually fronts for capturing passwords and credit card numbers.

e-zine. Electronic magazine. Writing in the *Boston Globe*, June 5, 1996, Michael Saunders said, "The best e-zines offer deep content and take full advantage of the sound and video multimedia gewgaws that print magazines can't reproduce."

FAQ. Frequently asked questions. Most Usenet newsgroups maintain an FAQ document to keep newbies from wasting bandwidth asking about stuff everyone else already knows. As the newsletter *Internet Newsroom* put it, "Reading the FAQ is a good way to avoid getting flamed."

FCOL. For crying out loud.

finger. Internet software term for locating people on other Internet sites.

firewall. Combination of hardware and software separating a local area network (LAN) into two or more parts, for security reasons.

flamage. What newsgroup readers not involved in a FLAME WAR end up wading through.

flame. 1. An angry message, often a personal attack, posted on the Net. 2. To post such a message. Those who dare to post a note advertising their vitamin supplements or Amway products on the network risk being "flamed" with sharp messages from other users who resent such commercial intrusions. More recently, "flame" has come to refer to any derogatory, witless, or crude comment.

flame bait. A posting intended to trigger a FLAME WAR or flurry of nasty replies.

flame out. To anger someone.

flame war. What you get when one flame begets another. At their worst, flame wars have been known to take over entire newsgroups. They tend to erupt easily, sometimes over very little—mistakes in grammar, for example—burn brightly for a time, and then die out. It can be unsettling to be flamed, but it's one way norms are enforced on the Internet.

forum. Electronic subdivision, where many users discuss one topic. Forums often contain "rooms" for more subtopics.

FTP. 1. File transfer protocol, an Internet procedure that allows you to download text and programs from computers all over the world. Whether you want business software, games, educational programs, or digital photos of *Sports Illustrated* models, FTP lets you transfer the contents of an Internet computer library to your personal computer. 2. Also a verb, as in "I'll FTP that new game from Berkeley."

F2F. Face to face. One of the rules of Net etiquette is to behave as if you are F2F even if you are a world apart.

F2F world. The world outside the Net.

G. Grin or giggle. See also SMILEY.

GAL. Get a life.

gate crashers. Users who barge into a conversation with a bogus message.

gateway. Machine or machines used to relay packages from one network to another.

Say, What?

Punc Speak

Tilt your head slightly to the left to read these punctuation-based "faces."

:) or **:-)** Smile, smiley face, or happy face.

D or **:D** Big smile; laughing.

:-)) Very happy.

:-)))) Keep smiling.

:-o Surprised or shocked.

:-} Ironic smile.

:-> Impish grin.

:/) Not funny.

:-(or **:(** Sad; frowning.

>:-> Angry.

() Hugging.

((())) Lots o' huggin'.

[!] A hug.

:* or **:-*** Kiss.

::** Returning kiss.

:-J Tongue in cheek.

:-? Licking your lips.

8-) Wearing glasses, or grin with glasses.

B:-) Wearing glasses on head; designer glasses on head.

x-> Laughed so hard my glasses are crooked.

[x x]
^ Laughed so hard my contacts fell out.

 # -) Punker in shades.

| - | No way, buster.

O:-) Angel.

:+> Blushing sheepishly.

:-$ Biting one's tongue.

:-P or **:P** Sticking out her tongue at you.

:-! Foot in mouth.

:-# or **:-Z** or **:-X** or **:-x** My lips are sealed; zipped lip.

8(:-) A propeller head.

L:-) Just graduated.

[:-) Wearing a Walkman.

5:-) Writer is Elvis.

;-) or ;) Winking; winking smile.

:-@ Screaming.

:-O Shouting.

:-| Strictly neutral.

:-{ Alas, too bad, sorry.

:-Q Nyah, nyah.

:-Q I'm a smoker.

:-] Grim smile.

>:-> Devil.

:-& Twisted, wry expression.

:+< Hard night last night.

:-@ Grrr, grrr.

:-o Whispering.

:-0 Put a sock in it.

=(:o+ Mr. T.

:-p Razzberry.

:-3 With handlebar mustache.

:-? Humphrey Bogart, talking out of the side of his mouth with a cigarette in place.

:-B Tongue in cheek.

||<| The Cylon face.

;^) Woodhead's mark.

Fe) Ironic grin.

:E Vampire.

|:#/ Groucho.

:-u Aside, by the way.

:=| Person with a deviated septum.

:-[Severe displeasure.

- () About to vomit.

>:-o So shocked or surprised that one's hair stands on end.

=):-) Uncle Sam.

=|:-) Abe Lincoln.

:-; Disgusted.

:-B Drooling.

=:) Punker.

(o)(o) Breasts.

°V° Penis.

:-c or **:<** Bummed out.

<:-) or **<:-(** Feeling stupid, or asking a dumb question.

gif. Stands for graphic interchange format. A type of file allowing one user to upload a scanned image, usually a photo, so others may download and view it.

GMTA. Great minds think alike.

going postal. To send something by SNAIL MAIL.

google. To use Google or another SEARCH ENGINE to search for something on the Web. "I googled his name and got over a hundred hits."

GR8. Great.

G2G. Got to go.

Hacker. Traditionally, an avid user of computers, but in the context of the Internet it refers most generally to any traveler on the Net.

ham. Good e-mail. Not spam.

homepage. The first page of a Web site or document, an electronic front door that often includes a list of links to pages with further information.

Icon. A small symbol displayed on the computer screen used to access a program or file.

IMHO. In my humble opinion. Variation: IMHO WIVH, In my humble opinion, which is very humble.

infobahn. Information superhighway, a play on the German *Autobahn* highway system.

information superhighway. A Clinton administration buzzword for the convergence of communications technology. It comprises the Internet, telephone communications, and cable television.

Internaut. User of the Internet.

Internetter. User of the Internet.

IRC. Internet relay chat. Service that allows you to "chat" in real time with anyone on the Internet. Your comments appear on one side of the screen, the other user's comments on the other. This is the Net's "party room," a forum that allows real-time conversation with a variety of users.

I-way. Information highway, for short.

Jpg. Stands for joint photographic experts group and is pronounced "jay-peg." A type of file allowing one user to upload a scanned image, usually a photo, so others may download and view it.

Kevork. To ban electronically from a site or bulletin board. From the name Jack Kevorkian, a doctor who assisted suicides.

Kibo. Central deity in the parody religion Kibology, created by James Parry, a Net prankster who goes by the username of Kibo. Believed to be an acronym derived from "Knowledge in, bull out."

Line noise. Electronic transmission interference that results in a meaningless jumble of characters.

LMAO. Laughing my ass off.

LOL. Laughing out loud. Used in "chat" to show that someone has made you chortle.

LSHITIWMP. Laughing so hard I think I wet my pants.

lurker. Someone who reads a forum conversation but doesn't contribute.

lurkerly. Characterized by lurking—the first citation of this term in *American Speech* (Winter 1994) is from an Internet message.

luser. Online loser. Blend of loser + user.

Mailbomb. 1. To send or urge others to send massive amounts of e-mail to a single system or person, especially with the intent to crash the recipient's system. 2. To fax an endless sheet of black paper to a target, thereby using up his paper and ink (toner) supply. 3. Self-multiplying computer notes.

MAM. Middle-aged man / men, describing a male mindset that is the bane of Internet help desks. According to *The Glossary of Internet Terminology and Slang*, by Mike Bowen, the significance of this term is this: "For the same reason men cannot stop at service stations and ask directions until their wives threaten to get out of the car and walk, MAM (the age varies from about 19 to just over 106) cannot call the help desk and ask for assistance until they are so frustrated and mad, they are ready to bite the heads off chickens."

mash-up. To combine two Web services to create a third, for example, a site that pairs apartment rental ads from Craigslist with MapQuest to form an apartment locator. Borrowed from rap and hip-hop, where it refers to the vocals from one recording with the backing from another.

MEGO. My eyes glaze over.

modem. A device installed in a computer that allows it to connect with other computers or bulletin boards over a telephone line.

MUDs. Multi-user dimensions or multi-user dungeons are virtual suites (or cities) where you can "walk" from room to room. These electronic hang-outs allow dozens of people to gather in the same place. Most are used for conference discussions or role-playing fantasy adventure games.

murk. "A fake disclaimer at the end of a spam e-mail assuring the reader that the message complies with a bill" regulating spam that was introduced by former Alaska Senator (now governor) Frank Murkowski, reported *Inc.* magazine in October 2005. The bill didn't pass.

Navigate. To move from place to place on the Internet.

net. A network. Usually refers to the Internet or Usenet.

Netiquette. Online etiquette. One basic rule: All caps are rude. YOU DON'T HAVE TO SHOUT, SO DON'T DO IT. OK?

Netizen. Citizen of the Net, newbie and old-timer alike. The term tends to be used in terms of a collective Net consciousness, as in this line from the May 25, 1995, *Computing* magazine: "Netizens are not deterred by the fear, uncertainty and doubt (FUD) factors related to some alleged snippers or hackers on the highway." Blend of the words Net + citizen.

net.personality. One who posts regularly enough to become famous within a newsgroup or newsgroups.

Netrash. Junk sent over the Internet.

Netrock. Strident complaint sent over the Internet.

Netter / Nettie. Internet user.

Netwriter. One who uses the Internet to send messages.

newbie / newbee. One new to the Net. As in "Read the FAQ, newbie!"

newsgroup. Any Usenet topic group, usually designated by discussion type (e.g., "comp." for computer-interest groups, "rec." for recreational groups, etc).

NIFOC. Nude in front of computer.

nuts on the Net. Anarchists, plotters, and saboteurs on the Internet. In a *Washington Times* article, "Internet Becomes Haven for Anarchists" (May 14, 1995), by Arnaud de Borchgrave, the following revelation was made: "'Secret Service agents scanning the Internet even before the Oklahoma City bombing had identified what the computer experts considered were 11 credible plots to assassinate President Clinton, according to one of the agency's cybersleuths.

nuts on the Net. (*continued*) Thousands of other threats are simply discounted as the work of nuts on the 'Net,' said the investigator, who spoke on condition his name not be used."

nyetwork. A network, when it is acting flaky or is down—from the Russian *nyet*, for "no."

OTOH. On the other hand.

Pharming. Directing a consumer to an impostor Web page where he will be scammed.

phishing. Using deceitful e-mail or directing people to fake Web sites to fool them into divulging personal information so that criminals can access their accounts.

phreaking. Using the Net to crack telephone long-distance codes and the like.

pink. Anything spam-related, as in "That subject heading looks a little pink." It alludes to the pink color of Spam, the food.

PITA. Pain in the ass.

place. A page in hyperspace.

PLOS. Parents looking over shoulder.

p-mail. Physical mail, as opposed to e-mail.

posts. Messages posted on the Net.

PUMG. Puking up my guts—laughing really hard.

Quux. An expression of mild disgust.

Remailer. Computer that retransmits e-mail messages without identifying the sender.

ROFL. Rolling on the floor laughing, e-mail-ese for "I find this rather droll."

ROTFLOL. Rolling on the floor laughing out loud, that is, "That was very funny."

Satan (acr). Security administrator tool for analyzing networks. It is a tool that has given crypto-anarchists an alarming edge over the intelligence community. This "scout" enables assorted troublemakers on the Internet to find vulnerabilities in seemingly impenetrable electronic FIREWALLS. In a *Washington Times* article titled "Internet Becomes Haven for Anarchists" (May 14, 1995), by Arnaud de Borchgrave, an unnamed security specialist commented on satan, "There is much disinformation on the 'Net specifically designed to overload the circuits of the intelligence and law-enforcement communities and send us scurrying for clues," he said. "And yet you never really know what you're dealing with."

scriptkiddy. Hacker who disrupts a system for the fun of it rather than financial gain.

search engine. Software enabling user to find things of interest among the hundreds of thousands of Web sites.

send storm. A deluge of private messages received while a user is trying to do something else online.

server. A shared computer on the network that can be as simple as a regular PC set aside to handle print requests to a single laser printer.

shilling. The practice of sellers either bidding up their own items or using an alternate registration or associate to do so. e-Bay advises: "Don't even think about doing this. It can get you suspended. If you feel you have uncovered evidence of shilling by another user, please email the details to safeharbor@ebay.com so that it can be confidentially investigated."

.sig file. An elaborate signature, usually involving a quote or ASCII illustration, that is automatically appended to a user's post.

site kill file. Hypothetical means of blocking messages from a certain computer or part of the network.

smileys. Any facelike illustration made with punctuation marks used to convey emotion or satirical intent. See EMOTICON.

snail mail. The U.S. Postal Service, to those using e-mail.

spam. To deploy mass postings on the Net to unwilling recipients. Considered in extreme bad taste. Said to derive from the Monty Python song, "Spam, spam, spam, spam," although others insist it is from the fact that the canned meat, Spam, splatters messily when hurled. Spam is a registered trademark of the Hormel Corporation and is a blend of spiced + ham.

spambot. A robot used to collect e-mail addresses.

spamhandling. Begging via spam. Electronic panhandling.

spamhaus. A site devoted to sending out spam.

spider. Software that traverses the Web to find sites of interest to the user.

spim. Spam via instant message.

surfing. The act of skimming through the Web, following trains of thought from one Web site to another by means of links.

sysop (acr). System operator, the programmer in charge of a bulletin board.

TAFN. That's all for now.

tagging. A word that puts a Web page or image into a category that can be searched for by a search engine. A tag can be a proper name, verb, adjective, etc.

TAH. Take a hint.

thread. A series of postings on the same subject to an electronic bulletin board.

TIA. Thanks in advance.

TLA. Three-letter acronym, common in online communications. See XTLA.

traveler. One navigating the Net.

trolling. Sending a tongue-in-cheek message intended to irritate others.

TTFN. Ta-ta for now! Usually used at the end of a message before signing off.

TTYL. Talk to you later.

twit filter. Computer program that identifies e-mail from unknown senders and files it in an electronic mailbox. Same as BOZO FILTER.

Upload. To move a file from your computer to another computer or to a bulletin board via modem. See DOWNLOAD.

URL. Uniform resource locator, what the address of a Web page is called.

WB. Welcome back!

Web. The World Wide Web. An information space on the Internet, unified by a common addressing system and the ability for sites and documents to be connected via electronic links.

Web browser. 1. One who browses the World Wide Web. 2. Software application used to locate and display material on the World Wide Web. Popular examples: Mozilla, Internet Explorer, and Netscape Navigator.

Webhead. One addicted to searching the Web.

Webmaster. Person in charge of a Web site; modeled on the word "postmaster." In the May 1996 newsletter *The Editorial Eye*, Keith C. Ivey reports, "By the way, webmaster seems to be a gender neutral job title."

Webmeister. Super Web expert; a guru.

worm. An Internet virus transmitted by e-mail. "We Eat Worms for Money" was the headline for an ad for IBM's e-mail security service (*Financial Times*, November 22, 2005).

WTG. Way to go!

www. Electronic address for the World Wide Web.

XTLA. An extended TLA (three-letter acronym).

Zombie. 1. A computer infected by and under the control of another. 2. A computer that has been hacked to send spam to other computers.

20 THE GREAT OUTDOORS

In the Wilderness, in the Air, on (and Under) Water

I've dwelt in the surfurbs for more than six months now. But straight out, I'm an inland squid, a barney, a kak who's totally clueless about Big Mama. So last week I decided to do something really gnarly. I rang up a rad locie boardhead at Secret Spot Surf Shop and flowed a stokin' lesson—yea, a lesson. I know real surfers think lessons are bogus.

—Lane Thomasson, "A Surfin' Squid's Crashing Adventure," *Virginian-Pilot* (Norfolk, VA), September 20, 1992

Fresh air seems to foster slang, especially as we invent and discover new sports and activities to pursue out of doors. What follows is a potpourri of outdoor slang from backpacking, biking, climbing, cycling, fishing, gardening, hang gliding, hunting, ice fishing, lifeguarding, skating, skiing, snowmobiling, and surfing.

Liberally salted in this glossary is the language of "extreme" sports, a new class of high-energy pursuits starting with board sports (skateboarding, snowboarding, and wakeboarding), BMX biking, and in-line skating. They are to more traditional sports what hip-hop and punk rock are to music. They are cutting-edge pursuits at the cutting edge of competition, and of language—practitioners invent their lingo as they push the envelope of the physically possible.

For good measure, here is also a smattering of the slang of park rangers, tree surgeons, meteorologists, and the racetrack and a special lesson on how to talk like a birder.

Acid drop (skateboarding). Basic street trick used to jump down from something.

aerial bodyboarding (surfing). Move in which the entire board extends above the crest of a wave.

after-film period (fly-fishing). The era that followed the 1992 release of the movie *A River Runs Through It*, which created a large number of converts to the sport.

aggro (rock climbing). Aggressive; driven.

air (snowboarding). How high the boarders get from the vertical wall of snow, as in "I caught a lot of air on the first hit."

alley-oop (snowboarding). When the snowboarder goes straight up in the air, makes a turn, and comes back down. "Hey, that guy just did a front-sided alley-oop."

also-ran (horseracing). Describing a horse that finishes out of the money—comes in fourth or worse.

amped (surfing). Overdoing it, overenergetic, making loud or sudden movements.

angling (fishing). Taking a fish by hook and line.

asphalt surfer (surfing). Skateboarder.

auger (ice fishing). A tool used to drill a fishing hole in the ice. Some augers are hand drills, and some are gasoline-operated. Others are electric, but if you can't park nearby, carrying a heavy battery for the electric auger is no fun.

Aunt Emma (croquet). Cautious, uninspired, dull player.

à vue (rock climbing). French for "on sight." If a route is climbed with absolutely no prior information other than the grade and there are no falls, it is considered a true a vue ascent.

axel (ice skating). One of the more difficult jumps, the only one that takes off from a forward position. Takeoff is from the forward outside edge of the blade, and the landing is on the back outside edge of the other foot's blade. The turn comes in midair and the skater lands backward. It was named for its inventor, the Norwegian skater Axel Paulsen, who was dodging snowballs the first time he did it.

Backdoor (surfing). Going with your back facing the wave.

backhand surfing (surfing). Riding with one's back to the wave (also GOOFY FOOT).

bacon-in-the-pan (in-line skating). When you wipe out badly on a ramp and slide back down to the bottom.

Bake (surfing). Someone from Bakersfield in the Central Valley of California, as in "What a Bake!"

banana hammock (lifeguard lingo). Men's bikini-style bathing suit.

barney (surfing). A poor, clumsy surfer (from *The Flintstones* but certainly reinforced by the purple dinosaur).

base-area stone grinder (skiing). A novice who is unable to stop until he or she is sprawled out on the ski area parking lot.

BASS. Bass Anglers Sportsman's Society. The group's decal, attached to thousands of vehicles across the country, shows a substantial largemouth bass below "B.A.S.S."

BASSCAR. Blend of BASS + NASCAR to coin a term used to show the many parallels between competitive bass fishing and stock-car racing. An article in the *Pittsburgh Post-Gazette* (July 27, 2005) on bass fishing suggests that the term is sometimes used disparagingly: "The boats also are festooned with brightly painted sponsor logos and names, giving some credence to those who disparage the sport of competitive bass fishing with the nickname 'BASSCAR.'"

bassin' gals (bass fishing). Female anglers who participate in professional competition.

bat (horseracing). A jockey's whip.

bathtub (skiing). Mark left in snow from falling on one's butt—a *Sitzmark*.

beach Betty (lifeguard lingo). Bikini-clad bathing beauty.

beach break (surfing). Waves breaking close to a beach on a sandbank.

beached (surfing). Stuffed from eating.

belay (rock climbing). Procedure of securing a climber by the use of a rope.

belly (fishing). The midsection of a fly rod.

beta (rock climbing). Information about a route, ranging from required gear to movement sequences.

BICO (meteorology). Baby, it's cold outside.

biff a crash (mountain biking). Wipe out, as in "I biffed and then wiped away the blood."

Bird-Speak 101

By William Young

Millions of Americans watch birds, and birding enthusiasts have developed their own lingo. These enthusiasts call themselves **birders** rather than bird watchers, because birders listen to birds as well as watch them. The hobby is **birding**, and the verb form is **to bird**. **Birded out** can apply to a person exhausted from a lot of birding, or to an area a birder has so thoroughly explored that nothing new is likely to be found.

Many birders keep a **life list**, which includes all the birds seen in their lives. Some also keep **year lists**, **state lists**, **county lists**, **country lists, day lists,** and other list types. A species a birder has never seen before is a **lifer** or **life bird**. A **tick** is a species a birder can check (tick) off a list. A **lister** is a birder whose primary interest is to get as many ticks as possible. Some listers are **chasers,** chasing after rare birds they can tick off their lists—usually birds showing up outside their normal range. A birder who travels somewhere to see a particular species and fails to see it is said to **dip** on the species; the species in question is called a **target bird**. A birder who goes to an area hoping to see a number of target birds and sees them all is said to have **cleaned up**. Some birders might have a **jinx bird**, a species they have never seen even though it is not especially uncommon. **Trash birds** are exceedingly common species; a species uncommon in one area may be a trash bird in another. A **yard bird** is a species seen by birders at their own homes. Birders might attempt a **big day**, an attempt to see and hear as many species as possible during one day.

Birders use slang for various types of birds. A sharp-shinned hawk is called a **sharpie**. Hooded mergansers and wood ducks are called **hoodies** and **woodies,** respectively. Yellow-rumped warblers are called **butter-butts**. Certain species of small sandpipers collectively are called **peeps**, while certain small, plain songbirds are called **LBJs**, or little brown jobs. Sometimes, initials are used: a **GBH** is a great blue heron, and a **TV** is a turkey vulture. Ornithologists who do fieldwork use four-letter species codes, some of which have spilled into recreational birding: a mourning dove is called a **modo**, a blend of mourning + dove. A raptor called the goshawk (related to the sharpie) is the reason some birders jocularly refer to airplanes as **gashawks**.

Birders sometimes are afflicted with **warbler neck**, a soreness after spending long periods looking at warblers and other songbirds in the tops of trees. This condition can become acute during the spring migration if there is a **fallout**, a large number of songbirds who land in an area at the same time because of a storm or other weather condition. Birders sometimes **pish** or **spish** to entice songbirds to come closer; this is done by loudly whispering either "pish" or "spish," which causes some birds to investigate the sound. Birders might be able to identify a species by its **jizz**, which includes its posture, shape, wingbeat, behavior, and other nonplumage characteristics.

The most important piece of equipment for most birders is their binoculars.

Many birders use the shortened form **binos** (rhymes with winos) or **bins**. Technically, the instrument is *a binocular* and not *a pair of binoculars*, but the incorrect plural form is now so common that it has become an acceptable usage.

big mama (surfing). The ocean.

birder. Affectionate name for bird watcher.

birling. Log rolling.

blast-off (bass fishing). The launching of boats at the start of tournaments.

blasted (surfing). To wipe out. Normally getting blasted is the product of riding too deep in a TUBE or getting blown off your board by the spray coming out of a tube.

blind eye. Of a beach or other public place where nudity is allowed.

blitz (lifeguard lingo). A multivictim rescue.

blowdown (backpacking). Large trees that have fallen across the trail.

blur spin (bungee jumping). At the bottom of a stretch, the jumper spins like a figure skater.

boards (skiing). Skis.

bobhouse (ice fishing). An ice-fishing shelter.

bog down (surfing). To be unable to accelerate because of equipment design, lack of skill, or poor wave quality.

bonk (mountain biking). Total exhaustion caused by lack of sufficient food during a long race or ride.

boom (logging). A long string of logs connected end to end.

bouldering (rock climbing). Climbing on rocks that are small enough so that ropes aren't necessary. It often serves as a means of practicing difficult climbing moves.

bowl (surfing). Wave shape that occurs when the wave encounters a section of reef that causes it to break with more than usual suddenness and force.

breakaway (competitive cycling). A group of racers who get ahead of the main pack.

breaking maiden (horseracing). A jockey scoring his or her first career win.

breaking the barrier (rodeo). Starting before the flagman gives the signal. The penalty: ten seconds added to the rider's time.

bridge (mountain biking). To leave one group of riders and join another group that is farther ahead.

buck pocket (hunting). A spot where male deer gather, usually in high country.

buckle bunny (rodeo). Woman who loves to hang out with male performers; rodeo groupie.

buffasaurus (lifeguard). One who is in shape and looking good.

bug gulp. To swallow an insect whole, a play on the "big gulp" of convenience-store fame.

bugboy (horseracing). Apprentice rider.

bulldog (rodeo). To wrestle a steer to the ground by seizing its horns and twisting its neck until the animal falls. Bulldogging is one of the standard events in rodeo.

bulletproof (skiing). Icy surface so dense that it could bounce a bullet.

bumbly (rock climbing). Any climber who isn't as good as you are.

bumping (in-line skating). Skating down stairs; can be done forward, backward, even sideways. Also called bashing.

bunny-hop. To jump a mountain bike over a log, rock, or other obstacle without dismounting.

burly (snowboarding). Impressive.

butt floss. Thong bikini.

Cabbage patch (skateboarding). Thick weed patch above or below the water.

camel (ice skating). One of the most popular spins and it's upright. Starts on forward outside edge, spinning on toe, then dropping onto flat of blade. Variations include low camel, flying camel, back camel, and the Hamill camel.

camp robbers (backpacking). Jays, crows, pigeons, and ravens that frequent camp and steal your food.

Casper (surfing). A beachgoer with a very pale complexion, from *Casper the Friendly Ghost.*

cement (skiing). Wet, heavy snow.

chainsuck (mountain biking). When the chain becomes caught between the chainstay and the rear wheel, whether due to mud buildup or poor frame design.

chalk horse (horseracing). The favored horse in a race.

chalk people (surfing). People who live far from the beach; inlanders.

chasers (competitive cycling). Racers trying to catch a group that has gotten ahead of the main pack.

chasing the cans (rodeo). Barrel racing.

chicken heads (rock climbing). Small knobs of rock used to get a handhold.

cloon (mountain biking, skiing, and snowboarding). Slamming into the ground, resulting in a ringing head, or a delay in the action.

coming down (surfing). Warning cry to anyone taking off in front of you on a wave.

conditional instability (meteorology). It may rain—or it may not.

crankling (backpacking). Hiking at a fast pace.

crashing (skateboarding). Using heavy weight to cast hard into cover that must be penetrated to reach the target area.

crater (rock climbing). A fall in which the climber hits the ground so hard he leaves a small crater. "Poor form and to be avoided," say climbers.

creamed (surfing). To be caught by the CURL of a wave and violently tossed off one's board.

critical section (surfing). A section of wave that is very difficult to ride—usually deep within the CURL.

cross-over (ice skating). Primary method of gaining speed and rounding corners. The cross-over begins on a curve, when the free foot is passed in front of the other foot. Forward (clockwise) cross-overs begin on the left foot; backward, or reverse (counterclockwise), cross-overs begin on the right foot.

curl (surfing). The upper part of a wave's crest, which forms the TUBE in a large wave. Riding the tube is the holy grail of surfing.

Dally (rodeo). To wrap the end of the rope around the saddle horn immediately after the animal is roped.

day money (rodeo). The amount of prize money paid to the winners of particular events after each go-round, or attempt.

death cookie (skiing). Loose, icy lumps of snow or ice, often the result of using grooming machines in humid, freezing conditions.

death spiral (ice skating). A mandatory move for pairs. The male skater pivots (toe pick in the ice, circling around it), holding the partner's hand. She is parallel to the ice, spinning horizontally on one edge.

deck (board sports). Platform of the board.

dialed in (mountain biking). When a bike is set up nicely and everything works just right.

ding (surfing). A damaged spot on a surfboard.

dirt dive (skysurfing). Practicing a freefall performance on the ground.

dog (rock climbing). Short for hangdog. Climbing a route by hanging on to the rope, sometimes spending more time hanging than climbing. Not a good thing.

domestique (competitive cycling). A racer who sacrificially works for the team leader to ensure that he or she is in contention to win.

drafting (bicycle racing). Riding closely behind another rider to save energy by using that racer as a windbreak and being pulled by his draft.

drill (surfing). To wipe out. Normally this involves hitting the bottom, looking like you are going to hit the bottom, or being tossed over rocks.

drill and fill (tree-doc slang). To hollow out and fill a diseased part of a tree.

drop in (surfing). Riding another surfer's wave. One surfing Web site defines the term: "Dropping in is a crime in the surf world. A drop-in is where a surfer catches a wave where he/she does not have priority, i.e. there is already a surfer on the wave . . . Remember—it's a CRIME!"

drop-knee bodyboarding (surfing). Kneeling on a body board (usually with one knee) while moving on the wave face.

Earring down (rodeo). A method of subduing a wild horse by twisting its ears.

echelon (competitive cycling). A staggered line of racers taking orderly turns at the lead. The echelon is determined by the crosswinds.

Elvis syndrome (rock climbing). When a climber stands on a small hold for too long and starts trembling and twitching from the waist down. Also called "sewing-machine leg" or "Elvis leg," because it's all shook up.

end-to-ender (backpacking). Someone who hikes from the start of a long trail to the finish.

epic (surfing). Really good or large surf, as in "I had an epic session" or "I shoulda been here yesterday, the surf was epic!"

escrow. Birder term for sighting a bird that has not been made a distinct species in anticipation of its change in status. It can be added to one's life list when accepted.

Ethel. The human butt, to lifeguards. Ethel exposed is an alert.

extreme gardening. Name for those who grow enormous vegetables and enter them in competitions.

Face angel (skiing). After a FACE PLANT, (a sudden face-first fall), flapping one's arms and making like it was planned. A takeoff on snow angels made in new snow by kids.

face plant. Landing on your face. Hitting the ground face-first, as in "Joe hit a tree root and did a spectacular face plant." Also called auger, digger, soil sample, spring planting.

face shots (skiing). Splashes of powder in your face when the powder's so deep and light that it's flying everywhere as you ski down the fall line.

fat air (hang gliding). Preferable flying conditions.

feeding (competitive cycling). When the team manager hands up a bag containing food or liquids or both to a racer during a long race.

fetch (surfing). 1. The distance the wind blows over open water to create a swell. 2. The distance waves travel without obstruction.

field (competitive cycling). The main group of riders, also called the bunch, pack, or peloton.

fish stick. An ice-fishing pole. It has a place where the line is wound, a point so that it can be jabbed into the ice, and an eyelet on the other end for the line to go through.

fish storm (meteorology). A storm that stays far out at sea.

fishing (rodeo). When the roper has thrown the rope at an animal and misses, but then by accident or by flipping the rope turns it into a legal catch.

flag (ice fishing). A device for indicating when a fish has bitten. Being "flagged" is getting a message while watching one's flag(s) from a distance.

flank (rodeo). Strap with a self-locking buckle wrapped around the flank of the bronc or bull that is pulled tight as the animal leaves the chute. In an effort to get rid of the flank strap, the bronc bucks higher and harder.

flapper (rock climbing). A large piece of torn skin; a skin flap. It is often reattached (or at least held in place) with SuperGlue or tape.

flash (rock climbing). To climb a route on the first try without ever physically touching it before. Less of an accomplishment than À VUE, but still good.

fletching (archery). Feather or plastic vanes on an arrow, which guide the shaft.

flip. 1. From ice skating, a toe-assisted jump, taking off from the left foot going backward and landing on the right foot. 2. From horseracing, a jockey inducing vomiting to keep his weight low.

flip joint (ice skating). A move in which the takeoff is from the back inside edge and the landing is on the opposite back outside edge.

fluff and buff. Of a lifeguard, to get ready for duty: shave, shower, and make sure your male member has not become a victim of shrinkage.

flyer (mountain biking). A surprise burst of speed designed to leave others behind.

forehand surfing (surfing). Riding while facing the wave.

free climbing (rock climbing). To climb using hands and feet only. The rope is used only for safety, not for upward progress.

freshies (skiing). The first tracks in fresh powder.

Gaper (rock climbing). A nonclimber who watches climbers.

geriatric ski school (skiing). A group of older students.

gnarly (surfing). Treacherous, dangerous, hairy.

goat boat (surfing). A surf ski.

gobs (skiing). Geeks on boards.

goby (rock climbing). A flesh wound, usually from crack climbing.

goofy foot (surfing, snowboarding). Surfing with one's right foot forward.

granny gear (mountain biking). The third and smallest chain ring on a mountain bike, combined with the biggest sprocket. This is the lowest gear, used for extremely steep climbs. Also called "pixie gear" or "weenie gear."

grinding (in-line skating). Jumping up onto a curb and sliding across it on your skates.

gripped (rock climbing). Extremely scared, from knuckles white from gripping.

grommet (surfing). Adolescent or preadolescent surfer.

ground money (rodeo). If all the contestants in an event fail to qualify so that no one wins, the purse and entry fees for the event are split equally among its entrants.

grovel (surfing). To maintain speed on a broken wave in an attempt to find an area that has a face on it.

gumby (skiing). A novice skier with no muscles. Also, a "wet noodle."

gutter bunny (mountain biking). A bicycling commuter.

Hack-and-whack (gardening). A landscaper who massacres a garden that was in good shape.

hair (surfing). Nerve or courage.

haken (surfing). To go surfing (pron. "HAWK-in").

halfpipe (snowboarding, skateboarding, inline skating). U-shaped high-sided ramp or runway.

hammer (mountain biking). Riding hard; going all out.

hammered (mountain biking). Exhausted, beaten to a pulp, wiped out.

hammerhead (cycling). Biker who always rides at top speed and is unable to ride casually.

hammering (competitive cycling). Very strenuous pedaling.

hand plant (skateboarding). A half-pipe trick in which a skater reaches for the coping with one hand.

hang-up (skateboarding). When the front or back of the skateboard catches on an obstacle, usually causing a fall.

hangers (skiing). Novices who lose their skis while on the lift.

hangtags (gardening). Tags put onto plants and trees by nurseries containing information about the plants' care.

Hawaiian pullout (surfing). A way of pulling out of a wave involving pushing the nose under the wave face in much the same manner as in a duck dive.

hawg. Big bass, to a bass fisherman ("bassin' man").

heads. What skateboarders call each other.

headstand. In zoos, what they call it when an elephant squashes its victim with its massive head. They also can do quite a bit of damage with their well-muscled, 180-pound trunks, and even their relatively tiny tails pack the punch of a baseball bat.

heat seekers. Park rangers who specialize in firefighting, law enforcement, and emergency medicine.

herbs (skiing). Strange, nerdy people who take up skiing; derived from the guy named Herb who used to appear in Burger King commercials.

hit (snowboarding). A point on a vertical wall of the halfpipe where the snowboarder's board hits. "That first hit is awesome."

hitten (surfing). Adjective describing something of extreme goodness.

home run (in-line skating). A fall in which one or both axles scrape on a curb or other surface and both feet slide out from under you, as if you were sliding into home plate.

honey hole. An outstanding fishing hole where bodacious bass are bumping into each other.

hook (competitive cycling). When one racer, either on purpose or accidentally, moves his back wheel against the front wheel of the racer behind him.

hoolihan (rodeo). Illegal method of downing a steer in bulldogging competition by leaping on it in such a way as to drive the horns into the ground and flip the animal over on its back.

hot box (meteorology). The area of land covered by a severe storm warning.

hot camp. A hunting camp with running water.

hot saw (logging). In timber sports, a souped-up chain saw. Some utilize an engine taken from a power mower or snowmobile.

hydrant lift. In pairs ice-skating, when the male throws his female partner over his head while skating backward and catches her. Includes a half-turn. If all goes well, she should be facing him when it ends.

In lily whites. A race horse with his legs wrapped in white bandages.

invert (skateboarding). When a skater gets upside down and puts his hand on the coping.

involuntary dismount (mountain biking). A crash.

involved (gardening). A bug-ridden plant, as in "Don't touch that bush; it's involved."

Jam (snowboarding). A congregation of snowboarders, usually in the HALFPIPE. "Let's jam to see who can get the best hit."

Jams (surfing). A brand of colorful swim trunks, almost knee-length and usually loose to the point of bagginess. Trunks that look like genuine Jams often share the name.

jaybirds. Naked beachgoers.

JDLRs. To park rangers, park visitors who just don't look right, as in "I've got a carload of JDLRs up here. I'm going to pull them over and check them out."

jig and pig (bass fishing). A lure combination of lead weight jig with a piece of pork trailer.

jingus (rock climbing). Anything you don't like is automatically jingus, and probably heinous to boot.

Joe Baywatch (lifeguard lingo). Overly earnest lifeguard who isn't any fun—from the television show *Baywatch*.

joey (skiing). Obnoxious show-off typically wearing Day-Glo outfit and bragging loudly in the lodge; known to flash money; doesn't own chains.

juice heads (lifeguard lingo). Compulsive bodybuilders who look like they are on steroids (juice), whether they are or not.

jump (mountain biking). A quick acceleration usually developing into a sprint.

junk fishing. Going out fishing without a game plan.

Kelphead (surfing). A beginning surfer who spends most of the time with his or her head in the kelp.

kick (competitive cycling). A final burst of speed that provides the main acceleration in a sprint.

kneel-and-reel (fishing). A style of retrieve where the angler kneels in the boat with the rod tip in the water, causing a bait to dive deep.

kneelo (surfing). Kneeboard rider.

Latronic (surfing). See you later, as in "Latronic, dude" (pron. "lay-TRON-ic").

lawn carp (birding). Urbanized Western Canada Geese.

layback (ice skating). Upright spin, usually performed by women, in which the head and shoulders are dropped backward. Not to be confused with laid back.

lead-out (competitive cycling). A move where the designated contender for the win rides behind a "worker" until just before the finish and then speeds around his sacrificing teammate for the final sprint.

ledged out. Park ranger slang for when a tourist tries something really stupid, like trying to retrieve a souvenir over the edge of, say, the Grand Canyon, and needs to be rescued.

Leroy (fishing). The big one.

lethal projectile (skiing). A student who is out of control but doesn't know it.

lid kid (surfing). Usually a young bodyboarder.

lip (surfing). The crest of a wave; the part of the wave that pitches and falls out in front or spills forward down the face.

lipping. Using your thumb and forefinger to hoist a bass out of the water by its mouth.

loop jump. In ice skating, a move that begins and ends on the back outside edge of one foot. The directionally challenged applaud its simplistic design. In a toe loop, the movement is the same but the toe pick strikes the ice when the skater is jumping and landing.

loopy. When a skateboarder crashes really hard and is dazed.

lull (surfing). A period of time between SETS when waves are at their least intense.

lunker. A large fish.

lutz. An ice-skating jump that is similar to a flip. The skater starts in one direction and finishes in the other. The takeoff is from the back outside edge; the landing is on the opposite back outside edge.

Manky (rock climbing). Almost worthless, as in manky protection.

market animal (rodeo). Livestock bred for food rather than competition.

mashed potatoes (skiing). Snow, in warm weather.

max out (surfing). To go over the limit.

mazurka. In ice skating, a jump that takes off from back outside edge, the right foot crosses in front of left, a half-turn, right toe pick hits ice, onto left forward outside. Now do the hokey-pokey and turn yourself around.

mctwist (skateboarding). An inverted upside-down spin usually described with the degree of rotation—a 90° mctwist, for example.

moist tongue (meteorology). A ribbon of high humidity.

moto (mountain biking). Your bike. Also, clunker, cruiser, beater, bomber, fat-tire flyer.

mount money (rodeo). Payment for exhibition roping, riding, or bulldogging, not for competition.

mudder (horseracing). A horse who runs his best on a muddy or soft racing surface.

munchie (skateboarding). A cut or scrape gotten from falling off one's skateboard. Inspired by the feeling that the pavement is "munching" on one's skin.

mushy (surfing). Poor-quality small surf.

Nailed (surfing). Wiping out. Getting nailed normally involves some sort of impact, such as the crest of a wave falling on your head, your head hitting the bottom, or someone else hitting you.

neutercane (meteorology). A tropical storm that has hurricane potential.

never ever (skiing). A beginner.

never will be (skiing). A student who is and always will be a beginner.

nuking (gardening). Spraying plants with large amounts of pesticides.

nuts / tapers / camming devices (rock climbing). Metal devices that are temporarily placed in cracks to aid climbers. Such devices have virtually replaced pitons, which can damage the rock.

Oatmeals (surfing). Little mushy waves.

off the lip (surfing). Any move pulled by hitting the breaking crest of a wave.

off the Richter (surfing). Very good; an allusion to the Richter scale, for measuring the intensity of an earthquake.

ollie (skateboarding). Trick in which skaters lift the board off the ramp without using their hands.

Oral Roberts (skiing). A student who is hurt one moment but fine the next. The term refers to the evangelist and healer.

organ donor (biking). Rider who refuses to wear a helmet.

Passmodious (surfing). Really tired.

patch (figure skating). A space on the ice rented by a skater or a pair of skaters to practice figures.

peak bagging (mountain climbing/hiking). To climb and list as many peaks as possible. For example, many hikers aim to climb all of the forty-eight peaks over 4,000 feet in the White Mountains of New Hampshire.

pearling (surfing). Burying the nose of the board in the water; from "diving for pearls."

pegging (rodeo). Technique by which a steer wrestler throws a steer by driving one of the horns to the ground.

petal pushers (gardening). People who sell plants at garden shows.

pickup man (rodeo). Cowboy who helps the saddle bronc and the bareback riders get out of harm's way if they fall.

pigging string (rodeo). A short piece of soft rope with which a roper ties together the feet of a roped calf or steer.

pink (foxhunting). Scarlet livery of the staff of the hunt, so called not because of the color but rather to honor a famous British tailor named Pink.

pishing (birding). Scolding sound made by birders to keep intruders out of an area—such as keeping owls away from small birds. A newspaper description of pishing (*Washington Post*, December 31, 1995): *"pish, pish, pish; tchich, tchich, tchich."*

platter lift (ice skating). Move in which the man raises partner over his head, hands on her hips, leaving her horizontal to the ice and backward to him.

pogo (mountain biking). 1. To bounce on a full-suspension bike like a pogo stick. 2. For a full-suspension bike to bounce annoyingly and uncontrollably.

poodles (skiing). Instructors who wear expensive ski clothes.

positive vorticity advective (meteorology). It's going to rain.

potential (lifeguard slang). Possible drowning, as in "We've got a potential out there by the jetty."

power barf. To vomit after eating a PowerBar.

power fishing. Aggressive use of heavy rigs to catch fish in weedy or murky habitat.

pretzel / taco (mountain biking). To wreck a wheel.

prime (competitive cycling). See SPRINT.

pull (competitive cycling). To take a turn at the front of an echelon, breaking wind for the followers.

pull off (competitive cycling). To move to one side so that the next racer can take a turn at the front.

Rads (rock climbing). Sport climbers.

rail slide (in-line skating). Sliding on your skates down a handrail.

rainbow jersey (mountain biking). The coveted rainbow-striped jersey awarded to world champions in each of cycling's disciplines.

ramp pizza (barefoot water-skiing). What you will be if you fall on the ramp.

rank (rodeo). Of an animal who's history suggests you're going to get your butt whipped, as in "He is the rankest bull I've ever been on in my life."

rappel (rock climbing). To descend a rope by means of mechanical brake devices.

rental rodents (skiing). Kids on skis.

rev-head (surfing). One who thinks cars are more important than surfboards.

'rhoid buffing (mountain biking). Going down a hill so steep that your butt touches the rear wheel.

rig (fishing). The setup that attaches to the fishing line, including a hook, sinker, and swivel.

riprap (skateboarding). Rocks piled along river channels to thwart erosion.

road rash (in-line skating). Any wound associated with unintentional momentum reduction induced by contact with pavement.

rock (lifeguard lingo). Swimmer without the bod for the beach. Also, "stone."

rock dance (surfing). Walk over sharp, moss-covered rocks to recover a surfboard.

rogue (horseracing). A bad-tempered horse.

rooster tail. 1. (snowmobile) The snow thrown up behind a racing snowmobile. 2. (surfing) Spray thrown in an arc from the back of a surfer's board going into a good turn.

rough-stock events (rodeo). Events based on scores: bull riding, saddle bronc riding, etc.

rowel (rodeo). The circular, pointed part of a spur, often shaped like a star or a notched wheel, which protrudes behind the heel of a cowboy boot.

Sailing a bird (hunting). When you hit a bird and it flies 100 yards before falling.

salchow (ice skating). A single or double jump, fairly easy but requiring height. Starts on back inside edge and finishes on opposite back outside edge. Named for its creator, Sweden's Ulrich Salchow (pron. "sal-cow"), who won Olympic Gold in 1908.

scitz / skitch (in-line skating). To hold on to a moving automobile to get a free ride across part of town or up a hill. "I scitzed a ride on a Mercedes this morning."

scraping paint (horseback racing). Running along the rail, which is the shortest distance around the track.

screamer (rock climbing). A long fall.

scud (meteorology). A low, fast-moving cloud.

scud missiles (skiing). Tips of jagged rocks flush with the snow surface that tear up your skis' bases.

set (surfing). A group of waves that is larger than most.

set an edge (surfing). Dig the rail into the edge of a wave face.

shin-bang (skiing). The pain caused by constant pressure of the boots on the shins.

shoulder (surfing). Part of a wave to the side of the broken section that is steep enough to surf on.

shred (snowboarding). To ski powerfully, as in "I'm going to go out and shred the slopes."

sinker (lifeguard lingo). Drowning person.

sit spin (ice skating). The body is low to the ice, with the skating (spinning) knee bent and the free leg extended beside it.

skinhead (hunting). A young deer with no antlers.

skying out (hang gliding). Reaching a ceiling of 18,000 feet, the highest altitude permitted by the Federal Aviation Administration in uncontrolled airspace.

slackpacking. Giving your pack to someone else who drives ahead and meets you later. The hiker gets to walk easily without his pack.

slipstream (competitive cycling). An area of reduced air pressure behind the leader which helps following racers so they need less energy.

smokin'. Going very fast, in all racing and downhill sports.

snakebite (mountain biking). Most common type of flat tire. Caused by hitting an obstacle so hard that the inner tube is pinched against the rim, resulting in a double puncture that resembles two fan holes. Also called a "pinch flat."

snow pigs (skiing). The ski patrol.

specking out (hang gliding). Flying so high that you're a speck in the sky.

spike camp. A bare-necessities hunting camp with no running water.

spinner bodyboard (surfing). A 360-degree turn that is achieved while still moving on a relatively straight course.

spinning (competitive cycling). Fluid, fast pedaling.

spore (acr; skiing). Stupid people on rental equipment.

sprint. A special bonus prize given to the first racer across the line on a designated lap of a specific point on a road race. Also known as "prime" (pron. "preem").

squirrel chasers (skiing). Cross-country skiers.

squirrels (tree-doc slang). Workers who climb the tallest trees.

squirrelly (competitive cycling). A nervous or unstable racer.

steed. One's bike.

steer wrestling (rodeo). Bulldogging; bringing a steer to ground.

stick-up (bass fishing). A structure sticking up out of the water.

sticky wicket (croquet). A particularly tight wicket that is difficult to clear without getting stuck.

stoked (surfing). Happy. This word has entered general usage, but it originated in the surfing community.

street course (in-line skating and skate-

Say What?

That old myth about Eskimos having scores of names for snow has, alas, been disproved. But skiers are working on their own vocabulary of snow:

champagne powder. Light, small-flaked powder snow that has a low water content.

corn. Pellets that have frozen or thawed in the spring.

mashed potatoes. Heavy snow with high water content; typical of spring conditions; very hard on the thighs.

New England powder / New England clam powder. Bulletproof powder, a.k.a. solid ice. Icy pellets the size of small clams.

Portland cement. Northwest heavy snow, a.k.a. Cascade cement.

Sierra cement. Sierra tends to be very wet and after a freeze takes on the hardness of cement.

street course. (*continued*) boarding). Sporting area with ramps, rails, and box jumps as obstacles.

street luge. Competitors—solo or in four-man teams—race sleds on wheels that travel up to sixty mph.

suck milk (surfing). To wipe out, drink whitewater.

suck-up (surfing). A wave shape caused by a shallow spot over a sandbar, a rock, or any submerged object. It hinders the water flow and creates a nonsmooth spot on a wave.

sunfishing (rodeo). When a bull, calf, or horse twists its body in midair, rolling its belly upward toward the sun.

surf hamburger (lifeguard lingo). Swimmer who gets banged up in the undertow and comes out of the water with many red marks and bruises.

switchback (mountain biking). A tight, zigzag turn on the face of a mountain.

Tackle. Fishing gear.

tailwhip. Trick where a biker spins the entire bike underneath himself, while his body stays stationary in the air.

tea-bagger (surfing). Bodyboarder.

textile. A clothed person, in a nudist camp.

through the boilermaker (hunting). A shot to the heart—best because it kills quickly.

thru-hike. To hike the entire Appalachian Trail, from Springer Mountain in Georgia to Mount Katahdin in Maine, in one journey.

timber sports (logging). Work turned to play in such events as the "run, roll, and drive" competition.

tip-up (ice fishing). The pole that a fisherman sets up outside a fishing shelter. It's a self-contained fishing unit that signals the fisherman when there is possible action on

What the Blazes?

There is a special lingo associated with hiking the Appalachian Trail (AT). Here is an insight into that world derived from various trail sites (such as whiteblaze.net) and several articles on the trail, most important, an article called "Trail Lingo" in the *New York Daily News*, March 6, 2005. The trail markers are white blazes (rectangles 2 by 6 inches painted on trees, posts, or rocks to mark the AT) and blue blazes (rectangles painted on trees, posts, or rocks to mark the way to water, viewpoints, shelters, privies, or side trails from the AT). Much of the unofficial AT lingo plays off the blaze terminology.

aqua blaze. To substitute a river for a stretch of the AT.

brown blaze. The trail to the privy. Also sometimes refers to stain in underwear.

yellow blaze. To substitute a car ride for a section of the AT. The yellow alludes to the yellow lines painted down the middle of roads. **Yellowblazing** is hitchhiking to skip a section of the AT.

greenblazing. Bushwhacking through sections of woods to get from one point of the trail to another.

Pinkblazing. Hiking nude. The official day for that is June 21, the first day of summer.

the line. When a fish worries the bait, a flag goes up.

tires (in-line skating). Skate wheels.

toads (acr; surfing). Take off and die syndrome, when a late takeoff results in a heavy wipeout.

top roping (rock climbing). A BELAY from above. It protects the climber from falling even a short distance.

tourons (park ranger slang). Tourists who act like morons when they enter the park.

toxics / toxic socks (backpacking). Hiker's socks after a few weeks on the trail.

trads (rock climbing). Traditional climbers.

trails. The competitive bass-fishing circuit.

trash (hang gliding). 1. Turbulent air. 2. To be done in by turbulent air, as in "I was trashed today."

tree injection (skiing). Hitting a tree, as in "That hot dog is just asking for a massive tree injection."

trumps (gardening). Wealthy people who want instant gardens without having to work on them.

TTTC. (meteorology). Too tough to call.

tube (surfing). The curve of a wave within which a surfer gets a superior ride.

twitching (birding). Hard-nosed "combat" birding in which discomfort and danger do not deter. A line from *Sports Illustrated* on fanatical British birders stated, "In 1990 two twitchers were killed by Shining Path guerillas who doubtless had their own interpretation about what non-Latinos with binoculars were doing in backwoods Brazil."

two bubbas in a boat. Old-school noncompetitive bass fishing.

Valley cowboys. Inland surfers.

victory at sea (lifeguard lingo). Choppy waters. No swimming.

Wack / bonk (hang gliding). To drop the nose of the glider sharply when landing, causing a crash.

wad (street luge). A crash involving a large group of lugers.

wakeboarding (extreme sport). Surfers performing stunts in the water while being pulled by a motor-powered vehicle.

wang (hang gliding). A "wing-over" maneuver involving a sharp ninety-degree turn. Looks very impressive.

wanker two-planker (snowboarding). Derogatory term for a snow skier.

washy (horseracing). A horse that becomes so nervous that it sweats profusely before a race.

watch the water. To be on active duty as a lifeguard.

wheelsucker (competitive cycling). A cyclist who refuses to take a turn at the front of the pack, breaking the wind for the rest his team.

whipper (rock climbing). A long or violent fall in which the climber hits the end of the rope and is snapped like a whip.

widow maker (tree-doc slang). A large dangling tree limb that could fall off and kill someone.

wipe out (surfing). To fall off your board while riding on a wave. (See also DRILL, NAILED, and BLASTED.)

woodpecker snack bar (tree-doc slang). An insect-infested tree.

worked (surfing). Beaten up by a wave.

Yabow. A nonbirder who scares all the birds off (or lets his or her dog do it).

yahoo (hang gliding). What gliders yell as they step off a precipice. Like paratroopers' "Geronimo!"

yard dogs (gardening). Nursery employees, as in "Make the yard dogs water the begonias."

yard sale (skiing/mountain biking). Major crash that leaves you on the ground with assorted bits of equipment spread out all over.

yogi-ing (backpacking). Acting like Yogi Bear to persuade strangers to share their food with you.

21

PERFORMING SLANG

From the Mosh Pit and the Green Room

There is a Gresham's law in language as in economics. Bad currency once admitted will tend to drive the good out of circulation. The bilge of Hollywood will sink the language of Churchill and Lincoln.

—Lord Conesford, "You Americans Are Murdering the Language," *Saturday Evening Post*, July 13, 1957

The newspaper that transmogrified American slang.

—*Variety*, described by Nan Robertson in the *New York Times*, November 10, 1987

Show business slang is influenced by special forces. One of them is "Yinglish," a term coined by the lexicographer Leo Rosten for the combination of Yiddish and English, which has long been the argot of many in show business. Another force is the trade weekly *Variety*, which has influenced not only show-business talk but the total body of American slang. Many *Variety*-isms have lost their currency, such as "passion pit," for a drive-in movie lot, and "gams," for female legs, but others are still very much with us. "Sex appeal" was originally coined by *Variety* for the quality of being attractive to audiences owing to sexual aura.

However, other influences pale in comparison to the overall impact of television on performance argot. It has had a singular impact on language in general, and in the process, has taught us its own internal lingo. What's more, television lets us in on the slang of the rest of show business. Legitimate theaters have had green rooms—the room, of any color, where actors hang out when not on stage—for generations, but it was not until the goings-on in the green room became a topic of conversation on the *Tonight Show* that we all became aware of it.

What helps distinguish television from the rest of show business and other fields of endeavor is its compulsion to air its internal business. For this reason terms routinely pop up in televised conversation such as the following: segues, ratings periods, lavaliere mikes, booms, wipes, fills, rim shots, pans, minicams, voice-overs, feeds, simulcasts, laugh tracks, promos, overnights, outtakes, remotes, spin-offs, residuals, TelePrompTers, and so much more.

We are, in fact, treated as if we were all part of "the business" (as opposed to the movies, which is "the industry"), and addressed as if we really cared if the station we're watching is an indy, an affiliate, or an O&O (owned and operated by the network), or that some executive has decided that it sounds better if called an "encore presentation." Newspapers don't tell us what went on in the composing room, magazines don't report their front-of-the-book meetings; but television revels in the off-camera. So much on-camera chat about the green room has entered American mythology that many of us believe it is where all the really funny lines are spoken and all the really good gossip is traded. And now, with the advent of the DVD and its extra features, we are getting new insights into moviemaking.

Above the line. The cost of a movie before the camera begins to roll. See BELOW THE LINE.

actcom. Action comedy, in televisionland. The actcom has been defined as a sitcom (situation comedy) that starts with a disruption of the status quo and then follows the central character's action as he or she tries to bring things back to normal. By this definition, *I Love Lucy* was the prototypical actcom.

AFTRA. American Federation of Television and Radio Artists, a performers' union (pron. "AF-tra").

Alan Smithee. Name used by directors who are unhappy with the films they have created and choose to remain anonymous. Smithee's name is used extensively on the *Variety* Web site in hypothetical examples. For instance, the glossary on the Web site illustrates the use of the word "pen" with "Alan Smithee has been inked to pen the biopic about Abraham Lincoln."

alternative. Short for "alternative rock" and generally connoting any pop style too uncompromising, arcane, or intense for mainstream consumption.

ankle. To quit or depart. A term from *Variety.*

apple box. Wooden device used in filming to make a person or object appear taller.

arc. TV scriptwriter's term for a character who stays in place for a string of episodes rather than one show; those who help define the arc of the story.

auspices. Television-programmer talk for writers and producers. A show may have outstanding auspices but less than leading ratings.

ax. Horn or other instrument, but most commonly refers to the saxophone.

B. Second-rate, as in B-material or the B-western of yore.

back end / back-end money. The final profits in a film after all expenses have been met.

backer. Investor.

bankable. A star whose presence in a film virtually guarantees investors and audiences.

barn. Name for an old-fashioned movie theater in the era of multiplex boxes no larger than big family rooms.

begathon. TV or radio fund-raiser for a public television or radio station, which can go on for as long as a month.

below the line. Describing the actual costs of producing a movie. See ABOVE THE LINE.

best boy. In the motion-picture business, the gaffer's first assistant.

bester. Name for female BEST BOY.

bi-modal appeal. In television program-

bi-modal appeal. (*continued*) ming, describes a show that appeals to both children and older viewers.

big planet. Television-programmer talk for a huge show around which SATELLITE HITS may cluster.

billing. Order in which actors' names appear in ads, on marquees, and in film credits.

Black Rock. CBS corporate headquarters in Manhattan, from the dark gray color of the building.

bloom. A sudden flash of light on television, from light reflecting off objects.

blue material. Comedy-club slang for dirty jokes.

blunting. In television, competing with a show on another network by programming a similar show on your network, say, running a movie musical against a music special. See COUNTERPROGRAMMING.

boffo. A box-office hit. A term from *Variety.*

bofs. In the record business, albums that feature "the best of."

bookers. In talk radio and television, the people who arrange for guests. The term is a misnomer in the case of the major television news shows, whose bookers do more than book guests but also chase daily after the powerful and provocative.

bootleg. Record industry term for a recording that is unofficially and illegally released.

box bible. *TV Guide.*

break. Moment at which a motion-picture distributor breaks even and starts to amass profits.

broadcast flag. 1. Logo in the lower right-hand corner of a television image to identify the source of the programming. 2. Invisible data tag that a network can attach to its shows to prevent pirating.

buck. In Hollywood, $100,000. William Safire may have been the first to report that when a movie mogul says "ten bucks" he is talking about a million dollars.

bucket of blood. Comedy club slang for dives complete with hecklers and the smell of stale beer.

bumper. Prerecorded radio or television station identification with something extra—music, a jingle, or sound effects.

burned location. Place where film crews are not welcome because of the behavior of earlier crews.

burnt. Term used by disc jockeys to describe a tune that has been played once too often.

business, the. Television; as contrasted with film, which is called THE INDUSTRY.

bye-bye. Broadcasting term for phrases such as "We now take you to . . ."

Cart. Radio talk for a cartridge, usually an eight-track containing the prerecorded BUMPER.

chop socky movie. Karate and kung fu genre. A term from *Variety.*

clapper. Person who holds the hinged black-and-white-striped device that is used to "slate" each movie shot, sync the visual and sound tracks, and identify the shot.

comeallye. Folk music term for the scores of songs beginning with the words "Come all ye . . ."

confrontainment. Staple of TRASH TV in which people are pitted against one another for high ratings; blend of confrontation + entertainment.

contest pig. Disc jockey term for listener using a speed dialer to win giveaways.

continuity. Movie name for person in charge of making sure that all actors and crew have scripts, that there is continuity from scene to scene, and that all script changes are made. Previously known as script girl.

counterprogramming. Offering different television programming in an effort to attract a different audience, for instance, programming a comedy against a news special. See BLUNTING.

cradle to grave. Television-programmer talk for a show or event that appeals to everyone from teenagers to their grandparents.

Rare, but applicable to Olympics, the NCAA basketball Final Four, and the World Series.

crash and burn. Comedy club slang for a bad set with zero laughs.

crash TV. Quasi-sports shows emphasizing sex and violence. The pioneer examples of the genre, which *Newsweek* has labeled as "rough, tough and rotten": *RollerGames* and *American Gladiators.*

crawl. The rolling of credits at the beginning or end of a television show. See CREEP.

creep. Same as CRAWL.

crossover artist/crossover star. Performer who can move from one realm to another, such as from country and western to pop music or the movies.

crushed the crowds. Comedy club slang for "made them laugh."

Dead air. Broadcast silence, the great anathema of radio.

***Die Hard* on a _____.** Any of the many cinematic clones of the high-adventure *Die Hard* series. For example, *Under Siege* was known in Hollywood as *Die Hard* on a ship.

dish. Ground terminal that receives satellite signals.

DIY CD. Do-it-yourself homemade CD.

docudrama. Theatrical depiction of a historical personality or event.

dolly grip. In movies, the person in charge of the camera dolly, the four-wheel platform on which the camera rests.

DOR. In the music business, dance-oriented rock.

downtown set. A cheap television game-show set.

dramedy. Dramatic comedy, in television. *M*A*S*H* and *All in the Family* are classics of this genre.

drive time. Radio broadcast periods during which commuters are in their cars.

drooling. Unrehearsed conversation used to fill out time allotment in radio and television.

drop. Cable TV term for the actual cable that runs from the pole to the house.

Ear candy. Light syrupy music billed as "easy listening."

ECU. "Extreme close-up," a film image so close to the viewer's eye that it often stirs unsettling, even painful emotions.

elevator music. See EAR CANDY.

eye web. The CBS television network, in *Variety*-speak.

Fade. To raise or lower the volume of sound slowly.

fannies. 1. Seats sold. 2. Ardent fans of television personalities who send in nude photos of themselves.

favored nations. Agent's term for getting a stipulation in a contract that no other performer will get a better deal. An agent for a big star might say, "This contract has got to be favored nations."

film at eleven. TV news tout that has become general term for anything bold or flashy.

first-look. Arrangement by which a particular studio has the first option on a filmmaker's projects.

fish job. Running TV cables inside walls.

flagging. When there is a diagonal shift of the top portion of a television picture, causing the picture to bend to the right or the left.

flash and trash. During ratings periods, derogatory name for local news specials that tend to feature especially sexy or violent topics as well as non-news tie-ins to network features.

flop sweat. Nervous reaction to failure or impending theatrical doom.

fluffer. In the X-rated film business, the name for the woman who keeps the male talent enthused between scenes.

flyover people. Television term for the people who live between New York and Los Angeles, the two cities in which the vast majority of television shows are produced.

four-walling. Renting a theater to show a movie. Under such an arrangement, the renter pays all expenses and takes all the box-office receipts.

Freddy Krueger room from hell. Comedy club slang for a horrible audience.

front end. Money made before or during the production of a movie, as opposed to money from profits determined later, the BACK END.

f/x. In film, special visual effects.

Gaffer. The chief electrician on a movie set, responsible for everything that has "juice" running through it. This term and GRIP are slang that has long appeared in movie credits.

Golden Gater. In Hollywood, a script that is so bad that it is suicidal; akin to jumping off the Golden Gate Bridge.

gorilla. An enormous hit (movie, play, record); a blockbuster.

green light. The go-ahead for a film to be made. A film that has been so blessed is said to be greenlit.

green room. Place in which actors, actresses, television-show guests, etc., wait to go on and relax while not performing.

grip. Technician or handyman on a movie set. Hollywood's version of the Broadway stagehand.

gross player. Movie actor who is a big enough star to be able to demand a percentage of a film's gross income.

grunge. Rock style generally associated with alternative metal bands from the Seattle, Washington, area. It is similar in feel to hard rock but different in attitude, drawing more from punk-rock ennui than heavy-metal anger.

gypsy run. Final dress rehearsal, on Broadway.

Hammer. A handyman on a movie set.

hammock. To program a weak television show between two strong ones.

hammock hit. Television show that has good numbers but only because it is programmed between two hits.

hardcore. 1. J. D. Considine, music critic of the *Baltimore Sun*, defines hardcore as "the purest and most demanding music in any pop style; that which appeals only to the most knowledgeable and devoted fans; e.g., 'Eschewing pop, he only listened to hardcore rap.'" 2. Considine adds: "Hyper-fast and determinedly inaccessible form of punk rock, originally referring to early-'80s punk-rock scenes in Los Angeles and Washington, D.C."

heat. In Hollywoodese, either box-office power or word of mouth.

hell gig. Comedy club slang for an engagement sans crowd.

hick-hop. Edgy in Nashville—honky-tonk cum hip-hop.

hint (acr). Happy idiot news team, or happy idiot news talk, inside references to banter and chitchat between segments of the local TV news.

hitting the post. Disc jockey term for talking over the musical introduction to a song and ending just as the lyrics begin.

hoofer. Dancer.

house. Name for a funkier, electronically advanced version of disco that came on the scene in the late 1980s.

house nut. The operating and overhead expenses of one who shows a movie. It must be overcome before a profit can be posted.

housewife time. In radio, name for the period from ten A.M. to three P.M. Compare with DRIVE TIME.

hurban. Hispanic + urban, a radio format.

HUTs and PUTs (acr). Television-programmer talk for "homes using television" and "people using television." A *New York Times* article of June 6, 1993, about programmer lingo gave this example: "There was snow all over the East, so the HUTs and PUTs were up."

Idiot cards. Cue cards, sheets of cardboard on which a performer's lines are written.

if it bleeds it leads. Motto of local television news, especially during SWEEPS.

in the can. A movie that has been shot but is still not ready for distribution.

industry, the. The motion-picture business; Hollywood. Compare with THE BUSINESS.

indy. Independent, in show business, whether it be an independent television station or movie maker.

indyprod. Hollywoodese for "independent producer."

Jacuzzi jazz. Derogatory term used by musicians to describe the commercial, pop jazz of artists like Kenny G.

juicer. Electrician, in Hollywood.

jump the shark. The moment at which a television series strains credibility and begins its downward spiral. The term comes from the show *Happy Days*, when Fonzie water-skied over a shark.

Key grip. The head of the grip department, which on a motion-picture set is in charge of positioning camera equipment and devices that create shadows—all the equipment that does not have a plug (things with plugs are controlled by the gaffer).

kidvid. Television or home video for children.

kudocast. *Variety* term for an awards show such as the Academy Awards.

Lavaliere. 1. A small microphone used in television that fits around the person's neck or can be clipped to the person's lapel or dress. 2. To attach such a microphone: "Lavaliere the lady for the cooking demo."

legs. Strength and longevity at the box office.

letterboxed. Videotaped movie with dark bands to preserve the film's wide-screen proportions.

liner. A broadcasting term for the statement that identifies a station, its place on the dial, and its format. "You're listening to 101.7 WKIX, Middletown, the best in contemporary country."

linguini in clam sauce. Hitting a bad note in jazz, according to an article in *USA Today*, June 19, 1992, on a New York jazz festival.

loop. The central rhythmic phrase on a rap recording.

lunar rotation. Disc jockey term for a record that is played infrequently, as in "once in a blue moon."

Maggot. Call-in radio hosts' or producers' name for a caller who is always on the line with a boring or repeat message.

major. One of the top distributors of movies (Universal, Columbia, Paramount, etc.).

market. Broadcasters' way of saying where you are from or are currently working. "He is a credit to this market" are the words of a radio producer talking about an on-air personality.

megadoc. Big multipart documentary, such as Ken Burns's *Civil War* and *Baseball*.

megaplex. Movie theater with more than sixteen screens, as distinguished from a MULTIPLEX, which has three to sixteen screens.

mersh. Recording industry slang for commercial. The *Boston Globe*, August 15, 1991: "Well, here it is, finally. On their long-awaited fifth album Metallica, reigning kings of smart thrash metal, goes mersh. That's industry slang for commercial."

mike sock. Foam-rubber sleeve that fits over the business end of a microphone. It helps cut down on the extraneous sounds created by wind, heavy breathing, and the like.

mini-major. Big film production companies that are smaller than the majors, although some (Miramax, Polygram, and New Line) compete directly with the big studios. *Variety*: "The producers are in talks with several studios, including the mini-major New Line."

mitting. Applause, in *Variety*-speak.

mix. To combine sound from different sources.

moldy fig. A fan of old school pre-bebop jazz.

MOR. Middle of the road; appealing to middle-class, middle-aged Americans—light rock, for instance.

mosh. Dance favored by thrash fans, who hurtle against one another while flailing

mosh. (*continued*)
arms and bobbing in time; usually includes stage diving, in which audience members leap onto the crowd from the stage, and crowd surfing, where the stage-diver is passed over the heads of moshers in apparent gratitude for not having killed anyone.

mosh pit. Area of crowd in which moshing takes place.

Mouse House. The Walt Disney Co., a reference to the company's signature animated character, Mickey Mouse.

multiplex. Movie theater with more than two screens but less than sixteen.

Nix. To refuse, ban, overrule. A term from *Variety*.

no quote. In the film industry, this term is used to describe an artist willing to work below his or her normal fee, or quote.

nonpro. Person outside the movie industry.

nostril shot. Unflattering camera angle, on television.

numbers. Receipts, in Hollywood. A movie that is grossing a lot is said to have "good numbers."

O&O. A station that is owned and operated by the network, as opposed to an affiliate.

oater. Movie western, from the oats that horses eat. A vintage term from *Variety* that still comes into play when someone plans to film a western.

open mike. Entertainment in which people perform without auditions or other qualifications. Comedy clubs and places featuring acoustic music often have open-mike nights.

out of the box. Disc-jockey-ese for playing a new recording the day it is released.

outsider art. Folk art by self-styled visionaries.

overnights. The overnight ratings, in television.

Parrothead. Jimmy Buffett's Margarita-swilling, cheeseburger-chomping, faithful fans. Members of Parrothead Nation are given to shark, flamingo, and parrot hats for the men and coconut and seashell bras for the women. According to Jim Knippenberg, writing in the *Cincinnati Enquirer* (August 19, 2005), the term was coined in 1985 at a concert when a Buffett band member, Timothy B. Schmit, looked out at a crowd of tropically attired fans said something along the lines of "You guys are all a bunch of parrotheads."

pasadena. In many show business realms, a pass, for example, a person who is passed—rejected—for a television game show will be labeled "pasadena."

pasta-tute. Slur for one who has sold out his or her Italian culture and heritage for money. Invoked most recently for *The Sopranos*.

payola. A term coined by *Variety* for an illegal cash payoff made to get airtime for a record.

people meter. Device for registering in-home response to television.

Pepsi skating. Movie-theater staff term for people moving across a soft-drink-covered floor.

personality. One who appears as him- or herself on radio or television. A man who does a music and talk show for commuters on their way to work is known as a "morning personality."

phoner. 1. Radio talk-show interview conducted by telephone. 2. A false, or phony, plot device, whether in Hollywood or on Broadway.

picknickers. Movie-theater staff name for people who bring their own snacks to the theater.

piggybacking. Video retailing term for the special displays and packaging linking other products to just-released videos. The hit movie *Dances with Wolves* was first sold at McDonald's, for example.

plugola. Noncash gifts given to radio disc jockeys for playing songs. A free trip to Hollywood or Vegas is a common bit of plugola. It is distinguished from PAYOLA, which is a monetary gift.

podestrian. Person walking around wearing iPod earplugs.

points. Percentage of ownership in a movie or play.

pour. Cocktail party, Hollywood style.

PPV window. In video retailing, the guaranteed period of time when video has exclusive rights to a film before it can be shown on pay-per-view and cable TV.

prequel. Movie slang for film whose story line comes before rather than after a hit—the opposite of a sequel. Or, as one wag put it, "If we'd known the first picture was going to gross $289 million, we wouldn't have killed off the stars."

PSA. Public service announcement on radio or television.

Q. Recognition. It comes from TV-Q, a system that rates actors by the level of recognition by television viewers. A performer with a high Q gets more money.

quote. In Hollywood, the amount of money that an actor made on his or her last contract, as in, "What was Whoopi's quote?" See also NO QUOTE.

Rave. All-night dance party featuring oddly dressed, energetically undulating ravers, brutally loud techno music, and hypnotic lighting.

reality catchphrase. The final elimination line in the world of reality television shows. Cheesy, curt, and memorable, the most famous include "You're fired" (*The Apprentice*), "America has spoken" (*American Idol*), and "The tribe has spoken" (*Survivor*).

reggaeton. Spanish-language fusion of reggae, hip-hop, salsa, merengue, and other Carribean influences. On August 5, 2005, *USA Today* called it "the vanguard of a broader Latin urban music movement that could continue to grow for years."

riggers and juicers. Crew of electrical assistants who work on a movie set to set up and control lights.

rim shot. Comic punctuation from a drummer, it comes immediately after the punch line of a joke.

riot grrrls. J. D. Considine, music critic of the *Baltimore Sun*, wrote that this is a "post-feminist pop movement drawing from bands like Bikini Kill and Babes in Toyland, focusing on aggressive feminine pride and flouting of sexual stereotypes; generally easier to find in newspaper or magazine trend stories than in nightclubs or concert halls."

rip and grin. Describing the usher who takes tickets at movie theaters.

robo-anchor. Inside the TV business, term for a TV anchor who reads, but does not understand, the news.

rockumentary. Documentary film about rock 'n' roll or rock musicians.

running W. Trip wire used to make horses fall at critical moments in the making of a motion picture. The cruel device, responsible for the deaths of many animals, has been outlawed.

SAG (acr). Screen Actors Guild.

satellite hit. Television-programmer talk for a show that is secondary to a big hit, or BIG PLANET.

scrambler. Device used to keep cable-television subscribers from getting pay stations and events without paying for them. A decoder is required to unscramble a scrambled channel.

scrim. 1. To soften the intensity of a light. 2. A screen or curtain used to create the effect of mistiness onstage or on the screen.

second-unit work. Film work that involves no principal actors, such as shooting exteriors of buildings.

segue. 1. To move from one thing or shot to another. 2. Transition, as in "that was a nice segue." The word is Spanish (pron. "SEG-way").

shark club. Club that charges young musicians and groups to play. For instance, a shark club may require a group to buy a hundred tickets to their own performance.

shock jock. Radio disc jockey whose specialty is off-color material and general irreverence and rudeness.

sideman. A session musician.

sitcom. Situation comedy. A term from *Variety.*

ska. A precursor to reggae; essentially it's a faster version of the same sound.

skitcom. Skit-based comedy show.

slasher movie. As defined by the film critic Roger Ebert, "Movies starring a mad-dog killer who runs amok, slashing all of the other characters."

sleaze TV. Talk shows featuring sex, gore, and sensationalism. The same thing as TRASH TV.

slot. Time period, in television programming.

slugline. The slogan that appears in motion-picture advertising.

snapper. In drama or comedy, the talent's exit line.

SNL. *Saturday Night Live.*

soca. A style of music that is a blend of soul and calypso.

sound bite. A quotation recorded on location that is used in a later radio or television newscast as part of a larger report.

special. Anything not in the normal television schedule of programs. Television commonly puts its mistakes and visual typos into prime-time "bloopers" packages and calls them specials.

speds (acr). Stupid, pretentious English directors.

sping. Vocalizing that sounds more like speaking than singing. A spinger is different from a rapper, in that he is not doing rhythmic rhyming, just spinging. It is a blend of speak + sing.

splatter movie. One in which there is a lot of blood and gore.

spot. Prerecorded broadcast announcement.

staffer. Radio or television staff announcer.

stepping on it. Term used by disc jockeys to describe the gaffe that occurs when their introduction to a song runs into the first words of the lyrics.

street date. A video industry term for the day designated by studios and distributors when stores can begin to rent a title.

stretch. An actor reaching or working hard to fit into a part, as opposed to a natural fit. This term has become part of a common talk-show question: "Was that a stretch for you or did it come easy?"

stunting. Television tricks used to hook an audience at the beginning of the year or during a rating period. The tricks include special two-hour episodes, guest appearances, and tie-ins with other shows.

sudser. Soap opera.

sweeps. Periods during the year when the nation's 1,500 local television stations are rated for audience share. TV news often uses its sleaziest and most salacious items for sweeps weeks or sweeps months, in an attempt to boost their ratings.

Talent. Performer, as in "Do we need limos for the talent?"

tejano. Spanish for "Texan," the word is believed to be derived from an Indian word for allies or friends. Now "tejano" refers to a movement of young Texan musicians of Mexican descent who typically bring modern pop instrumentation and presentation to a mixture of traditional tunes and new songs sung in Spanish.

tent pole. 1. Movie that a studio expects to be its best-grossing blockbuster of the season. 2. Television-programmer talk for a show, usually a comedy, that stands in the middle of the prime-time lineup, usually at 9:00 ET, and holds up everything around it. *Cheers* was the classic tent-pole show.

Tex-Mex. The music played for social dancing along the Texas-Mexico border. The accordion-led music sounds like a cross between the polka, brought to Texas by Eastern European settlers, and Mariachi and other Mexican musics.

30-mile zone. The union-defined thirty-mile-radius zone, often measured from the Beverly Center in West Hollywood, within which a production company can shoot without paying travel expenses. In 2005 AOL created an entertainment service entitled TMZ.com, which stood for "Thirty-Mile Zone."

30 Rock. Headquarters of the National Broadcasting Company, which is at 30 Rockefeller Plaza, in New York City.

thrash. J. D. Considine, the music critic of the *Baltimore Sun*, wrote that this is a form of heavy-metal rock favoring jackhammer instrumental lines and brutally fast tempos, with lyrics generally devoted to death, doom, and destruction. Thrash bands include Metallica, Megadeth, Anthrax, Nuclear Assault, and Biohazard.

thrashcore. THRASH with hardcore punk, making the music more politically informed but less listenable than regular thrash.

three-sheet. Bragging; excessive promotion in show business. From the old forty-one-by-eighty-one-inch movie posters, called three-sheets by printers, and the most

Say What?

Seinfeld and Dave and Friends

TV has brought us lingos within lingos, shows that create their own lexicons—for example, Trekkie talk from *Star Trek.* Here are a few examples from three of the most popular network shows of the past decade and a half: *The Late Show with David Letterman, Seinfeld*, and *Friends.* A few prominent examples:

baldist (Sein). One who will not date bald men. George accuses Elaine of being a baldist.

commando (Friends). Without undies.

double crunch (Sein). Cereal Jerry consumes in vast quantities. Fictional.

double dipping (Sein). Sticking a chip back in the dip for the second time. George did this at a funeral.

Festivus (Sein). Holiday invented by Frank Costanza (George's father) to protest the commercialization of the other December holidays. The Festivus dinner begins with the Airing of Grievances.

home base (Dave). Dave's desk.

my boys (Sein). Jerry's name for his genitals; George's name for his sperm.

nostril penetration (Sein). The criteria for determining a true nose picker.

on the bus (Dave). Describing guests who get bumped when the show goes on too long.

re-gifting (Sein). Repackaging a gift and giving it to someone else.

shrinkage (Sein). What happened to George's hapless member in cold water.

snappies (Dave). One-liners.

so not true (Friends). False.

sponge-worthy (Sein). A deserving sex partner.

three-sheet. (*continued*) common size for movie posters. Twenty-seven by forty-one inches is a one-sheet.

toilet. A second-rate or small-time nightclub or comedy club, in the parlance of stand-up comics.

topline. To get top billing in a play or movie.

topspin. Momentum, in Hollywood.

traction. Television-programmer talk for a show that attracts the same faithful viewers week after week.

trades, the. The magazines and newspapers that serve the entertainment industry.

trash TV. Talk shows featuring sex, gore, and sensationalism. The same as SLEAZE TV.

turnaround. In Hollywood, the dropping of a project by one studio, which makes it available to another.

tweeny. Brief element of dialogue between the sex scenes in a porno film.

Up-front exposure. Money put up to get a film started, regardless of whether it is actually made.

uptown set. Glitzy television game show set with lots of lights and good carpeting.

V-chip. An electronic lock that prevents young eyes from viewing sex and violence on their television screen.

VOC. Voice-over credits, in television parlance.

VOD. Video on demand. From *Variety*'s Web page: "Home Shopping Network has been developing a VOD division that will allow customers to order specific programming."

voice-over / VO. A commercial or other television item on which the voice of an announcer is heard but the person is not seen.

Wackies. Term coined by David Letterman's staff for skits that employ elaborate props and site gags, like a volcano that spews creamed corn.

weeper. Sad movie.

weight. Clout that an agent or artist has in Hollywood, as opposed to HEAT, which is a star's clout at the box office.

went up in flames. Comedy club slang for really bombed.

wide / wide break. Big exposure, of a movie. A film that opens "wide" is likely to debut on close to two thousand screens.

wipe. 1. A technique to bring one scene in on top of another, in film or television. 2. To fire a person.

wrangler. In Hollywood, a person who is in charge of animals that will appear in a film.

Yawner. Boring show. A term from *Variety.*

Zit-com. Comedy for the young.

22

REAL ESTATE

Vocabulary to Go with a CNTRY KIT, 3BR, 2BA, W/DD, ALRM, C/V, GRDN & RFDK, for $1,495,000

How much would you pay for a neo-traditional SF home with 4BR, GTRM, OFF, WBF and HMOD? Not sure? Don't feel bad, because real estate lingo throws many buyers for a loop. The shorthand language used in home listings can be challenging for even seasoned home buyers. How many consumers would translate the above example to mean a single-family home on a small lot with a garage in the alley out back, four bedrooms, great room, office, wood-burning fireplace and handicap modifications?

—Chris Sicks, *Washington Times*, January 26, 2001

In his novel *Independence Day*, Richard Ford makes poetry out of real estate terminology, doting on descriptors such as "three-bedroom, two-bath, expandable, no fplc."

The lingo does have its own melody, tuned to and fueled by contracts, liens, easements, and the like—legal paperwork. This guarantees that much real estate jargon sounds identical to legal jargon. On the other hand, there is the fancy-schmancy real estate sales talk that can turn a covered parking space into a porte cochere, a covered patio into a lanai, and any corner with a sink and a stove into a kitchenette.

If you are in the market for a home, you also need to know the particular brand of ad-speak used to sell houses, which tends to be highly euphemistic. Real estate slang combines the legalese of contracts and titles with the bloated language of the sales brochure. It sounds like this—and increasingly contains hints of the realities of urban sprawl.

Accordion ARM. An adjustable-rate mortgage (ARM), in which the length of the loan expands when rates go up and compresses when rates go down.

alligator. Investment property whose income does not cover insurance, mortgage, and taxes. The presumption here is not only that an alligator "eats" capital but that one is

alligator. (*continued*)
up to one's ears in alligators—long-established slang for being mired in trouble, as in "It is difficult to drain the swamp when one is up to his ears in alligators."

alligator farm. Locales with an abundance of plots that consume expenses but create no income. Charlotte County, Florida, according to the *Sarasota Herald Tribune* of July 18, 2004, has 143,000 plotted undeveloped lots. Many who bought these lots have stopped making payments on them.

anchor. Major commercial establishment around which a shopping center or mall is built. Depending on the size of the development, an anchor might be one or more major department stores, a supermarket, or a large discount store.

ARM. Adjustable-rate mortgage. ARMs have interest rates that change every year. The rate is usually tied to one-year Treasury bills. The loan usually starts with a very low interest rate, then increases annually between one and two points. The loan usually can't rise more than two points a year and more than six points over the life of the loan.

Balloon. A final payment on a loan or mortgage that calls for an unusually large amount of money. It is one that balloons at the end.

banana (acr). Build absolutely nothing anywhere near anything. In Britain, a banana council is a do-nothing housing council.

barracuda. Very aggressive real estate agent.

Bart Simpson house. House with a castle-like architecture, complete with turrets. So called because they look like the cartoon character's hairstyle.

BI. Built-in—a BICC is a built-in china closet and BIBC is a built-in bookcase.

big box. Immense retail operation. The rule of thumb is that a big box has a footprint large enough to encompass two football fields.

binder. Payment that keeps a property from being sold for a specified period of time.

birdbath. Paved area that holds water—but was not meant to.

biz 'burbs. Former bedroom communities—suburbs—that have been transformed into job centers through massive commercial development. Once suburbs, they now are industrialized; also referred to as edge cities. See 'BURBS.

blue roof. Tarp-covered house.

blue-roof city. Post-hurricane name for a city or town where a large number of houses have blue tarps serving in the place of lost or damaged roofs. The term had particular relevance after the 2005 hurricane season and the triple punch of Katrina, Rita, and Wilma.

boilerplate. Time-tested language in deeds, leases, and other agreements.

bonus room. Name for extra room without a name or obvious function in luxury housing. Sometimes known as a hobby room or teen den.

bottom feeder / bottom fisher. One who tries to purchase a home for the lowest possible price in a weak market. Defined in a *Washington Post* real estate page article of early 1991: "The bottom fishers are out in force in the Washington area these days, hoping to snare the weak or financially faltering home seller or builder by offering a rock-bottom price and the chance to get out from under a crippling financial obligation."

bridge loan. One that lets the borrower close on a new home before the old house is sold.

bulldoze. A teardown, especially when the land is worth more than the structure sitting on it.

'burbs. Suburbs.

buydown / buydown mortgage. Arrangement under which a buyer is allowed discounted, below-market interest rates for the first few years of a long-term, fixed-rate mortgage.

buyer from the East. West Coast term for naive purchaser; what car salespeople call a "barefoot pilgrim."

buyer's broker. Person hired by the buyer to represent his or her interests and negotiate for the buyer in a real estate transaction.

CAC. Real estate ad lingo for central air conditioning.

CACH. Central air/central heat.

carriage house. A single-family house plan with a second unit on the garage.

cashtration. A house purchase that leaves the buyer financially impotent.

category killers. Big box stores—such as Best Buy and Circuit City (electronics), Bed Bath & Beyond (household linens), and Barnes & Noble and Borders (books)—that destroy business for smaller establishments selling the same category of merchandise.

catslide. Term used in some parts of the South for the style of house that is called saltbox Colonial or saltbox in the rest of the country.

CC&Rs. Covenants, conditions, and restrictions—the limitations placed on deeds.

charm of yesteryear. Ad-speak for lead pipes, no air conditioner, frayed wiring, no insulation, and so forth.

charmer. Home of little substance but that looks cute.

charming. Old, in ad-speak.

chef's kitchen. The trendy way to describe a kitchen that may offer little more than a large gas range.

choke point. Point at which mortgage interest rates prompt strong resistance by potential home buyers. The choke point for most consumers is about 13 percent.

clear title. Ownership without an encumbrance; see CLOUD.

close to nature. Ad-speak for squirrels in the attic.

cloud. An outstanding encumbrance, such as an unpaid tax lien. It comes from the concept of something that has "a cloud over it."

CMA. Comparative market analysis, a comparable sale, or a comp. "Run a CMA on it" is what an agent will say that about a property up for sales negotiations.

code-plus. Term for a structure that goes beyond local building codes to a higher standard. Code-plus houses are beginning to appear in affluent neighborhoods and are built to minimize damage from hurricanes and earthquakes.

combo condo. A building that has a combination of condominium units and town houses.

comp. Comparable sale. See CMA.

condo. Condominium.

convenient to everything. Ad-speak for next to the interstate and abutting train tracks.

country living. Ad-speak for in the middle of nowhere.

cozy. Small.

cramdown. The reduction of mortgage debt by a judge in a bankruptcy proceeding.

crank. Refinancing an existing mortgage obligation.

creampuff. Property in tiptop condition.

creative financing. Unconventional loan.

curb appeal. Describing a property that because of such things as fresh paint and a manicured lawn appeals to potential buyers who are viewing it from their car.

DG. Realtors' sly way of saying that a house is not a good one: a DOG.

dirt value. The value of a property if the existing house is torn down to make way for a new and larger one.

DLR. Double living room.

dockominium. A marina that is run like a condominium, with each member owning his or her own boat slip.

dog. Inferior or unsellable house, in the eyes of realtors and lenders.

dollhouse. Ad-speak for cramped.

DOM. Days on the market, an index used to tell how hot or cold a local market is based on the number of days an average house stays on the market.

double-end. Deal listed and sold by same agent.

downstroke. Seed money for an investment.

dragnet clause. Provision in a mortgage that pledges several properties as collateral. Default could lead to foreclosure on any of the properties in the dragnet.

Earnest money. Cash used to bind a sale.

ego pricing. 1. Extravagant price set by seller which seems to be tied to self-esteem. 2. Too-high price demanded for a property because of the value the seller places on improvements and decor.

embassy-sized. Realtors' term for gargantuan rooms in the larger of the new McMansions.

empty-nesters. Couples with grown children who no longer live at home.

Face-lift. Cosmetic changes to the appearance of a property that may improve the selling price.

Fannie Mae. Nickname for Federal National Mortgage Association.

farming. Real estate lingo for cultivating customers in a particular neighborhood. Many agents who farm choose an area with about two hundred homes. The idea is that neighbors will call that agent when they decide to sell.

FDR. Formal dining room.

first. A first mortgage, used to distinguish it from a SECOND.

first base. First home; starter home.

fixer-upper. Property that requires a lot of work.

fizzbo / fsbo. Realtors' pejorative term for "for sale by owner."

flex room. In small, entry-level houses, an optional room that can be used for a den, home office, guest bedroom, or dining room.

flip. 1. A series of real estate sales among partners in which the purchase price is inflated to unrealistic levels. The partners then sell the property to someone who obtains a mortgage for an amount greatly exceeding its true value. It is illegal and fraudulent, as underscored by this *Boston Globe* headline of 1991: "10 Charged in Fraud for Brockton-Area Real Estate 'Flips.'" 2. A quick and legal buying and selling of a property.

flipper. One who buys a house strictly to make a quick profit.

frog (acr). Furnished room over garage.

front foot. The property line that abuts the street, a body of water, a public way, etc.

front money. Down payment.

Garbage fees. Legal fees charged by lenders at settlement, such as messenger and document charges, that are often viewed as excessive. When in 1993 an article appeared in the *Los Angeles Times* on real estate terminology, one writer wrote to the paper to comment on this term: "The term 'garbage fee' was invented by the first cheapskate who demanded first class service but was too sleazy to pay for it."

garden carpet. Floor covering that is so dirty that it could support a vegetable garden.

garden level. Basement.

gazump. Raising the price of a property after a deal has been struck (but no contract has been signed). This term, now current in America, originated in England, where it has been a major factor in the real estate market. "There are millions of people getting the gazump," a realtor told the *Chicago Tribune* in 2004. "It's been a year of very unhappy people."

GEMS. Growing equity markets—fixed-rate loans with payments that increase at regular intervals.

GI loan. In the real estate context, GI stands for generous in-laws.

Ginnie Mae. Nickname for Government National Mortgage Association (GNMA).

ginnies. Bond funds that invest in mortgage securities backed by GNMA; see GINNIE MAE.

good bones. Dated house that has good structural character inside and out.

grandfather. To allow a flaw or violation to remain that is illegal in new construction; from the term "grandfather clause."

granny flat. Small apartment above a home or garage.

grant gnats. People who earn their living securing federal and state housing funds.

Handyman special. In need of repair. This term has been applied to houses in such dire and dilapidated condition that it is now something of a joke.

hard money. Money put into ownership or equity. See SOFT MONEY.

haver. Person who owns, has, a property that will satisfy a buyer's needs.

holy-shit area. Describing an area of houses one more expensive than the other. It comes from the comments of sightseers touring the area in question.

horseback opinion. Quick preliminary estimate of the worth of a property—as if made while riding by on a horse.

house flipper. One who buys, fixes up, and sells quickly for a higher price. See FLIP.

house fluffer. One who comes in and gets a house ready for a sale. Real estate glossaries insist that the term comes from pillow fluffing, but it is just as likely that it comes from the fluffing done in movie production. A fluffer is a hired member of the crew of a pornographic movie or theatrical presentation featuring frontal nudity. The fluffer's role is to sexually arouse the talent before the camera rolls.

house on steroids. Small home transformed into a big one after major remodeling work.

house wrap. A polyethylene barrier wrapped around a house to save energy.

Inside lot. Lot that is not on a corner.

Jumbo loan. Mortgage loans over $202,300.

junior / junior lien. Claim against property that can only be exercised after a prior claim has been settled.

junior 4. One-bedroom apartment with separate small dining room or den, kitchen, and bath, especially in the jargon of New York City real estate. It is essentially a one-bedroom apartment that can be turned into a two-bedroom.

Kennel. Substandard house; a DOG.

kicker. Loan surcharges.

kiddy condo. Condominium that is bought by parents for a child to live in while in college.

knockdown. 1. Structure built from preassembled components. 2. House bought to be leveled to make way for a bigger house.

Liars' loan. House loans in which lenders require very little documentation as long as the borrower puts down a sizable down payment of more than 25 percent. These mortgages are common among those who say they earn a certain amount of money but whose income tax returns show their earnings are much lower.

locn, locn, locn. Ad-speak for "Location, location, location."

lonely Charlie. Business transferee with too little time to look for a new home awaiting the move of the rest of his family.

lookie-lookies. People who look and look but never seem prepared to buy.

Lookie Lou and Bea Bax. Couple that looks, promises to be back, and disappears.

low-doc loan. Mortgage given to people who find it difficult to document their income.

low-doc mortgage. Loans made with little or no paperwork (documentation), usually granted to repeat buyers with built-up equity.

lower level. The basement. In 1996 a realtor told a *Boston Globe* writer why ads contain phrases like "lower-level in-law apartment": "When you think of a basement you think of something that's dirty."

lulu (acr). Locally unwanted land use, such as a prison or a halfway house.

luxury condominium. All condominiums, as they are always advertised as "luxury."

lvl. Ad-speak for level lot.

Maggie Mae. Nickname for Mortgage Guaranty Insurance Corporation.

mall. A large regional shopping center. The development of many of these malls over the last twenty years has been referred to as the "malling" of America.

McMansion. Pejorative description of a particular style of housing which, as its name suggests, is as ubiquitous as McDonald's fast-food restaurants. Like their namesake they tend to look alike and seem totally disconnected from the structures around them. They also tend to overwhelm the lot on which they are sited. (The Mc- prefix has been attached to other ostentatious structures: McBoathouse, McGarage, etc.) Other names for the same type of housing include Beltway Baronial, Starter Castle, Tract Mansion, Big Hair House, and Faux Chateau.

meeting of the minds. Mutual agreement at the time of contract.

mingling. Term for those who share properties—apartments, condos, house—to help pay for the cost of housing.

monkey. Mortgage, sometimes phrased as "monkey on the house" or "monkey with a long tail."

move-downs. Nervous about lean economic times, these folks move into smaller houses to lower their housing costs.

must-see. Code for dwelling that looks better on the inside than outside: a property that does not have CURB APPEAL, but is much more attractive on the inside.

Neutron-bomb loan. A low, teaser-rate adjustable mortgage that can kill the borrower but save the lender.

new price. Ad-speak euphemism for "reduced."

new security system. Ad-speak for located in high-crime area.

nimby (acr). Not in my backyard. Rallying cry of those who oppose halfway houses and recycling plants in their neighborhoods.

no perc. Describing a property whose soil is so poor it would not support a septic system, and the local municipality won't let you install any kind of septic system. In other words, water won't percolate through the soil.

nouveau-prairie style. An architectural style of tract house that has a Frank Lloyd Wright look.

Old world charm. Ad-speak for house needs work.

OP. Realtors' term for overpriced.

open house. Time when a property can be viewed without an appointment.

OPNG. Realtor's term for overpriced and no good.

OPT. Realtor's term for overpriced turkey.

Paper road. Said of a house in a development that exists only on blueprints or paper maps.

pedestrian pockets. A mixed-use community that stresses walking and bicycling instead of parking lots and the automobile.

penthouse. Has become a favored term of brokers because it sounds so much more swank than "top floor," however bland the top-floor unit may be.

pink-house syndrome. Term for the tendency of some people to do something to their house to make it more salable but that actually makes it harder to sell—such as painting it pink.

pioneer buyers. Buyers willing to trade mega-commutes for a shot at affordable housing.

PITI. Principal, interest, taxes, and insurance—the monthly payments on a property. Pronounced "pity."

pocket listing. Unlisted property known to realtor.

podmall. Small convenience-oriented shopping center serving a neighborhood; a strip center.

points. Fee charged by lender for making a loan. Points are over and above the cost of interest. One point is equal to 1 percent of the mortgage amount.

power center. A shopping center with a collection of big box stores. It might also have movie theaters as a draw for younger people.

premie. Not prematurely born baby, but a new house buyer.

puffing. "Misleading but not wholly untrue statements that are sometimes made to sell real estate" (Thomas and Charles F. Hemphill, *Essential Dictionary of Real Estate Terminology*).

Pullman kitchen. A kitchen in an apartment where all of the major kitchen appliances are lined upon one wall, like a narrow train wagon—especially in the parlance of New York City apartment advertising.

Quaint. Ad-speak for small and old.

qualifying. Process by which real estate agents eliminate nonbuyers and concentrate on those eager and able to buy.

Railroad flat. Apartment set up with one room after another so that you have to pass through one room to get to the others.

ranchberger. Traditional one-story ranch-style house.

ranchplex. Two-story units with no basement.

real estate grass. Annual rye, which quickly sprouts to a lush dark green. It sells houses but is only good for one season.

red light words. Terms that advertisers started to avoid in the 1990s for fear of being charged with fair-housing violations. A *Washington Post* article of May 29, 1994, by Dale Russakoff, told of realtors avoiding such terms as "executive" (could be construed as racist), "master bedroom" (suggesting slavery), and "sports enthusiasts take note" (could discourage the disabled). Now includes informal ban on terms like "bachelor" and "mother-in-law."

redlining. Lending policy that denies loans to minorities in certain areas. It is an illegal tactic used to thwart racial integration in housing.

rehab. Rehabilitate.

rehabber. One who rehabs dwellings.

Sandwich / sandwich lease. Three-party rental agreement between landlord, the original tenant, and a tenant who is subletting the property.

sausage house. One built right on the front of the lot line with only one or no side yard.

second. A second mortgage on a property that already has a mortgage, known as a FIRST.

shy. Secluded, in contemporary ad-speak, as in an ad in the *Seattle Post-Intelligencer* of September 2005: "MERCER ISLAND $1,875,000: Better than new 4br/3.5ba nestled on a shy 1 acre lot."

sleeper. Nice, well-priced house that attracts little attention.

smart streets. A planning scheme for new towns where technology such as fiber-optics is built into the infrastructure just like water lines and sewer and storm drains.

snout house. A house with the garage thrust to the front of the main body of the building and typically projecting out closer to the street than the front door like a snout. Built largely during the 1980s, neighborhoods of them are sometimes called *snoutscapes*.

soft money. Money put into paying the interest on a mortgage. Compare with HARD MONEY.

soft-money lender. Traditional lender such as a bank or mortgage company that deals in low to moderate interest rates.

spacious. Average size.

stager. Person, often an interior decorator, who comes into a house and makes it as attractive as possible to prospective buyers.

starter castle. McMansion, a play on the next entry.

starter home. Cheap, low-end home. It is one of the most common examples of the coded vocabulary of real estate advertising. In too many cases the term "starter home" actually means dilapidated and worthless.

step-saving kitchen. Ad-speak for a kitchen so small that it is hardly large enough for one cook, let alone too many.

strip. To build a small community shopping

strip. (*continued*) center; a convenience mall. "Stripping" is "malling" on a smaller scale. See MALL.

sweat equity. Hard work invested in a property to improve its value.

sweetener. Added incentive.

Tail wagger. Bad house; a DOG.

tear-down. House sold with the presumption that the new owner will immediately knock it down to make way for a larger home or homes.

teaser rate. A first-year mortgage rate that is below the going rate, also known as a "starter rate." They are offered to make adjustable-rate mortgages more attractive.

thirty-year fixed. Thirty-year mortgage based on a fixed rate of interest for the life of the loan. First-timers usually feel more comfortable knowing the interest rate will not change. Fixed-rate mortgages can also be taken out for ten, fifteen, or twenty years.

***Titanic* stairwell.** Oversize stairs that recall the scene in the film *Titanic* in which Kate Winslet comes down the ship's dining room staircase to meet Leonardo DiCaprio.

TLC. Tender loving care. "Needs TLC" in a real estate ad means the house is in need of major repairs.

TND. Traditional neighborhood development, with conventional main street and a small-town atmosphere.

toad (acr). Temporary, obsolete, abandoned, or derelict site.

TOD. Transit-oriented development, one built around bus or rail lines.

tornado bait. House trailer or trailer park, especially in areas prone to severe weather.

two-steps / two-step mortgages. Also called 5/25s or 7/23s, these mortgages offer two interest rates—a fixed rate for five years or seven years, then an annual adjustable rate or another fixed rate for the balance of the loan.

Uncle Louie. Any relative of the buyer who is going to "help" inspect the house.

upgrades. Improvements.

upside-down. Said when prices drop so much that a loan on a house exceeds its value.

W-2ers. Lender term for the preferred kind of home buyer who gets yearly

SY WHT?

"WBFP" is one of many common real estate abbreviations that are part of realtors' language of their own. Most "abbrs." are easy to get, but some are puzzlers for the uninitiated: ROW, RHFP, BBHA, and FHW stand for right-of-way, raised-hearth fireplace, baseboard hot air, and forced hot water, respectively.

As a service to readers, the *Boston Globe* real estate section translated this ad: "13 Bond St. Beauty. Unique & Wonderful. Immac. Cond. DLR w/WBF (Vict. mirror). Cntry kit., FDR, 3 BR, 2 1/2 BA, W/D, Alrm, C/V, Grdn & Rfdk. $495,000. Excl."

Translation: The ad was for a clean South End home with a double living room, a wood-burning fireplace with a Victorian mirror hanging above it, a large kitchen, formal dining room, three bedrooms, two and a half bathrooms, a washer-dryer, alarm, central vacuum, garden, and roof deck, listed exclusively with the advertiser.

statements of income on W-2 forms. Self-employed individuals who don't get W-2 forms have a much tougher time getting a loan.

WBFP. Wood-burning fireplace.

wide-body lots. Wide but shallow building lots that save land and permit builders to pack more houses onto smaller sites.

ww. Wall-to-wall, as in "ww crpt."

Yield. To surrender or give up a property.

Zero lot line. Describes a portion of a property where there is no yard; where the edge of the building is the front edge of the property.

zipper lots. A version of the wide-and-shallow lot with the garage on the side that lines up with the backyard of another lot in the rear.

23

THE SULTRY SLANG OF SEX

R-Rated Terms You Probably Won't Find in Your Junior Dictionary

"You can hardly assert that their inclusion would ruin the morals of the multitude?"

—Eric Partridge, quoted in the *Times Literary Supplement* (London), November 28, 1975, as asking an editor of the *Oxford English Dictionary* why the words "cunt" and "fuck" had not been included (they now are)

First came sexual euphemism. In the 1800s, Dr. Thomas Bowdler cleaned up Shakespeare's works for family consumption so that "a gipsy's lust" became "a gipsy's will." And there were the writers of the nineteenth century who could not bring themselves to write words like "trousers" and "breeches" and settled for terms like "inexpressibles" and "unmentionables."

Slang of the most forthright kind came forward to replace all of this coyness. It was there all the time, but soon occupied center stage. Linguistically, we let it all hang out, and modern speakers and writers held nothing back—"today an asterisk in a book is as rare as a virgin in life," said one startled critic not that long ago. When the smoke cleared, all the old dirty words and their hyphenated variations were in standard dictionaries, and Hollywood started vetting scripts by making sure these words were included, not excluded. (Is it my imagination or is there a law that requires all movies made after 1965 to have the word "asshole" in the dialogue?) Small-town theaters offered X-rated movies with titles like the redundant *Sluts in Heat*, and couples went shopping for sexual toys as if they were out to buy a Cuisinart.

Of late, however, it has become apparent that the words that the Federal Communications Commission used to call the "big six," those that could not be used on the radio ("piss," "fart," "shit," "fuck," "cock," and "cunt"), will always be with us and for all intents and purposes are no longer slang, but part of standard English. Many of them have little or nothing specifically to do with sex or elimination anymore but are what kids used to call "curse words."

Modern sexual slang, on the other hand, does not make the dictionary and tends to be more of a throwback to euphemism than four-letter-word directness. We have hung on to some of the Victorian urge to euphemize. In 1990 it was still common to ask a woman visitor if she "would like to powder her nose," and there are those who call a graveyard a "garden of remembrance." Euphemism has made the universe a little less perilous and harsh. Without a little euphemism, labor strikes would be harder to avert, fights would be harder to avoid, and parents would be dumbstruck when it came to explaining "the birds and the bees."

Here are a number of the terms—old and new—that are part of today's sexual slang. It also includes some slang from the sexual minorities who now are the self-described LGBTQ, an initialism standing for lesbian, gay, bisexual, transgender, and queer.

Abigail. Nickname for a middle-aged gay man who is still in the closet, or who has a conservative approach to love and life.

adult. Dirty; sexually explicit.

ass bandit. Homosexual male.

Aunt Flow. Woman's period, as in "Aunt Flow is in town."

aural sex. Phone sex.

Baby batter. Semen.

bag. Condom.

ball. A copulative verb; to have sex with.

balls. Testicles, from the much older Anglo-Saxon "ballocks."

basher. Someone who physically or verbally assaults a homosexual solely because he is gay.

baster baby. Reproduction by artificial insemination, sometimes said to have been achieved with the aid of a turkey baster, though this is not really feasible.

bazongas. Breasts.

BC. Birth control

beard. Woman who dates or marries a gay man to provide cover for his homosexuality. The term is also applied to a man who does the same for a lesbian woman. Such relationships are termed "bearded."

bearded clam. The female genitalia.

the beast with two backs. A couple during intercourse.

beauty spot. The female genitalia.

beaver. The female genitalia.

bed-hop. To sleep around.

belly ride. Copulation.

bi / bicycle. Bisexual.

bif. Bisexual female.

big brown eyes. The breasts.

big daddy. Penis.

Big Jim and the twins. Male genitalia.

bikini stuffers. Breasts.

bim. Bisexual male.

blow your top. Achieve sexual climax.

blue steeler. A particularly virile erection.

bobbitt. To cut off a penis, from the case in which Lorena Bobbitt performed this act on her husband. An early use of this verb occurred in the *Washington Post* for January 28, 1994, in a movie review by Rita Kempley in which a character in the film "picks up a carving knife and threatens to Bobbitt Sebastian."

body-rub shops. Massage parlors, a term used more commonly in Canada than the United States.

boinng. The sound and act of having an erection. In 1981 the *New England Journal of Medicine* carried an article on the

boinng. (*continued*)
subject entitled "Falling in Boinng Again." A letter to the editor in the May 20, 1982, issue took issue with the notion that boinng was an affliction: "Boinng is not an affliction. On the contrary, boinng, like love and watermelon, is one of life's genuine pleasures."

boner. As always, an erection.

boobiferous. Busty.

boobs. Breasts.

bouncers. Breasts.

bouncy-bouncy. Sexual act.

box tonsils. To kiss passionately, among collegians.

breeder. Homosexual term for a heterosexual; derogatory.

brush the beaver. To masturbate (female).

buckets. Breasts.

buff the helmet. To masturbate (male).

bugger. 1. To practice anal sex. 2. One who practices anal sex.

buns. The buttocks. An ad for a Cleveland health club is headlined "All rolls and buns drastically reduced."

burping the worm. To masturbate (male).

butch. Lesbian who wears a suit, motorcycle jacket, or other male clothing.

Cadet. Condom.

cakes. The buttocks, especially on men who wear them well. When the handsome Jim Palmer pitched for the Baltimore Orioles in the 1980s, his nickname was "Baby Cakes."

camel toe. The vulva, especially in the context of clothing which is so tight that it is immodest. Also known as "vaginal profiling." The term got a major workout in the 2005 film *The Weatherman*, when a concerned father, played by Nicholas Cage, is confronted with the fact that his teenage daughter is nicknamed Camel Toe at school.

carpet munching. To give oral sex to a female.

catcher's mitt. A diaphragm.

choking the chicken. To masturbate (male).

Cincinnati Bengal. Pickup slang for a woman with a good uniform (body) and an ugly helmet (head).

circle jerk. Group masturbation among boys.

cliterati. Female porn writers.

coin purse. The male scrotum.

Coney Island whitefish. Condom.

cork. Tampon.

crack of heaven. The female genitalia.

cream sauce. Semen.

cuddle party. Event where people gather to experience nonsexual touch and talk about intimate things. An article on such events in the *Morning Call*, August 12, 2005, says they are a national phenomenon: "Born from a belief that society's rigid rules about touch are creating a nation of lonely individuals, they exist so we can spit—gently—in the eyes of our repressed Puritan ancestors and reclaim a little humanity." It adds that the rules are simple: "Always ask before touching. No sex. No dry humping . . ."

cum. 1. Semen. 2. To ejaculate.

cut. Circumcised.

cybersex. Sex conducted over the Internet.

cyberslut. Woman who offers sex on the Internet.

Daisy chain. Three or more people linked sexually at the same time. The term has been applied to a nonsexual business application in which three or more companies gratify each other while ripping off the public.

dating. Increasingly, means having sex with a person. The *Houston Chronicle*, November 23, 1994: "[Richard Gere] confronted Sylvester Stallone at a recent London party thrown by Elton John and asked if he were dating [Cindy] Crawford only he didn't say date." This term, says the lexicographer Charles D. Poe, was once, and in many quarters still is, "used in such a way as to conjure up an Archie-and-Veronica, movie and malt shop kind of vision."

diddle. 1. Play with. 2. Copulate with.

disc drive. Female genitalia.

diva. A term of respect accorded a drag artist, especially one who sings.

DOM. Dirty old man.

doot. Female genitalia.

down there. One's genitalia.

dragback. Person of opposite sex brought back to one's house for sex, usually at the end of a long evening.

dry run. To bring to climax without undressing.

Ear sex. Phone sex; aural sex.

eleventh finger. The penis.

enema bandit. Homosexual.

exhaust pipe. The anus.

Fag hag. A heterosexual female who surrounds herself with gay men as friends.

fag stag. A straight male who enjoys the company of gay men.

family. A code word implying someone is homosexual, as in "You think he is family?"

family jewels. Male genitalia.

fanny. Female genitalia.

fart knocker. A braggart.

f-bomb. Euphemism for "fuck."

feigle. Yiddish slang for gay, derived from the word for bird.

femme. Lesbian or gay man who dresses and acts effeminately.

fern. Female genitalia.

fish skin. Condom.

flamer. A gay man, outrageous in his feminine characteristics both in private and in public.

flash. 1. To expose oneself. 2. Increasingly, for women to lift up their tops, revealing their breasts.

flesh session. Copulation.

44s. Breasts.

French embassy. Place where gay sex is available.

French letter. Condom.

French tickler. Condom.

friend of Dorothy. A gay man, referencing the many gay men who were devout fans of Judy Garland, whose death was strongly felt in the gay community.

frig. Sex between women involving the rubbing of the genitals with fingers.

fun bags. Breasts.

fur pie. The vulva.

fuzzy taco. Female genitals.

f-word. Widely used euphemism for the word "fuck."

G spot. An erotic zone or point of passion. Originally used to refer to a specific spot supposedly on the vaginal wall and named for its founder, the German gynecologist Ernst Grafenberg, it is now used generically. The G now seems to stand for something closer to gee whiz than Grafenberg.

garden of Eden. The female genitalia.

gay. In his *New Dictionary of American Slang*, Robert Chapman notes that use of the word in that sense may date from seventeenth-century England, when "gay" was used as an adjective to describe people addicted to "dissipations and social pleasures." The *Oxford English Dictionary* cites its use in the same sense in James Shirley's 1637 play *Lady of Pleasure*.

gaydar. Internal radar instinct for detecting who is, or is not, gay, no matter how well closeted; a blend of gay + radar.

getting your plumbing snaked. Having sexual intercourse. Similar terms for the same thing include getting your drain cleaned, getting your rocks off, getting your ashes hauled, and getting some mud for your turtle.

glove. Condom.

go over the mountain. Achieve sexual climax.

golden mound. Female genitals.

group grope. An orgy.

guyatus. A hiatus from guys.

Half dyke. Bisexual woman.

hard-off. Woman arousing no male sexual interest.

hard-on. Male erection.

hee-haws. Breasts.

helmet. Circumcised penis.

herotica. Female erotica.

heteroflexible. A straight person with a gay mind-set.

hide the salami. Copulate.

hobble. To have sex.

hobbler. Slut.

hogans. Breasts.

honeypot. Female genitals.

hookup. Sexual encounter with a stranger or acquaintance that includes anything from kissing to intercourse but usually doesn't result in a relationship.

hooters. Breasts.

horizontal bop. The sex act, among collegians.

horse. Condom, specifically a Trojan (from the Trojan horse).

hot beef injection. Coitus.

hot box. Female genitals.

Hudson River whitefish. Condom.

huevos. Testicles (Spanish for "eggs").

hump. To engage in sexual intercourse.

hung. 1. Describes a well-endowed male; big, as in "hung like a bull," "hung like a horse," etc. 2. More generally, how endowed, as in "hung like a mouse" or "hung like a cricket."

hunk. Handsome macho man.

In the life. Gay. The Internet glossary "Queer Slang in the Gay 90s" states that this term is most common in the black community.

intersex. Person born with partial organs of both sexes or ambiguous genitalia. About one in two thousand infants is born intersex. This word replaces "hermaphrodite," a blend of the names Hermes + Aphrodite, which is now considered derogatory.

Irish dowry. The female genitalia.

ISO. "In search of," in personal ads.

Jack off. To masturbate (male).

jill off. To masturbate (female).

Jimbo. Penis, allegedly the term of preference of President Lyndon B. Johnson.

jo-bag / jolly bag. Condom.

Johnnie. Penis.

joy hole. The female genitalia.

jugs. Breasts.

Kazoo. Anus or vulva.

knob. The meatus.

knocking boots. Coitus.

kosher. Circumcised.

Labonza. Buttocks.

lap dancing. For a naked stripper to rub her body against the crotch of a male customer, usually to orgasm and for a fee.

lay pipe. To have sexual intercourse.

lay your cane in a dusty corner. To have sexual intercourse. This metaphor acknowledges that the participants may be old.

lech. Lecherous man.

les. Lesbian.

LGBTQ. Collective expression for lesbian, gay, bisexual, transgender, and queer—grouping all alternative sexual lifestyles in one term.

lipstick lesbian. A homosexual female who exhibits very feminine qualities.

Little Elvis. The name Elvis Presley gave to his penis.

load. Semen.

love glove. Condom.

love juice. Semen.

love purse. Female genitals.

lubie. Lubricated condom.

Magnum. Oversized condom or penis.

main vein. Penis.

Manhattan eel. Condom.

maracas. Breasts.

marital aid. Sexual toy, such as a vibrator or dildo.

Mary. A name used by gay men with one another as a substitution for someone's real name.

master of ceremonies. Penis.

mattress mambo. To have sexual intercourse.

maypole. Sizable penis.

McQ. Quickie, borrowing the Mc from the fast-food franchise.

meat rack. Gay male cruising area.

mooning. Displaying one's butt for shock value.

morner. Sex in the morning—before a NOONER.

mount joy. The female genitalia.

mouse. Vulva.

Mr. Happy. Penis, a term given added currency because it has been used by Robin Williams in comedy routines.

muff diving. To give oral sex to a female.

mustache ride. Oral sex. Sideburns are "thigh ticklers."

Napkin ring. Penile ring.

night crawler. Penis.

night crawler in a turtleneck. Uncircumcised penis.

nookie / nooky. 1. Sexual intercourse. 2. Female genitalia.

nooner. Sex at noon. It would be irresponsible to fail to point out that the sentence "Sex at noon taxes" is a palindrome—it reads the same forward and backward.

O. Orgasm.

one-eyed wonder. Penis.

one-night stand. One-time sexual encounter.

OTR. On the rag; menstruating.

outing. Uncloseting gays without their permission.

over the shoulder boulder holder. Bra.

own it. To have sex.

Paddling the pink canoe. To masturbate (female).

parallel parking. The sex act, to collegians.

parsley patch. Pubic hair. By extension, to make love is to take a trip around the parsley patch.

parting the red sea. To masturbate (female).

personals. Classified ads which serve as a means of attracting others.

Peter, Paul, and Mary. Ménage à trois.

pink dollar. Money spent by gays and lesbians.

pink palace in the Black Forest / pink pleasure palace. The vulva.

pitch a tent. Get an erection.

plan B. Morning-after birth control pill.

play pocket pool. To masturbate (male).

plug. Tampon.

pluke. Have sexual intercourse.

pocket pal. Condom.

Polari. A secret gay underground language used before the decriminalization of

Say What?

Roberta B. Jacobson, Ph.D., kindly created and offered a decryption of the codes and phrases that appear in personals. It is reproduced here with some additions from other sources, including the author's reading of these ads.

A. Asian.

after my release. I'm in prison.

animal lover. I have four large dogs who all sleep with me in the bed.

A-NS / A-ns. Absolutely nonsmoker.

B. Black.

BIF. Bisexual female.

BIM. Bisexual male.

C. Christian.

Call my work number. I'm married.

CBB. Currently behind bars.

Confused about love. Not sure of my sexual preference.

DF. Divorced female.

DM. Divorced male.

first-time try at this. All my previous personals were published in other cities.

fit. I own a pair of sneakers.

GF. Gay female.

GM. Gay male.

H. Hispanic.

health-oriented. I have been accused of being a hypochondriac.

independent. I have my own phone line at my mother's house.

into jeans scene. Informal type of person who some might call a slob.

into leather scene. Into S&M.

J. Jewish.

LD. Light drinker.

let's meet for a drink. I'm too cheap to buy you dinner.

LTR. Long-term relationship.

M. Male.

mysterious. Nutty as a fruitcake.

natural. I don't believe in deodorants.

neg. Tested negative for HIV.

NK! No kids.

no financial considerations / not interested in financial considerations. I want sex but am not willing to pay for it.

no home phone. I'm married.

no responses to letters without photos. My prime consideration is what you look like.

nonmaterialistic. I am something of a cheapskate.

not into bar scene. Reformed lounge lizard.

NS. Nonsmoker.

P. Professional.

PA. Party animal.

personable. Will talk your ear off.

pleasant. Ugly as sin.

plump. Fat.

pos. Tested positive for HIV.

S/s. Smoker.

seeking companion. I am impotent.

seeking good times. Am only interested in sex, not a relationship.

seeking someone who loves children. I've got five (or more) kids.

seeking well-established . . . You must be rich.

SF. Single female.

SM. Single male.

to turn my life around. I'm a compulsive gambler, alcoholic, etc.

traditional. Finally through running around.

video fan. Couch potato.

W. White.

Wi. Widowed.

Polari. (*continued*) homosexuality in Britain back in the 1960s, which made a comeback as a curiosity in the gay community. A blend of Italian, Spanish, Yiddish, and Romany as well as Cockney rhyming slang. According to a Web site explaining the argot, it produces sentences like "How bona to vada your dolly old eek again!" The site explains: "In this outrageously camp world, 'bona' means good, 'vada' is to see and 'your dolly old eek' is your lovely face."

pood. Penis; rhymes with "wood."

pop one's cookies. Ejaculate.

popsicle. Penis.

porking. Copulation.

Port Said garter. Condom.

propho. Condom.

prunes. Testicles. This term suggests some strange comparisons. In Joseph Wambaugh's 1984 novel *Lines and Shadows* we read, "Manny's prunes were big as honeydews. Manny Lopez had balls to the walls."

pud. Penis.

punchboard. Promiscuous female.

purple-headed monster / purple monster. Male genitalia.

Queen bee. A wealthy woman who surrounds herself with young homosexual men.

quickie. A fast sexual interlude.

quief. Sound of air escaping from vagina after intercourse.

Rack. Breasts.

raincoat. Condom.

Roman. A person with a proclivity for orgies; used in personal classified ads.

roto rooter. Penis.

rough rider. Ribbed condom.

rubber duckie. Condom.

Safe. A condom. This is an old term given new meaning in the context of "safe sex."

Sex and the City Glossary

When *Sex and the City* ended its run in February 2004, in its wake was a new dating language. Some terms will survive—especially now that the show is in syndication—and others will die.

ADD. Another dating disaster.

all righty. An unromantic response to a marriage proposal.

frenemies. Friends who often act more like enemies.

goody drawer. Place where sexual accessories are kept.

manthrax. Men too poisonous to be around.

modelizers. Guys who date only models.

toxic bachelor. Commitment-phobic serial seducer.

trysexual. A lover who'll try anything once.

zsa-zsa-zsu. Spark that makes a romance work.

schwanz. Penis (*Schwanz* is German for "tail").

sex worker. Gender-free term for prostitute.

she-inal. Urinal for women allowing them to urinate while standing.

shoot your wad. Achieve sexual climax.

shower cap. Condom.

shtup. To copulate with.

size queen. Gay male especially interested in partners with large penises.

skanky. Slutty.

skin. Condom.

slam. 1. Sexual intercourse. 2. Female genitalia.

slap the salami. To masturbate (male).

snatch. The female genitalia.

sock. For a male to put a sock or other bulking agent in his genital area. "Put on a clean shirt and sock yourself and you'll be set for the night."

spank the monkey. To masturbate (male).

sperm napping. Suffered by men whose partners stop using contraception without their knowledge.

squirrel trap. Female genitalia.

stern-wheeler. Homosexual.

strange. Sex with a stranger or out-of-towner, as in "Got me some strange."

stray. A heterosexual male who everyone secretly thinks is gay. Blend of straight + gay.

switch-hitter. Bisexual.

T&A. Tits and ass.

tatas. Breasts.

tea. 1. Gossip, in the gay world. 2. Dances where gays can meet.

threesome. Sex involving three people.

tickle the tack. To masturbate (female).

tink. Penis.

titskis. Breasts.

titty shake. Topless bar.

tongue wrestle. Deep kissing.

tonsil hockey. Deep kissing, to collegians.

toys. Sexual aids and pleasure enhancers.

trouser trout. Penis. By extension, masturbation is fishing for trouser trout.

tube steak. Penis.

turtleneck. Uncircumcised penis.

TS. Transsexual.

TV. Transvestite.

twig. Vibrator with a slender business end.

twink. A derogatory term for a younger gay man who tends to be thin and preppy.

Ubersexual. Word coined in 2005 for men who are attractive and dynamic and whose masculine heterosexual attributes are totally unambiguous.

udders. Breasts.

umbrella. Condom.

unit. Penis.

Vanilla. Describing conventional sex.

Vatican roulette. The rhythm method of birth control, which attempts to avoid conception through timing. Named for the Vatican's opposition to mechanical means of contraception.

v-card. Virginity used as a credential.

Venus mound. The female genitalia.

Wake and bake. Sex on awakening in the morning.

wall job. Stand-up sex.

wane. Female genitalia.

W/E. Well-endowed, in the code of the personal classifieds.

well hung. Describes a male with large genitals.

wet deck. Describing a woman in a state of arousal.

whisker biscuit. Female genitals.

wide-on. Female version of HARD-ON; aroused.

wiener wrap. Condom.

whore d'oeuvre. "A slutty girl who is always the first to arrive at a party," as defined in an article on chick-speak in the *New York Times*, August 22, 2004.

woodie. An erection.

XXX. Particularly graphic and explicit depiction of sex.

Y, the. The crotch. Oral sex is sometimes described as having "lunch at the Y."

Zhush. Making something striking or flamboyant, especially among gays.

zipless fuck. Quick sexual encounter with someone you have never seen before, a term made popular in Erica Jong's *Fear of Flying*.

24
THE SLANG OF SPIN

Ad-speak, PR, and BR

Advertising, for its part, has so prostrated itself on the altar of word worship that it has succeeded in creating a whole language of its own. And while Americans are bilingual in this respect, none can confuse the language of advertising with their own.

—William H. Whyte, Jr., *Is Anybody Listening?*

There was a period in the late 1950s when the nation went gaga over the slangy metaphoric hyperbole of Madison Avenue. These expressions were dubbed "gray flannelisms" (from Sloan Wilson's 1955 novel *The Man in the Gray Flannel Suit*, about a Madison Avenue executive) by the syndicated columnist Walter Winchell, while another columnist, Dorothy Kilgallen, called them "ad agencyisms." Such talk was convoluted and many typical ad-speak formulations were about whether or not something—an ad, a campaign, a slogan—would work. The most famous flannelism was "Let's send it up the flagpole and see if they salute it," but there were hundreds more that columnists and TV personalities repeated with relish:

Let's pull up the periscope and see where we're at.
I see feathers on it but it's still not flying.
Let's toss it around and see if it makes salad.
Let's guinea pig that one.
Let's roll some rocks and see what crawls out.
Well, the oars are in the water and we're headed upstream.
Let's drop this down the well and see what kind of splash it makes.

Were these really used or were they created to get a line in a newspaper column? It would seem that most were genuine, not hype. No less an observer than John Crosby, of the old *New York Herald Tribune*, deemed them "the curiously inventive (and, in some cases, remarkably expressive) language of the advertising industry." This is not to say a few were not created for outside consumption.

In late 1957, when the Soviet Union put a dog in orbit, the metaphoric handstand that attracted attention was "Let's shoot a satellite into the client's orbit and see if he barks."

That fad has passed (at least the public side of it has) and things are a little less colorful in advertising and public relations, but plenty of ad slang remains, and there is something new on the horizon: the vast potential for advertising on the Internet. Cyberadvertising already boasts its own nascent slang, replete with terms such as "banner," "button," "click-through," "hit," "impression," and "traffic tracking."

Account side. The half of an ad agency that attracts and keeps clients. The other half is the CREATIVE SIDE.

ad. Print advertisement, as opposed to a COMMERCIAL, which appears on radio or television.

advid. Advertising video.

advertorial. An advertisement that sells an editorial point of view, as opposed to a product or service.

agency copy. Material printed or broadcast just as it was when it came from an advertising or public relations firm.

art. Any graphics—photography, typography, illustration—in advertising; everything else in an ad or commercial is COPY.

Banner. On the Internet, online advertising term for the most common type of online ad. Banners are usually rectangular or oblong and run at the top or bottom of a page. They carry short messages and act as a live link to promotional material from an advertiser or a Web site. The first big user of banners was the Coors Brewing Co., which used the Internet to help launch Zima, the clear malt beverage targeted at Generation-X drinkers. Coors put Zima banners on HotWired and NSCA in late 1994 and soon had spots everywhere.

beauty shot. A well-staged and -lit view of a product in a commercial.

bleed. An ad, photo, or illustration that extends to the very edge of a page.

boob-ads. Ads for bras and other female undergarments.

book. A magazine or other periodical. The front of the book is the portion of the magazine before the main editorial section, and the back of the book follows the main section.

boutique. Small ad agency, often noted for its creativity.

branding. The process by which the character and purpose of the company or organization is communicated clearly and indelibly.

brandstanding. Supporting a race car or sponsoring a rock tour or some other "special event" to promote one's product.

button. An online ad, smaller than a BANNER.

Click-through. In online advertising, the percentage of people viewing a Web page who click on an advertiser's banner. Consumers who "click-through" an ad banner to the information beyond are coveted because they're the best candidates to buy a company's goods or services, akin to people who respond to direct-mail ads. Also called click rate.

clutter. The collective name for the many advertising spots on television.

co-branding. The practice of using two established brand names to create a new product. Two examples are MSNBC and AOL/Time Warner.

co-op. A cooperative advertisement, jointly paid for by the manufacturer and the retailer.

commish. A commission paid to an ad agency.

comp. Short for comprehensive or complimentary.

copy. Written or typewritten text in an ad or commercial. See ART.

CPM. Cost per thousands of readers (the "M" is the Roman numeral for thousand). Print publications' ad rates are based on CPM, and many online publications are following in their footsteps.

creative side. The people in an advertising agency who actually create ads. The other side is the ACCOUNT SIDE.

customer golf. Term for recognizing the fact that an agency has to go along with and not "beat" the client. It is based on the notion that you don't go out to play golf with your best customer and whomp him on the fairway.

Dinfo (acr). Defense information—the Pentagon's public relations office. Also the function of that office.

dog-and-pony show. Press conference, or any other carefully prepared performance.

door buster. Heavily discounted premium item offered to the first people through the door.

double truck. A two-page ad.

Equity. A theme that has worked over time and increases in value.

Face. A particular alphabet or typeface.

flack / flak. 1. A public relations person. 2. To push a product, service, or story.

frame grabber. A celebrity who is the center of attention at all events.

Greek. Garbled letters used to indicate text in a dummy ad.

Hand-holding. Reassuring an advertising or PR client.

hits. In online advertising, the cumulative number of contacts made to a Web page, including graphics files and live links. Counting hits was the first accepted method of measuring a Web site's popularity. It's now considered inaccurate, but some Web publishers still use it.

hot-dogger. Publicity seeker.

hymns (acr). Hidden messages.

hype. Deception through inflated promises in advertising and or promotion.

Impressions. Number of people who have looked at a given page on the Internet. Web publishers use impressions as a basis for setting ad rates, and advertisers use them to choose the best Web pages to place their ads.

ink. Press coverage; a goal of public relations.

Jaboney. An accessible expert who makes frequent media appearances.

jingle. Short musical refrain used on radio or television commercials.

Kickapoo. The customer's product.

kotex. A free newspaper "shopper," which is seldom read but is scanned for ads.

Live tag. Voice at the end of a commercial that gives current or local information, such as "Opens Wednesday at the Cineplex 6" at the end of a movie commercial.

loose cannon. Client who talks too much and without restraint and, for this reason, must be kept away from the press.

Magalog. Blend of magazine + catalog, for a catalog that acts like a magazine in that among its own ads it also carries ads for other companies and their products.

media. In advertising, the ad space or time one buys. Not to be confused with "media" to refer to broadcast and print journalism.

mention. A short item in the press. Publicists like to be able to say, "Did you see this morning's mention in the *Wall Street Journal*?"

Nose hair. Client, especially a demanding one, to some folks in advertising.

Online malls. Collective name for the Internet as an advertising and marketing medium.

overexposure. What happens to a celebrity who endorses too many products and thereby becomes ineffective.

PA. Public affairs. This is what some companies and almost all government

PA. (*continued*)
agencies call their public relations operations, usually PAOs, for public affairs office, to avoid the PR label, which is seen as manipulation of opinion.

peg. Newsworthy or notable nugget in a press release or campaign. Also a SLANT or HANDLE.

pickup. The use of a press release, photo, etc., by the media; public relations placement.

pixels. The basic element of measurement on a computer screen (blend of picture + element). Online ads are measured by the pixel, so a banner could be, say, 260 pixels long and 80 pixels deep.

place. To use public relations techniques to get a favorable mention or story in the media.

placement. The process by which name-brand products appear in movies and on television, such as getting an expensive branded piece of diagnostic equipment on *ER* or a box of Kellogg's cereal on *Seinfeld*.

plug. In public relations, a favorable positioning for a product or service.

pluggery. A PR firm.

PR. Public relations, both as a noun and a verb. To PR the public is to put a message across.

praisery. A PR firm.

product PR. Publicity gained for an item rather than a person or a company. Product publicists work to get their products shown on television or in the movies.

puff piece. A flattering article in the press about a client or product.

puffery. Exaggerated claim or promise given for a product or service. Calling something the best that money can buy is often regarded as pure puffery.

pull. 1. The ability to create sales, which is said of the most effective ads. 2. To remove an ad or kill an advertising campaign.

put on the map. Successfully promote and advertise a relatively unknown product or service.

Release. 1. A press release. 2. In advertising, a written okay to use a person's face, voice, or name commercially.

remnant space. Odd page spots sold at a discount.

Sandwich man. A human billboard; a person wearing a huge sign fore and aft, making a human sandwich—less common today than they once were. The term is still used as an image of disparagement: "We'd be better off with a sandwich man."

score. A public relations coup.

shelf shout. The ability of a product to create immediate impact by means of its packaging.

shop. An ad agency.

shot. A publicist's attempt at placement.

shout and sell. Crude, low-budget infomercials.

sizzle. Image, from the advertising maxim that you should sell the sizzle, not the steak.

slant. The attitude or opinion that a publicist is trying to put across. For instance, a PR slant on nuclear power might be that it is essential to America's future.

sonic branding. The association of a piece of music with a product, company, or broadcast program.

space. Paper or airtime that has been purchased for a client. Space can also be obtained through public relations.

spin / spin control. In public relations and politics, the ability to present a client or situation in a certain light and with a certain SLANT; to control how others view the client or event.

spin doctor / spin master. PR person with the proven ability to put a certain slant or story across.

spokesweasel. Derogatory name for a spokesperson who tends to weasel out of giving answers.

stink bomb. A high-profile failure, in the world of public relations.

stunt. An event staged as news for the purpose of public relations.

suck wind. In PR terminology, an unsuccessful attempt to get publicity for your client or boss.

sweeps. Periods during which television shows are rated and ranked by audience size. The outcome determines the advertising rates for the show in question.

Teaser. Ad or announcement that arouses interest without naming the product, as in, "Coming soon, the movie of the year."

thirty. A thirty-second commercial.

throwaway. Handbill or other printed ad that the advertiser assumes will be looked at for a few seconds before being thrown away.

tip-on. Promotional item such as a magnet, DVD, or game piece affixed to a page in a magazine.

trade out. Goods or services given for ad space or broadcast time, for instance, meals given in exchange for a restaurant ad in a directory.

traffic tracking. Statistical analysis of activity on a Web site or page in online advertising. Companies such as Nielsen/IPRO, WebTrack, and NetCount sell traffic-tracking services, which Web publishers use as the basis for determining advertising rates.

tub-thump. To make an obvious appeal or pitch for a client or product.

Up-cut. To edit a television show, usually a rerun, to fit in one or more extra commercials.

USP. Unique selling proposition, one that distinguishes a product or service from its competitors.

Video cart. Recently introduced type of grocery shopping cart with a video screen that plays commercials for the customer while shopping.

virgin. Focus-group first-timer, in market research. Becomes a "recycled virgin," "semi-virgin," and "retread."

VO / voice-over. Narration in a commercial by a person not seen.

White-coat rule. Nickname for the Federal Trade Commission prohibition against commercials that claim or imply that the person on the screen is a doctor.

Zoo (acr). Zero on originality. To work for a zoo agency is to work for one lacking innovation.

25

SPORTS SLANG

Of Balls, Bats, Clubs, Rackets, and Pucks

What am I supposed to believe when some TV announcer talks about a nose guard making a key tackle? Come on. A nose guard is a piece of equipment. And what is this nickel defense? I used to know a guy named Floyd Nickel. Pretty good athlete. You don't suppose? No, no. He went into auto insurance.

—Michael Kernan, "Learning to Understand the Game in One 'Ese' Lesson: Football Made 'Ese,' "
Washington Post, September 11, 1982

The strong influence of sports on the American language is stunning and at the beginning of the twenty-first century appears to be at an all-time real and metaphoric high.

Senators throw "softball questions" (i.e., easy) at confirmation hearings and everyone seems to be willing to settle for a rough "ballpark figure," while the president reckons his legislative "box score" with Congress. We "play for keeps" (marbles), get "faked out" (football), and sometimes "get the benefit of the doubt" (fencing). "Inside baseball" has gained popularity outside baseball as a way of describing inner-sanctum goings-on, and just about everybody seems to be playing "hardball" (which, as it turns out, appears to be from handball, not baseball). When all else fails, we "fall back and punt."

This creeping sports-ese began its advance years ago. In fact, the transfer has not always been welcomed. "Hit and run" is a baseball term that upset many when it was first used for an automotive felony in the 1930s. Other terms are so much a part of our daily language that we are largely unaware of their sports origins. "Charley horse" is a baseball term that has become so standard for the ailment it describes, a cramp in the thigh muscle called the quadriceps famoris, that even medical doctors now use the baseball term.

Sports slang is in a class by itself. It is so vast and extensive that its individual components are counted in the thousands. A baseball dictionary I authored in 1989 contained more than five thousand terms, of which the vast majority were slang. A second edition had over seven thousand, and now I am working on a third, with more than ten thousand terms.

And that is just baseball. What about a pastime as humble as marbles—about the only game that I excelled at as a kid. I have begun a collection of marble terms because they are fast becoming archaic and will soon be "lost," and I have already come up with more than three hundred. There are more.

Here I have compiled a sampling of slang from various sports, labeled for the sport the term comes from if it is not general jock talk.

Ace. 1. (tennis) A serve which one's opponent fails to return. 2. (golf) A hole in one.

ad (basketball). You've got the ad, or advantage, when tight, up.

air pass (basketball). What occurs when the dribbler throws or taps the ball in the air and then touches it before it reaches the floor.

air war (football). Offense staged by a good passing team, as contrasted to a GROUND WAR.

airball / air ball (basketball). Shot that misses the rim of the basket.

aircraft carrier (basketball). The big man; a driver whose dominance can make a team a winner.

alibi-itis. An ailment characteristic of players who offer an excuse or alibi whenever they do not make the correct play.

all airport (basketball). Big, well-dressed player who looks good off the court but adds little to the team's effort on the court.

all net (basketball). Nothing but bottom. Also BIC, SCOOP, STRING MUSIC, SWISH.

alley-oop (basketball). A high lobbed shot or pass that is tipped in by a player near the basket.

allusional pitch (baseball). A pitch named for the characteristics of famous people. There's the Linda Ronstadt fastball, one with such speed that it "Blue Bayou," in sharp contrast to the Peggy Lee fastball, a reference to her jaded lament, "Is That All There Is?"

alphabet string. In health clubs, garment suggested for women too large for the traditional G-string.

also-ran. A competitor who is defeated in a race.

anchor. 1. (basketball) A shot likely to go "clang." Also known as a BRICK. 2. A member of a team, heavily depended upon, who is the last to perform in a relay race, as in track or swimming. The anchorman in bowling is the last to perform for his team.

apple. The ball, especially basketball and baseball.

arbiter. An umpire, in baseball and softball.

armchair quarterback. Fan of televised sports who thinks he has most of the answers; not restricted to football, or even sports (one can, for example, be a political armchair quarterback).

around-the-world (basketball). A schoolyard shooting game in which players try to match each other shot for shot along an arc.

audible. Football play that is called verbally by the offensive team after it has positioned itself over the ball.

Baby J (basketball). Short, smooth jump shot.

back-bounce pass (basketball). A bounce pass made in a backward direction toward a teammate. It may be a blind pass or the passer may peer over his shoulder at the receiver.

back nine (golf). The last nine holes on an eighteen-hole course.

backdoor (basketball). A cut toward the basket by an offensive player when he or she is being overplayed.

backdoor play (basketball). A play directly under the basket and behind the backs of the defenders. An offensive player sneaks in behind the backs of the defenders and takes a pass from a teammate under the basket for a backdoor play.

bag (baseball; softball). A base. Also called sack, hassock, pillow, canvas.

bagel (tennis). Zero. To win a set 6–0 is to give your opponent a bagel.

ball hawk. Basketball player who specializes in recovering loose balls. An aggressive defensive player who dives for and recovers loose balls, blocks passes and shots, and makes steals and interceptions.

ball hog. A basketball player who is not very popular for the simple reason that he or she doesn't like to pass the ball.

ball out (baseball; softball). To draw back from the plate in order to avoid being hit by a pitched ball.

Baltimore chop (baseball). A batted ball that strikes home plate or the ground near home plate to rebound high into the air. The batter can often beat out a Baltimore chop for a base hit.

bang (basketball). To hit the boards hard.

bangboard (basketball). The glass, metal, or wood surface above and to the sides of the basket, used for carom shots taken from an angle, particularly layups.

banger. A clumsy, ineffective pool or billiards player.

bank board / bankboard (basketball). Another term for backboard, so called because many players use the backboard to "bank" their shots toward the basket. See BANGBOARD.

bank's open, the (basketball). An interjection uttered while releasing a shot off the backboard.

baseball pass (basketball). A long one-handed pass to a receiver upcourt. Used mainly by centers starting a fast break for distance and speed or both.

barnburner. An exciting contest.

bases drunk (baseball). Bases loaded.

basket catch (baseball; softball). A catch of a fly ball at waist level, the glove and the bare hand cradling the ball.

basket-hanging (basketball). Staying in the offensive area of the court when the rest of the players have moved to the other end. The basket hanger hopes to receive a long pass and take an uncontested shot. Also called CHERRY PICKING.

basketball Jones. Playground basketball addict. On the street, a "Jones" is an addictive habit.

batboy shot (baseball). A term attributed to the Yankees' Oscar Gamble for a home run that is hit so hard that the batter simply hands his bat to the batboy. Similarly, in August 2005 the broadcaster Tom Marr, in attempting to describe the magnitude of a John Lowenstein home run, simply noted, "They show movies on a flight like that." These big homers have also been called moon shots.

battery (baseball; softball). The pitcher and the catcher.

bean (baseball). To hit the batter on the head with a pitch.

beanball (baseball). Pitch aimed at a batter's head.

bedposts (bowling). The 7–10 split.

bell lap (track; cycling). The last lap of a race.

bench jockey. A player who rides (heckles) opposition players from the bench or dugout.

bench warmer. Player who is seldom brought into the game; a substitute.

best ball. When golfers play as partners, each one using his own ball, the better ball on each hole is their score for that hole.

bic (basketball). A successful shot that touches no iron; popular in the D.C.-Baltimore area.

big ball. One of a number of names for softball.

Big Dance, the (basketball). The NCAA tournament, when the Big Player can hit the

Big Shot and later sign a sneaker deal for the Big Bucks.

big man. The center on a basketball team.

bird cage. Protective face mask.

birdie (golf). One under par for a hole.

biscuit. The hockey puck. The object of hockey is to put more biscuits in the net (the goal) than the opposition.

blackout. To prohibit the telecasting of a sports event in a specific area.

bleeder (baseball; softball). A batted ball that just trickles past the defensive players for a "weak" base hit.

blind pass (basketball). A pass in which the passer does not see his receiver but expects him to be there.

blind side. The side where a player is not looking.

blitz. 1. (basketball) To win a pickup game in straight baskets, usually by 9–0. Also SKUNK. 2. (football) A massive attempt by the defense to penetrate the offensive line and ground (tackle) the quarterback.

block, on the (basketball). Where a player sets up to receive the ball near the basket.

blocker. A hockey glove that generally has a foam-padded shield attached, worn on the stick hand.

blooper. A batted ball that arches over the heads of the infielders and drops in front of the outfielders for a base hit.

blue. Any baseball or softball umpire, from the color of his or her uniform. It is used in lines like "Oh, come on, blue" after a dubious call.

blue-collar ballet. Professional wrestling.

blueliner. Hockey defenseman, from the fact that he defends the area behind the blue line, which is sixty feet from each goal.

board 'n' cord. A basketball shot banked off the backboard.

boards. Backboards, in basketball.

bob and weave (boxing). To move one's upper body from side to side and forward and back in an effort to avoid an opponent's punches.

bobble (baseball; softball). Juggling the ball while attempting a catch, or dropping the ball for an error.

body nazis. Hard-core exercise and weight-lifting fanatics.

bogart (basketball). A strong move inside.

bogey (golf). A score of one stroke over par on a hole.

bomb (football). An extremely long pass.

boo-yah. Exclamation used following a good play.

boobird. Disruptive fan who boos frequently at sporting events.

boogie (basketball). To drive fast.

book. 1. To run fast; to BOOGIE. 2. Data on an opponent.

bootleg. In football, an offensive play in which the quarterback conceals the ball at his hip, and hurries to one side to run or pass.

bow (basketball). Shorthand for elbow; to bow is to elbow an opponent.

bowling pass (basketball). A one-hand pass thrown with an underhand motion similar to that used by a bowler. It is an air pass.

box out (basketball). To keep an opposing player behind you so he cannot rebound the ball; a screening tactic used by the defense to gain control of the ball.

break the ice (basketball). The custom, common on some playgrounds, of not keeping score until at least one basket has been made.

breeze (basketball). Air ball, as in the ball created a breeze.

brick (basketball). A misfired shot with little chance of going in. Also ANCHOR.

brush back (baseball; softball). To attempt to move a batter away from the plate by pitching the ball high and inside.

brush block (basketball). A combination of a block and a screen in which an offensive player rubs against a defensive player while on the move.

bucket. 1. (basketball) Two-point field goal. 2. (hockey) Helmet. 3. (bowling) A spare in which the 2-, 4-, 5-, and 8-pins are left standing.

Bugs Bunny change-up (baseball). Slow pitch that looks like a fastball but because of the grip (the ball is held firmly in the hand against the palm), it comes in anywhere from 10 to 20 mph slower. To work, everything has to look the same as a fastball: the angle of the arm, the speed of the arm motion, the release point. From a Bugs Bunny cartoon in which the character is able to get strikeouts by throwing balls so slowly that the batter falls asleep.

bulk up. To add to muscle size by exercise and weight lifting.

bump and run (football). For a pass defender to bump into a potential receiver (which is legal) to upset his balance and then run alongside him.

bunker (golf). They come in two varieties, both of which are to be avoided. The first is a depression in the course covered with deep grass. The second is a depression filled with sand, the sand trap. It is considered a hazard.

bunny (basketball). Layup without a nearby defender.

burn. 1. (basketball) To make a move that takes advantage of an opponent defensively. 2. To win convincingly, in any sport.

burner. 1. Pinched nerve. 2. (football) Speedy wide receiver, who can "burn" the opposition.

bus stop (basketball). A jump shot. Also THE J, joint.

bush. Short for "bush league," i.e., dishonorable, gutless, or without class.

bust (basketball). An explosive drive to the hoop.

butcher (basketball). 1. A physically abusive defensive player. 2. To inflict physical punishment on another player.

butt-ending (hockey). To hit an opponent with the handle end of the stick. Illegal.

butterfly (hockey). The method by which a goalie becomes very active—diving, flopping, and falling to his knees to make saves.

buttonhook. 1. (football) Forward-pass play in which the receiver runs downfield and then stops to turn evasively (hook) toward the passer. 2. (basketball) To go in one direction and then turn sharply and double back.

buzzer shot (basketball). A shot made in an attempt to score as the buzzer sounds.

Cabbageball (softball). One more name for a Chicago sixteen-inch softball.

cage (hockey). A one-piece helmet with a mask. Many goalies have pictures painted on it.

cager. A basketball player; derived from the original playing area, the cage. In the early days of basketball, games were played with a cloth or wire netting around the floor to prevent the ball from going into the crowd. It also served to prevent unruly spectators from harming players and officials.

cagey. Describing a smart, experienced basketball player who has basketball savvy. This term probably originated in the days when basketball was played in a cage.

camel toe. Volleyball ball struck with knurled fingers.

camp (basketball). To establish a position in the low post for extended periods of time.

can the shot (basketball). To score a basket.

card. Scorecard.

casual water (golf). Water not supposed to be on the course; puddles.

cellar. Last place.

center cut (baseball). Fastball down the middle.

chalk talk. A lecture or discussion conducted by the coach, often with the use of a blackboard.

charity stripe (basketball). The foul line where one goes to take a free—charity—shot.

chaser (basketball). Normally the man nearest midcourt in a zone defense. His job is to harass or chase the man with the ball.

chatter (baseball; softball). The continual encouragement (to your team) and the discouragement to the other team that goes on during a game, such as offering your pitcher ritual lines like "No batter here" and "They're scared of you out there."

cheap shot. An act of deliberate violence against an opponent, and one that is committed when the opponent is not expecting it and is not able to defend himself; unsportsmanlike conduct.

check. 1. (hockey) To impede the progress of an opponent by use of the body (body check) or the stick (poke check or stick check). 2. (basketball) A blocked shot.

check up (basketball). To play defense.

cheese. (pool and billiards) Luck.

cherry-pick (basketball). To remain near the basket while play is at the other end of the court in hopes of getting a long pass and an undefended basket.

chippie (basketball). An easy shot.

choke. To misplay, usually in a crucial moment in the game, because of anxiety, apprehension, or tension.

chopped ball (baseball; softball). A swing of the bat in which the batter strikes downward with a chopping motion so that the ball bounces high into the air. The purpose of a chopped ball is to allow the runner to reach first base by beating the throw.

chops (boxing). The jaw.

chucks. Classic Chuck Taylor basketball sneakers.

Cinderella team. A team with little hope at the beginning of a season or tournament that goes on to unexpected success. Among the most notable college basketball Cinderella teams were Utah's 1944 NCAA champions, CCNY's 1950 NCAA and NIT champions, and Texas Western's 1965 NCAA champions.

circus catch (baseball). Any catch that is characterized by a sensational element, such as diving and rolling on the ground.

cliff-hanger. A game or other event that is so closely contested that its outcome is uncertain until the very end.

clinch. 1. To win a championship before the end of the season by building a lead so great that it cannot be overcome by an opponent. 2. (boxing) To hold an opponent with one or both arms so as to prevent or hinder his punches.

clothesline. 1. (football) To strike an opponent, often a pass receiver breaking downfield, across the face or neck with an extended forearm. Clotheslining is illegal. 2. (basketball) Hard foul in the head and neck area.

coast to coast. (basketball) Taking a rebound and single-handedly taking it to the other end of the court for a basket. Going baseline to baseline.

cobra. 1. In a health club or gym, a person with a big muscular back that tapers down to a narrow waist. 2. (volleyball) A ball struck with straight, locked fingertips.

cocktail frank. Junior hot dog.

coffee (golf). The tee, what else?

cold hand (basketball). A player who has trouble making shots is said to have a cold hand.

combination (boxing). A series of punches delivered in rapid succession.

combo coverage. Defensive football in which man-to-man and zone defenses are combined.

cookie monster (bowling). A 5–7–10 split.

cords (basketball). The net below the rim of the basket. A quotation by Dave DeBusschere displayed at the Basketball Hall of Fame in Springfield, Mass., says, "It's kind of nice to get out there and make a couple of shots and hear the cords sort of talk back to you when you make a good jump shot."

counter (football). A play that goes in the opposite direction of its original movement.

counterfeit (basketball). A shot with a dubious chance of going in.

CORNHOLING: THE NEXT MAJOR?

The emerging game of cornholing involves tossing corn-filled bags into holes from a distance. Also referred to as baggo, softshoes, or 'hole, the game has become a popular pastime in bars and backyards in the Midwest. In fact, the *Cincinnati Post* in 2005 called it the "cornhole craze" in the city where many believe the game originated. The game is played in innings. Just like in baseball, the side that starts the game is the top of the inning while the side that follows is the bottom.

According to the rules posted on playcornhole.com, the cornhole boards face each other and are placed twenty-seven feet apart. Players throw from either side of the board while not going past the front of the board (the foul line). A bag on the board scores one point and a bag in the hole, three points. However, points cancel each other out. A bag on the board must cancel a bag on the board and the same goes for a bag in the hole. Any points scored that aren't canceled by an opponent's count toward that round's score.

An article in the *Roanoke Times* (Virginia), October 20, 2005, on the new sport identified an emerging cornholing slang:

blocker. Blocks the front of the hole, preventing the slide-in toss.

cornatopia. When your team is throwing really well and you have nothing to do but drink beer and throw 'hole.

cornucopia. Eight bags in the hole—basically an overflowing hole.

double dipper / triple dipper. When there's a bag or two on the board and you throw a new bag, pushing two or three bags in with one toss.

hooker. When you toss the bag with a lot of "Frisbee" spin to catch a corner of an existing bag on the board, which curls it around and into the hole (usually around a blocker).

wash. When neither team gets any points.

cousin (baseball). A pitcher that a batter usually finds he can hit well.

crackback (football). Blocking maneuver by a pass receiver who runs downfield and then turns around to clear out the man covering him.

crawling (football). An attempt by a ball carrier to advance the ball after he has hit the ground.

crease (hockey). The protected area in front of the net, also known as the goalmouth. Goalies can use its markings for positioning and to help with the angles. No other player is permitted in the crease before the puck arrives.

cross training. Using one sport to practice the techniques of another; for example, using Rollerblading to improve skiing skills.

cup. A hard cup-shaped device for protecting the male genitals.

cut. 1. In basketball, football, and other team sports, to make a quick change of direction in an effort to elude an opponent. 2. To drop a prospective player from a roster or team.

D. Defense.

day (basketball). Caucasian or white, as in "The dude's game is strictly *day*, man."

dead (basketball). Having completed a dribble, being forced either to shoot or pass.

deadwood. Bowling pins that have been knocked down but remain on the alley or in the gutter. In tenpin bowling, deadwood must be removed before the ball can be rolled. In candlepins, deadwood remains on the alley and is in play.

death valley (basketball). The foul lane.

deef (tennis). Default.

deke. 1. (ice hockey) A fake by the puck carrier that enables him to stickhandle around an opponent. 2 (baseball) To decoy an opponent, such as by giving a false signal.

deuce. Two, as in you've got to win by a deuce.

dinger (baseball). A home run.

dink. In tennis, volleyball, and other net games, a softly hit ball that goes just beyond the net.

dish. 1. (basketball) To pass off neatly; to make a deft pass, usually for an assist. 2. (baseball) Home plate.

ditchers (basketball). The back men in a zone defense.

divot (golf). A piece of sod cut and lifted out of the ground by the clubhead.

doctor (basketball). A player who scores from the inside in a showy manner—from the notion of one who operates well and makes HOUSE CALLS.

does windows (basketball). Can dunk the ball.

dog. 1. (football). To rush the passer, the same as RED DOG. 2. (pool and billiards). To blow a shot; one who blows shots.

dog it. To play lackadaisically; to goof off.

dogleg (golf). A sharp turn on the fairway.

double clutch / double pump (basketball). A move that involves bringing the ball up and down after leaving your feet, yet still shooting it before traveling.

double-team. To guard one offensive player with two defensive players, to prevent a shot, pass, or dribble.

downtown (basketball). Deep. A three-point shot will come from downtown.

drill (basketball). Nail a field goal.

drive in (baseball; softball). To bat in a run with a hit ball.

duckets / ducks. Tickets.

duffer (golf). A player who lacks skill and experience.

dunk / dunk shot (basketball). A shot blasted into the basket with the release coming after it has entered the cylinder.

Dutch 200 (bowling). Rolling a 200 game with alternative strikes and spares.

Eagle (golf). Two strokes under par.

eat the ball (football). For a potential passer to hold on to the ball and be tackled (for a loss of yardage) rather than throw it.

elbow (basketball). Corner of the painted area under the basket. A player may shoot from the elbow.

empty-net goal. A hockey goal scored when the goaltender has been pulled.

enduro. Endurance race.

enforcer. Hockey player whose forte is intimidating the opposition. Frank Luksa of the *Dallas Morning News* defined the term in 1993: "Player with an I.Q. equivalent to temperature of ice. His only forte is fouling to intimidate. He plays 80 games, scores two goals, spends 2,500 minutes in the penalty box. Don't invite him home. He will spear your house pet."

Face (basketball). 1. Respect and honor—that intangible at stake in any man-to-man playground encounter that makes even single plays memorable. When face is at stake, one can do only one of two things: save it or lose it. 2. An emphatic dunk or shot right in the face of an opposing player. Also used to urge a fellow player to stop his man, as in "Get in his face."

face job (basketball). An individual offensive or defensive move so captivating that it wins for one moment the karma of FACE.

fade (football). To gradually move backward or laterally.

fake. To indicate intention to go in one direction without actually doing so.

faker. A basketball player who feints or fakes.

farm out. To send a player to a farm, or feeder, team.

favorite. Team or entry in a contest who seems to be most likely to win, especially common to horse racing.

Faye Dunaway (basketball). A fadeaway shot.

feeder (basketball). The player "feeding" the ball to his teammate, who will try to drive in and score a basket.

finger roll (basketball). A basket that is made as the ball rolls off the tips of the shooter's fingers.

firehorse basketball (basketball). Game action that employs fast breaks, long passes, and one-handed shooting from angles; common in the sixties and early seventies.

five-hole (hockey). The sometimes-open area between a goalie's legs. Less common terms are one-hole (over the left shoulder), two-hole (over the right shoulder), three-hole (left side), and four-hole (right side).

flake. A player known for his eccentric conduct.

flanker (football). An offensive player set into a position beyond the end before the ball is put into play.

flash cut (basketball). A sudden cut into the lane for a possible pass in and easy score; then, if the ball is not passed, jumping back out on the side from which entry was made.

flats (football). The areas on either extremity of the line of scrimmage and extending about five yards into defensive territory. A "flat pass" is one thrown into this area for short yardage.

floater (baseball; softball). A ball that stays in the air for a long time, appearing to float.

flood (football). To put two or more receivers in one zone.

flopper (ice hockey). A goalkeeper who frequently falls to the ice to smother the puck.

flow (football). The direction in which the players are moving after the play has begun.

flush (basketball). To score.

fly hack (rugby football). The wanton kicking of a loose ball by a panicky player.

footer (basketball). Big, slower player.

fork ball (baseball). A pitch delivered with the index and middle fingers that drops as it nears the plate.

4A (baseball). Describes a player who is better than triple-A but still not good enough to make the cut for the majors.

free trip (baseball). Base on balls.

freelance. Players with an individual style rather than a team game with a one-for-all attitude. Originated on the playgrounds.

freelance play. An offense allowing individual choices, as opposed to a set play.

freeze. To attempt to retain possession of the ball or puck for an extended period of time without making an effort to score.

frontliners (basketball). Collective term for the two forwards and center.

frostie (softball). Slow-pitch pitch that arcs above twelve feet—a facetious allusion to the frost that appears at higher altitudes.

funk dunk (basketball). Any sort of DUNK that showcases flair or leaping ability.

fungo (baseball). A practice fly hit to a fielder by tossing the ball in the air and hitting it as it falls.

furniture (tennis). Racket frame.

Game face. Looking mean and determined; the term may have been created to describe the former New York Knick Bernard King.

game full of leather (baseball; softball). One characterized by good fielding.

game point (basketball). The juncture in a game where one score can win it.

garbage (basketball). A loose ball or rebound that results in a layup or short jumper.

garbage time (basketball). When the players play individual basketball rather than a team game and try to fatten their statistics.

gift of grab. The skill of a pickpocket in being able to steal the ball.

Ginny (tennis). The Virginia Slims tennis tour, for short.

give-and-take (hockey). A technique in which the goalie gives the shooter an open target, then quickly closes (or takes away) the hole when the opponent shoots.

golf widow. A woman whose husband spends a great amount of time on the golf course.

good cheese (baseball). Blurring fastball. Fastballs are, or have been, called breezers, aspirins, smokers, sizzlers, soakers, rivets, and steamers.

good hands. The ability to catch a ball.

good wood (baseball; softball). When one makes solid contact with the ball, despite the fact that, outside of the pros, hardly anyone uses wooden bats anymore.

googan (pool and billiards). A recreational pool player.

gopher ball (baseball; softball). A pitch that is hit for a home run.

gorilla juice. Steroids.

grand slam (baseball; softball). A home run with the bases filled.

granny shot (basketball). An underhand free throw.

grass cutter (baseball; softball). A hard-hit ball that skims along the green.

graveyard (bowling). Low-scoring lane.

grease it (basketball). A cry heard from shooters whose shots are hanging on the rim.

gridiron (football). The field itself, from the appearance of its horizontal lines, which are spaced five yards apart.

grips. Shoes. Everything from blinking L.A. Gears to Kmart specials and Doc Martens. It ain't the shoes, contrary to Spike Lee's ad pitch—it's the player in the shoes.

groove (baseball; softball). To pitch the ball right in the middle of the strike zone.

ground war (football). Offense staged by a good running team.

gun shy. Overly cautious, especially after an injury, such as a baseball player who has been hit by a ball.

gunner (basketball). Someone who shoots a lot. Also chucker, heaver, pump.

gusjohnson (basketball). To dunk so ferociously that rim is separated from backboard. (Ex-pro Gus Johnson did it once.)

gutter ball (bowling). A ball that rolls off the alley and into the gutter, or trough. A gutter ball is a dead ball and counts as a turn.

gym rat. A regular.

Hack (basketball). Hitting a player across the hands or arms as he tries to dribble or pass the ball.

Hail Mary (football). A pass thrown into the end zone into a crowd of receivers and defenders. This is a desperation play commonly attempted in the last few minutes of a game by a team that is losing.

handle (basketball). A player with good ball-handling skills is said to have a good handle.

hang (baseball; softball). Said of a pitch that fails to break.

hang time. 1. (basketball) The period of time a player hovers in the air—hangs—while driving to the basket. 2. (football) The amount of time a punted ball remains in the air.

harrigan (pool and billiards). A lucky shot.

hat trick. Three goals by one player in one game. The term is common to ice hockey and soccer.

headhunter (baseball). Pitcher using fastball to settle grievences, real or imagined.

heady (basketball). Adjective applied by announcers to short, slow players who can't shoot.

heave (basketball). A "hope," or desperation, shot where the player does not take the time or have the room to aim the ball properly.

hipping. To hit an opponent with your hip.

hit the dirt (baseball; softball). To slide.

hold court (basketball). To remain in successive pickup games by virtue of consecutive victories.

hole (basketball). The basket.

hole high (basketball). Ball position parallel to the circle, wheel, arc, or area surrounding the free-throw line.

homebrew. Locally bred player.

hook (golf). When the ball curves toward the body, it is hooking. For a right-handed golfer, that means to the left.

hoop (basketball). The metal rim of the basket, eighteen inches in diameter. Also called the CAGE or the BUCKET.

HORSE (basketball). Basic playground diversion, in which each player must match the successful shot of any previous player. If your predecessor misses, you're free to shoot from anywhere. Anyone who misses after someone else's make is assessed one letter of the word "horse." Spell H-O-R-S-E and you are one. If life's hectic, just play PIG.

hospital pass (rugby football). Dangerous pass that could, as they say in Britain, "put you in hospital."

host. To be the home team.

hot corner (baseball; softball). Third base.

hot dog. 1. One who shows off. 2. To show off.

hot hand (basketball). The player who is having a good night with his shooting and "can't miss" from the field.

house ball (bowling). A ball that is provided by the bowling center.

house call (basketball). A showy move.

house on (basketball). To be shown up; dunked on.

hung him out to dry (basketball). A player driving around his defender for an easy two points. It usually suggests that the offensive man had no trouble in getting by his opponent.

hustler. An individual who seeks to induce persons less skilled than himself to gamble at pool or billiards.

Ice time (ice hockey). The amount of playing time accumulated by a player during a game or season.

iceman. Hockey player.

in-and-out (basketball). A term used to describe a shot that appears to be ready to drop into the basket but is just a fraction off line and bounces off the rim or spins out.

in the refrigerator (basketball). The term applied to a game so far out of reach that the team ahead will win the game. It's "in the refrigerator."

in-your-face (basketball). Describing a disrespectful or disdainful style of play.

inside (football). The interior line; between the tackles.

iron man / woman. One who chooses to play though injured.

J / the J. (basketball). The jump shot. Also BUS STOP, joint.

jab (boxing). A quick, straight blow, usually delivered to the opponent's head with the lead hand (the left hand in the case of a right-handed boxer).

jack. In lawn bowling, the small white ball, two and a half inches in diameter, that serves as the bowler's target.

jam. 1. (baseball; softball) To pitch inside to a batter, usually very close to his hands, to prevent him from hitting the ball solidly. 2. (basketball) See DUNK.

jam up (basketball). When a defensive team clogs up the middle of the court. (A zone or floating defense may do this.)

jock. 1. An athletic supporter or jockstrap, for short. 2. An athlete. 3. Athletic in nature, as in "jock school" or "jock fraternity house."

juice. Steroids.

juice monkey. One bloated or otherwise affected by steroids.

juke. 1. (basketball) An awkward or unusual shot. 2. (football) To fake an opponent, especially a potential tackler, out of position.

jumper (basketball). A jump shot.

junk. 1. (basketball) A sudden move used by either an offensive or defensive player, usually as a decoy. 2. (baseball) Pitches that are regarded as being of inferior quality, usually slow curveballs. 3. (volleyball) Off-speed shots.

K. (baseball; softball). A strikeout. The letter *K* is used in scoring a game to indicate a strike.

keeper. 1. (football) Offensive play in which the quarterback holds on to and runs with the ball rather than passing it or handing it off. 2. Goalkeeper, for short.

kegler. A bowler. From *kegeln*, German for "bowling."

key. To watch and take one's cue from a player on the other team.

key/keyhole (basketball). The entire free-throw area, including the free-throw lane and the free-throw circle.

keystone sack (baseball; softball). Second base.

kill shot. 1. (football) Extremely aggressive tackles of a severity that means the man tackled will have to be aided from the field. Lawrence Taylor of the New York Giants defined the term on the eve of Super Bowl XXI in 1987: "A kill shot is when snot's coming from his nose and he's quivering on the ground." 2. (tennis) In tennis and other racket games, a shot hit with such force that it is virtually unreturnable. Sometimes called a smash.

kill the clock (basketball). Sneakers.

killing the clock. Another way of saying "freezing the ball."

kip (gymnastics). In swinging from a horizontal bar, a movement at the end of the swing in which the performer snaps the legs back and straightens them, then raises the body to an arm support position.

kiss. In basketball, banking the ball off the backboard into the basket. In billiards and pocket billiards, a shot in which the cue ball rebounds from one object to another.

kitchen (shuffleboard). Space in which a player loses ten points. Players work hard to put their opponents in the kitchen.

kitten ball (Softball). One of a number of historic names for softball. The term still has application as sixteen-inch players talk disparagingly about folks who play with a twelve-inch ball. A line from a 1976 issue of the periodical *Windy City Softball* tells of a "Kittenball team from Indiana" being introduced to Chicago-style ball (and being whomped).

knife (golf). The one-iron—the hardest tool in the bag to use successfully.

knock-hockey player (basketball). A bank-shot artist.

Lane (basketball). The area between free-throw boundaries, and from the end line to the free-throw line. Also called the alley, crease, well, or hole.

last bullet (softball). Slang softball term for the upcoming third out in the last inning for the losing team.

laugher. Lopsided victory; a blowout—so easy that the winning team has fun. One big laugh.

laxman / laxwoman. Lacrosse player.

layup (basketball). A shot made close to the basket in which the ball is played off the backboard.

leader board (golf). Scoreboard on which the rankings of golfers in a tournament are listed.

leatherman (baseball). A good fielder; one who uses the leather in his glove to advantage.

lemonade (pool and billiards). To deliberately play below your true level of ability, as one might do at the beginning of a hustle.

like money in the bank (basketball). Safe. A sure shot, such as a slam dunk by Michael Jordan.

li'l' help (basketball). The playground S O S. If your ball rolls away toward a neighboring game or gets stuck in a tangled chain net, this alerts others that you'd like them to retrieve it, or offer their ball so you can jar yours free.

line-drive shot (basketball). Some players favor hard, low trajectory shots at the basket. But often this is a hard shot to make unless the player is extremely proficient. The shot also has a lot of velocity.

links. A golf course.

lock. A certainty.

look (basketball). A pass, usually inside, that leads to a basket. Also DISH or find.

lose the handle (basketball). To lose control of the ball and turn it over to the other team.

Magic number. In baseball, football, and other sports in which league championships are decided on a won-lost basis, the magic number is the combined total of wins for the league-leading team and losses for the second-place team that will mathematically assure the league leader of the championship. For example, if Team A leads the league by seven games over Team B with ten games remaining on the schedule, Team A's magic number is four.

maiden. A racehorse that has never won a race.

man on (soccer). Beware, you are being closely defended—you have a man on your back.

Meminger's law (basketball). An edict promulgated by the former pro and New York playground habitué Dean Meminger: if you don't play ball, you can't hang out.

mitts (hockey). The special gloves players wear.

mixer (bowling). A ball that causes the pins to bounce around.

moguls (skiing). Washboard ridges created by other skiers' skiing at an angle.

mojo. Magic.

mombo (basketball). A series of head, shoulder, or ball fakes.

Monday morning quarterback. Sports fan with all of the answers the day after the game.

money player. A player who comes through in key situations, when money is at stake, such as in the playoffs and championship games. Also used to describe big-salaried rookies who sign pro contracts for financial packages estimated in the many millions of dollars.

monster. Great inside player: Shaq.

mopped. Blown out.

move the ball (softball). Hit the ball. It is used in the fast-pitch game.

Mr. Kodak. A vain pro player, one who poses for press photographers.

mulligan (golf). A free shot given a player after a poor one.

mush ball (softball). 1. The sixteen-inch softball, to distinguish it from the smaller twelve-inch version. 2. The sixteen-inch game. 3. A name for softball.

mustard came off the hot dog. Used to describe a player's action when he tries a fancy play, as in "The mustard came off the hot dog on that pass."

my bad (basketball). My mistake. An expression of contrition, uttered after an air ball or an air pass goes out of bounds.

my house (basketball). My territory; the free-throw lane, as in "Don't bring that weak (stuff) into my house!" (Peter Corbett, *Phoenix Gazette,* August 14, 1994).

Nail. Line drive, swish, perfect pass, close to the pin, etc.

naked bootleg (football). Play in which the quarterback is completely unprotected as he moves in the opposite direction of the flow of play.

next level, the. Where college players want to go after they leave school, e.g., the NBA.

nickel defense (football). Strategy in which an extra defensive back is put in the backfield to defend against a pass, making five (a nickel) defenders rather than four.

no harm, no foul (basketball). One of the original Chick Hearn phrases. A play involving physical contact, but not enough to warrant a foul being whistled.

no huddle (football). Continuous offense play without regrouping, a tactic meant to surprise the defense.

no-man's-land. In tennis and other net games, a midcourt area between the baseline and the service line from which it is difficult to make an effective return. The player is too far from the net to volley properly, and not back far enough to execute solid baseline strokes.

nose guard / tackle (football). A guard or a tackle who stands in front of—nose to nose with—the opposing center during certain plays.

nosebleed country (spectator). Seats high above the action.

nosebleeder. Basketball player who can go high in the air for rebounds.

nothing but net (basketball). Describes a basket in which the ball does not hit the rim.

nurse (billiards). A playing technique in which the shooter keeps the balls in position for consecutive shots by striking them very softly.

nutmeg (soccer). To push the ball between the defender's legs, run around him or her, control the loose ball, and continue dribbling. It is very embarrassing to a defender to be nutmegged.

Office pool. A gambling exercise in which you try to pick the winner of every game in a tournament. Called a pool because you get soaked for whatever fee is needed, and you never win. "Invariably, the winner is someone's 12-year-old kid who picked the winners according to the most popular college jackets in middle school. The biggest entertainment value comes in seeing the office basketball expert lose his national champion in the first round to an upset by the Sally Struthers School of Career Advancement" (Ray Frager, *Baltimore Sun*, March 17, 1995, NCAA Preview).

ohfer (baseball; softball). A batter who is hitless in a game, as in "He was oh-for-four."

old boys (rugby football). Players who are thirty-five years old or older.

o-line (football). Offensive line.

on deck (baseball; softball). Scheduled to bat after the present batter.

110 percent. Extra effort.

OT. Overtime, in clock-based sports.

Paint (basketball). The free-throw lane, usually painted a different color than the rest of the court floor. "In the paint" indicates that a player is in the lane area near a basket. So named because the lane is often a different color from the rest of the floor.

paint the corners (baseball; softball). Pitch that crosses the inside or outside part of home plate for a strike.

palm (basketball). 1. To hold the ball in one hand, usually for show. Obligatory for most varieties of FUNK DUNK. 2. The illegal dribble on which there's no prohibition in the speakeasies of the schoolyard.

palming (basketball). Losing control of a dribble and—for a split second—carrying the ball in the palm of the hand. If a referee spots it, the other team gets the ball. Also called carrying.

pancake (football). Throwing a block that plants an opponent on his back.

paste. Defeat.

PAT (football). Point after touchdown.

pepper (baseball). Played with one batter and one or more fielders. The batter either bunts at or takes a half swing at the ball tossed by the fielder immediately after he or she fields the ball. The ball is continually thrown, batted, and fielded in rapid succession.

physical (football). Rough or dirty. A team that is "very physical" is very nasty.

pick (basketball). Stationing oneself so that the defensive man guarding the ball handler will be unable to stay with him, having run into the picker.

pick-and-roll (basketball). An offensive play where one man sets a pick, then moves or rolls around the defender and heads toward the basket to receive a pass (Zander Hollander, *Encyclopedia of Sports Talk*). A play in which the player setting a screen for a teammate with the ball suddenly cuts toward the basket for a pass.

pickup. Unorganized, spontaneous ball game, as in pickup game, pickup team. Also called drop-in, free play, ratball.

pigskin (football). 1. The football. 2. Relating to football, as in "pigskin preview."

pillow ball (softball). The sixteen-inch softball, to distinguish it from the smaller twelve-inch version.

pillows (hockey). Oversized leg pads to provide not only protection but defense. Once stuffed with horsehair, they now contain synthetic material. There are no metal parts.

pipes (hockey). The posts to both sides of the goalie that support the net. The pipes are six feet apart.

pit (football). The area along the line of scrimmage where the two lines clash.

playing the angles (hockey). Refers to the goaltender's position in the net in relation to the puck. When playing back in net, goalies have to move farther to make a save. Playing out front cuts down on the area to cover. See FIVE-HOLE.

pluggers (football). Linebackers.

poach. In doubles play in tennis and other court games, to cross into one's partner's court to cut off a shot and volley.

poodle (bowling). To roll the ball into the gutter.

pork chop. One who is overweight.

post (basketball). Another term for the pivot man's spot on the court. It is "high" when he plays near the free-throw line and "low" when he plays near the basket (Zander Hollander, *Encyclopedia of Sports Talk*).

prayer. A shot let go in such desperation that it seems only divine intervention will put it in the basket.

pressure cooker. A close, important game that goes down to the final minutes of play when everything is on the line (from "Chick's Lexicon"—i.e., one from Chick Hearn).

PT. Playing time.

puckhead (hockey). Fan.

pulling the goaltender (hockey). This usually happens late in games that are one-goal differences to allow the team trailing to add an extra skater. See EMPTY-NET GOAL.

pump shot (basketball). An overhead two-hand shot taken in midair. The shooter lifts the ball over his head, then cocks (pumps) his arm and shoots the ball before hitting the floor (William T. "Buck" Lai, *Winning Basketball*).

pumpkin (hockey). Your head.

punch on (basketball). To score on a defender.

punk dunk (basketball). A sort of dunk in which the dunker attempts to humiliate the dunkee.

puppy. Beginner at the health club.

Quarterback. The player who generally supervises his team's tactics and gives signals.

Rabbit dunk (baseball). A baseball that is livelier than normal, and thus one capable of being hit a long distance.

rack, the (basketball). The basket. Also called the cup, dog, or HOLE.

radio pitch (softball). As described in *Softball Player's Magazine*, "Batters can hear it, but can't see it." It has been used to describe the fastball of Debbie Doom of El Monte, California.

rainbow shot (basketball). A high arcing shot, usually from the outside over the heads of tall defenders.

rat race (basketball). A high-scoring game.

rattle (basketball). A successful shot in which the ball hits the inside of the rim several times before dropping through.

red dog (football). Defensive play in which the linebacker crashes through the line to kill the offensive play before it begins. In an earlier time this was known as rushing the passer.

redshirt (football). A college player who has been withheld from competition for a year so as to extend his eligibility to play.

ref. Referee.

rep (basketball). Reputation.

ribbie (baseball; softball). Improved way of saying RBI for "runs batted in," as in "He's got fifty-seven ribbies and it's still June."

ring his bell. To hit someone hard in a contact sport.

ringer. 1. Illegal player; a contestant entered dishonestly into a race or contest. 2. In horseshoe pitching, a horseshoe that is thrown so as to encircle the stake; is worth three points.

rip (basketball). A successful shot, usually a SWISHER.

ripped to the bone. Describes one who is all muscle—also roped and inside out.

roid. 1. A hemorrhoid 2. Steroid. 3. One on steroids; a JUICE MONKEY.

rookie. A first-year player, a novice. An apparent corruption of "recruit."

round-tripper (baseball). A home run.

rugger (rugby football). 1. The game of rugby. 2. One who plays the game.

rugger hugger (rugby football). A rugger's date or spouse.

run a clinic (basketball). 1. To execute a play crisply. 2. To win convincingly.

run-and-gun (basketball). Describes an open style of play in which direct assaults are made on the basket.

run it back (basketball). The request of a pickup team that has just been beaten to get an immediate rematch.

running game (basketball). Fast-break play. It features a quick pass from the rebounder to an outlet man, usually on the side of the court. The objective is to have as many players as possible breaking for the basket with the defense out of position.

Sack. 1. (football) A tackle of the quarterback behind the offensive line, usually as the result of a BLITZ. 2. (football) To tackle the quarterback. 3. (baseball) A base.

sandbagger (bowling). An individual who purposely keeps down his average in order to receive a higher handicap than he deserves.

sandwich (football). To trap an offensive player between two defenders.

school (basketball). To take advantage of someone by pulling a deft offensive move—from the notion that the person is being taught how to make the move.

scissors cut (basketball). When two or more players crisscross each other's path.

scrambler (football). A quarterback with a reputation for moving around to avoid being tackled.

scratch hit (baseball; softball). A ball, usually weakly hit, which none of the fielders can reach in time to retire the batter.

scrimmage. Gamelike practicing with two sides and scores, but sometimes fewer than the normal number of players on a side.

second effort. Sudden display of power and determination by an individual or team following a setback.

second wind. A renewal of energy after a period of exhaustion.

sewer (basketball). A basket so loose that anything going near it goes down it.

shag (baseball; softball). Chasing down and catching batted fly balls during batting or fielding practice.

shaggers (softball). Youngsters who are hired to retrieve over-the-fence home runs in slow-pitch softball tournaments and bring them back for reuse. In a major tournament such as the Smoky Mountain Classic or the Twitty City, as many as a thousand balls will go over the wall.

shake (basketball). To elude an opponent, usually by duping him with a stutter-step, or JUKE, and then breaking away.

shake and bake (basketball). To feint, fake, and ultimately score with a graceful move.

shirts vs. skins / shirts 'n' skins. Means of distinguishing one team from another in pickup games: one team wears shirts while the other is bare-chested.

shoestring. At or near ground level. Catching any ball just as it is about to hit the ground is a "shoestring catch," and a "shoestring tackle" in football is one made just above the knees.

shoot for it. The shooting of fingers, or the shooting of a shot, to decide who'll get possession when a jump ball or another quandary arises.

shoot the boot (rugby football). To fumble the lyrics of a rugby song at the postmatch bash.

shovel / shovel pass (football). A forward pass tossed underhand.

showboat. A player who shows off; a hot dog.

shuffle cut (basketball). After the player has made a pass; he then moves away from the pass by cutting around a teammate who has set a pick for him.

sin bin (ice hockey). Penalty box.

sixth man (basketball). The player who is regularly used as the team's first substitute.

skate save (hockey). To stop the puck with a skate.

skinned (softball). The proper condition and description of a softball infield, which is devoid—skinned—of grass.

skull practice. Practice involving the mental rather than the physical nature of the game in question.

skunk (basketball). To win a pickup game in straight baskets, usually by 9–0.

skunk rule (softball). Proviso encounters in which a game is ended if a team is ahead by a certain number of runs at the end of an inning.

sky (basketball). Not merely to jump, but to sail—in pursuit of hoops, bounds, rejections, or just a whiff of rarer air. Also: rise, talk to God.

skyhook (basketball). A high hook shot taken from an altitude above the level of the basket.

skywalk (basketball). An aerial stroll.

slab (baseball). The pitcher's rubber.

slam dunk (basketball). A dunk shot of unusual force and spectator appeal.

slants (softball). Pitched balls, especially in fastball parlance.

slap shot (ice hockey). A hard shot made by bringing the stick into a high backswing, then forward, hitting the ice and puck simultaneously, causing the puck to be lifted from the ice.

slashing (hockey). According to Frank Luksa of the *Dallas Morning News* in 1993: "Not to be confused with tripping, hooking, holding or cross-checking. Slashing employs the stick as a scythe in a hacking motion to cause a rival to fall down. When prone, he is easier to skate over and leave blade tracks across the chest."

sledgehammer (pool and billiards). A heavy stroke, especially on the break.

sleeper (basketball). An easy basket. Normally the offensive player is all alone under the basket. Also called an easy bunny.

slice (golf). When the ball curves away from the body. For a right-handed golfer, to the right.

slingshot (softball). Fast-pitch delivery in which the arm, gripping the ball, leaves its position at the waist and is whipped backward to the stretching point, then moved forward with as much speed and force as possible.

slump. A period of time in which a player or team lacks effectiveness.

smile. Golfer's lingo for the crescent-shaped scar left on a ball's surface by a badly aimed swing.

snakebit. A team or individual athlete that seems to attract an inordinate amount of bad luck.

southpaw. Left-hander; originally a baseball term but now used in all sports.

span (bowling). The distance between the thumb hole and finger holes over the surface of a bowling ball.

spar (boxing). To box, usually in a practice session.

spearing (hockey). The illegal use of a stick to poke another player.

spears reverse dribble (basketball). Bringing the ball back toward oneself prior to switching hands on the dribble, thus protecting it before taking it across the body in front of the defender.

spike. 1. (baseball) To slide with one's baseball shoes, or spikes, high so as to hurt the man defending the base. 2. (football) To celebrate a touchdown by slamming the ball into the ground of the end zone.

split the post (basketball). Two players crisscross around a post player and into the lane.

sportoons. Name given by Joseph P. Kahn of the *Boston Globe* to *RollerGames*, *American Gladiators*, and other shows "masquerading as a sporting event."

spotter. 1. A person who assists a television or radio broadcaster by identifying the players on the field. 2. (gymnastics) An instructor who assists by supporting, lifting, or catching the gymnasts as a stunt is being performed during a practice session.

spread, the. The number of points by which one team is believed to be better than another for the purpose of wagering. If the spread is five, it means that the stronger team is favored by five points.

squad (basketball). A total of twelve men in pro basketball. Of the five on the floor, one is a center, two are forwards, and two are guards.

stand-up (hockey). The method by which a goalie remains in an upright position, using his stick and skates to makes saves below the waist.

starting five (basketball). The five regulars on a basketball team who are in the starting lineup.

stick save (hockey). To stop the puck with a stick.

stick-um (football). Sticky substance that a pass receiver puts on his hands to hold on to the ball.

string music (basketball). Sportscaster Joe Dean's term for a shot that bottoms out—*swish*.

stroke (basketball). Shot or shooting motion. Larry Bird had a stroke of genius.

studfish (basketball). Someone who can play.

stuff (basketball). Dunk; also to block someone's shot.

stuff shot (basketball). Stuffing the ball into the basket from above after a leap high toward the basket. See DUNK.

stunting (basketball). Sometimes referred to as multiple defenses. The strategy of changing defenses in order to confuse opponents.

stutter step (football). Shuffle or quick step that is used to deceive a defender by giving the illusion that the runner is about to stop or turn. It is also used by pass receivers trying to stay inbounds as they catch sideline passes.

sucker pitch (softball). Short pitch which a player throws with exaggerated motion hoping that the batter will mistime his or her swing.

sudden death. An overtime period in which the team that scores first wins the game.

suit up. To dress to play.

Sweatlanta. Name for Atlanta, coined by the Olympic athletes during the 1996 Games.

sweep (football). An attempt to carry the ball around the defensive end.

sweet spot. The spot toward the end of a baseball bat, on the face of a golf club, or at the center of a paddle or racquet on which the ball is best hit.

swingman (basketball). A versatile player who can play two different positions, almost always guard and forward.

swisher (basketball). A successful field-goal attempt (usually from long range) that apparently does not touch the basket rim.

swivel hips (football). Attribute of a player who is particularly hard to catch and tackle.

Tailor (basketball). Someone deft not only at blocking shots but at altering them, too.

take the train (basketball). A less-than-diplomatic suggestion that someone has traveled.

taste that (basketball). After blocking an opponent's shot, say this to remind him of what he can do with it.

taxi squad (football). Reserves who can be activated on short notice to replace others who are injured.

tenant (basketball). Player who tends to stay too long in the shooting lane, where one is allowed only three seconds.

tending (basketball). Goaltending.

Texas leaguer (baseball; softball). A fly ball that drops between an infielder and an outfielder for a hit.

thin. Said of a team without reserve players.

throwbacks. Term for old-fashioned facsimile uniforms worn by professionals for a game to commemorate an anniversary or special event.

tick (basketball). Shot.

tight (basketball). Tied.

toilet-seater (basketball). A shot that rolls around the rim several times before dropping through or spinning out.

tomahawk (volleyball). Hitting the ball with the back of one's forearms; a reverse bump.

tools of ignorance (baseball). The catcher's paraphernalia.

top shelf (hockey). The area where a puck enters the net just below the crossbar. See FIVE-HOLE and PLAYING THE ANGLES.

touch (football). Game in which tackling is forbidden and a player is considered "down" when he or she is touched below the waist.

touches (football). The number of times a player touches the ball during a game.

trailer. In ice hockey, basketball, and other goal games, a player who follows behind the player who is in possession of the puck or ball to be in a position to receive a pass.

transcon (basketball). See COAST-TO-COAST.

trapper (hockey). Used by the open hand, this glove is used mostly to catch the puck.

trash talk. Aggressive talk on the court or playing field.

traveling (basketball). Walking with the ball, or taking too many steps without dribbling. Results in loss of possession.

tree (basketball). A tall player.

trifecta (basketball). Three-point goal.

trim (basketball). To make a shot.

triple-double (basketball). Single-game performance in which a player gets double figures (ten or more) in terms of points, rebounds, and assists.

tude (basketball). Attitude.

turkey (bowling). Three consecutive strikes.

turnaround (basketball). A play with several options that is used by a pivot man.

turnover. The loss of possession of the ball, in football, basketball, and other ball games.

twig. Hockey stick.

twine (basketball). The net. Root for the expressions "twine time" and "twine twinkler."

two-bagger (baseball; softball). A double.

Ump. Baseball umpire.

Uncle Charlie (baseball). A fine curveball; also called a yakker and occasionally the yellow hammer.

undercutting (basketball). A dangerous and, when intentional, unsportsmanlike practice consisting of running under another player when he is already in the air attempting a shot.

uprights (football). The vertical posts that support the crossbar in a goalpost.

V-ball. The game of volleyball.

Waffle (hockey). Blocker pad on goaltender's stick hand.

waggle (golf). To move the clubhead back and forth with short, quick motions when addressing the ball.

walk-off home run (baseball). Game winner: one that allows the batter to walk off the field after hitting it.

walk-on. A player who shows up for a tryout on a college team who has not been recruited. A walk-on is drawn to the school by academics and does not have an athletic scholarship.

walking (basketball). Traveling with the ball.

walkover. An easy victory.

wallyball. Volleyball played on a squash court.

wave, the. The visual effect of a human wave or surge created as fans rise quickly to their feet as the swell passes through their section of the grandstand.

weak hand (basketball). The off hand.

weak side (basketball). The side of the lane away from where the ball was when a play or pattern was initiated; usually a minority of the offensive players are stationed on this side (Jim Pruitt, *Play Better Basketball*).

wear it (baseball). Instruction to a player to suffer through being hit by a ball no matter how painful.

Western Union (basketball). The telegraphing of a pass or a shot so that a steal or block results.

wet ones (baseball). The latest name for illegal spitballs, from the name of a commercial moist towelette.

wheel (basketball). Ankle.

wheels. Legs of a player with exceptional running speed.

white-knuckler. A close game; one that goes down to the wire.

white man's disease (basketball). A chronic inability to jump. Sometimes referred to as "the dread disease."

whitewash. To hold an opponent scoreless; to shut out an opponent.

wiff (golf). To miss the ball entirely.

wig-wag (football). Hand signals, as opposed to instructions brought into the huddle by a player.

wild-card team. In professional football, basketball, and soccer, a team that qualifies for playoff competition by virtue of having the best record of all the teams within the conference that did not automatically qualify.

Wimby (tennis). Wimbledon.

wind sprint. A short run.

windmill (softball). The name for a fast delivery that begins with a full circle.

window (basketball). Backboard.

wipeout (basketball). To win by a big margin.

wishbone (football). Offensive scheme developed in the 1950s and once the most overpowering idea in the game. It places three runners behind the quarterback to make a Y formation in the backfield.

wood (basketball). The court. Short for hardwood, but applies to all surfaces.

woof (basketball). To address an opponent in an intimidating fashion.

wraparound (hockey). When an offensive player tries to skate around behind the goal and attempts to wrap the puck around the goalpost under the goalie.

X's and O's. Diagramming plays on a chalk- or clipboard.

Yips (golf). Pressure that affects a player; usually referred to as "the yips." To CHOKE.

yo-yoing / yo-yoing up and down (basketball). A guard dribbling the ball upcourt so that it looks like the ball is a yo-yo. Consequently, the guard is yo-yoing the ball up and down.

yolked. Describes a health-club habitué with low body fat and plenty of muscles.

your world (basketball). You're all alone, take your shot.

Zamboni. The four-wheeled vehicle that is used to vacuum excess water from a field with an artificial surface before a contest is played; also the vehicle that is used in resurfacing an ice hockey rink. The Zamboni lays down a thin film of water that freezes to become the new surface.

zebra. Referee in any sport in which that person is distinguished by a striped shirt.

zip. A score of zero.

zone (basketball). A style of team defense in which each player is assigned to guard a designated floor area, rather than a specific player or opponent.

zoning (tennis). Excellent play.

zoom (basketball). To defend.

26

TEEN AND HIGH SCHOOL SLANG

A Dialect of, Like, Many Subcultures

One cannot keep up with slang, especially the slang of the young, which is designed to be unintelligible to adults, and, once decoded, since today's young reject history, has turned into vapour or unspeak.

—Anthony Burgess, *Times Literary Supplement* (London), December 5, 1986

In this the age of *South Park*, hip-hop, and a multitude of cliquish cultures, teenage slang is probably no more subversive than it ever was. However, its cultures are more diverse, comprising hip-hoppers, industrial-music fans, grunge-ophiles, gangstas, metal-heads, ravers, surfers, skaters, skiers, and snowboarders. Some teen slang is universal, whereas other terms vary from one ethnic group to the next: Hispanic teens use some Spanish-language terms, while African American teens throw around words such as "kickin' " (hanging out) or "gerpin' " (trying to find a date).

While each subgroup and culture comes with its own set of words, some youth slang is spread wide; it comes from movies or song lyrics and catches on nationwide. But other slang is geographical; kids on the western or southern side of Santa Clara Valley, California, have words and phrases that are exclusive to their cliques or peer groups. And you may catch surfer teens in Santa Cruz, California, calling girls "birds" or referring to great waves as "epic."

Despite all of this is there is a middle ground, a general teen argot that we can at least try to capture, especially when blended with chapter 13 on hip-hop and the skateboarding and other of extreme-sports entries in chapter 20.

What links the generations is that much teen slang tends to be about the same things. Today there are a host of words for "cool"—including "cool"—and another batch for nerds and dorks—including "geeks" and "dorks"—just as there was for the class of '57. Other terms, including "groovy" and "funky," now mean the opposite of what they did to the flower children of the sixties.

What was once barfing or losing one's lunch has grown into a rich vocabulary of vomit synonyms. When *USA Today* wrote about teenage slang in 1988, a fourteen-year-old reader wrote to say that she knew fifty-three different terms for blowing rainbows. Some terms that were once reserved for the young have now slipped into standard English—for instance, "hassle," "put-down," and "uptight."

What all of this proves is that the slang of the young is mercurial, unpredictable, and somewhat allergic to print. If a noted linguist is quoted in the papers as saying that "bad" no longer means good, the term seems to come back with a vengeance. If teachers start using a term, it is likely to either die or have its meaning change radically. "Teen speak—the language of youth—is as fickle as fashion," wrote Leslie Rubinkowski of the *Pittsburg Press* (California) in late 1992. "Just when you latch on to enough words to communicate, the entire vocabulary changes. And tomorrow, this entire primer on teen-age slang will be history. In fact, among some teens it already is dust."

In other words, if you are a teenager and need this list, you're "ass out."

Abusak. Elevator music, a blend of abuse and Muzak, a brand name of canned music.

ace-high. The best.

acid. Steroids.

aggresso. To act assertively; an act of aggression.

aggro. Great; good.

agro. Mad; pissed off.

air guitar. Imaginary guitar played along with real music or without.

air mail. Garbage thrown out the window.

airhead. 1. One who is empty-headed, dumb. 2. Someone who is out of it. This term dates from a time when many of today's teenagers were infants, but it still hangs on.

all-nighter. A party or study session that lasts all night.

all that and a bag of chips. Very attractive, very fine, very cool.

all that and then some. Usually used when talking about a member of the opposite sex; he or she is everything that defines great, and more.

Andy. The person in a band who is such a zero that no one gives a care about him. Origin: Andy Taylor of Duran Duran. Usage: "Danny Wood is the Andy of New Kids on the Block. Adam Clayton is the Andy of U2. Mick Mars is the Andy of Mötley Crüe."

arbuckle. Dingbat.

as if! 1. To the contrary. 2. No way.

ass out. In trouble.

attitude adjustment. High on drugs or booze.

atwood. Canadian synonym for wedgie. Usage: "This worn-out, old pair of underwear is giving me an atwood."

Audi. 1. Good-bye, I'm leaving. 2. I'm out of here. I'm Audi. 3. To run. All of these are from the name of the imported German luxury car, the Audi. Variation on all of this is "I'm Audi five thousand."

awesome. Great; good; okay. This term is passé in some circles, current in others. Can be elevated to "totally awesome" or "mega-awesome" for emphasis. (Pron. "AAH-some.")

B. Frisbee: "Let's play some B."

bad. Good. People keep saying that this term is verging on the edge of the archaic, but it just keeps hanging on.

bag. Kill; stop.

bag some rays. Same as "to catch some rays"—to get some sunshine.

bail. 1. To cut a class; bail out; to leave, thereby blowing off some distasteful task or event. 2. A general put-down—"Bail that!" is used like "Screw that!"

bail out. To leave.

bake. To smoke marijuana.

baked. Really stoned.

bald. Bad; terrible.

Baldwin. 1. Attractive guy. 2. A male BETTY.

ballin'. Going fast, as in, "I was really ballin' down the highway."

B&B. Beavis and Butt-head.

banjaxed. Demolished, ruined (as a car).

bank. Cash; money itself. This term is common in rap-music lyrics.

Barney. 1. Unattractive guy. 2. Not a BALDWIN.

bat-caver. Person wearing black.

b-boy / b-girl. Rap-music devotee. The *b* in these terms stands for "beat."

b-boy stance. Defiant pose typically taken by crossing both arms across the chest, a term and posture common to rap music.

B-boys. Beavis and Butt-head.

beach whistle. A tampon tube washed up on the beach.

beat. That's terrible.

beauteous maximus. A good deal; a good job.

beef. A butt fall, in skateboarding.

beeper. A coded means of conversation for those not able to afford actual text messaging.

being styling. Being dressed up: in high style.

bencher. An old person, such as is found sitting on benches in shopping malls.

Betty. An attractive female, as in Betty Rubble of the television show *The Flintstones.* Also: fly houchy, freak mama. See BARNEY.

bifftad. A preppy. A 1988 article in the *San Francisco Chronicle* on local high school slang reports that it is from quintessential preppy names like Biff and Tad.

biggums. Overweight.

biscuit. Easy.

bitchen-twitchen. Excellent; great; classy.

biters. People who copy from others.

bizotic. Weird, a blend of bizarre + exotic.

Black & Decker. A real grind; any power tool.

blaze. To leave, as in "Let's blaze."

bliss ninny. A silly, disoriented person.

blow it out. Forget it; let's move on.

boarder. Skateboarder.

boarding. Riding a skateboard.

bogue. 1. Smoke a cigarette. 2. To be stood up, as in "I was bogued last night."

bogus. Phony; bad.

bonzai. Large or massive.

boogerhead. Affectionate nickname for a friend.

book / book it. To move fast; to run like crazy, as in "He's really bookin' 'round the bases."

boom. A stereo, especially a car stereo.

boot. To vomit.

bounce. Go.

bowhead. A Texas teen defines this one as a bouncy cheerleader type who "ignores her intelligence, is superficial, and wears bows in her hair."

box. 1. Large portable stereo tape/radio combination. 2. Large woman.

boxie. Bleached blonde.

Brady. Not cool, from *The Brady Bunch.*

brainiac. Intelligent student.

brew. Beer.

babe. A good-looking girl.

brick. To be scared, as in "We saw their front line and bricked." Probably from the expression "to shit a brick," be scared shitless.

Beeper-ese

This report first appeared in the August 9, 1996, *Virginian-Pilot*: "So not only do 20th century teens have their own dialect, but their beepers do too. Don't freeak. It's not a 911 situation. Here's the 411 on the digits to comprehend the communication:

143. I love you.

411. Need information; want to give information.

911. Emergency call now.

07734. Turn the pager upside down and it reads "hello."

617173. Good (6) nite (17173)

***.** A space.

The pager alphabet:

A. 8

B. 8

C. 0

D. 0

E. 3

F. 94

(because of the "ph" sound)

G. 6

H. 4

I. 1

J. 7

K. 15

L. 7 or 1

M. 177

N. 17

O. 0

P. 9

Q. 2

R. 12

S. 5

T. 7

U. 11

V. 11

W. 111

X. 25

Y. 4

Z. 2

Some people have an identification code; some use their name using the beeper alphabet; others use their birth date or little numeric idioms such as '007.'"

buff. Muscular; tough.

buggin'. 1. Being upset. 2. State of relaxation.

bum-rush. To come in; to break down the doors—a common rap term.

bummer. A bad break; a nasty experience. This term has been in use since the days when it was used to describe a "bad trip."

bump'n. Of the highest quality; such as clothes or music (pron. "BUM'pun"). Sometimes extended to "bump'n like a mug," for emphasis.

bunk. Uncool.

burly. A hard thing to accomplish.

burn. 1. To put down. 2. A put-down, as in "What a burn dad."

burn-out. One who abuses drugs or alcohol.

burnt. Terrible; tough; strict.

bus-head. What one looks like after a long school field trip or away game.

bush. One's real boyfriend or girlfriend; one with roots. Compare to SCOPE.

bust. 1. To be in trouble, such as getting busted by one's parents over homework. 2. A rude insult, commonly stated as "Bust you out." 3. A good shot, especially in basketball.

bust this. Watch this.

busted. When a teen gets caught doing something.

butter. Something good.

buttons. Remote-control device for TV.

buzz crusher. A killjoy.

buzza. What's up?

Caj / cas. Casual.

calendar. One month.

camel toe. Noun. This is what you get when your jeans are too tight in the crotch area, as in "Buffy, perhaps you shouldn't wear those size four jeans. They give you camel toe."

cameo. A type of haircut popular among young black males. The hair is trimmed short on the side and flat or angular on top.

cap. To put down; to insult.

cashed. Used up; finished.

catch one. To get drunk on beer.

check you later. Bye.

checking. Pulling down another's outerwear boxer shorts from behind as a surprise.

cheesehead / cheese meister. A jerk.

cheesy. 1. Phony. 2. Tacky. Mostly passé.

cherry. Something good; cool.

chick with a stick. Girl jock, presumably a reference to softball and field hockey.

chief. Form of address for virtually anyone.

chill / chillin'. 1. To calm down; to become cool; to relax. 2. Calm, cool, or laid back. 3. To stand up for a date—common in rap-music lyrics.

chill out. To settle down; to quiet down; to get cool.

chill with you later. See you later.

chilly most. Someone who is very cool; a paragon of chill.

chomp. To copy.

chopped. Physically unattractive or obnoxious.

chuborian. Fatty.

circle of death. A bad pizza.

click. A clique.

clockin'. Bringing in; acquiring.

clueless. Describing someone who doesn't know what is going on, who doesn't have a clue.

Clydesdale. A stud; good-lookin' guy.

cob. Not cool; stupid.

cold-blooded. Very cool.

cook. Cool.

cool. Fine; first-rate; copasetic. It is a term that has displayed remarkable staying power.

costing. Expensive, as in shoes that look "costing."

coyote-ugly. Extremely ugly.

cozy. Dull or lacking in interest. Precious, special, and quaint mean the same.

crankin'. Excellent, especially in music.

crazy. Good; hip.

creepers. Thick-soled black shoes.

crew. One's circle of friends.

crewby. Crew; that is, rowing jock.

crib. Home.

critical / crit. Cool.

cruisin'. driving around town, with no real destination.

cruising. Searching for a date.

crunchy. It's an adjective for someone who is overly earth-loving, probably from the characterization "crunchy granola."

crush. The person you really like, but they don't know it. "I was walking down the hall with my head down, and I smacked right into my crush!"

crush'n. What looks good, especially clothes.

cujine / cujette. Cousin, male and female. Same as HOMEBOY but in an Italian neighborhood.

cut down on / cut on. Insult.

Da bomb. great, awesome.

daddy mac. An attractive male. Synonyms are mac daddy, freak daddy.

daddylac. An expensive car that has been given to a young driver by his or her parents.

dag. To slow down, especially on a skateboard.

daisy dukes. Short shorts.

dap. Well-dressed.

death. Very appealing; to die for.

decent. Excellent.

decorate your shoes. To vomit.

def-fest. The best; the coolest.

demoto. Someone who is unmotivated and not doing well in school.

dexter. Nerd.

dibs. Residence, in hip-hop parlance.

digit head. One who studies too much, or works too long in front of a computer.

digits. Telephone.

dippin'. To listen in on somebody else's conversations for the purpose of obtaining gossip.

dipstick. Idiot; jerk; loser.

dis / diss. To show disrespect; to harass. This term is common in rap-music lyrics. It is commonly believed to have been clipped from "disrespect," although some teenagers insist that it is short for "dismiss."

disconcur. Disagree.

dissin'. Treating a person with disrespect.

ditz. Female airhead.

ditzy. Silly or goofy.

do. Hairstyle.

do the do. Have sex.

doable. 1. Sexually attractive. 2. Has mate potential.

doe. Cool.

dog. 1. To intentionally ignore. 2. To criticize or bother. 3. To work hard, as in "dog it." 4. To crumble under pressure, in skateboard talk. 5. To have sexual intercourse. 6. To beat up.

dogess. Bitch.

donnez-moi un break. Give me a break. A sixteen-year-old from Connecticut explained: "It's a French-class thing. Anyone with a minimal French background will recognize 'give me a,' and they assume that 'break' means break. 'Break' is French for station wagon; however, it makes a cute joke expression."

dooky. Excrement, as in "He smells like dooky."

dope. Great; superb—a common rap term. Synonym: fresh.

dopey. Hip.

dorky. Stupid. Old, totally passé slang given new life by Beavis and Butt-head of MTV fame, whose vocabulary is limited to "that sucks," "this is cool," and dork-related remarks like "Look at this dork."

double bagger. Person so ugly he or she needs two bags over his or her head instead of just one.

down with. A kid who is "down with" is high.

drain a pain / drain the main vein. For a male to urinate.

drive the porcelain bus. To throw up into a toilet.

driveby. To drive in a car and check out a situation.

drop science. To give important information, say something people should listen to (rap origin).

drop some iron. To spend some money.

du. Hairstyle, from "hairdo."

dual. Good.

duckets. Money.

dude. 1. Originally a guy, but now genderless. This term is a tricky one, because it can be applied to someone who is especially well-dressed or, cynically, to one who is a mess. 2. A form of address, as in "Hey, dude." 3. A friend.

Many people believe the term "dude" originated with surfers, as in "Yo, dude, what's up?" In fact, says Albert Lewin of Los Angeles, coauthor with his wife, Esther, of *The Random House Thesaurus of Slang*, the term, spelled "dudde," dates from Shakespearean days. It eventually came to mean an overdressed Easterner who went west (hence dude ranches).

duggy. Stylishy dressed. "I'll be lookin' duggy on the first day of school." Sometimes written as Doug E.

duker. Massive bowel movement.

dust. Verb meaning to get rid of, dump, as in "My boyfriend was treating me like dirt, so I dusted that old troll at the prom."

dustup. A fight.

dweeb. Loser; nerd; person you would not want to have to share a locker with.

Ear duster. A gossipy person.

easy. Asking someone to calm down, pronounced by saying the letters E-Z.

eat chain. Drop dead; short for "eat a chain saw."

eating in hell. Dining at Taco Bell.

egg. To smash raw eggs on a car, house, or other large object. The practice is called egging.

ends. Money.

express. In the mood to party.

Face paint. To fall off a skateboard onto one's face.

faced. Put down; having lost face.

fan (it). Forget it; let's not do it; pass. One father, Walt Gianchini, says that his daughters are likely to say, "Let's fan on that" after he has suggested something like a Sunday picnic.

fat. Nice; good.

fave. Favorite, the best, in their opinion.

fetus. A real loser.

fierce. Terrific.

file. Dangerous.

filthy. Hip.

fine. Describes a cute person of the opposite sex.

fire on (someone). To hit or punch.

fired up. Excited.

five-O. Police, from the old *Hawaii Five-O* television show, presumably recaptured in reruns.

flail. To do poorly on or fail a test; to mess up.

flake. To miss an appointment or not show for a date.

flamin'. To become infuriated, mad.

flares. New term for bell-bottom pants.

flash! As in "News flash!," which basically means you just said something really stupid.

flex. To leave.

floppy disk. One who studies too much.

flu. Fine; good, the same as FRESH.

fly. 1. Cool, as in "John's threads are fly." But you wouldn't use this term alone, as in "Cool!" 2. In the know; street-smart.

fly-boy / fly-girl. Attractive young man / woman.

for real even? Are you serious?

fork the lawn. To vandalize a property by sticking hundreds of plastic forks in the lawn on a cold night, which will be frozen in place by dawn.

Fred. An unattractive or unintelligent male, like Fred Flintstone of *The Flintstones.* Synonym: BARNEY, as in Barney Rubble, of the same show.

Fred Smith. The imaginary perfect boyfriend, the one who does everything right. As in, when the flesh-and-blood boyfriend seems inadequate, "Oh yeah? Well, Fred Smith would never say such an unsupportive thing."

fresh. Fine; very good. When a writer for the *Detroit News* discussed this term in a 1985 article on teenage slang, he said, "Possibly the most difficult new slang term to define, 'fresh' can encompass an individual's attitude, a state of mind, a mode of dress, or an enlivening influence or situation."

front. Confront.

frontin'. Lying, a phony person, in hip-hop lingo.

full hank. Nerd.

full of acid. Describing a well-built guy who looks like he is on steroids.

fully-on / fully. Perfect; the best possible.

funky. Someone who thinks he or she is cool but definitely is not.

Gaffle up. To confuse, mess up, hurt.

gag. Valley girl, from "Gag me with a spoon."

gangsta. A person in a gang.

gank. Flirt.

gapo (acr). Giant armpit odor.

gaucho. To expose one's buttocks at someone, usually through a window (also known as "mooning").

gay. Not cool; totally stupid.

geed. Looking good.

geek. Loser, nerd. A rare perennial in the ephemeral realm of teenage slang. "Geekoid" is used in some circles.

gel. To relax.

generic. Dull; out of it.

gerbil. To spill. "I just gerbilled my diet Pepsi all over my desk."

get a life. Get your act together; stop bothering me.

get horizontal. To lie down (alone or with someone else).

get naked. A way to say "Let's go."

get up!. Good job!

getting off with your bad self. Obviously feeling good about something that you have done.

gimp. A loser.

girlfriend. Used in greetings and conversation mostly between two girls, as in "What's up, girlfriend?"

glam. Glamorous; it's a style, "the glam look."

glitterbag. Flashy female given to shiny clothes, hair piled high with Aqua Net, and gum chewing.

gnarly. Disgusting; gross. But in some circles and in some situations it also means good, cool, hip.

god box. Remote-control device for TV.

godly. Cool.

goob / goober. Nerd, loser. But "to goober" is to spit through one's two front teeth.

gooey. Girlfriend.

gorpoblorcho. Imaginary chemical used by chemistry teachers.

GQ or **Q.** Nice clothes, from the fashionable men's magazine Gentleman's Quarterly.

granola. One who dresses and shares the

preferences of the 1960s. This term has gotten a significant boost from the *Bloom County* Bohemian character Lola Granola.

grille. Face, from the grille of a car. "How'd you'd get that scrape on your grille?"

grindage. Food, a term popularized by the comic Pauly Shore.

grip. Money.

gritch. To complain; blend of gripe + bitch.

grooviness. Now instead of something being groovy, it is full of grooviness.

groovy. Stodgy, old-fashioned; 1960ish. But also sometimes used in its original sixties meaning of "cool."

ground. To punish by keeping at home, as in "I'm grounded for the week because of my report card."

guidette. Female who is likely to use much hairspray to keep her hair piled high and poufy. See also GLITTERBAG, GUIDO.

guido. Male characterized by slick hair, gold jewelry, a hairy chest (exposed), acid-washed jeans, and a fondness for Bon Jovi music. A sixteen-year-old from the Bronx says that although this started out as a stereotype of "cool" Italian American guys, it now includes any group or nationality—for example, there are Greek and Jewish guidos.

gumby. An unintelligible person.

guns. Muscles.

gutter wear. Very hip, punky clothing.

Hack. To get rid of undesirable people quickly.

ham. Any alcoholic beverage.

hane. Heinous, or gross.

hang. Relax; hang out.

happy camper. Someone having fun, although this is often phrased in the negative, as in "not a happy camper."

hard. Tough; authentic—a common rap term.

hard way to go. Sympathetic response to somebody's sad story.

hardcores. Tough courses.

harsh. 1. Strict; bad. 2. To abuse someone, give them a hard time, as in "Readers were really mad at Mike when he harshed on Nelson."

hawking. Searching for a date.

headbanger. Heavy-metal fan.

hecca / hella. "Heck of a" and "hell of a," as in a hella good time. Also prefix for "very," as in "hellacool."

hein. Person who is ugly or possessed of a rotten personality.

hellified. Super.

hellish. Horrible.

hello. 1. I heard that. 2. Used to get someone's attention. If one says something stupid, the other says, "Hello, is anyone at home?"

high-jack. To take something trivial, almost borrowing.

high postage. A conceited woman.

hippy witch. Girls who dress in black and wear sixties-style clothing.

hit me on the hip. Page me.

hit up. To ask someone where they are from.

hittin' / hit'n. Something that tastes good.

ho! Great; good-looking; "Look out world!" A seventeen-year-old informant says that this term got a boost from the movie *Biloxi Blues*.

ho / hootchie. A slut, and an obvious play on the word "whore."

holler at / hollerat. Talk to.

holmes / homes / homie. Derivations of HOMEBOY and HOMEGIRL which mean the same thing; a common rap term.

homeboy / homegirl. Friendly term of address for someone from the same neighborhood or school; a neighborhood friend.

homiez. Friends; preferred spelling for homies, short for HOMEBOYS or HOMEGIRLS.

'hood. Neighborhood.

hook. Catch on.

hook up. Once upon a time this meant to begin a relationship; now it means to have sex.

hooptie. Car, in hip-hop lingo.

hoovering. Getting an abortion.

horn. Telephone.

hosebag. Slut.

hot. Extremely appealing or good-looking; very cool.

hottie. Cute person of the opposite sex: a hot one.

house. 1. To have a major success; to bring down the house—a common rap term. 2. To steal.

house ape. Small child.

hubba. Stupid.

hype. Great.

hyped. Full of energy.

Illin'. Stupid; un-chillin'. This term is common in rap music lyrics.

I'm sideways. Good-bye.

iron pimp. School bus.

it ain't all that. You're overstating; don't exaggerate.

it rules. It is awesome.

Izod. Preppy guy or girl.

Jack shit. Nothing, as in "I'm doing jack shit."

jack up. To kick in the rear end.

jacked. Happy.

jag. A loner, a nerd.

jam. In the world of rap, a concert, party, record, good time.

jammin'. Music that sounds good.

jank. All-purpose noun.

jeepin'. 1. Having sex in the backseat. 2. Socializing in a jeep.

jingus. Bogus.

joanin'. To insult publicly, as in "They were joanin' me about my car." When this term was reported by the *Washington Post* in 1987, it was suggested that it might be derived from Joan Rivers, but a number of readers wrote to point out that the term was an old one that was common in the black community when Rivers was still waiting for her first break.

jockin'. For a girl to hang on a guy.

johnny. Cop.

joint. 1. Marijuana. 2. Jail. 3. A fight.

joints. Any popular brand of sneakers, in hip-hop parlance.

juco. Junior college.

juice. Power, influence, respect, in hip-hop lingo.

juicer. Steroid user.

juke. 1. Elude. 2. To make a direct hit.

jump his / her bones. To have sex with. Almost always phrased conditionally, as in "I'd like to . . ."

junks. Basketball shoes, especially expensive ones.

Keepin' it real. Being serious, or an effort to be serious.

kegger. Party with beer, from the notion that these parties often feature kegs of brew.

keystone. The police, from the comic Keystone Kops.

kick back. To relax.

kick it. To relax, to CHILL OUT.

kickin'. 1. Hanging out with friends. 2. Great, as in "That movie was kickin'."

kickin' it. Doing something, even if it's just hanging out.

kill. Really good.

killer. 1. Good, like killer shoes. 2. A very tough course, especially in college.

kirk. To go off, lose control—an allusion to *Star Trek*'s Captain Kirk.

knob. A loser.

knocking boots. Having sex.

L-7. Square, from the shape formed by those two characters in instant messaging.

L-12. Stupid times 12.

lame. 1. State of boredom. 2. Stupid or nerdy. A lame time would be a dull party.

lame-out. Really dumb or boring, as in a total lame-out.

lardo. Fat person.

later. So long; good-bye.

law, law. I don't believe it.

left hanging. Stood up.

let's cruise. Let's go.

like. To say, as in "I'm, like, good-bye." This linguistic development netted an article in the *New York Times* ("For 'Teenspeak,' Like Another Meaning for the Multipurpose 'Like,'" August 25, 1988).

living large. Doing well, in rap talk. A ghetto kid who gets rich.

load. Car.

loadies. 1. Drug abusers. 2. Acquaintances whom you might party with but wouldn't want to be one of.

loaf. A fat person.

loose. A senseless daring act.

lop. A nerd or dork.

lost between the bells. Late for class.

lunchin'. Characteristic of one who is out to lunch.

Macking. Searching for a date.

mad. thumbs-up.

magnet. 1. A DWEEB who won't even move from his or her seat; a "glue-bottom." 2. A school or school program created to attract students so that racial or enrollment imbalances can be corrected voluntarily.

major. Extremely important.

majorly. 1. Very. 2. Totally, furiously.

mall crawler. Teenage girl who spends almost all of her spare time at the mall.

maw. To kiss; to pet.

maxin'. Relaxing.

mega-. Prefix of emphasis; see MUNDO-.

melba. Odd or unusual.

mellow up. Calm down.

mental. Describing any strange person.

mersh. Commercial.

mesoza. A group of small, wormlike, parasitic animals. Usage: "The mesoza hanging on the street corner harassed Karen when she walked by in her miniskirt."

mess 'em up. Good luck; the equivalent of "break a leg."

mess up. To screw up; to fail.

metal mouth. Teenager with braces.

Mickey D's. McDonald's. The company now uses this name in some of its ads, which are obviously aimed at the young consumer. Other slang fast-food names include "the BC lounge" for Burger Chef and the perennial "DQ" for Dairy Queen.

mint. Good, great; same as KILLER.

mobile. Attractive.

modeiant. Of or pertaining to the rock group Depeche Mode; something worthy of them.

molded. Embarrassed.

momaflage. To conceal an item from one's mother in a suitcase.

Monet. 1. Looks fine from a distance but really a mess up close. 2. Not a babe, really.

money. Friend.

mother's nightmare. Describing a punky look and feel.

moto. Someone who is motivated and doing well in school.

Muffie and Biff. Charactronyms for preppies, used by high schoolers.

muffin-head. Really nice-looking guy. Coined by a crazed, chameleon-headed friend of mine who enjoys baked goods almost as much as she enjoys a good man. Use it like so: "Henry Rollins is such a muffin-head. Pity that he's twice my age." Any pastry item available at the bakery will work just as well. "Croissant" and "crumpet" are two of my personal favorites.

mug. Guy.

munch on. To treat unfairly; to come down on.

mundo-. Prefix of emphasis. Something that is very strange, for example, is "mundo-bizarro." See MEGA-.

my bad. My mistake.

my peeps / my rents. My parents.

Narc. Loser; nerd. Once a term for a narcotics agent or someone giving an agent information.

neat whistle. Person wearing odd or weird clothing.

nectar. A good-looking girl.

ned. Marijuana.

nice du. Slur aimed at a bad or odd hair-style.

nitro. Very good; better than DOPE—a term associated with rap.

no-brainer. A thought or idea considered extremely obvious and easy to comprehend.

no duh. No kidding.

nog. To come into contact with.

nooks. Pain, especially to a high school jock.

not! Interjection used to show disapproval or label as stupid. "You may use NOT! but only in a highly ironic sense, aware that you are making fun of *Wayne's World* and all it represents," Leslie Rubinkowski wrote in the *Pittsburg Press* (California) in 1992. "If you took such a concept seriously, you would be nothing but a follower. You would be, in the world of Wayne, a sphincter boy."

not hard. Thumbs down; bad (as in the "bad" sense of "bad").

nuke. 1. To destroy; "I was nuked by that chemistry exam." 2. To microwave.

Oc. Out of control.

offie. Nerd.

old boy. Father.

old girl. Mother.

ollie grab. To kick a skateboard up, catch it, and then jump back on it.

omigod! "Oh my god!" compressed into a single word.

on hit. Good, exciting. Synonyms: COOL, FUNKY, DOPE, KICKIN'.

on the strength. Really great, in the rap lexicon.

organ recital. Sex-education class.

Pager. Annoying person.

party hats. Erect nipples. You get these when you're cold. "Margie, I would advise you to throw a sweater on over that thin little T-shirt, as your party hats are on full display."

PDA. Public display of affection. Common in schools, as there are rules prohibiting them.

perpetrators. The executor of an action—any action, not just crime.

petunia. Man or boy who pays a great deal of attention to his appearance.

phat. Good, cool; but less common now than previously (pron. "fat").

pick no squares. Don't fight.

pick up your face. Response to somebody who has just done something stupid or embarrassing.

piece. Junk. Probably from "What a piece of shit!"

pig sniffer. Radar detector.

played out. Tiresome, boring.

player. 1. Person who two-times or flirts, as in "Look out, she's nothing but a player." 2. Promiscuous person.

po po. Police.

podestrian. A pedestrian seen wearing the ubiquitous iPod.

pond scum. Grease on hair.

poser. Someone who tries to act and dress like people in another group but is considered a phony by that group. In punk circles: punkster wannabe.

posse. A group of good friends.

postal. 1. A state of irrational, psychotic anger and disorientation. 2. Wacko, flipped. Gained notority in the 1995 film *Clueless*. At the time the movie was released, eleven disgruntled postal workers had killed thirty-five supervisors and coworkers in the prior twelve years.

preps. Kids that are really into school; from college prep.

pseudo. 1. Person you think little of, such as pseudo-hippie, pseudo-jock, etc. 2. Anything that is suspect.

psych. To exaggerate wildly; to put somebody on momentarily.

psychotic. Really great; good.

Quality. Lousy; bad—the opposite of the real meaning of quality.

queef. Fart.

queer. Stupid or odd; it has nothing to do with sexual orientation.

queeve. To run out of energy, in the parlance of skateboarding.

Rack. 1. Sleep. 2. To sleep.

rack monster. A bed.

rack up. To kick somebody in the rear end.

rad / radical. Cool.

radical to the fifth dimension. Terrific.

raggin'. 1. Well-dressed. 2. Beating up on somebody. 3. Beating someone or winning ("He ragged on him in the race"). 4. For a girl to be having her period. 5. Make fun of.

raging. A good time; a lot of fun.

rags. Clothes, but most likely concert T-shirts.

ralph. To vomit. It has been pointed out that the name Ralph mimics the sound of regurgitation.

ranker / rank out. One who backs out; to back out.

rat. One who hangs out at a place. A "gym rat" hangs out in gymnasiums; a "rink rat" spends spare hours at a skating rink; a kid who caddies is a "bag rat"; anyone who hangs around shopping centers is a "mall rat." Ancient in terms of this kind of slang, "rats" seem to be a constant.

raw. Great; very good; good-looking.

real slice, a. A bad day

reeks. Smells really bad.

rents. Parents.

rickety-raw. Good-looking.

ride. A car, as in "My ride is outside."

ride / ridin'. 1. To make fun of; verbal jockeying. 2. To flatter, such as praising a teacher to get a better grade.

ride the slow train. To not want to party.

rider. Very negative term for someone who tags along when unwanted; a copycat. It is probably short for "ball rider."

rip. 1. A rip-off; a bad deal. 2. To be cheated or robbed.

ripe. It means you smell.

rita. A girl, from señorita.

road dog. Best friend.

roasted. Drunk.

rock. Really good. "Hanson rocks!"

rock and roll. To do something rowdy or noisy.

rock your world. 1. To beat you up. 2. To delight.

rocker. Anybody who is into heavy-metal music.

roll. A fat person.

rouge. To steal.

rude. Out of sight; cool—the same as rad or radical; totally good.

rude boys. People who like ska bands.

ruff. Neat, cool.

rush. To confront someone in a hostile or violent mood.

Ruth. Girls' bathroom, perhaps from the "House of Ruth" as a female sanctuary.

Salty. Angered, as in "My dad was totally salty on the phone."

sappnin'. What's happening?

saucy. Attractive.

scam. To lie, as in "I had to scam my way out of it."

scamming. Flirting.

scarf. To consume quickly; for example, to scarf up a pepperoni pizza.

school. The opposite of MOTO.

scoop. To kiss someone.

scope. 1. To hunt for something, as in "Let's see if we can scope a party." 2. To ogle. "Why you scopin'?" translates into "What are you looking at me for?" 3. Possible boy- or girlfriend; a person one is scoping out.

scrappin'. Fornicating.

scribe. Writing utensil.

scurb. Suburban skateboarder; one who skates on streets and curbs.

seven digits. Telephone number.

sev's. 7-Eleven store.

shady. Someone who's lying.

shagging. Picking somebody up by their underpants.

ship to shore. Cordless telephone.

shot who? What? Pardon me.

shout at one's shoes. To throw up.

shun it. To go with it.

sick. Good; awesome, as in "It was a sick party."

skanky. Rank or gross. Sometimes used specifically to describe a teenage girl who is so skinny that she is "gross-looking." One sixteen-year-old adds, "Would be pretty if she gained weight."

skater / skate rat. Skateboarder. See RAT.

skaters. Skateboard types: with long hair, long shorts, alternative T-shirts/music.

sketch. To mess up on a skateboard.

skidder. Backwoods teen in New England; after the name of a piece of logging equipment. "A skidder," says a western Maine teen, "has a mean dog and a broken snowmobile in his yard."

skin it. Slap hands; new way of saying "Gimme five!"

skinz. A well-built woman.

slacker. Lazy person, not someone who tries but can't do something.

slacking. Not keeping up with one's duties.

slam. To cut down, verbally.

slap-down. 1. To embarrass. 2. An embarrassment.

slaps. Rubber-thonged sandals.

slice up. To criticize or cut down.

slick. Can mean something is good or can be sarcastic, like "Oh, real slick."

sloshy, loopy. Drunk.

slutty. Describes sloppy inanimate objects, as in "Mmmm, I can't wait to eat a big, slutty burrito when I get to Benny's."

smit. To skip.

smokin'. 1. Looking great. 2. Crazy or severely misguided, as if from smoking pot. Usage: "If you think Warrant is a good band, you must be smokin'."

smokin' up. Smoking marijuana.

snake. To steal.

snap. To break a promise. A snapper is one who breaks promises.

sounds. Music.

spacin'. Not paying attention; being off in space. Spacin' usually occurs in class.

spack. Stupid, dense, spacy.

spazz. To become overly excited.

spent. Cash.

splockenin'. Egging a car or house.

spoink. An indefinite unit of measure. ("It was, oh, three spoinks high. I don't know.")

spud. A jerk.

spun. Cool, as in "John's threads are spun." Not used alone, as in "Cool!"

squash that / squash that melon. Forget it.

squid. Nerd, someone with tape on their glasses. Sometimes used as a joke with friends. By extension, a computer room or center is a "squid tank."

step off. Leave.

stick. Skateboard.

sticks. Needles used to inject steroids.

stoked. Excited; psyched.

stole. To punch out; "I stole him" is to hit him with a knockout punch.

stud. Once a sexy male, increasingly a male who thinks he is cool/hot/fresh but is not. Loser; person who is strong and athletic but still a loser.

stud-muffin. An immodest good-looking guy.

stuffies. Stuffed animals.

stupid. Cool.

stupid fresh. Outstanding or spectacular—more than plain fresh—in rap terminology.

stylin'. Someone who dresses well.

sucky. Not good; that which sucks.

s'up / 'sup. Greeting. From "Whassup?" for "What's up?"

sure you're right. Said of someone not telling the truth.

sweat. 1. To trash; to break something. 2. To give someone a bad time.

sweet. Good; cool. Just as "sweet" means good, as in "That's sweet." In a typical show of ingenuity, it can also mean just the opposite.

sweet hookup. A good deal.

swillmobile. Car full of empty beer bottles or cans.

swivel neck. Nerd.

syke. Same as PSYCH.

syndicate. Group of friends. Synonyms: POSSE, houser.

Take a chill pill. Calm down.

take the L train. To lose at something.

talk out of the side of your neck. To bullshit.

talking. Going out. If you're talking, you're not really together, though. You're getting to know each other.

tamale time. Embarrassment.

'tard. Someone who is moving or acting slowly, from "retard."

TBF. Top-button fag, a goofy guy. One so described is likely to wear his shirt buttoned to the top.

teepee. To cover a house, tree, car, or other large object with toilet paper, from the initials TP.

that bites! That stinks.

that's a plan. Confirmation or agreement of a suggested action.

that's casual. A statement of acceptance.

thrash. 1. To spin a skateboard in midair; to make any good move on a skateboard. 2. To be really good at something.

thrashed. The state of being exhausted or otherwise depleted mentally or physically.

thrasher. 1. Skateboarder. 2. Skateboarder who doesn't give a damn.

thrashin'. Dancing.

three-ring circus. A fashion disaster, such as one's father in some unspeakable plaid Bermuda shorts, black sneakers, and white tube socks with three rings encircling his leg just below the knee.

tight. Good.

tin grin / tinsel teeth. Braces.

to the curb. Dumped by one's girlfriend or boyfriend.

tool. One who studies; a grind.

toss chow. To eat quickly.

totally. Fully. MTV's brain-dead dude, Pauly Shore, whose film *Encino Man* introduced the nondude population to words such as "buff" (cool), once predicted that someday the written part of driving exams

totally. (*continued*) may replace "true" and "false" with "totally" and "not even."

touron. Annoying tourist; apparently a blend of tourist + moron.

tow up. 1. Tore up, in bad condition. 2. Trashed, toast.

toxic. Astonishing.

toy cop. School or mall security officer.

trashed. Drunk.

trife. The wrong way. Living trife is living the wrong way; said of a bad person. "This may come from the Yiddish word *treif* (pron. "trayf"), meaning not kosher," says Robert S. Greenman of Brooklyn, who picked the term up from his students.

triffin. Nasty.

trip. An experience on or off of drugs—same as in the sixties.

trip-out. One who is out of it; a space cadet.

trippy. Neat; weird; far out.

'tsup. Catsup. A "clipped" form. See also ZA.

tubaruba. TV.

tube / tube out. To watch TV.

tweaked / tweaked out. Spaced out.

tweet. Teacher.

twillie. Noun. A fool.

twink. Loser; nerd.

Uh. Bad, ugly. "That shirt Todd is wearing is so uh."

units. Parents.

unruly. Gruesome, a term beloved of skateboarders, who talk of unruly spills.

up the ying-yang. A ridiculous amount; for instance, "I have homework up the ying-yang."

upper story / upstairs. The mind; the brain.

Vamp du. Slur aimed at a bad or odd hairstyle. Also, NICE DU. See DU.

veg / veg out. To do nothing; to vegetate.

vid. A hassle or a bother.

Wack. Bad; lousy.

wail. To beat somebody up.

wakilana. Adjective meaning crazy, wacky, nutty, zany, madcap. Usage: "We had to reshoot the fashion photos because they weren't wakilana enough."

waldo. Out of it.

wanna be / wannabe. An emulator; one on the periphery. The term is sometimes applied to a white who seems to be emulating blacks or a black who is emulating whites.

wassup? What's up?

wasted. Drunk or high on drugs.

wastoid. Person throwing it away on drugs or booze.

waver. New Wave teen who goes to clubs, wears black, and "evolutionized" from punk.

way. Plenty; accentuated, as in "way dumb" for very dumb.

weak. Not good; poor.

wedge. Food.

wench. Girlfriend.

whoa. Cool, or anything that attracts your attention.

wicked. Cool.

wig out. State of agitation.

wiggy man. A cop.

wild. Cool.

Wilma. Unattractive female, as in Wilma Flintstone of *The Flintstones*.

wingnut. Not all there.

winner. Loser; a put-down when you have done something stupid.

wit. What you say when a bad joke has been told; delivered as if it were "nitwit."

woebetide. Bad news.

woodsy. Outdoor party.

woof. To brag.

woofie. Wimp.

Whitmanese

It is probably true that no two schools have the same body of ever-changing slang. In late 2005 a teacher at Walt Whitman Middle School in Alexandria, Virginia, sent me a list of slang terms used in her school with a note that said in part: "Being an eighth-grade English teacher, I am always looking for ways to bring pop culture into my classroom and show the students how their lessons have real-life application. Middle school is a culture in and of itself, and going hand in hand is the jargon indigenous to the students."

The teacher and her students prepared a list of slang to give a taste of Walt Whitman Middle School jargon. She added, "Their generation has an overwhelming amount of words, abbreviations and slogans that are a part of their everyday speak. It is a gruesome task for an English teacher to have the students seamlessly shift to 'school-speak' so every little justification helps."

Here is the middle schoolers' unedited list; clearly they have been heavily influenced by the slang of instant messaging, e-mail, and wireless communication.

2. "To," used when writing a note to a friend.

4. "For," when addressing a note to someone.

:). Smiley face, used after a sentence when you are saying something exciting.

?. "What" or "why" . . . saying that you have no idea!

@. At.

4rm. From.

aight. All right.

B cuz. Because.

bf. Best friend or boy friend.

bff. Best friends forever.

bling bling. Flashy jewelry.

bro. brother, used when addressing a male friend.

busted. Messed up, as in beaten up.

c. Standing for "see" in closing a letter, i.e., "See you later."

c'mon. Come on.

comin. Coming.

cuz. Because and cousin.

da. Shortened form of "the."

dawg. "Pal," found in the greeting "what is up dawg."

dude. By changing the pronunciation, it can be "man" or "hello."

fa sho. "For sure," meaning I am positive about it.

fo shizzle. "For sure," meaning I am positive about it.

goin. Going.

gonna. Going to.

gtg. Got to go—I have to leave.

h8r. Hater—someone who is jealous.

h8. Hate.

homes. "Friend," used primarily by Spanish-speaking people.

homie g. Friend.

holla bac. "Holler back" at the end of a letter means "Write back."

hw. Homework.

idk. I don't know.

ily. I like you.

jk. Just kidding.

k. Okay or yes.

kool. Cool, written with a *k* just to be defiant.

l8r. Later or good-bye.

lol. Laugh out loud, used after something is funny or when a joke has been told.

luv. Love.

lyk. Like.

lylas. Love you like a sister, when you are talking to a close girl friend.

np. No problem.

OMG. "Oh my god!" Used when you see or hear something cool.

pops. Used when you are insulting someone and calling them old.

ppl. People.

sis. Sister, when you are talking about your sister.

sk8r. Skater, referring to someone who skateboards.

skool. School.

sm1. Someone.

snap. Oh my goodness!

sum1. Someone.

sike. Just kidding.

ty. Thank you.

ttfn. Ta ta for now—good-bye.

u. You.

wanna. Want to.

wut up. What is up? What is going on?

wut up son. What is up, son. Used between males to say hello.

y. Why?

yea. Yeah, meaning yes.

yo. Hello, a form of greeting.

wooshie. Soft; fuzzy.

word. 1. When one cannot think of a word. It comes from rap music, where "word" is used when no rhyming word has been thought of, as in "That girl is fine. Word." 2. I agree; agreement.

word up. To affirm "that's the truth," coined in the song "Word Up" released in 1986 by a band called Cameo.

worn. Exhausted. "Man, I'm worn." Derived from "worn out."

wreck. To fight.

wuss. Wimp or coward.

wylin' out. Acting crazy.

X-ing. Tripping on the drug Ecstasy, or X.

Yawn in technicolor. Vomit.

yea / yeay. Imprecise unit of measurement, as in "He's yeay tall."

yen. Money of any kind.

yesterday. Out of date; outmoded. "Don't call someone a babe because that is, like, so totally yesterday."

young. Something small or undersized, particularly an article of clothing. "Look at that young shirt he's wearing!"

'Za. Pizza. A major "clipping" formation, in which only the word's last two letters remain.

zappening. What's happening?

zing. Zinger; quick comeback or line.

zit. Pimple.

zoiks. An expletive employed when there is nothing else to say. It is without meaning.

zun. Pimple; possible reaction to the coopting of ZIT by the commercial producers of skin preparations.

zup. What's up?

27

UNIVERSITY AND COLLEGE SLANG

A-OK, but Not Always PC

A large part of the struggle for group harmony for college students is internecine verbal skirmishing; and the terms for negotiating the struggle are slang.

—Connie Eble, *Slang and Sociability: In-Group Language Among College Students* (University of North Carolina Press, 1996)

College and university slang is a vibrant species, but it is not quite as ephemeral and ever-changing as is commonly assumed. Some of it is long-accepted ritual talk, and students will still be "pulling all-nighters" for generations to come. Go back to the 1930s and one finds that wolfing was snaking another's date, hanging the hardware was getting pinned by a fraternity, and quilling was kidding a professor along, which was known as apple waxing a generation earlier.

Back in 1937 an erstwhile professor at the University of Washington was able to uncover a host of student terms that were simultaneously quaint and graphic. His terms for a kiss or kissing included "a gab goober, a honey cooler, lollygagging, a mug muzzle, parksology, a paw, a pitch-honey, rottenlogging, a smootch, and tonsil swabbing." "Tonsil swabbing," indeed! A 1989 UCLA slang collection offers "tonsil hockey" and the 1991 University of North Carolina list features "suck tonsils."

An earlier look at Johns Hopkins University slang, reported in the *Baltimore Sun* in 1932, included oiled, phutz around, and bozo, which all mean the same thing as they do today. Your homely co-ed circa 1938 was a muddy plow, and one of a number of terms used for an easy course was a letter-writing course and to go to a movie was to hit a flick. If there is a national expert on all of this, it is Connie Eble, associate professor of English at UNC and the author of *College Slang 101*, She has been collecting slang from her English students since 1972 and has put out annual lists of that which is current and in season.

Eble believes that campus slang is predominantly national, with a lot of local variation, especially when places and local customs are alluded to. For instance, a cradle hag at UNC is a female who spends vast amounts of time at a place called the Cat's Cradle. At Brown University a certain piece of school-issue furniture is called a chastity bed because of its narrow dimensions; a DePaul girl who is too trendy is called a troll; at Delaware a girl from New Jersey with teased black hair is known as a fluff monster; and unappealing guys at the University of Alaska are known as groovers. Emeroids is what students at Emory call themselves, while Reedies work at Reed and Mawters at Bryn Mawr.

Meanwhile, alumni magazines and college newspapers are featuring glossaries of slang indigenous to a given campus, and at Dartmouth new students are given their own book of campus slang, called *Dartspeak*. With such help you can determine the local term for the person who studies too much. For instance, a recent article on slang in the *Tufts Criterion* says that the term of choice on that Massachusetts campus is still "throat," which is short for cutthroat and refers to any grind or person out for grades.

In fact, this interest in college slang is not all that remarkable and may simply be further evidence of a general national interest in various slangs, jargons, and dialects. College slang has been around for generations and seems to have been a constant for most of the twentieth century.

What *is* remarkable about it is that while it seems to be ever-changing and subject to different influences, it always seems to retain the same goofy, irreverent tone.

ABD. All but dissertation—Ph.D. students who have finished all their graduate work except the dissertation.

aced. Did very well on a test.

all that. Beyond good—something that's "all that and even more."

apes. Fraternity brothers.

artsy-fartsy. Describes an arts-and-crafts major.

Bag. 1. To sleep with. 2. To cut, to blow off, as a class.

bagger. Stereotypical fraternity member, a.k.a., fratty bagger.

baggers. Prospective freshmen (visiting on "sleeping bag" weekend).

baggy. When campus dining facilities are filled with BAGGERS.

bail. Leave somewhere or skip a class.

baked. As has been the case for many years, collegiate for drunk or stoned.

be a Wendy. To be like the stereotypically waspy Wellesley woman.

beans. Townspeople.

beast, the. Milwaukee's Best beer.

beauteous maximus. A good deal, a good job.

beaver / beav. Used as an adjective, not as a derogatory noun, means you're looking "hot."

beer bong. A tube through which beer rushes down into the mouth.

billies. Local men who do not attend the university but may be seen at sporting events and college bars.

bitchin'. Good. Long-standing slang that originated in California and swept eastern

bitchin'. (*continued*) campuses in the early 1960s as mock-Californian.

black. Incomprehensible course material.

blitzed. Became very intoxicated.

blizz. A crazy or unrestrained action.

blow off. 1. To cut, to not go. 2. To ignore an otherwise important thing. 3. Very easy, simple, requiring little work. 4. (University of Pittsburgh) Slack off, quit, break off relationship.

blow shit. To tease someone.

blunted. Stoned—high.

bogel. To pass time without having a plan or destination.

bogus. Not as bad as HANUS.

bomb. Fail.

bone. To sleep with.

book. Also bookin'. Used sarcastically to say you are definitely going to do something.

boot. Get sick from drinking.

boxing. Engaging in sexual activity.

brutal. Difficult test or assignment.

buff. Muscular.

bump. Throw out, skip, or drop ("I bumped the class").

bungee. Very, as in "Joe has a bungee awesome smile."

buttloads. Large amounts. "I can't stay out too late—I have buttloads of work to do."

Cabbage. For many years, collegiate slang for money (green).

cack. To play a joke or prank on somebody.

cake course. Easy-A class.

call the cops. Something wrong has been done to me.

cancer stick. Longtime slang for cigarette.

cheese. Software.

cheesebox. A computer.

cheezy. Corny, stupid.

chiphead. A person who is familiar with computers.

chog. An individual from New England.

cholo. Very macho. This term used to be used for a Mexican gang member. Now it is used as a description of anyone who is macho.

chug. Still, to drink beer quickly.

Cincinnati Bengal. "Coed with a good uniform (body) and ugly helmet (head); refers to colorful National Football League team uniform," according to the "College Slang Glossary," *Chicago Sun-Times*, March 18, 2005.

circle of death. Bad pizza.

clicky-windy. A photography major.

clue. Someone not aware of what's going on; "She really is a clue."

clueful. To have a clue; be aware of what's going on.

clueless. To not know anything about something.

college communists. Young Republicans, a term used derogatorily by campus liberals.

cool beans. Great, very pleasing.

cool deal. Longtime collegiate for great, outstanding.

corporate fascist. Person in interview mode, especially when dressed for an interview.

cows. Sorority sisters.

cracker jack. Prejudice.

crash. 1. To enroll in an overenrolled class. 2. To sleep.

crash and burn. To fail in a pickup attempt.

crewtons. Those who row for the school.

crib. Someone's home or abode.

crumb snatcher. Dependent woman or child. "My name is John. I'm thirty-two, single, and don't have any crumb snatchers following me around."

cut. Skip a class intentionally. It is so well entrenched that the only alternative to it is to "consciously avoid."

cutty-pasty. A fine arts major.

Daddy, the. The best.

DDFMG. Drop dead fuck me gorgeous—a very attractive member of the opposite sex.

deal. Cope. "She said she couldn't do the paper as well as the visuals, but I told her to deal."

dickweed. Jerk.

dig. In the 1990s, as for decades, college slang for understand.

digithead. Computer sciences major.

do the ______ thing. Yuppie locution; for example, "Give me a call sometime—we'll do the lunch thing."

dog. 1. A male who treats females poorly, particularly by being unfaithful. 2. A friend, buddy.

dormcest. Sex with a student living in the same dorm.

double. Two all-nighters in a row.

down with that. I understand or that is cool.

dramats. Drama majors, in general. Also known as the "ones wearing black."

drinking B's. Consuming cans of beer.

duck. 1. Person who teaches an easy course. 2. Easy course.

Earth biscuit / earth muffin. Environmentalist; one who clings to the styles and causes of the sixties. Also known as granola, green, hippy, flower child, and Woodstock wannabe.

ease. Become less aggressive, less tense, less nervous.

erg. A training exercise done by members of a crew team (male or female).

Fabulous. Cool; good. Said in three stressed syllables, accompanied by finger snapping.

facebook. To participate in the Facebook Web site, a hugely popular friend-of-a-friend (FOAF) network for college students.

fade. Take advantage of; to use for one's money.

fake bake. An artificial tan acquired from the use of a tanning booth or bed. "The fake bake business is always good right before spring break."

fattie. Marijuana cigarette.

fine speci-men. Good-looking males. "The bar is filled with fine speci-men tonight."

flailed. Blew it in a big way.

flame. One who is annoying.

fly. Cool.

forclempt. All choked up. This comes directly from a Mike Myers character, Linda Richman, on *Saturday Night Live*. From Yiddish and German, *verklemmt*.

forty. Any forty-ounce container of an alcoholic beverage.

foton. A word meaning really flashy, almost neon. To describe a guy or girl who deserves the spotlight.

freshling. First-year student.

frick. Exclamation of anger, frustration, condemnation. "Frick! I've got a paper, a project, and other homework to do over our fricking spring break."

from the ninth circle. Very tough or exacting, it alludes to Dante's *Inferno* and the various circles of hell. One of Eble's students provided this example: "My prof assigned a paper that's due the same day as her midterm. She's from the ninth circle." It does the same job as "from hell"—as in "midterm from hell," an expression of the late 1980s.

frosh. First-year student; freshman.

froshtitutes. Freshmen women eager to hook up.

fruits. Students in the college of fine arts.

fugly. Extremely ugly, presumably a blend of fucking + ugly.

funneling / to funnel. Drinking one to six (average) beer(s) in one swallow through a funnel.

Garden tool. Sexually promiscuous female; from "hoe," the dialect pronunciation of "whore."

gaungy. Very big.

GDI. Goddamned independent; widely used.

gear. Clothes.

geek box. A box (usually a tackle box) carried by electrical engineering managers. Contains myriad electronic components needed in lab.

geeking out. Expression of sympathy.

get shafted. To be required to write an extremely difficult paper.

ghoul. Person who studies to excess and haunts the library.

go grungy. Go out without showering.

going shopping. Cruising for dates.

gone. Became very intoxicated.

got reamed. Did very poorly on an exam.

granny panties. Big cotton underpants.

grubbin'. Eating good food quickly, as in "That was really grubbin', man!"

grunt. Army ROTC cadet.

Gucci girl. Gold digger.

gunslinger. Female who rudely rejects a man. "Man, that girl just dissed me—she's a gunslinger."

gut. An easy course, on many campuses.

Hack. 1. A prank. 2. To "explore," i.e., go places where students aren't supposed to be.

haint. Country bumpkin; backward ignorant person.

hammered. As has been the case for many years, collegiate for extremely intoxicated.

hangtime. Time spent waiting before something happens. "I'm ready, but I have thirty minutes hangtime."

hanus. Really, really bad, an alternative spelling of "heinous."

hatin' it. Expression of commiseration. First student: "My professor really dicked me on that grade." Second student: "Hatin' it."

heater. A cigarette.

heinous. Ugly, repulsive. See HANUS.

helmet. Women.

herb. A geek, loser.

herbalistic. Really stoned.

here's bread in your face. Forget it!

Say What?

Generically there are dozens of well-established terms covering snap courses, starting with the traditional snaps, guts, and cakes. They are also widely known as mick courses (from Mickey Mouse) and slides (by extension, a professor known for easy classes is likely to be known as Dr. Slide). Depending on the campus you are on, they are also variously known as crip courses, or crips, loan-savers, blow-offs, easy A's, sleep courses, cruise courses, fluffs, bluffs, punts, puds, and skates. Rare but in use are the terms "sop" and "bunny."

According to *Lisa Birnbach's New and Improved College Book*, schools tend to come up with their own names, so what is a cakewalk at Pepperdine is a cake at George Washington University. Some places have constructed their own easy-course vocabulary. The journal *American Speech* carried an article in 1980 on the "boat" courses at landlocked Gettysburg College—the ones you could "sail through." A yacht was a superboat and a professor who taught boats was known as an admiral. One prof, aware of his status as an admiral, greeted his class with a hearty "Welcome aboard" and an announcement that the course was about to set sail. A final extension of the metaphor terms a pop quiz or a tough exam that sinks the boat a jap.

high postage. A conceited female.

hit the slot machine. Obtained money from the ATM machine.

ho train. A group of provocatively dressed women parading across campus.

home skillet. A good friend.

hook up / hook up with. To be with someone romantically, or to have sex with someone. There is much variation in this term. The October 4, 2005, issue of *Newsweek* defines "hooking up" as anything from "gentle touching" to intercourse.

hose. Description of a test or exam that is going to be or was impossible.

hosed. Failed to achieve something; was rejected.

In the house. Present, here. "Tom is in the house, so let's say hi."

ITZ. In the zone—to excel, be in the zone.

Jet. To leave.

jimmy / jimmie. Condom.

jock. For a female to seek out a male athlete for sexual pleasure. "That girl is always jockin' someone."

jock'n. Nagging.

Keg is kicked, the. The keg is empty.

keggin'. Good.

Ken. Guy who cooks a lot!

key, the. Important, current.

kickin' dancing. Country-western dancing.

kicks. Shoes.

kind, the. Drug slang used to refer to whatever type of marijuana or other drug one is into. "Do you have any of the kind for me today?"

Lame. Longtime college slang for less than top quality: pitiful.

lesbigay. A blend of lesbian + bisexual + gay. Not derogatory. Used as an adjective or noun.

long nose. A liar.

Marinate. Relax.

mash. 1. To kiss, neck, make out, etc. 2. Some sort of sexual activity.

meat market. Sorority row, where boys pick up girls.

mint. Really cool.

momaflage. To hide an item in your suitcase or knapsack that you don't want your mom to see; blend of mom + camouflage.

Monet. Person of the opposite sex who, like an Impressionist painting, looks better from afar.

moneygrip. Person who has money and flaunts it.

mouley. Derogatory yet endearing term used among males.

mutant. Math major, especially theoretical math. Sometimes applied to theoretical physicists as well.

Nappy. Unhappy, disgusting.

narfs. Stupid freshmen, or Republicans.

nasty. Sexual intercourse, as in "So you two been doin' the big nasty."

nerd. Same as TOOLING, but especially when one is turning down an opportunity to PUNT.

nerd kit. A breadboard with power supply and a small set of integrated circuits for the digital lab courses.

nerd path. Dirt path worn across campus grass.

nerd whomper. Dork.

new school. New trends, new phases.

nipply. Very cold weather.

no can do. I'm sorry, I can't help you.

no way. I don't believe it.

nuke. 1. To destroy or delete. 2. To pull a prank on someone.

Occifer. Longtime college slang for "officer," but spoken by one under the influence.

o'river. Good-bye, mock pronunciation of the French *au revoir*.

ozone. Out of it, hungover, wasted totally.

Peachy. Fine; for example, "How are you?" "Just peachy!"

penis. Derogatory epithet used by a male to another male. A pseudo-scientific way to call someone a "dick," "dickhead," or "prick with ears."

plasma. Caffeine, in any of its forms.

pound a beer. Drink the beer quickly.

power sludge. Strong coffee

powertool. To cram or study intensely.

prospies. Prospective students.

psych! Just kidding.

pulling a Sue. Telling someone what you really think of them, an allusion to the blast that Sue Hawk gave to Kelly Wigglesworth in the final council of the first *Survivor* series.

punt. To cut class, skip a problem set, or otherwise avoid doing academic work.

Rack. To sleep.

rage. To party to excess.

reality-impaired. Unintelligent; an airhead.

rent-a-cop. Campus safety.

rip, to. To do well in.

rocked. Did very well on an exam.

Rocks for Jocks. Geology 101 for nonmajors at many colleges—an easy course favored by those who spend much of their time on the athletic practice field.

roll. To cut class, at Oklahoma State.

Salt sucker. An individual from the Midwest who forgets to close his or her mouth when he or she swims in the ocean.

sauce. Beer.

scam. To go looking for guys or girls: cruise.

scoping. Looking for possible members of the other sex to date, etc.

scrod. To have been screwed over, the past tense of screwed not to be confused with a young cod, also scrod.

scrump. To have sex with someone.

seppo. Really bad. Short form of "septic."

sexile. The state of banishment from one's room while one's roommate is with his significant other; a blend of sex + exile.

shack. To stay at the apartment, dorm, frat, or sorority of your significant or not so significant other overnight.

shack pack. 1. Three-pack of condoms. 2. Supply packs given by some sororities to pledges, often as a joke, that contain essentials for shacking, like hairbrush, mouthwash—and condoms.

shacker sheets. Linen hung around a bed so no one can see a roommate having sex inside.

shooting the shabookie. 1. "Taking it all" in the card game hearts. 2. Anything particularly destructive.

slip 'er the Woodrow, to. To sleep with.

slore. Woman you dislike; blend of slut + whore.

slort. To go to class with the express purpose of sleeping through it.

sog. Spend a lot of time with a woman, implying that the male is slightly pussy-whipped.

sohority. Sorority with a reputation for sexually adventurous members.

spoink. An indefinite unit of measure; "It was, oh, three spoinks high; I don't know."

squid. 1. Navy ROTC (Reserve Officer Training Corps) cadet. 2. Someone who always studies, especially on Friday nights. The local etymology of this at Wesleyan University is that it comes from the glass-sided Science Center Library, where students studying late at night look like squid in an aquarium.

step. To back off (used as a warning).

step off. To get away (used mostly as a warning).

stoked. Happy, elated, etc. Excited, pumped up.

stride of pride. Early-morning trip a male student makes back to his room after sleeping overnight at a female's place.

Say What 101?

Tradition dictates that easy courses get their own nicknames, which they are likely to carry for decades. Some of the more common examples include "Nudes for Dudes" (art), "Gods for Clods" (comparative religion), "Nuts and Sluts" (abnormal psychology), "Monday Night at the Movies" (film), "Baby Shakes" (introduction to Shakespeare), "Monkeys to Junkies" (anthropology), "Betty Crocker" (home economics), "Clapping for Credit" (music appreciation), "Chem for Cro-Magnons" (general chemistry, also "Kinder Chemistry"), "Art in the Dark" (introduction to art), and "Math for Trees" (mathematical studies). Even the places with the toughest academic reputations have their "Heroes for Zeroes" (Harvard's "Concept of the Greek Hero"), "Breathing for Credit" (Dartmouth's "Breathing Voice for the Stage"), and "Moons for Goons" (Oberlin's "Planets, Moons and Meteorites"). These easy-course names follow an old tradition of giving all sorts of nicknames to courses, including the ever-popular rhyming formation: "Cut 'Em and Gut 'Em" for anatomy courses, "Bag 'Em and Tag 'Em" for field anatomy, "Hicks and Sticks" (for local rural history), and so forth. A few other real-world examples:

Princeton—"Architecture 204" = "Architorture"

Purdue—"Engineering 100" = "Sleep 100"

Berkeley—"Astronomy 10, Self-Paced General Astro" = "Astro Without Stars"

Carnegie-Mellon—"Statistics" = "Sadistics"

Rochester Institute of Technology—"Anatomy and Physiology" = "A and P"

Georgetown—"Modern Foreign Government" = "Mo-Fo Go"; "Problem of God" (an introductory theology course) = "God's Problems"

superslamonic. The girl gets around!

suzie. Stereotypical sorority member. "My business class is full of suzies."

SWAG. Scientific wild-ass guess. Answer to homework or exam question usually written down minutes before it is due.

sweet. Good, fine, superb. This is a term with staying power on campus.

Tag. To mark, as with graffiti. "Look, they're tagging that wall."

taking the L train. To lose at something; get rejected by the opposite sex.

tea-bagger. One who is left hangin', or looking stupid.

Tensor-ghoul. One who secretly studies after everyone else is asleep, from high-intensity Tensor lamp.

that's sweet. That's really, really nice, awesome, terrific.

thes. To work on one's thesis.

they're buzzin'. They're clueless—like, when drunk.

throat. Someone who studies to excess; lives in the library; a study geek. A clipped form of "cutthroat," it can be used as a verb: "to throat for an exam."

tighty-whities. Men's brief-type underwear.

Say What?

Oldies but Goodies—The Top Forty, 1972–1993

Connie Eble, who conducts an annual survey of slang terms at the University of North Carolina at Chapel Hill, came up with this ranking of the most popular terms on campus between 1972 and 1993:

1. **sweet.** Excellent, superb.
2. **chill / chill out.** Relax.
3. **slide.** Easy course.
4. **blow off.** Neglect, not attend.
5. **bag.** Neglect, not attend.
6. **killer.** Excellent, exciting.
7. **jam.** Play music, dance, party.
8. **scope.** Look for partner for sex or romance.
9. **wasted.** Drunk.
10. **clueless.** Unaware.
11. **diss.** Belittle, criticize.
12. **pig out.** Eat voraciously.
13. **bad.** Good, excellent.
14. **crash.** Go to sleep.
15. **cheezy.** Unattractive, out of favor.
16. **hook / hook up.** Locate a partner for sex or romance.
17. **trip / trip out.** Have a bizarre experience.
18. **dweeb.** Socially inept person.
19. **buzz / catch a buzz.** Experience slight intoxication.
20. **cool.** Completely acceptable.
21. **grub.** Kiss passionately.
22. **geek.** Socially inept person.
23. **granola.** One who follows the lifestyle of the 60s.
24. **homeboy / homegirl / homey.** Friend, person from home.
25. **not!** No, sentence negation.

26. **ace.** Perform well, make an A.

27. **dude.** Male, any person.

28. **the pits.** The worst.

29. **bagger.** Fraternity member.

30. **flag.** Fail.

31. **hot.** Attractive, sexy.

32. **slack.** Below standard, lazy.

33. **trashed.** Drunk.

34. **veg / veg out.** Do nothing.

35. **word / word up.** I agree.

36. **awesome.** Excellent, superb.

37. **book.** Leave, hurry.

38. **turkey.** Socially inept person.

39. **fox / foxy.** Beautiful, sexy.

40. **sorority sue / sue / suzi.** Sorority member.

toast. What you are if you do badly on a test.

toasted. Became very intoxicated.

tool. 1. To study. 2. Someone with political or business ambitions, usually a Woodrow Wilson School major. 3. Someone you pick up, use, and put back when you're done.

torque. To hit on someone.

trashed. Overworked, tired, drunk. More often the former.

triple. Three all-nighters in a row.

tuna. A heterosexual woman who keeps company mainly with young gay men, as in "Steve, Shane, and their tuna are going clubbing on Saturday." Also, "fish."

turkey. Undesirable person.

Un. An undesirable or unlikable person.

Undue Perversity. Purdue University.

Vegetables. Science and engineering students.

virtual. Almost but not quite real; from "virtual reality." "He has a virtual job."

Walk. When a professor decides not to have class; sometimes used to describe cutting.

walk of shame. The stroll back to your room after hooking up, wearing the same clothes you had on the day before.

wank. 1. A person who is logged on for a huge amount of time. 2. To log on, to stay logged on, and to hack your brains out while drinking lots of Jolt or Mountain Dew. 3. Having the properties of a wank.

wasted. Overworked, tired, drunk. More often the former.

wat up? How are you doing?

wigging. Stressing, going crazy.

woody. An erection.

wookie. Word taken from the *Star Wars* character to mean a hairy or slovenly person.

word. Any hint on what might be asked on an exam by a professor.

X-kegger. Party at which a specific number of kegs of beer were consumed. An 8-kegger, for example.

Zone / zone out. Lose contact with the world, e.g., daydream in class. To lose concentration.

zoo. To fail.

zoomie. Air Force ROTC cadet.

28

WAR SLANG

Terms for a Time of Terror

Today is ArmForDay, the culmination of HawMilWeek, when civvies say thanks to all the pork chops, bubble heads, zoomies and gun bunnies who protect our butts all year long.

—Editorial, *Honolulu Star-Bulletin*,
May 21, 1994, Armed Forces Day

For Americans, the face of war was forever changed on September 11, 2001, with attacks on American soil aimed at killing large numbers of civilians who were the vast majority of the casualties. Suddenly the terms of war were both civilian and military. Even as the initial shock of the attacks on the World Trade Center and the Pentagon began to wear off it was clear that all Americans—in uniform and out—were living in the "new normal," a state of "low-level anxiety" in which we worry that "evildoers" or "sleeper agents" could set off "dirty bombs." When the home front becomes the war front, things change and distinctions between civilian and military language blur, and the language discussed in this chapter represents that blurring.

This attempt to capture the language of the late 1990s, the early years of the War on Terrorism, and the days leading up to March 2006, when this chapter was written, is one that by its nature is destined to be out of date quickly. But it does show what the language was up to before that impending conflict that journalists were already calling Gulf War II. Many terms from the first Gulf War and earlier wars were still very much in use, some adapted to new times. GI Joe was joined by GI Jane and the term MRE (meals ready to eat) no longer carried the old stigma of "meals rejected by everyone."

What makes all of this collecting easier and more relevant is the help of online services. One Web site entitled "GIJargon.com," no longer functioning as of 2006, described itself as "a place for the Military, Police, Coast Guard and the fire service community to share stories, news and ideas. Dedicated to men and women everywhere who put their lives on the line to protect our country. God, guts, guns, and Frosted Flakes!" Reporters and soldiers in the Middle East had access to the Internet and the slang of American forces in the field was sent back as quickly as other information was sent to the front. "With Internet access, my wife is able to send me digital pictures of my 8-month-old baby," is how one soldier described his communicating ability from Kuwait in early 2003. As the war progressed, more and more war fighters, as they are now called by the Pentagon, created their own blogs—or, as they are called in this case, warblogs—allowing anyone to read what amount to editorial diaries about a war as it is being fought.

Above my paygrade. A retort, a way of saying, "Don't ask me, I'm too low on the totem pole."

ace face. Red lines left on a pilot's face by a tight oxygen mask.

across the fence. Across a border.

acting jack. Acting noncommissioned officer.

ADA. Air Defense Artillery.

adopt-a-pilot. Ground forces' name for the urge to cheer aviators who would presumably soften up the resistance to a ground invasion.

agency, the. The CIA.

agent defeat. Describing a class of penetrating bombs aimed not at blowing things up but rather at incinerating stocks of chemical and biological agents. Precision-guided agent defeat bombs are intended to puncture the warheads with titanium rods, then incinerate the agents inside without allowing vapor to escape.

a-gunner. Assistant gunner.

Air Force salute. A shrug of the shoulders.

airborne copulation. Euphemism for "I don't give a flying fuck."

airwing Alpo. A variety of field rations including corned-beef hash and meatballs with barbecue sauce. From the name of a popular brand of dog food.

al-Canaeda. Pejorative post-9/11 term for what was at the time described as "America's terrorist-riddled, porous-bordered neighbor to the north"; a blend of al Qaeda + Canada. This term was short-lived. The impact of September 11 and subsequent events on slang was sometimes fleeting. Clever as it sounded at the time, "shoe-icide bomber" (someone who tries to blow up an airplane with explosive-filled sneakers) was only around for a matter of days, as was the redundant "facial profiling."

ALICE pack (acr). All-purpose, lightweight, individual carrying equipment pack, a field backpack that at its most basic is a squarish, green nylon bag with an aluminum frame. Still very much in use in 2003, but being replaced by the even lighter-weight MOLLE (modular lightweight load carrying equipment) plastic-frame pack.

alligators inside the boat. Problems and screwups; modern military metaphor for "snafu" (situation normal all fouled up).

already in the clouds. Assuming one is dead after being injured.

Amazon. Female soldier; not absolutely pejorative in that it is the name for the tribe of women warriors in Homer's *Iliad*; but can be regarded as a slur, especially in a negative context.

American Siberia. The northern-tier Air Force bases in winter, such as Malmstrom (Montana), Minot and Grand Forks (North Dakota), F. E. Warren (Wyoming), and Ellsworth (South Dakota).

AMF. Adios (or Aloha), Mother-Fucker—in other words, good-bye. A popular and long-running television ad for the "Greaseman," a Washington, D.C., radio personality, ends with the "The Grease" waving and yelling "AMF."

ammo humper. Artilleryman.

amped-out. Fatigue after being under the influence of combat drugs and certain amphetamines.

angel. False radar image.

angels. Air intercept and close air-support code word meaning aircraft altitude (in thousands of feet).

animal. A soldier who is able to endure all manner of hardships and pain in pursuit of the mission. Also "maniac."

ape. Air Force Air Police, from the initials AP.

applesauce enema. Mild criticism. Defined in *A Dictionary of Soldier Talk*: "To give a chewing out (the enema) to a subordinate, but to do it so tactfully and gently that he goes away feeling better for the experience."

Army brat. Long-standing name for the son or daughter in a regular Army family.

artichoke suit. The brown and green "Woodland" BDU (battle dress uniform) of the Gulf War.

artie / arty. Artillery.

ashtray. The desert, because institutional ashtrays (hotels, military institutions, etc.) feature sand.

asymmetric warfare. Shorthand used by the U.S. military for unorthodox attacks on an enemy's weakness, such as the attacks on the USS *Cole*, or the U.S. embassies and the World Trade Center. "The term," said lexicographer Anne Soukhanov after the 9/11 attacks, "has been in military lexicon for more than a decade, but the general public never heard of it until the past three months."

at the tip of the spear. Describing the leading unit in combat.

at zero. Having an enemy fighter on your tail.

ate up. Describing a soldier who has no clue about what's going on; a state of stupidity. According to a contributor to the GI Jargon Web site, "a soldier who is always slacking, uniform trashed, boots unshined."

auger in. To crash a plane, but especially apropos of jet planes which resemble an auger, or boring tool, as they drill into the earth.

AWOL (acr). Absent without leave. An "AWOL bag" is a small piece of luggage.

Axis of Evil. Iran, Iraq, and North Korea, collectively. When President Bush first used "Axis of Evil" in his State of the Union address in January 2002, the phrase instantly entered the lexicon of contemporary politics. Bush called the three states that because they were "seeking weapons of mass destruction" and posed a "grave and growing danger." The construction has led to other axes, such as one declared by antiglobalists, an axis consisting of the International Monetary Fund, the World Bank, and the World Trade Organization. The pejorative "Axis of Weevils" was applied to American allies (notably France and Germany) that did not support the war against Iraq in early 2003.

Baby shit. Mustard.

backdoor draft. Filling military positions through reactivation or mandatory extensions of enlistments or reserves' active-duty time through "stop-loss" orders.

bad paper. Discharge other than honorable.

bag matching. Security procedure by which airline passengers must be linked to their luggage.

Baghdad. Official Iraq, in the same vein that Washington represents U.S. officialdom, as in "Washington believes." A headline of February 26, 2003, in the *International Herald Tribune*: "Baghdad Studying UN Order on Arms."

banana clip. A curved ammunition clip designed to hold thirty rounds.

Band-Aid. Medical corpsman.

bandit. Hostile aircraft.

bandwidth crunch. Term applied to the ability of modern remotely piloted vehicles to use up massive amounts of the finite supply of bandwidth. U.S. forces could fly only two unmanned Predator planes over Afghanistan at any one time because of the limited bandwidth.

bang out. To eject oneself from an aircraft; to literally blow yourself out of the plane.

bare-ass. Barracks.

basic. Basic training; boot camp.

battle rattle. Kevlar helmets and flak jackets, collectively.

battlespace. Where the action happens, in the jargon of the twenty-first century.

BCD. 1. Bad conduct discharge, as in earlier wars, but now, after the first Gulf War, also the facetious "big chicken dinner." 2. Birth control device, referring to military-issue spectacles that are so ugly, they inhibit conception. They are also known as BCGs, for "birth control glasses."

BDO. Battle dress overgarment.

be in deep kimshi / kimchi. To be in serious trouble, synonymous with "to be in deep shit." The term "kimchi," for the traditional pickled cabbage dish, survives from the Korean War to the present day and is found in many novels about the military, as in, "We'll be in deep kimshi with Sundown if we lose another bird," by Richard Herman, Jr., *The Warbirds*. Herman adds in a 1992 letter, "Being in 'Deep Kimshi' is indeed 'Bad Juju' (black magic)."

beach. 1. The desert; fighting terrain. 2. Also, as reported by Harry Levins in the *St. Louis Post-Dispatch*, January 27, 1991, "A new way of saying boondocks, the old GI term for anyplace excessively rural or uncivilized."

beans, bullets, and Band-Aids. Everything troops need to fight.

beat your face. To do pushups.

beehive. Nickname for an artillery cannister that is essentially a giant shotgun shell. It harks back to the days when grapeshot was a standard load for cannon. It contains a load of metal balls or finned darts (flechettes), which are fired from the muzzle at a reasonably high velocity into infantry formations, making a buzzing sound, which has prompted the nickname.

B-H. Bosnia-Herzegovina.

big blue 82. The BLU-82, or daisy cutter, a 12,540-pound bomb creating tremendous blast overpressure. BLU is military shorthand for "bomb live unit."

big chicken dinner. See BCD.

big red. The brutal desert sun, as in "Me and big red don't get along real well."

Big Red One. Nickname for the 1st Infantry Division.

big twenty. Army career of twenty years.

bird. Aircraft, but usually used for helicopters.

bird colonel. Full colonel, whose insignia are eagles.

birdfarm. Aircraft carrier.

birdland. Quarters for senior officers.

blade time. The time a helicopter is in the air.

blood stripe. Rank achieved at the expense of others.

bloods. Black troops.

blooper. The 40 mm grenade launcher and, less often, the soldier detailed to fire it; from the distinctive sound of the weapon when fired.

blow away. Kill.

blow smoke. To confuse; to cover up.

blue. A body of water, from its color on the map.

blue max. The Medal of Honor, from its blue field.

blue on blue. Friendly fire or shooting at one's own soldiers by mistake. This term stems from NATO exercises where the two forces were blue and red.

blues. An airmobile company.

bogey / bogie. Aircraft suspected to be hostile.

bohica (acr). Bend over here it comes again. A GIJargon.com contributor added, "You would use bohica primarily when you are screwed or going to be screwed."

bolo. A soldier who flunks his rifle qualifications. A first-person witness, the writer Joseph C. Goulden, reports, "As punishment at Fort Chaffee, Arkansas, circa May–July 1956, such a cluck was given a 'bolo,' a crude southern scythe, and put to work cutting grass on the entire firing range."

bolo badge. A Purple Heart, the long-established medal awarded to soldiers wounded in combat. The term "bolo badge" was most likely to be used when the wound was, as a *New York Times* dispatch put it, "foolishly acquired."

boloed. Destroyed; killed.

bone domes. The high-tech Kevlar helmets that became standard equipment during the war in the Persian Gulf.

bonedaddy / bonemama. Slang for someone suffering from starvation.

boobies. Boobie traps.

boogie out of Dodge. To get out, beginning with the Gulf War, as in this quote from a Marine captain that appeared in the *Boston Globe*: "We move in quick, hit hard and then boogie out of Dodge. By the time he hits back, we ain't there." Dodge is Dodge City of the Wild West and means anyplace where there is the potential for gunfire.

boonie rat. Soldier who has spent a lot of time in the field.

boonies. Backwoods; the jungle.

boot. 1. Soldier just out of boot camp. 2. New and untested. At one point in *Rumor of War*, Philip Caputo writes, "I was alliteratively known as the 'boot brown-bar,' slang for second lieutenant."

bottle-cap colonel. Lieutenant colonel, from the insignia, which looks like the tinfoil on a bottle cap.

bought the farm. To be killed. In *Soldier Talk* (1982), First Sergeant Frank A. Hailey, a veteran of World War II, Korea, and Vietnam, says that this term was coined by Americans during the Korean War and had the same meaning that "bought it," a term borrowed from the British during World War II, did during the Vietnam War.

bouncing Betty. A land mine that, when triggered, pops up waist high and sprays shrapnel.

box, the. Pilots' slang for Iraqi airspace.

box kicker. Supply clerk, especially in Marine Corps parlance.

brace. An exaggerated position of attention that recruits and cadets are sometimes required to adopt. In *The Boo*, a novel about the Citadel, a military school, Pat Conroy describes plebes bracing: "Their chins are tucked in, their shoulders thrown back, and their backs are rigidly straight."

brew. 1. Coffee. 2. Beer.

bring smoke. To attack or punish.

broken down. Disassembled.

brown bar. Second lieutenant, who wears a single gold bar.

buckle. To fight.

buff (acr). Big ugly fat fucker, nickname for the B-52 bomber. A number of war glossaries in family newspapers during the Gulf War reported that this stood for "big ugly fat fellow," and more recently it has been treated as a nickname for the plane being buff.

Bumfuck, Egypt. Remote site of hardship assignments; also known as East Overshoe.

bunker-buster. Bomb designed to penetrate the concrete shelters housing military communications networks, especially those controlling ballistic missiles. By extension, the term is being used to describe anything heavy-handed. A book reviewer talks about a writer who "is at her best when she unearths the scientist's life with a trowel instead of bunker buster." Earlier this term described a satchel charge composed of C-4 explosives and a short-fuse detonation cord, developed in Korea and used extensively in Vietnam.

burp. A Marine, especially to an infantryman.

bush. 1. The field or the boonies. 2. Ambush, for short.

bust. To reduce a man in rank or grade.

bust caps. To fire rapidly. In *Nam*, Mark Baker says that it is "probably derived from the paper percussion caps used in toy guns." See also CAPPING.

Butcher of Baghdad. Saddam Hussein.

butter bar. 1. Second lieutenant, from the brass bar indicating that rank. 2. The bar itself.

buy it / buy the farm. To die.

CamelBak. A tough water bottle with shoulder straps that can be worn like a pack and is favored over traditional canteens by troops in Afghanistan and the Middle East. Its long sipping tube can be pinned to a lapel or strap near the mouth to allow troops to drink while on the move.

cammies / camos. Camouflaged clothing.

Camp X-ray. Located in Guantanamo Bay, Cuba; since late 2001 it has been the name for the high-security home of suspected Taliban and al Qaeda prisoners.

canker mechanic. A medic.

cannon cockers. Soldiers whose area of specialty is artillery. A character in Philip Caputo's *Rumor of War* is described as a "cannon-cockin' Texas shitkicker."

capping. Shooting at.

care package. Goodies (candy, cookies, etc.) from home.

catbox. The Middle East.

Cav. Air cavalry.

C-DAT. Computerized Dumb Ass Tanker.

cell. A small terrorist group, affiliated with a larger one but not in direct contact.

CENTCOM. The U.S. Central Command, in Qatar.

chairborne. Describing a military bureaucrat or paper pusher—a play on the term "airborne."

chalk. A helicopter squad, as in Mark Bowden's *Black Hawk Down*: "Before him, arrayed on both sides of the sleek UH-60 Black Hawk helicopter, was Eversmann's Chalk, a dozen men in tan, desert camouflage fatigues."

chalk leader. The person responsible for loading and unloading every aircraft. Usually the platoon leader designates a soldier to open and close the door of the helicopter.

charlie tango. Control tower.

chatter. Intercepted conversations. To the public it amounts to nonspecified message traffic whose intensity is measured as an indication of possible attack. Increased "chatter" will cause increased security and a heightened level of alert. This is a term that was once innocuous but has taken on ominous overtones in the post-9/11 world.

cheap charlie. Skinflint.

check six / check your six. Pilot parlance for "Watch your tail," alluding to the fact that six o'clock describes the area directly behind an aircraft.

cheese / cheeser / cheese dick. A person who sucks up to a superior; brownnosing.

cherry. New man in unit.

chicken cach. Packaged chicken cacciatore, served to the troops day after day. "The Spam of the 1990s."

chicken / chickenshit. Petty.

chicken guts. Looped braid on officers' dress uniforms.

chicken plate. Personal armor, such as the kind that helicopter pilots wear across their chest and groin.

chicken soup casualty. A post–Gulf War term for mild battle fatigue—the kind treated by a few hot meals and a secure place to sleep.

chicks in tow. Fighters lined up behind a tanker for midair refueling.

chopper. Helicopter.

chow. Food.

Cinderella liberty. Period of freedom that ends at midnight.

civil serpent. Civil servant, especially one who works with the uniformed military.

clerks 'n' jerks. Support staff.

click. Kilometer; also KLICK.

clobber. 1. To attack a ground target from the air. 2. To defeat decisively.

Club Dead. The Guantanamo Bay, Cuba, detention camp for Taliban and al Qaeda members, which the *Washington Post* described as "the only tropical hideaway with a suicide watch."

cluster fuck. A totally screwed-up situation.

clutch belt. Cartridge belt worn by Marines.

CNN effect. The fascination and disruption created by extensive live television presence in combat zones.

CO. Commanding officer.

coal burner. Any older jet with smoky engines. A member of the Air Force on the GI Jargon Web site adds "Early KC-135's, B-52's and F-4's come to mind."

COB. Close of business; the end of the day, as in, have that on my desk by COB tomorrow.

cold, cold, smoked the bitch. Pilot's terse report on shooting down an enemy plane.

column. A batallion.

commfu. Completely monumental military fuckup.

commo. Communications in general, but often specificially used for radio.

connect the dots. Cliché of the War on Terrorism for coming to a conclusion based on far-flung information.

connex. Large metal box for shipping and storage.

contact. Firing or being fired upon; engaging in combat.

'copter. Helicopter.

cots. Apricots. During the Vietnam War a superstition developed among Marine tankers that apricots, an ingredient in some rations, brought bad luck. The word was "No cots."

C [plus 2] V. Shorthand for windowless armored command-and-control vehicle, hermetically sealed against chemical attack, which can travel at 30 mph. The commander in this vehicle looks at a bank of computer screens, which shows the locations of all his units, current satellite imagery, and intelligence data, even as he cruises near the front lines.

crapper. Latrine.

C-rats / Cs. C-rations, which the military began phasing out in 1978. The new rations are called MRES, for "meal, ready to eat."

crease. To wound, as in "We just creased him and all it did was make him mad."

crew served. Very large, very powerful, as in "I've got a crew-served headache."

crispy critters. Enemy personnel killed by napalm or other incendiary device.

Crotch, the. The U.S. Marine Corps.

crunchies. Ground infantrymen.

cuff 'em and stuff 'em. Policy of quick detention and transport taken toward noncombatants who might get in the way of military operations.

cunt cap. Narrow green Army cap.

CYA. Cover your ass.

cyber warfare. Officially, "Any act intended to compel an opponent to fulfill our national will, executed against the software controlling processes within an opponent's system," it boils down to attacks on computers, networks, and the Internet and ranges from massive assaults to stealing e-mail or taking password lists from a mail server, introducing viruses and overloading of systems through e-mail (e-mail overflow). Sometimes shortened to CyW.

DADT. "Don't ask, don't tell." It alludes to the the nonprovocative, passively permissive policy toward gays and lesbians in the U.S. armed forces.

daisy cutter. The BLU-82, a 15,000-pound bomb that earned its nickname because when it is detonated about three feet above ground it incinerates everything within 600 yards. First used by the Air Force in the final year of U.S. involvement in Vietnam, it was often employed to clear thick jungle areas to create instant helicopter landing zones. Daisy cutters were dropped on Taliban positions in Afghanistan after the 9/11 attacks. In December 2001 the American Dialect Society voted it the "most euphemistic" term in its annual "word of the year" awards, "because it doesn't actually cut daisies. It atomizes them—and everything else." About the size of a minivan, the BLU-82 combines a watery mixture of ammonium nitrate and aluminum with air, then ignites to create a huge fireball. The shock wave can be felt miles away.

day the eagle shits, the. Payday. The eagle is the federal government.

Dear John / Dear John letter. Letter from a girlfriend announcing that it's all over.

decapitation. The process of overthrowing a government from the top by bombing strategic targets and removing the leadership.

DEFCON. Defensive readiness condition. Officially, DEFCON 5 = normal peacetime readiness; DEFCON 4 = normal, increased intelligence and strengthened security measures; DEFCON 3 = increase in force readiness above normal readiness; DEFCON 2 = further increase in force readiness, but less than maximum readiness; DEFCON 1 = maximum force readiness. The term is parodied in constructions like "SniffleCon 5."

denied area. Nation or region with no means of covert access on the ground. At the beginning of 2003 Iraq was considered a "denied area," with no U.S. access to insiders, no U.S. offices in the country, and limited opportunities to contact Iraqi officials when they traveled abroad because they were usually chaparoned.

deros (acr). Date eligible to return from overseas or date of expected return from overseas. In his *Everything We Had*, Al Santoli called deros "the sweetest word in the military language."

deuce and a half. A two-and-a-half-ton truck; a medium cargo truck.

devil doc. Marine Corps doctor ready to go to the front lines to treat troops. In the *Miami Herald* in February 2003, the war correspondent Juan O. Tamayo wrote, "They are combat doctors, the docs of war, the men Marines, who like to call themselves 'Devil Dogs,' count on to save their lives and who are reverentially nicknamed the 'devil docs.'"

devil dog. Member of the U.S. Marine Corps. This nickname, first established during World War I, has come back into common use.

dich. Vietnamese for dead, and one of the terms used for enemy killed: "We got twenty-nine dead dichs up here and another seventeen hurtin'" (pron. "dick").

dicks in the dirt. Enemy dead. An article by an anonymous Marine in Iraq which appeared in the *Washington Times*, November 22, 2005, contains a review of the M-240 machine gun as "worth her considerable weight in gold. The ultimate fight-stopper, puts their dicks in the dirt every time."

diddy-bopping. Walking carelessly.

dilligaf (acr). "Does it look like I give a fuck?"

dink. Derogatory term for an Asian.

dirty bomber. Bomber using nonconventional weapon such as radiation bomb. Term first applied to Jose Padilla, who allegedly was scouting fresh attack targets in the United States.

dirty officer. Duty officer.

do-rag. Bandanna or scarf worn over the head and tied at the back in lieu of regular headgear.

dog him out. To criticize; to chide.

dog tags. Identification tags worn on chain around neck.

doghouse. A protuberance or blister that houses an instrument or instruments on an otherwise smooth skin of a drone or missile.

dogs. Feet.

dome of obedience. Kevlar helmet.

Dover test. The level of war dead that will be tolerated by voters, named for the Dover Air Force base in Delaware, which is the official entry point for America's war dead.

DOW. Died of wounds.

dream sheet. Official forms on which officers and enlisted members indicate their preference for their next location and job.

dry hole. Any target where you don't find anything and nothing finds you.

dumb bombs. Sometimes called "iron bombs," they are traditional freefall bombs, as constrasted with "smart bombs." The daisy cutter is the largest dumb bomb in the U.S. arsenal. First used in the later days of the

Gulf War. Advances in technology have made the distinction between smart and dumb all the more important.

DuPont lure. A grenade or C4 plastic explosive, used for fishing.

dust-off. 1. Medevac helicopter. 2. To be lifted out by chopper.

E-bomb. Microwave bomb that flashes millions of watts of electricity in a microsecond, capable of wiping out large power grids. Described as "a lightning bolt in a cruise missile," their existence was made public in early 2003 as a weapon with a massive surge of energy designed to fry Saddam Hussein's computers, radar systems, weapons launchers, radios, cellular phones, and even the ignition systems of Iraqi tanks.

echelons beyond reality. Higher command; the source of orders and directives. Implied by this term is the suggestion that those at this high level of command are out of touch with reality—"beyond reality." It first showed up during the Gulf War.

EGS. Everything goes to shit.

eight. A master sergeant who is in pay grade E-8.

Eighth and I marine. A member of the Marine Corps assigned to ceremonial duties at the White House and elsewhere. In 1994, this term came to light when two marines from Virginia ran for the Senate. The challenger, Oliver L. North, attempted to put this label on Senator Charles S. Robb, who had in fact been assigned to the White House but also had spent eighteen months in Vietnam.

el-tee. Second lieutenant. Also called louie, butter bar, and the missing link.

embed. Journalist who has been assigned a slot within a combat unit. In late February 2003, on the eve of the Iraq War, over 350 news organizations had applied for 600 correspondents to be embedded in military units. "The word is 'embed.' Short, sweet and utterly bland," wrote Verne Gay in *Newsday* on February 23, 2003, "but in a few weeks—maybe sooner—'embed' will enter the language in a new and dramatic way. Already, this is the word that everyone in TV news is talking about, the word they toss about as effortlessly as if it had always been a fundamental part of their life and vocabulary."

E-nothing. One at the bottom; an imaginary pay grade below E-1; a recruit.

EPW. Enemy prisoner of war.

evak'd. Evacuated.

Face-shot. Air-to-air missile fired on an enemy aircraft. Also known as IN THE LIPS.

face time. Getting in to see and talk with a person at a higher command level.

fangs out. A gung-ho fighter pilot itching for combat; like a serpent.

fart sack. Bedroll.

fast movers. 1. Primarily high-performance jet aircraft but also M1 Abrams tanks and M2 Bradley Fighting Vehicles. 2. Jet fighters, usually F-4's.

fat. Describing a unit that is over its authorized strength. In *A Rumor of War*, Philip Caputo talks of a fat battalion.

fatty-gews. Fatigues.

FBCB2. "Force XXI Battle Command, Brigade and Below," the Internet-based communications system that was tested in Bosnia during the 1990s with promising results. The Tactical Internet, as FBCB2 is called, takes data collected from thousands of global positioning satellite sensors aboard vehicles and aircraft and integrates them with battlefield intelligence from a range of sources.

field expediency. Using what you have for what you need. For example, using the wrappers and cardboard containers for MRES as targets for rifle practice, scratch pads or, in a real pinch, toilet paper.

field first. An NCO rank that does not exist in any regulations; the field first is the sergeant who runs the company while the first sergeant is in a rear area.

fieldcraft. The art of real combat, as opposed to training and theories. It seems to be a parallel construction to the intelligence term "tradecraft."

FUBAR FLASHBACK

Steven Spielberg, in an interview given at the time of the 1998 release of his realistic epic *Saving Private Ryan*, said the expression almost got left out of the movie. Spielberg admitted he was unfamiliar with that authentic piece of Army slang until his father, a World War II vet, brought it to his attention. "My dad said, 'Do you have the word 'fubar' in this film?' And I said no," Spielberg recalled. "He told me what it meant and he said, 'We used to say it all the time,' so we wrote the scenes in. The whole thing came from my dad." One character spends much of *Ryan* trying to learn what "fubar" means.

figmo (acr). "Fuck it, got my orders."

fire base. Remote artillery base.

fire in the hole. Explosives about to be detonated deliberately, such as a satchel charge being dropped into a suspected enemy HIDEY-HOLE.

five by. Loud and clear, five being high quality, one being low.

flapjacks. Looters, a term from the American operation in Somalia.

flash-to-bang time. The interval between a gun's recoil and the shell's explosion. In combat, the shorter it is, the better.

flopper. Person unable to make a decision—one who flips and flops.

fly. Pilot. Not the most respectful term; a modern incarnation of "flyboy."

flying a desk. Air Force pilot working an office job.

flying butterknife. Winged bayonet patch worn by paratroopers.

FNG. Fucking new guy.

fobbit. Soldier in a secure position; one who does not leave base. May have replaced REMF in Iraq.

fog of war. The ages-old condition of combat confusion that modern digital military technology is aimed at lifting. "You will never, ever get rid of the fog of war," Marine Colonial Tom Bright told reporters from a command center in Qatar in early 2003: "War is a personal business—inside each commander's mind is what he intends to do." But, he said, "the new technology will allow operational chiefs to see more clearly and more quickly a 'mosaic of information' that will better inform war-fighting decisions."

Fort Living Room. Home. Duty station one goes back to after discharge or, in the case of reservists, after a period of active duty.

four-deuce. A 4.2-inch mortar.

fourth point of contact. One's ass, as in "Your head is stuck in your fourth point of contact." The other three points are (1) feet, (2) knees, (3) elbows.

fox. To fire, from the old phonetic alphabet. To report "fox one" is to say that a pilot has fired his first missile.

frag. 1. Fragmentation grenade. 2. To grenade; to wound or kill with a hand grenade.

freak. Short for radio frequency.

freedom bird. Airplane returning soldiers to the United States.

friend-of-a-friend e-mail. Name given to the post-9/11 Internet rumors, which often began with information collected from a "friend of friend." Typical was a warning from a friend of a friend who said that he or she had information that shopping malls were to be attacked on Halloween 2001 or that certain groups were forewarned of the

9/11 attacks and told to stay home from work.

friendlies. Allies, both military and civilian.

frog hair. Mythical unit of measure denoting a very small distance, such as "Lay that two frog hairs to the right." Same as RED CUNT HAIR.

fruit salad. Two or more rows of campaign ribbons.

FTA. Fuck the Army.

fubar (acr). "Fouled/fucked up beyond all recognition" was, along with snafu, "situation normal all fouled/fucked up," one of World War II's most enduring slang constructions. Fubar is a term with postmillennial legs used commonly in Kuwait.

full bird. A colonel, from the eagle insignia.

funny papers. Maps.

fur ball. 1. The frenzy of air combat; the hectic tangle of the dogfight. 2. The dogfight, or close air battle, itself.

Garritrooper. Term invented during World War II by the cartoonist and writer Bill Mauldin to describe a soldier who was "too far forward to wear ties and too far back to get shot." The term survived, and Charles D. Poe has noted, "On Barry Sadler's album of Vietnam songs [*Ballads of the Green Berets*] there is one entitled 'Garet Trooper,' and the song's lyrics suggest that Sadler had in mind pretty much the same kind of soldier that Mauldin was describing."

gate rage. Post-9/11 reaction to intense airport security; akin to road rage.

gate rape. A full-body search at an airport security area.

GENIE (acr). Genetic imagery exploitation, a program that can identify hidden weapons in X-ray images of carry-on baggage.

gerbil launcher. M203 grenade launcher.

get some. Kill.

get your gut right. To eat; also to TAKE IT IN THE FACE.

getting mopped up. Donning chemical-warfare gear. The mission-oriented protective posture, or MOPP, gear provides complete encapsulation, which includes suit, hood, gloves, boots, and filtering mask.

getting short. Coming up on the end of one's tour of duty.

ghosting. Special Forces term for hiding out so you don't get put on a shit detail.

GI Joe or GI Jane. New sexually inclusive personification of a service person, replacing the solo characterization of GI Joe. The generic GI for a member of the armed forces is just as common in the era of the War on Terrorism as it was in World War II, when it was first used to describe an Army enlisted man, from the World War II term "government issue." The fact that this term, which came into being about 1940, is still used illustrates the power of slang over officialdom. In 1951 the Pentagon actually issued an edict prohibiting further use of "GI" within the military, stipulating that the proper term was "soldier."

GI shower. Cleaning oneself when water is scarce. For troops amassing in the Kuwaiti desert in early 2003, the definition was "baby wipes."

giant voice. A public address system that broadcasts messages across a military base or flightline.

GIB. Guy in back, term used to describe a radar intercept officer who flies in the backseat of certain aircraft.

Gitmo. The U.S. Navy station at Guantanamo Bay, Cuba, in Navy slang. Tucked away on the remote southeastern end of the island nation, it is America's oldest overseas installation and a key patrol point for the Atlantic Fleet watching the Caribbean and South America. Now America's largest detention center and the only U.S. military base on Communist soil.

giving a warm fuzzy. According recognition to new sensitivities and sensibilities in the military. Tony Allen-Mills of London's *Sunday Times*, in a 2001 article from Washington aptly titled "Fix Bayonets and Hug,"

giving a warm fuzzy. (*continued*) says, "Warmth and fuzziness are not normally associated with the U.S. military, but times are changing and even soldiers are having to learn how to be politically correct."

glad bag. Body bag.

go 911. To panic; to become terrorized, from the 911 emergency telephone number and the attacks of 9/11.

go bag. Prepackaged items for evacuation. On February 14, 2003, the *Washington Post* reported that "members of Congress were told to gather a 'go bag' of supplies, sensitive documents and key phone numbers in case of an attack."

go pills. Amphetamines, in military parlance, the equivalent of "uppers" in civilian slang. They have been given to pilots for decades, for it was thought that they are vital for keeping aviators alert on extended missions. But a "friendly-fire" incident in April 2002 in Afghanistan—a bombing that left four Canadian soldiers dead—has brought new scrutiny to the practice. Now, many are questioning the safety of giving dextroamphetamine, or Dexedrine, to pilots. Go pills' sleep-inducing counterparts are NO-GO PILLS.

goat rope. A confused situation, as one would experience trying to rope goats.

goat screw. A real mess. It means "Someone's gonna get it for this!"

goat screw on ice. Quite a bit worse than a GOAT SCREW.

golden BB. American name for the antiaircraft doctrine that says that when you put enough ordnance in the air, an enemy plane or two will be hit. Not a new term, it was used in the Iraq War as a derisive description of the Iraqis' emulation of Soviet antiaircraft defenses. The term "golden bullet" had limited use as a synonym for golden BB.

gone Elvis. Lost; missing in action.

good end. Conclusion denied to many in the military in the First Gulf War and used on the eve of the Second Gulf War as a goal for the second campaign against Saddam Hussein.

good to go. Fit, competent, and ready to perform.

gook. Derogatory term for an Asian, from Korean slang for person.

gorilla snot. Popular name for yellowish-brown contact cement that cures to form an instant asphalt-like landing field. Cited in dispatches from Kuwait on the eve of the Iraq War. This is also a trade name for a commercial substance sold to musicians to keep a grip on guitar picks and drumsticks.

goya (acr). Get off your ass.

gravel agitator. Infantryman.

grease. To kill. "Brother or not," says a character in Alfred Coppel's *Apocalypse Brigade*, "you come out now or we grease you on the spot."

greased. Killed in action. These gruesome lines appear in John Skipp and Craig Spector's *The Scream*: "The A-gunner's brains blew all over him. His squad was getting greased."

green bait. Reenlistment bonus.

green beanies. U.S. Army Special Forces (from the Green Berets). To call a member of the Special Forces a green beanie is to risk personal injury.

green machine. The U.S. Army.

greenbacks. American money.

ground hogs / ground pounders. The infantry.

Ground Zero. The sixteen-acre site of the wreckage of the World Trade Center and, by extension, the site of of any disaster. The official pre-9/11 Army definition: "The central point of a nuclear detonation (or other large blast). Refers to the point on the ground below or above a nuclear detonation if the device is triggered in the air or underground." That meaning changed overnight: "It's metaphor," Donna Jo Napoli, a linguistics professor at Swarthmore College, said in early 2002 of the new usage. "It wasn't a nuclear attack, but it leveled the place. And it had a nuclear effect on us as a nation."

grunt. Old term with new explanation: government reject unfit for normal training.

gun bunny. Artilleryman.

gung ho. Overzealous; driven.

gunny / guns. Marine gunnery sergeant.

gunship. Armed helicopter.

gut ripper. Antipersonnel mines and grenades used by either side.

gyrene. Marine.

Hack it. To stand it.

haji mart. Flea market, bazaar, etc., to troops in Iraq and Afghanistan; play on Wal-Mart and Kmart.

hash mark. Diagonal uniform bars, each signifying four years of military service.

HDR. Humanitarian daily ration, variant of the MRE used to feed a malnourished person for one day with 2,300 calories in a two-meal packet. In the first year of the American presence in Afghanistan under Operation Enduring Freedom, 3.8 million HDRs were distributed.

headquarters pukes. Administrative personnel removed from combat areas.

heart. A Purple Heart, the medal that signifies a combat wound. In *Fields of Fire,* James Webb reported on the "three Heart rule," which was in effect in Vietnam. It stated that any Marine wounded three times within one combat tour was immediately removed from the combat zone.

heavy metal. Loosely applied term alluding to heavy artillery, naval arms, etc., and a clear reapplication of a term from a form of rock 'n' roll with considerable popularity among the soldiers in the Gulf War.

helitrooper. Soldier who jumps from a helicopter.

hero gear. Battle souvenirs.

hesperophobia. Fear of the West, an obscure term given new relevance in the twenty-first century.

hidey-hole. Any hole scratched into the ground or into the brow of a hill where a soldier can take refuge.

hillbilly armor. Scavenged metal used to harden military vehicles in Iraq.

Hilton. Name of fancy hotel chain invoked ironically for places totally unlike Hiltons. When Bob Hope returned from Vietnam in 1967, he noted, "Every broken-down hut, hootch, or Quonset hut is called the Chu Lai Hilton, or the Hilton East, or the Hilton something." The most famous Vietnam Hilton was the infamous Hanoi Hilton, a prison in which many American POWs were held.

hitch. A period of enlistment or reenlistment.

hog. 1. The A-10 or Thunderbolt II aircraft, sometimes called the WARTHOG. 2. Helicopter gunship of the UH-Huey series.

hog-60. The M-60 machine gun.

homeland. Washington's term of choice for the United States in the post-9/11 world, which in its early applications was used mostly by the bureaucrats charged with defending the country and by security merchants. Tom Ridge, head of the Department of Homeland Security and the person most closely connected with the term in its early years, was not even sure how the choice came about. "Etymology unknown, don't have a clue," Ridge told Elizabeth Becker, a reporter from the *New York Times*, in 2002.

homesteading / homesteader. Remaining at one military base for a long period of time; soldier who manages to stay in one assignment for a long period of time.

honcho. A leader, boss, or man in charge. This very common item of Korean War slang soon entered general American slang. It's from Japanese *han*, squad, and *cho,* leader, reports Stuart Berg Flexner in *I Hear America Talking*, literally "squad leader," a corporal or sergeant. A common definition given during the war, number one man, suggested this Japanese lineage.

honey box. Portable toilet.

hoo-ah. An all-purpose, all-terrain mostly-Army term for "Yes, roger, ready"; a military exclamation of positive exuberance. Mark Kinkade, in an April 9, 1996, article in *Stars and Stripes*, said of this term, "Nobody's quite sure how to define it, but everybody knows what it means." Another writer,

hoo-ah. (*continued*) William H. McMichael, has written, "In the Army, the expression 'hoo-ah' has, as the Chinese say, a thousand different meanings. 'It's basically the answer for everything,'" Sergeant Scott Lachut of the 6th Battalion at Fort Eustis told McMichael. It may be an all-purpose greeting; anything and everything except "no"; good copy, solid copy, roger, good, great, message received, understood; amen. It's an upbeat word, one that can be used to describe any military situation where the speaker is alive and well. For instance, it was almost invariably used to greet mail call. It has also been written URAH and OOH RAH and was called "the signature call of the American forces" by the *Houston Post*. It is also known as YEE-HAH. Indeed, an energy snack bar, named HooAH!, for the Army's ubiquitous expression, was created by the Army's Soldier Systems Center in Natick, Massachusetts. Unlike commercial energy bars, the Army version will last for three years at 80 degrees and six months at 100 degrees. CranRaspberry is one of five HooAH! flavors.

hooch. Hut or simple dwelling.

hop and pop. "Wake 'em up and move 'em out."

hose down. To shoot with automatic fire.

hot line. A real or imaginary line that separates contaminated from uncontaminated areas in nuclear-, biological-, and chemical-warfare situations.

hot LZ. Landing zone under fire.

hot skinny. Information.

hotel alpha. Radio call to "get out of there"—phonetic equivalent of Haul Ass.

hotel warrior. Term from the First Gulf War for journalists who did their reporting from the roofs of their hotels. The term is not pejorative.

hots. Hot meals.

Howard Johnson. Fire base built with future occupancy in mind.

HQ. Headquarters.

Huey. Nickname for the UH-1 series of utility helicopters, which one reporter described as a combination of "shuttle bus, supply truck, ambulance, and weapon of war." It comes from the official term "helicopter, utility," or HU.

human shield. A civilian positioned at or near a military target as a deterrent to attack by the enemy.

humma. Et cetera; whatever.

Humvee / Hummer. 1. The successor to the Jeep and the most common military vehicle in the Gulf. Don Kirkman, of Scripps-Howard News Service, wrote of the vehicle: "President Bush's Thanksgiving dinner was served on the hood of a Hummer. Bob Hope and his troupe of entertainers bounced from base to base in Hummers. The humble Hummer seems to be in the background of every news clip about troops in the field." 2. Much less commonly used as a nickname for the Navy's Hawkeye early-warning aircraft. 3. Marque of vehicles sold by General Motors.

hundred and worst. The 101st Airborne.

hurtin'. Injured or dead.

I&I. Intercourse and intoxication; a clear play off the expression R&R.

IED. Improvised explosive device, the jury-rigged roadside bombs used against U.S. troops in Iraq and the cause of one third of all American deaths by the end of 2005.

ilities. Survivability, mobility, and lethality, for short. Weapon systems are judged on their ilities.

illum. An illumination flare.

in-country. Country outside the United States to which one is assigned. During the Vietnam War it meant being in Vietnam: "After R&R in Bangkok, I was back in-country." As this is written, it refers to Iraq and Afghanistan.

in the lips. Air-to-air missile shot taken directly at an enemy aircraft. Same as FACE-SHOT.

incoming / incoming mail. Hostile artillery fire.

Indian country. Unsecured territory.

indigs. Indigenous people.

ink blot. A fortified enclave for supplies and weapons.

intel puke. Person in intelligence, especially one working far from the front.

intervasion. Term for the 1994 U.S. incursion into Haiti (Operation Uphold Democracy); a blend of intervention + invasion.

Irish pennant. A loose thread, strap, etc.

iron fist. The heavily armored U.S. Army Third Infantry Division.

Jack-off flare. Handheld tube-shaped flare about a foot long that is fired by striking the bottom. The projectile comes out trailing a bunch of sparks.

jacket. One's official permanent service record.

jafdip (acr). Just another fucking day in paradise.

jafo. Just another fucking observer, derogatory Air Force slang for anyone there to observe the actions and progress of the troops; usually this means a squad will have to babysit an officer or corporate rep into the bush.

jay-dog. Joint detention operations group commander, the man in charge of detainees at Guantanamo.

JDAM / jay-dam. Joint direct attack munition is a smart weapon using global positioning system (GPS) technology. Because of its accuracy and low cost it has become the wildly popular "Ford Mustang of smart bombs."

Jesus nut. The bolt that holds the rotor blade to a helicopter.

Joe. Any U.S. enlisted soldier. Contraction of World War II's GI Joe.

john. Lieutenant; hence "first john" and "second john," for first and second lieutenant.

John Wayne High School. The U.S. Army Special Warfare School at Fort Bragg.

John Wayne. 1. To act heroically. 2. Soldier who "acts it up" for the media, especially the camera.

Jolly Green Giant. The CH-47 double-rotor helicopter. Also LOG.

junk on the bunk. Inspection in which one's field equipment is laid out and displayed on one's bunk.

Kaserne. German for "military camp," this is now used to describe a military base anywhere in the world.

K-bar. A military knife.

keyboard jockey. Any member of the Armed Forces whose job causes that person to be on a computer all day.

khaki tit. The Army as provider. A regular Army person is said to suck the khaki tit.

KI pill. Potassium iodide, treatment used on the thyroid for radiation exposure.

KIA. Killed in action.

kick. Dishonorable discharge.

kill. A downed enemy aircraft. This term has been in use since World War II, replacing the equivalent "victory" of World War I.

kill box. Rectangle on aircraft radar screen on which target is seen blowing up.

kill-fire. A burst of gunfire that is so effective it leaves nobody to return fire.

killer bees. Attack aircraft; from the name of a species of African bee much discussed in the United States at the time of the First Gulf War.

kiss-and-cry area. Area designated for departing troops to bid farewell to family and friends. Term first used to describe the area where competitive figure skaters await their final grades.

kiwi injections. A swift kick in the ass with your highly shined boots, from the name of a popular brand of shoe polish.

klick. Kilometer. Also CLICK.

KP. Kitchen police; mess-hall duty.

K-pot. Standard-issue Army Kevlar helmet; analogous to the STEEL POT of the Vietnam era, the then-standard Army helmet, which consisted of a fiber helmet liner and an outer steel helmet.

KYPIYP. Keep your pecker in your pants.

Lanyard puller. Artilleryman, a reference to the time when cannons were fired by pulling a lanyard.

lay chilly. To freeze.

LCs. Line crossers; enemies who defect.

leaflet drop. Spending money on girls and booze with reckless abandon.

legos / legs. Unit that is neither airborne nor mechanized; ground soldiers, to airborne rangers.

let's roll. The phrase coined by Todd Beamer, a passenger on United Airlines Flight 93, who helped launch the attack against the hijackers over Pennsylvania on 9/11.

lick. A mistake.

lie dog. To go to cover and remain motionless while listening for the enemy. This is SOP for a recon team immediately after being inserted or infilled.

lifer. Career military person.

lifer juice. Coffee.

lima charlie. The letters LC, meaning "loud and clear."

liquid cork. Diarrhea medicine.

live large. To enjoy the maximum of creature comforts, a term applied to U.S. troops in Kuwait in early 2003, who, according to the Associated Press, "relax at umbrella-covered picnic tables on a wide field surrounded by eateries offering burgers, ice cream, pizza, and egg rolls. A huge gym boasts aerobics classes and state-of-the-art cardiovascular machines. Movies are shown on a wide-screen TV beside a game room with ping-pong and chess." This occasioned this comment from one of their officers: "They're living large right now, but if I put them out in a tent they're gonna be fine."

log. The CH-47 double-rotor helicopter. Also JOLLY GREEN GIANT.

long tom. Long-range .155 mm artillery.

lost-lieutenant finder. A handheld global positioning satellite (GPS) unit, which according to the defunct GI Jargon Web site, "is relied on entirely too much by butter bars who can't read a map or use a compass."

louie. Lieutenant.

love Scud. The penis (as guided missile).

lower than whaleshit. At the bottom of the ocean, in terms of rank and status.

LP. 1. Listening post. 2. Landing platform.

LPC. Leather personnel carrier (your boots), i.e., hoofing it on foot.

lum. Illumination flares.

lurp. 1. Special ration of food packaged

The MOAB Law of Unintended Consequences

Several days after ABC News revealed the existence of the MOAB., it carried a follow-up story that began, "The tiny town of Moab, Utah, has asked President George W. Bush not to use the acronym MOAB for a new bomb because it could damage the image of the city, best known for outdoor recreation." A letter from the Grand County Council to the White House said, "We realize that it is an acronym, but we are still concerned about the effects it may have on our community. Moab relies on tourism both domestic and foreign and has worked for many years and spent hundreds of thousands of dollars to create an image that 'Moab' is a destination." The name of the town in Utah was named after the biblical kingdom southeast of the Dead Sea.

for those on long-range patrol. 2. Ranger engaging in long-range reconnaissance patrols.

LZ. Landing zone.

Ma deuce. M2 .50-caliber heavy machine gun.

Maggie's drawers. 1. Red flag displayed from the target pit on the rifle range when a shot has completely missed the target. 2. A miss.

maggot. Clueless GI.

man up! Step up to the plate.

meals refusing to exit. Reinterpretation of the initials MRE, which actually stands for "meals ready to eat."

mechanical. Ambush weaponry triggered by the enemy; mines, flares, etc.

media puke. A journalist. Also called headaches, pencils, and JIB (joint information bureau) rats.

mess kit repair battalion. Mythical unit to which goofs and BOLOS are sent.

mess / mess hall. Dining facility.

Middle Eastern Theater. The Persian Gulf and nearby regions as a military area.

mike bag. Nickname for "modular lightweight load carrying equipment" (MOLLE), a backpack with a plastic frame. Also called MOLLY PACK.

mike mike. Millimeter, military jargon for firing a 20-millimeter cannon, as in "Lay down some twenty mike mike."

million-dollar wound / million-dollar zap. A noncrippling wound that is serious enough to warrant return to the United States; a ticket home.

missing link. Second lieutenant.

mission essential. Something vital.

misunderstandistan. The inability to differentiate among unstable Central Asian nations whose names ending in -stan (meaning "place where one stays," i.e., homeland or country). These country names—Afghanistan, Tajikistan, Turkmenistan, and Uzbekistan—are formed by adding -stan to the name of the tribe living in that country, so the country of the Afghani is Afghanistan.

MLR. Main line of resistance, a.k.a. the front line. Often used in the bravado sense of "I've got more time on the MLR than the REMF has in-country."

MOAB (acr). Massive ordnance air burst bomb or, as it was immediately dubbed, the mother of all bombs (pron. "MO-ab.") It is a bigger version of the 15,000-pound DAISY CUTTER used in Vietnam, the Persian Gulf War, and Afghanistan. When its existence was first disclosed in February 2003 MOAB, then still experimental, was described as a 21,000-pound bomb that will be pushed out the back of a C-130 transport and guided to its target by satellite. Because it is not dropped by parachute, as was the daisy cutter, it can be let go from much higher altitudes. It was first reported by ABC News, which said of it, "The MOAB's massive explosive punch, sources say, is similar to a small nuclear weapon." From the *New York Post:* "The U.S. military yesterday exploded a newly developed 21,500-pound monster weapon nicknamed the 'mother of all bombs'—and let Saddam Hussein know he will face its devastation in any war on Iraq."

molly pack (acr). MOLLE, modular lightweight load carrying equipment, a lightweight pack with a plastic frame; also called the MIKE BAG.

monkey suit. The fur suit used by World War I and II aviators flying at high altitudes. Now refers to the military uniform in general.

Monopoly money. Foreign currency.

MOOTWA (acr). Military operations other than war; refers to any regular armed forces used in a peacekeeping role.

MOPP suit. Mission-oriented protective posture, specially designed suits that go over one's uniform to prevent contamination and exposure; full-body protective gear.

mother of all bombs. See MOAB.

Mr. No-shoulders. A snake. The term originated with the troops in Vietnam, where snakes are common.

Mr. Zippo. GI operating a flamethrower.

MRE. Meals ready to eat, a staple for U.S. troops in the field. The MRE of the early twenty-first century was a far cry from the MREs of a decade earlier, which were widely lampooned as "meals rejected by everyone." In a nod to international cuisine, MREs may now be beef enchiladas, chicken in Thai sauce, jambalaya, and pasta Alfredo. The chemical smell of the earlier versions of the MREs is gone, there is more variety, and there are even vegetarian offerings. The 2003-version MRE is lightweight, compact, easily opened, able to withstand a parachute drop from 1,250 feet or from a helicopter at 100 feet with no parachute, endure inclement weather, and survive temperature extremes from minus 60 to 120 degrees Fahrenheit. They must have a minimum shelf life of three years at 80 degrees Fahrenheit and last for six months at 100, be highly acceptable, and meet the Office of the Surgeon General's nutritional requirements as identified in Army Regulation 4025, Nutritional Standards for Operational Rations. Still, there are those who find these meals hard to pass through the system, and to them they are "meals refusing to exit."

mule. Small motorized platform used to carry arms, but sometimes also supplies and troops. Sometimes called a "mechanical mule." In Philip Caputo's *A Rumor of War*, a mule is described as "a heavy-weapons carrier that looked nothing like a mule, but rather resembled an oversized toy wagon."

mummify. Fighters who bury themselves in loose dirt to surprise the enemy, used mostly in the desert. It was originated by Arab nomads.

mummy sack. Rubber body bag.

mustang. Officer who has come up through noncom ranks; also, one who has been given a battlefield promotion.

mystery meat. Mess-hall meat lacking clear identity.

Nam. Vietnam.

NBC. Nuclear, biological, and chemical weapons, as a class. "In the past, the troops would joke that NBC stood for No-Body Cares," a 10th Mountain Division soldier at Fort Drum's Nuclear, Biological and Chemical School told an AP reporter in 2002, "but we are never going back to the way war was. Chemical and biological threats are now something that will always be a constant."

newby / newfer. Replacement person.

news crawl. Headlines at the bottom of television screens, a staple of cable news channels in the post-9/11 world.

NICKA. Pentagonese for a computerized nomenclature procedure called the Code Word, Nickname and Exercise Term System. It keeps track of hundreds of two-word code names, which defense planners craft more carefully than some parents name their children.

Nintendo effect / Nintendo war. Videotapes of exploding buildings that made the Gulf War bombing look like a Nintendo video game.

9/11. September 11, 2001. 9/11 became universal shorthand for the attack—and everything related to it—within days. Using a number to denote the tragedy is unusual, because tragedies are usually named for their location. Pearl Harbor. Kent State. Oklahoma City. It has also been termed Terrible Tuesday, Black Tuesday, and, in Spanish, *negro once* ("black eleven").

98,000 tons of diplomacy. An aircraft carrier. Term spotted in a *Washington Post* article of November 28, 2002, in which the commanding officer of the USS *Harry S Truman* used this term to describe his ship.

no-clap medal. Good-conduct medal, from the belief that one will be given the medal if one avoids venereal disease.

No Such Agency. National Security Agency (NSA), so called because of its secret budget and ultrasecret methods.

no sweat. No trouble; I can handle it.

nods / nogs. Night-vision goggles (NVGs). They attach to the front of the helmet and transform night into green-tinted day, giving troops a big advantage over less sophisticated opponents. They run on AA batteries.

no-go pills. Drugs used to calm soldiers after combat. See GO-PILLS.

no-hope pope. Name for reserves; compare to the name for active-duty forces: "people with no lives."

nordo (acr). "No Radio," or radio failure.

not a problem / no problem. Standard response of troops to their officers in the Gulf and a far cry from lines like "Sounds like a personal problem to me" from the Vietnam War era.

november foxtrot whiskey. No fuckin' way, using the words that stand for the letters N, F, and W.

nuclear coffee. Drink prepared by taking the instant coffee, cocoa, creamer, and sugar contained in an MRE accessory package and mixing them in a canteen half filled with water.

nugget. A new pilot assigned to an aircraft carrier; a rookie at landing jets at sea.

number 1. The best.

number 10. The worst.

nylon. Parachute.

O-club. Officers' club.

officer material. Not officer material; a goof-off.

oh-dark thirty. Early in the morning—for example, 3:30 A.M.

on the economy. Living off-base.

one-wire. Navy electrician; a "two-wire" is an electronics technician.

oohrah. Marine Corps' version of the Army's "HOO-AH."

OP. Outpost.

Operation Anaconda. A U.S. offensive against dug-in al Qaeda and Taliban troops in eastern Afghanistan's Paktia province in March 2002. The operation officially ended when declared a success by General Tommy Franks, but a *Washington Post* article on slang suggested that "Op-An," from Operation Anaconda, was a new word for "total failure and defeat."

Operation Infinite Justice. Original name given to the United States' war on terror. It offended Muslims and was replaced by "Enduring Freedom."

opfor. Opposition forces.

optempo. Optimum tempo.

ossifer. Officer.

outgoing / outgoing mail. Friendly artillery fire.

outside, the. Civilian life.

outside the wire. Outside army authority.

outstanding. Term of mock enthusiasm for anything from the excellent to the barely passable.

over the beach. Naval aviation slang for missions over land—notably, routine patrols over the southern no-fly zone in Iraq.

over-two. More than two thirds of the way through a normal enlistment, which is three years.

oxygen thief. Totally useless person.

Palm. Napalm.

passover party. Gathering of officers who have been passed over for promotion to a higher rank.

patch guys. Highly experienced fighter pilots recognizable by the many patches signifying their awards, special schools, and experiences.

PBI. Poor bloody infantry.

pencil. Reporter without a camera crew; print journalist.

pencil whip. To make up a story for the record.

penguins. Air Force members and ground crews who don't fly (wingless birds). They're also called ground hogs, wing weenies, CHAIRBORNE rangers, pencil pushers, and desk jockeys.

PI. Political influence or political interest. For instance, a private whose father is an appointed judge would find the initials PI on his service jacket.

pick up brass. To leave; to move out. It comes from the rifle range, where soldiers are required to pick up their brass shell casings when they are done.

ping. To criticize.

pinger. Used by the guys in the electronics field, derogatorily, to describe a new guy in the unit. Derived from a training school prank in which the first project assigned to the trainee was to assemble a "pinger detector."

Play-Doh. Plastic explosive, after the trade name for child's modeling clay.

PMS. Premaneuver syndrome; condition that acknowledges that military married couples are prone to argue before shipping out because it is easier to say good-bye when you're angry with someone.

pocket leave. To take leave but stay on the post or base—probably because the leave papers never leave the leave taker's pocket.

pogue. A complainer.

pogues. Rear-echelon military personnel. Derogatory.

point. Forward man on a combat mission.

police. To clean up.

pop. To kill; to WASTE; a term that first saw use in Vietnam.

pop smoke. To ignite a smoke grenade to signal an aircraft.

porky. Someone carrying too much equipment or weaponry.

pos. Position.

POV. Privately owned vehicle—one's own car, as opposed to a GOV, or government-owned vehicle.

prang. To land a helicopter roughly.

prick-77. The standard battlefield radio, whose official name is the AN/PRC-77.

psywar. Psychological warfare.

ptomaine domain / ptomaine palace. Mess hall.

pucker factor. Level of anxiety experienced by air crews.

Puff the Magic Dragon. A C-47 transport plane armed with 7.62 mm machine guns that was used in support of ground troops.

puke. Somebody in a different career field from yours. For instance, an admin puke, headquarters puke, media puke, etc.

pull rank. To exercise the power of one's position or rank.

pull the pin. To leave, from the rapid exit one makes after pulling the ring on a hand grenade.

punch out. Eject or bail from an aircraft. Sometimes used to say you are going home for the day or leaving.

purple. Describing a condition where all military services come together, from the idea that the colors of the various uniforms blend to make purple. Term has been used in Operation Purple, a system of summer camps for the children of parents deployed by the military that was introduced in 2004.

purple hurt. Purple Heart.

purple vision. Night vision.

Quartermaster property. Dead, because burial is a job of the Quartermaster Corps.

Rack. Cot or bed.

rack time. Sleep.

rail. First lieutenant, from the single-silver-bar insignia of that rank.

Rambo. According to a March 20, 1989, *Houston Chronicle* article, this is a term "used derisively by soldiers for someone who is braver than he is intelligent."

R&R. Rest and relaxation, or rest and recuperation. In Vietnam, R&R was a three- to seven-day vacation from combat zones. "Rape and ruin" is just one of a number of unofficial translations of R&R.

ranger pudding. A combination of MRE cocoa beverage mix, coffee creamer, and water mixed to the consistency of pudding. When made with less water, ranger pudding also can be baked into a brownie. It is one of a number of dishes created from MRE ingredients.

rat fuck. Mission or operation that is doomed from the beginning.

ration drawer. Person who collects food, pay, and benefits without working for them.

ration of shit. A hard time.

re-up. Reenlist.

read. To hear or understand.

real estate. Territory lost or gained.

reckless rifle. Recoilless rifle.

recon. Reconnaissance.

red cunt hair. Bawdy unit of measure denoting a very small distance, as in "That is one red cunt hair out of alignment." Same as FROG HAIR.

red phone. Emergency telephone reserved for the direst of emergencies.

reefer. Refrigerator or refrigerated vehicle.

REMF. Rear-echelon motherfucker, or base-camp support troop.

repple-depple. Replacement depot, the casual camp where incoming soldiers, replacements, are processed.

rhip (acr). Rank has its privileges.

rifle. An infantryman.

rimbo. Female soldier, from Rambo.

rip cords. Loose threads.

roach wagon. Mobile canteen or snack bar.

roaches. Opposition forces dwelling in or operating from caves or tunnels.

road soldier (acr). From retired on active duty, anyone who spends a lot of time avoiding work.

rock and roll. 1. To fire an automatic weapon. 2. Automatic-weapon fire.

rockers. The lower stripes on an NCO's insignia, which look like the rockers that would be found on a rocking horse. For instance, a master sergeant (or E-8) wears three stripes and three rockers.

Rocket City. Nickname for any base under constant rocket fire.

roll out. To get up.

Rome plow. Bulldozer with a mammoth blade for jungle clearing.

rotate. To return to the United States after a period overseas.

rototilling. Carpet-bombing enemy territory with strategic bombers.

rusmow (acr). "Are you shitting me or what?"

Sack. Bed; RACK.

Sammy. Somalis, during Operation Restore Hope. Patrick D. McGowan, in *Outside the Wire: Confessions of an Infantryman*, added that it was reserved for certain Somalis: "Sammy was slang for any Somali citizen that stole from, badgered, or fought US forces. Another unique word heard was 'Sammy Stick,' a tool used as a head basher for vagrant Somalis that attempted to grab anything not tied down in a vehicle."

sandbox. Currently, Iraq; earlier it referred to Saudi Arabia.

S&D. Search and destroy.

Sandland. The Middle East.

sandpaper. Government-issue toilet paper.

sapper. Infiltrator.

sarge. Sergeant.

saw. Machine gun.

sci-fi. Generic label applied to the most advanced military technology—the E-BOMB, for example.

scope head. Radarman.

scorched-ocean policy. A military tactic of releasing crude oil and igniting it. It is a feared tactic modeled after the scorched-earth policy adopted by the Chinese when the Japanese invaded Manchuria in World War II.

scrambled eggs. Gold embellishment of senior officers' hat visors.

second balloon. A second lieutenant.

see pick (acr). Coalition Public Information Center, where U.S. commanders gave daily briefings that became a TV staple during Gulf War I.

seen the elephant. To have been under fire; to have been in combat. According to *A Dictionary of Soldier Talk*, by Colonel John R. Elting, Sergeant Major Dan Cragg, and Sergeant Ernest Deal, this phrase, which cropped up in Vietnam, dates back to the Mexican War. A longer earlier version was "I've heard the owl and seen the elephant."

self-kill mode. Built-in provision to battlefield electronic gear that causes the unit to self-destruct if it falls into enemy hands.

September tenth. Applied to someone who is naive or oblivious to new realities, as in "She's so September tenth."

sewer trout. Mess-hall fish.

shake-and-bake. Describing any sergeant who has earned rank quickly and without much time in the service, such as a graduate of NCO training school.

sham foo master. A soldier who manages to do nothing yet looks very busy all day.

shavetail. A new lieutenant. This is an old term dating back to a time when the Army used mules. New mules had their tails shaved so that their handlers could distinguish them from the trained mules.

shit on a shingle. Creamed beef on toast.

shithook. The CH-47 Chinook heavy-lift helicopter.

shock and awe. Tactic based on psychologically overwhelming the enemy and, by extension, the intimidation of the world's population. In World War II, Japan's fierce resistance crumbled after atomic bombs leveled Hiroshima and Nagasaki. In planning for war against Iraq, "shock and awe" envisioned hitting with a massive bombing campaign and simultaneous invasions from the north, south, and west.

shoot and scoot. Artillery-firing technique in which the unit is moved quickly after firing to avoid return fire.

short-arm inspection. Check for venereal disease.

short-timer. Term for one whose tour of duty or period of enlistment is nearing an end. Such a person is sometimes said to be "short."

short-timer's stick. Defined in Mark Baker's *Nam*: "[When] a soldier had approximately two months remaining of his tour in Vietnam, he might take a long stick and notch it for each of his remaining days in-country. As each day passed he would cut another notch in the stick until his rotation day, when he was left with only a small stub."

shotgun envelope. Manila envelope for interoffice mail, which is punched with holes (so that it is easy to see if anything remains in the envelope).

showstopper. Any condition that will keep a GI out of a combat zone. Bad teeth is a major showstopper.

sierra hotel. Pilot-speak for "Super hot!"

silk. Parachute.

silo sitters. Those assigned to missile sites.

single-digit fidget. Nervous condition of a single-digit midget, one with fewer than ten days remaining in a combat zone.

sitmap. Situation map, which shows the dispositions of friendly and enemy forces.

sitrep. Situation report.

SIW. Self-inflicted wound.

skag. Cigarette.

skate. Not working hard on the job.

skid lid. Kevlar helmet.

sky out. To flee or leave suddenly.

sky pilot. Chaplain.

sleeper cell. Covert location where terrorists await a signal or orders to move into action.

slick. Helicopter without rockets or other external armament; one used to carry troops and supplies.

slick sleeve. An airman basic.

SLJO. Shitty little job officer(s).

slop chute. An on-post beer hall for enlisted men not of NCO rank.

slope. A particularly derogatory term for an Asian, especially Vietnamese.

smadge. Term of address for sergeant major.

smart bomb. One that gains remarkable accuracy because it is guided by a laser beam or TV camera.

smokey bear. Drill sergeant.

smokies of the sea. The U.S. Coast Guard in a law-enforcement role.

smurf. Blue-helmeted UN forces, because of the similarity of color to the blue cartoon trolls.

snake. AH-1G Cobra attack helicopters.

snake eater. U.S. Army Special Forces soldier; Green Beret.

snatch. A capture or a rescue; an operation in which live subjects are brought back. A squad specializing in such operations goes on "snatch patrol."

sniffer-drone. Unmanned aircraft programmed to detect the first whiff of chemical terrorist gas attacks with nerve agents such as tabun, sarin, or VX.

SniffleCon 5. A mission on a cold, cold night necessitating layers and layers of clothing. Troops stationed in Udairi Range, Kuwait, at the end of 2002 told a reporter from the *Atlanta Journal Constitution* that preparing for such a night was "to go SniffleCon 5."

snowdrops. White-helmeted Air Force Security Police.

snowstorm. An enemy artillery or mortar attack.

snuffy. Recruit or low-ranking individual.

SOL. Shit out of luck.

SOP. Standard operating procedure, also standing operational procedure.

sorry about that. Ritual response to any bit of ill fortune, from the trivial to the tragic.

SOS. "Shit on a shingle"—chipped beef on toast.

spec. Specialist.

special feces. Special forces.

spit and polish. Attention to outward appearance and show; polished.

spoon. Cook (the mess sergeant is the head spoon).

spray and pray. Undisciplined machine-gun fire—usually on the part of the enemy.

spud gun. M203 grenade launcher.

squared away. Prepared; ready for action.

SRP. Soldier readiness processing, which involves checking medical and dental records, renewing vaccinations where needed, and providing short-term procedures such as tooth extraction.

stack pencils. To kill time.

Stan, the. Afghanistan, to U.S. troops posted there.

stand down. Rest period for a military unit when all operations, except security, cease.

stand tall. 1. To come to attention. 2. Ready.

stateside. The United States.

steel pot. A helmet.

stewburner. Army cook.

still pissing water from West Point. A young officer just out of the military academy.

stop loss. Policy preventing service members from retiring or leaving the service at their scheduled time. *Stars and Stripes* reported on February 21, 2003, "Active-duty soldiers whose units are part of a secret war plan involving Iraq now are prevented from voluntarily leaving the service, according to a stop-loss policy announced Thursday by Army leaders."

stop movement. Policy preventing permanent changes of station. A stop-movement order was issued in January 2003 in anticipation of the war against Iraq.

straphanger. A useless person; one who is only along for the ride.

strike. To barhop.

strings. Ropes, usually 120 feet long, tossed out of helicopters that soldiers can lash themselves to for a quick evacuation from an area where helicopters can't land.

stuck in the Stan. Remote posting to Afghanistan.

SWAT team. Seeds, weeds, and trash. A GI who got in trouble might be sent to the SWAT team.

swinging dick. Male soldier.

Tac air. Tactical air support.

tactical Internet, the. See FBCB2.

TAD. Temporary active duty.

take down / take out. To destroy.

take fire. To be shot at.

take it in the face. To eat.

tank killer. Apache helicopter.

tanker / tankerman / tankmen. Soldier in a tank unit.

TAP apron. Toxicological agent protective apron.

target-rich environment. Pilotese for more targets than bombs.

TDY. Temporary duty (pron. "teedee-Y").

tent peg. Stupid or worthless soldier.

terps. Interpreters to American forces in Iraq.

theoterrorism. Attacks on civilians for religious purposes.

thirty-year man. Career Army man; a lifer.

Thule coolies. Those on duty in Thule, Greenland.

ticks. Seventy-pound-plus rucksacks carried by Army Rangers, so called because they suck the life out of you.

tiger stripes. Tropical CAMO uniform.

titi / tee-tee. A little; a small quantity.

TLAR. That looks about right, used to describe seat-of-the-pants flying and other outside-the-box behavior.

toadsticker. Bayonet.

toe-poppers. Small land mines that can take one's leg off up to the knee—despite the cute name.

top. Top sergeant.

tore up. Messed up, broken, messy, unserviceable.

total goat fuck. Situation in which everything that could go wrong did go wrong.

tracer. Round of ammunition treated so that it will glow or smoke, so its flight can be followed.

track / tracks. Armored personnel carrier.

tracked Budweiser. An M2 Bradley, a reference to the fact that it's made out of aluminum.

trained killer. 1. A recent graduate of technical school or other nonweapons training, such as information technology, as in "He's an IT trained killer." 2. Soldier, usually applied facetiously and ironically to boys who seem to be anything but.

T-rations. Large tins of food such as spaghetti or chicken chow mein, heated and brought out in trucks.

tread-head. Soldier whose specialty is armor. A character in Harold Coyle's *Team Yankee* says, "Shit, don't they teach you tread-heads anything at Fort Knox?"

tree-eater. Special Forces soldier.

trip wire. 1. Booby trap. 2. Soldier with a knack for finding traps.

triple A. Anti-aircraft artillery, in Air Force slang, as in "We gave them a lot of triple A." Triple A was known as ack-ack in World War II.

tube steak. Hot dog.

tunnel rat. Soldier whose job it is to search underground for the enemy.

turn and burn. To service an aircraft quickly and get it airborne again. Also called a hot turn.

turret-head. An arguer; one who is always spouting off.

turtle. Kevlar helmet.

turtles. New replacements—so called because they take so long to arrive.

twidget. Person whose primary job is working with and maintaining military electronics.

twink. Second lieutenant.

two-digit midget. One with less than a hundred days of active duty left.

two hots and a Charlie. Combat fare of two hot meals and a C-ration.

Ultimate weapon, the. Infantryman.

un-ass. To get off of, or out of, a sitting position, as in "Let's un-ass this place!" It's a play on the official term "unasseting," which means emptying a helicopter of troops.

Uncle / Uncle Sucker / Uncle Sugar. Uncle Sam; the U.S. government.

unit. Military grouping: division, corps, aircraft carrier group.

use up. To kill.

Vampire. American sniper who stalks his prey at night.

WAFWOT. "What a fucking waste of time."

WAG. Wild-ass guess.

wait-a-minute-bush. Any bush that has thorns that you could get hung up on.

wand. To check for the presence of metal on a person's body by moving a wandlike electronic rod up and down.

wander. Any security enforcer who waves metal-detecting wands over others. Commonly applied to airport-security personnel.

war belt. Web belt worn in the field, from which to hang canteens, etc.

warblog. Weblogs written by those fighting wars in Iraq and Afghanistan.

warm body. Any soldier.

warmed over, hammered dog shit on a soda cracker. Hangover, Navy style.

warrior wipes. Certificates of achievement.

Warthog. Nickname for the airplane formally known as the A-10 or Thunderbolt II.

waste. To kill.

water buffalo. Tank of potable water behind a truck.

wax. To kill.

weaponize. To turn something that occurs naturally into a weapon, as in "weaponizing" anthrax or smallpox.

weapons-grade. Powerful enough to kill, say, weapons-grade uranium. Beyond the military it is used to describe something extreme ("weapons-grade salsa") or powerful (Bobby Hull's "weapons-grade slap shot").

wet read. To study a reconnaissance photo while it is still wet from processing.

wetsu (acr). 1. We expect this shit usually. 2. We eat this shit up (pron "wet-soo").

white sidewalls / whitewalls. Military haircut clipped so close to the sides of the head and high above the ears that the skin shows through.

whizo / wizzo (acr). Weapons systems officer, a.k.a. backseater.

WIA. Wounded in action.

wild geese. Mercenaries.

willy peter / willie pete. White phosphorus.

willy-peter bag. Bag for white phosphorus, alluded to in Philip Caputo's *A Rumor of War*: "They did not find enough of him to fill a willy-peter bag, a waterproof sack a little larger than a shopping bag."

wire. Perimeter where trip wires set off booby traps.

wire hangers. Troops who are so far out of the combat zone they can enjoy the luxury of hanging their clothes on hangers at night.

woofing / woof, woof. Meaningless talk, like barking; talking without saying anything.

word, the. The latest rumor.

word one. A single word. Someone who cannot get a chance to talk will say that they were unable to say word one.

world, the. In Vietnam, any place outside the area where the soldier happened to be.

WTFO. "What the fuck, over." According to an online informant, "Commonly used to describe a situation or position that is completely not what one expects. For example, cold weather gear humped to Kuwait, WTFO."

Yankin' and bankin'. Fighter-pilot term for aggressive aerial maneuvers.

yobo. Lover, from Korean; it usually is applied to a girlfriend.

Zap. Kill.

zebra. Noncommissioned officer in the higher grades (E-6 through E-9), because of their insignia stripes.

ZI. Zone of the interior, a nickname for the United States.

zulu. Casualty report.

29

WASHINGTON-SPEAK

Inside the Beltway: The Lingo of the Hill, K Street Lobbyists, the Slug Line, and Other Denizens of the Capitol City

What language do they speak around here?

—Sue Grabowski, *A Congressional Intern Handbook*

Most of what is said in Congress sounds like a foreign language and requires an interpreter . . . Congress becomes so entangled in vocabulary that people often have to work past midnight to figure out what they're doing.

—Susan Trausch, *Washington Post*, March 16, 1986

Washington is a city of slang and jargon—bureaucratese, Pentagonese, legalese. Fort Fumble is the Pentagon, "the sound of the city" is a reference to paper shuffling, and "reprogramming" is moving money from one place to another. Getting riffed—from RIF, reduction in force—means losing your job. The city is peopled with Beltway bandits, influence peddlers, superlawyers, and supply-siders.

Some terms go national in an instant, such as Trent Lott's 2005 "nuclear option," referring to the proposed Senate rule change to prevent filibusters of judicial nominations. Reports have surfaced indicating that the Republican code phrase for a plan to shut down a filibuster was "the Hulk."

Other terms show their age. Remember the Atari Democrat, a term for someone who foresaw a bright future in high technology? The phrase, an allusion to a successful computer-and-video-game company, was coined by the *New Yorker*'s Elizabeth Drew. Atari lost some of its appeal when it cut its U.S. workforce in 1983 and moved jobs to Taiwan.

Here are more words and phrases that constitute secret verbal handshakes that make things work "inside the Beltway."

AA. Administrative assistant, the top staff aide in a congressional office. Few on the Hill call someone by his or her full title, instead referring to "Congressman Smith's AA" or "the senator's LA" (legislative assistant).

across the river. The White House and Congress, to those in the Pentagon, and vice versa.

affair. Fund-raising event. Congressional affairs range from bull roasts to fancy dinners, and the cost of admission to one of them can range from $10 to $1,000.

ahead of the curve. Where astute players and politicians would like to be—in the position of anticipating problems before they surface. It's what Hedrick Smith, in *The Power Game,* called "one of Washington's most telltale phrases."

are they in / are they out? Questions asked to determine if Congress has reconvened (is in session) or adjourned (is out of session).

AstroTurf organization. Beltway slang for a pseudo-grassroots group that lends a veneer of moral legitimacy to a cause.

AstroTurfing. A PR/lobbying program which deliberately seeks to engineer the impression of spontaneous grassroots behavior.

atmospherics. Temporal considerations surrounding a campaign or an appointment, such as the atmospherics surrounding the nomination of a Supreme Court justice. The term got heavy play in 2005–2006 with the nominations of John Roberts, Harriet Miers, and Samuel Alito.

attack dog. Politician on the offensive. The term came into prominence during the 1991 Senate Judiciary Committee hearings on Judge Clarence Thomas's nomination to the Supreme Court. University of Oklahoma law professor Anita Hill accused Thomas of sexual harassment, and New York senator Alphonse D'Amato, among others on the committee, responded by attacking Hill's credibility. The *Washington Post* reported (December 18, 1991) that New York governor Mario Cuomo had branded D'Amato an "attack dog."

Back channel. An unofficial route that a government official can take, outside normal channels, to contact someone without the people above him in the chain of command knowing.

beauty contest. A nonbinding primary election; a vote that measures popularity but doesn't deliver delegates. For instance, the Vermont presidential primary is a beauty contest.

Beltway. Literally, the interstate highway that rings Washington, D.C., as it runs through the inner suburbs of Virginia and Maryland. It also refers to a state of mind that reigns in the capital but not outside the Beltway—a.k.a. the rest of the nation. The term was coined in 1951 to describe what to that point had been known as a "circumferential highway." With the advent of the Washington Beltway, the term was capitalized and used as a reference to this particular road. See INSIDE THE BELTWAY.

Beltway bandit. A consultant working out of one of the many think tanks and consulting firms in the Washington, D.C., area. It is more jocular than hostile and some of the ilk actually identify themselves as such.

big casino. The center ring, grand prize. In 1974 Ronald Reagan referred to the presidential election as "the big casino," according to William Safire, in *Safire's Political Dictionary*.

big tent. A term coined by late Republican political consultant Lee Atwater, who called for the Republican Party to accommodate a broader range of opinion; used recently by *Newsweek*'s Howard Fineman, who asserted that the deal by the GANG OF FOURTEEN "set off a food fight in the Big Tent."

big ticket. High-priced item in an appropriation bill, often military hardware such as the B-2 Stealth Bomber, which costs $860 million per plane.

blamestorming. What used to be called passing the buck.

blue dog. Conservative Democrat.

blue goose. The largest of the lecterns used by the president; it weighs several hundred pounds.

blue smoke and mirrors. Verbal sleight-of-hand used to sell a program to Congress or a candidate to the public. The independent presidential candidate John Anderson quipped that Ronald Reagan's economic policies would need "blue smoke and mirrors" to work. The journalists Jack Germond and Jules Witcover used the phrase as the title for their book on the 1980 presidential election.

boast writer. Derogatory name for a ghostwriter who has revealed himself.

BOB. (acr). Boy on BlackBerry. An up-and-coming politico who tells the world he has "arrived" by being on his BlackBerry 24/7 (especially on the Metro—we all know they're just playing solitaire). As in "I'm going out to drinks with one of the BOBs I met on the Metro."

body slam. A devastating political comment. The vice-presidential candidate Lloyd Bentsen's "Senator, you're no Jack Kennedy," during his debate with Senator Dan Quayle, still holds the body-slam prize.

bogeys. Spending targets given to the armed services by the secretary of defense.

boll weevil. Nickname for conservative Southern Democrats—pests who keep conservative pressure on the Democratic majority.

bork. To reject a political nominee, as in the Republican admonition not to "bork" John Bolton when his nomination as United Nations ambassador came up for Senate confirmation. The term comes from Robert Bork, nominated to the Supreme Court in 1987 by President Reagan but rejected in the Senate by a 58–42 vote after a nasty fight. See MIERED.

BR. Blogger relations, a new art form analogous to PR, or public relations. BR consists of finding the blogs and bloggers with the greatest impact and telling your story to them.

bridegroom at a wedding. Potential nominee about to go to a confirmation hearing, as in "Your role in this process is that of a bridegroom at a wedding: Stay out of the way, be on time, and keep your mouth shut." Coined by Tom Korologos, currently U.S. ambassador to Belgium.

bubba vote. Southern white conservatives, mainly rural males.

buckslip. A cover note used to forward a document or newspaper clipping to a recipient, often with a brief comment or explanation. It's usually about the size of a dollar bill—hence the "buck" in buckslip.

Cardinal. Informal title of the powerful chairman of each appropriations subcommittee in the House. Sean Farrell explains: "It comes from the idea that you, as a rank-and-file member, have to 'kiss the cardinal's ring' (as in the practice of reverence) in order to get what you want included in a particular spending bill."

casework. Dealing with the problems of constituents. It is a constant in the workings of a congressional office and commands a major portion of staff time.

caseworker. Staff member whose prime responsibility is dealing with constituent problems.

caucus. 1. A meeting of party members in either house to elect leaders and set the legislative agenda. 2. Any informal gathering of lawmakers working on a course of legislative action. 3. A group that meets regularly to monitor and advance the interests of a specific group.

Christmas express. The surge of congressional junkets just after Congress adjourns and just before Christmas.

Christmas tree bill. A bill that has been adorned with extra, often unrelated, pieces of legislation.

CIA. Insiders do not use the article: It is "CIA" rather than "the CIA." The same is true for NSA (National Security Agency).

clean bill. A new version of a bill, replete with a new number, prepared after a committee has reworked the original. It allows the bill to move on its own rather than having each revision voted on individually.

clinker. An amendment or rider to a bill that's so out of place that it stands out like a misplayed musical note. From the Dutch *klinker*, a vitrified brick that clinks when struck.

cloture / closure. Process by which debate can be limited in the Senate without unanimous consent. When invoked by roll-call vote, it limits each senator to one hour of debate.

coattail. The ability of a presidential candidate to help members of his party win seats in Congress.

code word. A word, such as "ultra" or "marketgarden," that gives certain people the right to see a document. More secret than top secret.

CoDel. Congressional delegation; usually designates a group but can refer to one Congress member traveling abroad on official business; as distinct from a StaffDel, the term applied when the traveler or group is congressional staff.

coin rusters. Homeless men who dive in the city's public pools and fountains to retrieve the coins that have been tossed in them by tourists for luck.

comity. A state of mutual harmony and civility. This word is the seldom-invoked buzzword for old-school Washington. The headline in *Roll Call* the day after the "nuclear option" was forestalled was "Despite the Deal, Comity Lacking."

cone. One of five career paths into which Foreign Service officers are grouped at entry into the Service: consular, economic, administrative, political, and public diplomacy. The word "cone" is used presumably because you rise and fall in the cone of your choosing, and there's less and less room as you reach the top.

convention bounce. Usual rise in polls after a candidate has won his or her party's nomination.

CR. Continuing resolution; Hill talk for legislation that keeps the government running on last year's budget when debt ceilings haven't been raised or appropriations haven't passed.

cubed out. Pentagon slang for "filled to capacity." The term may come from the trucking industry, where a truck is said to be cubed out when it's full.

Dark side of the moon. The House of Representatives, in Hill slang—implying that it is the lesser of the two houses. Increasingly, anything that's not desirable.

DCI. Director of central intelligence, to those who work for him.

Dear Colleague. Traditional salutation used in letters in which one member asks another for support or cosponsorship of a bill. Defined deftly in Sue Grabowski's *Congressional Intern Handbook* as a "hustle" in the form of a letter.

death-squad Democrat. Late-eighties label for Democrats who supported right-wing leaders in Latin America, such as those who supported aid to El Salvador.

death taxes. Taxes on estates, to those who oppose them.

demagogue it. To take a dramatic, grandstanding position on an issue without necessarily supporting or believing in the position; to mislead with spirit.

dirty dozen. List of members with the worst environmental records.

Dome, the. The Capitol. The "Insider" column in *The Hill* newspaper is called "Under the Dome."

dotgov. A government official. Based on the fact that government Web site addresses all end with a "gov" extension.

dove. Legislator who is against military intervention by the United States specifically and generally against increased military spending of any kind. His opposite number is the hawk, and a well-known congressional watering hole is the Hawk & Dove.

drop a bill. To file or introduce a bill in the House. The bill is dropped into a wooden box known as a hopper, which sits on the left side of the Speaker's rostrum. Members who wish to introduce a bill drop the signed text in the hopper anytime the House is in session. The Senate has no hopper; senators introduce bills by handing them to the bill clerk, seated at the front of the chamber.

duck. A pest or nuisance, from the decades-old notion of "being pecked to death by ducks."

Earmarks. Footnotes in spending bills to fund pet projects without public review; synonym for PORK. An anti-pork representative, George E. Brown, Jr., said in 1993, "Earmarks are like mushrooms—they grow best in the dark."

eat on receipt. "Top-secret" classification.

eighteen acres. Reference to the White House grounds, which comprise eighteen acres.

80-20 rule. Tom Korologos: "This is a rule that's told to all potential nominees going through a hearing. It means that if the senators are talking 80 percent of the time and you, the nominee, are talking 20 percent, you're winning. If it's 60-40, you're arguing. If it's 50-50, you've lost—immediately withdraw your name."

elevator phenomenon. The inflating of the egos of senators and representatives when they realize they have, among other perquisites, private elevators at their disposal. Noted by Mark Green and Michael Waldman in *Who Runs Congress?* (1984).

Everest committee. Any congressional team organized to investigate something because, like Mount Everest, it's there.

Fair-fight district. Congressional district which is configured to favor no political party.

Fifth Street bar. The collective term for lawyers who have offices near the D.C. courthouses and handle small cases.

fig leaf. Flimsy, insubstantial solution intended to hide an unpleasant reality; from the fig leaf used to cover the genitals of a nude statue. First invoked by Senator Jim Sasser, D-Tenn., during February 1992 debates over the economy; he called President George H. W. Bush's proposal a "fig-leaf economic growth plan."

filibuster. To delay or stop action on a bill in the Senate through constant talking. It is a time-honored technique which is almost always employed by a minority to defeat a measure favored by the majority.

527. An advocacy organization, such as Swift Boat Veterans for Truth or the Media Fund, that has been allowed to use unlimited contributions to run political commercials. Named for the section of the U.S. Tax Code permitting them. The term "527" is often paired with "attack."

foia (acr). Freedom of Information Act, a statute that requires much federal information to be disclosed to reporters and citizens (pron. "FOY-ya").

football. A heavy black bag containing military codes and secret national security information carried for the president by a military aide.

fresh legs. A rookie lobbyist who enjoys immediate recognition on the Hill; for example, a former White House special assistant.

frog march. The state of being hauled off under custody. The D.C. equivalent of New York City's "perp walk."

F-word. Filibuster.

Gang of Fourteen. The senators, seven from each party, who in May 2005 worked out the compromise that averted the antifilibuster "nuclear option." Partisans have been calling the Republicans who compromised on the matter the Magnificent Seven.

-gate. The common suffix for Washington, D.C., scandals since Watergate, as in Koreagate and Irangate. The Watergate scandal was named for the Watergate apartment complex where the break-in that opened the scandal took place. Also popular is the -scam suffix, as found in ABSCAM, Contrascam, and Debatescam. The original name was the FBI code name for its foray into the realm of congressional ethics. ABSCAM stood for AraB SCAM, a reference to the front group for the operation, the bogus "Abdul Enterprises."

gerrymander. To design or redesign a congressional district to unfairly favor the party in power on the basis of traditional voting and demographic patterns.

get. The hiring of a lobbyist from the Hill or White House; a firm will announce an important "get." The term is borrowed from TV news shows, where it refers to a desirable or hard-to-book guest.

ghost senator. Sometimes slang for a strong administrative assistant. See AA.

ghost speech. A speech that is never delivered but appears in the *Congressional Record* or the printed record of a committee.

go-go (acr). Government-owned, government-operated. A facility not under the ownership of an outside contractor.

goat. Derogatory slang for a constituent.

goat food. Shameless political posturing.

goo-goos. Forces of and for *go*od *go*vernment. The League of Women Voters is a perennial source of goo-goo-ism. Although the term sounds intensely derisory, it is often used with a certain degree of affection.

grassroots. The folks back home; people who are not in the business of politics.

grasstops. Community leaders who have influence; "grassroots" is deeper and broader.

gray ghost. A senator or representative's chief staffer.

greenies. Environmentalists. Derived from West Germany's Green political party and the international Greenpeace movement.

Gucci Gulch. Polished marble hallway outside the House Ways and Means Committee room in the Longworth House Office Building, where well-tailored lobbyists, who specialize in engineering tax breaks and loopholes for their clients, gather, especially while committee members are meeting in secret to deal with tax-reform matters.

gypsy moth. Republican moderate. According to William Safire in his *New York Times Magazine* column, "On Language," the term was created by Congressman Lawrence DeNardis (R.-Conn.), who said that the gypsy moth was as much of a nuisance in New England and the Great Lakes as the BOLL WEEVIL is down south.

Hammer, the. Tom DeLay's nickname as the most powerful man on the Hill—a tradition dating back to Speaker Thomas B. "Czar" Reed, who was known as the Terrible Turk. DeLay resigned in 2006 amid scandal.

hard money. Contributions by individuals or political-action committees to candidates; regulated by federal election laws.

headquarters. What CIA insiders call home base. Outsiders and spy novelists refer to it as Langley because of its Northern Virginia location. The offspring of CIA officers are known in-house as Langley brats.

HOH. "Heard on the Hill," a gossip column in *Roll Call*. The current writer of the column is Mary Ann Akers.

hot-button. An issue that is value-intense and controversial.

Idiot sheets. Questions to be asked of witnesses at congressional hearings, prepared for not-always-knowledgeable lawmakers by their staffs.

inside the Beltway. Popular metaphor for the parochialism and political intensity of Washington. It is a reference to the BELTWAY, the highway that rings the city. The phrase was coined in the 1970s by *Washington Post* columnist Mike Causey. The *Washington Post* defined outside the Beltway as "the so-called Real World, as perceived by those unfortunate souls doomed to live east of Seat Pleasant [a suburb in Prince George's County, Maryland] and west of the moon."

J books. Defense Budget Justification Books, the organizing documents from which congressional committees work during the authorization-and-appropriation process.

Jersey Barrier City. One of a number of nicknames given to Washington in the post-9/11 era as more and more concrete barriers ("Jersey barriers") are put into place around the Capitol and White House. A.k.a Fortress Washington.

junket. Derogatory term for an expenses-paid trip made by a member of Congress. A trip is a junket if paid for by public funds or by a special-interest group.

K Street. Washington's lobbying community.

kicker. A hidden, unsuspected section of a bill.

LA. Legislative assistant, the person in a congressional office who is in charge of legislation.

lame duck. 1. An incumbent who has lost an election but whose term has still not run out. 2. Congress after November elections and before the convening of a new Congress in January, i.e., lame-duck session.

lawyer's bill. Any bill that, if enacted, would create a lot of confusion and litigation.

leg counsel. Legislative counsel, for short.

Mangy dog. Legislation that has more flaws than a dog has fleas.

me wall. A wall covered with photos of Washingtonians posing with dignitaries. The phenomenon, a way of attempting to show one's proximity to power, is described in the novel *The Washingtonienne*, by a former Hill staffer, Jessica Cutler: "I noticed that a lot of people in the office kept a 'Me Wall' in their cubicles, these little photo galleries of themselves standing next to Congressman So-and-So, Senator What's-His-Face, and Governor Whoever. As if that was supposed to impress anyone. Like, 'Wow! You got to stand next to some unrecognizable person who is way more important than you are! That's awesome!'"

meat ax. Popular—and graphic—congressional metaphor for across-the-board budget cutting; it is often used in the context of the Gramm-Rudman Budget Reduction Act of 1986, which can bring the meat ax down evenly on domestic and defense expenditures. The opposite of meat-ax cuts would be selective, or "scalpel," cutting.

mego (acr). My eyes glaze over; bored.

miered. Rejected by an ally in the manner of the 2005 Supreme Court nominee Harriet Miers. The *Houston Chronicle*, October 30, 2005: "A contributor to *The Reform Club*, a right-leaning blog, wrote that to get 'borked' was 'to be unscrupulously torpedoed by an opponent,' while to get 'miered' was to be 'unscrupulously torpedoed by an ally.'" S. T. Karnick, coeditor of *The Reform Club*, elaborated. "If you have a president who is willing to instigate a big controversy, the prospect of being 'borked' will be the major possibility," he said. "But if you have a president who is always trying to get consensus, then it's much more likely that nominees will get 'miered.'"

motherhood bill. Legislation everybody supports immediately. From resolutions in support of Mother's Day and other noncontroversial subjects.

move the ball. To advance an election or legislative campaign.

MRE. Morally repugnant elite, term used by Peace Corps and some State Department personnel to describe ruling classes in certain countries.

murder board. Prehearing rehearsal sessions used to prepare a nominee for the worst-case set of questions.

Neverendum. Referendum that never seems to get finished.

Newt-speak. Direct way of speaking used by Newt Gingrich before, during, and after his House speakership.

990. To pull the tax forms of a nonprofit based on IRS form 990. By law, nonprofits that enjoy 501(c)3 tax-exempt status must furnish their tax returns upon request. If they don't do so, they risk fines of up to $10,000.

nonconcur. "Disagree," in bureaucratese.

nonpaper. A document with no identifying marks as to who wrote or proposed it. It can propose a shift in policy or a new policy, or it can simply serve as a backgrounder. See ONE-PAGER.

Old Europe vs. New Europe. A comparison made popular by Secretary of Defense Donald Rumsfeld to distinguish old loyalties with France and Germany from the distancing of the Iraq-war era.

one-pager. A cheat sheet. As defined by Bill Timmons, former aide to presidents Nixon and Ford, "a piece of paper containing all of the information on an issue, from geologic formations at Anwar in Alaska to complex tax proposals totally incomprehensible in their completed form. When Henry Kissinger once gave President Nixon two pages, Nixon told him, 'Henry, I want this on one page.' Kissinger turned to a secretary and said, 'Retype this on one page.'"

Newt's Distinctions

Newt Gingrich created his own method of verbal attack, using a partisan choice of words. In 1990, a GOP committee called GOPAC distributed a brochure filled with choice Gingrich buzzwords for describing one's own campaign and that of one's opponents.

You	**Your Rival**
Pristine	Sick
Tough	Pathetic
Pioneer	Traitor
Workfare	Welfare
Crusade	Crisis
Common sense	Ideological
Hard work	Cheat, steal
Confident	Insecure
Unique	Bizarre
Moral	Permissive
Pro-(issue)	Anti-(issue)
Activist	Radical

orange pouch. A marked mail sack for expedited delivery to a member of Congress's home district or state. Also known as a gold bag.

originalist. Name given to a judge or jurist who sees the Constitution as a set of rights and rules that were frozen in time when they were written. It is a term that Supreme Court Justice Antonin Scalia applied to himself in 2004 and it was used extensively in the confirmation hearings for John Roberts to the Supreme Court.

other end of Pennsylvania Avenue. One of the ways Congress refers to the White House, and vice versa.

other government agency (OGA). The CIA, in current government code when one doesn't want to mention the CIA by name.

Pacronym. An acronym for a political-action committee (PAC); a blending of PAC + acronym. Fannie Mae's pacronym is Fannie PAC.

PAYGO. Pay as you go, a rule that compels new spending or tax changes not to add to the federal deficit. New proposals must either be "budget-neutral" or be offset with savings derived from existing funds and programs.

pebble beach. An area covered with gravel on the White House driveway where TV crews congregate.

people's republic. Massachusetts or Vermont, because of those states' liberal legislation in favor of such causes as same-sex marriage and civil unions.

pigeonhole. To kill a bill by keeping it in committee and not reporting it to the larger body. The term comes from the cubicles—pigeonholes—in the old congressional desks.

placeholder. A section of a bill that's not substantive but inserted early in anticipation of later details being added.

player. One who operates effectively in Congress.

point man. Member who is moving a specific piece of legislation through Congress.

porcupine power. The power to block and obstruct.

pork. Government funds for projects benefiting a politician's constituents in exchange for their political support; from "pork barrel," the nickname applied to such appropriations since before the Civil War. Pork comes in all cuts, including academic pork—funds for influential universities. See also EARMARKS.

pork panic. A term applied to quick legislative activity that ensues when pork is threatened.

POTUS (acr). President of the United States, who is often in the company of FLOTUS, the first lady. The two are usually in CONUS (the continental United States), except when they're OCONUS (outside the continental United States).

prebuttal. Argument presented in anticipation of an opponent's argument; a pre-rebuttal.

public trough. The federal money supply, from which consultants, corporations, and other members' constituents feed greedily. It completes the metaphoric notion of politicians as pigs (pork). The porcine imagery continues in terms like slop-over, used pejoratively to describe the items found in the back of the *Congressional Record*.

pump priming. The process of using federal funds to stimulate the economy, whether the national economy or a local one.

push-polling. Poll that uses questions meant to influence a voter's position.

Queen of the hill. Refers to a special rule for sequencing, debating, and voting on competing amendments. If more than one version receives a majority of votes, the one with the largest margin—the queen of the hill—prevails. It is an allusion to the fact that the high school girl with the most votes is elected prom queen.

Railroad. To push or jam a bill through Congress.

rainmaker. 1. A lawyer who brings in big clients and cases. 2. A lobbyist capable of causing big dollars to flow into campaign chests and other important matters. 3. Anyone able to get things done legislatively.

red-headed Eskimo. Legislation tailored to benefit a tiny minority.

reg-neg. Negotiated rulemaking, a process that brings together those who would be significantly affected by a regulation, including the government, to reach consensus on some or all aspects thereof before the regulation is formally proposed by the government. The idea is that in exchange for having a hand in making a rule, the interests promise not to challenge it.

Republican L. An L-shaped stretch of conservative-leaning midwestern and southern states that are extremely hard for a Democrat to win. If a GOP candidate can hold the L, he wins the White House.

RINO. Republican in name only—for example, Senator Lincoln Chafee of Rhode Island.

robo. 1. A form letter congressmen use to answer some of their constituent mail; before computers, these letters were generated by a Robotype machine, which also provided a facsimile signature. 2. The Robotype machine itself.

RON. White House scheduling term for where the president will spend the "remainder of the night."

room lottery. A drawing for office space held every two years. Representatives choose according to rank. Offices are in one of three House office buildings: Cannon, Longworth, or Rayburn.

root-canal politics. The politics of pain, austerity budgets, and deep program cuts.

Rosemary's Baby. Any monstrous piece of legislation. The nickname comes from the book by Ira Levin and the subsequent Roman Polanski movie in which a woman unknowingly bears the devil's baby.

rug rank. High rank; refers to a uniformed military officer who rates a rug on his or her floor.

run the traps. To check out in advance all options and pitfalls in a course of action. According to William Safire, in *New Political Dictionary*, "A hunter will check his traps in the morning to see what animals were caught; a reporter will 'run the traps' of his sources to check out a story."

Safety net. Level of established financial support for individuals through Social Security, Medicare, welfare programs, and Veteran's Assistance.

sagebrush rebels. Informal but cohesive band of western legislators whose major concern since the late 1960s has been local control over the millions of acres of federal land that lie west of the Rockies.

sausage factory. Congress. The term dates to the old political axiom holding that people who love sausage and respect the law should never see how either one is made.

school uniforms. Weak, nonstarter issue; from the idea that school uniforms will bring discipline and better times to ailing public school systems.

seat warmer. A senator or representative appointed by a governor to fill a vacancy, with the understanding that he or she won't run in the next election.

SecDef. The secretary of defense, as in "The SecDef and his wife will be having dinner with us tonight." DASDEs (pronounced "das-dees") are deputy assistant secretaries of defense, who carry the workload of the ASDs (assistant secretaries), USDs (undersecretaries), and the DepSecDef, deputy to the SecDef.

sherpa. A high-level advance person sent ahead to prepare for a head of state's or cabinet minister's visit. Sherpas work out details of the trip, discussion topics, and public expectations. Named after the term for Nepalese mountain guides.

show horse. A member of Congress known for the ability to garner attention and publicity; a showboat.

six-pack Republican. Populist GOP member or candidate, sometimes known as Joe Six-Pack Republican.

slash and burn. Tactics used without consideration of the possible harm to others.

sleaze factor. Component of an administration or political party that is corrupt, unethical, controversial, scandal-ridden, or otherwise under a cloud.

slippery slope. What nominees find themselves on when a committee finds, and perhaps leaks, damaging information and support begins to erode.

slugging. Form of commuting in the Washington, D.C., area—sometimes referred to as "instant carpooling" or "casual carpooling"—unique because people commuting into the city stop to pick up other passengers, called slugs, even though they are total strangers. Commuters gather in "slug lines" at appointed locations to share cars with other commuters.

slush fund. Any covert, suspect, or otherwise tainted source of campaign money.

smoking gun. Metaphor used at either end of Pennsylvania Avenue for unequivocal evidence of guilt, as if one had discovered a man with a smoking gun in his hand standing over a bullet-ridden body. Just before the Senate report on the Iran-*contra* affair was released in 1987, Senator David Boren (D-Okla.) was quoted as saying, "There's no smoking gun."

snooker clause. A last-minute insert into a dense bill, hurriedly and after midnight, that, as noted recently in the *New York Times,* "if ever disclosed after passage, always leaves legislators shocked, shocked at how such an undemocratic bit of mischief ever came to be."

SLUG-ESE

Slugs have their own rules and vocabulary, found in the glossary of slugging terms on the official Web site of Washington slugs (www.slug-lines.com).

"Body snatching" is the taboo practice of drivers picking up slugs as they are walking to the slug line, which violates the "first come, first served" principle for the other slugs as well as the other drivers waiting in line.

"Will call," on the other hand, is a term describing "the driver's option to pick a particular slug not at the front of the line. This situation usually happens when a driver sees a friend in line and simply calls for that individual."

soft money. Money largely unregulated by federal law that is raised by the political parties for party-building activities such as get-out-the-vote drives, as opposed to money for a specific candidate's campaign.

softball. An easy question, which an experienced politician can easily hit out of the ballpark.

spin doctors. Experienced practitioners of "spin control," at either end of Pennsylvania Avenue. Spin is endemic during election campaigns, as both sides seem to push their own interpretation of events and discredit the other side's. According to the *Economist*, the term was coined in the Reagan White House during his first term and became important after the first 1984 Reagan-Mondale presidential debate in Louisville. By the time of the 1988 Bush-Dukakis debate at Wake Forest University, there were so many "spinners" working for each candidate that the *Washington Post* declared a post-debate state of "spinlock."

spy. Despite what they tell you at the International Spy Museum, this term is used by the Washington intelligence community only to describe enemy agents and traitors. CIA uses the term "agent"—thus, all of our so-called agent operations engage individuals, usually foreign nationals, in the conduct of intelligence work as guided and directed by CIA officers.

squish. The nickname for an uncommitted conservative.

stealth legislation. A law made quickly and quietly, often by adding an amendment to an unrelated bill.

sticker shock. Term borrowed from the auto showroom, facetiously used on Capitol Hill to describe the reaction to the unit cost of new weapons.

straphanger. A person who tags along to a briefing or on a trip even though his or her presence isn't required.

stud book. The State Department's *Biographic Register*, a publication giving biographical information on officers of the department.

sunset. To expire, as in "Sunset legislation is written with a built-in moment when it will sunset."

supp. Shorthand for a supplemental appropriation bill, usually under consideration after regular bills are completed.

Supremes, the. The justices of the U.S. Supreme Court as a group.

Tap dance. Briefing or testimony that is slick and pleasant but says little.

third rail. An issue to be avoided because of its controversial nature and its tendency to lose support for anybody who touches it. It comes from the electrified third rail on railroad tracks. Traditionally Social Security has been a third-rail issue.

three I's. Three countries with large demographic groups among the American population: Ireland, Israel, and Italy.

throw red meat. To please or appease one's constituency.

TMPMITW. The most powerful man in the world—the president—especially to bloggers.

train wreck. Fiscal or legislative mess in Congress.

Up or down. Yes or no vote; not a test vote, not a substitute or amendment, but the real thing.

Washington read. The act of looking first at a book's index to see if you're mentioned and then reading only those passages. Synonym: index surfing.

winger. A person on the far right or left politically. Also, wingnut.

world's greatest deliberative body, the. Name sometimes applied to the U.S. Senate.

WTO. Washington theater of operations, an ironic reference to the Pentagon.

Yellow dog Democrat. A Southern expression for a Democrat who will vote for whoever the party's candidate is, even a yellow dog.

Zen spin. Spinning a story by not doing anything to spin the story. A coinage of George Stephanopoulos, in *All Too Human*: "The benefits of spin were being canceled out by the press's resistance to it. Often we reacted by spinning even harder, but I was beginning to see the virtue in just letting stories go—Zen spin."

30

X-ERS, YUPPIES, SOCCER MOMS, AND OTHER MODERNS

A Field Guide to the Socio-tagged

There is nothing new about slang nicknames for groups of people who are classified by age or lifestyle—our flappers and beatniks, hippies and junkies, lounge lizards and drugstore cowboys.

During the 1980s, however, there was a whole new wave of these terms. Some were the creations of demographers looking for a handle to put on a group—even groups that had lived most of the century without a snappy name—while others were simply clever neologisms that took off. In any event, they collectively serve to show us a new form of slang that has established itself. For lack of a better description, it is the slang of groups and demographics. It is also unusual in that the British seem as obsessed with these terms as Americans—in fact, some are imports from the U.K.

Here, then, is a generous sampling of the crop that came on the scene in the last two decades of the twentieth century, many of which were acronyms or derived from them. The fad of creating new ones seems to have lasted a relatively short time, but many of the terms (save for the most convoluted) seem to have stuck. The trick here is to find the right tag. Anne Gowen and Sean Piccoli, in "A Generation Lost in Time: Rebellion? Twentysomethings Find It's Too Much Trouble" (*Washington Times*, October 15, 1991), pointed out the difficulty of naming the group then in their twenties: "They've been slapped with more stickers than a Deadhead's van: 13ers, baby busters, Generation X, the New Lost Generation, yiffies—yiffies?—young fogies, and, yes, twentysomethings."

Afterboomers. Those born in the decade after the post–World War II baby boom was over, from about 1965 to 1974. Contrast with BABY BUSTERS and POSTBOOMERS.

Baby boomers. The 78 million Americans born between 1946 and 1964. In 1986, when the first baby boomers turned forty, they started to be referred to as "aging baby boomers." They have been cited as

baby boomers. (*continued*) catalysts for many social changes, including this one suggested in a 1985 Knight-Ridder News Service headline: "Baby Boomers Urge Washington State to Make 'Louie Louie' Official Anthem."

baby busters. Children born from 1965 to 1974, after the baby boom subsided. This was an era of ecological concern and advocacy of zero population growth, and for the first time in history the population declined for reasons other than war or disaster. Sometimes shortened to "busters." See also AFTERBOOMERS.

bapple (acr). Baby of affluent professional parents (more common in the U.K. than in the United States).

biddies (acr). From "baby boomers in debt."

bimbos. Vacuous, sometimes sexy, females. An old bit of slang given new life in the eighties, with the help of such luminaries as Jessica Hahn (who publicly denied her bimbitude) and Tammy Faye Bakker.

boomer babies. Children born between 1965 and 1979, as BABY BOOMERS had babies of their own.

boomerang family. A household where grown children move back in after schooling is completed.

boomerang generation. Young adults who move back into their parents' homes.

boomers. Short for BABY BOOMERS. A 1996 ad for boomer paraphernalia (T-shirts, caps, etc.) proclaims: "You wore the coon skin cap. You wore the mouse ears. You wore the alligator and pony on your shirt. You are the 'Big Chill' generation 70 million strong setting the trend. Now you can wear the T-shirt and cap that will distinguish you as a charter member of this generation."

buppies (acr). 1. British urban professionals. 2. Black, upwardly mobile professionals.

BWKs. Boomers with kids.

Caboose baby. The last child born in a large family.

chuppie (acr). Chicano urban professionals.

collar ID. Identifying people by metaphoric color of shirt collar (usually blue or white).

couch people. Homeless families who live temporarily with friends on their floors or couches. Because they are not on the street they have also been dubbed "the hidden homeless."

couch potatoes. Those content to spend great amounts of their free time at home watching television. At first a term of derision, it was quickly embraced by those who took pride in their passive ways.

C-wasp. "Catholic wasp," i.e., affluent Catholic professional not much concerned with ethnicity (derived from WASP). Anne H. Soukhanov, in her 1995 book *Word Watch*, points out that this term was coined by Maureen Dezell of *Boston Business* in 1986: "C-wasps are defined by their business or professional status . . . But they have an added aura. They may lapse into [singing] 'Danny Boy' at private get-togethers on March 17 but they don't venerate that kind of gunk. Basically they'd rather be sailing."

Dagwood. Member of the SANDWICH GENERATION, from the sandwich-loving cartoon character in *Blondie*.

dewk (acr). Dual employed with kids. In 1998 the U.S. Census Bureau reported that for the first time since it began recording such data, the majority of all families were dewks—married couples, both employed, with children.

dik (acr). Double (or dual) income, kids. See DINK and SIK.

dimp (acr). Double (or dual) income, money problems.

dink / dinc / dinkies (acr). Double (or dual) income, no kids. The point of this category is that they have more disposable income than the average family. In her "Word Watch" column in *The Atlantic*, in June 1987, Anne H. Soukhanov pointed to the distinguishing characteristics of the dink: "The women usually retain their maiden names, the couples are very career-oriented, the husband is likely to cook the meals, and they usually own property in an upscale location."

The term seems to have first popped up in late 1986. (It was noted by the researcher Charles D. Poe that in the 1974 sci-fi film *Planet Earth* there is a female-dominated society in which males are turned into cowering slaves called dinks.)

dissident yuppie / DY. Young urban professional (YUPPIE) who does not fit the mold; nonconforming YUPPIE, or as one was quoted as saying, "Yeah, I want a BMW, but I don't necessarily like them."

domo. Downwardly mobile, specifically, those in their thirties who downscale their careers in order to find more meaningful work.

droppies (acr). Disillusioned relatively ordinary professional preferring independent employment situation.

dumpy (acr). Downwardly mobile, middle-aged professional.

dwems (acr). Dead white European men—the scourge of radical multiculturalists.

dwik (acr). Dual income with kids. This pseudo-acronym is used in place of DIK, which means the same thing.

Echo boomers. Those born after the 1965-to-1974 baby bust.

empty-nesters. People whose children have left home, so their homes contain empty bedrooms.

Flyers (acr). Fun-loving youth en route to success. Identified in 1987 by *USA Today* as a hip group aged thirteen to twenty-five.

folkies. Folk music musicians and their fans.

foodies. Ardent food consumers attracted to the hot, new restaurants and new cuisines.

frumpies (acr). Formerly radical upwardly mobile persons.

fruppie. Young upwardly mobile Jew who is religious and observes Jewish customs. Blend of the Yiddish *fromm* (religious) + yuppie.

fundies. Fundamentalist Christians. Likely to be seen as derogatory by those it is applied to.

Generation ADD. Name for those born from the late 1980s to the present, during which time large numbers of kids were diagnosed with attention deficit disorder. A review of a film in the *New York Times*, February 11, 2005, says of it: "Strategically packaged for generation A.D.D., with rapid-fire editing, flash graphics and a breathlessly upbeat vibe, the documentary fuses a melange of stag-loop snippets, educational-film guffaws and television news reports with a hit parade of talking heads."

generation D. Name for those born in the digital age.

generation Jones. Children of the late 1960s and 1970s, too young to be baby boomers but too old to be part of GENERATION X. From slang for yearning. Members of generation Jones are high-spending, influential adults who were raised on television. The term was created by Jonathan Pontell and described in his book *Generation Jones*. He told a reporter for the *Charlotte Observer* (December 19, 2000, "Meet the Jonesers"): "Generation Jones grew up witnessing the slow, hypocritical sellout between the lovefest of the '60s and the money grab of the '80s."

generation X. Those 59 million Americans born between the years 1965 and 1980. The term was coined in 1991 by the author Douglas Coupland in his novel of the same name. Born into a world of hype and family instability—40 percent were raised in broken homes—they grew up on MTV and PacMan, and were characterized as being both realistic and cynical.

generation XXL. Postmillennial term for the 15 percent of children aged six to nineteen who, according to the Centers for Disease Control and Prevention, were overweight in 2003, when the term was coined.

generation Y / generation why? Those born from 1980 and into the late 1990s, who, according to one commonly accepted definition, were born far enough before the events of 9/11 to grasp and remember those events.

generation Z. Proposed generational name for the children born after Y.

GI generation. Those born between 1901 and 1924 and therefore eligible for service in World War II.

glams (acr). The graying, leisured, affluent middle-aged.

gold collar. Group of young blue-collar workers who tend to live with their parents and work in low-level service jobs but who find solace in luxury goods—$300 Dior sunglasses, $12 Grey Goose martinis. In writing about them in September 2005, the *Kansas City Star* said: "A question remains about blue-collar men and women, well into their 20s, who have meatloaf jobs and truffle tastes. They lust after luxe, but why would parents put up with them?"

golden-agers. Old people; senior citizens. The U.S. National Park Service issues passes for discounts in national parks which are called "Golden Ager" cards.

grampies (acr). Growing retired active monied persons in excellent state.

grumpies (acr). Grown-up mature people.

grumps (acr). Grim, ruthless, upwardly mobile professionals.

guppies (acr). 1. Gay, upwardly mobile professionals. 2. YUPPIES with ecological concerns; a blend of green + yuppie. 3. Grown-up urban professionals.

Hookies. Derived from "Who cares?" Hookies are college students who espouse apathy and noninvolvement. The University of Utah, an apparent hotbed of political apathy, attracted press attention in 1988 because of its large hookie population.

humpy (acr). Horny upwardly mobile urban professional.

huppie. Blend of hippie + yuppie, for a person who is upwardly mobile but spends his or her spare time living unconventionally, in the manner of a hippie.

Juppies (acr). Japanese urban professionals.

Lampies. Those who have worked at the *Harvard Lampoon*, a group that includes such diverse folks as John Updike and Conan O'Brien. A.k.a. poonie.

latchkeys / latchkey kids. Children who are left at home alone for at least part of the day—an estimated five to seven million in 1988—while their parents work.

lips (acr). Low income, parents supporting (couples). Coined in the wake of DINK.

luppie. Latino urban professional or a lesbian urban professional; blend of lesbian + yuppie.

Maffies (acr). Middle-aged affluent folks.

mallies. Young people who hang around shopping malls.

marpies (acr). Middle-aged rural professionals.

mensans. Members of Mensa, an organization for people who score in the top 2 percent of standardized IQ tests. It is from the Latin word for "table" and connotes a meeting of minds.

millennial / millennial generation. People born after 1981 who came of age at the end of the millennium, in 2000.

mink (acr). Multiple income, no kids.

Moonies. Followers of the Reverend Sun Myung Moon.

moss (acr). Middle-aged, overstressed, semiaffluent suburbanite.

muppy (acr). 1. Medical urban professional. 2. Mature yuppie. 3. Mennonite urban professional. Presented as evidence of how far people have taken the YUPPIE premise.

NASCAR dad. A blue-collar white male, probably from a rural area, most likely the South, who tends to vote conservative and is against tax increases and big government. These men were once the backbone of the Democratic Party, but became Reagan Republicans in the 1980s as the Democrats became more culturally liberal.

never-nesters. Couples who never have children.

new-collar. Middle-class BABY BOOMERS in the context of the workplace. Also called "new-collar workers."

notch babies. Those born in and after 1917, who get a smaller Social Security check than those born earlier. They complain, sometimes bitterly, about this to Congress.

OAP. Old-age pensioner (U.K.).

oilies. American petroleum workers, but usually used in a foreign context, such as "one of the thousands of American oilies in Indonesia."

oink (acr). One income, no kids.

opals (acr). Older people with active lifestyles.

open-collar workers. People who work at home or telecommute.

Phonies. People hooked on talking on the telephone.

pink collar. Lower-level clerical workers, who are almost always women. The term connotes a level of employment that falls just short of white collar.

pink neck. Sophisticated first cousin of the redneck.

post-boomer. One born after the baby boom. Also, a member of GENERATION X and the THIRTEENTH GENERATION.

postie. A post-boomer.

posy-sniffers. Derogatory term for environmentalists, commonly shortened to SNIFFERS.

preboomers. Those born during or just prior to World War II, from about 1935 through 1945.

preppies. People who go to, or went to, private preparatory (or prep) schools.

puppies (acr). Poor urban professionals, or pregnant yuppies, or parent of yuppies.

Rubbie (acr). Rich urban biker.

rumpie (acr). Rural, upwardly mobile professional. *Longman-Guardian New Words* defines a rumpie as a "relatively affluent and basically conservative young person living in a rural area and engaged in a professional career."

Sandwich generation. Middle-generation couples who find themselves responsible for elderly parents and young children at the same time.

sik (acr). Single income, kids.

silent generation, the. Those born between 1925 and 1942 who came to political power during the Watergate era.

sippy (acr). Senior independent pioneer. Financially secure consumer aged fifty-five to eighty who has been married once and who is in good health. Sippies control a large segment of the discretionary money in the marketplace.

sitcom. Single income, two children, outrageous mortgage.

skippies (acr). School kids with income and purchasing power. Coined in the summer of 1987 by marketing people targeting this group.

skoteys (acr). Spoiled kids of the eighties.

slumpr (acr). Still living under Mom and Pop's roof—the coinage appeared in Bob Levey's July 18, 1995, *Washington Post* column.

sniffers. Derogatory label for environmentalists. Short for POSY-SNIFFER.

snowbirds. Northerners who head south in the winter to escape the ice, cold, and snow.

soccer mom. Suburban mom (or dad) who is affluent, probably owns a minivan, and is concerned about her children's education. The term emerged during the 1996 presidential election, when soccer moms constituted about 6 percent of the voting public; this group is thought to have assisted Bill Clinton with his second-term victory over the Republican Bob Dole. The American Dialect Society voted "soccer mom" its top new word for 1996.

sofa spuds. COUCH POTATOES.

spec taters. COUCH POTATOES.

suppies (acr). Senior yuppies.

Taffy (acr). Technologically advanced family—one who owns, at a minimum, several computers, all of which have high-speed Internet connections.

techies / tekky. Technicians, especially those associated with electronics and computers.

thirteenth generation, the. Those born between 1961 and 1981. A thirteener is a member of the thirteenth generation.

thirtysomethings. A name for yuppies in the late 1980s, from a television show of the same name.

3-D lifestyle. Delayed marriage, deferred childbearing, and divorce—a term that has been used to characterize many baby boomers.

tick (acr). Two-income couple with kids in school (and parents in retirement). The columnist Ellen Goodman termed this group the "most-wooed voters of the 1988 election."

tins (acr). Two incomes, no sex. According to the *Weekend Telegraph* of August 22, 1998, this term was being considered for the *Oxford English Dictionary*.

toolies. Technical folks (architects, engineers, surveyors, programmers, etc.) who are absorbed with numbers, science, and mechanical pencils (which they pull out in restaurants to make calculations). Given a boost in Stephen Clark's 1987 *Toolies: The Official Handbook of Engineers and Applied Scientists.*

truppie. A truck driver whose family travels in living space behind the cab of the truck. The quarters are configured like those of a house trailer and are ideally suited to husband-and-wife driving teams.

tweener. Those aged eight to fourteen years who are in a sociological limbo—no longer children, but not old or mature enough to be looked upon as true adolescents.

twentysomethings. Name given to those in their twenties in the early nineties, a hand-me-down from the yuppie generation and its now-canceled television show *thirtysomething*. Writing in the *New York Times* for December 2, 1990, Bret Easton Ellis wrote of this term, "Our style is assimilation, our attitude reaction, even if some visceral rebelliousness remains. While 'thirtysomething' has become high-concept, 'twentysomething' lacks coherence: we are clueless yet wizened, too unopinionated to voice concern, purposefully enigmatic and indecisive."

Un-yuppies. Term created for those who do not share YUPPIE values, who, for example, are young, upwardly mobile, and professional but don't care much about high-status European cars.

Uppie yuppie. Young urban professional living in Michigan's Upper Penninsula. Anyone from the U.P. is an Uppie.

ustabe. Has-been.

Wasp (acr). White Anglo-Saxon Protestant.

whappies (acr). Wealthy, healthy, older people.

whoopies / woopies (acr). Well-off older people.

wimps. 1. The weak, meek, and the cowardly. Old slang that was propelled into the new in October 1987, when it was applied to George H. W. Bush. *Newsweek* ran a cover story entitled "George Bush: Fighting the 'Wimp Factor.'" This so-called W-word picked up a quick set of derivatives, including these cited by the Los Angeles *Daily News*: wimpy, wimpish, wimpdom, wimpism, wimplike, wimp out, and wimpismo. 2. (acr) Weak incompetent malingering pussy (ca. 1985—military use). 3. (acr) Whining insecure male person (ca. 1995).

woofies (acr). Well off, over fifty.

woofs (acr). Well-off older folks.

X condition. Generation X attitude described by *Newsweek* on January 27, 1992: "This is the X condition in a nutshell. We're alienated from our own alienation."

X-er. Member of generation X; BABY BUSTER.

X generation. Member of generation X; BABY BUSTER.

X-speak. The slang of generation X. Example: a playpen is an apartment.

Yaps (acr). Young aspiring professionals.

yavis (acronym). Young, attractive, verbal, intelligent, and successful.

yeepie (acr). Youthful, energetic, elderly person involved in everything.

yiffie (acr). Young, individualistic, freedom-minded, and few—a 1991 creation of *Fortune* magazine.

Say What?

Anne Gowen and Sean Piccoli, in "A Generation Lost in Time: Rebellion? Twentysomethings Find It's Too Much Trouble" (*Washington Times*, October 15, 1991), attempted to pin down some elusive X-speak:

boinkers. Couples who privately argue all the time yet engage in excessive PDA (public displays of affection).

circular conversationalism. Endless discussion and analysis of would-be relationships and possible career choices. Participants generally female. Usually involves a cheap jug of wine.

eye-spys. Those who pretend to understand *Spy* magazine.

Gap cretins. Do all their shopping at you-know-where.

gradual school. Graduate school.

gradual-schoolers. Couples who remain together after college and marry out of fear and to have kids. Also known as wabbits.

Heineken factor. Intense lifestyle pressure exerted by beer ads.

lip-mitment. Stunted relationship characterized by shallow talk, malt liquor, and infrequent (but safe) sex.

paisleyites. Sixties/nineties cross-pollinators who wear tie-dyed shirts, flimsy prints, and leather thongs around wrists or ankles. Affiliation with sixties consciousness ends with clothing.

readers. Those who profess to have given up television in favor of the Sunday *New York Times.* Occurs mostly during Yom Kippur and Lent.

spokes. Bike couriers who aim to combine Lycra fitness with post-punk cool. Handlebar pouch mandatory. Riding gloves and bandanna optional.

units. Parents.

unnatural selection. Tendency to forgo real attraction to find an economically secure mate.

velvetina. Tall, frail girl with white skin and black clothes.

yippies (acr). 1. Members of the Youth International Party, known in the late 1960s for their civil disobedience and antiwar protests, especially at the Democratic National Convention in Chicago in 1968. 2. Young indictable professional person, a name born of the insider stock-trading scandals.

yoick. Young one-income couple with kids.

yorkie. A New York YUPPIE.

Y-people. Yuppies.

Yuppie-Fest

The term "yuppie" was first put in print and popularized by the writer Bob Greene in an article in *Esquire* (March 1983) on "networking parties" sponsored by the former radical leader Jerry Rubin. Writing in the newspaper *Newsday* (April 7, 1985), Erica Jong pointed out that it was a corruption of "Yippie," which was a member of Rubin's own Youth International Party.

The publication of *The Yuppie Handbook*, by Marissa Piesman and Marilee Hartley, in January 1984 gave the term a monumental boost. The concept and the term were said to have lost their relevance with the stock market crash of October 19, 1987.

Derivatives of the term include yuppification, yuppyesque, yupguilt, yuppieback (book aimed at the yuppie reader), yupsters (yuppie gangsters), yuppie tax (such as one put on health-club membership), yup-topia, yuppyish, yuppiegate (for any scandal involving yuppie greed), yuplet (Herb Caen's term for a child yuppie), yupiteria (for a restaurant catering to yuppies), and yuppity (a blend of yuppie + uppity).

The term contributed to some nice headlines. On June 7, 1989, an article about the popularity of tropical fish among young urbans that appeared in the *Baltimore Evening Sun* was titled "Yuppies Find Guppies Are Ideal Low-Maintenance Pets."

A yuppie slum refers to any neighborhood that is largely populated by a young, well-off crowd, but often has other connotations of gentrification and rising rental and dining costs in a previously low-rent neighborhood.

Yuppie food stamps are crisp twenty-dollar bills from ATM machines. Yuppie flu is a nickname for chronic fatigue syndrome and yuppie crack is high-quality, expensive coffee such as Starbucks, Peet's, etc.

yuca (acr). Young, upwardly mobile Cuban American.

yuffie (acr). Young urban failure, generally a BABY BOOMER making less than $20,000 a year. In her book *Too Smart to Be Rich: On Being a Yuffie*, Patty Friedman says, "The yuffie was born with the trappings of success and infinite potential—his daddy's rich and his mama's good-looking and his IQ's over 135. He'd be a yuppie if he weren't so smart. But he ran it all into the ground with the aplomb and finesse of a true genius."

yukkie (acr). Young, upwardly mobile communist—term created in the pages of the *National Review* to refer to Gorbachev's supporters.

yummie (acr). Young upwardly mobile mommy.

yumpie. Young upwardly mobile professional—YUPPIE who earns less than $40,000 a year (at least in 1984, when the term came on the scene). Like YUPPIE, added to the *Oxford English Dictionary* in 1986.

yuppie (acr). Young urban professional. Typically, with a taste for BMW's, Rolex watches, jogging suits, imported bottled water, and fashionable restaurants. Influenced by YIPPIE.

yuppie puppies. Children of yuppies.

yupple. Blend of yuppie + couple, for codependent yuppies.

LEXPIONAGE: SOURCES AND ACKNOWLEDGMENTS

One of the ways slang differs from conventional English is that conventional English is relatively formal and the other is determinedly informal. It seems, therefore, totally consistent to offer these informal working notes on sources. Much of my slang collecting comes from many hours of eyeballing newspapers and magazines looking for terms. In the months leading up to completing this third version of *Slang*, I spent hours sitting in front of immense piles of newspapers, magazines, and newsletters, many of them in the Library of the National Press Club in Washington, where I had access to newspapers from all over the country. This access was especially useful in certain subject areas, such as real estate, where one can consult real estate sections from far-flung newspapers.

Another major source of information was friends and other slang collectors who keep me abreast of the latest sightings. They are mentioned by name in the notes to the individual chapters.

Then there is Google News, which is especially useful when it comes to looking for the latest coinages. Erin McKean, of *Verbatim* magazine and Oxford University Press, taught me how to find the latest in slang in the news by Googling for such phrases as "also known as" and "coined by," as well as terms such as "lingo," "slang," and "jargon."

My greatest single source of historical material was the Tamony Collection at the University of Missouri, Columbia. Put together over the course of a long lifetime by the etymologist Peter Tamony, this collection gives the United States its own archive of native slang. Tamony was considered to be the leading twentieth-century lay expert on American slang, and his collection is the only thing like it anywhere. It has been a major factor in giving this small book its authority and strength, and will fuel other such efforts for many years to come.

Introduction: Slang 101

The genesis of this chapter and all that follow was eight file drawers of material on slang and American English and a large collection of books on the subject, many of which are now part of the Espy Library in Oysterville, Washington.

Chapter 1: Auctionese

The following people (I have included the license number of the auctioneers among them) helped me in the collection of auction terms: Daniel W. Andrews (Me. 0385); Elsie M. Andrews (Me. 0389); Bill and Virginia Cressey; Frank Dingley; Barbara Hardenbrook; Susan Kenney; Patricia McIlvaine, M.D.; Joe Reilly; and Norman Stevens. Additional material came from the auction files in the Tamony Collection. I was helped considerably by reading *Maine Antique Digest*, a fine monthly tabloid published in Waldoboro, Maine. An early version of this glossary appeared in the April 1990 issue of the late, lamented *New England Monthly*. Thanks go to Richard Todd for his help. A particularly good book on the subject is E. C. Janes, *I Remember Cape Cod* (Brattleboro, Vt.: Stephene Greene Press, 1974).

Online auction slang can be found in various online locations, including the eBay site. A good article on eBay slang by Gary Neubert, "You Say You Want a Revolution? Try Selling on eBay," appeared in the *Palm Beach Post*, June 25, 2003.

Last but not least, the most important source of help for this chapter was my son Andrew Dickson, whose eBay persona is the superslick AC Dickson, PowerSeller. Andrew has turned this persona into a powerful performance art piece that has been acclaimed on both sides of the Atlantic. I have relied on his small primer *AC Dickson's Guide to eBay PowerSelling*. The glossary from that work as well as direct help from AC himself has contributed much to this glossary.

Chapter 2: Automotive Slang

The most important source for this chapter was my old friend Joseph C. ("Stroker") Goulden, who has been dutifully clipping and forwarding racing terms for lo these many years. John Rush, Norman Stevens, Tom Dalzell, Roberta B. Jacobson, James W. Darling, the Tamony Collection, and Gary B. Van Voorhis of the Daytona International Speedway have also contributed, and the late Robert Chapman's files were valuable especially for hot rod terms (see "Slang Dictionaries," p. 382). The "Winston Cup Glossary," published in October 1994, and the NASCAR *Pocket Guide* to the 2001 season were very helpful, as were Montie Tak's *Truck Talk* (Philadelphia: Chilton, 1971) and the weekly newspaper *NASCAR Scene*, which can be found at www.scenedaily.com. Tony Swan's "Talk Like a Gearhead: A Primer on Automotive Lingo," in the February 29, 2004, issue of the *Cleveland Plain Dealer*, was the best of many newspaper articles on car slang I drew on for this compilation.

Chapter 3: Aviation and Space

A remarkable collection of NASA acronyms and terms appears in NASA Reference Publication 1059, *Space Transportation System and Associated Payloads: Glossary, Acronyms and Abbreviations*. A good source of commercial-aviation slang shows up as a glossary to Jay David's *Sex and the Single Stewardess* (Chicago: Playboy Press, 1976). A small but important collection of commercial aviation slang appears in a short unsigned glossary, in the July 3, 1989, *Newsweek*. A large collection of aviation and aerospace glossaries in the Tamony Collection proved invaluable, as did suggestions from the late Ralph Hamil, Dave Matheny, and Tom Dalzell, who was able to find a first-rate collection of aviator slang on the Internet.

Bill Adair's "His Airplane, Your Life" (*St. Petersburg Times*, January 19, 1997) and a glossary of Atlanta airport terms from the *St. Petersburg Times* of July 25, 1993, were most useful. A good source of material on ballooning slang appeared as a glossary attached to Hugh Hart's "Free as a Bird: Ballooning Blossoms in the Midwest" (*Chicago Tribune*, June 5, 1998).

Bob Skole reviewed this chapter and made many important suggestions for its improvement.

Chapter 4: Bureaucratese

Beyond the fact that I have spent the last twenty years of my life inside and just outside the Beltway and am by now fluent in the capital's lingo, the sizable file on bureaucratese in the Tamony Collection was most helpful, as were the suggestions from Chris Keller, Norman Stevens, Bill Young, and others both inside and outside the beast.

Chapter 5: Business and Finance

The late Irving Hale and Stephen Brent Wells provided much help in the preparation of this chapter. This glossary was also built from a mammoth pile of clippings from the financial pages, magazines including *Forbes*, and a large collection of financial and business glossaries found in the Tamony Collection. Help was also rendered by *Lamont's Glossary*, prepared by Lamont & Partners of London, a first-rate contemporary guide to the financial terminology used on both sides of the Atlantic. It was helped to some degree by my year in a brokerage firm back when "Bessie" was the nickname for Bethlehem Steel and there was only one phone company. Also useful for the latest in business slang is Ron Sturgeon's *Green Weenies and Due Diligence: Insider Business Jargon—Raw, Serious and Sometimes Funny* (Lyndon, Wash.: Mike French Publishing, 2005).

Chapter 6: Computerese
Richard Danca, writer and computer journalist, Ross Reader, Norman Stevens, and David Broome, the king of hacker acronyms and initialisms, provided invaluable help in the preparation of this collection. Although it is fast becoming dated, the key work on computer slang is Eric S. Raymond's *New Hacker's Dictionary*, third edition (Cambridge, Mass.: MIT Press, 1996), which was originally produced by a team of six professional computer wizards led by Guy L. Steele, Jr., and published in 1983. Alan Freedman's *Computer Glossary*, ninth edition (New York: AMACOM, 2001), was also useful, along with Brian Pfaffenberger's *Webster's New World Computer Dictionary* (New York: Hungry Minds, 2001).

Chapter 7: Crime, Punishment, and the Law
The holdings of the Tamony Collection were a great help in the preparation of this glossary, as was the eagle-eyed journalist Joseph C. Goulden, who scanned many a newspaper police story for examples. Among other things, he sent along a carbon copy of a piece he did thirty-five years ago for the *Dallas News* on South Dallas cop and perp slang. Russell Mott, Charles D. Poe, Edward O'Brien, Mike Stackpole, and Suzy Nace were all of great help. Letters from convict #63760 at the Colorado Department of Corrections, convict #80535 at the Louisiana State Prison in Angola, Louisiana, #381867 in the Texas Department of Criminal Justice in Amarillo, and several other insiders made most helpful contributions, as did an Internet convict slang glossary updated through August 10, 1996.

It should be noted that a particularly useful and fascinating glossary of police terminology appears in the back of Carsten Stroud's *Close Pursuit: A Week in the Life of an NYPD Homicide Cop* (New York: Bantam, 1987). An especially good article on Los Angeles Police Department slang by Chip Johnson appeared in the *Los Angeles Times* of December 19, 1994; a glossary of current prison slang appeared in the February 7, 2000, issue of *Texas Lawyer*; and another excellent source was an article from the *Baltimore Sun* on the language of the new police chief, "Baltimore's New Chief Gives Police N.Y. Accent: Norris Adds Touch of Big Apple Jargon" (July 3, 2000).

Several inmate Web sites can be accessed with a simple Google or Yahoo search for "prison slang."

Chapter 8: Cube-speak
Many newspaper articles informed this chapter, ranging from "Phrases from the Cube Farm" (*Los Angeles Times*, September 27, 1999) and "Lexicon Valley" (*Boston Globe*, July 15, 1997) to articles in the free weekly arts papers given away in most cities. Many cube-speak terms have made their way overseas, appearing, for example, in the *Times* of London ("Business World Has a Blamestorm," March 4, 2003). Other sources include Eric S. Raymond's *The New Hacker's Dictionary*, third edition (Cambridge, Mass.: MIT Press, 1996); Ed Krol's *The Whole Internet User's Guide and Catalog* (Belmont, California: Integra Media, 1996); and online versions of *Microspeak*, an unofficial guide to Microsoft corporate lingo said to have been compiled by the staff of *Micronews*, the company's weekly internal corporate newsletter. A host of online slang sites were valuable, most notably the Microsoft Lexicon, Netlingo, The Ultimate Silicon Valley Slang Page, Galileo International, Metamor Technologies, SPR, and Streams Online Media.

Chapter 9: Drugs
The major ongoing attempt to maintain an up-to-date accounting of drug terminology is available through the White House Office of National Drug Control Policy (ONDCP), unofficially called the office of the drug czar. This office posts new terms as soon as they are spotted. The ONDCP, whose softball team is named "We Czar the Champions," can be reached at http://www.whitehousedrugpolicy.gov. The glossary can be found at http://www.whitehousedrugpolicy.gov/streetterms/Default.asp. An earlier glossary was most useful: "Street Terms," a list compiled by the Federal Drugs and Crime Data & Clearinghouse and distributed by mail and over the Internet (contact: askjncjrs@ncjrs.aspensys.com).

Esther and Albert Lewin's *Thesaurus of Slang* (New York: Facts on File, 1988) and J. E. Schmidt's *Narcotics Lingo and Lore* (Springfield, Ill.: Charles C. Thomas, 1959) were most useful in the preparation of this listing. An anonymous person familiar with California's drug scene helped authenticate some of these terms; the late Charles D. Poe located many references in newspapers and novels; Joe McCabe was the first to point out that the Justice Department was compiling crime-related slang; and the Tamony Collection provided many examples. Virginia Scallis also contributed.

Lana Berkowitz's article "Here's a Hint: It Doesn't Refer to April 20" appeared in the April 20, 2005, *Houston Chronicle*. An exhaustive "Meth Glossary" appeared in the *Lewiston* (Idaho) *Morning Tribune* of May 22, 2005. It was compiled by a group of local social workers, police, and court officials.

Chapter 10: Fantasy, the Future, Science Fiction, Potterdom, and Cyberpunk

Earthlings who helped with this glossary are the writer and game designer Mike Stackpole, the futurist Ralph Hamil, and the book editor Michael Dirda. Many of Stackpole's definitions have been quoted in their entirety, especially those from his memos on game and cyberpunk terminology. Martin Kottmeyer of Carlyle, Illinois, read the original version of this glossary and made important suggestions for its improvement. The second edition of Robert Runté's *Fanspeak Glossary* (available from the author: P.O. Box 4655, Postal Station South Edmonton, Edmonton, Alberta T6E 5G5), and a fanzine glossary produced by Mike Gunderloy, editor of *Factsheet Five*, of Rensselaer, New York, were very useful in decoding sci-fi-speak. David C. Kopaska-Merkel, of Tuscaloosa, Alabama, suggested and defined more than a dozen new terms for this edition.

A series of glossaries pulled from the Internet by Tom Dalzell were the source of most of the cyberpunk entries. Of these, the best glossaries are Jes Wulfsverg Nielsen's Shadowrun & Shadowpunk Glossary; Logan Graves's Shadowpunk Glossary; Definition of Slang Used in Cyberpunk, compiled by Ocelot, also known as HighRider; the Glossary of Slang in 2054, courtesy of the World Wide Word Watch. Newspaper articles that provided entries were Colin Covert, "Star Trek Glossary" (*Star Tribune*, November 22, 1996); "Potter-Speak Glossaries" (*Newsweek*, July 17, 2000); "Welcome to Potter-Speak" (*USA Today*, July 14, 2005); "Glossary Provides Guide for Understanding of Wizard's World" (*Florida Times Union*, July 7, 2000); and "Wizard Glossary" (*Sunday Mail* [UK], July 10, 2005).

Chapter 11: Food and Drink

Phyllis Richman, a former *Washington Post* food critic, was most helpful, as was the food file in the Tamony Collection. "Short-Order Musts" in the September 24, 1991, *New York Times* is an invaluable source of short-order cooking slang, and Janey Milsead's piece on bartender slang in the April 23, 1993, *Los Angeles Times* Sunday magazine is especially good.

David Hawley's "Pizza Speak Glossary Dishes Up Some Crusty Slang" (*Detroit Free Press*, October 14, 1996) is the definitive source on the subject. Sheryl Julian's "Kitchen Talk Is Enough to Burn Your Ears" (*Chicago Tribune*, October 1, 1989) is a good source of wait-speak. The magazine *Food Arts: The Magazine for Professionals* is a great source of inside food slang and terminology. Roberta B. Jacobson and John Clarke also contributed.

Chapter 12: Gaming Slang

Roberta Jacobson, Joseph C. Goulden, and the files of the Tamony Collection were most useful in preparing this chapter. More than a score of newspaper stories on gambling and its language were consulted, including most prominently the *Chicago Tribune* (which has a regular poker column), the *St. Petersburg Times*, the *New York Times*, and the *Las Vegas Review-Journal*.

Chapter 13: Hip-hop and Like That

Dozens of articles were consulted for this section, several of which are cited in the text. They range from as far back as "Rap Primer" (*Washington Post*, September 1, 1986) and "Words to Rap By" (*New York Times*, August 22, 1988) up through the latest articles on Google News. The best hip-hop Web site by far is the long-established online Rap Dictionary (www.rapdict.org), which bills itself as "the oldest and ultimate resource for looking up hip-hop slang" and which contained 2,967 content pages as of May 2006. The dictionary has now officially gone "wik-wik-Wiki!" which means that readers can now edit virtually anything, giving it a certain vitality.

Chapter 14: Java-speak

Web sites that were most useful were Brian Connors's "Coffeehouse Dictionary," "A Seattle Lexicon: Coffee & Espresso Lingo" (www.geocities.com/connorbd/coffee/coffeewords.html, www.calihan.com/seattle/coffee.htm), and Starbucksian.com. Articles of particular help were Mark Peters, "Coffee as a Second Language" (*Buffalo News*, August 28, 2005) and Alan Woods, "Starbucks Prints Guide to New Coffee Lexicon: 'Hold the Whip'" (*National Post* [Canada], January 9, 2004).

This chapter was also informed by personal visits to the Bean Bag, Caribou, Green Mountain, Seattle's Best, Torrefazione, Coffee People, Peet's, Stumptown Roasters, Brewed Awakenings, Dunkin' Donuts, Seattle Gourmet (and their drive-thru espresso stands), Elliot Bay, Starbucks, and others.

Chapter 15: Media and Publishing Slang

Dave Metheny of the Minneapolis *Star-Tribune* provided the major boost for this chapter in a series of memos on newsroom slang. Thanks also to Russell Ash, Hal Davis, Sam Freedenberg, Tom Gill, Joseph C. Goulden, Arnold R. Isaacs, Charles D. Poe, Dan Rapoport, Dorothy Repovich, James E. Farmer, Bob Skole, Anthony A. Spleen, David Streitfield, Elaine Viets, Tony Wynne-Jones, and Bill Hickman for their help.

Two articles I consulted on this subject were "Journalism Slang" (*Newsweek*, September 4, 1989) and Arthur C. Norris's column on the subject (*Writer's Digest*, January 1932). Bob Skole, Thomas B. Allen, and Jim Srodes read the chapter for accuracy and supplied additions of their own.

Chapter 16: Medical and Emergency Room Slang

Thanks to P.B.P., M.D.; F.M., M.D.; Joseph Morales, M.D.; and Reinhold Aman, M.D., who publishes a journal, *Maledicta*, with many interesting articles on medical terminology: "Milwaukee Medical Maledicta," by Sue Ture (*Maledicta* 8, 1984–85), "Not Sticks and Stones, but Names," by Lois Monteiro (*Maledicta* 4, number 1, Summer 1980), "Common Patient-Directed Pejoratives Used by Medical Personnel," by C. J. Scheiner (*Maledicta* 2, 1978), and "More Common Patient-Directed Pejoratives Used by Medical Personnel" (*Maledicta* 7, 1983). The *Newsweek* "Buzzwords" sections were a good source (see the issues of February 19, 1990; May 28, 1990; July 9, 1990; and April 29, 1991). Sheilendr Khipple, "Word for Word/Hospital Lingo: What's a Bed Plug? An L.O.L. in N.A.D." (*New York Times*, May 13, 2001) and a piece on NPR's *All Things Considered*, "*ER* Writers and Doctor Slang," on March 7, 1996, were most helpful.

Ross Reader pointed me in the direction of a variety of sources for U.K. medical slang, including the BBC's *Radio Times*, June 17–23, 2000, which contained a good collection of ER terms; and David Millward's "Doctor, We've Got a Nasty Case of the Grollies" (*Daily Telegraph*, December 20, 1997). In his excellent *Weekend Telegraph* "Wordplay" column of November 2, 1991, Fritz Spiegl lifted the curtain on the deepest secret of British medicine, the letter code. See also "Hospital Lingo" (*Daily Record* [Glasgow], October 13, 2004) and Camillo Fracassini, "What's Up Doc? Am I a Bundy or Just Foddo?" *Scotland on Sunday*, September 1, 2002.

Chapter 17: Mental States

Robert D. Specht, Bob Skole, Roberta B. Jacobson (who sent along not one but two compilations), Joseph C. Goulden, Robert C. Norris, James W. Darling, the late Charles D. Poe, and Joseph E. Badger all helped with the compilation of this list. The best list of "westernisms" that I have seen was compiled by David McQuay and appeared in the *Denver Post* of August 25, 1985, and the best article on the subject to come to my attention is Robert Fulford's "Never at a Loss for Marbles Metaphors" (*Toronto Globe and Mail*, November 30, 1994).

Chapter 18: Nautical Slang

Bill O'Neill, Dick Dana, James Darling, the late Charles D. Poe, and the Tamony Collection were all of help in compiling this glossary. Don Kowet's "Seafaring Terms You Won't Find in the Dictionary" (*Washington Times*, June 21, 1990) and "Boatloads of Fun—Summer on Lake Michigan Looks a Lot like Spring Break" (*Chicago Tribune*, July 20, 2003) were of use, as were several nautical Internet sites. The nautical writer Paul Clancy reviewed and embellished the chapter.

Chapter 19: Net-speak

Most helpful to the preparation of this chapter were Internet Literacy Consultants' "Glossary of Internet Terms"; "The Glossary of Internet Terminology and Slang," copyrighted by Mike Bowen; an unsigned "Web Terminology Glossary"; and a half dozen additional online Internet glossaries. Some definitions are drawn from *Downsizing Information Systems* (Carmel, Ind.: Sams Publishing, 1992), one of a trio of valuable reference books written by Steven L. Guengerich and other experts at BSG Consulting, a systems-integration company based in Houston. The Winter 1994 issue of *American Speech* (volume 69, number 4) contained a listing of Internet terms in the "Among the New Words" section, by John and Adele Algeo. A number of sources were used in gathering the emoticon collection: *Newsweek*, March 9, 1992; Mike Stackpole's files; and the August 1995 issue of *Boston Computer Currents*. The "Spam Glossary" that appeared in the October 2005 issue of *Inc.* magazine was very helpful.

Chapter 20: The Great Outdoors

Some of the jargon used by modern rock climbers came from an article by Will Gadd in the July-August 1993 issue of *Rock & Ice* magazine and an article by Hal Mattern in the August 8, 1993, *Arizona Republic* titled "Arizona Climbers Rock! Scaling Vertical Walls Is Down-to-Earth."

Terms for mountain biking come from the Internet site provided by *VeloNews: The Journal of Competitive Cycling*, based in Boulder, Colorado.

Many skiing terms were scooped up from the Internet. A particularly useful horse-racing glossary appeared in the *Shreveport* (Louisiana) *Times* of April 26, 1991. Trevor Cralle's *Surfin'ary: A Dictionary of Surfing Terms and Surfspeak* (Berkeley, Calif.: Ten Speed Press, 1991) is the first and last word on the subject. The best online surfing glossary I could find was http://www.surfing-waves.com/surf_talk.htm#D. A superb snowboarding glossary appeared in the *Hagerstown* (Maryland) *Herald*, and a number of articles on bass fishing were consulted, including Don Hopey's "Fishing Contest a Far Cry from 'Two Bubbas in a Boat'" (*Pittsburgh Post-Gazette*, July 27, 2005).

Chapter 21: Performing Slang

The Tamony Collection provided special help in the preparation of this chapter, as did several columns by William Safire that originally appeared in the *New York Times*. The late Charles D. Poe made major contributions. A number of articles were of special use, including "A Lesson in Radio Lingo" (*Christian Science Monitor*, April 20, 1993); "Hut's, Putt's and Traction: Television-Programmer Talk" (*New York Times*, June 6, 1993); and a number of *Newsweek* "Buzzword" columns: see November 13, 1989 (agents); May 7, 1990 (TV news); August 27, 1990 (talk radio); and June 28, 1993 (Letterman slang).

The first and best "Sein" lexicon appeared in the April 9, 1993, *Entertainment Weekly*. The writing of J. D. Considine, music critic of the *Baltimore Sun*, provided a valuable assist on pop music terminology.

Chapter 22: Real Estate

Gina Creepy, Roberta Jacobean, and Norman Stevens helped with this chapter. Work by Bradley Unman in the *Sacramento Bee* and Warren Boron in the *Bergen County Record* provided the latest list of the popular real estate lexicon used by architects, lenders, planners, and builders. Dale White's "Sprawl Scopes? Snout House? Privatopia? Southwest Florida's Landscape Is Full of Illustrations of a New Urban Sprawl Vocabulary" (*Sarasota Herald-Tribune*, July 18, 2004) was especially useful in detailing the language of sprawl. Many real estate sections from assorted newspapers were read and marked for this section, ranging from the *New Canaan Advertiser* to the *Las Vegas Review-Journal*. Bob Skole made many valuable additions to this chapter.

Chapter 23: The Sultry Slang of Sex

This collection was aided with material found in *Maledicta; Journal of Verbal Aggression; Playboy*; the Tamony Collection; and *Modern English*, by Jennifer Walters (San Francisco: Last Gasp Press, 1985). Important help came from the late Robert T. West, Leonard Ashley, the modest J.B.W., Norman D. Stevens, and the late Charles D. Poe. Scott Callis also contributed. Bob Skole vetted and improved the chapter in early 2006. The Internet site for "Queer Slang in the Gay 90s" (copyright 1986 Gay-MART Enterprises, Vancouver) was most helpful, as were a number of other online glossaries. *Wired* magazine's article on the language of phone sex, "Best Phone Sex Ever" (July 2005), was a good source, as was Virginia Braun's "'Snatch,' 'Hole' or 'Honey-Pot'? Semantic Categories and the Problem of Nonspecificity in Female Genital Slang" (*Journal of Sex Research*, May 2001).

Chapter 24: The Slang of Spin

A good source of "flannelisms" is two articles by John Crosby on Madison Avenue-ese which appear in B. A. Botkin's *Sidewalks of America* (New York: Bobbs-Merrill, 1954). Material in the Tamony Collection was of great help in preparing this glossary, as was Michelle V. Rafter's "World Wide Sell: The Web Is Becoming the Place to Advertise" (*Los Angeles Times*, December 17, 1995). Janet Kinosian's "Publicist Patois" (*Los Angeles Times*, April 24, 1994) was useful for Hollywood PR talk.

Chapter 25: Sports Slang

Webster's Sports Dictionary (Springfield, Mass.: Merriam-Webster, 1976), Tim Considine's *The Language of Sport* (New York: Facts on File, 1982), and Harvey Frommer's *Sports Lingo* (New York: Atheneum, 1979) are just a few of the many sources of sports slang. Asphalt argot from Chuck Wielgus' *The Back-in-Your-Face-Guide to Pick-up Basketball* (New York: Dodd Mead, 1987) and William T. "Buck" Lai's *Winning Basketball* (New York: Stadia Sports, 1973) were also important.

My best source for cornholing was an article in the October 20, 2005, *Roanoke Times*.

The Tamony Collection lays particular emphasis on sports.

Chapter 26: Teen and High School Slang

I am indebted to Ashley E. Miller and her students at Walt Whitman Middle School in Alexandria, Virginia, and to Gretchen Howard and her students at John F. Kennedy High School in Rockville, Maryland, for their major contributions. Walt Giachini, guidance counselor at Wallenberg High School in San Francisco, obtained contributions from his four daughters, Julia, Brooke, Gina, and Kate. The teacher and writer Richard Lederer, the writer Geof Huth, and the late researcher Charles D. Poe helped, as did Willy Risser and Andrew Dickson.

Robert S. Greenman, teacher and journalist, was kind enough to query students at the Columbia Scholastic Press Association summer workshop in June 1989. In addition, a number of recent newspaper articles on teenager and college slang were consulted, from the *Los Angeles Times*, the *New York Times*, the *Washington Post*, the *Detroit Free Press*, *New York Newsday*, the *Concord* (N.H.) *Monitor*, *USA Today*, the *San Francisco Chronicle*, and the *Fort Lauderdale Sun-Sentinel*.

Chapter 27: University and College Slang

UCLA Slang: A Dictionary of Slang Words and Expressions Used at UCLA, edited by Pamela Munro (occasional collections published privately). The UCLA book reemerged in 1991 as the highly publicized *Slang U* (New York: Crown, 2005). Then there was Steve Zweig's *Unofficial College Dictionary* (Minnetonka, Minn: Meadowbrook, 1990), which let us know that a party where no girls show up is properly called "a male-bonding event." Other valuable sources are Tom Dalzell, *Flappers 2 Rappers: American Youth Slang* (Springfield, Mass.: Merriam-Webster, 1996) and Connie C. Eble, *Slang and Sociability: In-Group Languages Among College Students* (Chapel Hill: University of North Carolina Press, 1996).

Meanwhile, *Lisa Birnbach's New and Improved College Book* (New York: Simon and Schuster, 1992) provided a new feature for a college guide: the slang indigenous to each college. Birnbach and her staff even let you know where blow-off courses are called "skates," "guts," and any of a number of other variations.

The official Usenet dictionary of college slang created by Jennifer Doyle was most useful, and many of the entries sent to her from colleges around the country appear in this glossary. The 1993 Merriam-Webster survey of hot words on campus was also a major source. Useful articles included "College Sex Glossary" (*Chicago Sun-Times*, March 18, 2005), James R. Petersen's "Words to Baffle Your Spell Check" (*New York Times*, April 24, 2005), and "Hanging Out and Hooking Up" (*Hampshire Gazette*, November 26, 2005).

Chapter 28: War Slang

Thanks to David K. Barnhart, Joseph C. Goulden, John Koopman, Jesse H. Moore V, the late Robert F. Perkins, the late Charles D. Poe, and Bob Skole for their help. Also thanks to the defunct GIJargon.com. It also relies to a significant degree on my own book *War Slang: American Fighting Words and Phrases Since the Civil War* (New York: Pocket Books, 1995—revised edition, Dulles, Va.: Potomac Books, 2003); Tony Allen-Mills, "Fix Bayonets and Hug" (*Sunday Times* [London], June 24, 2001); Jim Auchmutey, "The Power of Language" (*Atlanta Journal-Constitution*, October 21, 2001); Elizabeth Becker, "Prickly Roots of 'Homeland Security'" (*New York Times*, August 31, 2002); "Buzzwords" (*Newsweek*, May 10, 1993); Dick Polman, "This Homeland Is Your Homeland, This Homeland Is My Homeland" (*Milwaukee Journal Sentinel*, December 8, 2002); and Emily Wax, "In Times of Terror, Teens Talk the Talk: Boys Are 'Firefighter Cute,' Messy Room Is 'Ground Zero' in Sept. 11 Slang" (*Washington Post*, March 18, 2002).

Chapter 29: Washington-speak

Years of reading about Congress have led me to valuable contributions for this chapter, from the *Washington Post*, *The Hill*, *Hill Rag*, *Congressional Quarterly*, *National Journal*, the *Washington Times*, the *Congressional Record*, and *Roll Call*. I also relied on research conducted with Paul Clancy for his book *The Congress Dictionary: The Ways and Meanings of Capitol Hill* (New York: Wiley, 1995). Individuals who helped with the preparation of this section included the writers Thomas B. Allen, Joseph C. Goulden, Grant Barrett, Douglas Evelyn, James Srodes, and John McArdle of *Roll Call*; the U.S. ambassador to Belgium, Tom Korologos; Bill Timmons, chair emeritus of the lobbying firm Timmons & Co.; former undersecretary of defense Dov S. Zacheim; and the late Philip Merrill, Jack Limpert, and Bill O'Sullivan of the *Washingtonian*. Maura Brackett, Sean Farrell, and Roslyn Johnson also contributed.

Chapter 30: X-ers, Yuppies, Soccer Moms, and Other Moderns

The grackels (acronym: generous researcher and contributor of key elements) for this chapter were the late Charles D. Poe, Ross Reader, and Robert Greenman. John and Adele Algeo's "Among the New Words" section in *American Speech* (especially the winter 1992 issue, volume 67, number 4) was most helpful, as was Anne Gowen and Sean Piccoli's "A Generation Lost in Time: Rebellion? Twenty-Somethings Find It's Too Much Trouble" (*Washington Times*, October 15, 1991).

General Sources: A Bibliography

Slang Dictionaries

There are a number of very good dictionaries on the market today. Here are the best:

The Random House Historical Dictionary of American Slang (2 vols., New York: Random House, 1994–), edited by J. E. Lighter, is the first authoritative historical dictionary of American slang. Volume I is a 1,006-page tome that is seen as the beginning of the definitive work on American slang, comparable to the *Oxford English Dictionary* in importance. It covers entries from "A"—a euphemism for "ass"—to "gytch," to steal. Volume II of the dictionary covers the letters H to R. Among other things, Lighter's opus disproves the commonly held belief that slang is transitory; terms such as "out of sight" and "sweat it out" date back to the 1800s. Use of the word "bad" to mean good isn't new, either, Lighter tells us; he found such references as early as 1877.

Robert L. Chapman's *The Dictionary of American Slang* (New York: Collins, 1998) is a new book that builds on earlier Chapman dictionaries and on Harold Wentworth and Stuart Flexner's earlier

Dictionary of American Slang (New York: Thomas Y. Crowell, 1960). The last edition of Chapman's work was published in 1998 with a lot of new examples ("greenmail," "bean counter," "glitterati") and some purging of old terms (Gypsy and carnival slang get short shrift). Chapman died shortly after the 1998 edition of his book was published.

Eric Partridge's *The New Partridge Dictionary of Slang and Unconventional English*, edited by Tom Dalzell and Terry Victor (2 vols., New York: Routledge, 2005), is a totally updated version of *A Dictionary of Slang and Unconventional English* (8th ed., New York: Routledge, 1990), by Eric Partridge and edited by Paul Beale. A gigantic book, containing over 65,000 entries, *The New Partridge* details the slang and unconventional English of the English-speaking world since 1945 and through the first years of the new millennium, with the same thorough, intense, and lively scholarship that characterized Partridge's original slang dictionaries.

Richard A. Spears has written more than forty-five dictionaries, many of slang, with the most recent being *The McGraw-Hill Dictionary of American Slang and Colloquial Expressions* (New York: McGraw Hill, 2005) and *Slang American Style: More Than 10,000 Ways to Talk the Talk* (New York: McGraw-Hill, 1996). His work *Slang and Euphemism* (New York: Signet, 2001) is not a general slang dictionary but a book of the taboo, as trumpeted on its dust jacket: "a dictionary of oaths, curses, insults, sexual slang and metaphor, racial slurs, drug talk, homosexual lingo, and related matters"—with nary a page lacking at least an R rating.

Joseph A. Weingarten's *An American Dictionary of Slang* (privately published, 1954) is a fascinating and almost impossible-to-find work.

Jonathon Green's *Cassell's Dictionary of Slang* (London/New York: Cassell's, 2006). First published in 1998, the newest edition covers English-language slang from the British Isles, the United States, Australia, New Zealand, Ireland, South Africa, and the anglophone West Indies.

Tom Dalzell's *Flappers 2 Rappers: American Youth Slang 1920–1990* (Springfield, Mass.: Merriam-Webster, 1996) and *The Slang of Sin* (Springfield, Mass.: Merriam-Webster, 1998) cover all kinds of sin, not just what you are thinking of. Dalzell is the lead editor on the new Partridge dictionary discussed above. He is also at work on a single-volume American Partridge for 2008.

John Ayto's *Oxford Dictionary of Slang* (New York/Oxford: Oxford University Press, 2003).

Slang Thesauri

Lester V. Berrey and Melvin Van Bark's *American Thesaurus of Slang* (New York: Thomas Y. Crowell, 1952) is a monumental work that covers everything. Recent and somewhat more limited efforts are the excellent *Thesaurus of Slang*, by Esther Lewin and Albert E. Lewin (New York: Facts on File, 1988) and Jonathon Green's *The Slang Thesaurus* (London: Elm Tree Books, 1986).

New Words Books

By their nature, books about new words are great sources of new slang. Two that I found to be most useful: *New Words*, edited by Simon Mort (London: Longman Guardian, n.d.), and *The Facts on File Dictionary of New Words*, by Harold LeMay, Sid Lerner, and Marian Taylor (New York: Facts on File, 1989).

Outstanding in this genre, however, is Anne H. Soukhanov's *Word Watch: The Stories Behind the Words of Our Lives* (New York: Henry Holt, 1995).

INDEX

NEW EDITIONS OF THIS BOOK

I am planning to keep *Slang* current with contemporary examples by updating it in the second decade of the twenty-first century. I would like very much to hear from those with suggestions for terms—and topics—that could be included in the monumental fourth edition.

I can be reached at P.O. Box 280, Garrett Park, MD 20896-0280.

A NOTE ON THE AUTHOR

Paul Dickson, the coauthor (with Thomas B. Allen) of *The Bonus Army: An American Epic* and *Sputnik: The Shock of the Century*, has written numerous books on American English, including *War Slang*, *Family Words*, *The Congress Dictionary* (with Paul Clancy), *Words*, and *The New Dickson Baseball Dictionary*. He is a former consulting editor at Merriam-Webster, Inc., and a contributing editor for the *Washingtonian* magazine. He lives in Garrett Park, Maryland.